O9-ABF-228

Becoming Visible
Women in European History

Becoming Visible
Women in European History

Edited by

Renate Bridenthal
Brooklyn College
Claudia Koonz
Holy Cross College

Houghton Mifflin Company Boston
Atlanta Dallas Geneva, Illinois Hopewell, New Jersey
Palo Alto London

Printed in the U.S.A.

Library of Congress Catalog Card Number: 76–11978

ISBN: 0–395–24477–3

Contents

Preface

This book was conceived in the turmoil of the early seventies. On August 26, 1972, thousands of women marched exuberantly with banners demanding "our rights and nothing less!" Consciousness-raising groups formed in hundreds of homes, bringing women together to share their life experiences. Sharing and discussing brought to light the patterns of discrimination, the repeated violations of women's integrity by home, school, and workplace. Many of the conveners moved from anger into action and started working for equality. Their solutions varied, but the questions they asked were the same: Why are women treated differently from men? Why should that inequality continue? Part of the solution lay in an understanding of history. This made it important to ask how that inequality came to be.

This set of essays grew out of that questioning and is a contribution to the shared goal. It is both an individual and a collective venture. The contributors have been informed by a common purpose: to understand the history of women and to bring it into the mainstream of Western civilization. Yet they have brought their own individualities to this book, their own viewpoints, methods, and styles of writing.

The editors take full responsibility for the final result. We selected a chronological, rather than a thematic, approach as being the most appropriate both to the state of research in the field at this time and to the needs of a college audience using standard historical works. We originally planned not to burden the undergraduate with a monograph-style scholarly apparatus, but simply to distill essential facts and ideas. Several contributors disagreed with our pedagogical intent, and so some chapters have heavier documentation than others. We trust that this diversity, along with the occasional diversity in the findings of the articles themselves, will not hamper understanding, and will even increase it by stimulating discussion.

In bringing this book together, we were enormously vitalized by our contact with many different and interesting authors, as well as with each other, and we have a keen sense that the finished product stands for collective effort. Our work on *Becoming Visible* gave us as much insight into social process and human relations as did the material with which we were working.

We want to thank the staff at Houghton Mifflin Company for their dedication and helpfulness, especially in the urgent last days of manuscript preparation. Most of all, we are grateful to Brenda Steinberg and Hobart A. Spalding, Jr., whose intellectual comradeship, love, and support helped bring this book to life. And from Renate to Hoby, my companion in growth and the unfolding of self, a special acknowledgement of the gift of sharing.

Becoming Visible
Women in European History

Introduction

Challenging accepted views of women, contemporary feminists are questioning our most fundamental social institutions and assumptions. Critical of the present, we have turned simultaneously in two directions — toward a future ideal and back into the past to understand the origins of sex-role stereotyping and of crippling patriarchy. The canons of traditional history, however, provide few guideposts for this quest. Until the development of women's history, historians recognized only those women who most resembled men or those who fulfilled male expectations of the "ideal" woman. One widely used textbook limits its discussion to four women (Jane Austen, Catherine II, Fatima, and Isabella of Castile), three female deities (Athena, Isis, and Mary) and Alice in Wonderland.[1] Until recently, the average woman of the past has remained obscure, almost invisible.

The essays written for this volume seek both to restore women to history and to explore the meaning of women's unique historical experience. Brushing aside the few, and often derogatory, portraits of women that characterize traditional histories, we begin to see the real women of history emerge — beyond deification and vilification. Women as a force in politics: reformers, revolutionaries, and feminists, searching for a political identity in their nation, their class, themselves. Women as producers: peasant wives, artisans, cottage and factory workers, domestic servants, corporate drones, and marginal professionals. Women in their roles as wives and mothers in changing family structures: from indispensable helpmeets to conspicuous consumers. Women in organized religion, seeking a niche in patristic tradition or rashly denouncing it: nuns, witches, and pious wives.

A chronicle of women's history points inevitably to a new feminist perspective. We depart from male-centered models and literally bring to our study a new point of view, although theorizing about women's history itself is not new. In *The Second Sex* (1949), Simone de Beauvoir constructed a general theory to explain women's chronic powerlessness. Passive onlookers in the historical drama of great events, women have, in her theory, acted in the service of patriarchy. Therefore, they have created no history of their own. Others have disagreed. Mary Beard, in *Woman as Force in History* (1946), called attention to the fact that women, despite formidable obstacles, have made far greater contributions to human history than is commonly recognized. They have been active, not merely passive; independent, not just ancillary. Both Beard's and de Beauvoir's categories are important, but they are too crude to aid us in interpreting the complexity of women's history.

Other analytic approaches attempt to depict women's history as an upward or downward curve, moving relentlessly toward liberation or more intensive oppression. The liberal tradition of Mary Wollstonecraft, Condorcet, John Stuart Mill, and Harriet Taylor Mill argues that history shows a steady progress of women from slavery to emancipation. Marxists see precisely the opposite development: from relative sexual equality under conditions of primitive society to relatively greater exploitation under capitalism. But again these notions of linear improvement or decline are too simple. A highly technological capitalist society differs so fundamentally from a nonliterate, communal one that relations of power, family, and the economy defy simple comparisons. Yesterday's abbess is not today's woman priest; the medieval alewife is not the modern barmaid; and the preindustrial wife is not the alienated drudge described by Betty Friedan.

We hope, through the essays in this volume, to destroy simplistic notions about women's passivity or activity, progress or regress. Women must be seen within the complexity of their specific cultural contexts. Inevitably, as research in women's history continues and methodology becomes more sophisticated, controversies intensify. In these essays we evolve no consensus on several key issues, such as the impact of the Christian legacy, the romantic image of womanhood, and industrialization of women. But if change affected women differently from men — and it did — these controversies themselves will enrich our search for an understanding of our human past.

Where can we find the lost women of earlier cultures? Central to our search is the discovery of new sources and the reevaluation of traditional ones. The primary and secondary materials most commonly available to historians have been written by men. Often these sources tell us more about male needs and attitudes than women's realities. Starting with the very earliest written records, we find a bifurcated female image. Men have seen women as either passive and good or evil and powerful. The pedestal and the stake represent the polarities of men's views of women's place. Such a stereotypic vision masks the real women of the past and deprives them of their ordinary human strengths and frailties. The ensuing distortion serves several purposes: it rationalizes inequality, limits competition for wealth, power, and status, and displaces responsibility for social malfunctions. The polarized image of women makes it difficult for us to understand the complex realities of past societies and last, but not least, it prevents women from perceiving themselves as whole human beings capable of acting in and upon their environment. The stereotype is a self-fulfilling prophecy: women have rarely written their own history.

Now that we have begun, we have to decide how properly to use conventional, male-centered sources, which, despite their bias, contain valuable clues. Rather than discounting this material, we can reinterpret it. Many misogynistic accounts, for example, are merely symbolic; they may be pseudo-explanations of other conflicts perceived in social relations. We are learning to decode such accounts by placing them in their appropriate setting. For example, changing literary images of women in classical and Renaissance Europe provide us with a fresh perspective on changing relations between the sexes and concomitant transformations in the political and economic structures. We ask not only what the image of woman was and whether it corresponded to reality, but who created it and what function it served in a larger social setting.

Just as we have begun to reevaluate old sources, we find that we must redefine the categories within which we analyze history. Past politics, for example, that most traditional of all forms of history, appears at first glance to be an almost totally male preserve. On the rare occasions when women did actively participate in politics, historians have tended to perceive them as disruptive. To many observers, the very presence of women in politics provides an index of social decay. This view is rooted in a narrow definition of politics as the overt and recorded activity of officially recognized leaders operating in the public arena. But women rarely have a place in the formal organizations of power, particularly not at its highest levels. When they do, by accident of birth and circumstance, they are "exceptional" women, who managed to survive and flourish in a male world. Historians have been fascinated by these women because of their pseudo-maleness. Thus, they attract special scrutiny for being unnatural: men in women's bodies at best, monsters at worst. In no case are they considered representative of women generically. This is a realistic assessment. The "exceptional" women viewed themselves as atypical; frequently they rejected or ignored contemporaneous efforts to advance women's status. Their lives remain exceptions that prove the rule and do not help us to understand the common experience of women in politics.

Politics more broadly and correctly defined, however, extends beyond the activity of a few dazzling personalities or the agreements made by a handful of leaders. It is a complex set of conflictual power relations between classes, regions, and religious systems struggling for control over scarce resources. Such a conceptual framework greatly expands the nature of the sources we have to draw upon. The letters, diaries, and memoirs of aristocratic and bourgeois women show their intense involvement in the affairs of their family, property, and class. Their strength waxes and wanes in relation to the degree of independent control they exert over property and the size and centralization of the state. This influence can be traced through firsthand reports, changes in family and property law, church history, and women's recorded political activity.

The political expression of peasant and working-class women, like that of all historically inarticulate classes, must be sought in other sources. Absent or underrepresented in formal organizations of power, frequently illiterate, these classes usually are noticed only when they protest. Women's role in rebellion, religious upheavals, or political revolutions can be traced through eyewitness accounts, police records, newspapers, pamphlets and broadsides, minutes of meetings, and organizational records. Women's revolutionary demands included both proposals for change and complaints about the status quo. Interestingly, the latter often reveal important material losses over time, not merely nostalgia for a glorified past. Further, the study of political activities by women in revolutionary situations provides us with a new perspective on the revolutionary process itself. Women's participation in protest movements follows a recurrent pattern. In the early stages of a movement, women are welcomed for their selfless dedication. But at the moment of victory, their enthusiasm is rechanneled from disruptive to stabilizing activities, consigning them once more to the home. Revolutionary men attempting to establish a liberated new order have clung to patriarchal values and traditional domestic arrangements. The social relation between the sexes appears to resist change unless women organize among themselves, even within revolutionary movements.

In the nineteenth century, women began to organize themselves somewhat independently of kin networks. Only then do we see sustained female political activity. This movement began among middle-class women, whose leisure, affluence, and social position permitted them partially to escape the confines of their homes. Beginning with charitable and religious causes, they gradually progressed to more self-oriented activities. This first wave of feminism deserves the attention given it for its major achievements: the expansion of women's education, property-law reform, and the suffrage victory. Yet these accomplishments must also be evaluated in their total historical context. Suffrage, for example, is more important when it is limited and linked to property ownership. It carries less weight in highly developed political systems than in loosely structured, decentralized ones. With massive, bureaucratized parties on the one hand and manipulation by corporate interests on the other, the modern voter lacks the real political power wielded by the landed aristocrats and merchants who selected representatives in nineteenth-century parliaments. At the legislative level, women's voice grows feebler still. The "club" system of parliamentary bargaining remains largely a male preserve and the proportion of female leaders remains insignificant. One might hypothesize that the general expansion of the political base has produced a decline in women's political influence relative to their male counterparts. We do not intend to imply that women have achieved no political gains, but only that we must assess these achievements in context rather than as absolutes. We ask, also, if these gains translate into practical, economic benefits.

A recurrent theme throughout several of the essays in this book suggests that while formal political action has won major advances, women's lives have been more profoundly affected by structural changes in society. Economic and social institutions appear to develop according to their own dynamic, relatively inaccessible to political manipulation. To discover the sources of change in women's roles and status, we are drawn to the study of the family.

In preindustrial society the most common mode of political activity for women has been family strategy for social mobility, an important nexus between politics and economics. The changing nature of such a nexus is itself a historical problem. Preliterate societies exhibit no clear division between political and economic, public and domestic spheres. "Domestic" activities (involving the home, its space, its members, and its work) were "public" and shared by the entire community. The clan was at once an economic and political entity, whose members shared its wealth and governance on a remarkably egalitarian basis. With the development of private property and political institutions to safeguard it, inequalities developed inside the clan, between families and along sex lines. The development of commercial classes, capitalism, and concomitant changes in production and social relations further widened the gap between public and domestic functions. Responsibilities formerly assumed by the family were surrendered to specialized public institutions. The consolidation of capital wealth by a few eroded the economic and political power of the average family, and women's role within the family declined commensurately. The political significance of the family contracted.

This erosion of women's familial power was paralleled in economic areas as well. In preindustrial society, the major concern of every generation was to preserve, augment, and transmit to future generations family property and status. More fundamentally, the family, often through the efforts of its women, provided its own subsistence. As economic and technological developments transformed society, the structure and functions of the family gradually shifted. The family in industrial society became a nonproducing collectivity of consumers, whose major responsibility was to provide emotional security for its members.

In both the producing and consuming forms of the family, women have played an active part. They have contributed to family income, allocated it, transformed it into consumable goods. They have influenced family inheritance and social mobility through birth control, the education of their children, selection of marriage partners for their children, and maintenance of kin networks. These functions, however, are not traceable in official chronicles or codified laws. One source of information on women's role in the family is demographic data, which note changes in age at marriage, criteria for selection of marriage partners, numbers of children born and surviving infancy, methods of birth control from infanticide through contraception, changing family life cycles, and migration statistics. Our best sources for demographic change are recent, since census data were not collected regularly until the nineteenth century. For earlier periods we must research indirect reports like baptismal certificates, hospital and asylum records, indices of nutrition and health such as harvest and butchering records, deeds, wills, tax registers, marriage contracts, and burial records. Using such sources, supplemented by first- or second-person reports, we can trace women's impact on family economy and, conversely, the effect of broader social patterns on women's experiential reality.

The search for women's role in past societies leads us to still other problems when we try to assess women's control over property and over their own labor. The sexual division of labor becomes more exaggerated with the accumulation of property in the hands of a new business elite. Not only does women's work become more distinct from men's, but it changes in a way that reduces women's ability to accumulate property and wield power. We ask therefore: What kind of work have women done? How was it evaluated? How did it fit into the total mode of production? of reproduction? How did women's expectations of work affect mechanization and specialization in specific industries? How did women's work relate to technological innovations, capitalization of manufacturing and trade, and the organization of production?

By focusing on these questions we add a new dimension to the debate on the Industrial Revolution. Although the impact of industrialization on women was uneven and depended on a multitude of variables, it now appears that the Industrial Revolution seriously reduced women's effective participation in production. An overview shows that women often predominate in stagnating industries while modernizing sectors engage men in new skills. If women do enter a new area of manufacturing, they do so at the bottom of its hierarchy. Thus, during the early stages of industrialization, women were eagerly recruited into the work force because their labor was so cheap. But male factory workers steadily replaced women even in the "women's" trades of spinning and weaving. An analysis of the impact of industrialization on women, however, cannot be limited to a study of factory women. Recent scholarship makes it clear that factory work occupied only a tiny fraction of all women. Far more important were changes that occurred in those sectors that traditionally employed large numbers of women: domestic service, agriculture, and the "sweated trades."

As indicated by the essays in this volume, a lively debate continues over the ultimate benefits of industrialization for women. Single women, it seems, did enjoy expanded economic opportunities. This, in turn, gave them at least the potential to increase their leverage within their families, save money for their own dowries, and choose husbands more independently. Working-class women generally also gained the opportunity to join together in extrafamilial alliances. Some women mobilized for collective action by establishing their own unions or cooperative societies. Others joined predominantly male unions — although women's low wages made them objects of considerable resentment by male workers. Still other women responded to the appeal of socialism, not only by joining the rank and file but also by participating actively as organizers and intellectuals in the international movement.

These opportunities for working-class single women must be balanced against new difficulties created for married women. Because the workplace moved away from the household and into the factory, married women with children found it nearly impossible to harmonize their domestic duties with gainful employment. Moreover, the scope of women's responsibilities in their households diminished. The wife no longer produced her family's food and clothing but instead purchased it with the wages earned by other members of her family. The caricature of the spendthrift woman arises from this shift in women's functions — as does our contemporary ambivalence about the value of homemaking.

The technological and social changes that swept through nineteenth-century Europe affected the atmosphere and internal politics of the middle-class home. While bourgeois women found themselves increasingly relegated to the domestic sphere, they also discovered new outlets for their energy and idealism. Nowhere is this double trend better illustrated than in the areas of charity and social work. Middle-class women, liberated from the more menial tasks of homemaking, ministered to the larger family of humanity. In so doing they created an escape for themselves and their daughters. In the twentieth century this area of social caring became a state-run occupation whose policies were determined by men. Again, a modernizing influence opened up new opportunities for women in its initial stages and then pushed them out of responsible positions. Yet in the long run, the impact of an expanding public-service sector on middle-class women paralleled the effect of industrialization on working-class women. Both developments provided some women with paid occupations, giving them the possibility of greater bargaining power in family decision making and the option of living independently of the traditional family altogether. However limited, new career options did encourage more permanent employment patterns and sponsored women's adherence to unions and professional associations. The second wave of feminism can be attributed in large measure to this heightened consciousness.

We are interested, however, in assessing the trends of women's work not only in relation to its own linear development and in relation to men's but also in relation to other aspects of women's lives. More questions crowd in: How does change in women's work patterns affect the internal dynamics of their families and their other social behavior and attitudes? Does it affect their wish to bear and care for children? their feelings about sexuality? their relations with each other? the development of their wider abilities and interests?

In the area of reproduction, we see first that as the total economic context changed, so did family economy, the contributions of family members to it, and, therefore, women's life cycles. Thus, in preindustrial times, work and family life were relatively integrated. Production and reproduction meshed, and women's lives suffered little hiatus from childbearing. With the development of the factory system, the home was eventually displaced as the workplace, so work and family life *dis*integrated.

For bourgeois women, the split tended to relegate them to the home, for which there developed a "science of domestic economy" enhanced by the "cult of true womanhood." For working-class women, the split was mirrored in the double burden of wage labor and housework, which could be assumed simultaneously or serially. Typically, the working woman dropped out of the work force during her childbearing years. For both middle- and working-class women, the social ideal now emphasized childrearing over childbearing. This shift from quantity to quality occurred for several reasons. For one, family size decreased with urbanization. With the decline in child labor required by an agricultural society, multitudes of children became liabilities rather than assets — mouths to feed rather than extra hands for work. The spread of public education further limited children's contribution to the family economy. Besides these incentives to reduce family size, more children survived infancy, guaranteeing family continuity with fewer pregnancies.

These demographic changes, plus women's restriction to the home, resulted in major emotional reorientations. As earning became the responsibility of the father, parenting became increasingly the task of the mother. She became the emotional facilitator for her family and the repository and guardian of society's morality. Bourgeois mothers had the time and standard of living to aspire to such a role and gradually the middle-class ideology of motherhood became the norm for the working class. This process was accomplished through various media, including the social work of the very women whose time had been freed by their exclusion from productive work and their own rejection of a purely domestic role. Although they themselves chose to leave the confines of their homes, these social workers still preached bourgeois values — which included a glorification of the home. Ironically, they became an important factor in the dissemination of the cult of domesticity to the working classes.

Similar contradictions have produced the recent crisis of identity experienced by women. The public assumption of functions that earlier were considered domestic and feminine has deprived the housewife of many traditional responsibilities. As "mother's work" is taken over by institutionalized education, health care, social work, and psychological counseling, women experience diminishing status within the home. Conflict is inevitable. Women who have opted for public roles will view the family as the source of potential oppression for all women; women who choose to remain identified with domestic responsibilities will resent institutional encroachments on their sphere. They will view feminist criticism of the family as endangering their feminine identity and role integrity.

Even more basic is the conflict women find within themselves as they confront their own feelings about these dual sources of identity. Self-doubt is inevitable whichever response women choose. Some will retreat from the problem by entrenching themselves even more firmly within the renewed mystique of homemaking and wifehood — seeking to escape the conflict by reaffirming their belief in their traditional role. These women may join the backlash against feminism. Yet at the same time an increasing number of women and men have begun to question the usefulness of a sexual division of labor and of personality traits. Why at this time have people begun to doubt the age-old stereotypes? Most obviously, the brute strength that traditionally defined masculinity loses its importance as machines assume most tasks requiring heavy labor or warfare. An increasingly managerial society requires socialization and skills once labeled "feminine," such as tact and the ability to empathize with and manipulate others. Whether closing a corporate merger, dealing with protesting workers, or lobbying for legislative proposals, psychological finesse is decisive. Society is forced to define masculinity along more androgynous lines. A similar androgynous movement has resulted from women's struggles to fashion a new identity. Besides learning to value themselves for their feminine attributes, women have adapted traits previously ascribed to men: ambition, competitiveness, and leadership. Even when women enter occupations and professions closely related to traditional female concerns (such as health care, social work, and education) they need "masculine" detachment and goal orientation in order to succeed. As a result of this integrative process, polarities of masculine and feminine traits dissolve and woman's bifurcated image likewise merges into a single human personality.

The gains of previous struggles — education, suffrage, increased civil equality — have helped to create a new woman, restive with her remaining disabilities and appalled by her historical losses. We, the "new women," are searching for a new identity with freer attitudes toward work, sexuality, family relationships, individual development, and sisterhood. We are trying to create a new social matrix that will allow, even nurture, realization of this identity. In this quest, we need to understand what brought us to this place. This book is in the service of that goal.

Notes

1. Berenice A. Carroll, "Mary Beard's *Woman as Force in History:* A Critique," *Woman: An Issue,* Little, Brown, Boston, 1972, p. 126.

1

Women in Egalitarian Societies

Eleanor Leacock

Inequality between the sexes in the present has necessarily been the starting point of any investigation of its origins. That is, one asks whether or not inequality has always existed and to what degree. We can never have full knowledge of the earliest social relations, but the outlines may be partially reconstructed with archaeological and anthropological data. Eleanor Leacock here attempts such a reconstruction through comparative examination of European archaeological evidence and anthropological studies of American Indians. The material suggests that these early societies practiced a primitive form of communism, marked by egalitarian economic and social organization. In spite of sexual division of labor, the entire group shared decision making and responsibility for children. The transformation into unequal and stratified societies was achieved by a social process in which sharing developed into barter, barter developed into trade and specialization of labor, and these in turn led to individually held wealth and power. This materially and culturally enriching process had the unforeseen result of changing the structure of human relations from egalitarian to hierarchical and exploitative. The communal kin group was undercut by conflicting economic and political ties. It was replaced by social strata composed of individual family units having parental responsibility for children. Women's role was relegated to private service. The first and most important step in the process that created social inequality between the sexes had taken place. The process itself set the outlines of a pattern that recurred, in more complex form, in later times.

Montagnais-Naskapi woman setting a rabbit snare. (Photo by Richard Leacock)

Popular images of the relations between women and men in primeval society are epitomized by the club-carrying "cave man" of the *New Yorker* cartoon who drags off his woman by the hair of her head. At a higher, supposedly scientific level, the writings of Robert Ardrey, Desmond Morris, and the like reinforce this image.[1] Behind the laughter at the cartoon, or behind whatever picture is being woven from bits and pieces of ethnographic data pulled out of context, the message remains basically the same: humans have always been aggressive and competitive, and men, being more so than women, have always been "dominant." The theme repeats, with variations, that our "primitive" or "animal nature" reflects the "law of the jungle," whereby might makes right. Our social problems arise because a fundamentally brutish human nature — so the argument runs — lies beneath the superficial gloss of "civilization," with its Golden Rule of "do unto others as you would have them do unto you," and the value our culture claims to place on human life and human individuality.

When, however, we weigh the data of social and physical anthropology, archaeology, and primatology in their entirety, rather than selecting from them arbitrarily, they tell a different story. Sociality, curiosity, and playfulness, not assertive competitiveness and aggressiveness, made it possible for a fairly small and defenseless creature to evolve into the human being that created many different ways of life around the world. Sociality, that is, an abounding desire to be close to others of the same species and an overriding interest in them, characterizes our primate relatives. Fighting and scrapping occur as subsidiary, not primary, motives. Humanity did not evolve from an innately aggressive forebear as postulated by Thomas Hobbes. By hindsight it is clear that it *could* not have done so. The basis for the successful evolution of human beings was the group life that both required and made possible cooperative patterns. In turn, cooperation led to and became dependent upon the development of refined tools and utensils, and the elaboration of language.[2]

Much has been written about the fact that our primate ancestors turned to hunting for meat as a supplement to foraging for vegetable foods. One reads that the killing of animals at an early stage in human history led to deeply embedded aggressive drives. The argument has been persuasive, especially since it can be used to rationalize the dominance drives of ambitious politicians and the powerful financiers who back them, by blaming their actions on *our* human nature. People forget that, among animals, to kill other species does not lead to killing their own kind, but that to kill one's own species is specifically *human.* One must ask, what significance does killing animals actually have for people who depend on hunting to live?

A few peoples, beyond the reaches of industrialization, until recently sustained themselves largely by gathering wild vegetable foods and by hunting. They paid great attention to hunting skills, but aggression as we know it in our society was played down. Hunting was usually hard work — certainly at times an exciting challenge, but also drudgery. The feeling for the animals killed, especially for large animals, did not resemble our egoistic pride in conquest; it revealed instead attitudes of gratitude and respect. Animal gods were commonly honored, and in stories humans and animals interacted closely; they intermarried, gave birth to one another, taught one another, and entered into compacts sealing their relations. Such peoples cooperated in the obtaining of meat and shared the animals procured. From the Bushman gatherers and hunters of the Kalahari Desert in southwest Africa to the Eskimo sea mammal hunters of the Arctic, the social arrangements of foraging peoples were similar. Societies that lived by gathering and by hunting (and fishing) were cooperative. People shared food, and thought of greed and selfishness much as we might think of mentally ill or criminal behavior. People made and valued fine possessions, but as much to give away as to keep.

People did not follow a single leader but participated in the making of decisions important to them. Social codes stressed the importance of muting animosities and of restraining jealousy and anger. Sometimes personal enmity was ritualized, as in the Eskimo drum duel, where two opponents hurled insults back and forth at one another in song. People criticized each other through banter and teasing, which usually led to outbursts of laughter in which even the person being criticized joined. When serious fights led to a person hurting or killing another, atonement, not punishment, was sought. Warfare was rare or unknown. When it occurred, it took the form of short-lived raids, not organized conflict for lands, slaves, or tribute. Two hunting peoples have recently been filmed and written about, the gentle and cheerful monkey-hunting Tasaday of the Philippines, and the unfriendly and grimly competitive Ik of Kenya.[3] It is the Tasaday, until recently living their own free life, who give us the better approximation of our gathering and hunting forebears, for the Ik have been removed from their hunting lands and, totally demoralized, they seem bent on collective suicide.

Private property, social stratification, political subjugation, and institutionalized warfare with standing armies are all social inventions that evolved through the course of human history. They do not automatically express some innate human nature. Otherwise the vast majority of us today would not seek so hard to work out some minimally satisfying, secure, and friendly way of living but would wholeheartedly revel in the competition, aggression, and violence allowed and encouraged by our social structure.

The institutionalized inequalities so familiar to us, the dominance hierarchies and the constant concern with large-scale warfare, first arose in the fourth millennium B.C. during what has been called the *urban revolution.* In the long course of human history, various egalitarian gathering and hunting, and later horticultural, societies elaborated ritually on various forms of social and ceremonial rank, but still maintained, as far as can be determined, the equal right of all to basic sources of livelihood. Then, as a result of human ingenuity and inventiveness, specialization of work gradually developed and removed part of the population from basic food production. Barter became transformed into commerce and traders into merchant intermediaries. Priest-chiefs increasingly manipulated the goods that were stored with them for redistribution, and what had been ritual rank was transformed into exploitative elitism. Equal access to land became restricted as free lands were turned into privately controlled terraced, irrigated, fertilized, or otherwise worked fields. In short, class systems were created, although not quickly or without resistance and attempts to preserve cooperative mores. Fully stratified societies emerged first in southwest Asia and northeast Africa, in Mesopotamia, Egypt, Jerusalem, Persia. In the Western hemisphere, urban, stratified societies evolved independently among the precursors of the Incas, Mayas, and Aztecs. In subsequent millennia, mercantile urban centers with stratified, competitive social and political forms repeatedly developed from societies that had been organized around egalitarian clans, as reconstructions of early history in Africa, Asia, Europe, and the New World indicate.

Nearly 5,000 years after cities arose in Asia and Africa, the next major social transformation, the Industrial Revolution, took shape. Inextricably bound up with European colonial and imperial expansion, the Industrial Revolution brought to a close the relative autonomy of the earth's myriad cultural traditions. Gradually, the peoples of all continents became enmeshed in a single world system of military, political, and economic exploitative relations. A constant theme recurs in careful ethnohistorical reconstructions of the many lifeways developed by different peoples. Archaeological data, accounts by early explorers, missionaries, and traders, as well as later ethnographic material, reveal that systematized cooperativeness has repeatedly been undercut by systematized competitiveness. Fortunately, increasing numbers of the world's people are now seeking to create new forms of cooperation. It is urgent indeed that we succeed, lest we render our planet unfit for life.

Women in Classless Societies

Where does this leave us in relation to the social status and role of women in classless societies? What insights do anthropological data offer us in the effort to understand the basis for women's present low status and the sources for change?

The dictum most commonly expressed in contemporary anthropological writings is blunt: the general egalitarianism of nonstratified societies did not fully apply to women. Anthropologists agree that women in such societies were by no means oppressed in the ways that developed in the classical patriarchal societies of the Mediterranean world and the Orient. Nonetheless, in the view of most anthropologists who write on the subject, women have always been to some extent subordinate to men. Hence, one may read such statements as: "It is a common sociological truth that in all societies authority is held by men, not women"; "Men tend regularly to dominate women"; "Subordination of females happens to occur with remarkable persistence in a great variety of cultures"; "Men have always been politically and economically dominant over women"; and "Regardless of the form of social structure, men are always in the ascendency." [4] It is admitted that the widespread institution of matrilineality — the reckoning of descent through women — enhanced women's status, but, it is argued, matrilineality merely substituted the authority of maternal uncles and elder brothers for that of fathers and husbands. A rough and ready equality of the sexes is generally seen as existing among foragers, but men are still said to have slightly higher status. "Men's occupations are always the focus of greater cultural interest and prestige. . . . Women can exert influence outside the family only indirectly through their influence on their kinsmen. Therefore, however important the woman's work may be to the domestic economy, it does not elicit the public esteem accorded the work of men." Women's role is always "private," men's "public," it is asserted.

> Women's work is . . . bounded by the domestic framework, concerned with the familial, private sectors of society. Roles within the public sphere are the province of men, and the public sphere is the locus of power and prestige. . . . In effect, whatever the nature of women's work, or its economic value, it is never invested with glamour, excitement, or prestige.[5]

Contemporary studies of women in history and society promise to force the revision of such views. The thesis that a stage of egalitarian economic and social organization — primitive communism — preceded the emergence of stratification in human history has only recently become widely accepted by anthropologists — not long ago such a notion was laughed at as nineteenth-century naiveté. Careful analysis reveals the influence women held in such societies and the great measure of autonomy with which they functioned. It is hoped, then, that the next decade will see the stereotyped characterization of women's roles in terms of the cliché of male dominance discredited.

Four main distortions perpetuate confusion about women in classless societies. First, societies that are not part of the specific historical traditions of either Europe or the Orient are commonly lumped in a single category, designated "primitive." Yet stratified and urban societies had emerged or were emerging in many parts of the world at the time of European expansion. Only a few of the societies called "primitive" retained fully egalitarian institutions at that time. Therefore, general statements about women's status in "primitive" society reflect the wide variations that existed around the world and deflect attention from the analysis of their status in truly egalitarian societies.

Second, the cultures that anthropologists describe are not autonomous for the most part, but exist in the context of a colonial world. Generalizations about tribal cultures are too commonly drawn from twentieth-century ethnographies without account being taken of colonialism and imperialism and their worldwide effects. The societies that American Indian elders described to early anthropologists also do not represent aboriginal life in unchanged form. Trade with Europeans, conquest and resistance, work and in some cases enslavement, intermarriage, and missionizing, all created problems with which native Americans have been dealing for the last 400 years or more. In Africa, for two, three, or four hundred years (depending upon the region) peoples were willy-nilly involved, directly or indirectly, in the development of capitalist Europe and an imperialist world order. They traded and politicked; went to work on plantations and in mines to pay newly imposed taxes; were missionized or themselves became missionaries; were conquered or enslaved or otherwise subjugated; and resisted and fought for political independence.

Patriarchal practices and attitudes brought by the Europeans who imposed imperialist control accelerated the decline in the status of women in several ways. Public positions of prestige and influence were relegated to men, first informally by European emissaries and traders, later formally by colonial administrators. Women's rights to land were eroded or abolished altogether. Reciprocal economic ties within clans and lineages were undermined, and women and children became dependent on individual, wage-earning male family heads. Finally, missionaries extolled European ideals and exhorted women to obey and be sexually faithful for life to a single man.

The third impediment to an objective cross-cultural analysis of women's roles is the bias that books like this are seeking to overcome. Anthropologists have on the whole been men who interview other men, and assume that the data collected thereby are sufficient for understanding a society. Women anthropologists have generally gone along, and only recently have begun in any numbers, as women, to examine the distortions that have resulted. As a group of women anthropologists recently put it:

> Anthropology, at its present stage of development, is lacking a theory of women that is complex enough to account for almost anything we do. Our mostly male colleagues have been content to describe women's behavior as men would like it to be. A lot of essential questions have never been asked — the result of male anthropologists' chewing the fat with male informants has been a view of women that proceeds almost directly from male norms. In part, this state of affairs grows out of the lack of semantic differentiation for what women do and are. But, beyond this, it involves the startling failure of some anthropologists to comprehend that women are as much people as men are . . .[6]

The fourth difficulty in arriving at a clear picture of sex roles and functions in preclass societies follows from an ethnocentric approach to social organization. Two pervasive and misleading assumptions are: 1) that male-female dyads exist as the core of basic social-economic units in all types of societies and function with respect to dependent children much as they do in Western society; and 2) that social action is everywhere divided into a public, formal, and politically crucial male sphere, and a private, familial, and informal female sphere, much as it is in our society. Where data are thin, the ethnographer can always dispatch the discussion of women's activities with a paragraph or two about producing and preparing food and caring for children and home. In monograph after monograph such allusions recur with a lack of rigor or explicitness, although the restriction of women to these activities may be belied by a close reading between the lines of the monograph itself. The practice perpetuates the conventional wisdom reflected in casual generalizations about, in the words of one text, the "normal importance of men."[7]

Given these problems, is it possible to define with any certainty what the role of women was in egalitarian societies? The answer is yes; the foundation for an adequate definition of women's roles cross-culturally is now being laid as anthropologists (mostly but not exclusively women) turn to collecting new data on women's participation in different kinds of societies and to reexamining allusions to women scattered through old data. The picture that emerges falls, in my estimation, within the broad outlines proposed by Frederick Engels in his now classic *Origin of the Family, Private Property and the State*: the initial egalitarianism of human society included women, and their status relative to men declined as they lost their economic autonomy. Women's work was initially public, in the context of band or village collectives. It was transformed into private service within the confines of the individual family as part of the process whereby, through the specialization of work and increase of trade, both women and men lost direct control of the food and other goods they produced and economic classes emerged. The process was slow, and one that women apparently banded together to resist in various ways, judging from what we know of West African women's organizations and of patterned hostility between the sexes in Melanesia and other areas.

In Europe, no enclaves of foraging or horticultural peoples were left by the urban and industrial revolutions as direct representatives of egalitarian lifeways. For such cultures we have only archaeological evidence. Written historical records, however, indicate two broadly differing streams in the later social history of Europe: 1) that of the Mediterranean world, where, as the following chapter indicates, the classical patriarchy of the ancient Middle East finally succeeded in submerging what had been the formal public participation of women in social, political, and religious matters; and 2) that of the northern European periphery described by Tacitus, where women, though far from equal to men, nonetheless retained a relatively higher status than in Mediterranean cultures, a status that persisted long enough to have its effect on early medieval society. Tacitus noted that the "Britons make no distinction of sex in their appointment of commanders," and his assessment of the "reverence" felt for women leaders among the Germans is interesting. He referred to it as "untainted by servile flattery or any pretence of turning women into goddesses," which suggests a real respect, rather than the self-serving pattern of placing women on a pedestal as evidence of upper-class status.[8]

Mediterranean patriarchal traditions and northern traditions that suggested earlier, more egalitarian mores were both late, of course, in terms of human history as a whole. Archaeological remains indicate that they were preceded by egalitarian horticultural societies, that were in turn preceded by societies based on some combination of fishing, hunting, and gathering of wild vegetable foods. In order to make educated guesses about women's changing roles among these past European peoples, it is necessary to describe societies in parts of the world where egalitarian forms were not destroyed as early.

In the Western hemisphere, urbanization and stratification developed in Mexico and the Andes, but by the time of Columbus's voyages had not engulfed the far-flung peoples of what are now the northern United States and Canada. Therefore, we can look to these groups for an understanding of how egalitarian societies functioned. I shall take as examples the Montagnais-Naskapi hunters of the Labrador Peninsula in eastern Canada and the Iroquois villagers of northern New York State, for early writers gave some indication of how these peoples lived in early colonial days before their lives were completely transformed. This is particularly true of the Montagnais-Naskapi, for in the winter of 1633–1634 a Jesuit missionary, Paul le Jeune, lived with a Montagnais band and wrote a detailed account of his experiences in his mission report to his superiors in Paris. Le Jeune's letters afford an invaluable record of the mores and ethics of an egalitarian people, and he made explicit references to the prestige and autonomy of all individuals, women as well as men.

The Montagnais-Naskapi, Native Americans

The Montagnais-Naskapi lived almost entirely on fish and game in pre-Columbian times. The collecting of roots and berries was minimal. People moved camp many times during the winter, but during the short summer fairly large numbers came together at lake and river shores, to visit and court, and to prepare snowshoes, canoes, and clothing for the next winter. Some fifteen or twenty people, several nuclear families, lived together in a large skin- or bark-covered lodge. In the winter two or three lodge groups traveled and camped together or somewhat near each other. They would join with others from time to time for short periods of feasting if hunting was good or would turn to one another for help if the hunt was poor.

There was no division of labor except by sex, and all adults participated in the procuring of food and manufacture of equipment necessary for life in the north. In general, women worked leather and bark, while men worked wood, with each making the tools they needed. For instance, women cut strips of leather and wove them onto the snowshoe frames that were made by men, and women covered with birch bark the canoe frames the men made. Women skinned game animals and cured the hides for clothing, moccasins, and lodge coverings. Everyone joined in putting up lodges; the women went into the forest to chop down lodge poles, while men cleared the snow from the ground where a lodge was to be erected.

All able-bodied members of the camp, women, men, and older children, participated in collective hunts, when migrating caribou were driven into compounds or across rivers to be speared from canoes. Men in twos and threes hunted solitary game in the forests. Women hunted occasionally when they wanted meat and the men were away, or if they wished to join their husbands on a hunting trip. Both sexes procured small game around camp, setting traps and snares. Cooking also involved the cooperation of both sexes. Large animals were roasted in pits with hot stones placed on top, or cut in chunks to be skewered on stakes held over the fire, or boiled in bark dishes into which heated stones were placed. With the advent of the copper pot, a valued trade item from the sixteenth century on, meat could be simmered over an open fire without requiring much labor or attention. Everyday cooking fell to the women, although men helped prepare food for feasts or cooked for themselves when on a hunt.

Virtually everyone married, although divorce was easy and could be obtained at the desire of either partner. An inept or lazy person might have trouble keeping a spouse, and a man might be ridiculed for doing work usually done by women as evidence that he could not keep a wife. Some men had more than one wife, a practice that the seventeenth-century missionaries deplored. Le Jeune wrote, "Since I have been preaching among them that a man should have only one wife, I have not been well received by the women; for, since they are more numerous than the men, if a man can only marry one of them, the others will have to suffer." [9]

Children observed almost the entire gamut of work, recreation, and religious life that went on around them; their training was therefore largely informal as they played, helped, listened, and watched. While the care of infants devolved mainly on their mothers, fathers were not inept or impatient with small children. Le Jeune wrote of a man soothing a sick baby with what he considered "the love of a mother" as well as "the firmness of a father." [10] Over three centuries later, I observed the unquestioning patience with which a man sat cradling his sick and fretful infant in his arms, crooning over it for hours, while his wife occupied herself at the long and demanding task of smoking a deerskin.

Le Jeune wrote of the "patience" shown in daily life, and of how well people agreed. "You do not see any disputes, quarrels, enmities, or reproaches among them," he stated, as people went about their work without "meddling" with one another.[11] During the summers of 1950 and 1951, I myself witnessed an ease in the course of daily interaction that persisted despite the fact that the economic basis for Indian autonomy was fast being whittled away, and there were growing reasons for new anxieties. Not that everyone was at peace: a woman in one camp had a reputation for always scolding; a man in another became drunk whenever he could procure molasses or sugar for making beer. But it was beautiful to see the sense of group responsibility that still obtained for children, and the sense of easy autonomy in relationships unburdened by centuries of training in deferential behavior by sex and status.

Not surprisingly, however, there was an evident feeling of constraint when whites were around. In an earlier period, this had not been the case. Le Jeune described the bawdiness, the banter and kidding, the love of sharp talking and voracious eating that characterized relaxed periods in the daily life of the Montagnais-Naskapi in the early seventeenth century. "They have neither gentleness nor courtesy in their utterance," he wrote, "and a Frenchman could not assume the accent, the tone, and the sharpness of their voices without becoming angry, yet they do not." [12] To his dismay, both sexes indulged freely in language that had "the foul odor of the sewers," [13] and in the ribald teasing that to his surprise was usually taken with great good humor by the victims themselves. Today we understand ridicule as an important means of reinforcing group mores in a society devoid of formal controls. As le Jeune saw it,

> Their slanders and derision do not come from malicious hearts or from infected mouths, but from a mind which says what it thinks in order to give itself free scope, and which seeks gratification from everything, even from slander and mockery.[14]

Some observers said of Montagnais-Naskapi women, as they said of other native American women, that they were virtual slaves. Their hard work and the lack of ritualized formalities surrounding them contrasted sharply with ideals of courtesy for women in the French and British bourgeois family and were taken as evidence of low social status. Those who knew the Indians well reported otherwise. "The women have great power here," le Jeune wrote, and exhorted the men to assert themselves. "I told him then that he was the master, and that in France women do not rule their husbands." [15] Another Jesuit father stated, "The choice of plans, of undertakings, of journeys, of winterings, lies in nearly every instance in the hands of the housewife." [16]

It is important to recognize that these decisions about movements were not private family affairs but were community decisions about the main business of the group. There were no formal chiefs or superordinate economic or political bodies to which people had to defer, either with or without direct orders being given. In fact, the Jesuits bemoaned the independence of Indian life. Le Jeune complained, "Alas, if someone would stop the wanderings of the Savages, and give authority to one of them to rule the others, we could see them converted and civilized in a short time." [17] Recurrent themes in the seventeenth-century letters and reports of the *Jesuit Relations* were the attempts to establish the authority of elected chiefs over their bands and of husbands over their wives.

Spokespeople for a group vis-à-vis outsiders were those respected for their rhetorical abilities. Their influence was personal only. They would be ridiculed if they tried to exert any power in their group. Le Jeune wrote that the Indians "cannot endure in the least those who seem desirous of assuming superiority over the others; they place all virtue in a certain gentleness or apathy." [18] Knowledgeable people would come forth to lead the hunting groups, but their responsibilities as temporary chiefs would terminate with the end of a hunting trip. Shamans, religious practitioners who communicated with the various gods, held no formal power, but merely personal influence. Formerly, women as well as men became shamans. One Jesuit father tried to stop a powerful female shaman who was rallying her people to fight against the Iroquois. She drew a knife and threatened to kill him if he did not stop interfering.

A lack of formalized authority was possible since the small groups that lived together and depended upon each other shared common interests in group survival and well-being. Also, people could easily leave one group and join another if they wished, a flexibility that enabled those who felt animosities toward others to move away before too great discomfort or disruption occurred. Anger might burst out in violence or even lead to murder, but it could be handled by separation. At worst, then, personal animosities functioned at a distance. Illness was sometimes attributed to the manipulation of supernatural forces by a personal enemy.

The kind of power over others familiar to our society did not govern egalitarian societies. Since we find it difficult, however, to interpret how such societies did in fact function, we commonly project the terms of our own social order upon them, an error especially common with respect to the status of women. As noted before, by failing to collect adequate data on women or to interpret data from the vantage point of women, anthropologists may all too casually distort the true state of affairs. The kind of statement le Jeune has made available remains rare; most of the time one must read between the lines of ethnographic accounts for indications of women's actual roles. When one does, assumptions about brutal men pushing women around among hunting peoples become revealed for what they are — contemporary mythology.

Early Hunting Peoples of Europe

In Europe, the few hints left about the life of even very early humans, the Neanderthal people who preceded modern humanity there as elsewhere, confirm the essentially social nature of human evolution. Several families shared single large dwellings in the community sites that have been found, and the infirm were cared for, as shown, for example, by a skeleton of a relatively old arthritic cripple in one site, and in another, one of an older man whose right arm had been amputated when young. Writing of an unusually rich find in Iraq, where one Neanderthal was buried with flowers and six others were found, the archaeologist Ralph Solecki makes a comment that applies as readily to Neanderthal sites in eastern Europe:

> The picture of the lone stalker cannot be ruled out in the case of the Neanderthal but, since these people lived in a communal setting, it would

> be more natural for them to have engaged in communal hunting. And the fact that their lame and disabled . . . had been cared for . . . is excellent testimony for communal living and cooperation.[19]

Cannibalism in some instances may have been practiced, but ceremonial group burials suggest it was highly ritualized. Ritual cannibalism in later times has been practiced widely, sometimes on respected enemies, sometimes as part of the funeral service of dead relatives.

The cave paintings executed by early modern humans, the Cro-Magnon successors of the Neanderthals, tell us more. They reveal a respect for the animals that were hunted and an appreciation of their beauty that concurs with what we know to be felt by recent hunters. Some contemporary theorists stress the ritualization of the hunt and the importance of male hunters, to the detriment of women, among our early ancestors. However, cave paintings suggest a ceremonial life in which both women and men participated, and the numerous female figurines, ranging from very fat to almost sticklike but always very stylized, indicate the ritual importance of women. No comparable male figurines were made, though paintings of men were. It could well be argued that female figurines need not imply women's high status; ubiquitous representations of the Virgin Mary in Catholic countries do not, nor do the endless representations of the female form in our own media. However, the link between ideology and behavior is necessarily far more direct among egalitarian peoples than in hierarchical societies, where the glossing over of inequality and exploitation with ambiguous and contradictory ritual and rhetoric is elaborately institutionalized. Upper Paleolithic society was egalitarian; burials yield no evidence of appreciable status differences. All told, we have every reason to assume that autonomy and prestige for women obtained among early European hunters as they formerly did among other hunting and gathering peoples.

Generally, foraging and hunting as ways of life eventually gave ground to agricultural and/or pastoral economies. In the Middle East, the domestication of plants was developed some 13,000 years ago, presumably by women who gathered and processed wild seeds. Horticulture as a way of life spread northward into Europe, as evidenced by village remains of grain-growing peoples. These societies retained their earlier egalitarianism; the class distinctions revealed by differences in dwellings and burials took time to develop.

What kind of life did early European villagers lead? What roles did women play? The individual histories of different peoples and their cultures vary widely, yet certain broad similarities in social structure characterize known egalitarian horticultural societies. For an ethnological insight into such a society, we turn to a group whose history is better documented than that of most horticultural peoples — the Iroquois, native Americans of New York State.

The Ho-de-no-sau-nee, or People of the Long House

The People of the Long House, known as the Iroquois, included from west to east in New York State the Nun-da-wa-o-no, or Great Hill People (Seneca), the Gwe-u-gweh-o-no, or People at the Mucky Land (Cayuga), the O-non-da-ga-o-no, or People on the Hills (Onondaga), the O-na-yote-ka-o-no, or Granite People (Oneida), and the Ga-ne-a-go-o-no, or People Possessors of the Flint (Mohawk), as well as later, to the south of the Oneida, the Dus-ga-o-weh-o-no, or Shirt-Wearing People (Tuscarora). Recently, a group of Mohawks, along with members of other Indian nations, has moved back onto a piece of former Mohawk land in the Eagle Lake area of the Adirondack State Park. They wish to return, in their words, "to the cooperative system of our ancestors," and to re-create "a people's government" with broad community participation in decision making. These contemporary pioneers come from urban as well as rural areas, but they differ from other cooperative movements primarily in their sense of their history and former traditions.

At the time of European intrusion in the sixteenth century, the Iroquois lived in villages of 2,000 people and more, and worked as gardeners and hunters. The women farmed, using digging sticks and hoes with deer scapula blades. They planted some fifteen varieties of maize, as many as sixty different kinds of beans, and eight types of squash. They also collected wild fruits and nuts, roots, and edible or medicinal leaves. The men hunted deer, bear, and small game, and fished and took birds, using a variety of snares, traps, and nets, as well as bows and arrows. Both sexes worked together to build the fairly permanent large, bark-shingled frame houses that were shared by up to twenty-five families. These longhouses had anterooms at either end for storage and a row of fireplaces down the center. Families that lived across from each other used the same fireplace, and back from the fireplaces, family sleeping quarters were set off from each other by partitions.

During the course of the sixteenth and seventeenth centuries, the Iroquois became heavily involved in the fur trade, and when they exhausted the beaver in their homelands, they either acted as intermediaries in the trade with outlying peoples or fought with them to extend their own sphere of operation. They became the enemies of the Montagnais, and in the competition between the French and English for control of American lands that came to a head during the eighteenth century the Iroquois allied with the English and the Montagnais with the French.

By the nineteenth century, when the anthropologist Lewis Henry Morgan wrote *League of the Ho-De-No-Sau-Nee or Iroquois,* published in 1851, longhouse life was a distant memory, although the longhouse remained a strong symbol of the still functioning Council of the Confederacy. Fundamental changes had been taking place in Iroquois society since the sixteenth century, following from the fur trade and the warfare engendered by competing colonial powers and by the loss of Indian lands to them. The confederacy of the six tribes acted as a powerful unifying force, and the formal powers of the council increased in order that it might deal effectively with the political and economic rivalries and pressures of the Dutch, French, and British. At the same time, however, the fur trade enabled economically independent entrepreneurs to detach themselves from responsibilities toward their people. The effect was eventually to undermine the previously unchallenged communism practiced by the families sharing a longhouse, a process aided both by missionary teaching and governmental policies. Descriptions of Iroquois society, therefore, and especially of women's position, abound in contradictions, as people with different viewpoints and sources of information make judgments at different points in time.

That women at one time held a relatively high status in Iroquois society, however, no one questions. The Iroquois counted descent matrilineally, a common practice among horticultural peoples, and usufruct rights to clan lands passed down from mother to daughter. A man usually moved into his wife's household when he married and could be sent home if he displeased her. The matrons of a longhouse controlled the distribution of the food and other stores that made up the wealth of the group; they nominated and could depose the sachems or chiefs that represented each tribe in the Council of the Confederacy; and they "had a voice upon all questions" brought before the clan councils.[20] Women and men held in equal numbers the important positions of Keepers of the Faith, influential people who admonished others for moral infractions and sometimes reported them to the council for public exposure. Compensation to her kinfolk for a murdered woman was twice that for a murdered man. An early eighteenth-century missionary, Lafitau, writing either of women among the Iroquois or the similar Huron, or both, stated that "All real authority is vested in them. . . . They are the souls of the Councils, the arbiters of peace and of war." [21] Well over a century later, Reverend Wright, a missionary to the Seneca, wrote:

> The women were the great power among the clans, as everywhere else. They did not hesitate, when occasion required, "to knock off the horns," as it was technically called, from the head of a chief, and send him back to the ranks of the warriors.[22]

In his book *The Inevitability of Patriarchy,* however, Steven Goldberg three times makes reference to the statement made by Lewis Henry Morgan that "the Indian regarded women as the inferior, the dependent, and the servant of man, and from nurture and habit, she actually considered herself to be so." [23] Morgan also wrote that women's influence

> did not reach outward to the affairs of the gens [clan], phratry [grouping of clans], or tribe, but seems to have commenced and ended with the household. This view is quite consistent with the life of patient drudgery and of general subordination to the husband which the Iroquois wife cheerfully accepted as the portion of her sex.[24]

How do these statements square with the previous account of women's high status among the Iroquois?

Part of the answer lies in the changes that took place as women's control of the longhouse became replaced by their dependence on wage-earning husbands in the context of the individual nuclear family. Such institutions as the dormitories where adolescent girls had lived and courted their lovers, alluded to disapprovingly in sixteenth- and early seventeenth-century accounts, were not even a memory by Morgan's time. Chastity had since then been enjoined for unmarried women, along with the double standard and the public whipping of women for adultery.

Part of the discrepancy in evaluations of Iroquois women's status also lies in the failure to understand their control over the household in its full significance. In modern times, to speak of women's high position in the household and of their prestige and influence in male councils would imply no more than the usual power behind the throne, whereby women manipulate their families to gain some measure of control over their lives in a fundamentally patriarchal society. In the Iroquois case, however, the fact that the households constituted the communities meant that women's decision-making power over the production and distribution of food and other goods gave them a large measure of control over the group economy itself. Such decisions did not have the private character they have in our society, where production and distribution of any importance are carried on by corporate business, and power lies with complex and formidable institutions far beyond the community.

Council decisions were not backed up with the kind of power held by a modern state, but rather expressed group consensus in relation to inter-village affairs and policies toward outside groups. In a paper on women's position among the Iroquois, Judith Brown gives an example of the practical power inhering in their economic role: they could choose to support or to restrain a proposed war party by agreeing to furnish, or by withholding, necessary supplies. Were societies like the Iroquois, then, matriarchal? The answer is yes if the term means that women held public authority in major areas of group life. The answer is no if the term alludes to a mirror image of Judeo-Christian and Oriental patriarchy, where power in the hands of men (or an occasional woman) at the top of hierarchical structures is reflected in the petty power men exercise over their wives in individual households.

In precolonial Iroquois society, it was necessary to regularize the production and distribution of food by and among hundreds of villagers who lived together. This must have lessened somewhat the kind of personal autonomy that characterized Montagnais-Naskapi life. Nonetheless, Iroquois society remained basically communal and egalitarian. The artistic, ritual, and other cultural elaborations that a settled life made possible were participated in by everyone according to interest. People of personal prestige and influence lived, worked, and ate along with everyone else. At worst, prisoners of war who were adopted into a clan might have to do the more tiresome chores for a while, but they partook of the same food and housing as the others and could with time win a respected place in the group. In his classic work *Ancient Society,* Morgan wrote:

> All the members of an Iroquois gens were personally free and they were bound to defend each other's freedom; they were equal in privileges and in personal rights, the sachems and chiefs claiming no superiority .... [This] serves to explain that sense of independence and personal dignity universally an attribute of Indian character.[25]

Morgan, however, referred to the Iroquois gens as a "brotherhood"; although he recognized the high status of women in such a society, he did not perceive the full significance of their parallel "sisterhood."

Horticultural Society in Europe

The archaeological remains of the European horticultural societies that preceded what is known from written history look much like the remains of Iroquois-type villages. The Danubian I peoples of the early third millennium B.C. in central Europe were horticulturalists who used stone tools, and, in the words of the eminent European prehistorian V. Gordon Childe, lived in "commodious and substantial rectangular houses from 10 to 40 m in length and 6 to 7.5 m wide." Childe stated that "the 'household' must have been more like a clan than a pairing family," and he described the culture as "peaceful" and "democratic." There were few weapons, and "no hint of chiefs concentrating the communities' wealth." Some of the early northern European peoples, such as those of Denmark in the first part of the second millennium B.C., also dwelt in large frame houses. Others lived in clusters of small one-room houses. In both instances, remains indicate egalitarian societies.[26]

Successors of egalitarian villagers, however, began to show evidences of stratification, with chiefly dwellings and burials much more elaborate than those of the common folk. Metal tools became important and were traded from the south, and warfare increased. Childe wrote of the central European Danubian III peoples of about 2000 B.C.:

> Settlements were often planted on hilltops as well as in the valleys, and were frequently fortified. Competition for land assumed a bellicose character, and weapons such as battle-axes became specialized for warfare. The consequent preponderence of the male members in the communities may account for the general disappearance of female figurines. Part of the new surplus population may have sought an outlet in industry and trade; imported substances such as Baltic amber, Galician flint and copper began to be distributed more regularly than heretofore. Warriors would appreciate more readily than cultivators the superiority of metal, and chiefs may already have been concentrating surplus wealth to make the demand for metal effective.[27]

The accounts by Tacitus of central and northern European societies described women's position as higher than in the classical patriarchies of the Mediterranean world, though below that of men, a decline that presumably developed slowly over the some two millennia following Danubian III times. In connection with certain Danubian III sites, Childe stated that the female figurines, so common in earlier levels, "are no more in evidence." He continued, "The old ideology has been changed. That may reflect a change from a matrilineal to a patrilineal organization of society." [28] In Europe, then, as in so much of the world, women's position was transformed from early autonomy and equality to one of lesser status and, subsequently, of oppression. What was responsible for this transition?

The theme that innate human drives toward dominance, and especially the aggressiveness of males, have determined human history threads through most answers given to this question. Precise formulations vary, but in general, arguments run along the following lines: Human populations recurrently grow to the limits of their different environments, given the technical skills at their disposal. This leads to competition for resources, and to warfare. As the technological means for producing food and other necessities improve, populations grow, and so does the competition for land. Warfare increases, which enables the more ambitious and aggressive men to acquire surplus wealth and assert dominant status over others in their group and over women, as well as over other groups. From the viewpoint of recent history, the assumption seems reasonable enough. From the perspective of cultural history as a whole, however, the argument turns out to be oversimplified to the point of serious distortion; it does not really work.

The Transformation of Egalitarian Society

As mentioned earlier, everything known about foraging life indicates that human hunters and gatherers were not engaged in an unremitting struggle with each other for survival as they wrested food from a stingy world and faced the problem of population always growing to the very limit of its resources. Human society evolved through the application of ingenuity and the expression of sociality, not merely some drive to dominate. With skills and knowledge, early humans were able to use an extremely wide variety of plants and animals, and they moved into new environments as they learned how to handle new resources. Fighting was apparently disliked and avoided by foraging societies, and such societies persisted far longer than have the warring societies that succeeded them. All indications are that there was abundant leisure for the sheer fun of talking, joking, and storytelling in foraging/hunting societies, and for artistic and ritual pursuits. Le Jeune complained of the Montagnais that "their life is passed in eating, laughing, and making sport of each other, and of all the people they know." [29]

Furthermore, group size and composition was apparently maintained at a level well within the limits of environmental resources. All evidence points to conscious population limitation in egalitarian societies. A variety of means was employed, some more, some less effective: periods of abstinence, prolonged lactation, herbs for birth control or abortion, mechanical attempts at abortion, and, as a last resort, infanticide. Infants who followed siblings so closely as to overburden the mother, and hence the group, were not allowed to live. The Jesuits commented on the early Montagnais families, with two, three, and rarely more than four children, by contrast with the large families of the French.[30]

The transformation from egalitarian society to societies built on inequality and stratification was not due to a psychobiological combination of dominance drives and population pressures. Instead, a profoundly *social* process — sharing — sparked the change, for sharing developed into barter, which in turn developed into the systematic trade and specialization of labor that eventually led to the innovation of individually held wealth and power. The exchange of resources from different areas is as old as human society itself. In ancient sites, seashells occur many miles from ocean shores. Flint, obsidian, and other desirable stones have wandered far from their original locations. Such rarities as fascinatingly beautiful amber have been passed from hand to hand great distances from their sources. In the course of human history, the increasingly stable village life made possible either by agriculture or by unusually dependable seasonal supplies of wild foods (such as the salmon runs that supported the coastal villagers of British Columbia) called for more and more regularized exchange both within and among groups. In turn, specialization became common in the production of goods to be traded for luxury items and special tools and foods. The process enriched life and promoted skill. As an unforeseen result, it ultimately transformed the entire structure of human relations from the equality of communal groups to the exploitativeness of economically divided societies.

Networks of exchange relations were originally egalitarian in form, for profit was not involved. However, the production and holding of goods for future exchange created new positions and new vested interests that began to divide the commitments of some individuals from those of the group as a whole. The role of economic intermediary developed and separated the process of exchange from the reciprocal relations that had bound groups together. Concomitantly, the holders of religious and chiefly statuses, traditionally guardians of produce that was redistributed as needed, acquired novel powers from the manipulation of stores of locally unavailable and particularly desirable merchandise. As Engels outlined in his *Origin of the Family, Private Property and the State,* the seeds of class difference were sown when people began to lose direct control over the distribution and consumption of the goods they had produced. Simultaneously, the basis for the oppression of women was laid, as the communal kin group became undercut by conflicting economic and political ties. In its place, individual family units emerged, in which the responsibility for raising future generations was placed on the shoulders of individual parents, and through which women's public role (and consequent public recognition) was transmuted into private service (and loss of public esteem).

Contemporary analyses of the structural components of women's social status indicate the critical role played by their degree of control over goods and resources. In an article comparing twelve societies with respect to women's position, Peggy Sanday wrote that for this sample "the antecedent of female political authority is some degree of economic power, i.e., ownership or control of strategic resources." [31] The importance of control over resources is illustrated by Judith Brown's comparison of early Iroquois society with the nineteenth-century Bemba of Zambia. Among the latter, women no longer controlled their produce and they held relatively lower status. Among the Iroquois, Brown wrote, the hospitality of women in the dispensing of food redounded to their own prestige; among the Bemba it reflected the prestige and power of the male household heads. In Bemba society, inequality and individual family units had replaced communal groups, and a man's right to his labor was "subject to the superior claims of certain older relatives and ultimately to that of the chief himself." [32] Chiefs held and distributed food to reinforce their own economic and political power.

Karen Sacks compared four African societies, the hunting/gathering Mbuti of Zaïre, the horticultural Lovedu and pastoral/agricultural Pondo of South Africa, and the stratified Ganda of Uganda. She showed the relative decline in women's status as the societies moved from "collective social production by women, as against that by men: equal in Mbuti and

Lovedu, unequal in Pondo, and absent in Ganda."[33] These differences persisted in spite of the effects, both direct and indirect, of colonialism.

Where women were traders and marketers, as in many West African societies, they retained greater economic autonomy and resultant status than when trading was carried on by men. The Ibo of Nigeria afford an unusually well-documented example of women marketers. When their status became threatened by the external economic ties — negotiated by men — that expanded rapidly following World War I, women protested publically, rioting and demonstrating, first in 1919, then again in 1925 and 1929. Accordingly, women's organizations among the Ibo were studied in detail, while elsewhere we have only hints of their existence. Women sat together in public meetings, and through their organizations, they made their "own laws for the women of the town irrespective of the men," regulated the markets, protected women's interests, and negotiated legal cases where women and men were both implicated. Their protests emphasize the close relation between their economic position and their personal rights vis-à-vis men. Issues included both proposed new taxes by the British and the threat to the traditional right of women to have sexual relations with men other than their husbands.[34]

African political and social systems were either destroyed or subverted to the service of colonial administrations. But oral history and early accounts both indicate many parallels with the state societies that arose in the Mediterranean area. In West Africa as in the Mediterranean, specialization of labor and commodity production were tied in with far-flung trading and kingdoms that rose and fell according to the geographical availability of routes and resources and other accidents of history. In both areas there was a long-term strengthening of economic classes and a decline in the status of women, accompanied by conflicts over lineality, over land rights, and over family and kin commitments. This is the point at which written allusions to women in European history begin.

Notes

1. Robert Ardrey, *African Genesis: A Personal Investigation into the Animal Origins and Nature of Man,* Atheneum, New York, 1961, and *The Social Contract,* Atheneum, New York, 1970; Desmond Morris, *The Naked Ape,* Dell, New York, 1966.

2. For an evolutionary summary and further references, see Eleanor Leacock's introduction to "The Part Played by Labor in the Transition from Ape to Man," Frederick Engels, *The Origin of the Family, Private Property and the State,* ed. Eleanor Leacock, International Publishers, New York, 1972. Were humanity by nature that disposed to fighting, we would all be fully involved in the contemporary melee with great enjoyment. Instead, despite our competitive socializa-

tion, most of us try to find some reasonably peaceful niche in which to gain some pleasure from life.

3. Colin Turnbull, *The Mountain People,* Simon & Schuster, New York, 1972.
4. T. O. Beidelman, *The Kaguru: A Matrilineal People of East Africa,* Holt, Rinehart & Winston, New York, 1971, p. 43; Walter Goldschmidt, *Man's Way: A Preface to the Understanding of Human Society,* Holt, Rinehart & Winston, New York, 1959, p. 164; Marvin Harris, "Women's Fib," *Natural History* (Spring 1972), and *Culture, Man, and Nature: An Introduction to General Anthropology,* Crowell, New York, 1971, p. 328; E. E. Evans-Pritchard, *The Position of Women in Primitive Societies and Other Essays in Social Anthropology,* Faber & Faber, London, 1965, p. 54.
5. Dorothy Hammond and Alta Jablow, *Women: Their Economic Role in Traditional Societies,* Addison-Wesley Module in Anthropology, No. 35, Reading, Mass. 1973, pp. 3, 8, 26, 27.
6. Ellen Lewin, Jane F. Collier, Michelle Z. Rosaldo, & Janet S. Fjellman, "Power Strategies and Sex Roles," paper presented at the 70th Annual Meeting, American Anthropological Association, New York, 1971, pp. 1–2.
7. John Honigman, *World of Man,* Harper & Row, New York, 1959, p. 302.
8. Tacitus, *The Agricola and the Germania,* Penguin, New York, 1971; pp. 66, 108.
9. R. G. Thwaites, ed., *The Jesuit Relations and Allied Documents,* vol. 12, Burrows Brothers, Cleveland, 1906, p. 165.
10. Ibid., vol. 11, p. 105.
11. Ibid., vol. 6, p. 233.
12. Ibid., vol. 6, p. 235.
13. Ibid., vol. 6, p. 253.
14. Ibid., vol. 6, p. 247.
15. Ibid., vol. 5, p. 181; vol. 6, p. 255.
16. Ibid., vol. 68, p. 93.
17. Ibid., vol. 12, p. 169.
18. Ibid., vol. 16, p. 165.
19. Ralph S. Solecki, "Neanderthal Is Not an Epithet but a Worthy Ancestor," *Anthropology, Contemporary Perspectives,* eds. David E. Hunter and Phillip Whitten, Little, Brown, Boston, 1975, p. 30–31.
20. For a summary statement of the position of Iroquois women, see Judith K. Brown, "Iroquois Women: An Ethnohistoric Note," *Toward an Anthropology of Women,* ed. Rayna R. Reiter, Monthly Review Press, New York, 1975.
21. Ibid., p. 238.
22. Lewis Henry Morgan, *Ancient Society,* ed. Eleanor Leacock, Peter Smith, Gloucester, Mass., 1974, p. 464.
23. Lewis Henry Morgan, *League of the Ho-De-No-Sau-Nee or Iroquois,* vol. 1, Human Relations Area Files, New Haven, 1954, p. 315; Steven Goldberg, *The Inevitability of Patriarchy,* Wm. Morrow, New York, 1973, pp. 40, 58, 241.
24. Lewis Henry Morgan, *Houses and House-Life of the American Aborigines,* University of Chicago Press, Chicago, 1965, p. 128.

25. Morgan, *Ancient Society*, pp. 85–86.

26. V. Gordon Childe, *The Dawn of European Civilization*, Random House, New York, 1964, pp. 106–107, 109, 182–183.

27. Ibid., p. 119.

28. Ibid., p. 123.

29. Thwaites, vol. 6, p. 243.

30. Ibid., vol. 52, p. 49.

31. Peggy R. Sanday, "Female Status in the Public Domain," *Woman, Culture, and Society*, eds. Michelle Zimbalist Rosaldo and Louise Lamphere, Stanford University Press, Stanford, 1974, p. 193.

32. Quoted by Brown from Audrey I. Richards, *Land, Labour and Diet in Northern Rhodesia*, Oxford University Press, London, 1939; pp. 188–189.

33. Karen Sacks, "Engels Revisited: Women, the Organization of Production, and Private Property," Rosaldo and Lamphere, *Woman, Culture, and Society*, p. 215.

34. G. T. Basden, *Among the Ibos of Nigeria*, Barnes & Noble, New York, 1966, p. 95. See also G. T. Basden, *Niger Ibos*, Seeley, Service, London, 1938, and C. K. Meek, *Law and Authority in a Nigerian Tribe*, Oxford University Press, London, 1937.

Suggestions for Further Reading

Engels, Frederick. *The Origin of the Family, Private Property and the State.* Edited and Introduction by Eleanor Leacock. International Publishers, New York, 1972.

Leacock, Eleanor. "The Structure of Band Society." *Reviews in Anthropology*, 1 (May 1974).

Lebeuf, Annie M. D. "The Role of Women in the Political Organization of African Societies." *Women of Tropical Africa*, ed. Denise Paulme. University of California Press, Berkeley, 1971.

Liebowitz, Lila. "Changing Views of Women in Society, 1975." *Reviews in Anthropology*, 2 (November 1975).

Martin, M. Kay, and Barbara Voorhies. *Female of the Species.* Columbia University Press, New York, 1975.

Murphy, Yolanda, and Robert F. Murphy. *Women of the Forest.* Columbia University Press, New York, 1974.

Reid, John Phillip. *A Law of Blood: The Primitive Law of the Cherokee Nation.* New York University Press, New York, 1970.

Reiter, Rayna, R. *Toward an Anthropology of Women.* Monthly Review Press, New York, 1975.

Rohrlich-Leavitt, Ruby, ed. *Women Cross-Culturally: Change and Challenge.* Mouton, The Hague, 1975.

Turnbull, Colin. *The Forest People.* Doubleday Anchor, Garden City, N.Y., 1962.

Washburne, Heluiz Chandler, and Anauta. *Land of the Good Shadows: The Life Story of Anauta, an Eskimo Woman.* John Day, New York, 1940.

2

Women in Transition: Crete and Sumer

Ruby Rohrlich-Leavitt

The first dim outlines of the development of private property, social stratification, and political forms indicate how the subordination of women began; surviving historical records of the earliest civilizations in the Near East suggest a continuing trend. Ruby Rohrlich-Leavitt discusses the relationship between contrasting social structures of Neolithic Anatolia, Minoan Crete, and Sumer, and how these affected the role and image of women. She hypothesizes that in the earliest societies of this region, egalitarian clans provided the basis for women's social, economic, and political importance, much as they did for North American Indians. In urbanized Crete, peace and prosperity under favorable geographical conditions obviated the establishment of a centralized political state, allowing kin groups and women's high status to persist. In Sumer, by contrast, rivalry among economic elites for control over scarce resources led to increased centralization of the state and to militarism. First a priesthood, then a powerful kingship steadily eroded egalitarian clan structures and reduced women to being property. Here we see the first historically traceable systematic subordination of women, as a result of material conditions, in a pattern that recurs in the classical world and throughout the formation of the European states.

Ivory and gold snake goddess, ca. 1600 B.C., unknown provenance. (Courtesy, Museum of Fine Arts, Boston. Gift of Mrs. W. Scott Fitz.)

Anthropologists now generally concede that women invented agriculture. However, civilization itself, so the argument goes, was a totally male accomplishment, and therefore all civilizations are patriarchal in structure. Implicit in this view is the assumption that civilization is the ultimate goal of all human social endeavor, rather than a particular level of cultural development.

Moreover, it is typically contended that, because of the immutable biological and psychological differences between the sexes, men are superordinate not only in civilizations but in all types of society. In the preceding chapter, Eleanor Leacock documents the egalitarian relationships between the sexes in gathering/hunting and horticultural societies. And the evidence presented in this chapter indicates that Minoan Crete, the first European civilization, was a matriarchy. This term emphasizes the political role of women in society but also includes economic, social, and religious privileges that give them greater authority than men. Minoan Crete fulfills these criteria for a matriarchal society.

But the Cretan matriarchy was not a mirror image of the contemporaneous Sumerian and Egyptian civilizations. These became patriarchal as male elites gained control over the means of production and the masses of people, eventually changing all human relationships, especially those between women and men. Male supremacy, social stratification, and the emergence of private property were then confirmed and extended by a militaristic policy of territorial expansion that was absent in Minoan civilization from its beginnings, c. 3000 B.C., until its destruction by earthquakes some 1,500 years later. Concomitantly, the gynocentric institutions that germinated in the earlier Neolithic societies not only survived but flourished.

Catal Huyuk: Anatolian Antecedents

The settlement of Crete was begun early in the seventh millennium B.C. by immigrants who came in successive waves primarily from Anatolia, part of present-day Turkey. Bringing few of their material possessions as they crossed the Aegean Sea in their small open boats, they successfully adapted their antecedent institutions to the habitat of Crete. Their way of life in Anatolia has been brought to light by archaeological discoveries that indicate that Neolithic society reached an advanced stage earlier in this area than in any other Middle Eastern region, as exemplified particularly by Catal Huyuk. The excavations of this site, directed by James Mellaart, show that in the seventh millennium B.C., Catal Huyuk was a town economically and culturally midway between Neolithic village and Bronze Age city. Its economy was based on well-developed agricultural practices, extensive trade in raw materials, and occupational specialization with, however, few signs of social stratification. Like other Neolithic societies, the communal clan-based structures, with production for use and direct exchange, were egalitarian, democratic, and peaceable.

Women played a very important part in this society. From all indications, their political status in the typical Neolithic council of elders was at least equal to that of men, and in the economic, social, and religious spheres they predominated.

The economic role of women was crucial. They cultivated an amazing variety of indigenous plants for food and medicine. Apparently, women also participated in hunting the many species of wild animals that roamed the plains. A goddess was associated with wild animals, probably reflecting her ancient role as the provider of food for a hunting population and as patron of the hunt. This indicates that the earlier participation of women in both gathering and hunting continued into the Neolithic period. Since most of the meat consumed at Catal Huyuk for much of its existence was supplied by hunting, animals were domesticated primarily for their milk, wool, and leather.

With the grain they grew, women baked bread in huge communal ovens. They tanned animal skins and sewed the skins and fur into clothing. With the loom, that great mechanical invention of Neolithic women, they wove the earliest textiles yet to be discovered anywhere. Their cotton and wool garments and rugs were strikingly patterned and dyed with a full range of pigments, as shown on the wall paintings in the houses. Out of wheat straw, they made carpets, mats, and the oldest known baskets. They also made pottery, again the earliest so far found, having learned to heat certain types of clay to the proper temperature and shape them into receptacles for cooking and storage.

Women's social preeminence at Catal Huyuk is clear. Among the house platforms used for working, sitting, and sleeping, the small corner platform belonging to the man was often moved about, but the much larger main platform, which belonged to the woman, never changed its place. The clan was unmistakably matrilineal and matrilocal (i.e., both kinship and residence were established with reference to the mother rather than the father). The children were buried either with the women or under the platforms, but never with the men. Representations of adults and children in order of importance showed this order to be: mother, daughter, son, father.

In religion women also predominated. Not only was the goddess the principal object of worship in the earlier period, but it was women who ministered to her cult. Out of a total of about 400 skeletons found at the site, only eleven, all female, were painted with the red ocher or cinnabar that symbolized "blood and life" as far back as 100,000 years ago. Moreover, these skeletons were found in the shrines, the burial places of those who had enjoyed respect and authority. The shrines themselves comprised about a fourth of the living rooms at the various building levels and could be recognized by their elaborate wall paintings, plaster reliefs of deities and animals, rows of bulls' horns, and groups of statues. On the plaster reliefs the goddess is depicted in human form and the male is represented by bulls and rams. Since these animals symbolized male sexual potency in many cultures, we might ask: Were the men of Catal Huyuk valued as sex objects?

The goddess is shown in a variety of ways that reflect the activities and attributes, actual and symbolic, of women in secular life. She is shown as fat and slim, giving birth to humans and animals, running and dancing and hunting, surrounded by the patterns of women's activities in agriculture and weaving. The statues include a male deity, but statues of the female deity far outnumber those of the male who, moreover, is not represented at all any more after 5800 B.C.

Sometime during the fifty-eighth century B.C., agriculture triumphed over hunting, and with its triumph the power of women increased. But because hunting had for so long persisted as an important activity, the Catal Huyuk people retained their respect for all forms of animal life, an attitude that remained typical of hunting/gathering societies even after they had learned to domesticate animals. The site contained no altars or tablets for bleeding sacrificed animals and no pits for their blood or bones. Nor do human skeletons show signs of violence between individuals or groups within the society or of warlike activities directed against other people. Although their housing seems to have been designed for defensive purposes, with access by ladder through the roof, there is no evidence of any sack, massacre, or deliberate destruction at Catal Huyuk during the 800 years of its existence. Matriarchy and peace appear to have reigned.[1]

Neolithic Crete: 7000–3000 B.C.

The innovations of the Anatolian Neolithic peoples were adapted to the island environment of Crete and reached their apogee there. Prehistoric Crete is described by Arthur Evans, its discoverer, as an island offshoot of an extensive Anatolian region through which Neolithic culture spread to Europe. The Neolithic peoples of Anatolia and the Aegean shared the same or closely related non-Greek languages. In both Anatolia and Minoan Crete, the palace was at once an economic, royal, and sacerdotal abode, featuring the worship of the goddess and the prevalence of the *labrys,* the double ax. Associated only with the goddess and never with a god, the labrys was a symbol equivalent in importance to the cross in Christian buildings. It probably became sacred through its use in cutting down trees and clearing the land.

The settlers found many natural advantages on the island. Much of it consisted of mountains and forests, the sources of its valuable timber. The plains and valleys were fertile, water was plentiful, good harbors abounded, its climate was ideal, and its isolation in the Aegean provided protection from invaders. On the low hill that later became the site of the palace of Knossos, the center of Minoan civilization, a village was settled before 6000 B.C. that became one of the largest settlements in Neolithic Europe and the Near East. Built out of fired mud brick, this village of close-packed houses came to cover as much as eleven acres.

Equipped with the technical knowledge of their homeland, the pioneers began their life on Crete at a relatively advanced stage of Neolithic culture. They cultivated wheat and barley, grapes and olives, figs and apples. They hunted the wild animals that roamed the island and raised cattle, sheep, goats, and pigs. Since Crete lacked the flint needed to make cutting and piercing instruments, such as knives, sickles, and awls, obsidian was brought in from Anatolia; already in Neolithic times long sailing voyages were organized for overseas trade.

The village women not only cultivated the fields and wove cloth but they also made excellent pottery, as well as the female figurines that appear in all phases of the Cretan Neolithic culture. These images range from voluptuous forms with broad hips, full belly, and squatting posture to abstract ones that are tall, slender, and small-breasted. Expressing a religion characteristic of Neolithic cultures all over the European-Mediterranean world, the prevalence and variety of the goddess images suggest that the women of Neolithic Crete played roles as important as those of their Anatolian foremothers. The power of religions represented by the goddess, so deeply rooted in agricultural life in which women remained prominent, never died out in Greece:

> It may have been outlawed, made unofficial, transformed, suppressed, harnessed, set in political balance with newer religions, but any archaeologist of religion will recognize in it one of the primary gifts of the Neolithic . . . to its heirs in Greece and the Near East.[2]

Minoan Crete: 3000–1500 B.C.

The transformation of Neolithic society into the cultural level defined as civilization first took place, according to the archaeological record, in Sumer. This is the ancient name for southern Mesopotamia (now called Iraq), situated between the Tigris and Euphrates rivers in the region of southwestern Asia known as the Middle East. Here, occupational specialization and the exchange of commodities had, by about 3500 B.C., reached the stage where social stratification and the political state had emerged, city life had come into being, constant warfare was an integral part of life, and the status of women was declining. These processes took place in a number of areas in both the Old and New Worlds during the Bronze Age, when metal supplanted stone for tools and weapons.

About 3000 B.C., Crete also began to undergo these processes. This principal stage of Cretan civilization was named "Minoan" by Arthur Evans, after Minos, a later ruler of the island. But Minoan Crete differed in important ways from the other Bronze Age civilizations. Although urbanization and social stratification existed, the Minoan state was not a strong centralized entity, warfare was absent, and the status of women apparently became even higher than it had been during the Neolithic era. The factors that gave rise to the brilliant and original civilization of Crete also underlay the central position of Minoan women; the factors that were responsible for the decline in women's status in the other Bronze Age societies brought about those societies' eventual decay.

Diodorus Siculus, an ancient Greek historian, noted that Crete lay in a most fortunate position for travel to all parts of the ancient world, at a point where the great trade routes crossed. The island flanks the southern entrance to the Aegean basin and forms a bridgehead from Asia and Africa to the Greek mainland and so to Europe. Although Cretan civilization was undoubtedly influenced by Sumer and Egypt, at the very beginning of the Bronze Age, Crete may already itself have been a center for the diffusion of civilization throughout the Aegean area.[3]

Cretan civilization developed out of relatively autonomous processes: trade and commerce, both local and long distance, strong links with tribal systems, and indigenous craft traditions. While these processes were also basic to the emergence of the other Bronze Age civilizations, in Minoan

Crete trade was not superseded by military conquest as the primary means of gaining access to important resources, and the kin-based clan structures were not radically transformed to serve the state. Thus, the island remained at peace both at home and abroad, and Minoans in the several social strata continued to live relatively independent lives within the clan system, in which women played crucial roles.

The character of the economy in the Minoan urban centers militated against political centralization and the internecine strife typical of the Sumerian cities. The walls that began to surround the Sumerian towns from around 3000 B.C. symbolized the ever-expanding militarism that drained their human and natural resources and benefited only the elites. But the Cretan towns developed primarily out of settlements that grew up around harbors, and the marketplace was the center for the peaceful exchange of commodities as well as the hub of religious and social activity. Minoan towns and cities were unfortified, the approach to the palace of Knossos, for example, being a great bridge, a viaduct, without a drawbridge or high defensive walls.

Good harbors and an abundance of timber enabled the Cretans to take advantage of their maritime position long before the Bronze Age began. By the second millennium B.C., Cretans were the equal of any people with a stake in Mediterranean commerce. They traded manufactured goods, such as ceramics, metal products, and textiles, for the raw materials needed by their industries: gold, silver, tin, lead, copper, ivory, and lapis lazuli. Minoan goods were traded in Egypt, Anatolia, Syria, Cyprus, and the Greek mainland, and in time Crete achieved economic and cultural hegemony in the Aegean.

In the *Iliad,* Homer speaks often and admiringly of "Crete of the Hundred Cities." The rapid growth of the towns prevented concentration of power in the hands of large landowners who, in Sumer, were at the same time the religious and secular authorities. There were shrines in the Minoan palaces, but no temples in the towns. In the palaces, the workshops and storehouses are more conspicuous and take up more room than those in the major temples of Sumer, showing that commercial enterprise was not subordinated to the priesthood. Thus, the urban revolution affected traditional society far less in Crete than in Sumer:

> The typical Minoan town clustered round an open space adjoining the palace of a prince, one who was high priest as well as governor, but primarily a merchant prince, with other merchants living close by in mansions only less rich . . . and with nothing to segregate . . . them from the rest of the community.[4]

The towns surrounding the palaces were well designed for "civilized living" with the streets paved and drained. The Town Mosaic, a series of panels set into the sides of a wooden chest excavated in Knossos, depicts the residences of average middle-class families: houses of two or three stories, with six to twelve rooms, built out of sun-dried bricks bound by wooden beams, on a stone foundation, and facing inward onto a central open patio. Aside from the core of palace and marketplace, cities were unplanned, building patterns continuing the Neolithic tradition of adding structures of different sizes to one another. The haphazard cellular growth of the towns, their very planlessness, testifies to the lack of central control and corresponding greater freedom in Minoan Crete than in other Bronze Age civilizations.

The basic social unit in Minoan Crete continued to be the kin-based clan, with its communal land tenure, as reflected in the communal burials that persisted through much of Minoan history. A whole community shared the same burial place, used by many generations, sometimes for 500 years or more. The most distinctive type of tomb architecture in Crete was the large, circular, vaulted stone structure known as the *tholos,* modeled on the dwelling place of the clan. The tholos was filled with the bones of a whole clan, rather than of any ruling dynasty, indicating the lack of unified control in Crete. The cemetery of the Sumerian city of Ur also contained communal burials, but of a vastly different nature:

> The burial of the kings was accompanied by human sacrifice on a lavish scale, the bottom of the grave pit being crowded with the bodies of men and women who seemed to have been brought down here and butchered where they stood.[5]

The nature of agricultural production in Minoan Crete also inhibited political centralization. Since military conquest and defense were not overriding considerations, the people, consisting mainly of farmers, were not heavily taxed or drawn into military service and forced labor, as were the Sumerian peasants. Moreover, since the palaces depended much more on industry and commerce than on agricultural production, agriculture was apparently never directed from a single center but was left to develop according to environmental conditions. As a result, a form of garden tillage was favored by skilled specialists with an independent social tradition. The surplus produced — of grain, barley, meat, fish, olive oil, wine, raisins, honey, herbs, and fruit — maintained the noble and priestly classes, the merchants and sailors, artisans and artists, and swelled the cargoes of the merchant ships.

Farmers and fisherfolk benefited from the specialization of the artisans in the neighboring towns. The remains of Gournia, a small town excavated on the bay of Mirabello, were packed with the houses of potters, carpenters, smiths, and oil pressers, who lived above their basement storerooms. They were all well equipped with the tools of their trade and must have served the needs of their customers efficiently while making a decent living even in the provincial towns not dominated by the palaces.

Sooner or later, the Bronze Age civilizations created writing systems out of the need to keep economic records, and Crete was no exception. Arthur Evans discovered three principal forms of writing that developed on the island over a period of a thousand years. In the middle of the third millennium B.C., a system of pictorial hieroglyphs was used, mainly on stone beads and seal stones. The second type, a cursive script, Linear A, in a language that has not yet been deciphered, originated around 1900 B.C. and by the seventeenth century B.C. was being used for the palace records. The third form, Linear B, apparently was developed out of Linear A around 1450 to 1400 B.C. by the Mycenaeans who invaded Crete at this time.

What was perhaps the first schoolroom in Europe was discovered in the palace of Knossos and dates from the sixteenth century B.C. Situated near the queen's suite, close to the workshops of the artisans, the room contained baked clay tablets inscribed with Linear A. At the top of each tablet was a sentence written in a firm hand, while underneath an uncertain hand had tried to imitate the signs above. Judging by the prevalence of the script not only on art and craft objects, but also in the form of graffiti, literacy during this period in Cretan history was not limited to the elites, as it was in the other Bronze Age civilizations.[6] Except for Crete, all of them used writing to adorn their palaces and the tombs of important people. Also lacking in Minoan Crete is the equivalent of the great literary epics of Sumer, in which the Sumerian king uninhibitedly recites his own virtues and achievements. Even more important, as early as the Bronze Age, the elites began the practice of using writing to record as history those events that perpetuated their rule and to distort and suppress those not serving this purpose:

> Writing provides the ruling classes with an ideological instrument of incalculable power . . . an official, fixed and permanent version of events can be made. . . . Those people who *could* write, the scribes and priests . . . were rarely disposed to record the attitudes of those they taxed, subordinated and mystified.[7]

If writing played little part in the embellishment of the Minoan palaces, the same cannot be said of the arts and crafts. An important class, which must have made up an appreciable part of the urban population, consisted of the artisans and artists who provided the goods and services for the aristocracy, as well as for the cargoes of the merchant ships. But while in Sumer specialists who became dependent on the priests and kings lost the social prestige and artistic freedom they had gained in the Neolithic period, in the Minoan palaces specialized production resulted in a fresh gain of such prestige and in creative invention.

The gifted women and men who won court patronage were artisans and artists of genius. Construction and hydraulic engineers built networks of paved roads, aqueducts, viaducts, irrigation channels, and harbor installations that were among the best in the Bronze Age. Sanitation engineers constructed drainage systems that anticipated the most modern scientific sanitation methods. Architects built palaces that outshone those of the Orient. The palace at Kato Zakro in east Crete showed craftsmanship surpassing that of contemporary Egypt. Metalworkers alloyed metals of great strength and were particularly skilled at molding bronze. Minoan sculptors were the first to use gold and ivory for statues; the potters invented the technique of faience, coating clay with a glaze; the fresco painters were unrivaled. Using a great variety of media, painters, jewelers, and seal cutters created masterpieces in miniature, an important source of information about Minoan life.

Sober scholars exclaim over the contrast between the motifs and styles of art in Minoan Crete and in the other Bronze Age civilizations. Minoan art was realistic, yet imaginative and exuberant, and drew on every aspect of the natural environment and social life, both everyday and ritual. Artists showed women and men, animals and plants, in free and close communion with each other. They also showed that the female figurines of the Neolithic period had become those of the impressive and pervasive goddess, as well as those of queens, priestesses, and votaries. What *was* the influence of women in this unusual civilization?

Women in Minoan Crete

Minoan Crete was a paradoxical society. It was socially stratified but not politically centralized. Wealth derived principally from trade and commerce, and political power was widely dispersed, mainly among the merchants. Peace endured for 1,500 years both at home and abroad in an age of incessant warfare. Wealthy patrons left artists and craftspeople singularly free to create their masterpieces, and small-town artisans made an adequate living from the neighboring farmers and fisherfolk. Farmers were left to develop their agricultural expertise and grow their surplus products within the framework of their ancient clan structures.

The artifacts provide clear evidence that the status of women in this relatively rich and free society was very high. Women were the central subjects, the most frequently portrayed in the arts and crafts. And they are shown mainly in the public sphere. In the Grandstand Fresco and the Blue

Fresco, "the women alone are fully drawn, in the foreground. . . . In the background are a large number of small conventional squiggles representing eyes, noses, and hair. Those are the men." [8] The mature women in these scenes (to whom one archaeologist refers as "gossiping girls") are relating to each other warmly and intimately, by touch as well as speech. They are comfortable and relaxed with each other and would obviously have no difficulty cooperating in their common interests. Are they talking about affairs of state, their economic investments, their triumphs with the bull, the dances they choreographed, the music they composed, the pottery they decorated, the religious rituals they led?

Merchants and navigators could as easily have been women as men. Even in patriarchal Sumer, women carried on long-distance trade in their own names. On the Ring of Minos, a woman is steering a ship. A gold signet ring, found in a grave on Mochlos, shows another woman disembarking from a ship, carrying a tree. She may have been a merchant prince trading in timber.

The crucial roles played by Neolithic women were apparently continued by women farmers in Minoan Crete. As noted earlier, the fact that agriculture and irrigation systems were not centrally controlled meant that modified forms of garden tillage persisted. Thus, the farmers maintained, relatively unimpaired, their independent social traditions, in which women were preeminent. One scholar has remarked:

> In view of the marked surviving traces of matrilineal descent in historical Crete, it may be that any tendency for the work of agriculture to be transferred to the men, with consequent transition from matrilineal to patrilineal descent, was complicated by factors operating in reverse.[9]

Crete was renowned for growing fruit, and orchard cultivation became increasingly important as the produce from olive, grape, fig, and apple trees was traded abroad, as well as consumed locally. This helps to explain why the tree, usually shown associated with women, is considered sacred and is so prevalent in Minoan religion. Again and again, women are shown, on rings and seals, tending fruit trees.

Using plants to heal and cure, as well as for food, the women were of course the midwives and probably the general practitioners as well. The lily, poppy, crocus, and iris, favorite subjects of Minoan painters, potters, and seal cutters, were especially sacred, associated with the goddess in her aspect as deity of vegetation, and in secular scenes. The lily was used to check menstruation and the poppy seed was used for religious as well as medical purposes. On one seal, a seated woman is holding three poppy seed heads, and a late figurine shows a woman wearing three seed heads, cut as for the extraction of opium, in a crown above her head. No one knows whether these images depict the goddess or a flesh-and-blood woman, perhaps a doctor involved in healing or a priestess performing rituals.

Minoan women probably had equal access to professional status in the arts and crafts, particularly as potters, an occupation they developed in Neolithic times. Minoan Crete was famous for its fine ware throughout the ancient world, especially after the potter's wheel was introduced around 2000 B.C. The pottery was as thin as porcelain and decorated with dynamic geometric patterns of flowers and leaves, shellfish and flying fish, birds and animals and dancing women. There is no evidence that men took over the craft with the introduction of the wheel; indeed, a statue of a woman potter dates from this period.

The Minoans had a passion for dancing. Legend insists they were great dancers and the record left by Minoan artists suggests that women did most of the dancing. Again and again, on the frescoes, seals, and signet rings they are shown dancing in meadows and groves, before the goddess and her altars, in front of large audiences, singly and in groups. Women were also expert tumblers and musicians, playing the flute and the lyre. The Minoan chorus always consisted only of women, led by a priestess.

Minoan women also hunted, as they did in Neolithic Crete and Anatolia, and are shown sometimes with bows and arrows, sometimes driving chariots. One of the end panels on a limestone sarcophagus found in a chamber tomb near the palace of Hagia Triada shows two women standing erect, holding the reigns of a horse-drawn chariot, presumably hunting wild animals. On the opposite panel, two goddesses are driving a chariot drawn by griffins, eagle-headed lions of fable. Above all, women and men together, entrusting their lives to one another, hunted the wild bull with staves and nooses and played a most dangerous game, that of bull grappling or bull leaping, in public arenas. In one fresco, a young girl is shown hurling herself upon a bull's head. A scene on one of the gold Vapheio cups shows a male hunter thrown by the bull while the other hunter, a woman, grasps the animal's horns in an effort to bring it down.

Androgynous attire accompanied the role sharing in Minoan society. While the woman bull leapers wore the loincloth and codpiece of the men, in funerary rites women and men wore identical sheepskin skirts. In other rituals in which both sexes took part, men donned long flounced robes, initially the garb of the priestess and usually worn by women. Both women and men wore metal belts around their very slim waists; both used a great deal of jewelry — bracelets, armbands, collars, and headbands; both wore their hair the same way — long and curly, falling down their backs, with locks hanging in front of the ears. Clothes accentuating the penis and female breasts are equally revealing, indicating a frank acceptance of the human body.

But it was above all their roles in religion, the institution that integrated Bronze Age life, that attested to the predominance of women in Minoan

Crete. By about 2000 B.C., a time when the position of Sumerian women had declined considerably, the Minoan goddess had become pervasive, and she or her priestesses or votaries were pictured in almost every aspect of the natural and social ambience of Crete:

> with animals, birds and snakes; with the . . . pillar and the sacred tree; with the sword and the double-axe. She is a huntress and a goddess of sports; she is armed and she presides over ritual dances; she has female and male attendants; she has dominion over mountain, earth, sky and sea; over life and death; she is household-goddess, vegetation goddess, Mother and Maid.[10]

The one religious shrine found in the palace of Knossos contained faience figures of the Snake Goddess, a skillful and commanding figure, with snakes wreathed around her wrists, waist, and head. In Crete, as elsewhere, nonpoisonous snakes were a symbol of protection, since they exterminate vermin, and Minoan houses contained tubes made expressly for snakes to crawl into. The snake charmer was thus a person of significance.

The goddess-queen priestess had male as well as female attendants, and men are also depicted in various roles and activities. They are the farmers on the Harvester Cup; they are acrobats, boxers, and wrestlers, bull hunters and bull leapers, participants in funerary rites and other ceremonies, artisans, and artists. But when they are associated with the goddess or her earthly representatives, they are shown in worshiping and respectful postures. These are particularly evident in the procession scene on a fresco in Knossos, where two lines of men, some carrying vases, are depicted advancing from both sides toward the central figure, the queen or priestess. A picture of a longhaired youth, unarmed, naked to the waist, wearing a headdress of peacock plumes and walking among flowers and butterflies, was painted on a plaster relief in the Great Corridor of the palace of Knossos. Modern scholars have dubbed him the Young Prince and sometimes refer to him as the Priest-King, but in fact no single representation of a king or a dominant male god has yet been found.

Who, then, occupied the one throne, placed between a pair of griffins painted in brilliant colors on a wall of the throne room in the palace at Knossos? A number of scholars are convinced that Crete was matriarchal, a theocracy ruled by a queen-priestess. The absence of portrayals of an all-powerful male ruler, so widespread in the Bronze Age, backs them up; so does the religious prominence of women.[11] But if queens occupied the Minoan throne, who was Minos, the king for whom this matriarchal society was named? Increasing evidence indicates that he was a member of the dynasty established at Knossos by the Achaeans from Mycenaean Greece, who entered Crete after its coastal towns had been devastated by tidal waves and earthquakes, floods, and fires, sometime between 1500 and 1400 B.C. These catastrophes resulted from a tremendous volcanic eruption that destroyed Thera, now known as Santorin, an island eighty miles from Crete. The Mycenaeans overran the weakened Cretans, colonized most of the fertile parts of their island, and enslaved many people. Thus, "Minoan" is a misnomer for the earlier period.

The Achaeans were an Indo-European people who, by the sixteenth century B.C., had made Mycenae the wealthiest and strongest kingdom on the mainland. Long influenced by Minoan culture, by 1400 B.C., they had thoroughly mastered Minoan techniques and taken over Minoan economic and cultural activities. However, the martial character of the Achaeans, as revealed in the fortification of their citadel, the abundance of weapons, and the popularity of battle scenes in art, was altogether foreign to the Minoan spirit. Although the Achaeans had adopted the cult of the goddess and many of her symbols, they also worshiped male gods who were more than her inferior consorts. By about 1250 B.C., the Homeric Achaeans under Agamemnon conquered Troy, but only about fifty years later, the Mycenaean Age — indeed, the Bronze Age itself — came to an end with the invasion of the Dorians, another warrior people. As one writer eloquently put it:

> Behind the work of the humane poets who composed the *Iliad* and *Odyssey* lies an age of brutality and violence, in which the bold pioneers of private property had ransacked the opulent, hieratic, sophisticated civilization of the Minoan matriarchate.[12]

Sumer

The processes involved in the decline of the position of women in the Bronze Age patriarchal civilizations are illustrated in the development of Sumer from a land of small city-states to the empire ruled by Hammurabi. Essential to the consolidation of private property and the political state (institutions that first came into being in Sumer) was the breakup of the corporate kinship group based on communal land tenure and the centrality and freedom of women. Thus, the destruction of the kinship group and the subordination of women were inextricably linked. As private ownership of land, political centralization, and militarism gained momentum, the elites increasingly became male, and male supremacy pervaded every social stratum, providing men who were themselves exploited with a place in the power structure. Women became a form of private property, deprived of decision making power in the major aspects of living. But the expulsion of women from their high status, and their social and legal subordination and degradation, must have been accompanied by great resistance on their part, and took a relatively long time to complete. More than a trace of matriarchy can be found in the early Sumerian city-states.

In Sumer, pictographic writing, which began about the middle of the fourth millennium B.C., the Protoliterate period, had by about 2500 B.C. evolved into a cuneiform system in which records of economic transactions, myths, epics, dynastic lists, and royal proclamations provide the basis for the modern reconstruction of Sumerian political history. Thus, historical documents, along with archaeological finds, furnish the data on women's status.

By Protoliterate times the small city-state was a well-established feature of the Sumerian landscape. The impetus to urbanization in Sumer was different in some respects from that in Crete. The fertile alluvial plain between the Tigris and Euphrates rivers lacked stone, timber, and metals, which were obtained by extensive trade very early in the settlement of Sumer. But the farming communities, with their surpluses of food and other material, were vulnerable to invasion by nomadic herders, so the villages drew together into larger social units that could more easily be defended.

The significance of religion in social integration here led to the domination of the town by the temple, with the high priest, the *en* or *patesi,* exercising religious, economic, and political functions. The temple was not only the center of ritual but of surplus food redistribution in time of need. Here also, writing developed out of account keeping and so did crafts that depended on the importation of raw materials from distant sources. Most of the surplus labor, food, and other material went into building and maintaining the temple, the first type of monumental architecture in Sumer. A considerable amount of this surplus was retained by the priests, who soon became an elite group, owning and controlling large tracts of land.

By early dynastic times, around 3000 B.C., many of the cities were enclosed by walls, defensive fortifications against nomadic raiders and rival cities. The cities conflicted primarily over border areas and canals. Lagash and Umma, for example, fought each other for more than 150 years over the fields and canals between their borders. As warfare became endemic, the descendants of earlier war leaders gained power and influence at the expense of the priesthood. Eventually they emerged as kings — *lugals,* literally "great men" — who provided leadership for the forces committed to a policy of military control over the lands containing valuable resources. By the middle of the third millennium B.C., the patesi was in a position of dependence on the lugal.

The key change arising out of the struggle between the priests and the military was the transformation of the corporate kinship groups as they became encapsulated in social organizations that had become rigidly divided along class lines. While these corporate groups continued to own and work large tracts of land, their internal autonomy and cohesiveness were eroded as they adapted to buying and selling land that had hitherto been inalienable. The foundation of the clan system was also shaken as farming and herding, the two staple industries in Sumer, came under the control of the emerging state.

Constant warfare was significantly related to the centralized control over both farmers and agricultural production. While the walled cities provided relatively greater security, they led to heavy demands for taxes and military and corvée service. In addition, defensive considerations would have encouraged cultivating areas close to the city walls, which probably resulted in irrigation works to enlarge and sustain agricultural output. Whether state control over irrigation systems preceded or followed the institutionalization of warfare, it was certainly one means of gaining control over human labor and basic natural resources, and in the process the state was strengthened.[13]

The new elites used the structures of the clan to organize craft guilds, militias, and corvée squads, and the clan leaders became part of an autocratic hierarchy. The state also took over from the priesthood and the kinship groups the distribution of food during droughts and famines, and some part of the tribute it received from conquered peoples. The ruling family gave land and booty to the soldiery, gave or sold war captives as slaves to the owners of the great estates, and underwrote the cost of religious festivals to celebrate military victories.

Trading was of the utmost importance in establishing routes to the essential raw materials. The principal goal of warfare was commercial, to control the trade routes and sources of supply. When trade routes also became tribute routes, garrisons provided security for the long-distance merchants. As a class, the merchants prospered greatly, and were organized under an official with superior status who enjoyed a very close relationship with the ruling families. The merchants who handled the intercity trade under royal control were included in the lists of individuals receiving rations and allotments of land.

As the kings gained ascendancy over the priesthood, they established an independent economic base, building palaces on the land they acquired. To buttress their essentially secular authority the kings assumed priestly functions, built temples crowned by massive ziggurats, claimed divine origin, and set up a system of hereditary succession. The lavish tombs of the kings of Ur, where many members of their retinue were sacrificed when the rulers died, represent another tangible aspect of royal wealth and power.

The extent of territorial conquest was continuously broadened, and by about 2600 B.C., Sargon the Great of Akkad unified Sumer with northern Mesopotamia. He and his successors acquired vast quantities of land in an unprecedented pattern of extended territorial control. Thenceforth, deities who had been patrons of agriculture were depicted as celestial warriors. Enlil, the "farmer," the "lord of the plow," became "lord of all lands," or "he who breaks enemy land as a single reed." Sargon's conquests marked the beginning of an imperialism that culminated with the empire of Hammurabi, which extended from the Persian Gulf to the Habur River. In 1750 B.C., Hammurabi established his dynasty at Babylon, and with the rise of Babylonia the history of Sumer came to an end.

Women in Sumer

The differences in economic and political organization in Sumer and Crete are striking, as are the resulting differences in the role of women, though even with the militarization of Sumer we find traces of a prior matriarchy. During the First Dynasty of Ur, which began shortly after 3000 B.C., the royal tombs indicate that in the ruling class the status of women may have been higher than that of men. Here two graves have been found, those of Queen Shub-ad and her supposed consort. But only the queen's name was inscribed, and her grave, even more than her consort's, shows the astonishing wealth of the rulers. In northern Mesopotamia, the woman Ku-Bau, an innkeeper, had risen to power, founded the Third Dynasty of Kish, ruled for a very long time, and become a legendary figure. One Baranamtarra, bearing the honorific title "The Woman," ruled the city of Lagash with her husband Lugalanda, the patesi; kept her own court, "The House of the Woman," distinct from her husband's court, "The House of the Man"; and her chief minister was styled "Scribe of the House of the Woman." Shagshag, referred to as "The Goddess Bau," wife of the next patesi, Urukagina, who ruled Lagash beginning around 2630 B.C., also kept her own court and was served by the "Scribe of the Goddess Bau." Does this title mean that the queens were also deified in their own lifetime and that the patesis were merely consorts, the real authority being vested in their wives? In both reigns official documents were dated in the names of the women.[14]

In the mercantile class, both married and unmarried women engaged in trade freely and made contracts in their own names. They sometimes carried on long-distance trade and ran businesses, particularly inns and taverns. Women kept their right to inherit land and their names sometimes appear on land deeds and ration lists as heads of households. Documents recording purchases of land in which multiple sellers are in a corporate relation to one another refer to "sons of the field," a category that sometimes included women.[15]

Women also retained the right to practice certain professions, particularly that of medicine, and an old Babylonian text from the city of Larsa, as late as Hammurabi's reign, refers to a woman physician at the palace. In

Mesopotamia surgery and medicine were divine functions exercised by the goddess Bau. The earliest Sumerian medical text, dating from the latter part of the third millennium B.C., is altogether free from the irrational and mystical elements that entered medicine later, when women began to be ousted from the profession.

Both girls and boys were trained to be scribes in the schools attached to the earlier Sumerian temples. Some of these scribes continued to live in the temples, performing religious tasks such as preparing the books for the services, keeping temple accounts, and recording the details of the legal actions brought before the priestly courts. Some even did original research, copying out old inscriptions on brick or stone that cast light on the past, still a major source of information for us today. But there is no question that the invention of writing in Sumer, which fairly soon led to the establishment of a formal educational system, benefited mainly the members of the ruling classes. A school, dating back to about 1780 B.C., found in a priest's home in Ur, was attended principally by upper-class male students. In striking contrast to the virtual absence of physical punishment in preclass societies, one school official was "the man in charge of the whip." The goals of Sumerian education have a very familiar ring:

> The competitive drive for superiority and preeminence played a large role in Sumerian formal education, which entailed many years of school attendance and study. Together with the whip and the cane, it was consciously utilized by both parents and teachers to make the student exert himself to the utmost to master the complicated but far from exciting curriculum in order to become a successful scribe and a learned scholar.[16]

While a few upper-class women in early Sumerian cities were rulers, priestesses, doctors, and scribes, their lower-class sisters were factory workers, prostitutes, wives, and slaves. Probably the first record of women factory workers dates from the Third Dynasty of Ur, 2278–2170 B.C., but it does not state whether they were slaves or free. The women spun and wove the raw wool, an indispensable trade item, brought to the temple by country people. Already in the earliest Protoliterate tablets, about 3500 B.C., signs appear for "slave girl." Male slaves appear later and in far smaller numbers. Slaves were war captives and people who had committed some offense. Also, in payment of debt, a man might give his wife and children to his creditor for three years of slavery. Slaves were owned even by ordinary artisans, farmers, and petty officials, but they played a far more important economic role on the great estates and the temples. The Bau archives of Lagash show that in a community of about 1,200 people there were 250 to 300 slaves, mainly women. One tablet alone lists 205 slave girls and their children, who were probably put to work weaving, milling, brewing, cooking, and doing other closely supervised indoor work.

The slave was regarded as property and could therefore be branded and flogged, with more severe punishments for attempts to escape. A female slave had to give her buyer not only her labor but her body. He could, if he wanted, turn her into a prostitute. However, a free man who took a slave as his concubine and had children by her could not sell her, and on his death both she and the children became free. If a free woman married a slave, the children inherited half the father's property when he died and the mother's freedom. In a document dating from the end of the early dynastic period, the Sumerian word for "freedom," *amargi,* meaning literally "return to the mother," appears for the first time. This phrase refers to the earlier matrilineal clan system.

Male domination was more and more reflected in religion. The goddess who pervaded all aspects of life in Crete, as in earlier Sumerian society, was replaced by a hierarchical pantheon headed by a male god. Judging by the recorded prayers, and ritual and mythological texts, women were ousted from their public roles and many of the functions of the goddesses were assigned to gods. For example, when the patron of the scribes changed from a goddess to a god, only male scribes were employed in the temples and palaces, and history began to be written from an androcentric perspective. The harems of the gods reflect the harems of the palaces, and the royal right to every woman's virginity dates back almost 5,000 years, as shown in the epic of Gilgamesh.

> As king, Gilgamesh was a tyrant to his people.
> He demanded, from an old birthright,
> The privilege of sleeping with their brides
> Before the husbands were permitted. . . .
>
> Gilgamesh was a godlike man alone
> With his thoughts in idleness except
> For those evenings when he went down
> Into the marketplace to the Family House
> To sleep with the virgins, . . .[17]

The contempt for women that accompanied their degradation is expressed by Gilgamesh when Inanna, the patron deity of his city, proposes marriage to him. When Gilgamesh asks, "What would I gain by taking you as wife," her reply, "Love and peace," is answered by: "You are an old fat whore, that's all you are."

The roles of the priestesses also changed to reflect the secular status of women in class-stratified Sumer. By the time of the Third Dynasty of Ur, 2278–2170 B.C., they had become members of the god's harem, concubines and prostitutes in the temples. The organization of the temple priestesses, the Sal-Me, was headed by the priestess who was the god's "true wife," and who might be the eldest daughter of the reigning king. At the bottom of the hierarchy were very many common temple prostitutes. In between were the god's concubines, some of them princesses, who might bear the children of unknown fathers but were not permitted to bear children to a legal husband who owned property and carried on business in their own names. Later, the Code of Hammurabi restricted the activities of the priestesses, but not, apparently, of the priests. A priestess opening a wine shop or even entering one was to be burned.

Laws also codified changes in women's status in the family. Long before Hammurabi's reign, the Sumerian kings brought the family under their control and changed the status of wives and mothers. The increasing prevalence of private property required the imposition of monogamy, in practice for women only; the woman's isolation, in the nuclear family, from her kinship group; the inventions of adultery and illegitimacy, and the harsh punishment, usually only of women, for these "crimes." Hence, the development of the legal means by which property could be kept in the family, transmitted from father to son. What is perhaps the first Sumerian law code contains a provision forbidding women, under pain of being stoned, any longer to take two husbands, a practice that had apparently had been common in the period of the matrilineal clan.

Once married, the Sumerian woman had some legal protections, especially compared with the later Babylonian laws. Her dowry was her inalienable property, which she could bequeath to her children. Her husband could not dispose of their joint property without her consent. She could keep and dispose of her own slaves, and give witness in a court of law. Upon her husband's death she inherited the same amount of property as each of the children and could marry again if she wished, taking her dowry with her. On the other hand, only the wife suffered from certain legal disabilities. As noted earlier, a husband could sell his wife under certain conditions and hand her over as a slave for three years in payment of a debt. He could divorce her on very slight grounds, but she could obtain a divorce only with great difficulty and only if her conduct was above reproach. Docility was brutally enforced:

> If a woman said to a man "....." [unfortunately the text is unintelligible at this crucial point], her teeth were crushed with burnt bricks, [and] these burnt bricks [upon which her guilt was inscribed] were hung up in the great gate [for all to see].[18]

If a woman was barren, her husband could divorce her or take a second wife, and to prevent this the wife could give her husband one of her own slaves as a concubine. If childlessness was due to the wife's refusal of conjugal relations, she was thrown into the water and drowned. The same penalty attached to adultery by women. The Code of Hammurabi carried to their ultimate severity the penalties for offenses against "the sacredness of the family tie":

> A flagrantly careless and uneconomical wife [to be drowned]. A wife causing her husband's death, in order to marry another [to be impaled or crucified]. . . . A worthless wife became a slave in her own house if her husband took another wife.[19]

Conclusion

The evidence for women's status in Minoan society is mainly archaeological, while for Sumer it is both archaeological and historical. A comparison of the archaeological data shows that Minoan arts and crafts reached heights not attained by any other Bronze Age civilization, in a society that left the artists, and the people as a whole, relatively free to be creative and innovative. In Sumer art reached its zenith sometime around 3500 B.C., and thereafter became more and more stereotyped and static as private property, political centralization, and militarism became increasingly dominant. The differences in the development of the arts reflect the differences in the socioeconomic processes in Minoan Crete and Sumer, particularly as they relate to the status of women.

In preclass Sumer, as in Neolithic societies generally, the communal ownership of land by the corporate kinship group was integrally related to the preeminence of women. As the kinship structures were radically changed to fit a rigidly hierarchical system, increasingly based on private property and the centralization of political power in the hands of military leaders, women were pushed out of political decision making. With no voice in the laws that were passed primarily to protect the wealth and power of the elite groups, they were deprived of education and ousted from lucrative and prestigious professions. Segregated from the kinship group, they were made totally dependent on the male heads of the patrilineal family. Women could be divorced on the slightest pretext, in which case they had few alternatives to prostitution, or they could be sold into slavery. Finally, they could suffer the death penalty not only for the new crime of adultery but also for minor acts of independence.

In Minoan Crete the high status of women derived from their interdependent relationships with the corporate kinship group and from their strong association with other women. Although Minoan society was socially stratified, women appear to have had access to all occupations. In the absence of warfare, they participated at least equally with men in political decision making, while in religion and social life they were supreme. The prominence of women in the brilliant civilization of Minoan Crete is in the sharpest contrast to their subordination and degradation under Sumerian civilization toward its close.

Notes

1. James Mellaart, *Catal Huyuk: A Neolithic Town in Anatolia,* McGraw-Hill, New York, 1967, p. 77.
2. Emily Vermeule, *Greece in the Bronze Age,* University of Chicago Press, Chicago, 1964, p. 21.
3. Sinclair Hood, *The Home of the Heroes: The Aegean Before the Greeks,* McGraw-Hill, New York, 1967, p. 35.
4. George Thomson, *The Prehistoric Aegean,* Citadel, New York, 1965, p. 28.
5. Sir Leonard Woolley, *The Sumerians,* W. W. Norton, New York, 1965, p. 39.
6. Agnes Carr Vaughan, *The House of the Double Axe,* Doubleday, Garden City, N.Y., 1959, p. 138.
7. Stanley Diamond, *In Search of the Primitive,* Transaction Books, New Brunswick, N.J., p. 304.
8. Leonard Cottrell, *Lion Gate,* Evans Brothers, London, 1963, p. 199.
9. R. F. Willetts, *Cretan Cults and Festivals,* Barnes & Noble, New York, 1962, p. 20.
10. Ibid., p. 76.
11. Jacquetta Hawkes, *Dawn of the Gods,* Random House, New York, 1968, p. 76; Hood, *Home of the Heroes,* p. 81; C. G. Thomas, "Matriarchy in Early Greece: The Bronze and Dark Ages," *Arethusa,* 6 (Fall 1973); Cottrell, *Lion Gate,* p. 199.
12. Thomson, *Prehistoric Aegean,* p. 430.
13. Robert M. Adams, "Patterns of Urbanization in Early Southern Mesopotamia," *Man, Settlement and Urbanism,* eds. P. J. Ucke, Ruth Tringham, and G. W. Dimbleby, Schenkman, Cambridge, Mass., 1972, pp. 743–744.
14. Woolley, *Sumerians,* p. 66; Thomson, *Prehistoric Aegean,* p. 161.
15. Robert M. Adams, *The Evolution of Urban Society,* Aldine, Chicago, 1971, p. 83.
16. Samuel Noah Kramer, *The Sumerians,* University of Chicago Press, Chicago, 1963, p. 266.
17. From *Gilgamesh: A Verse Narrative,* translated by Herbert Mason (Boston: Houghton Mifflin, 1970), pp. 5–7. Copyright © 1970 by Herbert Mason. Reprinted by permission of Houghton Mifflin Company.
18. Kramer, *Sumerians,* p. 322.
19. J. B. Bury, S. A. Cook, and F. E. Adcock, "The Law of Ancient Babylonia," *Man in Adaptation: The Institutional Framework,* ed. Y. A. Cohen, Aldine, Chicago, 1971, pp. 154–157.

Suggestions for Further Reading

Adams, Robert M. *The Evolution of Urban Society.* Aldine, Chicago, 1971.

Diamond, Stanley. *In Search of the Primitive.* Transaction Books, New Brunswick, N.J., 1974.

Engels, Frederick. *The Origin of the Family, Private Property and the State.* Introduction by Eleanor Leacock. International Publishers, New York, 1972.

Evans, Arthur. *The Palace of Minos.* Vols. 1-4. Macmillan, London, 1921–1935.

Hawkes, Jacquetta. *Dawn of the Gods.* Random House, New York, 1968.

Mellaart, James. *Catal Huyuk: A Neolithic Town in Anatolia.* McGraw-Hill, New York, 1967.

Morgan, Lewis Henry. *Ancient Society.* Edited by Eleanor Leacock. Peter Smith, Gloucester, Mass., 1974.

Redfield, Robert. *The Primitive World and Its Transformations.* Cornell University Press, Ithaca, 1953.

Willetts, R. F. *Everyday Life in Ancient Crete.* G. P. Putnam's Sons, New York, 1969.

Woolley, Sir Leonard. *The Sumerians.* W. W. Norton, New York, 1965.

3

"Liberated" Women: The Classical Era

Marylin Arthur

Classical Greece and Rome continued in the direction of social and political differentiation with a corresponding reduction in women's role. Culture also became more sophisticated in its rationalization of these trends. Marylin Arthur shows us how literature and art can be decoded to give us insights not only into the daily reality of the ancients, but into their psychic lives as well. The classical Greek polis *justified the evolution of its patriarchal social structure in myths that civilization had been a hard-won victory over nature, with male moral authority triumphing over female irrationality. This misogynistic sentiment arose during the transition from an aristocratic to a more broadly based society.*

In the period when a new class of commercial entrepreneurs came into being, the nuclear family assumed a more important role in creating and transmitting wealth. The oikos, *or household, was the basis for citizenship, so women's role as mother and wife assumed legal and moral dimensions: their main function was to ensure the legitimacy of heirs. They themselves, however, were merely wards of the male heads of their households. Thus, relative democratization was gained for the class partly through the subordination of its women and also, of course, its slaves.*

In the Hellenistic period that followed, the empire gained importance at the expense of both the household and the polis, in which women, ironically, now regained some independence. As the gap between public and personal life widened, people increasingly turned for satisfaction to the latter and accepted female sexuality, previously feared as threatening to civilization and rationality. Women's position improved in law, life, and literature, and misogyny waned. Rome underwent a similar transformation from republic to empire, resulting in an emergent middle class, smaller families, subordination of women, and evolving misogyny, though the last did not have as deep historical roots as in Greece.

Left: Perseus slaying Medusa, vase early fifth century B.C. *Right:* Mask of Medusa, sixth century B.C. The myth of Perseus and the Medusa illustrates the familiar Greek theme of male triumph over female monstrosity. The monster Medusa ("ruler" in the feminine gender), who turned men to stone by her glance, was slain by Perseus with the help of the goddess Athene. Athene's ambivalent allegiance to both male hero and female monster was shown by her use of the mask of the Medusa on her armor. Here Medusa's potential survived, but in a form that subordinated it to the control of the patriarchal state. (Vase from the Metropolitan Museum of Art, Rogers Fund, 1906. Mask from the Metropolitan Museum of Art, Fletcher Fund, 1931.)

As a general proposition: Social advances and changes of periods are brought about by virtue of the progress of women towards liberty and the decadences of the social order are brought about by virtue of the decrease of liberty of women. . . . The extension of privileges to women is the general principle of all social progress.[1]

CHARLES FOURIER

This chapter will treat one historical stage that, in our view, has peculiar and important ramifications for women: the transition from the aristocratic to a more egalitarian form of the state. This transition is a recurrent one in history; it appears later most notably as the passage from feudalism to capitalism, and occurs in antiquity in the course of the development of the Greek and Roman states. In outlining the general historical forces that brought about this transition in both Greece and Rome, and in correlating in some detail the concomitant change in the status and cultural evaluation of women, we expect to show, as Fourier put it, "the progress of women towards liberty" as a measure of both the general character of human relations and of the relationship between human beings and the natural world.

We shall proceed by first discussing the correlation between the ideological evaluation of women in ancient Greece and their social position; second, we shall present the transformation that both the attitude toward women and women themselves underwent in the Hellenistic period, when the social and political organization of the state was transformed; third, we shall examine the Roman situation and the dynamics behind the alteration in women's status and in the attitude toward them in the course of the transition from republic to empire.

Aphrodite Denied: Classical Greece

In his epic poem *Theogony,* Hesiod explains the origins of the cosmos through myths describing the births of the gods. His narrative centers on a series of succession myths that conform to a single pattern: the youngest son enters into an alliance with his mother to overthrow his father. In the first stage the female goddess Earth (Gaia) generates Heaven (Ouranos) and together they produce the Titans (gigantic monsters). Ouranos attempts to prevent the birth of his children by holding them in Gaia's womb, and she retaliates by arming her youngest son Kronos with a sickle and setting him in ambush against his father. Kronos castrates Ouranos and thereby establishes himself as ruler of the gods. In the second stage of the succession myth Kronos and Rhea generate the Olympian gods. Kronos, afraid of losing his supremacy to his son, swallows his children as Rhea brings them forth. But she, upon the advice of Gaia and Ouranos, deceives her husband by giving him a rock wrapped in swaddling clothes instead of her youngest son, Zeus. When Zeus grows to maturity he and Gaia trick Kronos into vomiting up all of the children. Zeus establishes his supremacy over the universe by defeating the Titans in battle and escapes from the succession cycle by swallowing his wife Metis (Intelligence). He thus gains control over her powers of reproduction. His first child is the goddess Athene, who in Greek religion remains affiliated with her father and symbolizes male dominance of the universe. Zeus's wives bear his other children, but these represent no threat, since the birth of Athene establishes the principle of male dominion and female subordination. These children (Justice, Good Order, Peace, etc.) betoken Zeus's sponsorship of a moral order associated with civilized life. In addition, since they were all female, they signify the beneficence of the female principle when subjected to regulation by patriarchal authority.

Hesiod's model for the evolution of the cosmos and the birth of civilization thus involves a progression from a world dominated by the generative powers of the female to one overseen by the moral authority of the male. Associated with the early era of female dominance is the primacy of Nature in her most uncontrolled, spontaneous, and violent form: Gaia sends forth both rampant vegetation and monstrous, semihuman creatures. The triumph of the male deity signifies the subjugation of the procreative power of Nature to some form of control that renders it useful to civilization and the restraint of her more violent, chaotic, and destructive aspects.

The struggle Hesiod portrays is a pervasive theme in Greek thought. In the "Homeric Hymn to Delphian Apollo," for example, Apollo has to contend with the schemes and monsters bred by the indigenous female deity before he can establish the famous oracle at Delphi. The sculptural ornamentations on many classical Greek temples, including the Parthenon, depict the battles of the Olympian gods against the Titans and of the Athenians against the Amazons. Both the Olympian gods and the Athenian state stand for the forces of order, control, and harmony; the Amazons and the Titan giants symbolize chaotic monstrosity and hostility to political and social order.

This mythological scheme applies also to the conflict underlying the foundation of the Greek city-state (*polis*). The *Oresteia* of Aeschylus celebrates the birth of civil society and the triumph of the rule of law over the more primitive forms of tribal justice and represents this victory as a divine vindication of Orestes's murder of his mother Clytemnestra. She had killed her husband Agamemnon when he returned victorious from the Trojan war, bringing with him the Trojan priestess Cassandra as his concubine. In the trial with which the trilogy culminates, the Olympian divinity Apollo, son of Zeus, takes Orestes's side and the Furies, foul, animallike creatures who pursue and torture Orestes, defend Clytemnestra's rights. The characters themselves present the confrontation as the struggle between two systems, one old and one new, one associated with mother-right, the other with the authority of the father. Apollo, in pleading on Orestes's behalf, affirms the superiority of the father by disparaging the female's part in generation:

> The mother is no parent of that which is called
> her child, but only nurse of the new-planted seed
> that grows. The parent is he who mounts. A stranger she
> preserves a stranger's seed, if no god interfere.[2]

Athene, who settles the dispute by casting her vote for Orestes, proclaims herself partisan to the male for the following reasons:

> There is no mother anywhere who gave me birth,
> and, but for marriage, I am always for the male
> with all my heart, and strongly on my father's side.[3]

The moral and legal underpinnings of the Greek polis are thus represented as the result of an evolution from mother-right to father-right. Further, the patriarchal form of society is proclaimed as the necessary correlate to a higher form of civilized life. The goddess Athene is the ideal symbol for the new state, for as a female she embodies the dynamic principle of growth and generation, but her subordination to her father means that her potential finds expression in a socially useful form. She is a masculinized deity, for what is essentially female about her (the power of generation) never achieves expression: she remains a virgin goddess. She is also the major deity of ancient Greece. None of the other goddesses achieves Athene's preeminence in the art and literature of classical antiquity. When Aphrodite finally displaces her in the Hellenistic period there is a correlative change in both the status of and attitude toward women.

The threat women presented to the Greek mind emerges with particular clarity when the struggle is transferred to the arena of the individual human psyche. Euripides's *Hippolytus* is a drama played out between the inner and outer forces that compete for domination of the souls of the protagonists, Hippolytus and Phaedra. Aphrodite and Artemis symbolize the two extremes — one, the goddess of the passion that disrupts life and conflicts with social values; the other, a virgin goddess who stands for denial and control of instinctual urges. Aphrodite inspires in Phaedra not merely passion but an overwhelming and illegitimate desire for her stepson Hippolytus. Artemis, whom Hippolytus adopts as his patron, supports his hatred for the female sex and total rejection of sexuality. Phaedra, the character who in the play represents the sexuality Hippolytus has denied in himself, acts as the instrument of his destruction. The excess of Hippolytus's attack upon the female sex leads Phaedra to retaliate by accusing him of rape; the false accusation results in Hippolytus's death.

Euripides does not suggest a resolution of competing claims in the manner of Hesiod or Aeschylus. The action in the play moves between two irreconcilable opposites. The polarity is thus represented as an opposition between two autonomous goddesses: there is no longer a male deity to symbolize the possibility of transcendence. There remain only the alternatives of sterile repression, symbolized by Artemis, and the free reign of the instincts for which Aphrodite stands. The action of the play demonstrates that these instincts are by their nature uncontrollable, irresistible, and totally without regard for the limits of social custom and moral law. Insofar as they are exclusively associated with women in Greek thought, women themselves come to represent all that is opposed to civilized life, the whole world of the instincts and passions that must submit to restraint and modification in order for civilization to survive.

From Hesiod to Euripides and beyond, Greek thought contains a consistent and systematic association of the world of nature (including human nature) with female potency both expressed (as by Aphrodite) and denied (as by Artemis or Athene). Misogynistic sentiment, therefore, generally expresses a feeling of being at war with nature. We often encounter these two themes together. The most famous example of misogyny in Greek literature, for example, is the long diatribe against the female sex by Semonides of Amorgos that associates the various types of women with different animals. Characteristically, in the only other long fragment of this author that survives, Semonides portrays man as a helpless victim of divine caprice and the unpredictability of the natural world.

In Sophocles's tragedy *Antigone* this theme is even more explicit. The famous hymn to mankind takes the form of a catalogue of the ways in which man, by his ingenuity and will, has bent nature to his needs. Of particular interest to us is the praise of man's subjugation of the female earth:

> And she, the greatest of gods, the earth —
> ageless she is, and unwearied — he wears her away
> as the ploughs go up and down from year to year
> and his mules turn up the soil.[4]

This celebration of man as tamer of nature reveals the extent to which man, in his most human aspect, was conceived by the Greeks as something alien to and opposed to nature. He therefore asserted himself most fully as man and as human through the control he exercised over the natural world. Insofar as woman was identified with this world she was conceived of as hostile to man; if the Greeks thought of civilization as a triumph of man over nature, it was a triumph of man over woman no less.

A remarkable and peculiarly Greek manifestation of this notion of woman's fundamentally antisocial disposition was the theory and practice of Dionysiac religion. Dionysos (who became Bacchus in the Roman pantheon) was a fertility god associated with the growth of the vine, and hence with wine. "The Greeks," as Plutarch explained it, "think that Dionysos presides, not only over the wine, but over the whole realm of the wet element." The latter included plant sap, life blood, and semen. But more important, Dionysos was a wild and potentially destructive god, worshiped especially by women. His savage nature was revealed in the practice of the *omophagia* ("eating raw," usually animals and sometimes children) associated with his worship. His followers, the maenads, celebrated their devotion to Dionysos in a state of ecstatic possession. The worship took the form of frenzied dancing that could lead to violent acts of brutality like the *sparagmos* ("tearing apart") of animals or children.

The worship of Dionysos was a regular part of Greek social life and did not ordinarily involve savagery. But the poetry, drama, and art of the classical period kept alive the wild potentiality of the cult and its worshipers. In cases dealing with religious themes there is hardly a motif so common as the maenad, alone or with the god or his attendant satyrs. She rushes forward barefoot, her hair and clothing disheveled; snakes swirl about her head and arms, animal skins hang from her shoulders, and her neck strains backward into the curve of ecstasy. In her hand she wields the tree branch that was a symbol of the cult. The maenad was thus a constant reminder of women's close association with the natural world of rampant vegetative growth and wild animal drives.

How can we account for such ideas as women's fundamental hostility to civilized life? The answer, we suggest, is that such ideas represent a configuration of themes that ordinarily arise at a particular moment in history: that of the transition from an aristocratic or feudal to a more egalitarian type of society in which the nuclear family, for reasons we shall explain, assumes sudden and overwhelming importance.

Aristocratic or feudal society is usually dominated by a landholding nobility defined by birth whose social relationships preserve many of the features of tribal society. In such societies every social relationship finds concrete expression in an exchange of objects, including women. Aristocratic solidarity is maintained by these ties among men; women, as the medium of exchange, remain outside the principal social grouping.

In the midst of this society a class of commercial entrepreneurs arises. They derive from all social and economic groups: wealthy landowners interested in trade, younger or illegitimate sons of the nobility involved in maritime ventures, craftsmen and other specialists, and wealthy, independent peasants. In archaic Greece the rise of this class was associated with the discovery of iron, whose ready availability made possible small-scale cultivation of land and thus transformed the method of production. The artisans worked the new metals, the merchants traded in it, and agriculture was intensified through its use. This new middle class was thus still strongly tied to the land (the economic base of society was agricultural throughout all of antiquity), but it was a larger and more diverse group than the landowning aristocracy. At this point in history the small household emerged as the productive unit of society, and any head of a household (who was simultaneously a landowner) automatically became a citizen or member of the state. Conversely, the state itself, the polis, was defined as the sum of all individual households.

The more inclusive and more egalitarian state that resulted from these shifts in political and economic strength in the eighth and seventh centuries B.C. was thus bound up with the increasing importance of the *oikos*, or household, which was a small holding corporation composed of its male head, his wife, their children, and the slaves who served it and worked the land that was its economic base. The legal rights over this property were vested in the male head and transferred to his son to assure the continuity of the individual oikoi. The whole of the productive output of this small corporation was appropriated by its male head as the basis for his claim to participate in the state.

The transformations that occurred in Greece in the political, economic, and social arenas were internally consistent and marked the beginning of a new and important phase of human development. For the transition from aristocracy to democracy was not merely one in a series of historical advances but a stage in which the character of society was qualitatively altered. Property holding in the form of household units was the first advance over tribal ownership; the corresponding legal system that came into being at this time was the first step in the dissociation of the state from civil society; finally, the myth of a struggle between male and female gods culminating in the establishment of a patriarchal reign was the first articulation of an ideological pattern that, ever since, has accompanied such transformations. We shall see, for example, that in Rome a conceptual scheme like that of the Greeks, which implies women's basic hostility to civilized life, did not arise until historical conditions paralleled those under which it arose in Greece.

The new importance of the oikos in the Greek democracy had important ramifications for the position of women. For the woman was a necessary part of the oikos: she produced the sons who kept it together, and she supervised its day-to-day activities. The nuclear family, which in tribal and aristocratic society had existed only as a biological and social unit, now became a political and economic reality. The functions of wife and mother that women had always performed were now construed as a necessity and a duty, and their failure to perform them had legal and moral consequences.

The laws of the new democratic state therefore imposed restrictions on women's freedom designed to insure their subservience to the needs of the state. The patriarchal orientation of Greek society is nowhere more clearly demonstrated than by the legal system, which prohibited women from ever achieving the status of fully autonomous beings. Throughout her life a woman remained the legal ward of the head of her oikos, who was called her *kyrios* (or lord) and who might be her father, husband, or male child. His consent and supervision was necessary for any legal action undertaken on her behalf. Women could not engage in transactions involving property valued at over one *medimnos* (Greek bushel), about three days' wages for a skilled laborer; this restriction allowed women to trade and barter on a small scale but prevented them from transferring any landed property and therefore from interfering in the political and economic operation of the oikos. A woman could not inherit family property outright (with one exception discussed below). Her share consisted instead of her dowry, a sum provided by her father to insure her maintenance. When she married it was added to the oikos of her husband, and the wife herself could not ever dispose of it. It remained a legally separate piece of property, however, and her husband was liable for its repayment to the oikos of his wife's father in the event of divorce.

The word for marriage in ancient Greece betrays its function and character. It was called *ekdosis,* loan, and so marriage was a transaction whereby a woman's father lent her out to the head of another oikos so that she might perform for the latter the functions of wife and mother. The children of the marriage belonged to the oikos of the husband. The marriage itself was quite ordinarily contracted with a near relative (an uncle or cousin on the father's side). Divorce was a simple procedure for either the husband or the wife and returned the wife to the oikos of her father.

Behind all of these laws and restrictions there lay one primary principle: the inviolability of the individual oikos unit. A woman's procreative function was a duty owed ultimately to the oikos of her birth, should it ever be in danger of passing out of existence for want of an heir. A woman who was the only child in an oikos was in a special situation and was called an *epikleros,* "heiress." She "inherited" the oikos property but was legally obligated to contract a marriage with the next of kin on her father's side. Strictly speaking, then, she inherited only the right to transfer ownership of the property, and the laws required that it be transferred to a male member of the same family to whom it had already belonged (usually to her father's brother). The unbreakable bond between a woman and the oikos of her birth thus insured against the disappearance of that oikos.

This contrasts with earlier aristocratic practice, which allowed women to transfer ownership of property they might inherit to their husbands regardless of family affiliation. For marriage in aristocratic society entailed the forging of a powerful political, economic, and social bond between two houses. The upwardly mobile lower classes in aristocratic society therefore commonly regarded the right of intermarriage with women of the upper classes as an important privilege. In the democratic polis, too, marriage might lead to the political and economic advancement of the husband, since he gained an affiliation with the woman's family and the right to manage her dowry, which could involve a considerable amount of property. But there were some crucial restrictions: he could not dispose of the dowry; and if by marriage he acquired rights over the property of the woman's oikos (i.e., if she were an epikleros), he forfeited his rights to inheritance within his own family line. Further, he was not registered as kyrios of the newly acquired oikos until he had produced a son to inherit it. The state thus limited individual freedom to dispose of property to prevent its conflicting with the higher principle of the inviolability of each oikos. This primary principle, in turn, derived its force from the Greek idea that, as Aristotle put it, "the best form of political society is one where power is vested in the middle class." And it was essential to the definition of this group that "its members should possess a moderate and adequate property" (i.e., neither the large estates of the aristocratic class nor the impoverished farms of the peasants).

The centrality of the oikos to the polis caused a revaluation of the crime of adultery. Since adultery threatened the integrity of the oikos it became a crime against society rather than a personal transgression. The state, therefore, regulated the sexual lives of citizen women. Adultery of a free Athenian woman made her liable to exclusion from participation in religious ceremonies and festivals, and her husband had to divorce her. The adulterer could be killed with impunity. Men who raped or seduced unmarried free women were punished with a fine; an unmarried daughter caught with a man could be sold into slavery. The schedule of penalties shows that in this area of Greek life, too, the sanctity of the oikos dictated law. Adultery was punished more severely than rape or seduction because that crime threatened the preservation of the household by casting doubts on the legitimacy of its heir. Such a penalty was tantamount to loss of citizenship for a woman, since religion and marriage were the only two areas where the citizen woman was privileged.

Although men suffered heavy penalties for committing adultery with citizen women, their sexual lives were in other respects far less circumscribed than those of their wives. Prostitutes and courtesans were available in addition to homosexual partners. A famous statement by the orator Demosthenes distinguishes three kinds of women: "We have *hetairai* [courtesans] for the sake of pleasure, prostitutes for the daily care of the body, but wives to bear us legitimate children and to be the trusted guardians of our households." Demosthenes's description of the wife's function summarized her importance to the state and demonstrated that this importance was conceived of in terms of her role in the oikos. This subordination of women to their husbands in the interests of the oikos whose prosperity benefited them both was a unique feature of middle-class democracy. And so the relationship between man and woman in ancient Greece became the model for the relationship between citizen and state. For the polis required the subordination of man's individual and private self to its interests, and it was even proposed that the proper relation of the citizen to the state was that of a "lover": "I want you to feed your eyes upon Athens every day, and become filled with passion for her . . ." said Pericles in his Funeral Oration.

Regardless of her subordination to her husband, the married woman was held in high regard in ancient Greece. The association she formed with her husband was a kind of partnership; each party made a contribution to the oikos that was their mutual concern. The woman's job, aside from bearing children, was to supervise the household. She lived almost entirely in the private sphere and did not ordinarily participate in her husband's social activities. In the everyday life of the polis, however, the contributions of women were recognized by the important role they played in the celebration of religious festivals. For example, in the Parthenon frieze that depicts the Panathenaic procession in honor of Athene, young girls carry the sacrificial vessels, and the more mature women of the city, both married and unmarried, bear to the goddess the robe they had woven for her. The presentation of this robe climaxed the procession. The women's prominent role in this important celebration reveals that their contributions to the state were recognized and honored, even though women were not granted commensurate legal and economic privileges.

Noncitizen women lived a very different kind of life in ancient Greece. For example, the hetaira whom Demosthenes mentioned was a professional. She might be free or a slave, but she was only infrequently a citizen woman. Prostitutes, by contrast, were invariably slave women. The hetaira's job was to entertain at male drinking parties (*symposia*); this is the "pleasure" to which Demosthenes refers. The hetaira was educated in poetry and music with an eye to the enjoyment her presence could provide for the men at their symposia; she was thus more cultivated than cultured, although this fact has often led to the misrepresentation of courtesans as a highly educated, almost scholarly elite. Some, like Aspasia, the mistress of Pericles, formed liaisons with the leading poets, philosophers, orators, and statesmen of the day, but ordinarily a free woman resorted to courtesanship only out of financial necessity.

Other professions lower-class free women and slaves practiced were those of wool working (spinning and weaving), nursing, midwifery, retail selling of such wares as the garlands used in religious sacrifice, cobbling, and vase painting. Household slaves mainly spun yarn and wove cloth and performed other menial tasks. Even in households that could not afford male slaves, there would always be a few female slaves.

The Greeks themselves realized that women's lot was not an enviable one. The theme of the incapacities under which women must labor recurs throughout classical literature. Medea, for example, in Euripides's play of the same name, complains:

> We women are the most unfortunate creatures.
> Firstly with an excess of wealth it is required
> For us to buy a husband and take for our bodies
> A master; for not to take one is even worse.
> And now the question is serious whether we take
> A good or bad one; for there is no easy escape
> For a woman, nor can she say no to her marriage.
> She arrives among new modes of behavior and manners,
> And needs prophetic power, unless she has learned at home,
> How best to manage him who shares the bed with her.
> And if we work out all this well and carefully,
> And the husband lives with us and lightly bears his yoke,
> Then life is enviable. If not, I'd rather die.
> A man, when he's tired of the company in his home,
> Goes out of the house and puts an end to his boredom
> And turns to a friend or companion of his own age.
> But we are forced to keep our eyes on one alone.
> What they say of us is that we have a peaceful time
> Living at home, while they do the fighting in war.
> How wrong they are! I would very much rather stand
> Three times in the front of battle than bear one child.[5]

In what remains to us of the lyric poetry written by women, laments over lost virginity are a frequent theme. Several of the most beautiful fragments of Sappho treat this idea:

FIRST VOICE	Virginity O my virginity! Where will you go when I lose you?
SECOND VOICE	I'm off to a place I shall never come back from Dear Bride! I shall never come back to you Never![6]

Erinna addressed a hexameter poem to her childhood friend Baucis, who died shortly after marriage, and whom the poet gently chides for having transferred her affections to her new husband:

> O Baucis!
> the delights of a husband's bed,
> the magic of white sheets
> rustling
> charmed your heart
> into forgetfulness of childish
> pleasures
> Aphrodite
> has stolen you away
> into death.[7]

Such poetry, clearly, refers less to some supposed sexual trauma than to the jolt to their emotional and personal lives the sudden transition to the married state brought for women. This is the message of the lament of Procne in Sophocles's drama *Tereus,* who bewails her marriage to a barbarian Thracian king:

> Now I'm nothing — and all alone. . . . But I've given some thought to this life we women lead and what nothings we are. I think we're happiest as young children in our fathers' homes, where we lead the lives of human beings, and our nurses are carefree joys. But once we're grown to youth and reason — then we're thrown out of our family and country. Some of us go off to strangers, some to barbarians, some to be treated gently, some to be abused. And once one night has yoked us to this lot, we're obliged to commend it and think it fine! [8]

Aware though they may have been of the shortcomings of women's social role in the polis, the Greeks clearly regarded it as a necessary concomitant to the city-state. And so, whenever a modification of that role was proposed, it was always as part of a plan for a wholesale transformation of the state. Plato's *Republic* is the famous example, and his advocacy of equality between the men and women of the upper, or guardian, class is often cited as an example of liberated thinking. But the Greeks never advanced such ideas for the sake of their intrinsic merit; they always saw a change in family relations as a necessary but secondary issue. Plato, for example, proposed a return to an earlier era: the luxurious or aristocratic state was to be purified of those features that led to its transformation into the democratic polis. *The Republic* displays great similarities to the state of Sparta, which was peculiar in the Greek world precisely because it stopped developing in the seventh century. Its aristocratic form was preserved by a set of laws that maintained it as a military aristocracy instead of leading it toward a democracy.

The equality between the sexes Plato proposed really entailed the very different idea of "holding wives and children in common," as in the aristocratic state. Women, as the exchange objects, were to be held in common by the men of the class as a whole. The proverb with which Plato introduced this idea, "friends' possessions are held in common," refers to a system of free exchange within a restricted group. This ideal is a poor alternative indeed to counterpose against the Greek ideal of married life as exemplified in the relationship between Odysseus and Penelope in the *Odyssey* of Homer:

> It's a great strength and a fine thing
> when a man and a wife share their household
> as they share their thoughts:
> enemies gnash their teeth, friends are happy —
> and the two of them know it.[9]

This praise of women in the marriage relationship does not invalidate the idea that the fundamental attitude of the Greeks toward women remained misogynistic. As social beings, women in the polis entered into a partnership with men that fostered civilization, and only in this relationship did women gain favor. As we have seen, the misogyny of the Greeks originally sprang from the association of women with the world of instincts and passions, which was hostile to civilized life. Unlike man, the woman of the polis was regarded as a hybrid creature, a domesticated animal who could be adapted to the needs of society but whose fundamental instincts were antagonistic to it. Woman, says Euripides in an unidentified fragment, is a more terrible thing than the violence of the raging sea, than the force of torrents, than the sweeping breath of fire. Thus, her very existence was a testimony to the gods' hatred of mankind. This is the Greek view of women; this is the way in which women's ties with nature manifest themselves; this, finally, is the supreme articulation of man's alienation from the sources of his own essence as a natural being.

The Triumph of Aphrodite: The Hellenistic Era

On the east frieze of the Parthenon the twelve Olympian gods watch the solemn Panathenaic procession. Of all the gods in this pantheon, the only two who survived as important deities into the Hellenistic period were Aphrodite and Dionysos, just those two gods who sat most uneasily in the solemn assembly. For both deities shared an eastern origin that, in the context of classical Greece, always caused them to appear as intruders, outsiders, usurpers. In order to assimilate them into the Olympic pantheon their barbaric heritage had to be suppressed or overcome through some kind of ritual of adoption or rebirth. In the Hellenistic period this eastern origin reasserted itself, as the interests of the time turned in the direction of mystery religions and fertility cults. Aphrodite became one of the most important subjects of artistic representation as the ideal form of the female, now seen nude for the first time. Unlike her classical predecessor she does not stand cool and detached, but more usually bends or crouches to display more fully the elaborate curvature of her body. Dionysos became in this period the most important Greek god outside of Greece. He was the patron of artistic guilds, and he supplanted other deities in established religions such as that of the Orphics; one of the Ptolemies planned to make him the chief god of the empire.

The cultural transformations of the Hellenistic period, of which the increased importance of Aphrodite and Dionysos was only one sign, brought a change also in the attitude toward the relation between men and women. Here, as in the case of the classical Greek world, man's evaluation of nature and of his relation to it correlated with his attitude toward women. Let us therefore examine first the political and social organization of the Hellenistic world, then some of the very concrete ways in which women's position improved during this period, and finally the relation between the human and natural worlds.

After the death of Alexander the Great in 323 B.C., his vast kingdom was divided up into four distinct empires, each of which was still huge. The Ptolemaic empire was the most important. It included upper Egypt, extended over to the area along the Gaza strip, and took in the island of Cyprus. The kingdom contained a diverse population, but the government was highly centralized. Although ultimately the king controlled everything, the vast bureaucracy included a complex system of checks and counterchecks. The main business was agriculture, and the state monopolized oil and grain production. The native population, a pool of forced labor, performed all of the manual work. Their overseers were mostly Greeks or other foreigners, but the native Egyptian aristocracy maintained its position of social influence and power.

Alexandria, its capital, exemplified the characteristics of the empire as a whole. It was a conglomeration of individual settlements: there was an Egyptian village, a Jewish *politeuma* (corporation), a Greek polis modeled on the classical type and inhabited by Greeks, and a settlement of foreign soldiers. The Greek polis was the most important subunit and it, like the others, kept its own constitution but was overseen by a royal official who worked closely with the magistrates of the polis. Ethnic affiliation thus replaced national identity, and by the second century B.C. Greeks no longer identified themselves by the name of their polis (e.g., as Athenians) but called themselves simply "Hellenes," Greeks. In such an atmosphere clubs and associations of all sorts grew up. Many of the philosophical schools of this period were more like exclusive clubs than the schools of the late classical period, the great Academy of Plato and the Lyceum of Aristotle.

Under this centralized pluralism a new kind of individualism found expression. In the Hellenistic city citizenship no longer depended upon membership in a family, and the laws therefore ceased to concern themselves so exclusively with women as childbearers. The household as a social unit did not pass out of existence, however. Quite the contrary, it began to serve more truly the partnership ideal. And so, in the Hellenistic period, the marriage contract reflected both the new humanistic bias that treated each person as an autonomous unit and an emphasis on marriage as a compact between two persons, each with separate duties and responsibilities. One such contract from the Ptolemaic period (92 B.C.) runs as follows:

> Let Apollonia be the wife of Philiscus, having been persuaded by him that it is fitting for her to be his wife, and let her have mastery in common with him over all their possessions. And let Philiscus provide for Apollonia all the things that she needs and her clothing and all the rest that it is suitable for a married woman to have provided for her — and let him do this wherever they live, according as their means allow. And let him take no other wife but Apollonia, and no concubine, and let him have no boyfriends or beget children from any other woman so long as Apollonia is living nor inhabit any other household than the one over which Apollonia rules; nor let him repudiate her or do violence to her or treat her badly or alienate any of their property in a manner which is unfair to Apollonia. If he is caught doing any of these things . . . then let him pay back immediately to Apollonia her dowry of two talents and four thousand drachmas of bronze. By the same token, let Apollonia not be permitted to spend the day or the night away from the house of Philiscus without his knowledge, nor may she sleep with another man, nor may she squander their common household property, nor may she disgrace Philiscus in the ways in which men get disgraced. But if Apollonia willingly does any of these things, let her be sent away from Philiscus, and let him repay to her the dowry simply within ten days of her departure.[10]

This contract represents to a very significant degree the fulfillment of that ideal of mutuality the classical Greeks had originated, but failed to translate into reality. However, the double standard persists, and common threats to the relationship are indicated by the proscriptions.

With the breakdown of the link between citizenship and property ownership, women were not only freed from the restrictions imposed by their function as legitimizers of the heirs of family property but they became property owners themselves. Other evidence for women's improved position are the scattered references to women who performed duties or held offices previously restricted to men. Women were granted citizenship as a reward for outstanding service of one kind or another; a first century B.C. inscription from Asia Minor indicates that a woman named Phyle held the highest state office there and constructed a reservoir and aqueducts for her city. Another inscription describes a woman who served as *archon* (high magistrate) of her city, Histria. And an inscription from Delphi cites the honors, including the right to own land, conferred upon Polygnota, a female harpist, and her nephew, as a reward for her services to the temple. Hipparchia, wife of Crates, the cynic philosopher, exemplifies the women of this age. She was a woman of high birth who threatened her parents with suicide if they would not betroth her to Crates, to whose philosophy she was attracted. She married Crates and defended herself to a critic of both her style of life and her presence at symposia as follows: "Do I seem to you to have been advised poorly about myself if I have devoted my time to my education instead of wasting it at the loom?" [11]

Women figure in this period as the subject matter of poetry, as they had in the classical era. But women no longer appear as the antithesis to the cultural ideal, because the focus has shifted to the private realm with which women are traditionally associated. This is nowhere more clearly shown than in the literary mime, a form popular with cultured Alexandrian poets. The poet Theocritus illustrates the genre in his fifteenth idyll:

GORGO: Is Praxinoa in? PRAXINOA: Gorgo dear! it's about time — yes, I'm in.
It's a wonder that you're here now. Get her a chair, Eunoa,
and put a cushion on it. GORGO: It's just fine. PRAXINOA: Do sit down.
GORGO: What a foolish thing I am — I barely saved my soul getting here,
Praxinoa, what with the huge crowd, the huge number of chariots,
boots everywhere, everywhere men in soldiers' cloaks.
And the road was unending. You certainly live far out.
PRAXINOA: It's because of that husband of mine; he comes to the ends of the earth
and buys a pig-sty, not a house, so that we can't be neighbors,
whether out of bitterness or evil jealousy — he's always the same.
GORGO: Don't talk that way about your husband Dinon, my dear,
when the little one's around; see, woman, how he's staring at you.
It's all right, Zopyrion, sweet child; she's not talking about daddy.
PRAXINOA: The baby understands, by the goddess! GORGO: Daddy's nice! *

The sixth mime of Herodas illustrates a new attitude of acceptance and freedom toward women's sexuality. In this piece two women discuss the fine qualities of one cobbler's wares:

> We're alone, so let me tell you about these dildoes:
> harder than men, softer than sleep and laced with wool.
> Now there's a cobbler who likes women! [12]

* From *The Idylls of Theokritos,* tr. Barriss Mills, Purdue University Press, West Lafayette, Ind., 1963, p. 54. © 1963, Purdue University. Reprinted by permission of Purdue Research Foundation.

The mystery religions and ecstatic cults that in the late classical period especially had attracted women now dominated religious life as a whole. The goddess Isis was the most important deity of the period, and she gradually assimilated the functions of every major divinity. In a catalogue of her divine prerogatives, Isis includes among her functions a wide range of activities:

> I gave and ordained laws for men which no one is able to change.
> I am she that is called goddess by women.
> I divided the earth from the heaven.
> I brought together women and men.
> I ordained that parents be loved by children.
> I revealed mysteries unto men.
> I caused women to be loved by men.
> I made an end to murders.
> I am in the rays of the Sun.
> I am the Queen of War.
> I am the Lord of Rainstorms.[13]

From this selection it is clear that Isis's realm included the whole of the human and natural worlds, and she herself came to symbolize their essential unity. The natural world was no longer viewed as the antithesis of the human sphere, and consequently women were seen in a more positive light. The realms with which they had traditionally been associated — marriage, sexual love, family life, the natural world — had become the common cultural concern.

In the mystery religions nature was the arena of the great cycle of birth and death, of the coming-into-being and passing away in which all existence shared. The common humanity that the mystery religions affirmed had as its basis the universal participation in the condition of mortality and the shared expectation of immortality in a life after death.

This same spirit and these same ideas also found expression in the philosophical schools of the Hellenistic period. The two most important philosophies were Stoicism and Epicureanism. Although opposed in other respects, both schools regarded nature as not only the biological but moral source of man's being. In the philosophy of the Stoics, for example, nature was the realm in which the ultimate rationality of the world was expressed, and it was animated by a divine being who was the quintessence of reason. A rational and moral life, therefore, was a life lived in conformity with nature.

Within the life of the individual, natural instincts, such as the sexual urge, no longer appeared as malign forces. Both the love experience and its deities were evaluated positively. The love deity was either Eros or Aphrodite, depending on whether the poet wished to focus on the playful, even devilish, aspects of the experience or on its pleasurable and beautiful quality. The following two epigrams, one by a male, the other by a female, poet, will illustrate the difference:

> Wanted: Eros, mischievous child — just now
> At dawn, he fluttered away from my bed.
> Description: fast, fearless, cute when he laughs,
> Gentle when he cries; on his back: wings and a quiver.[14]
>
> — MELEAGER
>
> "Nothing's sweeter or lovelier than love — everything else
> Takes second place; even honey: I spit it out."
> Nossis has this to say: the woman whom Aphrodite never loves
> Never discovers the rose among the summer flowers! [15]
>
> — NOSSIS

The theme of hostility between male and female as a model of the cosmic struggle has disappeared from literature. And in the sphere of politics and social relations women's range of activity was far greater than in the classical polis. But the productive system of this period rested upon the backs of the enslaved masses who performed the agricultural tasks; the more liberated, individualized mode of life in this world brought in its train a lowering in the standard of living that was ultimately fatal to it. As Nietzsche noted, this sunny world harbored a dark secret:

> Let us mark this well: Alexandrian culture, to be able to exist permanently, requires a slave class, but with its optimistic view of life it denies the necessity of such a class, and consequently, when its beautifully seductive and tranquilizing utterances about the "dignity of man" and the "dignity of labor" are no longer effective, it drifts toward a dreadful destruction.[16]

Our evaluation of the position of women in this world must ultimately be informed by the same cynicism. Women were free to own property, but property ownership no longer led to citizenship; women were citizens and officials of the polis, but the polis was no longer the dominant political form; women were no longer a testimony to the gods' hatred of mankind, but it was the gods who ceased to hate men, not men who ceased to hate women.

Venus Enthroned: The Roman Period

The political organization of the Roman state and in particular the principle of *patriapotestas* ("right of the father") guaranteed the Roman female citizen even fewer citizen rights than the Athenian matron. But because the Roman state was at all times a remarkable blend of indigenous with imported elements, of archaic with sophisticated features, women were actually freer in some ways than their Greek and Hellenistic predecessors. In this section we shall explore this paradox and, in particular, its different application in the republican and imperial periods. For in the area of women's position, as in every other sphere, the transition from republic to empire is the great dividing line.

Ennius, in his epic poem *The Annals*, written in the third century B.C., celebrated the history and rise of the Roman state. Ilia, the mother of Rome's founders, Romulus and Remus, was a fully developed character. She was not the passive recipient of the god's seed but an active participant in her own destiny. At one point she relates to her sister a dream that prophesies her destiny. It is interpreted to mean that she, like the traditional hero, will undergo a period of trial and suffering, but eventually her fortunes will be restored and she will be hailed as a founder of the race. Another reminiscence of early times occurred in a speech of Cicero, in which he reproached a contemporary noblewoman for failing to live up to her illustrious female ancestors. He describes the "womanly glory" of one who had achieved fame by pulling free the image of a goddess grounded at the mouth of the Tiber River. Another had defended her father against an attack by the Roman populace. These examples, common in Roman history, demonstrate that women's fulfillment of their traditional duties could be consistent with action in the political and social spheres.

The Romans, unlike the Greeks, did not see women as intrinsically hostile to the aims of civilized political life. On the contrary, within their limited sphere of action, they were as apt as men to serve the state and were honored and glorified for their contributions. Certainly, the tradition of individualism and humanism inherited from the Hellenistic era was responsible for some of this. Far more important, however, was the fact that the women of whom we hear all belonged to the aristocratic class and were all acting in defense of their class or family interests. Thus, the woman who defended her father was saving him from attack in a popular uprising against aristocratic oppression. The possibility of greater participation in society and politics for the Roman matron was, therefore, tied directly to the class structure of the Roman Republic.

The Roman Republic was an aristocracy, and so it shared certain features with the archaic Greek state. But it was a vital and adaptable form of the aristocratic state, so the history of the republic was not one of steady undermining of aristocratic domination and progress toward democracy, as in Greece. Rather, the aristocratic class in Rome adapted itself to new economic conditions and gradually absorbed the wealthiest and most prestigious plebeian (lower-class) families through intermarriage.

Family law and marriage regulations retained their aristocratic character throughout this period. The most striking feature of the legal system was patriapotestas, which gave to the legal head of the household absolute power, including the right of life and death and the right to sell into slavery, over all the members of his family: wife, children, slaves. A Roman woman, like her Greek counterpart, remained under guardianship for life, her father's or husband's if she was *in patria potestate* or *in manu,* that of a male specifically appointed for the purpose if she was not. However, unlike Athenian women, Roman citizen women could inherit and acquire real property and could dispose of it with the consent of their guardians. This privilege is characteristically associated with the aristocratic form of society, and its purpose is to maintain the strength of the class through the formation of powerful bonds between the families that make it up. Marriage in aristocratic society is a form of exchange between the male heads of families, and therefore entails the complete severance of the woman's ties with her original family. In Rome the oldest forms of marriage were of this kind. A woman was married either by *confarreatio* (a religious ceremony performed by a priest), or by *coemptio* (purchase), where the father "sold" (rather than "leased," as in Greece) his daughter to the prospective husband, or by *usus* (what we would today call "common-law" marriage). In all three cases the woman abandoned legal and religious ties with her original family and was virtually incorporated into her husband's family. Such a marriage delivered her into her husband's *manus* (power and legal authority), an authority equivalent to patriapotestas. As her guardian, her husband had absolute power over her, including the power of life and death. A woman who was an Athenian citizen, by contrast, was in such a position only as an unmarried daughter caught having intercourse with a man; otherwise, the laws of the state guarded her life and her well-being.

The continued aristocratic character of the state made appropriate the preservation of this archaic, crude, and even inhuman legal system. Yet, the sophistication of the Roman state and the heritage of Hellenistic moral philosophy caused a modification of some of the effects of the legal code. Guardianship, for example, originally restricted a woman's right to the free disposal of her property, but eventually became the means to insure this right. For a woman gradually acquired the legal right to dismiss her guardian if he refused to obey her will. Roman marriage practices provide another example of the ways in which the modification of restrictions benefited women. The institution of the *trinoctium* allowed a woman not to pass under the manus of her husband. If she absented herself from his home for three successive nights in any one year she retained her ties with her original family. This institution was probably an attempt to prevent a patrician woman's loss of her class standing in the event that she married a plebeian. But it quickly became women's principal means for acquiring freedom from the legal domination of either husband or father, for the woman could put herself under a guardianship she could more easily control.

The art and literature of the republican period demonstrate that the same principles that determined women's social and legal position informed their cultural evaluation as well. Republican literature does not employ the paradigm of a deep-seated opposition between man and woman to articulate a view of man's place in the world. In the poetry of the late republican period both sexuality in general and the sexual relations between men and women are evaluated positively. For example, Lucretius's philosophical poem *On the Nature of the Universe* gives a scientific explanation of the forces governing the cosmos. It opens with an address to Venus, "mother of the Roman race, delight of men and gods, dear goddess." Lucretius subsequently characterizes her as "the guiding power of the universe" and hence an apt inspirational deity for his poem. Venus was a socialized, but not masculinized, deity: her erotic and sexual aspects were not suppressed but transformed into her characterization as nurturing, sustaining mother. Such an adaptation would have been inconceivable for the Greek goddess Aphrodite, whose threatening aspect caused her instead to be relegated to the fringes of the Olympian pantheon. The Roman view of love, as of the world of nature in general, was far more tolerant. In the Roman mind man was not tragically but fortunately a natural being. His natural side was not, as it was for the Greeks, the opposite of his existence as a political creature. The Roman Venus was a benign goddess, and her world was a sunlit, joyous, and life-giving realm. She was the mother of the Romans as well, and therefore sanctioned their natural and divinely given right to rule.

In the love poetry of this period the women emerge as strong and lively, if secondary, characters. And the affair itself was typically evaluated in terms of traditional Roman moral standards; it became the arena in which to fulfill, rather than threaten, the conventional code. Catullus, for example, described his feelings for his beloved Lesbia as follows: "I loved you once not as men love women, but as a father cherishes his children and family." In a moment of cautious optimism about Lesbia, whose habitual unfaithfulness constantly troubled him, Catullus prayed to the gods that they might "link their lives together in an eternal treaty of sacred friendship." Propertius, a poet of later date but writing in the same tradition, expressed his love for Cynthia using a military metaphor: he has, he says, enrolled himself as a soldier in the service of love's army. Elsewhere he described the relationship as if it were a complete and traditional Roman family: "You, Cynthia, alone are for me a home, and you alone are parents for me."

This poetry manifested a more generalized notion of late republican thinking, which held that only in the private sphere of life could one find genuine happiness. In this context, the world of the passions acquires a new interest, as it did in the Hellenistic world under the influence of a new attitude toward nature. Within the love relationship all human emotions and intense feelings can be given full play and express their true range. This contrasts with the Greek view of passionate love, which construed its essential irrational character as dangerous. The chorus of Euripides's *Hippolytus* prays that it might never feel the "wild and measureless rhythms of love" that are the prelude to destruction. The Romans, by contrast, felt the pain and torture of love, but welcomed it as the means to communication with the emotional wellsprings of their beings. Women, in both cases, were associated with passion but were judged differently according to the prevailing cultural view of natural instincts.

There were dramatic changes on all levels of society when Augustus acceded to power in 19 B.C. as the emperor of Rome. In form Rome remained a republic governed by an aristocracy; in fact it evolved into an empire ruled by one man. Augustus's base of support was the newly developed bourgeoisie, local and provincial notables whose status derived in large part from their achievements in business or the military. Under Augustus's rule the power and influence of the old Roman aristocracy, which controlled the Senate, was considerably weakened.

The transition from republic to empire in Rome, therefore, involved the rise to prominence of the same class that in Greece had supplanted the aristocracy with the polis. Although in Rome the transformation was more gradual and did not feature the adoption of a new constitution, many parallel changes occurred. For instance, Augustus attempted to revive the official state cult, which had been neglected and undermined by ecstatic cults and philosophical speculation; similarly, the Athenian tyrant Pisistratos had inaugurated the Panathenaic festival. Augustus embarked upon an ambitious building program, also like the tyrants of the early Greek city-states. The system of property ownership was not altered, but the laws having to do with debt were, as in Solon's reforms in Greece. For example, laws allowing the sale of family property and its transfer to creditors were introduced. The Roman legal system was already highly developed by the time of the late republic, but under the empire some reforms occurred that strengthened the state's interest over that of private individuals. Crimes that had previously been civil offenses now became breaches of criminal, or public, law. Jury courts were set up to try offenders. One such crime was adultery, and Augustus himself introduced the use of jury courts to deal with this offense. This was part of a whole legislative program designed to promote the growth of the nuclear family and to undermine the authority of and allegiances among the few remaining aristocratic families.

The propaganda of the time hailed these laws as a kind of moral rearmament program for the dwindling aristocracy, but it seems clear from what we can gauge about the effects of these laws that the interest behind them was not the old but the new Roman state. The two most famous of these laws were the lex Julia of 18 B.C. and the lex Papia Poppaea of A.D. 9. These laws made marriage virtually compulsory; parents of three children received special rewards: the mother acquired a grant of independence in the management of her property. Some provisions restricted movement across class lines; this preserved the prestige of the old nobility while at the same time opening up for all other classes the opportunity to marry freedwomen. Adultery now became a criminal offense, and normally the two offenders were banished to different islands for life. Until the time of Constantine a wife could not prosecute her husband for this crime. As in Greece, husbands were required to divorce adulterous wives, and in addition the wife was penalized by the loss of one-sixth of her dowry and one-third of her property (the adulterer lost half of his property). The lex Papia Poppaea relaxed some of these restrictions, especially those having to do with property inheritance, and this mitigation of the laws' severity is usually interpreted as a response to widespread protest by the wealthier groups of landowning Romans.

We found in Greece that a change in the cultural attitude toward women accompanied the emergence of the polis out of aristocratic society. A similar transformation occurs in the literature of the early empire, where for the first time in Roman culture the idea appears that woman is hostile to civilization. Virgil expresses this idea most notably in the *Aeneid,* his epic of imperial destiny that embodied the ideals of Augustus's regime. One of its main themes is that women, or the female force as manifested by certain men, impede Aeneas from the fulfillment of his destiny. In Book II he risks his life and mission by returning for his wife Creusa, whom he discovers has perished in the assault on Troy. Aeneas leaves the ruined city with his aged father and young son. The famous trio symbolizes the salvation from Troy of the masculine element, the family and future conceived in exclusively patrilineal terms.

Aeneas's sojourn in Carthage and his affair with its queen Dido was the most famous instance of the female character of the obstacles he must confront. However, Aeneas must escape not women per se, but love affairs that are pursued for their own sake. So the new ideal of the Roman citizen repudiates the ideal of the Latin love poets. Dido herself was a thoroughly competent ruler of her city until she succumbed to passion; under its influence she destroyed herself and her city and nearly dragged Aeneas down with her.

When Aeneas finally arrives in Italy, he forms bonds of friendship with a rustic people whose royal house conveniently lacks women. His main opponents are the Latins stirred against him by the queen mother, who rejects Aeneas as a suitor for her daughter and objects to the use of Lavinia for a political alliance with the newcomers. The two are finally married, and the mother of all future Romans is the only woman in the book who has not uttered a word. On the three occasions when she appears in the narrative, she casts her eyes down modestly, or blushes with maidenly shyness, or leads the women in lamentation over a dead hero. We are very far at this point from Ilia and other early Roman heroines who served their class or country in an active way.

The historians of the period express similar attitudes. Livy was the first Roman to glorify the housewife who, according to the traditional formula, "watched over the household and spun the wool." The good wife had been admired before, but her admirable qualities were tied to her nobility of character. Most often this included devotion to the ideals of the state, political acumen, and even visibility on the political scene. In the Augustan period, however, a contrast developed that reminds us very strongly of themes we encountered in the poetry of ancient Greece. The assertive woman became identified as an immoral virago; the ideal wife increasingly assumed the attributes of silence, obedience, and submissiveness to her husband.

This pattern was developed most completely in the history of the empire as related by the historian Tacitus. He attributed the degeneracy of the empire and its rulers to the power of women in the royal households. The emperor Claudius, according to Tacitus's narrative, was merely simple, even naive. But his third wife Messalina was devious, immoral, and murderous. She had her female rivals prosecuted and compelled young men to be her lovers, even if this meant divorcing their wives. She was eventually executed, justly, as Tacitus thought, but with lamentable consequences, for Claudius was then open to the influence and control of all the women competing for the position of empress. The successful candidate, Agrippina the Younger, was also the mother of Nero, whose succession to the throne Agrippina plotted and achieved. In the narrative of Nero's reign Tacitus suggests that all of the famous outrages connected with that emperor's name were directly or indirectly the result of the female influence in his life.

From this period too comes our only surviving Roman diatribe against women: the sixth satire of the poet Juvenal. Juvenal, like his Greek counterpart Semonides, catalogued women's vices in a long poem, drawing his examples from contemporary life. Like Tacitus, he found corruption under the empire best demonstrated by its women. In the opening lines of his poem Juvenal invokes Cynthia and Lesbia, the lovers of Propertius and Catullus, to illustrate the decline in moral standards; and like Semonides he reproaches women most severely for their sexual appetites.

Virgil, Livy, Tacitus, and Juvenal provide evidence that there occurred in Rome, as in Greece, a revaluation of the attitude toward women at a particular moment in history. In both cases the shift in outlook can be correlated with political and social developments. The forces that brought into being the middle-class state, whether it be the Greek polis or the Roman Empire of the first century B.C., produced a focus of attention on the nuclear family and hence on women's social role. Cultural perceptions of the limitations on women's lives cast them as the symbol of social malaise. The form it takes depends on the particular society: in Greece they epitomized all that was untamed, irrational, and imperfectly assimilated to civilized life. In contrast, the absence of systematized misogyny from the cultural life of the Hellenistic world must be connected with a form of government that made the nuclear family politically meaningless. And in Rome, as the nuclear family became more important to the state, misogyny reappeared. But the Romans' tendency to see things in specifically social rather than metaphysical terms meant that women represented to them a more specific social threat. They typified the immorality of the age and were used as an index of degeneration. And the fact that the final stage of Augustus's victory was his defeat of Cleopatra invited the use of a model of the empire as the triumph of male over female forces. This same fact, however, enabled a sympathetic portrayal of the queen to stand for a noble and valuable aspect of life whose expression the demands of empire precluded. Horace makes the point most strongly in his "Cleopatra Ode," ostensibly a poem celebrating the triumph of Augustus:

> She sought a nobler death: no woman's fear
> turned her trembling from the sword, no coward's
> spirit winged her swift ships to secret shores.
>
> No — she could stand the sight of her realm's collapse.
> Cooly and firmly she grasped the bitter serpents,
> and fed her body full on their black poison.
>
> So fierce was she in her deliberate death!
>
> Stripped bare of her army's strength, she scorned the role
> of star in the Roman triumph's haughty parade.
> Cleopatra was no woman meant to crawl! [17]

Notes

1. *Design for Utopia: Selected Writings of Charles Fourier,* tr. Julia Franklin, Schocken Books, New York, 1971, p. 77.

2. Aeschylus, *Eumenides,* tr. Richard Lattimore, *Aeschylus I: Oresteia, The Com-*

plete Greek Tragedies, eds. D. Grene and R. Lattimore, University of Chicago Press, Chicago and London, 1953, p. 158 (lines 658–661). Copyright © University of Chicago.

3. Ibid., p. 161 (lines 736–738).

4. Sophocles, *Antigone,* tr. Elizabeth Wyckoff, *Sophocles I: The Complete Greek Tragedies,* eds. D. Grene and R. Lattimore, University of Chicago Press, Chicago and London, 1954, p. 170 (lines 338–341). Copyright © University of Chicago.

5. From *Three Great Plays of Euripides,* translated by Rex Warner (New York: New American Library, 1958), lines 231–251. Copyright © 1958 by Rex Warner. Reprinted by permission of the New American Library, Inc., New York, N.Y. Also from *The Medea of Euripides* translated by Rex Warner published by The Bodley Head.

6. Sappho, *Songs,* tr. Mary Barnard, University of California Press, Berkeley and Los Angeles, 1958, no. 32. Copyright © 1958 by The Regents of the University of California; reprinted by permission of the University of California Press.

7. Author's translation.

8. Author's translation.

9. Author's translation.

10. Author's translation.

11. Diogenes Laertius, *Lives of Famous Philosophers, VI,* 98 (translated by Marylin Arthur).

12. Author's translation.

13. From *Hellenistic Religions,* edited by Frederick C. Grant (Indianapolis: Bobbs-Merrill, 1953), pp. 132–133. Copyright © 1953, by The Liberal Arts Press, Inc., reprinted by permission of the Liberal Arts Press Division of The Bobbs-Merrill Company, Inc.

14. Author's translation.

15. Author's translation.

16. Friedrich Nietzsche, *The Birth of Tragedy and the Case of Wagner,* tr. Walter Kaufmann, Vintage Books, a Division of Random House, Inc., New York, 1967, p. 111. © 1967, Random House.

17. Author's translation.

Suggestions for Further Reading

Note: For this section I have selected both those books that have influenced my own point of view and those that are nontechnical enough to be of use to the general reader. Many of the sources are reprints of much older works, but all are cited in their latest available editions. With three exceptions, no work later than 1974, the date of completion of this essay, is cited.

Two thematic issues of the journal *Arethusa* are of particular interest: VI.1 (Spring 1973) was devoted to women in antiquity; VIII.1 (Spring 1975) treated Marxism and the classics. Both contain bibliographies, and the latter issue contains articles on the class structure of ancient Greece and on Sparta.

Perry Anderson's *Passages from Antiquity to Feudalism* (New Left Review Books, London, 1974) presents a good overview of ancient history from a Marxist perspective; Anderson is a nonspecialist and the book is therefore highly derivative but no less useful for that. Moses I. Finley, *The Ancient Economy* (University of California, Berkeley and Los Angeles, 1973) presents a controversial but coherent account of the economic structure of the ancient world that is a necessary framework for understanding the position of women. Sarah B. Pomeroy, *Goddesses, Whores, Wives, and Slaves* (Schocken Books, New York, 1975) is the latest and most complete account of women in the ancient world. Verena Zinserling, *Women in Greece and Rome* (Schram, New York, 1973) is valuable primarily for the quality and quantity of its photographic reproductions. Other books on the subject, e.g., Charles Seltman, *Women in Antiquity* (Collier, New York, 1962) are not only dated in their approach but highly misleading in their presentation of material on women's status. Those readers who desire current lists of the primary and secondary sources especially relevant to this subject should contact Leona Ascher, Department of Languages, Adelphi University, Garden City, New York 11530, for a collection of syllabi of courses on women in antiquity assembled by the Women's Classical Caucus.

The position of women in the Bronze Age of Greece is of interest because of a long tradition (dating from Bachofen's 1861 *Mother-Right*) associating matriarchy with this period. F. Engels, in *The Origin of the Family, Private Property and the State* (latest edition: International Publishers, New York, 1972), incorporates these theories into a general history of ancient society. The works of G. Thomson, especially *Studies in Ancient Greek Society* (Citadel, New York, 1965) and *Aeschylus and Athens* (Lawrence & Wishart, London, 1966), use Engels's scheme and amplify it with a good deal of concrete data. The historical accuracy of this model is disputed. The standard work on the period is Emily Vermeule, *Greece in the Bronze Age* (University of Chicago Press, Chicago, 1964).

Remains of the social structure of the early period in Greece appear to have been preserved in Sparta and Crete in the classical period. Current discussions of these two important societies are: for Crete, R. F. Willetts's *Aristocratic Society in Ancient Crete* (Routledge & Kegan Paul, London, 1955) and R. W. Hutchinson's *Prehistoric Crete* (Penguin Books, Baltimore, 1962); and for Sparta, P. Oliva's valuable *Sparta and Her Social Problems* (Academia, Prague, 1971). Aristophanes's *Ecclesiazusae* is a satire of utopian proposals such as those of Plato.

The archaic age of Greece is reviewed thoroughly by Andrew Robert Burn in *The Lyric Age of Greece* (Minerva, New York, 1968). A. Andrewes's *The Greek Tyrants* (Harper & Row, New York, 1963) deals with a phenomenon that in Greece was crucial for the passage from aristocracy to democracy. Much of the lyric poetry of this period deals with women, and some of it was written by women. Denys L. Page's *Sappho and Alcaeus* (Oxford University Press, London, 1959) is a scholarly work, but much of the discussion will be of interest to the general reader. Alcman's *Partheneion* (ed. Denys L. Page, Clarendon Press, Oxford, 1951) is a long choral song for Spartan women. A new edition of Semonides's misogynous poem on women, called *Females of the Species* (Noyes, Park Ridge, N.J., 1975), by Hugh Lloyd-Jones presents commentary and interpretation of the poem.

For the classical period in Greece the best historical survey is Victor Ehrenberg, *From Solon to Socrates* (Methuen, London, 1968). The same author's *The Greek State* (Norton, New York, 1964) discusses the political form of the state in archaic, classical, and Hellenistic times. Arnold Hugh Martin Jones, *Athenian Democracy* (Blackwell, Oxford, 1957) is also valuable, as is A. Andrewes's *The Greeks* (Hutchinson, London, and Knopf, New York, 1967). Moses I. Finley, *Early Greece: The Bronze and Archaic Ages* (Chatto & Windus, London, and Norton, New York, 1970) relates the early form of the Greek state to its later shape. The most relevant primary sources for this period are Plato's *Republic* and *Laws,* the *Politics* and *Ethics* (Book VIII) of Aristotle, and the *Oeconomicus* of Xenophon. W. K. Lacey, *The Family in Classical Greece* (Cornell University Press, Ithaca, 1968) is the most comprehensive recent treatment of this subject. A valuable corollary to the historical material is Philip Slater, *The Glory of Hera* (Beacon, Boston, 1968), which analyzes Greek family patterns and Greek mythology from a psychological point of view, stressing the antipathy between the sexes produced by inequality in the social order.

For the Hellenistic period William Woodthorpe Tarn's classic study, *Hellenistic Civilization* (Meridian, World Publishing, Cleveland and New York, 1961) is still invaluable. A useful supplement is Moses Hadas's *Hellenistic Culture* (Norton, New York, 1959). One particularly important literary source for this period is *The Greek Anthology,* which contains poetry by women. Several selections in modern translation are available by Dudley Fitts (New Directions, New York, 1956 [1938]), Kenneth Rexroth (University of Michigan Press, Ann Arbor, 1962), Andrew Sinclair (Macmillan, New York, 1967), Robin Skelton (Methuen, London, 1971), and others.

The study of the early period in Roman history presents many problems, principal among which is the dearth of source material. Much of what is relevant is collected in the Loeb Classical Library edition by Eric Herbert Warmington (4 vols.), *Remains of Old Latin* (Harvard, Cambridge, and Heinemann, London, 1957), which contains early literature, laws, and inscriptions. Fustel de Coulanges's classic work *The Ancient City* (Doubleday, New York, n.d.) discusses family and religion in both Greece and Rome but is fullest on Rome. Michael Ivanovich Rostovtzeff, *Rome* (Oxford University Press, New York, 1960) is a good general survey. Peter Astbury Brunt, *Social Conflicts in the Roman Republic* (Norton, New York, 1971) is a good treatment of republican politics and society. John Anthony Crook, *Law and Life of Rome* (Cornell, Ithaca, 1967) discusses the evolution of Roman law in its social and political context. Herbert Felix Jolowicz's *An Historical Introduction to Roman Law* (Cambridge University Press, New York, 1972) is still the standard work in this field.

Ronald Syme's *The Roman Revolution* (Oxford University Press, London, 1960) treats Augustus's rise to power and the transformations of the Roman state it entailed. Alban Dewes Winspear and Lenore Kramp Geweke, *Augustus and the Reconstruction of Roman Government and Society* (Russell & Russell,

New York, 1970) deals with the same phenomenon from a slightly different point of view. Svi Yavetz, *Plebs and Princeps* (Oxford University Press, London, 1969) is also a very important book in this field. The works of Tacitus (*Annals, Histories*) and Suetonius (*Lives of the Twelve Caesars*) treat the period of the early empire. Finally, J. P. V. D. Balsdon's *Roman Women* (Bodley Head, London, Sidney, and Toronto, 1974) is a very complete survey of both the daily lives of women and the biographies of individual Roman women. It can be supplemented with the relevant chapters in Jerome Carcopino, *Daily Life in Ancient Rome* (Yale University Press, New Haven, 1960), which focuses on the early imperial period. The standard historical reference work is *The Cambridge Ancient History*; see I. E. S. Edwards et al., eds., vol. I^3 (Cambridge University Press, Cambridge, 1961–1971), and J. B. Bury et al., eds., vols. IV^2–XII^2 (Cambridge University Press, Cambridge, 1923–1939).

4

Sanctity and Power: The Dual Pursuit of Medieval Women

JoAnn McNamara
Suzanne F. Wemple

Did the status of women in the ancient world shape medieval conceptions of women? Or did the additional dimension of Christianity determine women's role? JoAnn McNamara and Suzanne Wemple discuss the duality of the Christian tradition regarding women: negative perceptions of female nature mandated their subordinate role in ritual, yet theology proclaimed spiritual equality of all believers.

The egalitarian strand predominated during the Christians' early struggle for survival and later, when they expanded the frontier into northern and eastern Europe. Feudal relations, based on kinship, allowed aristocratic women a relatively wide scope for activity. As medieval society stabilized and flourished, however, and as other more specialized institutions took over public functions, the role of both the family and of women diminished.

This development in political history was paralleled in the religious institutions of the time. During the early medieval period, women had access to positions of considerable responsibility and power as abbesses. But by the later phases of feudalism, the status of nuns had declined sharply, as they came increasingly under the control of male monastic orders. As scholasticism grew to dominate the church's intellectual life, women turned more and more to mysticism — a further retreat from power.

Ladies of the nobility in the ninth century. (Detail from a miniature of St. Jerome dictating the translation of the Bible to his disciples. Paris. Bibl. Nat. Ms. 1, fol. 3v. Reprinted from a woodcut in Paul Lacroix: *France in the Middle Ages*. Published by Frederick Ungar, 1963.)

From the fifth to the eleventh centuries, the frontier age of western Europe, women played a vital and expanding role in laying the foundations of our modern society. By the twelfth century, institutions that were to endure into modern times began to emerge. With this development, women found their own spheres of influence beginning to shrink, especially in the upper reaches of political and economic power. The practical need for the talents of women, not merely as wives and mothers but as administrators, educators, and religious leaders, largely determined the attitudes toward them. This was more sharply pronounced in the changing laws and institutions of the time than in theological attitudes, which remained fairly constant.

Christian attitudes, however, were also equivocal in many areas. The early Christians aspired to create a spiritual revolution rather than a series of social changes. While they preached the spiritual equality of all, including women, they did not wish to scandalize their contemporaries by according women a position equal to men in the practical direction of the new religion. The idea that the weaker sex required restriction and support was not altogether absent from the writings of the Christian fathers and this attitude provided ammunition for those who sought to cloister women in home or convent. In the later Middle Ages, when ecclesiastical thought concerned itself more closely with the social and political conditions of society, women's participation in activities outside the home or convent was rarely viewed as a serious possibility.

The Early Christian Background

Informed by their founder's emphasis on the salvation of the individual soul, early Christians recognized the claims of women to partnership in the new covenant. Christ's words and deeds reinforced this position. His ready forgiveness of the woman taken in adultery contrasted dramatically with his condemnation of the sins of her would-be executioners (John 8:3–11). In a society where men could readily obtain divorce for trivial complaints against their wives, Christ preached in favor of permanent monogamy, which would enhance the security and dignity of women (Matt. 19:1–9). While the twelve Apostles were all men, several women were among his closest disciples. Despite the disapproval of his companions, he instructed a Samaritan woman in the divine mysteries (John 4:7–26). He supported Mary of Bethany's preference for religious edification over the demands of housework (Luke 10:38–42).

The women thus dignified proved staunch followers. Some of them accompanied Christ on the road to Calvary, and it was to women that he first announced his resurrection. During the embattled years that followed, women played an active role in sustaining and disseminating the new faith. The daughters of the Apostle Philip were preachers in their own right (Acts 21:9), and all the Apostles depended heavily upon their sister Christians to furnish material support to their mission and establish communal gathering places. The Pauline letters illustrate the importance of the sisterhood in maintaining the scattered congregations of the early Christians. Despite their recognition of these services, however, the letters expose the ambiguity of the apostolic attitude toward the female sex. They depart from Jewish tradition by admitting women to divine services with the men but command them to cover their heads (1 Cor. 11:5) and forbid them to teach men (1 Tim. 2:12). They proclaim the spiritual equality of the sexes (Gal. 3:28) but reiterate the traditional concept that the husband is the head of the wife, as Christ is the head of the husband and the church (1 Cor. 11:3; Eph. 5:22–33).

In later generations women preachers were viewed with increasing suspicion. While men tended to monopolize the teaching role, women grew active in the heretical sects that proliferated in the second century. (Irenaeus of Lyons complained about the activities of heretic priestesses.) Only before the lions, confronting the terrors of the public executioner, could early Christian women remain the full and equal partners of Christian men. But even this equality tended to dissipate once the church had been legalized and absorbed among the institutions of the Roman state of the fourth century. Martyrdom became rare; and the clergy, going professional, tended to exclude women from the higher places in the church.

On the lower levels of the newly emerging hierarchy, women retained their position as deaconesses, but these responsibilities as well were greatly eroded over time. According to the *Apostolic Constitutions,* the deaconess instructed female catechumens and, jointly with the deacon and the bishop, baptized women. As baptism by immersion gave way to the custom of sprinkling the head alone, it was no longer necessary for the deaconesses to be present. In later centuries, their duties were limited to auxiliary functions relating to the care and instruction of women. In the west, the post was generally reserved for aging widows.

Pragmatic considerations alone did not shape Christian life. The patristic authors who were concerned with the creation of a whole society operating on moral principles did not ignore the roles and needs of women. Three generalizations of the utmost significance for women emerge from the writings of the early fathers. First, there was no compromising on the moral equality of the sexes. Whatever her condition on earth might be, in eternity woman was the equal of man. The conventions of secular society might subject her to unequal laws, but her capacity for virtue, for spiritual achievement, and ultimate triumph was never in doubt. All the fathers agreed: what was forbidden to women was also forbidden to men. They sternly rejected the social conventions that supported a double moral standard, preaching that adultery or promiscuity in a man was as loathsome a sin as in a woman. The fifth-century preacher Caesarius of Arles taunted the so-called stronger sex for their failure to withstand temptations over which women were routinely expected to triumph.

Second, while commanding all Christians to be equally strong in shunning the same vices, the fathers seemed unconsciously to accept the stereotypes of their contemporaries when exhorting their congregations to virtue. In addressing themselves to the states of virginity and widowhood, they were theoretically dealing with men as well as women but, with rare exceptions, they fell into a pattern of feminine references. Virgins, wives, and widows were urged to embrace virtues universally recognized as suitable to women, such as modesty and meekness toward all. The vices singled out for criticism are commonly also associated with women: talkativeness, deceitfulness, and vanity. Women in every state of life were frequently counseled in the spirit of the *Apostolic Constitutions* to be

> meek, quiet, gentle, sincere, free from anger, not talkative, not clamorous, not hasty of speech, not given to evil-speaking, not captious, not double-tongued, not a busybody. If she see or hear anything that is not right, let her be as one that does not see, and as one that does not hear . . . and when she is asked anything by anyone, let her not easily answer, excepting questions concerning the faith, and righteousness, and hope in God, remitting those that desire to be instructed in the doctrines of godliness to the governors.[1]

Third, the fathers concluded that the traditional role of women as wives and mothers was vastly inferior to that of the virgin or widow who eschewed remarriage. Formerly, women had always been idealized within the family setting. But the early church fathers tended to emphasize the disabilities of commitment to a family, which limited the woman's freedom to commit herself to Christ. Though they upheld Christ's insistence on monogamy and taught the importance of the virtuous Christian matron in the proper conduct of the Christian life, the fathers were intensely suspicious of the conjugal bed. In his "Exhortation to Virginity," Ambrose of Milan noted that "since Adam had sinned and Eve was pricked by the serpent with the venom of lubricity, even if marriage is good it nevertheless comprehends certain things for which the spouses themselves must blush together." [2]

Augustine, too, exalted virginity, but also asserted the honorable place of marriage in the Christian scheme of life. He formulated the basic Christian attitude: Christian marriage provides a lawful channel for the relief of lust, results in the procreation of children, and establishes a Christian atmosphere for their rearing. The mutual faith and love of man and woman could provide the needful support to bring them both to salvation. Reluctantly recognizing the claims of marriage, the patristic writers were sensitive to its disadvantages for a woman: the humiliation of trying to attract and please a husband, the harassment of wordly care and vanities, and the risks and pain of childbirth. Jerome's description of a married woman's life, in the "Letter Against Helvidius," is one of the milder presentations:

> Do you think that it is one and the same thing to spend day and night in prayer and fasting, and to paint the face in anticipation of the arrival of a husband? . . . Add to this, the prattling of infants, the noisy clamoring of the whole household, the clinging of children to her neck, the computing of expenses, the preparing of budgets. . . . Like a swallow she flies over the entire interior of the house, to see if the couch is properly arranged, if the floors have been swept, if the drinking bowls have been set in order, if the dinner has been prepared. Tell me, I ask you, where is there any opportunity to think of God in the midst of all this? [3]

Through the centuries, the church fathers chanted the glories of the brides of Christ. Only the martyr's crown could equal the glories reserved in heaven for the triumphant virgin. Even for the woman who had married in her youth, widowhood provided a second chance. By the fourth century, monastic life attracted increasing numbers of women and men who strove for moral perfection through asceticism. Extravagant glory has always accrued to the great male founders of the early monastic establishments. They were praised as the heroes of an age, the pioneers of the religious expansion. But their sisters who shared their labors and presided over communities of women received few panegyrics. Only Macrina, the sister of Basil, received some credit. Her younger brother, Gregory of Nyssa, clearly attributes Basil's conversion to her example and strenuous persuasion.

The first monastic rule for Western women was written by Caesarius of Arles for the use of his sister. Although Caesarius does not say so, she probably advised him in his work: the lessons of experience show in the provisions regarding the strict cloistering of women to protect them from the dangers of the age and in the financial arrangements that secured the independence of the establishment. Though the nuns were advised to work in order to fulfill their own needs, they were prohibited from engaging in commerce. Furthermore, Caesarius exempted them and their sizable endowment from episcopal authority though he was generally known to be very jealous of the prerogatives of his own office.

Why were women's achievements widely ignored in these writings? We may find a clue in one of Jerome's letters. He acted as mentor to a circle of ascetic women who helped him with his intellectual labors, and their life is illustrated in his surviving correspondence. On one occasion, when he was absent from the community, he entrusted a female disciple with the task of answering inquiries regarding the correct interpretation of Scripture. Hearing that she had been attributing her answers to himself or to other men rather than take credit to herself, Jerome praised her for her unwillingness to do "a wrong to the male sex."

The Germanic Kingdoms: 500–750

Monasticism proved singularly suited to the needs of the chaotic age that followed the collapse of the Roman Empire in the west. In the sixth and seventh centuries, monks and nuns became the principal agents in the civilizing of tribes who occupied the former Roman lands. In contrast to the ascetics of the late Roman Empire, who rejected the secular world with its decadent institutions, the monks and nuns of the early Germanic kingdoms enthusiastically began to convert the world to Christianity. Although nuns, unlike monks, could not aspire to episcopal appointments, they made equal contributions in the establishment of monasteries in the wilderness. Monks and nuns alike preserved learning and counseled newly converted rulers. The lands they controlled and the people they governed gave the abbesses a practical power equal to that of abbots and sometimes even bishops. Among secular women, only queens exercised comparable power.

The social structure of Germanic tribes before their appearance within the Roman Empire and their conversion to Christianity is shrouded in the darkness of their own illiteracy. We must rely on the occasional comments of Roman observers and the retrospective writings of the early medieval chroniclers to gloss the mute evidence of archaeology. In the later first century, Tacitus glorified the purity of Germanic family life in order to rebuke Roman immorality. He admitted, however, that the royal families were polygamous and that wife purchase was a common practice, though he interpreted it to be a measure of the esteem in which the Germans held their women. Tacitus also testified to the high place of women as priestesses and seeresses among the tribes of his period. He noted the Germanic practice of bringing wives to the battlefield while, at a later period, Ammianus Marcellinus maintained that Germanic wives took an active part in the fighting itself. The Lombard ("longbearded") people, according to their eighth-century chronicler, believed that their name derived from a time when their women went into battle with their hair tied under their chins to delude the enemy.

Apart from these tantalizing glimpses of the early society of the Germanic tribes, information can be gleaned about the life of women from law codes. By the time of their compilation, however, contact with Rome and conversion to Christianity were already beginning to change the basic nature of Germanic society. On the whole, these early codes reflect a society that regarded women primarily as property belonging to their families. The highest bidder received a marriageable girl, although those codes that were influenced by Christian and Roman customs divided the bride price paid by the new husband between his wife and her nearest relatives. Unmarried women who allowed themselves to be abducted were severely punished. Germanic laws thus conflicted with Christian tenets; in questions of marriage Christianity placed the individual's choice over that of the family. Moreover, the Germanic codes put the highest cash penalties on the injury of a woman of childbearing age, demonstrating that they did not share the church's view that virgins and widows were vastly superior to wives and mothers. This opposition was never to be fully resolved and, at least until the ninth century, secular society and its values predominated.

Christian chroniclers of the sixth and seventh centuries were reluctant to depict pagan marriage customs but they clearly describe the role played by women in the Christianization of the new kingdom. In the late fifth century, Clothilde, the wife of the Frankish king Clovis, persisted in her efforts to convert her husband despite his anger over the death of her first son — immediately following his baptism. Through her efforts the Franks became the first tribe to embrace orthodox Christianity. Moreover, she continued to nourish the church with practical assistance. Many Frankish monastic foundations and churches owed their existence to her generous and ready good will. In the following century Bertha, the Frankish queen of Kent in England, prepared the way for Augustine of Canterbury to convert that land. A succession of princesses went out from Kent in the succeeding generations to marry other Saxon kings and to help convert their new people.

Formal conversion to Christianity, however, did not change the practical lives of these peoples for many generations. The sixth-century Franks described by Gregory of Tours were still very pagan in their practices. Though, to our knowledge, none of the Frankish sovereigns relapsed so far as to pay active homage to pagan gods (as did some of the English), their customs bore little resemblance to the Christian life preached by the fathers. Polygamy and incest characterized their marriages. The heavy compensation legally demanded for the abduction or injury of the daughters and wives of the Franks did not deter violence and rape. Widows, seized on the very field where their dead and defeated husbands lay, were forced to marry the victors. Daughters were dragged to the beds of their fathers' murderers. Such was the fate of the sixth-century Frankish queen Radegond, who was captured and forced to marry Chlotar I, the murderer of several of her relatives. Luckier than many of her contemporaries, she succeeded, after several attempts to escape from her polygamous mate, in gaining release from her marriage. She lived out her life in a convent she established at Poitiers, where she acted as a counselor to Frankish kings and spiritual companion of the poet Fortunatus.

A few Frankish women in those violent and unsettled times bent their circumstances to improve their status. Some slave and peasant women used their beauty and seductiveness to advance themselves on the social ladder. The slave Fredegonda, for whose sake King Chilperic murdered his Visigoth wife, became a queen and proved herself capable of holding her position after her husband's death. Her savage rivalry with her sister-in-law, Queen Brunhilda, dominates the history of the late sixth century. There is evidence that these socially mobile women sometimes remembered the less fortunate people from whom they came. Another slave who became a queen in the seventh century was Bathilda, wife of Clovis II. As regent for her sons, she actively opposed and alleviated the evils of the slave trade.

In the work of the English chronicler Bede, histories of violent queens and the wars they waged give way to lives of saintly virgins and widows and the great convents they established. The most popular type of establishment for women in the seventh century, both in the English and Frankish kingdoms, was the double monastery, in which religious men and women observed a common rule and obeyed a common superior — usually an abbess. Monks were attached to a convent in order to provide heavy labor, performance of priestly functions, and, in those troubled times, some degree of protection. The subjection of men to the rule of a woman was consistent with the Christian doctrine that men and women are spiritually equal. The Mosarabic *Liber Ordinum* of the fifth century instructed bishops to declare at the installation of abbesses that before God there could be no discrimination of sex and no disparity between the souls of the saints because men and women were equally called to participate in the spiritual battle. In addition, the position of women in most of the double monasteries of this age no doubt owed much to the fact that they were ladies of royal lineage.

By Bede's time, double monasteries had become so fashionable in England that he complained of nobles who built such institutions on their own estates, one for themselves and one for their wives, without any intention of observing continence. This type of establishment, however, was exceptional. Most of the convents that spread over seventh-century England were true religious centers. Bede suggests that a whole generation of women from the royal families of Anglo-Saxon England preferred the celibate life of the convent to marriage. Women fled from the world to the cloister before and after marriage and, in many cases, while their husbands were still alive.

The convent provided shelter from an unwelcome union but it also offered liberty and scope for the ambitious. The nuns of this period were far from totally cloistered. Many of them, filled with the spirit of adventure, undertook arduous pilgrimages to far flung centers of worship. When Abbess Bugga of Minster proposed to go to Rome in the eighth century, she was not deterred by Boniface's warning that the roads into Italy were lined with brothels staffed by English nuns who had failed to reach their destination. Abbesses ruled establishments that sometimes included thousands of men and women and vast amounts of territory. And they exercised influence commensurate with their functions. For example, Hilda of Whitby founded several monastic institutions, acted as a consultant to her royal relatives, and gave shelter to the great Synod of Whitby in 664, which submitted the English church to Rome. Five bishops received their training in her convent.

The correspondence of the great eighth-century English missionary Boniface with the nuns of Wimbourne shows the important role played by these women in the expansion of Christian civilization. Responding to repeated requests, the English sisters supplied him with books, money, and altar cloths. Most impressive was the copy of St. Peter's epistle, done in gold lettering by the abbess of Thanet, Eadburga. As soon as he had gained a foothold in pagan lands, Boniface requested that Tetta, Abbess of Wimborne, send him a mission of women to establish nunneries for his new converts. Heeding his call, the learned Leoba followed him into the wilderness to establish the first convent in German lands at Bischofsheim. In later years, when Boniface and Leoba engaged in the reform of the Frankish church, Leoba became the friend and confidante of Charlemagne's empress, Hildegard.

In 816 a Frankish bishop exhorted the abbesses within his episcopal jurisdiction to take care that the nuns were never idle. In addition to doing routine housekeeping, the bishop had noticed, nuns were distinguishing themselves by the production of fine cloth and needlework. Fearing the temptations to vanity inherent in too much attention to spinning, weaving, and embroidery, the bishop recommended reading as a preferable activity. Similarly, the Council of Cloveshove in England declared that nuns ought to occupy themselves with reading and singing the Psalter.

During these centuries of upheaval and brutality, neither men nor women produced a very large body of original literary or artistic work. Education for both sexes rarely expanded beyond a sturdy knowledge of the Bible and some acquaintance with the writings of the Church fathers. Yet, the nuns' contribution to the culture of the age was significant.

In every Christianized area of early medieval Europe learned nuns played a vital part in culture and learning. Radegond, in the sixth century, was widely admired for her familiarity with the writings of the Christian fathers. A century later, Hilda of Whitby helped to lay the foundations of the English poetic tradition by inspiring and instructing the herdsman Caedmon, the "father of English poetry." The eighth-century Belgian canonesses Herlinda and Renilda of Eika received their contemporaries' praises for their mastery of the techniques of copying and miniature painting. Manuscripts produced by the nuns of Chelles were among the finest of the age. The life of Radegond was written by the nun Baudonivia; Dominica, a canoness of Nivelles, produced the biography of the convent's founder, Gertrude; and Bertha of Vilich wrote the life of Adelheid. About 760 a nun at the convent of Heidenheim composed a biography of Wunibald's pilgrimage to the Holy Land. Leoba was one of several nuns who turned her hand to the composition of religious poetry.

The Carolingian Age

Saint Paul's injunction that it was improper for women to teach men was ignored through the eighth century because of the demands of the frontier situation in most of Europe. Convents and monasteries monopolized education and instructed children of both sexes, whether or not they intended to enter the monastic life themselves. Only in the late eighth and ninth centuries was an effort made to introduce segregation of sexes in monastic education. The position of secular women was simultaneously made more secure by social legislation that eliminated unilateral divorce by men. The Carolingians also enhanced the importance of women as wives by conferring official recognition upon their administrative and economic rights and duties. Thus, ninth-century women did not have to rely on sheer willpower or scheming to amass property and secure their position in the secular world.

In the late eighth century, Pepin the Short, the ruler of the Franks, invited Saint Boniface to reconstitute the decaying church in his kingdom. The reform was continued into the ninth century by his son, Charlemagne. Churchmen in Charlemagne's entourage reintroduced the principle that "the weakness of her sex and the instability of her mind forbid that [women] should hold the leadership over men in teaching and preaching."

In his effort to restore the monastic system to its pristine purity, Charlemagne invoked ancient prejudices against women that his predecessors had ignored. He legislated against too close an association of the sexes in monasteries. Nuns and canonesses had to be strictly cloistered. No longer could they assist priests in the celebration of the mass and the administration of the sacraments. Abbesses were placed under the control of bishops. Bishops could even interfere with decisions about life in the convent and the admission of new members. Indeed, bishops alone could consecrate new applicants — a right formerly exercised by abbesses.

The emperor prohibited nuns and canonesses from educating boys in their convents. This reform tended to be more detrimental for laymen than for laywomen because it became increasingly rare for the sons of the nobility to be educated in convents. This meant that laymen frequently received no literary education at all while noble ladies continued to be raised and educated in convents until they reached a marriageable age. For several centuries thereafter, it was not uncommon that a representative of the sex whose "instability" of mind made her unfit to teach boys might find herself wed to an illiterate husband. Charlemagne himself never ceased to regret his own illiteracy and strove to master writing even as an adult. Charlemagne's biographer, Einhard, notes that he insisted his daughters be educated with his sons at the palace school. His sister, Gisela, Abbess of Chelles, was a learned lady who corresponded with the master of the palace schools. Very often in the two centuries that followed, the scant efforts to establish secular centers of culture were promoted by educated women. For example, the founder of the Saxon dynasty of German emperors, Henry I, was illiterate, while his wife Mathilda, educated at Hereford, patronized learning and founded one of the chief literary and scholastic centers of the west at Quedlinburg. This singular disparity of education in the secular world may even in part explain why the knightly class described the learned monk as "womanish."

Within the monasteries, the level of learning was raised by the Carolingian reform of education, which introduced a curriculum based on the seven liberal arts. Hence the tenth-century nun Hroswitha of Gandersheim, who displayed great familiarity with the products of classical learning. Inspired by the Roman playwright Terence, then enjoying a vogue in German society, she wrote a series of dramas of her own, making her the only European dramatist for nearly five centuries. In addition, she produced two histories (one of the German imperial house and one of her own convent of Gandersheim) and short stories based on the apocryphal Gospel of Mary and various lives of the saints. The preface to her first volume of poetry paid homage to the nuns among whom she lived and especially to her abbess Gerberga. Her description of her writing, her first efforts and laborious revisions, gives the modern reader an astonishing picture of a true artist at work within the conventual atmosphere. As her confidence in her own talents grew secure, she portrayed women of courage and resourcefulness. One of her female characters, Sapientia, on the very brink of martyrdom, instructs her male persecutors in the finer points of philosophy, mocking their efforts to turn her from her faith. However, even she occasionally succumbed to stereotypes. Thus in one of her prefaces she referred deprecatingly to the "imbecility" of her own sex. Still, here is the authentic voice of a medieval nun, expressing the ideals and aspirations of her less gifted sisters across the centuries:

> There are many Catholics, and we cannot entirely acquit ourselves of the charge, who, attracted by the polished elegance of the style of pagan writers, prefer their works to the holy scriptures. There are others, who, although they are deeply attached to the sacred writings and have no liking for most pagan productions, make an exception in favor of the works of Terence, and, fascinated by the charm of the manner, risk being corrupted by the wickedness of the matter. Wherefore, I, the strong voice of Gandersheim, have not hesitated to imitate in my writings a poet whose works are so widely read, my object being to glorify the limits of my poor talents, the laudable chastity of Christian virgins in that self-same form of composition which has been used to describe the shameless acts of licentious women.[4]

Commanding a dramatic style ranging from melodrama to slapstick comedy, Hroswitha pursued the subject of chastity, its defense, its loss, and its restoration. Her heroines sometimes display the standard courage of the virgin martyr faced with death and dishonor. Sometimes they meet death with mockery and impudent humor or with resolution and self-sacrifice. In other plays, their resourcefulness and sense of diplomatic strategy bring them to a happy outcome. Her heroines are self-reliant and never hesitate to assert themselves against the lustful or bloodthirsty men who persecute them.

Hroswitha's dramas should not be regarded simply as heroic fantasies based on the events of times long gone by. Though she preferred a traditional historic setting for her work, contemporary examples of steadfast heroism were not lacking had she chosen to use them. In addition to the everyday demands of suitors and the hazards of warfare among Christians who did not always respect nuns' garb, a new wave of pagan invasions broke through Europe in the ninth and tenth centuries. The flourishing monastic culture of Ireland, England, and wide areas of Frankland was destroyed by the Vikings. Convents with their wealth, their women, and their lack of protection were favorite targets for these savage marauders. Women were dragged through the streets by the hair, raped, and tortured. A new generation of martyrs was in the making. Particularly dramatic is the story of the death of Saint Ebba and all the nuns of her convent. In 870, an army of Danes landed in Scotland and proceeded south, spreading terror, ruin, and rapine. The convent at Ely was burned, and the army headed for the nunnery at Coldingham. Seeing no hope of flight, Ebba took heroic measures to defend the honor of her sisters. As the Danes approached, the nuns gathered together and, following Ebba's example, slashed off their noses and upper lips to confront their would-be rapists with a line of ghastly, bleeding virgins. The horrified Danes burned the convent, and the sisters victoriously achieved the status of martyrs.

Women who found fulfillment in the convent were, of course, only a small proportion of the female population. In the early Middle Ages, as in most ages of human history, the majority of women lived in the secular world, married, and bore children. By the ninth century a complex series of social advances had produced a vastly improved situation for the individual woman vis-à-vis the family interest to which she had previously been subordinated. Women were able to ensure their independence within the limits of whatever social sphere they occupied by their control of some property of their own. The Germanic custom of bride purchase practically disappeared. Instead of giving a purchase price to the bride's family, the groom endowed her directly with the bride gift, usually a piece of landed property over which she had full rights. To this, he frequently added the morning gift following the consummation of the marriage. In addition to the economic independence derived through marriage, the women of the ninth century enjoyed an increased capacity to share in the inheritance of property. Women had always been eligible to receive certain movable goods from either their own relatives or from their husbands but now law and practice allowed women to inherit immovables. A reason for this trend may be discerned from a deed from the eighth century in which a doting father left equal shares of his property to his sons and daughters. He justified his act by explaining that discrimination between the sexes was an "impious custom" that ran contrary to God's law and to the love he felt for all of his children.

Women's ability to inherit property had far-reaching social effects, which modern demographers are still investigating. Although a young woman still could not marry a man against her family's will, her independence after marriage was greatly enhanced if she possessed her own property. After their father's death, Charlemagne's daughters were able to withdraw from the court of their brother and lead independent lives because Charlemagne had endowed them with substantial property. As widows, too, women acquired increased status if they were allowed to control their sons' and their deceased husbands' property. The most dramatic example of this permanently affected the political future of England. The daughter of Alfred the Great, Ethelflaeda, widow of the king of Mercia, devoted her long reign to cooperation with her brother in the pursuit of their father's policy of containing the Norse invaders. Together they established a strong, centralized kingdom centered on Wessex. After a life of campaigning against Danish, Irish, and Norwegian enemies, she succeeded in willing the kingdom away from her own daughter, the rightful heiress, and leaving it to her brother. This act destroyed the independence of Mercia with its rival claims to Anglo-Saxon supremacy and assured that the English kingdom would be dominated by Wessex and the line of Alfred. Ironically, Ethelflaeda's indisputable contribution to the future of England deprived another woman of her right to rule.

On the Continent, the Carolingian house imposed a relatively stable peace for over a century. This was an age not only of religious but also of social reform aimed at reconstituting a political order that had vanished with the Roman state. Inspired by the vision of Augustine centuries earlier, Charlemagne endeavored to devise an imperial system that would give expression to the City of God. To this end, he redefined the duties of the great officials and created some new positions. These reforms, however, did not favor the advancement of women. The government of his empire was vested in counts, bishops, and other local officials under the supervision of the traveling *missi dominici.* The counts received some assistance from their wives but it would never have occurred to the emperor or any of his advisers to appoint a woman.

The establishment of the Carolingian system of government barred women from the power they sometimes wielded under the earlier Frankish kings and were to possess again in the first feudal age, which began in the late ninth century. The more modest responsibilities of women as wives, in contrast, received formal recognition in the imperial period. To support their own rather dubious claims to the crown, the Carolingians had introduced the custom of anointment and solemn coronation with its overtones of divine sanction for the monarchy. From Pepin forward, their queens shared in this ritual: they were crowned in their own right and their names were included in the royal liturgies. As head of the royal household the queen was a real force in the economic administration of the kingdom.

In the ninth century no one distinguished between an office and the person who held it or between private and public authority. The ministers of state had the titles of palace servants and the ancient concept of the state was but a dim memory. The whole realm was regarded as the ruler's property. His finances and real power rested on the vast estates he owned directly. All the ninth-century sources agree that it was the duty of the queen to run the royal estates — that is, the finances and domestic affairs of the realm — in order to leave the king free for what were considered more important duties. In the *Capitulare de villis,* Charlemagne specifically endowed his queen with the power to run his estates: "We wish that everything ordered by us or by the queen to one of our judges, or anything ordered to the ministers, seneschals or cupbearers . . . be carried out to the last word."

The same pattern is repeated through the ranks of the aristocracy, where competent wives were trained and expected to administer the affairs of thousands of dependents in their extended "household." Occasionally, too, the lady entrusted with such responsibilities might not be working simply as her husband's supporter. We have one extraordinary example of a "professional" in the life of Saint Liutberga. Raised in a convent, Liutberga's intelligence and sweet disposition recommended her as a companion to Gisela, a wealthy widow who had inherited the broad lands of her father, Count Hessi of Saxony. Liutberga proved an apt pupil to her patron, who spent most of her time traveling to supervise her lands. On her deathbed, Gisela advised her son and heir, Bernard, to entrust the administration of the estates to Liutberga. He did so and under her management his family prospered. As she advanced in age, however, Liutberga became increasingly devout and possibly also increasingly weary of being exploited by this wealthy family. In any case, she withdrew from them and established herself as a recluse near the convent of Wendhausen. Here she was frequently visited by the great men and women of the area, who looked to her for counsel and elevating discourse. Due to her popularity, the convent attracted the attention of leading bishops and was showered with endowments, becoming one of the leading centers of education for young women.

The position of Carolingian women as wives was further secured by the introduction into secular legislation of the principle of marital indissolubility. The general position of the early church held that a wife's barrenness or illness was not sufficient cause for her repudiation. Her husband might find her repulsive but he could not put her away for a wife that suited him better. Only if she committed adultery could she be repudiated. But these principles lacked the power of enforcement in the early period. The Carolingians, who depended heavily on church support to secure their own power, worked steadily to bring their own laws into conformity with canon law. Charles himself, who in youth had repudiated at least one wife, became a model of marital decorum once he had issued his prohibitions against divorce. Despite the urging of his counselors, he refused to repudiate his unpopular queen Fastrada, and after the death of a subsequent wife, Liutgard, he did not again submit himself to the legal bonds of marriage.

The new laws met several dramatic tests under Charlemagne's successors but they were finally upheld. Louis the Pious, Charlemagne's son, succeeded in retaining his unpopular wife, Judith of Bavaria, by relying on synodal legislation, which entitled the accused woman to a trial in defense of her honor and position. An alliance of prelates and nobles, grouped behind the sons of the emperor's first marriage, had sought to drive Judith from her place with charges of adultery and even sorcery. They had succeeded in forcibly separating the royal couple and placing them in monasteries for repentance. When, however, Louis could reassemble his forces, he was able to force an ecclesiastical court to hear the case and accept the queen's successful purgation. The final test came later in the ninth century when Louis's grandson, King Lothar II of Lotharingia, attempted to repudiate his wife, Tetberga, and marry his mistress, Waldrada. Through a champion, the queen underwent the ordeal of boiling water and successfully negated his charges of adultery and incest. Ignoring the verdict, Lothar then dragged her before a series of ecclesiastical tribunals, one of which, manned by bishops he had appointed, found in his favor. This, however, drew upon the king the wrath of the leading Frankish prelate, Hincmar of Rheims, and finally of Pope Nicholas I. Even though the queen, exhausted and frightened, begged to retire into a convent, the pope insisted that Lothar take her back.

The church proclaimed that even adultery did not excuse divorce. To insure the utmost legal recognition for the wife, Hincmar advised a formal contract, parental consent, and personal vows with a blessing by the clergy. These formalities, however, were not indispensable. Through the five centuries that followed, the jurisdiction of the church over marital problems was steadily expanded. A body of legislation was built up aimed at applying the principle of indissolubility to common-law marriages, betrothals, especially where the couple had consummated their relationship, and even to promises made by seducers to their victims.

Although our information about the lives of ordinary people in this period is scant, it seems clear that they (like their royal and noble rulers) regarded themselves primarily as parts of family units. The new rules prohibiting divorce, for example, tightened family ties for them as well as for the elite. It must be remembered that for men and women of the Carolingian age, the provision of the necessities of life was a never-ending preoccupation. In the peasant class, burdened with the support of the entire society, the labor of each member of the family was indispensable for survival itself. Even without legal and spiritual compulsions, the most pressing necessities served to strengthen the marital bond. Moreover, what these women did, who they married, how they disposed of what small income came to them was a matter of concern to the lord who ruled them. The records of the great abbeys and other manorial documents specifically list the status of each man and woman on the estate with the exact obligations each individual owed in labor and in provisions. Even though bound to their husbands and to the land, the women were regarded with a certain respect in the manor rolls. They were sources of labor and therefore of wealth. Each person who could work was valuable, and no ideas about the infirmity of women excluded them from their place in a world of productive people.

The importance of peasant women was demonstrated by the attention Charlemagne paid to them in the same capitulary that laid out the authority of the queen. In addition to their general duties in their own family circles, the women of the royal domain, like their husbands, owed certain services to the lord. On the Carolingian estate, as in the manufacturing establishments of the later Middle Ages, their exclusive province was the making of cloth. To supply the emperor with the household linens and clothes he and his retainers needed, the women of his estates worked at set periods in the great hall, providing "linen, wool, woad, vermillion, madder, wool-combs, teasels, soap, grease, vessels and other objects." In addition, they performed duties related to the provision of food in the hall itself and probably participated in the preparation of the foodstuffs owed by the family to the lord: "lard, smoked meat, salt meat, partially salted meat, wine, butter, malt, beef, mead, honey, wax, flour."

The aspirations of all medieval men and women were limited by their class. Within those bounds, peasants, like their noble masters, pursued their own ambitions. The most important social fact of this age is the practical disappearance of ancient forms of slavery. Many factors combined to achieve this elevation of the lowest ranks among the agricultural workers. Since the peasants derived their legal status through their mothers, it has recently been suggested that by marrying free women dependent men achieved the freedom of their offspring.

The short-lived effort of Charlemagne and his descendants to achieve a structured society tended to deprive women of the powers they had exercised in the sixth and seventh centuries. In this sense the Carolingian period foreshadowed twelfth-century developments. As the control of church and state came increasingly to be vested in the hands of men, women's activities were restricted to the home and the cloister. Yet, the Carolingian age strengthened the position of women within the family. By enforcing the principle of marital indissolubility, the church protected women from the caprices of their husbands. Their contributions to the well-being of society were recognized at every level. Their right to enjoy the reward of their own labor was protected by their right to share in their patrimonial inheritance.

The First Feudal Age

Endowed with their own property and rights of inheritance, secure in their marital status, women were equipped to act with power and decision in the fluid society of the first feudal age, which followed the collapse of the Carolingian Empire in the late ninth century. The institutions of Charlemagne proved incapable of sustaining themselves under the dual assault of new invasions and the claims of blood that caused the emperors themselves to divide their dominions among their sons. Land, power, and title passed from one to another of their warring successors. Out of the ruins of the Carolingian state the family emerged as the most stable and effective element in a troubled world. Profiting from the almost unlimited power of their families, women for two centuries were able to play a central political role. Since land had become the only source of power, by exercising their property rights, secured in the Carolingian period, a growing number of women appear in the tenth and eleventh centuries as chatelaines, mistresses of landed property and castles with attendant rights of justice and military command, proprietors of churches, and participants in both secular and ecclesiastical assemblies.

By the middle of the tenth century, the most stable and secure power in Europe was the German kingdom of Otto I. The fate of Germany was changed forever by his imperial ambitions, which were furthered by his marriage to Adelaide of Burgundy, who had come into possession of large estates in the kingdom of Lombardy after the death of her first husband. Control of these lands laid the base for a possible renewal of the Roman imperial title. Competitors literally besieged the widow in order to win her hand and all that went with it. With Adelaide's marriage to Otto began the connection between Italy and Germany that lasted until the nineteenth century. In recognition of his wife's political power and prestige, the emperor issued diplomas with their joint signatures and minted coins with her portrait on them.

With most of Europe beset by violence and political disintegration, tenth- and eleventh-century Germany represented an oasis of culture and security. The great convents continued to flourish there as centers of learning. Under the rule of the Salian and Saxon emperors and the regencies of their wives, widows, and sisters, Germany prospered. Among the women who helped to rule this empire, one of the most interesting was the sister of Otto II, Matilda, Abbess of Quedlinburg. When her brother was occupied with his government in Italy, she ruled in his name and even presided over church councils. Even when acting only in her own name, she exercised the enormous political and economic power vested by Otto I and his successors in the great offices of the church. Her biographer used the word *metropolitana* (overseer of bishops), to describe her authority.

Outside of Germany, power and wealth tended to disintegrate throughout this period. The west broke up into a collection of small principalities or seigniories; the authority of each extended as far as its lord, with his limited resources, could enforce his will. The bonds of lineage represented the principal source of strength for the men and women of this anarchic age. With their dowries and their family connections, women could make a vital contribution to the advancement of their families. For example, in the tenth century, Hugh Capet defended his claim to the throne of France against his rival, Charles of Lorraine, with the argument that Charles had married beneath his station, the daughter of one of Hugh's own vassals, a mere knight. Hugh's wife, on the other hand, was the daughter of Empress Adelaide by her first marriage.

The age of the seigniory was characterized by the total confusion of public and private power. With the ownership of great estates went the sovereign rights of military impressment, justice, minting, taxation, and all the other responsibilities of government. Abbesses sent their knights to war. Noble ladies sat in judgment with their husbands and held the castle when the lord was in the field. Countess Almodis of Barcelona was named as co-author of the *Usages of Barcelona,* one of the earliest written law codes of the new age. Wherever one looks during this period there seem to be no effective barriers to the exercise of power by women. They appear as military leaders, judges, chatelaines, and controllers of property.

The independent and powerful women of tenth-century Italy shocked and appalled their monkish chronicler, Liutprand of Cremona. Everywhere he looked his world appeared to be in the grip of this horrible "pornocracy," government by prostitutes. Liutprand was utterly incapable of explaining the source of this power. Rather than attribute it to the possibilities of inheritance or to personal competence, he repeatedly suggested that when such a woman beckoned from her perfumed couch, no man could help but do her bidding. For example, he noted that the daughter of the Marquess of Tuscany and widow of the Marquess of Ivrea Ermengarde "held the chief authority in all Italy." But his only explanation was that "the cause of her power, shameful though it be even to mention it, was that she carried on carnal commerce with everyone, prince and commoner alike. . . . Ermengarde's beauty, in this corruptible flesh, roused the fiercest jealousies among men: for she would give to some the favours she refused to others." [5]

The holders of sovereign rights in the tenth century claimed control of the church as well. Regarding churches as their own property, they held it their right to appoint church officials — bishops, abbots, and even parish priests. In Rome itself, the great proprietary rights of the family of Theophylactus and the political influence attached to them passed into the hands of Lady Theodora and then to her daughter Marozia. The papacy itself lay under their control. Mistress to one pope, mother of another, Marozia, through her marriage to the king of northern Italy, nearly succeeded in uniting the whole peninsula under her influence until she was thwarted by the violent intervention of one of her sons. Not all chroniclers viewed this feminine influence as uniformly evil. Many a bishop, interested in reform and good government, relied on the influence of the ladies who controlled appointments to local churches and sought their assistance in restoring order to disturbed parishes and monasteries.

The Gregorian Revolution

By the mid-eleventh century, a more settled world began to emerge from the turbulent feudal society. Population was growing, invaders had finally been repelled, commerce was expanding, and the cities were reviving after their long neglect. The church took the lead in establishing the new tone of society, one that ultimately tended to restrict the wide variety of roles women had played in the tenth and early eleventh centuries.

With the help of interested and energetic patrons, including the Empress Agnes, the church sought to enter a period of self-reform. Centering upon a revived papacy, the Gregorian Revolution of the late eleventh century began to focus on several basic reforms that tended directly or indirectly to exclude women from positions of influence in the church. The first of these was the drive to impose celibacy upon the clergy. The correlative effect on their wives is obvious. What little we know about the wives of the ordinary clergy is enshrouded in the violent attacks aimed at them by reformers from the tenth century onward. The tenth-century Bishop Atto of Vercelli criticized them chiefly for diverting ecclesiastical revenues to their own use, taking church land into their own hands, distracting their husbands from pastoral duties, and involving priests in situations where they could not claim exemption from secular jurisdiction. If their dowries and their labor contributed to the effectiveness of parish and diocesan work, their critics chose to disregard it.

These women had few public defenders. Their husbands at one local council pleaded that their role in household management was essential to a sound parish economy. But the argument was ridiculed by the reformers. Some suggestion of their role in pastoral work is illuminated in the biography of Peter Damian. His mother, a woman of the lesser nobility, was weakened by too much childbearing and refused to suckle him, her thirteenth child. The infant stood in immediate danger of death and was saved only by the timely intervention of the priest's wife, who recalled the weary mother to her duty. In later life Damian became the leader of the movement for clerical celibacy. His tracts on the subject expose a hysterical virulence toward priests' wives symptomatic of the most unsavory aspect of the monastic mentality. One might suggest that he seems to have suppressed his hostility toward his mother by transferring it to the class of women who had saved his life. Doubly disturbing is the startling contrast between his attacks on the priests' wives and his romantic correspondence with Empress Agnes, whose powerful support contributed heavily to the success of the reform movement.

The second goal of the reform was the elimination of lay influence in the bestowal of church offices, which culminated in the drive to establish a hierarchical church under the control of the papacy. The aristocratic women of the earlier age had shared with the men of their class in the disposition and protection of ecclesiastical positions. With the destruction of this patronage, they lost that influence. Ironically, the success of the movement depended heavily upon the financial and military support of two women, Beatrice of Tuscany and her daughter Matilda. They gave Pope Gregory VII the strong secular protection that was essential to his successful defiance of Emperor Henry IV in claiming the sole overlordship of the ecclesiastical hierarchy. The central drama of the emperor's submission was played out in Matilda's castle of Canossa. After Gregory's death, Matilda continued for years to secure the papal victory on the battlefield. When she died, she left her Tuscan inheritance to the papacy, providing the base for much of the pope's landed power.

The achievement of these reforms took active control out of the hands of secular leaders and thus effectively deprived women like Matilda of their former influence. At the same time, the importance of the convent in the leadership of society began to decline, though an independent role for women as nuns continued to be possible throughout the Middle Ages. The center of church leadership was moving from the monastic system to the bishoprics and to Rome itself. The center of intellectual ferment in the twelfth and thirteenth centuries was not in the monasteries but in the cathedral schools and the universities, which excluded women. Even their familiar wifely roles were denied them in the halls of learning, for the universities were staffed by celibate clerks.

Nuns continued to study within the convent and to educate girls, but, like the monks of the twelfth and thirteenth centuries, they tended to turn toward mysticism. The last nonmystical literary composition by a nun is the *Hortus Deliciarum,* written in prose and poetry by Herrod of Heidenheim between 1160 and 1170. To be sure, mysticism contributed to the development of art in all its forms, and the works of the great female mystics of the later Middle Ages, Julian of Norwich, Margery Kemp, and Catherine of Siena, continue to claim a place in the literature of Christian Europe.

The Western Monarchies

In the twelfth century, secular society was quick to follow the lead of the church. With the proliferation of new, centralized institutions in church and state, the active influence of women was steadily restricted. Ecclesiastical and princely control did not progress evenly everywhere. In areas removed from centers of church and state power women continued to exercise their rights as proprietors of churches and feudal suzerains. But by th later Middle Ages, women were deprived of direct participation in the affairs of the church and were displaced from their political positions almost everywhere.

The extensive influence of women in the earlier period derived from the irregular powers vested in the great families, but the gradual increase of princely power and centralization restricted the independent political role that characterized the aristocracy of the first feudal age. Royal and princely power depended on the capacity of the greater lords to subject the lesser lords even if only nominally. By force, cajolery, or bribery, they sought to convert landed property from freeholds to fiefs that were held in exchange for loyalty and service. Lords made use of wardship of minor heirs and heiresses as a source of revenue and as a means of rewarding loyal vassals. They also exercised their right to control the marriages of heiresses to fiefs, whether the daughters or the widows of the vassal. The rebel barons who forced John of England to sign the Magna Carta restricted the abuse of wardship and defended a widow's right to remain unmarried. But the nobles did not presume to deny the king's right to determine whom the widow was to marry if she decided to remarry. The military obligations attached to the fief generally fell on the male vassal. As a result, the husbands of heiresses tended to take over the rights of their wives' fiefs along with their obligations.

Occasionally, princes barred women from holding fiefs altogether, for they feared the loss of control implicit in the power of women to convey property rights. The *Constitutio de feudis* of Emperor Konrad II in 1031 forbade the inheritance of fiefs by women, but two centuries later Barbarossa ignored the restriction, and elsewhere in Europe lords did not raise serious objection to the succession of females as long as they acknowledged their feudal obligations, including the lord's right to arrange their marriages.

On the other hand, the great families themselves increasingly excluded women from inheritance in order to halt the erosion of their power through the division and alienation of the patrimony. As the dual concepts of primogeniture and the indivisibility of patrimony became entrenched, daughters usually received a dowry at the time of their marriage in lieu of future claims of inheritance. More and more frequently, only those women without brothers could succeed to their father's patrimony. Even so, as late as the thirteenth century, the northern French customarily reserved only two-thirds of the property for the eldest son, the remaining third to be divided among the younger children. The history of France after the deaths of the sons of Philip the Fair dramatically illustrates the problem inherent in the unrestricted inheritance of women. The strict rules of blood succession would have given the crown either to a woman of doubtful legitimacy or to the son of the last king's sister: Edward III of England. To avoid both contingencies, the leaders of the nobility pretended to find in the ancient Salic law of the Franks a prohibition against any passage of the kingdom through the female line, and the convention continued.

In England, daughters could succeed to the throne if there were no sons. Their succession to private property, however, could be restricted by entail, which secured the perpetual movement of landed property to the nearest male relative, excluding all females regardless of degree of relationship. Moreover, both in England and on the continent, the transformation of the bride gift into the dower — revenue set aside for the maintenance of a widow in lieu of an outright gift of property to the wife — further restricted the economic power of women in the twelfth century. Everywhere, the integrity of the family's estate was maintained by the sacrifice of the economic independence of wives and the testamentary independence of widows.

The bureaucratization of government constricted the influence of aristocratic ladies. The development of treasuries, chanceries, law courts, and other branches of government was paralleled by the development of a professional class to serve in them. The centralization of government in many areas deprived local lineages of their prerogatives. Aristocratic men, to be sure, could often find compensation by taking a place in the lord's government, but their wives and daughters could not. Because of their sex, women could not get the education that would have equipped them for the professions. At best, they might hope to act as regents, surrogates for their men, or exercise an informal influence, but even this might be denied them. Eleanor of Aquitaine's hostility to her first husband, Louis VII of France, and her long conflict with her second husband, Henry II of England, were rooted in her belief that she did not have sufficient political power in the government of those kingdoms. Eleanor lived in a transitional period. The power she sought came to her during the reigns of her sons. Similarly, her granddaughter, Blanche of Castille, dominated the government of France during the reign of her son, Louis IX.

The next generation saw a dramatic change. In England, the household itself became institutionalized under Henry III. Blanche of Castille deprived her daughter-in-law of control even of her own son's education. Queens with a powerful and loving husband might still be provided a share of his power through his good graces. But by the fourteenth century, the position of royal ladies was further weakened by growing xenophobia. Queens normally were foreigners and often were cut off from their friends and retainers, who were suspected of pursuing inimical interests. During the Hundred Years' War, the "foreign woman" frequently became the focus of popular discontent, a scapegoat for the follies of her husband as often as the victim of her own thwarted ambition. The efforts of such queens as Isabelle of France, wife of Edward II of England, Marguerite of

Anjou, wife of Henry VI of England, and Isabeau of Bavaria, wife of Charles VI of France, to pursue their own political interests brought bloodshed and violence upon them and their subjects. By the end of the Middle Ages the glamour that had once surrounded queens and their personal influence over their husbands had all too often been usurped by that piquant figure, the royal mistress.

In the upper reaches of later medieval society, apart from bearing children and acting as sex objects, companions in social functions, and sources of religious or poetic inspiration, women lost their usefulness. Professional men took over the administration of their family's estates; nurses and tutors brought up their children. Among the lesser nobility and the middle classes, women continued to contribute to their family's economic well being. In the fifteenth century, Leon Battista Alberti cautioned men against confiding their business to their wives or heeding their counsel but he wrote at length about the family's comfort, which depended upon a hardworking wife. In the fourteenth century, Goodman of Paris wrote a handbook of housewifery for the instruction of his teenage wife to insure the proper management of the household economy. No known example of this instructional literature was written by a woman, but the letters of Margaret Paston clearly demonstrate how large a role was still left to the mistress of an estate. With her husband in London much of the time, Margaret ran the Norfolk estates with skill and efficiency, not hesitating, on one occasion, to defend them by force of arms.

Among the peasants and the workers of the cities, married and unmarried women shared in the labor of staying alive and perhaps gaining some degree of comfort. The records of most of the craft guilds indicate that the wives of the masters assisted in plying the craft and commonly carried on the business if widowed, though they were sometimes considered incapable of teaching the craft to others. In some guilds women predominated, especially in those relating to cloth work. So many women earned a living by spinning that the unmarried woman acquired the title "spinster." Women also found employment in the heavy work of the fields and in the coal- and iron-mining industries. On the assumption that women ate less than men, they were generally paid less, and the fourteenth century English Statute of Laborers, devised to control wages against too inflated a rise, also prohibited the hiring of cheap female labor in preference to men.

Women did not accept their exclusion from the learned professions, from the government of kingdoms and principalities, and from the active life of the church without protest. Unfortunately, the expression of their frustration must be inferred from sources that do not directly describe their reactions. The extensive role of women in the great heretical movements that swept through Europe in the twelfth and thirteenth centuries is widely acknowledged. Although their social and psychological motivations for turning away from the orthodox religion have not yet been satisfactorily explored, the appeal of heterodoxy was extremely broad and no doubt attracted different women for different reasons. The female *perfectae,* who preached and administered the sacraments of the heretical Cathari, resembled the early martyrs in their courage and capacity for sacrifice. Other women gave money, shelter, and support to the rebel heretics of southern France and died with them during the Albigensian Crusade. Some lower-class women, who followed heterodox preachers, joined prayer and study circles of dubious orthodoxy and finally faced the choice of the stake or a less independent form of worship. An even more obscure set of underground beliefs emerges from the confession of Na Prous Boneta to the inquisitors in 1325 that she expected to become the goddess of the new church as Mary was the goddess of the old. The trial of Joan of Arc, politically motivated as it was, strongly suggests that a male-dominated society had begun to associate "unfeminine" behavior with heresy and witchcraft. Joan's judges frequently seemed to be more disturbed by her habit of dressing like a man than by her religious beliefs.

At the end of the Middle Ages as at the beginning, then, courage and heroism in martyrdom were expressed by women. However, from the twelfth century on, female devotion frequently transferred its object from heaven to earth. Romantic love — all-consuming and all-absorbing — began to obsess many women and men. The sufferings of patient Griselda, the heroine of a popular tale written by men but read by women, were rewarded not by the martyr's crown but by the love of her husband. This new ideology disabled the lady who, as an object of man's devotion, found herself restricted to the occupation of a pedestal. But at least some women may have turned to love as an outlet for their frustration in an increasingly narrow life.

Love as a heroic endeavor was first expressed by one of the most astonishing women of the twelfth century. Héloise was a priest's niece, very possibly the child of one of those clerical marriages that had just been outlawed. In Paris, she had acquired some fame for her learning, achieved by private tutoring, since the Cathedral School barred women from attendance. Proud of the glory she won through her illicit love for Abelard, the foremost scholar of the age, she married him only after a debate in which she quoted all the scholars and fathers of the church to support her reluctance to bear the infamy of damaging his future. Finally, for his sake, she entered a convent, protesting that she was not the bride of Christ but the bride of Abelard. In her later correspondence with Abelard, Héloise insists repeatedly on the perfection of her love for him and the matchless quality of her devotion. But just as persistently, she maintains her claim to glory as her reward.

Less ecstatic ladies may have viewed the growing literature of love in a more practical manner. As listeners, patrons, and writers, women played a central role in the propagation of the concept of courtly love. The heated scholarly debate over the meaning and effect of this literature continues. It may never be possible to establish its true effect on the mores of society. But the debate takes on still another dimension through the suggestion that the creation of the ideal of courtly manners, molded to and molding in turn the tastes of women, may reflect an attempt by aristocratic ladies to carve out a sphere of competence for themselves in an increasingly specialized society.

For centuries, female leaders of society sought an outlet for their energies as arbiters of manners and taste. With varying degrees of success, wives, mothers, and mistresses of the men who ruled the world made the most of their personal influence. Sanctity and power were still within the grasp of a few fortunate and outstanding women. But it is no accident that many upper-class women of the twelfth, thirteenth, and fourteenth centuries, who could not accept the loss of their own power, involved themselves in heretical and romantic activities that were, by their very nature, subversive of the religious and social foundations of medieval society.

Intriguing as one may find the expressions of feminine aspirations in the literature of love, social manners, religious mysticism, and heterodoxy, one must not forget that such expressions reinforced the ancient stereotype of women as unstable creatures moved by willfulness and emotion and in need of protection. That women in the undeveloped frontier stages of medieval society had been able to take advantage of the broad opportunities to elevate themselves to positions of wealth and power was all too quickly forgotten. The most significant conclusion that emerges from the study of medieval women is that women are capable of carrying responsibilities equal to those of men. Their participation in Merovingian times in spreading Christianity and building a new society led to the legal recognition of their economic and marital rights in the Carolingian period. Secure in the knowledge of their indispensability as partners in the governance of the feudal world, the women of the tenth and eleventh centuries had an unprecedented opportunity to use their talents. However, with the growth of a more structured society, where church and state aimed at centralized control, women of the high and late Middle Ages (1100–1500) found their rights and roles increasingly curtailed and their ambitions frustrated. Women who held the most influential positions were the first to suffer from these restrictions, while women in the lower ranks of society continued to contribute their labor to the economy until modern times.

Notes

1. *Apostolic Constitutions,* Book 3, section 5, in *Ante-Nicene Christian Library,* vol. 17, ed. James Donaldson, T. T. Clark, Edinburgh, 1870, pp. 95–96.
2. Ambrose, "Exhortatio Virginitatis," 6, 36, J. P. Migne, *Patrologia Latina,* vol. 16, Paris, 1866, p. 362.
3. Jerome "Letter Against Helvidius," chap. 20, John N. Hritzen, *Dogmatic and Polemical Works,* Catholic University of America Press, Washington, D.C., 1965, p. 41.
4. Hroswitha, *Plays,* trans. Christopher St. John, Benjamin Press, New York, 1966, p. xxvi.
5. Liutprand of Cremona, *Antatapodasis,* Book 3, chap. 8, *The Works of Liutprand of Cremona,* trans. F. A. Wright, E. P. Dutton, New York, 1930, p. 113.

Suggestions for Further Reading

Perhaps the only aspect of the history of women in the Middle Ages that has been adequately studied is the legal rights of women. Such studies, however, were written mainly in French and German and are not available in English translation. Most important among these are Louis-Maurice-André Cornuey, *Le régime de la "dos" aux époques mérovingienne et carolingienne* (Ph.D. dissertation, Université d'Alger, 1929), which traces the transformation of the dowry into the dower, and Aimée Ermolaef, *Die Sonderstellung der Frau im französischen Lehnrecht* (dissertation, University of Bern, 1930), which analyzes the extensive powers women held under French feudal law. A discussion of the legal restrictions imposed upon Englishwomen in the twelfth century may be found in the second chapter of Doris Stenton's *The English Woman in History* (George Allen & Unwin, London, 1950). This work fails, however, to take into account similar developments on the continent and attributes changes for the worst to the Norman invasions. In her analysis of the power of Anglo-Saxon women, the author has heavily drawn upon Frank Stenton's study of place names, "The Place of Women in Anglo-Saxon Society," *Transactions of the Royal Historical Society,* 14th Ser., vol. 25 (1943), 1–113.

Local histories, in which the French excel, usually contain material on women. The overall conclusions of the grand master of this type of historical inquiry, Georges Duby, have been integrated into his general survey, *Rural Economy and Country Life in Medieval West,* trans. Cynthia Postman (University of South Carolina Press, Columbia, S.C., 1968). A fine example of American scholarship is Archibald Lewis, *Development of Southern French and Catalan Society* (University of Texas, Austin, 1956).

A modern approach to social history is through demographic study, which also yields information of importance for the history of women. Especially useful for our period are David Herlihy's "Land, Family and Women," *Traditio,* 18

(1962), 89–113, and Emily Coleman's "Medieval Marriage Characteristics: A Neglected Factor in the History of Medieval Serfdom," *Journal of Interdisciplinary History,* 2 (1971), 205–219.

For the history of medieval convents we still have to rely on two nineteenth-century works: Lina Eckenstein, *Woman under Monasticism* (Cambridge University Press, Cambridge, 1896), and Mary Bateson, "Origin and Early History of Double Monasteries," *Transactions of the Royal Historical Society,* 13 (1899), 137–198. These may be supplemented by Eileen Power, *Medieval English Nunneries* (Cambridge University Press, Cambridge, 1922), and M. P. Heinrich, *The Canonesses and Education in the Early Middle Ages* (Ph.D. dissertation, Catholic University of America, 1924). There are also histories of individual convents.

As biographies of medieval women are of varying quality, we would rather recommend the reading of collective biographies, such as Eileen Power, *Medieval People* (University Paperbacks, London and New York, 1966, new rev. ed.). An analysis of the role of queens is provided by Marion F. Facinger, "A Study of Medieval Queenship: Capetian France," *Studies in Medieval Renaissance History,* 5 (1968). For an understanding of developments in the later Middle Ages, the most essential study is Eileen Power, "The Position of Women," *The Legacy of the Middle Ages,* eds. G. C. Crump and E. F. Jacob (Clarendon Press, Oxford, 1926), pp. 401–434.

5

The Pedestal and the Stake: Courtly Love and Witchcraft

E. William Monter

Each essay in this collection discusses female stereotypes as well as social realities. E. William Monter's essay concerns itself with the most extreme versions of the eternal polarity between Eve and Mary. Of course, these images are opposites, but he stresses their close interrelationship. Both views of woman cast her in a passive role. The Virgin is honored not so much for what she herself does but for the courage, nobility, and grace she inspires in her masculine admirers. The witch wreaks destruction, but only because she has been unable to resist the temptation of the devil. What impact did both conceptions have on the lives of women? Monter says we will never be sure just how women's lives were changed by the courtly love tradition, because the significant literature was written by men. We do know, however, that for three centuries untold numbers of women did suffer execution and torture due to the negative image. The author concludes that the history of both courtly love and witchcraft belongs properly to the history of men's views of women, from which women's history can only be extrapolated.

Sixteenth-century German witches being burned at the stake. The devil, in the form of a flying serpent, comes to claim his reward. (Woodcut, 1555. The Mansell Collection.)

Medieval Christendom developed two basic feminine stereotypes, Mary and Eve; yet neither was invented in the Middle Ages, the Virgin being as old as Christianity and the legend of Eve being a good deal older. However, the topics of this chapter really are distinctly medieval. Both courtly love and witchcraft had antecedents, but both were essentially novel female roles. Neither was drawn directly from Christianity nor copied from older patriarchal stereotypes. The medieval version of courtly love was new insofar as it viewed human love as an ennobling emotion. This represented a radical break with both classical and Christian traditions that shared a basic view of love as at best a necessary weakness and at worst a kind of sickness. The medieval version of witchcraft was new because it viewed sorcery as an organized diabolical conspiracy, thereby reversing an older Christian tradition (also found in some classical sources), which viewed magic and sorcery primarily as superstitions and illusions. Precisely how these two traditions came to be reversed in European civilization during the high and late Middle Ages is mysterious; the changes are easier to describe than to explain.

Furthermore, we must emphasize that courtly love and witchcraft represented not only emotionally opposite feminine roles but also socially opposite roles. That courtly love was to be restricted to the aristocracy (of both sexes) was made clear by its first major theorist, Andreas Capellanus:

> If you should, by some chance, fall in love with a peasant woman, be careful to puff her up with lots of praise and then, when you find a convenient place, do not hesitate to take what you seek and to embrace her by force. For you can hardly soften their outward inflexibility so far that they will grant you their embraces quietly or permit you to have the solaces you desire unless first you use a little compulsion as a convenient cure for their shyness. We do not say these things, however, because we want to persuade you to love such women, but only so that, if through lack of caution you should be driven to love them, you may know, in brief compass, what to do.[1]

Throughout its long history, *courtoisie,* or courtly love, was a pastime confined to the upper classes, as its vocabulary makes clear: only "gentlemen" and "ladies" could play this game. On the other hand, witchcraft was almost completely restricted to the lower classes: modern historians accept the descriptions of medieval demonologists that portray the witch as usually poor, old, solitary, and female.

Courtly Love

Modern scholarship discovered courtly love in the 1880s and has created a large and confusing literature around it. One of the greatest difficulties is that there exists an almost total separation between historians and literary scholars about the real significance of courtly love. Again and again, historians describe the conventions of courtoisie only to cast doubt on its social effects; while literary scholars, with the huge corpus of medieval lyric poetry and romances to explore, tend automatically to accept it as a major cultural force. One can sense the caution of the historians whenever a great medievalist touches this problem. Eileen Power has noted that the social importance of courtly love was far less than its literary importance: "It is probable that the idea of chivalry has had more influence upon later ages than it had upon contemporaries." [2] And more recently, John Benton is even more skeptical:

> Courtesy was created by men for their own satisfaction, and it emphasized women's role as an object, sexual or otherwise. Since they did not encourage a genuine respect for women as individuals, the conventions of medieval chivalry, like the conventions of chivalry in the southern United States, did not advance women toward legal or social emancipation. When men ignored chivalry, women were better off.[3]

In contrast, literary scholars are generally optimistic about the influence of courtly love, simply because of the huge quantity of medieval poetry and prose devoted to its themes. Of course, there are some who deny the very existence of courtly love, but they are an embattled minority who see irony and sometimes satire behind every medieval romance. Most literary scholars line up behind C. S. Lewis, who once said of courtly love that "the most revolutionary elements in it have made the background of European literature for 800 years. . . . Compared with this revolution, the Renaissance is a mere ripple on the surface of literature." [4] This is the literary consensus, although there is still plenty of room for debate about possible Arabic influences, national crosscurrents, and the like.

The birth date for this major literary event has been fairly clearly established. Courtly love came into being during the third quarter of the twelfth century, either at the court established by Eleanor of Aquitaine at Poitiers in 1160 or at that of her daughter Marie in Champagne about a decade later. Its first acknowledged masterpieces, the stories of Chrétien de Troyes and the theoretical treatise *The Art of Courtly Love* by Andreas Capellanus, were both composed at Marie's court in Champagne. One explanation for the rise and popularity of courtly love relates it to the dynastic politics of the family of Eleanor of Aquitaine and to the rise of the Angevin Empire:

> The new courtly epic derived its "political" nourishment from three principal sources: Anglo-Saxon romancing, Celtic inspiration, and the doctrines of love and eroticism peculiar to Provence and southwestern France. These three fused to produce a superb work of art which was the hallmark of the Angevin Empire, that loose-knit assembly of lordships stretching from England to the borders of Spain, itself the supreme example of political artistry the Middle Ages has to offer.[5]

Certainly, the role of Eleanor of Aquitaine was important. She was the granddaughter of one of the greatest troubadours and a queen whose praises were sung by minstrels in French, English, Provençal, and German. And the rapid popularity of courtoisie, spreading out from Eleanor's and Marie's courts, is attested to by the survival of almost a hundred chivalric romances written between 1150 and 1220 in several European countries — as well as by the survival of the names of at least a hundred troubadours who were active during the century after 1150.

There were three distinguishing features of courtly love as it emerged in the twelfth and thirteenth centuries: first, this was a completely extramarital kind of love; second, it was not Platonic love; and third, this concept was *actively* influenced by women at several different points.

Andreas Capellanus stated clearly that this new and ennobling kind of love was utterly separate from marriage. "Everybody knows," he said, "that love can have no place between husband and wife," and he later repeated that "we declare and hold as firmly established that love cannot exert its powers between two people who are married to each other." [6] His position was reasonable, because in twelfth-century Europe marriages were and always had been unemotional business deals between families, arrangements for furthering mutual interests and for producing heirs to extend lineages. The medieval noblewoman, the much-honored lady of the minstrels, was merely an object on the marriage market whose value was not personal but the value of her fief. Medieval noblewomen were either married by their families (one must use the passive verb) or else required to enter a convent: unmarried noblewomen are scarcely mentioned in medieval law and literature outside the cloister. And marriage, although very nearly inevitable, offered very few real advantages to medieval women. Canon law permitted wife beating. Divorce was impossible; even obtaining a separation from a brutal or unwanted husband was extremely difficult. Of course, there were many happy marriages in the Middle Ages, and some women, like Chaucer's Wife of Bath, found ways to beat the system, but by and large medieval marriages were not intended to be emotionally satisfying for the women (or men) who entered into them. They were a necessity.

Although this new, ennobling kind of love was totally separate from marriage, it was not a purely intellectual or Platonic love. Here, too, its first theorist was unambiguous. "Love," he defined, "is a certain inborn suffering derived from the sight of and excessive meditation upon the beauty of the other sex, which causes each one to wish above all things the embraces of the other and by common desire to carry out all of love's precepts in the other's embrace." [7] This sounds like a romantic concept of love but hardly an ethereal one. Later, Capellanus defines "pure" love (as opposed to "mixed" love or venery) as something that "consists of the contemplation of the mind and the affection of the heart; it goes as far as the kiss and the embrace and modest contact with the naked lover" [8] — which could hardly have been reassuring to husbands or male kin. Courtly love, in its principal theoretical treatise and in some of its best-known stories, sounds like a set of rather elaborate rules for adultery — which it probably was, although it also became a great deal more.

Finally, it is worth noting that courtly love depended to a large extent upon the active participation of women. We have already seen how Eleanor of Aquitaine and her daughter Marie of Champagne presided over its creation: Marie's greatest court poet, Chrétien de Troyes, explicitly states that the plot line of one of his most famous stories, *The Knight in the Cart,* was given to him by Marie. But women's role was even more creative than this. Of the hundred known troubadours active from 1150 to 1250, almost twenty were women, including Countess Beatrix of Die and her daughter Tiburga. And one of the most important early poets of courtly love was a woman known as Marie of France, whom most scholars say was a Plantagenet princess, abbess of Shaftesbury between 1165 and 1190, who composed fairy tales and love poems dedicated to major personalities at Eleanor's English court. Women were more than passive objects on pedestals during the centuries of courtoisie. They were also judges of the man's worth as lover and had not only the freedom but the obligation to reject all unworthy candidates. Their role in Capellanus' dialogues is as important as the men's.

Of course, to help the ladies in this difficult job of screening out the unworthy lovers, theorists of courtoisie soon evolved an elaborate set of rules. They created a service of love much like the services a feudal vassal owed to his lord, a set of formal duties that a lover was obliged to perform before he could win his lady's love. To be acceptable, a nobleman had to possess the virtues that could kindle love. This meant in the first place the ordinary chivalric virtues of prowess and loyalty, which made for a good public reputation. But his private assets were at least as important. A courtly knight was also supposed to be handsome and always pleasant company for his lady — a good talker, preferably a good singer and dancer, capable of reciting poetry if not of writing it. After he had won his lady's affections, the courtly knight was required to demonstrate his love by serving her: this meant primarily performing some deeds of prowess in her honor, ordinarily by wearing her colors at tournaments. And — a very important literary point — the courtly knight must be discreet about his love, in order to keep his lady's reputation as pure as possible. In fact, he should respect all ladies and neither slander them himself nor permit any slander about them to go unpunished.

Perhaps it is the strain involved in trying to match these elaborate conventions and formalities with the recorded facts of daily life that makes historians so skeptical about the social effects of courtly love. There are at least three principal reasons for their skepticism.

First, iconographical evidence for the social reality of courtly love comes very late. Only in the fifteenth century (a time, as we shall see, when the pedestal theory came under severe attack) can we find a tournament shield depicting a knight kneeling before his lady. Before then, knights kneeled before the Virgin or perhaps a saint, but not a mortal woman. Furthermore, the only solid evidence for the existence of a Court of Love also dates from the fifteenth century, and (as we shall also see) its relation to the pedestal theory is ambiguous.

Second, there was very little improvement in women's legal position during the later Middle Ages, when courtoisie was most fashionable. Indeed, one historian has even argued that in England women's legal position declined steadily after the Norman conquest.[9] In French law, a comparison of women's legal rights in such matters as holding property, testifying in court, or making a valid will shows practically no change between the earliest Frankish kings and the Renaissance. We know that laws sometimes lag behind social customs; still, if courtly love produced no legal improvement for women in the countries where it was strongest, then its social power seems infinitesimal.

Third, the only surviving didactic treatise by a medieval nobleman intended for his daughters, composed in the late fourteenth century, includes a vigorous condemnation of courtly love. From the man's viewpoint, the author very much doubted that courtoisie helped inspire prowess or other useful knightly virtues. From the woman's viewpoint, courtly love was a useless pastime because it diverted her mind from religion. And it was dangerous, because even the innocent amenities of courtoisie might irreparably damage a lady's reputation and make her a social outcast.

In literary history, the concept of courtly love is interesting because it was both stationary and changing. Stationary insofar as the rules of courtoisie, the conduct of the courtly lover, varied little from the twelfth century through the end of the Middle Ages. But discussions about the nature of love, if not about the rules of courtoisie, took a new direction during the thirteenth century, at a time when the courtly romance began to grow to monstrous dimensions (a version of Lancelot's search for the Grail compiled between 1200 and 1235 runs to 4,000 printed pages). Specifically, this change was introduced by the most popular of all medieval treatments of love, the *Roman de la Rose,* begun about 1240 by Guillaume de Lorris and completed forty years later by Jean de Meun. (The popularity of the *Roman* is shown by hundreds of surviving manuscript copies and by fourteen printed editions before 1540.)

One of the most unusual major works of European literature, the *Roman* marks a turning point in the history of chivalric ideas. In its first 4,000 lines (Lorris's part), it offers a delicately woven allegorical tale in which the protagonist-lover is also the objective narrator, and the heroine as such does not exist but is distributed among a number of personified attributes. The story, which its author boasted contained the "whole matter of love," was broken off by Lorris's death. It was continued, for 18,000 rambling lines, by Jean de Meun, who permitted his narrator to pick the rose only after leading his readers through ten major digressions, most of them over 1,000 lines each. Jean de Meun did not merely inflate the length of the poem and tamper a bit with Lorris's allegorical scheme, he also changed the whole tone of the *Roman* by satirizing many of the conventions of courtly love. Where else does a major literary work begin as a highly conventional allegory and end as a huge, rambling satire on the same subject? Yet this is precisely what happened to courtly love in the single most important work about it. Jean de Meun includes a long, vigorous, and traditional tirade against women (lines 8467–9360) among his digressions; sometimes he shades off into gentler irony or even into sexual naturalism. What he cannot and will not do is return to the allegorical and conventional framework of courtly love.

Of course, Jean de Meun was not the only major writer on courtly love who satirized or ridiculed it. Andreas Capellanus's *Art of Courtly Love* contains a third section on "the rejection of love," which is a furiously misogynistic diatribe and completely contradicts his first two books. For that matter, Ovid, Andreas's model, tacked a final section about the "remedies for love" onto his *Art of Love.* Yet the whole problem of where medieval writers about courtly love are sincere, when they recommend it or when they attack it, is probably a false one. C. S. Lewis convincingly maintains that " 'cynicism' and 'idealism' about women are twin fruits of the same branch . . . and may be found anywhere in the literature of romantic love, and mixed in any proportions," adding that "the history of courtly love from beginning to end may be described as an 'amorous-odious sonnet,' a 'scholar's love or hatred.' " [10]

In any event, the apparently contradictory sentiments of the *Roman de la Rose* provided endless matter for debate about love and chivalry in the later Middle Ages, and set off a noisy literary quarrel, the *querelle des femmes,* in the fifteenth century. Many arguments, few of them new or interesting, were put forward. Perhaps the most unique feature of the quarrel was that it was conducted on both sides entirely by men, with one noteworthy exception (Christine de Pisan), who made the obvious point that women had a bad literary reputation because men wrote all the books: another detail confirming the impression that courtly love was created for women but by men. Consider also the famous Court of Love founded by the Duke of Burgundy at Paris in 1401, 700 strong: the pleaders in this court were all men, while the ladies' role was confined to distributing prizes. It is even more interesting to notice that among the members of this court were many men who defended Jean de Meun and attacked Christine de Pisan in the querelle des femmes. "Evidently," says Huizinga, "it was merely a society amusement." And he continues:

> Medieval literature shows little true pity for women, little compassion for her weakness and the dangers and pains which love has in store for her. Pity took on a stereotyped and factitious form, in the sentimental fiction of the knight delivering the virgin. The author of the *Quinze Joyes de Mariage,* after having mocked at all the faults of women, undertakes to describe also the wrongs they have to suffer. So far as is known, he never performed this task.[11]

Somehow, courtly love survived the *Roman de la Rose* and the querelle des femmes. It even outlived the Middle Ages. It was taken off horseback, out of tournaments, and endless knightly vows, and propelled into Renaissance manners largely because of the revival of Platonism and consequent vogue of Platonic love in Medicean Florence. The basic Renaissance text about courtly love, comparable in importance to Andreas Capellanus, is the third book of Baldassar Castiglione's *Book of the Courtier* (1528). Of course, its chivalric aspects also lingered on in many parts of Renaissance Europe, which saw a tremendous vogue for *Amadis of Gaul* and some other old romances, until this was finally killed by the ridicule of *Don Quixote.* It is the Renaissance Platonism version of courtoisie that survived in Europe as the code of correct behavior, proper treatment of women, and elegant (if not necessarily adulterous) flirtation until the Victorians and beyond: here is the source of the modern version of the lady as romantic object on her pedestal.

Witchcraft

One historian has recently suggested that witchcraft and courtly love might be causally connected:

> The rise in the status of ladies caused by courtly love and the cult of the Virgin may actually have encouraged the development of the witch image as a reaction. The basic mythological image of the female has both good and bad qualities, and when the good qualities are extracted, refined, and elevated to the status of a principle, the evil qualities that remain also attain the status of a principle. The witch is then the natural mythological counterpart of the Virgin.[12]

However, it is easy to raise objections to this line of reasoning. Christian mythology already had an evil female principle to set against the Virgin: Eve, the human cause of original sin. Furthermore, and more mundanely, while courtly love and the cult of the Virgin both originated during the twelfth-century Renaissance, the full development of witchcraft and its serious social effects came many centuries later. It is only toward the end of the fifteenth century, in the mountains of Austria instead of the court of Champagne, that we find the fully articulated theories of European witchcraft and the start of a massive persecution of witches.

Of course, the prehistory of European witchcraft goes much further back. The ingredients in the witch-maker's cauldron came from many different places: from classical antiquity; from bits and pieces of regional folklore; from the widespread human belief in the power of sorcery; and, to a considerable extent, from medieval concepts of heresy and heretical behavior.

The most important ingredients were very slowly fused together. The tradition of night-flying female cannibals or *strigae* gradually merged with the originally separate tradition of the malevolent sorceress or *malefica,* who could harm man or beast through magic herbs and spells. Both these stereotypes were, starting in the thirteenth century, assimilated into the Inquisition's stereotypes about heretics, who habitually met after dark to engage in secret orgies and who reputedly worshiped the devil. But some of the key elements in this new theory of witchcraft came only very late. For example, the fact that when the devil has sexual intercourse with witches his penis and semen are ice cold (a detail found in numerous theorists and witches' confessions in the sixteenth and seventeenth centuries) first appeared in witchcraft literature only in the 1460s, replacing an older tradition. (We should notice that this detail, like many others, appeared in witches' confessions *before* it was discussed in the theoretical literature about witchcraft; in this domain, "theory" consistently follows "practice.") The modern name for the Witches' Sabbath or *sabbat* also came very late and only appears in two of the numerous fifteenth-century treatises; the older term it replaced was *synagogue,* which strongly suggests the confusion between witches and Jews or other heretics. And some of the ingredients we now associate with witchcraft, such as the Black Mass, simply do not exist at all in the fifteenth-century theory. The process whereby witchcraft theory assumed its final form is a complex and fascinating tale, no less difficult to unravel than the prehistory of courtly love. Like courtly love, however, the theory of witchcraft underwent remarkably little change for several centuries after it reached maturity.

Finally, in 1486 appeared the book that stands as the basic text on witchcraft, just as Andreas Capellanus's work stands as the basic text on courtly love. Written by two Dominican inquisitors, it was called the *Malleus Maleficarum,* the "hammer of witches"; and already in its title it made "witch" a female noun. Among its many fascinating sections, the *Malleus* includes a lengthy discussion (Book I, Question 6) of why women were especially prone to witchcraft. The authors bring forward several reasons: women are more credulous than men; women are more impressionable; also, "they have slippery tongues, and are unable to conceal from their fellow-women those things they have learned by evil arts." Drawing on the old tradition of women's greater sexual appetite, they stress that lust is a major cause of witchcraft. Also, "a wicked woman is by her nature quicker to waver in the faith" (something they have already demonstrated by deriving *femina* from *fe* and *minus,* "less faith") and thus women are "quicker to abjure the faith, which is the root of witchcraft." They then summarize:

> Just as through the first defect in their intelligence they are more prone to abjure the faith; so through their second defect of inordinate affections and passions they search for, brood over, and inflict various vengeances, either by witchcraft or by some other means. Wherefore it is no wonder that so great a number of witches exist in this sex.[13]

And it is no wonder that they ended this Question by some unashamed self-congratulation: "blessed be the Most High who has so far preserved the male sex from so great a crime."

This manual on witchcraft was soon followed by other landmarks: in literature, by Fernando de Rojas's long play of 1499, popularly known as *La Celestina,* the first and best dramatic treatment of a certain kind of witch; in the fine arts, by Hans Baldung Grien's series of witch pictures, done between 1510 and 1530 (other masters such as Dürer did their witch pictures even earlier). By the time Martin Luther posted his theses, Europe already possessed excellent multimedia descriptions of its witches. And from this point until the eighteenth-century Enlightenment, European civilization was not only haunted by the idea of witches but also relieved its anxieties by killing them in massive quantities.

The exact number of victims of the witchcraft mania cannot be calculated. The likeliest guess is that the total number of trials exceeded 100,000, and the number of executions was somewhere below that figure. Some parts of Europe were much more heavily affected by witch trials than others. For instance, the kingdom of England — whose laws prohibited the use of torture, and where some basic demonological ideas such as the Witches' Sabbath appeared at a relatively late date — almost certainly executed fewer than 1,000 witches; but in the smaller kingdom of Scotland, which used torture and where the full demonological system was introduced before 1600, more than 4,000 witches were probably executed.

Some parts of Europe we might have expected to see blanketed with witchcraft trials actually had very few. This is especially true of Mediterranean Europe, Spain and Italy, the only lands where the much-maligned Inquisition retained jurisdiction over witchcraft trials: surviving records indicate that only a handful of people were ever killed for this crime by Inquisition tribunals, although many were tried for it. For instance, the Inquisition's courts at Toledo and Cuenca (Spain) put 500 people on trial for witchcraft in the sixteenth and seventeenth centuries, but none of them was condemned to death — even though the Inquisition could torture any suspect.

It seems clear that the epicenter of witchcraft trials and deaths was the Holy Roman Empire (which then included, at least in theory, present-day Austria, Switzerland, the Benelux countries, and parts of eastern France and northern Italy). Surviving records show about 3,500 deaths for witchcraft in the southwestern corner of Germany (Baden-Württemberg) alone, and approximately as many in Bavaria. Switzerland may also have accounted for as many as 5,000 deaths for witchcraft, and Austria was not far behind. Despite the fact that in many parts of the empire (such as the Imperial Free Cities, the French or Benelux frontier zones, or most of Switzerland) our evidence suggests that more than half of all people arrested for witchcraft were not put to death, the number of people who undoubtedly *were* killed as witches was greater in the empire than in the rest of western Europe put together. The real witchcraft panics, where hundreds of suspects were arrested in a single wave, very seldom happened outside the German parts of the empire — except in Poland, which has the dubious distinction of being the second most heavily afflicted European region and the equally dubious distinction of being the European region where witchcraft trials peaked latest (between 1675 and 1720), at a time when many of the more progressive governments of western Europe had stopped witch trials altogether. But we must emphasize that in the sixteenth and seventeenth centuries absolutely no part of Europe escaped the witch mania altogether; executions varied greatly from country to country and from province to province, but witch trials happened everywhere.

To give some idea of what these trials were like, let us briefly consider two of them, one early and one late, from the same place (Geneva).

Jeanette Clerc, wife of a peasant from a hamlet under the jurisdiction of the Republic of Geneva, was arrested and condemned for witchcraft in 1539 (hers is the third trial on record at Geneva and the second after the coming of the Reformation in 1536).[14] She was an unexceptional rural woman, neither a thief nor an adulteress, who was accused of witchcraft because her neighbor's cow died suddenly after eating some herbs Jeanette had fed it to cure it. Most of her other acts of witchcraft were of the same order: a horse she had bitten went mad; two oxen refused to work after Jeanette had quarreled with their owner; she gave an apple to a girl who got sick afterward; she fed a meal to a peasant who vomited things "as black as ink" afterward. The worst accusation (though dating from some time ago) was that she had killed one of her husband's relatives after a family feud by throwing some diabolical powder in his face.

Her trial, like those of most witches, was rapid. She was questioned four times within two weeks, until her confession was complete and acceptable. She explained to her judges that she had done homage to the devil and thus become a witch in a fit of rage after having lost a brand-new pair of shoes. She confessed all the *maléfices* (acts of witchcraft) of which she stood accused. And she gave a full account of the activities at her sabbath, or synagogue. First, she gave herself to a large black devil with a raucous voice, named Simon, who promised her all the money she wanted. When she agreed, Simon gave her a number of coins that next day became oak leaves. Next she rode off to the synagogue on Simon's back. There she had sodomitic intercourse with the devil ("in the rear, like animals"); his semen was ice cold. She did homage to him by kissing him on his left arm, which was also unnaturally cold; he then marked her by biting the right side of her face. She renounced God "in a loud voice, as she remembers well, as though she had done it today," and also the Virgin. In many ways the synagogue was pleasant; there was plenty of singing and dancing to tambourines, and the food (apples, white bread, white wine) was good, except for the roast meat, which was "pinkish and awful." When it ended Simon gave her a small white stick and a box of grease and told her how she could attend more synagogues by rubbing the grease on the stick and repeating the magic formula, "White stick, black stick, carry me where you should; go, in the devil's name, go!" Jeanette Clerc was beheaded and her property was confiscated by the Republic of Geneva.

More than a century later, Michée Chauderon became the last witch to be killed in Geneva.[15] She was the fifty-year-old widow of a silk carder, both of them immigrants from Savoy, who now made her living as a laundress. Her witchcraft was very different from Jeanette Clerc's; in fact, the charges against her reduced to only two cases of bewitching girls (both daughters of women who employed her as laundress) into a state of demonic possession, and one of these fits had taken place many years ago. Only the recent one, a twenty-three-year-old girl, really mattered in Michée's indictment. Her case was curious in some respects; for example, doctors examined the possessed girl and returned with an inconclusive, even negative report on the authenticity of her possession; and surgeons who then examined Michée for the special scar, the devil's mark, also made an inconclusive report that she had two marks "of an extraordinary nature, unlike other marks on the surface of the human body . . . although the said marks do not absolutely conform to all the conditions described by writers who discuss those which are customarily found on witches." The Genevan government solved this problem by importing two other surgeons from a nearby Protestant town, who promptly found the devil's mark without any equivocations. Meanwhile, Michée had been tortured and began to confess — although to a simpler type of witchcraft than Jeanette Clerc's. In 1652 the Genevan devil merely made a quick, unsexual agreement with the witch, marked her, and gave her some powder to bewitch people; there were no synagogues, no orgies, no magic formulae, no perverted sex — nothing but the aspect of diabolical possession, a single maléfice, remained. And the hesitations of Geneva's doctors and surgeons show why this was the last case where a witch was condemned at Geneva.

Apart from one type of maléfice and the role of the devil in promoting witchcraft, almost the only thing that links these trials together is the fact that both of the accused were adult women. Of course, there is nothing surprising in this. The *Malleus Maleficarum* had insisted that witches were almost invariably women. The artists and playwrights of Renaissance Europe had offered only female models. Legal records generally corroborate the preponderance of women among people tried for witchcraft, although their monopoly was not quite as complete as theory and legend would have us believe (see Table 5–1).[16] In some places, witch trials showed an almost complete monopoly of female victims, while other places — including Mediterranean lands, where Inquisitorial punishments were comparatively mild — showed a sizable minority of male witches.

Thus far, historians have spent a little time and energy explaining the role of women in the history of witchcraft but have paid no attention to

TABLE 5–1

REGION	WOMEN TRIED	MEN TRIED	PERCENTAGE OF WOMEN
Southwest Germany	1050	238	82%
West Switzerland	893	237	80%
Venetian Republic	430	119	78%
Castile	324	132	71%
Belgium (Namur)	337	29	92%
England (Essex)	267	23	92%

the role of witchcraft in the history of women. Yet both aspects are important. The significance of witchcraft for the history of women lies in the simple but eloquent fact that it was the most important capital crime for women in early modern Europe. Although retrospective studies of criminality are still in their infancy, it seems safe to predict that, from 1480 to 1700, more women were killed for witchcraft than for other crimes put together. The only other crime for which many women were put to death was infanticide, and in most regions it was far less common than the massive executions of witches. Insofar as history must be concerned with the social consequences of stereotypes, this fact becomes extremely important: misogyny takes many forms, but it has seldom provided a legal method for killing dozens of thousands of women (and a few men as well).

Considering the broad streak of misogyny in European religion and literature, it is not very difficult to see why women should have been accused of making hail, causing sickness and sometimes death in people and animals, engaging in diabolical orgies, and all the other practices of witchcraft. What must be explained is something subtler: why were they so accused and punished for it with death at the stake during only a certain period in European history? The reasons why women should have been prosecuted for witchcraft mainly in the sixteenth and seventeenth centuries are not easy to list or simple to evaluate. An important argument advanced recently says that the changing European marriage pattern, the shift to a system that delayed marriages and left a sizable minority of women permanently unmarried, first becomes visible in the sixteenth century, about the time when the first great witch hunts began.[17] If witch trials were primarily projections of general social fears onto atypical women (those who lived apart, without husbands or fathers to rule them), then the sudden growth of spinsters and an increased number of widows who did not remarry automatically provided a much larger range of witchcraft suspects than before. The advantage of this explanation is that it accounts for, and indeed begins from, the fact that many women accused of witchcraft were either widows or spinsters. Widows were particularly numerous (see Table 5–2).[18] It is almost certain that fewer than half of

TABLE 5–2

REGION	WIDOWS	OTHER WOMEN	PERCENTAGE OF WIDOWS
Neuchâtel	79	100	44%
Basel Bishopric	55	108	34%
Montbéliard	24	34	41%
Toul (Lorraine)	29	24	55%
Essex (England)	49	68	42%

all women accused of witchcraft were married at the time of their accusation. It is no accident that the typical witch of folklore should be an old woman dwelling off by herself in the woods.

A second approach argues that witchcraft was a recognized crime at a time when most major crimes were crimes of violence. The maléfices or evil doings attributed to witches were serious and often deadly; many witches were charged with killing people and animals in addition to causing sickness or destroying crops. Viewed from this angle, witchcraft becomes a *magical* form of violent revenge, practiced by exactly those persons who could not employ physical violence. Women, especially isolated women like widows or spinsters, fit these requirements perfectly. They had many grievances; they wanted revenge; yet recourse to the law often was beyond their economic power, and successful physical violence was beyond their physical power. Nothing remained except harming or killing by magic, with the devil's help. Another advantage of this argument is that it helps explain why the decline in witchcraft trials (which in many cases began after 1650) coincided with a more general movement in the history of criminality, visible both in England and in France, when crimes of personal violence began to be replaced by crimes against property, when theft replaced assault as the typical crime. In this perspective, magical violence by women merely declined together with physical violence by men at the beginning of the Enlightenment.

A third argument suggests that women were unusually defenseless during the time of the great witch trials because the social gap between men and women in rural villages was larger then than before or afterward. In order to prove the existence of such a gap, we must know much more than we do about relative male-female incomes in rural Europe and especially about male and female illiteracy in rural villages. There are a few interesting clues: in sixteenth- and seventeenth-century Languedoc, for instance, the wages of hired women farmhands relative to men were lower than in the later Middle Ages.[19] And although we are even more ignorant about rural literacy rates than about rural wages, it seems safe to predict that for sixteenth- and seventeenth-century Europe most male peasants were illiterate but virtually all female peasants were. In other words, this argument says that both the poverty gap and the literacy gap between rural men and women were especially great during the centuries of witchcraft trials, thus aggravating the vulnerability of women (particularly isolated women, widows, or spinsters) to charges of witchcraft.

Of course, these are only hypotheses, which at best can only complement and reinforce each other — and which can only offer auxiliary reasons why many suspected witches could be so easily found everywhere in Europe after the witchcraft stereotype had been assembled at the end of the Middle Ages. Much of the persecution of witches, of course, is simply attributable to the long misogynistic heritage in European laws and religion; it only required small triggering incidents to set witch hunts in motion once the crime had been defined.

There are scholarly doubts about witchcraft, just as there are scholarly doubts about courtly love. But the witchcraft doubts are of a different kind. With courtly love, almost everyone agrees that a theory existed, with enormous cultural consequences; it is the social effects of this theory that are in doubt. With witchcraft, it is impossible to doubt or underestimate the social effects of the theory, but it is also impossible to take the intellectual content of the theory seriously. Although both courtly love and witchcraft were created by medieval European patriarchy, their historical consequences were grotesquely different. The sad truth is that, in women's "real" social history, the pedestal is almost impossible to find, but the stake is everywhere.

Notes

1. Andreas Capellanus, *The Art of Courtly Love,* trans. John J. Parry, Columbia University Press, New York, 1941, p. 150.
2. Eileen Power, "The Position of Women," *The Legacy of the Middle Ages,* eds. G. C. Crump and E. F. Jacob, Oxford University Press, Oxford, 1926, p. 406.
3. John F. Benton, "Clio and Venus: An Historical View of Courtly Love," *The Meaning of Courtly Love,* ed. F. X. Newman, State University of New York Press, Albany, 1968, p. 35.
4. C. S. Lewis, *The Allegory of Love,* Oxford University Press, Oxford, 1936, p. 4.
5. Friedrich Heer, *The Medieval World: Europe 1100–1350,* Mentor, New York, n.d., p. 166.
6. Capellanus, *Art of Courtly Love,* pp. 100, 106.
7. Ibid., p. 28. In this and the next quote, I have changed Parry's wording slightly after consulting E. Trojel's critical Latin edition, Copenhagen, 1892.
8. Ibid., p. 122.
9. Doris M. Stenton, *The English Woman in History,* Macmillan, New York, 1957, p. 26.
10. Lewis, *Allegory of Love,* p. 145.
11. Johann Huizinga, *The Waning of the Middle Ages,* Anchor, Garden City, N.Y., n.d., p. 127.
12. Jeffrey B. Russell, *Witchcraft in the Middle Ages,* Cornell University Press, Ithaca, 1972, p. 284.
13. Montague Summers, ed. and trans., *Malleus Maleficarum,* Pushkin Press, London, 1928, p. 45.
14. R. Christinger and J.-E. Genequand, "Un procès genevois de sorcellerie inédit," *Genava,* n.s. 17 (1969), 113–138.

15. P. Ladame, ed., *Procès criminel de la dernière sorcière brûlée à Genève le 6 avril 1652,* Delehaye, Paris, 1888.
16. Table 5–1 is adapted from E. William Monter: *Witchcraft in France and Switzerland* (Ithaca, N.Y.: Cornell University Press, 1976), p. 119. Copyright 1976 by Cornell University. Used by permission of Cornell University Press.
17. H. C. Erik Midelfort, *Witch-Hunting in Southwestern Germany 1562–1684: The Social and Intellectual Foundations,* Stanford University Press, Stanford, 1972, pp. 183–186.
18. Table 5–2 is adapted from E. William Monter: *Witchcraft in France and Switzerland* (Ithaca, N.Y.: Cornell University Press, 1976), p. 121. Copyright 1976 by Cornell University. Used by permission of Cornell University Press.
19. E. Le Roy Ladurie, *Les paysans de Languedoc,* vol. 1, S.E.V.P.E.N., Paris, 1966, pp. 265–283.

Suggestions for Further Reading

There is a very useful "Selected Bibliography of the Theory of Courtly Love" on pp. 97–102 of the symposium *The Meaning of Courtly Love,* ed. F. X. Newman (State University of New York Press, Albany, 1968). Among the older works that offer the most helpful insights for the novice are C. S. Lewis, *The Allegory of Love* (Oxford University Press, Oxford, 1936); Sidney Painter, *French Chivalry* (Johns Hopkins University Press, Baltimore, 1940); and Friedrich Heer, *The Medieval World: Europe 1100–1350* (World Publishing, Cleveland and New York, 1961).

On witchcraft, see my bibliographical essay, "The Historiography of European Witchcraft: Progress and Prospects," *The Journal of Interdisciplinary History,* II (1972), 435–451. Recent works of major importance include Jeffrey B. Russell, *Witchcraft in the Middle Ages* (Cornell University Press, Ithaca, 1972); Keith Thomas, *Religion and the Decline of Magic* (Scribners, New York and London, 1971); H. C. Erik Midelfort, *Witch-Hunting in Southwestern Germany 1562–1684* (Stanford University Press, Stanford, 1972); and E. W. Monter, *Witchcraft in France and Switzerland* (Cornell University Press, Ithaca, 1976).

6

Did Women Have a Renaissance?

Joan Kelly-Gadol

In this essay, Joan Kelly-Gadol challenges traditional periodization in her very title — thus emphasizing, yet again, that women's historical experience often differs substantially from that of men. We note the reappearing interrelationship between changing property relations, forms of institutional control, and ideology. The author demonstrates that an emerging class created new forms of political and social organization that tended to reduce options for women. She examines how literature rationalized and perpetuated class interests and how it reflected political and sexual relations. She traces major changes in the courtly love tradition. Courtly love is first attributed to powerful feudal women, who made it responsive to their sexual and emotional needs, which harmonized with the needs of their class as a whole. In its Renaissance form, courtly love is attributed to powerful male princes and their courtiers, who had an interest in creating dependency in women. In this period, female chastity and passivity better suited the needs of the expanding bourgeoisie and the declining nobility. The modern relation of the sexes, with its subordination of women, makes its appearance. Like Marylin Arthur, Joan Kelly-Gadol uses literature as an index to the interaction of class needs, state forms, sexual and family relations, and ideology.

Agnolo Bronzino's *Portrait of Laura Battiferri,* ca. 1555. The poet Laura Battiferri was the platonic love of Bronzino, with whom she exchanged Petrarchan verses. Bronzino painted her with a volume of Petrarch's sonnets in her hand, and portrayed her very much as he described her in one of his sonnets — "all iron within and ice outside." (Alinari — Art Reference Bureau)

One of the tasks of women's history is to call into question accepted schemes of periodization. To take the emancipation of women as a vantage point is to discover that events that further the historical development of men, liberating them from natural, social, or ideological constraints, have quite different, even opposite, effects upon women. The Renaissance is a good case in point. Italy was well in advance of the rest of Europe from roughly 1350 to 1530 because of its early consolidation of genuine states, the mercantile and manufacturing economy that supported them, and its working out of postfeudal and even postguild social relations. These developments reorganized Italian society along modern lines and opened the possibilities for the social and cultural expression for which the age is known. Yet precisely these developments affected women adversely, so much so that there was no renaissance for women — at least, not during the Renaissance. The state, early capitalism, and the social relations formed by them impinged on the lives of Renaissance women in different ways according to their different positions in society. But the startling fact is that women as a group, especially among the classes that dominated Italian urban life, experienced a contraction of social and personal options that men of their classes either did not, as was the case with the bourgeoisie, or did not experience as markedly, as was the case with the nobility.

Before demonstrating this point, which contradicts the widely held notion of the equality of Renaissance women with men,[1] we need to consider how to establish, let alone measure, loss or gain with respect to the liberty of women. I found the following criteria most useful for gauging the relative contraction (or expansion) of the powers of Renaissance women and for determining the quality of their historical experience: 1) the regulation of *female sexuality* as compared with male sexuality; 2) women's *economic* and *political roles*, i.e., the kind of work they performed as compared with men, and their access to property, political power, and the education or training necessary for work, property, and power; 3) the *cultural roles* of women in shaping the outlook of their society, and access to the education and/or institutions necessary for this; 4) *ideology* about women, in particular the sex-role system displayed or advocated in the symbolic products of the society, its art, literature, and philosophy. Two points should be made about this ideological index. One is its rich inferential value. The literature, art, and philosophy of a society, which give us direct knowledge of the attitudes of the dominant sector of that society toward women, also yield indirect knowledge about our other criteria: namely, the sexual, economic, political, and cultural activities of women. Insofar as images of women relate to what really goes on, we can infer from them something about that social reality. But, second, the relations between the ideology of sex roles and the reality we want to get at are complex and difficult to establish. Such views may be prescriptive rather than descriptive; they may describe a situation that no longer prevails; or they may use the relation of the sexes symbolically and not refer primarily to women and sex roles at all. Hence, to assess the historical significance of changes in sex-role conception, we must bring such changes into connection with all we know about general developments in the society at large.

This essay examines changes in sex-role conception, particularly with respect to sexuality, for what they tell us about Renaissance society and women's place in it. At first glance, Renaissance thought presents a problem in this regard because it cannot be simply categorized. Ideas about the relation of the sexes range from a relatively complementary sense of sex roles in literature dealing with courtly manners, love, and education, to patriarchal conceptions in writings on marriage and the family, to a fairly equal presentation of sex roles in early Utopian social theory. Such diversity need not baffle the attempt to reconstruct a history of sex-role conceptions, however, and to relate its course to the actual situation of women. Toward this end, one needs to sort out this material in terms of the social groups to which it responds: to courtly society in the first case, the nobility of the petty despotic states of Italy; to the patrician bourgeoisie in the second, particularly of republics such as Florence. In the third case, the relatively equal position accorded women in Utopian thought (and in those lower-class movements of the radical Reformation analogous to it) results from a larger critique of early modern society and all the relations of domination that flow from private ownership and control of property Once distinguished, each of these groups of sources tells the same story. Each discloses in its own way certain new constraints suffered by Renaissance women as the family and political life were restructured in the great transition from medieval feudal society to the early modern state. The sources that represent the interests of the nobility and the bourgeoisie point to this fact by a telling, double index. Almost all such works — with certain notable exceptions, such as Boccaccio and Ariosto — establish chastity as the female norm and restructure the relation of the sexes to one of female dependency and male domination.

The bourgeois writings on education, domestic life, and society constitute the extreme in this denial of women's independence. Suffice it to say that they sharply distinguish an inferior domestic realm of women from the superior public realm of men, achieving a veritable "renaissance" of the outlook and practices of classical Athens, with its domestic imprisonment of citizen wives.[2] The courtly Renaissance literature we will consider was more gracious. But even here, by analyzing a few of the representative works of this genre, we find a new repression of the noblewoman's affective experience, in contrast to the latitude afforded her by medieval literature, and some of the social and cultural reasons for it. Dante and Castiglione, who continued a literary tradition that began with the courtly love literature of eleventh- and twelfth-century Provence, transformed medieval conceptions of love and nobility. In the love ideal they formed, we can discern the inferior position the Renaissance noblewoman held in the relation of the sexes by comparison with her male counterpart and with her medieval predecessor as well.

Love and the Medieval Lady

Medieval courtly love, closely bound to the dominant values of feudalism and the church, allowed in a special way for the expression of sexual love by women. Of course, only aristocratic women gained their sexual and affective rights thereby. If a knight wanted a peasant girl, the twelfth-century theorist of *The Art of Courtly Love,* Andreas Capellanus, encouraged him "not [to] hesitate to take what you seek and to embrace her by force." [3] Toward the lady, however, "a true lover considers nothing good except what he thinks will please his beloved"; for if courtly love were to define itself as a noble phenomenon, it had to attribute an essential freedom to the relation between lovers. Hence, it metaphorically extended the social relation of vassalage to the love relationship, a "conceit" that Maurice Valency rightly called "the shaping principle of the whole design" of courtly love.[4]

Of the two dominant sets of dependent social relations formed by feudalism — *les liens de dépendence,* as Marc Bloch called them — vassalage, the military relation of knight to lord, distinguished itself (in its early days) by being freely entered into. At a time when everyone was somebody's "man," the right to freely enter a relation of service characterized aristocratic bonds, whereas hereditability marked the servile work relation of serf to lord. Thus, in medieval romances, a parley typically followed a declaration of love until love freely proffered was freely returned. A kiss (like the kiss of homage) sealed the pledge, rings were exchanged, and the knight entered the love service of his lady. Representing love along the lines of vassalage had several liberating implications for aristocratic women. Most fundamental, ideas of homage and mutuality entered the notion of heterosexual relations along with the idea of freedom. As symbolized on shields and other illustrations that place the knight in the ritual attitude of commendation, kneeling before his lady with his hands folded between hers, homage signified male service, not domination or subordination of the lady, and it signified fidelity, constancy in that service. "A lady must honor her lover as a friend, not as a master," wrote Marie de Ventadour, a female troubadour or *trobairitz.*[5] At the same time, homage entailed a reciprocity of rights and obligations, a service on the lady's part as well. In one of Marie de France's romances, a knight is about to be judged by the barons of King Arthur's court when his lady rides to the castle to give him "succor" and pleads successfully for him, as any overlord might.[6] Mutuality, or complementarity, marks the relation the lady entered into with her *ami* (the favored name for "lover" and, significantly, a synonym for "vassal").

This relation between knight and lady was very much at variance with the patriarchal family relations obtaining in that same level of society. Aware of its incompatibility with prevailing family and marital relations, the celebrants of courtly love kept love detached from marriage. "We dare not oppose the opinion of the Countess of Champagne who rules that love can exert no power between husband and wife," Andreas wrote (p. 175). But in opting for a free and reciprocal heterosexual relation outside marriage, the poets and theorists of courtly love ignored the almost universal demand of patriarchal society for female chastity, in the sense of the woman's strict bondage to the marital bed. The reasons why they did so, and even the fact that they did so, have long been disputed, but the ideas and values that justify this kind of adulterous love are plain. Marriage, as a relation arranged by others, carried the taint of social necessity for the aristocracy. And if the feudality denigrated marriage by disdaining obligatory service, the church did so by regarding it not as a "religious" state, but an inferior one that responded to natural necessity. Moreover, Christianity positively fostered the ideal of courtly love at a deep level of feeling. The courtly relation between lovers took vassalage as its structural model, but its passion was nourished by Christianity's exaltation of love.

Christianity had accomplished its elevation of love by purging it of sexuality, and in this respect, by recombining the two, courtly love clearly departed from Christian teaching. The toleration of adultery it fostered thereby was in itself not so grievous. The feudality disregarded any number of church rulings that affected their interests, such as prohibitions of tournaments and repudiation of spouses (divorce) and remarriage. Moreover, adultery hardly needed the sanction of courtly love, which, if anything, acted rather as a restraining force by binding sexuality (except in marriage) to love. Lancelot, in Chrétien de Troyes's twelfth-century romance, lies in bed with a lovely woman because of a promise he has made, but "not once does he look at her, nor show her any courtesy. Why not? Because his heart does not go out to her. . . . The knight has only one heart, and this one is no longer really his, but has been entrusted to someone else, so that he cannot bestow it elsewhere." [7] Actually, Lancelot's chastity represented more of a threat to Christian doctrine than the fact that his passion (for Guinevere) was adulterous, because his attitudes justified sexual love. Sexuality could only be "mere sexuality" for the medieval church, to be consecrated and directed toward procreation by Christian marriage. Love, on the other hand, defined as passion for the good, perfects the individual; hence love, according to Thomas Aquinas, properly directs itself toward God.[8] Like the churchman, Lancelot spurned mere sexuality — but for the sake of sexual love. He defied Christian *teaching* by reattaching love to sex; and experiencing his love as a devout vocation, as a passion, he found himself in utter accord with Christian *feeling*. His love, as Chrétien's story makes clear, is sacramental as well as sexual:

> . . . then he comes to the bed of the Queen, whom he adores and before whom he kneels, holding her more dear than the relic of any saint. And the Queen extends her arms to him and, embracing him, presses him tightly against her bosom, drawing him into the bed beside her and showing him every possible satisfaction. . . . Now Lancelot possesses all he wants. . . . It cost him such pain to leave her that he suffered a real martyr's agony. . . . When he leaves the room, he bows and acts precisely as if he were before a shrine. (p. 329)

It is difficult to assess Christianity's role in this acceptance of feeling and this attentiveness to inner states that characterize medieval lyric and romance, although the weeping and wringing of hands, the inner troubles and turmoil of the love genre, were to disappear with the restoration of classical attitudes of restraint in the Renaissance. What certainly bound courtly love to Christianity, however, aside from its positive attitude toward feeling, was the cultivation of decidedly "romantic" states of feeling. In Christian Europe, *passion* acquired a positive, spiritual meaning that classical ethics and classical erotic feeling alike denied it. Religious love and courtly love were both suffered as a destiny, were both submitted to and not denied. Converted by a passion that henceforth directed and dominated them and for which all manner of suffering could be borne, the courtly lovers, like the religious, sought a higher emotional state than ordinary life provided. They sought ecstasy; and this required of them a heroic discipline, an ascetic fortitude, and single-mindedness. Love and its ordeals alike removed them from the daily, the customary, the routine, setting them apart as an elite superior to the conventions of marriage and society.

Religious feeling and feudal values thus both fed into a conception of passionate love that, because of its mutuality, required that women, too, partake of that passion, of that adulterous sexual love. The lady of medieval romance also suffered. She suffered "more pain for love than ever a woman suffered" in another of Marie de France's romances. As the jealously guarded wife of an old man, ravished by the beauty of her knight when she first saw him, she could not rest for love of him, and *"franc et noble"* (i.e., free) as she was, she granted him her kiss and her love upon the declaration of his — "and many other caresses which lovers know well" during the time she hid him in her castle.[9] So common is this sexual mutuality to the literature of courtly love that one cannot take seriously the view of it as a form of Madonna worship in which a remote and virginal lady spurns consummation. That stage came later, as courtly love underwent its late medieval and Renaissance transformation. But for the twelfth century, typical concerns of Provençal *iocs-partitz,* those poetic "questions" on love posed at court (and reflecting the social reality of mock courts of love played out as a diversion) were: "Must a lady do for her lover as much as he for her?"; or, "A husband learns that his wife has a lover. The wife and the lover perceive it — which of the three is in the greatest strait?" [10] In the same vein, Andreas Capellanus perceived differences between so-called "pure" and "mixed" love as accidental, not substantial. Both came from the same feeling of the heart and one could readily turn into the other, as circumstances dictated. Adultery, after all, required certain precautions; but that did not alter the essentially erotic nature even of "pure" love, which went "as far as the kiss and the embrace and the modest contact with the nude lover, omitting the final solace" (p. 122).

The sexual nature of courtly love, considered together with its voluntary character and the nonpatriarchal structure of its relations, makes us question what it signifies for the actual condition of feudal women. For clearly it represents an ideological liberation of their sexual and affective powers that must have some social reference. This is not to raise the fruitless question of whether such love relationships actually existed or if they were mere literary conventions. The real issue regarding ideology is, rather, what kind of society could posit *as a social ideal* a love relation outside of marriage, one that women freely entered and that, despite its reciprocity, made women the gift givers while men did the service. What were the social conditions that fostered these particular conventions rather than the more common ones of female chastity and/or dependence?

No one doubts that courtly love spread widely as a convention. All ranks and both sexes of the aristocracy wrote troubadour poetry and courtly romances and heard them sung and recited in courtly gatherings throughout most of medieval Europe. But this could happen only if such ideas supported the male-dominated social order rather than subverted it. The love motif could, and with Gottfried of Strasbourg's *Tristan* (c. 1210) did, stand as an ideal radically opposed to the institutions of the church and emerging feudal kingship. But in its beginnings, and generally, courtly love no more threatened Christian feeling or feudalism than did chivalry, which brought a certain "sacramental" moral value and restraint to the profession of warfare. While courtly love celebrated sexuality, it enriched and deepened it by means of the Christian notion of passion. While the knight often betrayed his lord to serve his lord's lady, he transferred to that relationship the feudal ideal of freely committed, mutual service. And while passionate love led to adultery, by that very fact it reinforced, as its necessary premise, the practice of political marriage. The literature of courtly love suppressed rather than exaggerated tensions between it and other social values, and the reason for this lies deeper than literature. It lies at the institutional level, where there was real agreement, or at least no contradiction, between the sexual and affective needs of women and the interests of the aristocratic family, which the feudality and church alike regarded as fundamental to the social order.

The factors to consider here are property and power on the one hand, and illegitimacy on the other. Feudalism, as a system of private jurisdictions, bound power to landed property; and it permitted both inheritance and administration of feudal property by women.[11] Inheritance by women often suited the needs of the great landholding families, as their unremitting efforts to secure such rights for their female members attest. The authority of feudal women owes little to any gallantry on the part of feudal society. But the fact that women could hold both ordinary fiefs and vast collections of counties — and exercise in their own right the seigniorial powers that went with them — certainly fostered a gallant attitude. Eleanor of Aquitaine's adultery as wife of the king of France could have had dire consequences in another place at another time, say in the England of Henry VIII. In her case, she moved on to a new marriage with the future Henry II of England or, to be more exact, a new alliance connecting his Plantagenet interests with her vast domains centering on Provence. Women also exercised power during the absence of warrior husbands. The lady presided over the court at such times, administered the estates, took charge of the vassal services due the lord. She *was* the lord — albeit in his name rather than her own — unless widowed and without male children. In the religious realm, abbesses exercised analogous temporal as well as spiritual jurisdiction over great territories, and always in their own right, in virtue of their office.

This social reality accounts for the retention of matronymics in medieval society, that is, a common use of the maternal name, which reflects the position of women as landowners and managers of great estates, particularly during the crusading period.[12] It also accounts for the husband's toleration of his wife's diversions, if discreetly pursued. His primary aim to get and maintain a fief required her support, perhaps even her inheritance. As Emily James Putnam put it, "It would, perhaps, be paradoxical to say that a baron would prefer to be sure that his tenure was secure than that his son was legitimate, but it is certain that the relative value of the two things had shifted." [13] Courtly literature, indeed, reveals a marked lack of concern about illegitimacy. Although the ladies of the romances are almost all married, they seldom appear with children, let alone appear to have their lives and loves complicated by them. Much as the tenet that love thrives only in adultery reflected and reinforced the stability of arranged marriage, so the political role of women, and the indivisibility of the fief, probably underlies this indifference to illegitimacy. Especially as forms of inheritance favoring the eldest son took hold in the course of the twelfth century to preserve the great houses, the claims of younger sons and daughters posed no threat to family estates. Moreover, the expansive, exploitative aristocratic families of the eleventh and twelfth centuries could well afford illegitimate members. For the feudality, they were no drain as kin but rather a source of strength in marital alliances and as warriors.

For all all these reasons, feudal Christian society could promote the ideal of courtly love. We could probably maintain of any ideology that tolerates sexual parity that: 1) it can threaten no major institution of the patriarchal society from which it emerges; and 2) men, the rulers within the ruling order, must benefit by it. Courtly love surely fit these requirements. That such an ideology did actually develop, however, is due to another feature of medieval society, namely, the cultural activity of feudal women. For responsive as courtly love might seem to men of the feudality whose erotic needs it objectified and refined, as well as objectifying their consciousness of the social self (as noble), it did this and more for women. It gave women lovers, peers rather than masters; and it gave them a justifying ideology for adultery which, as the more customary double standard indicates, men in patriarchal society seldom require. Hence, we should expect what we indeed find: women actively shaping these ideas and values that corresponded so well to their particular interests.

In the first place, women participated in creating the literature of courtly love, a major literature of their era. This role they had not been able to assume in the culture of classical Greece or Rome. The notable exception of Sappho only proves the point: it took women to give poetic voice and status to female sexual love, and only medieval Europe accepted that voice as integral to its cultural expression. The twenty or more known Provençal trobairitz, of whom the Countess Beatrice of Die is the most renowned, celebrated as fully and freely as any man the love of the troubadour tradition:

> Handsome friend, charming and kind,
> when shall I have you in my power?
> If only I could lie beside you for an hour
> and embrace you lovingly —

know this, that I'd give almost anything
to see you in my husband's place,
but only under the condition
that you swear to do my bidding.[14]

Marie de France voiced similar erotic sentiments in her *lais.* Her short tales of romance, often adulterous and always sexual, have caused her to be ranked by Friedrich Heer as one of the "three poets of genius" (along with Chrétien de Troyes and Gautier d'Arras) who created the *roman courtois* of the twelfth century.[15] These two genres, the romance and the lyric, to which women made such significant contributions, make up the corpus of courtly love literature.

In addition to direct literary expression, women promoted the ideas of courtly love by way of patronage and the diversions of their courts. They supported and/or participated in the recitation and singing of poems and romances, and they played out those mock suits, usually presided over by "queens," that settled questions of love. This holds for lesser aristocratic women as well as the great. But great noblewomen, such as Eleanor of Aquitaine and Marie of Champagne, Eleanor's daughter by her first marriage to Louis VII of France, could make their courts major cultural and social centers and play thereby a dominant role in forming the outlook and mores of their class. Eleanor, herself granddaughter of William of Aquitaine, known as the first troubadour, supported the poets and sentiments of Provence at her court in Anjou. When she became Henry II's queen, she brought the literature and manners of courtly love to England. When living apart from Henry at her court in Poitiers, she and her daughter, Marie, taught the arts of courtesy to a number of young women and men who later dispersed to various parts of France, England, Sicily, and Spain, where they constituted the ruling nobility. Some of the most notable authors of the literature of courtly love belonged to these circles. Bernard of Ventadour, one of the outstanding troubadours, sang his poems to none other than the lady Eleanor. Marie de France had connections with the English court of Eleanor and Henry II. Eleanor's daughter, Marie of Champagne, was patron both of Andreas Capellanus, her chaplain, and Chrétien de Troyes, and she may well be responsible for much of the adulterous, frankly sexual behavior the ladies enjoy in the famous works of both. Chrétien claimed he owed to his "lady of Champagne" both "the material and treatment" of Lancelot, which differs considerably in precisely this regard from his earlier and later romances. And Andreas's *De remedio,* the baffling final section of his work that repudiates sexual love and women, may represent not merely a rhetorical tribute to Ovid but a reaction to the pressure of Marie's patronage.[16]

At their courts as in their literature, it would seem that feudal women consciously exerted pressure in shaping the courtly love ideal and making it prevail. But they could do so only because they had actual power to exert. The women who assumed cultural roles as artists and patrons of courtly love had already been assigned political roles that assured them some measure of independence and power. They could and did exercise authority, not merely over the subject laboring population of their lands, but over their own and/or their husbands' vassals. Courtly love, which flourished outside the institution of patriarchal marriage, owed its possibility as well as its model to the dominant political institution of feudal Europe that permitted actual vassal homage to be paid to women.

The Renaissance Lady: Politics and Culture

The kind of economic and political power that supported the cultural activity of feudal noblewomen in the eleventh and twelfth centuries had no counterpart in Renaissance Italy. By the fourteenth century, the political units of Italy were mostly sovereign states, that, regardless of legal claims, recognized no overlords and supported no feudatories. Their nobility held property but not seigniorial power, estates but not jurisdiction. Indeed, in northern and central Italy, a nobility in the European sense hardly existed at all. Down to the coronation of Charles V as Holy Roman Emperor in 1530, there was no Italian king to safeguard the interests of (and thereby limit and control) a "legitimate" nobility that maintained by inheritance traditional prerogatives. Hence, where the urban bourgeoisie did not overthrow the claims of nobility, a despot did, usually in the name of nobility but always for himself. These *signorie,* unlike the bourgeois republics, continued to maintain a landed, military "class" with noble pretensions, but its members increasingly became merely the warriors and ornaments of a court. Hence, the Renaissance aristocrat, who enjoyed neither the independent political powers of feudal jurisdiction nor legally guaranteed status in the ruling estate, either served a despot or became one.

In this sociopolitical context, the exercise of political power by women was far more rare than under feudalism or even under the traditional kind of monarchical state that developed out of feudalism. The two Giovannas of Naples, both queens in their own right, exemplify this latter type of rule. The first, who began her reign in 1343 over Naples and Provence, became in 1356 queen of Sicily as well. Her grandfather, King Robert of Naples — of the same house of Anjou and Provence that hearkens back to Eleanor and to Henry Plantagenet — could and did designate Giovanna as his heir. Similarly, in 1414, Giovanna II became queen of Naples upon the death of her brother. In Naples, in short, women of the ruling house could assume power, not because of their abilities alone, but because the principle of legitimacy continued in force along with the feudal tradition of inheritance by women.

In northern Italy, by contrast, Caterina Sforza ruled her petty principality in typical Renaissance fashion, supported only by the Machiavellian principles of *fortuna* and *virtù* (historical situation and will). Her career, like that of her family, follows the Renaissance pattern of personal and political illegitimacy. Born in 1462, she was an illegitimate daughter of Galeazzo Maria Sforza, heir to the Duchy of Milan. The ducal power of the Sforzas was very recent, dating only from 1450, when Francesco Sforza, illegitimate son of a condottiere and a great condottiere himself, assumed control of the duchy. When his son and heir, Caterina's father, was assassinated after ten years of tyrannous rule, another son, Lodovico, took control of the duchy, first as regent for his nephew (Caterina's half brother), then as outright usurper. Lodovico promoted Caterina's interests for the sake of his own. He married her off at fifteen to a nephew of Pope Sixtus IV, thereby strengthening the alliance between the Sforzas and the Riario family, who now controlled the papacy. The pope carved a state out of papal domains for Caterina's husband, making him Count of Forlì as well as the Lord of Imola, which Caterina brought to the marriage. But the pope died in 1484, her husband died by assassination four years later — and Caterina made the choice to defy the peculiar obstacles posed by Renaissance Italy to a woman's assumption of power.

Once before, with her husband seriously ill at Imola, she had ridden hard to Forlì to quell an incipient coup a day before giving birth. Now at twenty-six, after the assassination of her husband, she and a loyal castellan held the citadel at Forlì against her enemies until Lodovico sent her aid from Milan. Caterina won; she faced down her opponents, who held her six children hostage, then took command as regent for her young son. But her title to rule as regent was inconsequential. Caterina ruled because she mustered superior force and exercised it personally, and to the end she had to exert repeatedly the skill, forcefulness, and ruthless ambition that brought her to power. However, even her martial spirit did not suffice. In the despotisms of Renaissance Italy, where assassinations, coups, and invasions were the order of the day, power stayed closely bound to military force. In 1500, deprived of Milan's support by her uncle Lodovico's deposition, Caterina succumbed to the overwhelming forces of Cesare Borgia and was divested of power after a heroic defense of Forlì.

Because of this political situation, at once statist and unstable, the daughters of the Este, Gonzaga, and Montefeltro families represent women of their class much more than Caterina Sforza did. Their access to power was indirect and provisional, and was expected to be so. In his handbook for the nobility, Baldassare Castiglione's description of the lady of the court makes this difference in sex roles quite clear. On the one hand, the Renaissance lady appears as the equivalent of the courtier. She has the same virtues of mind as he and her education is symmetrical with his. She learns everything — well, almost everything — he does: "knowledge of letters, of music, of painting, and . . . how to dance and how to be festive." [17] Culture is an accomplishment for noblewoman and man alike, used to charm others as much as to develop the self. But for the woman, charm had become the primary occupation and aim. Whereas the courtier's chief task is defined as the profession of arms, "in a Lady who lives at court a certain pleasing affability is becoming above all else, whereby she will be able to entertain graciously every kind of man" (p. 207).

One notable consequence of the Renaissance lady's need to charm is that Castiglione called upon her to give up certain "unbecoming" physical activities such as riding and handling weapons. Granted, he concerned himself with the court lady, as he says, not a queen who may be called upon to rule. But his aestheticizing of the lady's role, his conception of her femaleness as centered in charm, meant that activities such as riding and skill in weaponry would seem unbecoming to women of the ruling families, too. Elisabetta Gonzaga, the idealized duchess of Castiglione's *Courtier,* came close in real life to his normative portrayal of her type. Riding and skill in weaponry had, in fact, no significance for her. The heir to her Duchy of Urbino was decided upon during the lifetime of her husband, and it was this adoptive heir — not the widow of thirty-seven with no children to compete for her care and attention — who assumed power in 1508. Removed from any direct exercise of power, Elisabetta also disregarded the pursuits and pleasures associated with it. Her letters express none of the sense of freedom and daring Caterina Sforza and Beatrice d'Este experienced in riding and the hunt.[18] Altogether, she lacks spirit. Her correspondence shows her to be as docile in adulthood as her early teachers trained her to be. She met adversity, marital and political, with fortitude but never opposed it. She placated father, brother, and husband, and even in Castiglione's depiction of her court, she complied with rather than shaped its conventions.

The differences between Elisabetta Gonzaga and Caterina Sforza are great, yet both personalities were responding to the Renaissance situation of emerging statehood and social mobility. Elisabetta, neither personally illegitimate nor springing from a freebooting condottiere family, was schooled, as Castiglione would have it, away from the martial attitudes and skills requisite for despotic rule. She would not be a prince, she would marry one. Hence, her education, like that of most of the daughters of the ruling families, directed her toward the cultural and social functions of the court. The lady who married a Renaissance prince became a patron. She commissioned works of art and gave gifts for literary works dedicated to her; she drew to her artists and literati. But the court they came to ornament was her husband's, and the culture they represented magnified his princely being, especially when his origins could not. Thus, the Renaissance lady may play an aesthetically significant role in Castiglione's idealized Court of Urbino of 1508, but even he clearly removed her from that equal, to say nothing of superior, position in social discourse that medieval courtly literature had granted her. To the fifteen or so male members of the court whose names he carefully listed, Castiglione admitted only four women to the evening conversations that were the second major occupation at court (the profession of arms, from which he completely excluded women, being the first). Of the four, he distinguished only two women as participants. The Duchess Elisabetta and her companion, Emilia Pia, at least speak, whereas the other two only do a dance. Yet they speak in order to moderate and "direct" discussion by proposing questions and games. They do not themselves contribute to the discussions, and at one point Castiglione relieves them even of their negligible role:

> When signor Gasparo had spoken thus, signora Emilia made a sign to madam Costanza Fregosa, as she sat next in order, that she should speak; and she was making ready to do so, when suddenly the Duchess said: "Since signora Emilia does not choose to go to the trouble of devising a game, it would be quite right for the other ladies to share in this ease, and thus be exempt from such a burden this evening, especially since there are so many men here that we risk no lack of games." (pp. 19–20)

The men, in short, do all the talking; and the ensuing dialogue on manners and love, as we might expect, is not only developed by men but directed toward their interests.

The contradiction between the professed parity of noblewomen and men in *The Courtier* and the merely decorative role Castiglione unwittingly assigned the lady proclaims an important educational and cultural change as well as a political one. Not only did a male ruler preside over the courts of Renaissance Italy, but the court no longer served as the exclusive school of the nobility, and the lady no longer served as arbiter of the cultural functions it did retain. Although restricted to a cultural and social role, she lost dominance in that role as secular education came to require special skills which were claimed as the prerogative of a class of professional teachers. The sons of the Renaissance nobility still pursued their military and diplomatic training in the service of some great lord, but as youths, they transferred their nonmilitary training from the lady to the humanistic tutor or boarding school. In a sense, humanism represented an advance for women as well as for the culture at large. It brought Latin literacy and classical learning to daughters as well as sons of the nobility. But this very development, usually taken as an index of the equality of Renaissance (noble) women with men,[19] spelled a further decline in the lady's influence over courtly society. It placed her as well as her brothers under male cultural authority. The girl of the medieval aristocracy, although unschooled, was brought up at the court of some great lady. Now her brothers' tutors shaped her outlook, male educators who, as humanists, suppressed romance and chivalry to further classical culture, with all its patriarchal and misogynous bias.

The humanistic education of the Renaissance noblewoman helps explain why she cannot compare with her medieval predecessors in shaping a culture responsive to her own interests. In accordance with the new cultural values, the patronage of the Este, Sforza, Gonzaga, and Montefeltro women extended far beyond the literature and art of love and manners, but the works they commissioned, bought, or had dedicated to them do not show any consistent correspondence to their concerns as women. They did not even give noticeable support to women's education, with the single important exception of Battista da Montefeltro, to whom one of the few treatises advocating a humanistic education for women was dedicated. Adopting the universalistic outlook of their humanist teachers, the noblewomen of Renaissance Italy seem to have lost all consciousness of their particular interests as women, while male authors such as Castiglione, who articulated the mores of the Renaissance aristocracy, wrote their works for men. Cultural and political dependency thus combined in Italy to reverse the roles of women and men in developing the new noble code. Medieval courtesy, as set forth in the earliest etiquette books, romances, and rules of love, shaped the man primarily to please the lady. In the thirteenth and fourteenth centuries, rules for women, and strongly patriarchal ones at that, entered French and Italian etiquette books, but not until the Renaissance reformulation of courtly manners and love is it evident how the ways of the lady came to be determined by men in the context of the early modern state. The relation of the sexes here assumed its modern form, and nowhere is this made more visible than in the love relation.

The Renaissance of Chastity

As soon as the literature and values of courtly love made their way into Italy, they were modified in the direction of asexuality. Dante typifies this initial reception of courtly love. His *Vita Nuova,* written in the "sweet new style" (*dolce stil nuovo*) of late-thirteenth-century Tuscany, still celebrates love and the noble heart: *"Amore e 'l cor gentil sono una cosa."* Love still appears as homage and the lady as someone else's wife. But the lover of Dante's poems is curiously arrested. He frustrates his own desire by rejecting even the aim of union with his beloved. "What is the point of your love for your lady since you are unable to endure her presence?" a lady asks of Dante. "Tell us, for surely the aim of such love must be unique [*novissimo*]!" [20] And novel it is, for Dante confesses that the joy he once took in his beloved's greeting he shall henceforth seek in himself, "in words which praise my lady." Even this understates the case, since Dante's words neither conjure up Beatrice nor seek to melt her. She remains shadowy and remote, for the focus of his poetry has shifted entirely to the subjective pole of love. It is the inner life, *his* inner life, that Dante objectifies. His love poems present a spiritual contest, which he will soon ontologize in the *Divine Comedy,* among competing states of the lover poet's soul.

This dream-world quality expresses in its way a general change that came over the literature of love as its social foundations crumbled. In the north, as the *Romance of the Rose* reminds us, the tradition began to run dry in the late-thirteenth-century period of feudal disintegration — or transformation by the bourgeois economy of the towns and the emergence of the state. And in Provence, after the Albigensian Crusade and the subjection of the Midi to church and crown, Guiraut Riquier significantly called himself the last troubadour. Complaining that "no craft is less esteemed at court than the beautiful mastery of song," he renounced sexual for celestial love and claimed to enter the service of the Virgin Mary.[21] The reception and reworking of the troubadour tradition in Florence of the late 1200s consequently appears somewhat archaic. A conservative, aristocratic nostalgia clings to Dante's love poetry as it does to his political ideas. But if the new social life of the bourgeois commune found little positive representation in his poetry, Florence did drain from his poems the social content of feudal experience. The lover as knight or trobairitz thus gave way to a poet scholar. The experience of a wandering, questing life gave way to scholastic interests, to distinguishing and classifying states of feeling. And the courtly celebration of romance, modeled upon vassalage and enjoyed in secret meetings, became a private circulation of poems analyzing the spiritual effects of unrequited love.

The actual disappearance of the social world of the court and its presiding lady underlies the disappearance of sex and the physical evaporation of the woman in these poems. The ladies of the romances and troubadour poetry may be stereotypically blond, candid, and fair, but their authors meant them to be taken as physically and socially "real." In the love poetry of Dante, and of Petrarch and Vittoria Colonna, who continue his tradition, the beloved may just as well be dead — and, indeed, all three authors made them so. They have no meaningful, objective existence, and not merely because their affective experience lacks a voice. This would hold for troubadour poetry too, since the lyric, unlike the romance, articulates only the feelings of the lover. The unreality of the Renaissance beloved has rather to do with the *quality* of the Renaissance lover's feelings. As former social relations that sustained mutuality and interaction among lovers vanished, the lover fell back on a narcissistic experience. The Dantesque beloved merely inspires feelings that have no outer, physical aim; or, they have a transcendent aim that the beloved merely mediates. In either case, love casts off sexuality. Indeed, the role of the beloved as mediator is asexual in a double sense, as the *Divine Comedy* shows. Not only does the beloved never respond sexually to the lover, but the feelings she arouses in him turn into a spiritual love that makes of their entire relationship a mere symbol or allegory.

Interest even in this shadowy kind of romance dropped off markedly as the work of Dante, Petrarch, and Boccaccio led into the fifteenth-century renaissance of Graeco-Roman art and letters. The Florentine humanists in particular appropriated only the classical side of their predecessors' thought, the side that served public concerns. They rejected the dominance of love in human life, along with the inwardness and seclusion of the religious, the scholar, and the lovesick poet. Dante, for example, figured primarily as a citizen to his biographer, Lionardo Bruni, who, as humanist chancellor of Florence, made him out as a modern Socrates, at once a political figure, a family man, and a rhetor: an exemplar for the new polis.[22] Only in relation to the institution of the family did Florentine civic humanism take up questions of love and sexuality. In this context, they developed the bourgeois sex-role system, placing man in the public sphere and the patrician woman in the home, requiring social virtues from him and chastity and motherhood from her. In bourgeois Florence, the humanists would have nothing to do with the old aristocratic tradition of relative social and sexual parity. In the petty Italian despotisms, however, and even in Florence under the princely Lorenzo de' Medici late in the fifteenth century, the traditions and culture of the nobility remained meaningful.[23] Castiglione's *Courtier,* and the corpus of Renaissance works it heads, took up the themes of love and courtesy for this courtly society, adapting them to contemporary social and cultural needs. Yet in this milieu, too, within the very tradition of courtly literature, new constraints upon female sexuality emerged. Castiglione, the single most important spokesman of Renaissance love and manners, retained in his love theory Dante's two basic features: the detachment of love from sexuality and the allegorization of the love theme. Moreover, he introduced into the aristocratic conception of sex roles some of the patriarchal notions of women's confinement to the family that bourgeois humanists had been restoring.

Overtly, as we saw, Castiglione and his class supported a complementary conception of sex roles, in part because a nobility that did no work at all gave little thought to a sexual division of labor. He could thus take up the late medieval *querelle des femmes* set off by the *Romance of the Rose* and debate the question of women's dignity much to their favor. Castiglione places Aristotle's (and Aquinas's) notion of woman as a defective man in the mouth of an aggrieved misogynist, Gasparo; he criticizes Plato's low regard for women, even though he did permit them to govern in *The Republic*; he rejects Ovid's theory of love as not "gentle" enough. Most significantly, he opposes Gasparo's bourgeois notion of women's exclusively domestic role. Yet for all this, Castiglione established in *The Courtier* a fateful bond between love and marriage. One index of a heightened patriarchal outlook among the Renaissance nobility is that love in the usual emotional and sexual sense must lead to marriage and be confined to it — for women, that is.

The issue gets couched, like all others in the book, in the form of a debate. There are pros and cons; but the prevailing view is unmistakable. If the ideal court lady loves, she should love someone whom she can marry. If married, and the mishap befalls her "that her husband's hate or another's love should bring her to love, I would have her give her lover a spiritual love only; nor must she ever give him any sure sign of her love, either by word or gesture or by other means that can make him certain of it" (p. 263). *The Courtier* thus takes a strange, transitional position on the relations among love, sex, and marriage, which bourgeois Europe would later fuse into one familial whole. Responding to a situation of general female dependency among the nobility, and to the restoration of patriarchal family values, at once classical and bourgeois, Castiglione, like Renaissance love theorists in general, connected love and marriage. But facing the same realities of political marriage and clerical celibacy that beset the medieval aristocracy, he still focused upon the love that takes place outside it. On this point, too, however, he broke with the courtly love tradition. He proposed on the one hand a Neo-Platonic notion of spiritual love, and on the other, the double standard.[24]

Castiglione's image of the lover is interesting in this regard. Did he think his suppression of female sexual love would be more justifiable if he had a churchman, Pietro Bembo (elevated to cardinal in 1539), enunciate the new theory and had him discourse upon the love of an aging courtier rather than that of a young knight? In any case, adopting the Platonic definition of love as desire to enjoy beauty, Bembo located this lover in a metaphysical and physical hierarchy between sense ("below") and intellect ("above"). As reason mediates between the physical and the spiritual, so man, aroused by the visible beauty of his beloved, may direct his desire beyond her to the true, intelligible source of her beauty. He may, however, also turn toward sense. Young men fall into this error, and we should expect it of them, Bembo explains in the Neo-Platonic language of the Florentine philosopher Marsilio Ficino. "For finding itself deep in an earthly prison, and deprived of spiritual contemplation in exercising its office of governing the body, the soul of itself cannot clearly perceive the truth; wherefore, in order to have knowledge, it is obliged to turn to the senses . . . and so it believes them . . . and lets itself be guided by them, especially when they have so much vigor that they almost force it" (pp. 338–339). A misdirection of the soul leads to sexual union (though obviously not with the court lady). The preferred kind of union, achieved by way of ascent, uses love of the lady as a step toward love of universal beauty. The lover here ascends from awareness of his own human spirit, which responds to beauty, to awareness of that universal intellect that comprehends universal beauty. Then, "transformed into an angel," his soul finds supreme happiness in divine love. Love may hereby soar to an ontologically noble end, and the beauty of the woman who inspires such ascent may acquire metaphysical status and dignity. But Love, Beauty, Woman, aestheticized as Botticelli's Venus and given cosmic import, were in effect denatured, robbed of body, sex, and passion by this elevation. The simple kiss of love-service became a rarefied kiss of the soul: "A man delights in joining his mouth to that of his beloved in a kiss, not in order to bring himself to any unseemly desire, but because he feels that that bond is the opening of mutual access to their souls" (pp. 349–350). And instead of initiating love, the kiss now terminated physical contact, at least for the churchman and/or aging courtier who sought an ennobling experience — and for the woman obliged to play her role as lady.

Responsive as he still was to medieval views of love, Castiglione at least debated the issue of the double standard. His spokesmen point out that men make the rules permitting themselves and not women sexual freedom, and that concern for legitimacy does not justify this inequality. Since these same men claim to be more virtuous than women, they could more easily restrain themselves. In that case, "there would be neither more nor less certainty about offspring, for even if women were unchaste, they could in no way bear children of themselves . . . provided men were continent and did not take part in the unchastity of women" (pp. 240–241). But for all this, the book supplies an excess of hortatory tales about female chastity, and in the section of the dialogue granting young men indulgence in sensual love, no one speaks for young women, who ought to be doubly "prone," as youths and as women, according to the views of the time.

This is theory, of course. But one thinks of the examples: Eleanor of Aquitaine changing bedmates in the midst of a crusade; Elisabetta Gonzaga, so constrained by the conventions of her own court that she would not take a lover even though her husband was impotent. She, needless to say, figures as Castiglione's prime exemplar: "Our Duchess who has lived with her husband for fifteen years like a widow" (p. 253). Bembo, on the other hand, in the years before he became cardinal, lived with and had three children by Donna Morosina. But however they actually lived, in the new ideology a spiritualized noble love *supplemented* the experience of men while it *defined* extramarital experience for the lady. For women, chastity had become the convention of the Renaissance courts, signaling the twofold fact that the dominant institutions of sixteenth-century Italian society would not support the adulterous sexuality of courtly love, and that women, suffering a relative loss of power within these institutions, could not at first make them responsive to their needs. Legitimacy is a significant factor here. Even courtly love had paid some deference to it (and to the desire of women to avoid conception) by restraining intercourse while promoting romantic and sexual play. But now, with cultural and political power held almost entirely by men, the norm of female chastity came to express the concerns of Renaissance noblemen as they moved into a new situation as a hereditary, dependent class.

This changed situation of the aristocracy accounts both for Castiglione's widespread appeal and for his telling transformation of the love relation. Because *The Courtier* created a mannered way of life that could give to a dependent nobility a sense of self-sufficiency, of inner power and control, which they had lost in a real economic and political sense, the book's popularity spread from Italy through Europe at large in the sixteenth and seventeenth centuries. Although set in the Urbino court of 1508, it was actually begun some ten years after that and published in 1528 — after the sack of Rome, and at a time when the princely states of Italy and Europe were coming to resemble each other more closely than they had in the fourteenth and fifteenth centuries. The monarchs of Europe, consolidating and centralizing their states, were at once protecting the privileges of their nobility and suppressing feudal power.[25] Likewise in Italy, as the entire country fell under the hegemony of Charles V, the nobility began to be stabilized. Throughout sixteenth-century Italy, new laws began to limit and regulate membership in a hereditary aristocratic class, prompting a new concern with legitimacy and purity of the blood. Castiglione's demand for female chastity in part responds to this particular concern. His theory of love as a whole responds to the general situation of the Renaissance nobility. In the discourse on love for which he made Bembo the spokesman, he brought to the love relation the same psychic attitudes with which he confronted the political situation. Indeed, he used the love relation as a symbol to convey his sense of political relations.

The changed times to which Castiglione refers in his introduction he experienced as a condition of servitude. The dominant problem of the sixteenth-century Italian nobility, like that of the English nobility under the Tudors, had become one of obedience. As one of Castiglione's courtiers expressed it, God had better grant them "good masters, for, once we have them, we have to endure them as they are" (p. 116). It is this transformation of aristocratic service to statism, which gave rise to Castiglione's leading idea of nobility as courtiers, that shaped his theory of love as well. Bembo's aging courtier, passionless in his rational love, sums up the theme of the entire book: how to maintain by detachment the sense of self now threatened by the loss of independent power. The soul in its earthly prison, the courtier in his social one, renounce the power of self-determination that has in fact been denied them. They renounce *wanting* such power; "If the flame is extinguished, the danger is also extinguished" (p. 347). In love, as in service, the courtier preserves independence by avoiding desire for real love, real power. He does not touch or allow himself to be touched by either. "To enjoy beauty without suffering, the Courtier, aided by reason, must turn his desire entirely away from the body and to beauty alone, [to] contemplate it in its simple and pure self" (p. 351). He may gaze at the object of his love-service, he may listen, but there he reaches the limits of the actual physical relation and transforms her beauty, or the prince's power, into a pure idea. "Spared the bitterness and calamities" of thwarted passion thereby, he loves and serves an image only. The courtier gives obeisance, but only to a reality of his own making: "for he will always carry his precious treasure with him, shut up in his heart, and will also, by the force of his own imagination, make her beauty [or the prince's power] much more beautiful than in reality it is" (p. 352).

Thus, the courtier can serve and not serve, love and not love. He can even attain the relief of surrender by making use of this inner love-service "as a step" to mount to a more sublime sense of service. Contemplation of the Idea the courtier has discovered within his own soul excites a purified desire to love, to serve, to unite with intellectual beauty (or power). Just as love guided his soul from the particular beauty of his beloved to the universal concept, love of that intelligible beauty (or power) glimpsed within transports the soul from the self, the particular intellect, to the universal intellect. Aflame with an utterly spiritual love (or a spiritualized sense of service), the soul then "understands all things intelligible, and without any veil or cloud views the wide sea of pure divine beauty, and receives it into itself, enjoying that supreme happiness of which the senses are incapable" (p. 354). What does this semimystical discourse teach but that by "true" service, the courtier may break out of his citadel of independence, his inner aloofness, to rise and surrender to the pure idea of Power? What does his service become but a freely chosen Obedience, which he can construe as the supreme virtue? In both its sublimated acceptance or resignation and its inner detachment from the actual, Bembo's discourse on love exemplifies the relation between subject and state, obedience and power, that runs through the entire book. Indeed, Castiglione regarded the monarch's power exactly as he had Bembo present the lady's beauty, as symbolic of God: "As in the heavens the sun and the moon and the other stars exhibit to the world a certain likeness of God, so on earth a much liker image of God is seen in . . . princes." Clearly, if "men have been put by God under princes" (p. 307), if they have been placed under princes as under His image, what end can be higher than service in virtue, than the purified experience of Service?

The likeness of the lady to the prince in this theory, her elevation to the pedestal of Neo-Platonic love, both masks and expresses the new dependency of the Renaissance noblewoman. In a structured hierarchy of superior and inferior, she seems to be served by the courtier. But this love theory really made her serve — and stand as a symbol of how the relation of domination may be reversed, so that the prince could be made to serve the interests of the courtier. The Renaissance lady is not desired, not loved for herself. Rendered passive and chaste, she merely mediates the courtier's safe transcendence of an otherwise demeaning necessity. On the plane of symbolism, Castiglione thus had the courtier dominate both her and the prince; and on the plane of reality, he indirectly acknowledged the courtier's actual domination of the lady by having him adopt "woman's ways" in his relations to the prince. Castiglione had to defend against effeminacy in the courtier, both the charge of it (p. 92) and the actuality of faces "soft and feminine as many attempt to have who not only curl their hair and pluck their eyebrows, but preen themselves . . . and appear so tender and languid . . . and utter their words so limply" (p. 36). Yet the close-fitting costume of the Renaissance nobleman displayed the courtier exactly as Castiglione would have him, "well built and shapely of limb" (p. 36). His clothes set off his grace, as did his nonchalant ease, the new manner of those "who seem in words, laughter, in posture not to care" (p. 44). To be attractive, accomplished, and seem not to care; to charm and do so coolly — how concerned with impression, how masked the true self. And how manipulative: petitioning his lord, the courtier knows to be "discreet in choosing the occasion, and will ask things that are proper and reasonable; and he will so frame his request, omitting those parts that he knows can cause displeasure, and will skillfully make easy the difficult points so that his lord will always grant it" (p. 111). In short, how like a woman — or a dependent, for that is the root of the simile.

The accommodation of the sixteenth- and seventeenth-century courtier to the ways and dress of women in no way bespeaks a greater parity between them. It reflects, rather, that general restructuring of social relations that entailed for the Renaissance noblewoman a greater dependency upon men as feudal independence and reciprocity yielded to the state. In this new situation, the entire nobility suffered a loss. Hence, the courtier's posture of dependency, his concern with the pleasing impression, his resolve "to perceive what his prince likes, and . . . to bend himself to this" (pp. 110–111). But as the state overrode aristocratic power, the lady suffered a double loss. Deprived of the possibility of independent power that the combined interests of kinship and feudalism guaranteed some women in the Middle Ages, and that the states of early modern Europe would preserve in part, the Italian noblewoman in particular entered a relation of almost universal dependence upon her family and her husband. And she experienced this dependency at the same time as she lost her commanding position with respect to the secular culture of her society.

Hence, the love theory of the Italian courts developed in ways as indifferent to the interests of women as the courtier, in his self-sufficiency, was indifferent as a lover. It accepted, as medieval courtly love did not, the double standard. It bound the lady to chastity, to the merely procreative sex of political marriage, just as her weighty and costly costume came to conceal and constrain her body while it displayed her husband's noble rank. Indeed, the person of the woman became so inconsequential to this love relation that one doubted whether she could love at all. The question that emerges at the end of *The Courtier* as to "whether or not women are as capable of divine love as men" (p. 350) belongs to a love theory structured by mediation rather than mutuality. Woman's beauty inspired love but the lover, the agent, was man. And the question stands unresolved at the end of *The Courtier* — because at heart the spokesmen for Renaissance love were not really concerned about women or love at all.

Where courtly love had used the social relation of vassalage to work out a genuine concern with sexual love, Castiglione's thought moved in exactly the opposite direction. He allegorized love as fully as Dante did, using the relation of the sexes to symbolize the new political order. In this, his love theory reflects the social realities of the Renaissance. The denial of the right and power of women to love, the transformation of women into passive "others" who serve, fits the self-image of the courtier, the one Castiglione sought to remedy. The symbolic relation of the sexes thus mirrors the new social relations of the state, much as courtly love displayed the feudal relations of reciprocal personal dependence. But Renaissance love reflects, as well, the actual condition of dependency suffered by noblewomen as the state arose. If the courtier who charms the prince bears the same relation to him as the lady bears to the courtier, it is because Castiglione understood the relation of the sexes in the same terms that he used to describe the political relation: i.e., as a relation between servant and lord. The nobleman suffered this relation in the public domain only. The lady, denied access to a freely chosen, mutually satisfying love relation, suffered it in the personal domain as well. Moreover, Castiglione's theory, unlike the courtly love it superseded, subordinated love itself to the public concerns of the Renaissance nobleman. He set forth the relation of the sexes as one of dependency and domination, but he did so in order to express and deal with the political relation and its problems. The personal values of love, which the entire feudality once prized, were henceforth increasingly left to the lady. The courtier formed his primary bond with the modern prince.

In sum, a new division between personal and public life made itself felt as the state came to organize Renaissance society, and with that division the modern relation of the sexes made its appearance,[26] even among the Renaissance nobility. Noblewomen, too, were increasingly removed from public concerns — economic, political, and cultural — and although they did not disappear into a private realm of family and domestic concerns as fully as their sisters in the patrician bourgeoisie, their loss of public power made itself felt in new constraints placed upon their personal as well as their social lives. Renaissance ideas on love and manners, more classical than medieval, and almost exclusively a male product, expressed this new subordination of women to the interests of husbands and male-dominated kin groups and served to justify the removal of women from an "unladylike" position of power and erotic independence. All the advances of Renaissance Italy, its protocapitalist economy, its states, and its humanistic culture, worked to mold the noblewoman into an aesthetic object: decorous, chaste, and doubly dependent — on her husband as well as the prince.

Notes

I first worked out these ideas in 1972–1973 in a course at Sarah Lawrence College entitled "Women: Myth and Reality" and am very much indebted to students in that course and my colleagues Eva Kollisch, Gerda Lerner, and Sherry Ortner. I thank Eve Fleisher, Martin Fleisher, Renate Bridenthal, and Claudia Koonz for their valuable criticism of an earlier version of this paper.

1. The traditional view of the equality of Renaissance women with men goes back to Jacob Burckhardt's classic, *The Civilization of the Renaissance in Italy* (1860). It has found its way into most general histories of women, such as Mary Beard's *Women as Force in History* (1946), Simone de Beauvoir's *The Second Sex* (1949), and Emily James Putnam's *The Lady* (1910), although the latter is a sensitive and sophisticated treatment. It also dominates most histories of Renaissance women, the best of which is E. Rodocanachi, *La femme italienne avant, pendant et après la Renaissance,* Hachette, Paris, 1922. A notable exception is Ruth Kelso, *Doctrine for the Lady of the Renaissance,* University of Illinois Press, Urbana, 1956, who discovered there was no such parity.
2. See the essay by Marylin Arthur. The major Renaissance statement of the bourgeois domestication of women was made by Leon Battista Alberti in Book 3 of *Della Famiglia* (c. 1435), which is a free adaptation of the Athenian situation described by Xenophon in the *Oeconomicus.*
3. Andreas Capellanus, *The Art of Courtly Love,* trans. John J. Parry, Columbia University Press, New York, 1941, pp. 150–151.
4. Maurice Valency, *In Praise of Love: An Introduction to the Love-Poetry of the Renaissance,* Macmillan, New York, 1961, p. 146.
5. *"E il dompna deu a son drut far honor/Cum ad amic, mas non cum a seignor."* Ibid., p. 64.
6. Lanval (Sir Launfal), *Les lais de Marie de France,* ed. Paul Tuffrau, L'Edition d'Art H. Piazza, Paris, n.d., p. 41. English ed., *Lays of Marie de France,* J. M. Dent and E. P. Dutton, London and New York, 1911.
7. Excellent trans. and ed. by W. W. Comfort, *Arthurian Romances,* Dent and Dutton Everyman's Library, London and New York, 1970, p. 286.

8. Thomas Aquinas, *Summa Theologiae,* pt. 1–2, q. 28, art. 5.

9. Lanval, *Les lais,* p. 10.

10. Thomas Frederick Crane, *Italian Social Customs of the Sixteenth Century,* Yale University Press, New Haven, 1920, pp. 10–11.

11. As Marc Bloch pointed out, the great French principalities that no longer required personal military service on the part of their holders were among the first to be passed on to women when male heirs were wanting. *Feudal Society,* trans. L. A. Manyon, University of Chicago Press, Chicago, 1964, p. 201. See also, in this volume, the essay by Suzanne Wemple and JoAnn McNamara.

12. David Herlihy, "Land, Family and Women in Continental Europe, 701–1200," *Traditio,* 18 (1962), 89–120. Also, "Women in Medieval Society," *The Smith History Lecture,* University of St. Thomas, Texas, 1971. For a fine new work on abbesses, see Joan Morris, *The Lady Was a Bishop,* Collier and Macmillan, New York and London, 1973. Marie de France may have been an abbess of Shaftesbury.

13. Emily James Putnam, *The Lady,* University of Chicago Press, Chicago and London, 1970, p. 118. See also the chapter on the abbess in the same book.

14. From *The Women Troubadours,* trans. and ed. by Meg Bogin, Paddington Press, New York/London, 1976.

15. Friedrich Heer, *The Medieval World: Europe 1100–1350,* Mentor Books, New York, 1963, pp. 167, 178–179.

16. This was Amy Kelly's surmise in "Eleanor of Aquitaine and Her Courts of Love," *Speculum,* 12 (January 1937), 3–19.

17. From *The Book of the Courtier,* by Baldesar Castiglione, a new translation by Charles S. Singleton (New York: Doubleday, 1959), p. 20. Copyright © 1959 by Charles S. Singleton and Edgar de N. Mayhew. This and other quotations throughout the chapter are reprinted by permission of Doubleday & Co., Inc.

18. Selections from the correspondence of Renaissance noblewomen can be found in the biographies listed in the bibliography.

19. An interesting exception is W. Ong's "Latin Language Study as a Renaissance Puberty Rite," *Studies in Philology,* 56 (1959), 103–124; also Margaret Leah King's "The Religious Retreat of Isotta Nogarola (1418–1466)," *Signs,* Winter 1977.

20. Dante Alighieri, *La Vita Nuova,* trans. Barbara Reynolds, Penguin Books, Middlesex, England and Baltimore, 1971, poem 18.

21. Frederick Goldin, trans., *Lyrics of the Troubadours and Trouvères,* Doubleday, New York, 1973, p. 325.

22. David Thompson and Alan F. Nagel, eds. and trans., *The Three Crowns of Florence: Humanist Assessments of Dante, Petrarca, and Boccaccio,* Harper & Row, New York, 1972.

23. For Renaissance humanistic and courtly literature, Vittorio Rossi, *Il quattrocento,* F. Vallardi, Milan, 1933; Ruth Kelso, *Doctrine for the Lady of the Renaissance,* University of Illinois Press, Urbana, 1956. On erotic life, interesting remarks by David Herlihy, "Some Psychological and Social Roots of Violence in the Tuscan Cities," *Violence and Civil Disorder in Italian Cities, 1200–1500,* ed. Lauro Martines, University of California Press, Berkeley, 1972, pp. 129–154.

24. For historical context, Keith Thomas, "The Double Standard," *Journal of the History of Ideas,* 20 (1959), 195–216; N. J. Perella, *The Kiss Sacred and Profane: An Interpretive History of Kiss Symbolism,* University of California Press, Berkeley, 1969; Morton Hunt, *The Natural History of Love,* Funk & Wagnalls, New York, 1967.
25. Fernand Braudel, *The Mediterranean World,* Routledge & Kegan Paul, London, 1973; A. Ventura, *Nobiltà e popolo nella società Veneta,* Laterza, Bari, 1964; Lawrence Stone, *The Crisis of the Aristocracy, 1558–1641,* Clarendon Press, Oxford, 1965.
26. The status of women as related to the distinction of public and private spheres of activity in various societies is a key idea in most of the anthropological studies in *Women, Culture, and Society,* eds. Michelle Zimbalist Rosaldo and Louise Lamphere, Stanford University Press, Stanford, 1974.

Suggestions for Further Reading

On Renaissance women: Stanley Chojnacki, "Patrician Women in Early Renaissance Venice," *Studies in the Renaissance,* 21 (1974), 176–203; Susan Hoag Bell, "Christine de Pizan," *Feminist Studies,* 3 (Spring/Summer 1976), 173–184; Joan Kelly-Gadol, "Notes on Women in the Renaissance," *Conceptual Frameworks in Women's History* (Sarah Lawrence Publications, Bronxville, N.Y., 1976); Margaret Leah King, "The Religious Retreat of Isotta Nogarola," *Signs,* Winter 1977; Kathleen Casey, "Reconstructing the Experience of Medieval Woman," *Liberating Women's History,* ed. Berenice Carroll (University of Illinois Press, Urbana, 1976), 224–249. With the exception of Ruth Kelso, *Doctrine for the Lady of the Renaissance* (University of Illinois Press, Urbana, 1956), and Ernst Breisach, *Caterina Sforza: A Renaissance Virago* (University of Chicago Press, Chicago, 1967), all other serious studies stem from the first wave of the feminist movement. They form a necessary basis, although they concern themselves almost exclusively with "exceptional" women and are not sensitive to socioeconomic factors. Among them, Marian Andrews (pseud. Christopher Hare), *The Most Illustrious Ladies of the Italian Renaissance* (Scribner's, New York, 1904); Julia Cartwright (Mrs. Ady), *Isabella d'Este,* 2 vols. (Dutton, New York, 1903) and *Beatrice d'Este* (1899); Ferdinand Gregorovius, *Lucrezia Borgia* (Blom, 1968 reprint of 1903 ed.); E. Rodocanachi, *La femme italienne avant, pendant et après la Renaissance* (Hachette, Paris, 1922); T. A. Trollope, *A Decade of Italian Women,* 2 vols. (Chapman & Hall, London, 1859).

The most significant studies in demographic and social history bearing upon Renaissance women are those of David Herlihy, among whose several articles are "Mapping Households in Medieval Italy," *The Catholic Historical Review,* 58 (April 1972), 1–24; "Vieillir à Florence au Quattrocento," *Annales,* 24 (November–December 1969), 1338–1352; "The Tuscan Town in the Quattrocento," *Medievalia et Humanistica,* 1 (1970), 81–110; also, a forthcoming book on the Tuscan family. Two demographic studies on infanticide and foundlings in Florence by Richard C. Trexler are in *History of Childhood Quarterly,* 1, nos. 1 and 2 (1973); Gene Brucker has excellent selections from wills, marriage contracts, government minutes, legal judgments, etc., in *The Society of Renaissance Florence: A Documentary Study* (Harper, New York, 1971).

Histories of family life and childrearing among the courtly aristocracy of early modern France supplement very nicely Castiglione's portrayal of the courtier and court lady. Among them, Philippe Ariès, *Centuries of Childhood: A Social History of Family Life* (Knopf, New York, 1965), and David Hunt, *Parents and Children in History* (Harper, New York, 1972). Although he does not deal with Renaissance Italy, Lawrence Stone's *The Crisis of the Aristocracy, 1558–1641* (Clarendon Press, Oxford, 1965) is indispensable reading for information about aristocratic social life.

Primary sources on medieval and Renaissance love used in the text in English translation are: Andreas Capellanus, *The Art of Courtly Love* (trans. John J. Parry, Columbia University Press, New York, 1941); *Lays of Marie de France* (J. M. Dent and E. P. Dutton, London and New York, 1911); Chrétien de Troyes's Lancelot from *Arthurian Romances* (trans. and ed. W. W. Comfort, Dent and Dutton Everyman's Library, London and New York, 1970); Baldassare Castiglione, *The Book of the Courtier* (trans. Charles S. Singleton, Doubleday, New York, 1959); Dante Alighieri, *La Vita Nuova* (trans. Barbara Reynolds, Penguin Books, Middlesex, England and Baltimore, 1971). In addition to sources given in the footnotes and by E. William Monter in his essay in this volume, see F. X. Newman, *The Meaning of Courtly Love* (The State University of New York Press, Albany, 1967) for contemporary opinion and a good bibliography. The soundest and most sensitive study is still Maurice Valency's *In Praise of Love* (Macmillan, New York, 1961). Two fine articles on the literature of love, sex, and marriage in early modern Europe are by William Haller, "Hail Wedded Love," *A Journal of English Literary History,* 13 (June 1946), 79–97, and Paul Siegel, "The Petrarchan Sonneteers and Neo-Platonic Love," *Studies in Philology,* 42 (1945), 164–182.

7

Women in the Reformation Era

Sherrin Marshall Wyntjes

Renaissance women, with some exceptions, accepted their restricted and largely ornamental role in the established state of the Renaissance prince. But women in the Protestant Reformation found themselves participating in political and economic turmoil. Their emotional and practical support was essential to the Protestant cause. Consequently, they took on new roles in an unsettled situation. More often than not, Reformation women used their novel opportunities to fight for family, religion, and class, rather than to assert their rights as women. As with other religious and political movements discussed in this book, women were welcomed into the early stages and excluded as the movement triumphed and became institutionalized.

Image breakers in the Netherlands, 1566. (From Pieter Bor, *Oorsprongk, begin, en vervolgh der nederlandsche oorlogen,* Amsterdam, 1679. With the kind assistance of the Widener Library, Harvard University.)

The age of the Reformation was a time of upheaval. Throughout the sixteenth century, organized religion underwent momentous change. Society was in constant flux. Perhaps because established institutions were being forced to justify their very existence, women had the opportunity to assume different roles from those that were time honored. Women's roles will be contrasted here in two ways: as traditional roles or lifestyles and as extraordinary roles or lifestyles. The first of these encompasses the direction of the household, which, depending on the woman's social status, might include a good deal of participation in household tasks as well, such as cooking, laundering, gardening, sewing, child care, and doctoring; running a tradesman's or artisan's shop, either to help her husband or to take charge herself if she were widowed; or, if the woman were of noble birth or an aristocrat, the assumption of many or all of her husband's privileges and responsibilities on their estate if he were absent or deceased, and, to some extent in any case, the assumption of these on her own lands, depending on where she lived. Traditional roles or lifestyles took a woman no further than the world of her own household (which might include a shop as well) or estate. Extraordinary roles or lifestyles include the following: the extension of these traditional roles beyond the household or estate, and often on a much greater scale; careers chosen by aristocratic or noblewomen, such as those of patrons and protectors, which again carried her beyond the household or estate. Reaching out, or being forced to reach out, to the world beyond the household or estate provided the crucial distinction.

The roles that women played during this tumultuous time were intimately connected with their social position, and corresponded in many important ways with those of men of their own social class. Options available to women in preindustrial society were often class- rather than sex-oriented and might thus operate to a woman's benefit or detriment, depending on her social standing. Kinship groupings, ties of patronage and clientage, and corporate groupings provided the basis for personal identification more frequently than sex. Women viewed themselves as members of such a group or groups and tended to act accordingly with regard to religion and religious change.

What sort of religious life did women have on the eve of the Reformation? While Christianity was becoming established in Europe in the early Middle Ages, women, particularly aristocratic women, had opportunities for great freedom and the exercise of authority. They lost these as the church became more securely established and men came to dominate the positions of authority. By the sixteenth century, convents had often become a convenient repository for superfluous daughters of the aristocracy and wealthy urban classes. Inevitably, while many nuns were examples of spiritual dedication, many others had little sense of vocation. Women outside the religious orders were similarly excluded from full participation in religious life. They were sacramental participants but not full ecclesiastical participants in the rituals of religious services, for example. In social organizations within the extended church, such as confraternities, men were far more often members than women and enjoyed corresponding privileges, such as gala processions on saint's days and banquets.[1] As one result of this exclusion, women turned to reform movements or heresies. There, they could participate fully and receive their share of attention. Such movements appealed most strongly to middle-class women, who were not as likely to enter convents.

The Beguines, who appeared at the beginning of the thirteenth century and flourished in the Low Countries and Germany, represented one such nonestablishment reform movement. These laywomen lived communally and supported themselves by their own labor. Their work included nursing, weaving, lace making, and embroidering, and they ordinarily pooled their earnings. This way of life especially appealed to single, rootless women. The movement survived despite attempts of the religious authorities to discredit the Beguines as heretics, perhaps because of the extreme simplicity of their religious views, which often approached pious mysticism. Far more sophisticated intellectually were the tenets of the *devotio moderna*, practiced by the Brethren and Sisters of the Common Life in the fourteenth and fifteenth centuries. Unlike the Beguines, the Sisters of this group, which also spread throughout the Low Countries, were defended theologically by the Brethren. The founder of the Brethren, Gerhard Groote, had turned his parental home into a house for religious women in 1374. The Sisters took no binding vows, wore no distinctive habit (they felt both of these encouraged religious formalism), and belonged to no formal religious order. They said they served God through the "imitation of Christ," and were self-supporting. At its height, the Sisters had several hundred members, and wealthy aristocratic widows and poor servant girls worked side by side.[2] The authorities did not systematically persecute either of these groups; they were not heretics, although they often skirted that charge. Both demonstrated discontent with the church establishment, particularly with traditional religious orders, but worked within the framework of the established church all the same.

In contrast, true heretical movements, which appeared throughout the Middle Ages, presented a more direct threat to civil and religious authority and were persecuted vigorously. Lollardy, which presaged the Reformation, indicated such a dimension of discontent with the church establishment. The beliefs of the Lollards originated in the principles of John Wycliffe, an Oxford scholastic philosopher who wrote and taught in the second half of the fourteenth century. At first his teachings circulated among scholars, priests, and the propertied classes, all of whom approved of his attack on papal supremacy, but during his last years, Wycliffe became increasingly revolutionary. In fact, he anticipated almost all of the main issues that concerned the sixteenth-century reformers. These included advocacy of clerical marriage, the elevation of the temporal ruler above the pope (with the concomitant duty of reforming the church), attacks on monasticism as an institution, and a desire to see Scripture translated into the vernacular. After 1401, most of his early influential and literate followers recanted under threat of the death sentence. The movement went underground, abandoning most of Wycliffe's complex theology in the process. It now appealed to the lower classes, specifically men and women workers and artisans who felt discontented with the church. Throughout the fifteenth century, the authorities sporadically uncovered local groups. Then came a surge in popularity, despite intensified persecution, at the end of the fifteenth and beginning of the sixteenth centuries.[3]

The religious attitudes expressed by the Lollards during this later period were essentially negative. They did not offer a program for reform or even put forward a coherent doctrine. They were antipapal, referring to the pope as the Antichrist. They refused to believe in transubstantiation or in the efficacy of pilgrimages, images, or relics, and persisted in reading the Bible in English translation. Lollardy appealed to women, who often comprised up to one-third or more of the membership. Many Lollard women participated in the movement for lengthy periods of time and helped its growth in the same ways as did men. Margery Baxter, one of the East Anglian Lollards, suggested that it was lawful to withhold tithes from unworthy recipients, and that the money might better be given to the poor. She also said that she would rather eat leftover meat than go into debt to buy fish on fast days.[4]

Not only were such movements forerunners of the Reformation, they influenced the subsequent development of the Reformation as well. For example, the Lollards' disdain for images and relics is often seen as a precursor of Puritan ideas later in the sixteenth century in England. All of these movements emphasized in one way or another a personal, nonhierarchic, lay-dominated religion that looked to Scripture for its authority. In any such movement women would find a place.

The coming of the Renaissance in the north brought change in religious attitudes within the church as well. One way in which the Northern Renaissance differed from the Renaissance in Italy was in its commitment to religious reform as a logical consequence of humanism. This concern was integral to the movement known as Christian humanism, which developed around the end of the fifteenth century in England, France, and the Low Countries. The Christian humanists, most notably Desiderius Erasmus and Thomas More, intended that their writings be utilized not as esoteric treatises on spirituality but as practical handbooks of daily piety. Erasmus wrote in the *Paraclesis,* the preface to his Greek and Latin edition of the New Testament, that the "doctrine of Christ casts aside no age, no sex, no fortune or position in life. . . . It keeps no one at a distance." He went on to say:

> I would that even the lowliest women read the Gospels and the Pauline Epistles . . . [that] the farmer sing some portion of them at the plow, the weaver hum some parts of them to the movement of the shuttle, the traveller lighten the weariness of the journey with stories of this kind!

More believed that if the New Learning, as the new humanistic studies were called, was to be used as a basis for this lay piety, it would have to be brought to women as well as men. "Learning and morals go together," More insisted in a letter to the tutor of his daughters.

> Nor do I think that it affects the harvest, that a man or woman has sown the seed. If they are worthy of being ranked with the human race, if they are distinguished by reason from beasts; that learning, by which the reason is cultivated, is equally suitable to both. Both of them, if the seed of good principles be sown in them, equally produce the germs of virtue.[5]

More's children, three daughters and a son, learned Latin, Greek, logic, theology, philosophy, mathematics, and astronomy from an early age. More corresponded with his children into their adulthood in Latin.

His eldest daughter, Margaret, developed into a recognized scholar, and her translation of Erasmus's treatise on the Lord's Prayer was well known in England. One of her tutors, Richard Hyrde, wrote the introduction, and included a justification of the right of women to a scholarly education. More's pride in the accomplishments of Margaret, who continued her studies after her marriage, knew no bounds.

These attitudes were most important for women of the high nobility or of the upper classes. Only they had access to this kind of intensive educational program. For instance, Marguerite d'Angoulême, better known as Marguerite of Navarre, sister of Francis I, King of France, was won over to the philosophy of the Christian humanists. She not only encouraged and protected some of the outstanding representatives of the movement in France, such as Jacques Lefèvre d'Étaples, Guillaume Briçonnet, and

Guillaume Budé, but herself wrote the devotional works *The Mirror of a Sinful Soul* and *The Heptameron.* Catherine Parr, sixth and last wife of Henry VIII, was technically an Anglican because the English church had already been reformed, but considered herself a Catholic who supported the goals of the Christian humanists. She embraced their teachings both in her personal religious life and in her political life as queen of England. Both Marguerite and Catherine criticized the ignorance, superstition, and misunderstanding of Scripture they felt plagued the Catholic Church. Catherine went even further, because by the time she wrote, the Reformation had already occurred: she included a section on justification by faith in her treatise *The Lamentation of a Sinner.* Their general program of prayer and of a life guided by the Gospel does not seem too different from that of the Brethren and Sisters of the Common Life, except that these women were more learned, and more often from the nobility. The similarities become understandable if we recall that the ideals of the Brethren exerted strong influence on Erasmus. He incorporated the interaction between scholarly learning and practical living in his thought and writing, as did the disciples of the Christian humanists. The programs of Erasmus and Marguerite of Navarre both went beyond condemnation of the abuses of the church to offer positive guidelines for personal religious commitment. Although these attitudes predated the Reformation and did not indicate thorough institutional changes, they critically influenced the reformers, many of whom were humanists by training.[6]

The progressive Christian humanists legitimized new possibilities for women. First, they gave women educational parity with men. This educational trend accounts in large measure for the renowned erudition of many female rulers and aristocrats in the sixteenth century, such as, in addition to Marguerite of Navarre and Catherine Parr, Catherine of Aragon (first wife of Henry VIII), Elizabeth I, and Lady Jane Grey, to mention only a few. Women who benefited from this educational program patronized humanistic studies and incorporated them into their own court schools. Second, as an extension of women's spiritual equality came the assumption that concerned and knowledgeable women had the right to criticize the church just as men did. It became acceptable for women to function as outspoken critics of current religious practices. Women who did this were careful to preserve their "femininity," by voicing the platitude that they were "merely women" and had no presumptuous intentions. Originally, upper-class and aristocratic women took advantage of this right, but after the coming of the Reformation, middle-class women would also do so. The Christian humanists hoped that their doctrines would benefit all of Christendom and, although the pre-reform movements affected the upper classes almost exclusively, the Reformation, in one form or another, became everybody's Reformation.

There were not one but several reformations. The earliest began with Martin Luther's posting of his 95 Theses in 1517. Others followed, which can be grouped into two main types. First came those initiated by the magisterial reformers, who relied on the local judicial officials or magistrates for their authority and thus tended to work closely with secular government. They often differed with Luther in their thinking and actions, and usually affiliated themselves with a leading church, which provided them with a podium and a position of influence. The most important of the magisterial reformers, besides Luther, were Huldreich Zwingli and later John Calvin. They drew their broad support from the middle classes and, particularly later in the century, from the upper classes as well. The second main group of reforms was instituted by the radical reformers and became identifiable around 1525. The radicals consisted primarily of the forty or more Anabaptist sects, so called because of their insistence on adult baptism. They advocated wide-ranging social and religious changes, such as communal property holding, and were thus considered a threat to the established order and persecuted almost everywhere. Among Anabaptists there were a few notorious extremists, but the overwhelming majority were pious, industrious members of the lower classes.

The reformers, Luther in particular, did not aim to change women's role in society. But they focused on several targets of great significance for women. Clerical concubinage and fornication had been among the most blatant abuses in the church, which levied taxes on priests for the privilege of maintaining concubines and prostitutes. In Strasbourg, before the Reformation, the city fathers had felt that the "loose behavior of the canons, priests, and monks threatened the moral integrity of the community." In Holland, it has been estimated that approximately 25 percent of the clergy lived with a wife or concubine. Wives and sometimes children of canons often appear in genealogies, indicating the prevailing apathy with regard to this situation before the coming of the Reformation. These moral lapses seemed scandalous not only because they broke the vows of clerical celibacy but also because the church supposedly set moral standards for the entire community. Geneva, for example, had been an ecclesiastical principality before the Reformation, but the clergymen there never imposed any strict code of morals on themselves or the populace. Immoral behavior was regarded as inevitable. Prostitution, illegitimacy, and adultery were only sporadically punished.[7] The reformers addressed themselves to the entire atmosphere of hypocrisy the existence of this attitude signified.

The Reformation changed this situation not only for the clergy but for the general public as well. Even before Calvin had arrived in Geneva, ordinances of the city council decreed that all "fornicators and adulterers . . . abandon their wicked life" or be "whipped and punished." Systematic enforcement of these laws waited until Calvin's arrival and the consolidation of authority. During the 1550s the number of morals cases brought before the Genevan Consistory increased so rapidly that a delegation appeared before the council "to argue that the standards of sexual morality demanded by the consistory were humanly impossible, and to suggest that if the consistory continued to insist on such pure behavior, they feared their wives might all be tied in weighted sacks and thrown into the river (the punishment for flagrant adultery)." The consistory scolded them for being frivolous and imprisoned their leader. Although the emphasis on this statement is on the conduct of wives, in fact these laws regarding fornication and adultery put forward no double standard.

Laws regulating marriage also applied equally to men and women. Even more interesting were the grounds for rescinding a marriage. A marriage could be declared null and void if the man was physically impotent or if the woman "could not have intercourse with her husband because of some defect in her body, and she is unwilling to put it right." [8] If either husband or wife committed adultery or deserted and it could be proved, the other had the option of divorce and the freedom to marry again. Divorce had been rejected by the medieval church, which had only allowed separation from bed and board. This separation did not permit remarriage. Annulments were possible only if one could prove "consanguinity" — a blood relationship closer than that permitted by law. This frequently resulted in "zealous searching of the family tree or trumped-up testimony," providing one more form of hypocrisy against which the reformers reacted. Zwingli and Martin Bucer (who brought the Reformation to Strasbourg with Matthias Zell) advocated the more liberal proposals of Erasmus, based on civil law, which also granted divorce in event of madness and cruelty.

The reformers further asserted the right of the clergy to marry. Bucer, Zwingli, Zell, and Luther himself were all ex-monks who now accepted marriage as part of the ordinary life of ordinary people in the world. They undertook marriage as a duty to demonstrate the strength of their conviction. What sorts of relationships did they have with their wives? This question is as critical for us as a consideration of what the reformers said or failed to say regarding women. For one thing, none of them considered "women" systematically — they had no reason to do so — and are often attributed views that are small segments removed from the context of their entire work. Since this chapter considers the Reformation, it is useful to look at the ways in which the reformers influenced others by the example of their own lives as well as by what they wrote. At their best, they viewed marriage as a cooperative relationship of mutual responsibility and felt it to be a unity that God intended. Their theological training helped them to justify this condition: Since women had been made from men, argued Zell, men could only achieve full perfection or completeness in marriage.

Luther, who married the ex-nun Katherine von Bora, was initially dubious regarding the institution of marriage, but soon lost his reservations.

Over the years, the picture of their marriage that emerges from Luther's letters and table talk, his informal conversations, shows a mutual love and respect, with Katherine exercising a humanizing influence on Luther. Luther did indeed say that "men have broad and large chests, and small narrow hips, and more understanding than the women, who have but small and narrow breasts, and broad hips, to the end they should remain at home, sit still, keep house, and bear and bring up children." But he also said that "many good things come from a wife: the blessing of the Lord, children, community of all things and other things so good that they might overwhelm a man. Suppose there were no women, not only the house and household but even the state would perish. Even if we could beget children without women we could not get along without them." In 1538, he said of Hans Metzsch, the bailiff of Wittenberg of whose immorality he strongly disapproved,

> He who takes a wife ought to be a good man, but Hans Metzsch is not worthy of this divine gift, for a good woman deserves a good husband. To have peace and love in marriage is a gift which is next to the knowledge of the Gospel. There are heartless wretches who love neither their children nor their wives; such beings are not human. . . . The greatest blessing is to have a wife to whom you may entrust your affairs, and by whom you may have children.[9]

The wives of the reformers shared the concerns of their husbands, but chose for the most part to support their husbands' work more through the practical example of their daily middle-class lives than through the goals of individual activism evidenced by the Calvinist women later in the century. Luther, for example, was so generous with his possessions that Katherine had to keep track of his affairs and see that food was on the table. The wife of Matthias Zell, Katherine, championed her husband but spoke out only when Zell was excommunicated in 1527 for having married her. She discoursed on the sanctity of marriage and indicated that the bishop's opposition to clerical marriage came from purely financial considerations, since the loss of so-called "cradle taxes" levied on priests who kept prostitutes and concubines brought in far more revenue than the bishop could raise from honest married people. When she delivered an address on the occasion of Matthias's funeral, she denied "usurping the office of preacher or apostle." Rather, she saw herself as the "dear Mary Magdalene, who with no thought of being an apostle, came to tell the disciples that she had encountered the risen Lord." She claimed no intellectual pretensions, but indicated that she knew her Bible extensively by illustrating her arguments with examples from Scripture. Katherine Zell was the only woman in Strasbourg to expound such views publicly and may have viewed her role within the church as subordinate to that of her husband. Katherine von Bora certainly did. Both led exemplary lives filled with practical work.[10]

In addition to the traditional lifestyles already described, ministers' wives had to open their homes to others in need, such as ex-nuns and monks who needed shelter, students of their husbands who needed a place to stay, or like-minded Protestants fleeing repression. This might mean ten to eighty extra people in the parsonage at any one time. The vicissitudes of such an existence are well illustrated by the life of Wibrandis Rosenblatt. Wibrandis was married to a Christian humanist before the coming of the Reformation, and subsequently to three more reformers, all of whom she buried. Her third and best-known husband was Martin Bucer, whom she married when both had been recently widowed. She followed him into exile in England in 1549, moving her household, six children, and her own elderly mother along with her. Prior to this, she had managed for a year alone while her husband went off to establish the Reformation in Cologne. When Bucer died in England, she shouldered the financial responsibilities for her family. She wrote to various dignitaries in both German and English to request donations, and then moved the family back to Switzerland. She herself considered her conduct unexceptional. Thus, within the limits of supportive, traditional lifestyles, a wide range of extraordinary and independent behavior was encompassed and made acceptable through identification with the church.[11]

Although such women as Katherine Zell and other wives and daughters of ministers did not openly assume leadership roles, the situation of the Anabaptist women was different. The radical Reformation's insistence on freedom of conscience for all adult believers eliminated distinctions based on sex, and the doctrine of baptism or rebaptism for all believers became an equalizing covenant. Anabaptist priesthood included all members of the laity, both men and women, and some women, such as Ursula Jost in Strasbourg, attracted followings as prophets.[12]

On the whole, the radicals insisted on high standards of behavior and exercised strict control over their followers. Why, then, were they so persecuted? Inherent in Anabaptism was the principle of antinomianism, the idea that man's laws had no force for those whom God had saved. The Anabaptists wished to establish the Kingdom of Christ on earth, not in heaven, and to confine the church to the minority of true believers — those who had been saved, namely themselves. Carried to one possible extreme, this philosophy prompted the Anabaptists to withdraw from the world and settle in small groups. Some Anabaptist groups took another approach, however. They preached millenarianism, saying that the kingdom should be created here and now. They anticipated the end of the present world by bloodshed and violence. A small minority set this forth as their goal, and in their name all Anabaptists were persecuted. Interestingly enough, these extremists were particularly rigid and repressive with regard to women. The Anabaptist kingdom in Münster established in 1534 had a new legal code that made death the penalty for insubordination of wife to husband. It also introduced polygamy; what is less well known is that those who refused to support its establishment were executed, while all women under a certain age were compelled to marry. Since few unmarried men had arrived in Münster, this obliged women to accept the role of second, third, or fourth wife.[13] The fiery end of this community in 1535 marked the effective end of militant Anabaptism.

The pacific Anabaptists suffered guilt by association and were condemned by Lutherans, Calvinists, and Catholics alike. With few exceptions, Anabaptists came from the lower echelons of society. State and secular authorities everywhere, obsessed with the twin specters of anarchy and violent social revolution, viewed them as "rabble" and persecuted them zealously. The Anabaptists were often forced to flee and, when captured, were imprisoned and executed if they refused to abjure their faith. One of the countless who died was Elisabeth Munstdorp, executed at Antwerp in 1573. Shortly before her death, she wrote, or dictated, a letter to her month-old infant daughter:

> Since I am now delivered up to death . . . I must through these lines cause you to remember, that when you have attained your understanding, you endeavor to fear God, and see and examine why and for whose name we both [her husband had already lost his life] died; and be not ashamed to confess us before the world, for you must know that it is not for the sake of any evil. Hence be not ashamed of us; it is the way which the prophets and the apostles went, and the narrow way which leads into eternal life, for there shall no other way be found by which to be saved.[14]

She then admonished her daughter to live a just and pious life, working hard and living righteously. She concluded by reminding her that "if you follow that which is good, and seek peace, and ensue it, you shall receive the crown of eternal life; this crown I wish you and the crucified, bleeding, naked, despised, rejected and slain Jesus Christ for your bridegroom." Martyrdom was justified by faith for this woman and her husband alike. The Anabaptists as a whole had little opportunity to defend themselves because of their social position, but even well-to-do Anabaptists encountered difficulties. Anneken Jansdochter, the wealthy sponsor of Anabaptist leader David Joris, was executed for her heresy. Few Anabaptists could exert any influence whatever on the course of political affairs.

For Calvinist women, the situation differed both socially and politically. Knowledge of Calvin's teaching and of the example he had established in Geneva had reached into most areas of Europe by about 1550. Many circumstances combined to make Calvinism rather than Lutheranism the compelling force of Protestantism in the second half of the century. For one thing, Calvin was twenty-six years younger than Luther (who died in 1546) and thus represented the second generation of Protestant leaders.

Second, by this time the Catholic Counter Reformation had occurred. Many of the traditions of protest that were precursors of Protestantism can also be linked to the reform of the Catholic Church, which developed as a response to the Protestant encroachment. The Council of Trent, which met intermittently from 1545 to 1563, attacked the reformers unsparingly and uncompromisingly. The rise of a militant papacy, foundation of new religious orders, such as the Society of Jesus, and the use of weapons of repression such as the Inquisition and Index all indicate the thrust of the Counter Reformation. The church now took the offensive, attempting to win back the areas that were tending toward Protestantism and to halt the further spreading of the new doctrines. A vigorous, unified Protestant counterattack was called for.

Third, events of the 1540s and 1550s helped make Geneva the center of Protestantism. The fighting in Germany between Roman Catholic and Lutheran forces ended with the Peace of Augsburg in 1555, which provided that each territory follow the religion of its own prince. The toleration that each religion extended to the other did not include Anabaptism or, later, Calvinism. Thus, the cities in which Lutheranism was already firmly established, such as Strasbourg, became less open to new views from immigrants, and more vigorous in their orthodoxy.

Finally, political circumstances forced thousands of Protestants to leave France between 1547 and 1559, England from 1553 to 1558, and Scotland from 1546 to 1558. They fled to Geneva in great numbers. One of these exiles, the Scottish reformer John Knox, wrote effusively of life in Geneva:

> where . . . is the most perfect school of Christ that ever was in the earth since the days of the Apostles. In other places, I confess Christ to be truly preached; but manners and religion to be so sincerely reformed, I have yet seen in any other place.[15]

Such opinions were widely shared, and the exiles returned home imbued with the uncompromising zeal of Calvinism and driven by the desire to spread their faith. Calvinism provided a rigorous and convincing theology, which earlier forms of Protestantism had not. Calvin's *Institutes of the Christian Religion* are logical, systematic, and appeal only to the authority of Scripture — the word of God. His theology of predestination offered an assurance that his followers were God's elect, despite the persecutions that men might devise for them. Finally, the organization of Calvinism itself was effective for a subversive movement. Its congregations were self-sufficient, with participation by ministers and laymen alike. Geneva-trained pastors were particularly useful in France.

Calvinism was at its most militant when combined with political and social discontent. The wars of religion in the second half of the century were revolutions strongly shaped by religious forces. Religious expression and political action in Scotland, France, and the Netherlands were so interwoven that it is impossible to separate the two. In Scotland, this revolution proceeded quickly, due as much to the force of political as religious circumstances.

John Knox, who brought Calvinism to Scotland and saw it firmly established there, exemplifies the ambivalence the reformers showed toward women. However, looking at his writings on women out of context is particularly misleading. When in exile, he fulminated against the Scottish Catholic regent Mary of Guise with his well-known treatise *The First Blast of the Trumpet Against the Monstrous Regiment of Women.* This diatribe is often cited as evidence of his pervasive hatred of all women. After Elizabeth I came to the throne of England and rapidly took on the appearance of Protestant savior of Scotland, Knox recanted. It would have been impossible politically for him not to have done so, but Elizabeth was unforgiving and refused for a time to allow him to enter England, his paeans of tribute to her notwithstanding. His personal, as distinct from political, relationships with women are similarly revealing. His friend Anne Locke, who had probably been raised as a Protestant, joined Knox in exile in 1557 at his exhortation. In a letter to her, Knox wrote, "Ye wryt that your desyre is ernist to sie me. Deir Sister, yf I suld expres the thirst and langoure whilk I haif had for your presence, I suld appeir to pass measure." After her arrival in Geneva (without her husband, but with two infants), she translated some of Calvin's sermons into English, and after Knox returned to Scotland in the spring of 1559, channeled news from his letters to the other exiles. It seems evident that Knox's attitudes were greatly influenced by political exigencies and the personal attitudes of these various women toward him. Certainly, Mary Stuart (by now queen) was stubborn and hostile toward him. Knox marshaled every attack against her — as a monstrous Catholic, a monstrous ruler, and a monstrous woman. By the time of Mary Stuart's collapse in 1567, Calvinism as established by Knox was firmly entrenched in Scotland. This was more a commentary on Mary's unwise rule than on Knox's perspicacity.[16]

By contrast, in France as in the Netherlands, Calvinism met with vehement opposition. The high nobility of the country was divided into two hostile religious camps, with the Guise family supporting the Catholic position and the Bourbons the Protestant. Because Calvin recognized the dynamics of power in France, his native land, he sought to convert the high nobility and, if possible, the royal family itself to his cause. As a result, the converts to Calvinism from the ranks of the aristocracy and nobility were initially the most influential and important for the movement in France. Noblewomen, in particular, played a vital role in the formation of Calvinist policy in France between the late 1550s and 1572. Not only Calvin's doctrines but his relationship with these women, expressed through his correspondence with them, provided the impetus to conversion. The highest ranking and best known of these women was Jeanne d'Albret, daughter of Marguerite of Navarre and one of the leaders of the Calvinist party in France until her death in 1572. She was herself Princess of the Blood, Queen of Bearn and Navarre, and mother of Henri of Navarre, later to be Henri IV, King of France. She established Calvinism in her domains and exerted her influence to aid its foundation throughout France. Ministers sent from Geneva preached to and helped establish congregations of French Calvinists, known as Huguenots. They preached at open-air services as well, and it was at these preachings that the local authorities most often persecuted them. Noble ladies could often protect not only the preachers themselves but many of their less prominent converts from such hostility.

The balance of power between Catholics and Huguenots vacillated during a series of civil wars in France, but following the third civil war (1568–1570) and the St. Bartholomew's Eve Massacre in 1572, many thousands of Huguenots died. Those who survived formed a dissident minority utilizing what military strength was left to them. Women played little or no role militarily in the sixteenth century. As a result, if they wished to maintain their influence and religious faith as Calvinists, they often had to flee France.

Two of these prominent noblewomen, Charlotte de Bourbon-Montpensier and Louise de Coligny, ended up in the Netherlands and became, respectively, the third and fourth wives of William of Orange. Orange was a leader in the Dutch equivalent of the French civil wars, with the distinction that the Eighty Years' War was fought against Spain, a foreign power, as well as between dissidents in the Netherlands. The mothers of both women were themselves important in the Huguenot movement in its formative years and served as models for their daughters. Charlotte de Bourbon's mother, Jacqueline de Longwy, Duchesse de Montpensier, was not a convert herself, but was an influential intimate of Catherine de' Médicis and a champion of the Huguenot cause. Louise de Coligny's mother, Charlotte de Laval, was married to Gaspard de Coligny, who shared the leadership of the Calvinist party in France with Jeanne d'Albret. She corresponded with Calvin, converted before her husband did, and played an important regional role in the coming of the Reformation.[17]

The daughters pursued the interests of their mothers, demonstrating the way in which a strong faith had been transmitted. Charlotte de Bourbon had been a nun who fled the convent in 1571. With few possessions of her own she made her way to Germany and later to the court of William of Orange. Louise de Coligny fled to Germany after the St. Bartholomew's Eve Massacre, in which her father was murdered. After Charlotte's death in 1582, she in her turn married William and shouldered the responsibilities of administering his court and household and caring for his children, in particular the daughters of Charlotte. She and William had one child of their own, Frederick Henry, who became stadtholder of the Netherlands during its golden age in the seventeenth century.

In the struggle in the Netherlands, the Calvinists presented themselves as effective allies in the fight for national independence. Calvinism was to many Dutch not only a religious faith but a means by which they could defy Spanish Catholicism and what Spain represented to them as an oppressor. The Eighty Years' War had begun early in 1566 with the presentation to Marguerite of Parma, regent of Philip II of Spain, of a document known as the Compromise of the Nobility, urging the king to relax his enforcement of laws against heretics. Women were legally excluded as signers of this document. However, they not only directly influenced many men who signed but supported Calvinism as an extension of their political rights. One such influential lady was Petronella van Praet, Lady of Moerkerken and widow for ten years of Herman van Bronkhorst, Free Lord of Batenburg. As such, she exercised as lady dowager all the privileges of her husband's title although their eldest son had come of age. The family's lands, centered mainly near Nijmegen, had only within the past generation been brought under the hegemony of the Hapsburg king. They were considered a family of "rebels" even yet. Petronella was possessed of "more than ordinary independence." She saw in Calvinism, as did many of the gentry and nobility, a weapon against the encroachment of Spain on the traditional privileges her family exercised on their domains which encompassed the full administration of justice, civil and criminal, including the sentence of death and the issuing of edicts of law, levying of taxes, and appointing of various local officials. Petronella had been among the earlier Dutch converts to Calvinism. At his trial for rebellion against the Spanish crown in 1567 her son testified that for the past two or three years Calvinist preachers had frequented her castle. When the wave of iconoclasm swept the Netherlands in 1566, Petronella accompanied her son Dirk to the church that had been endowed by their family and supervised the destruction of the "images" there.[18]

When Calvinist rebels, both women and men, were condemned, their property and incomes were usually confiscated. Two annual rentals, for instance, were confiscated from Elisabeth van Rapenburch, who had fled along with her husband. These were properties that had come into the marriage from her side, and the total amount of 104 gulden was thus confiscated from her, "as it would be in fact for all Ladies [wives, in this sense] and Widows who had been condemned as fugitives, or executed."[19]

Women like Petronella van Praet and Elisabeth van Rapenburch, often widows, enjoyed a considerable amount of freedom of action; their first allegiance was to their families. In the Calvinist faith they found an ally against the Spanish king with the energy to carry on the fight for many years. An awareness of the importance of family connections, familial influence, and patronage are all integral to an understanding of the role of French and Dutch noblewomen in the Reformation.

What of middle-class women in these countries? Calvin had pitched his appeal to the ladies of the nobility in France, because he recognized the necessity of their support. Luther had the support of the princes in Germany, which was his primary concern, but his emotional appeal had been mainly to the middle class. Middle-class women were also early converts to Calvinism in France and the Netherlands, but have often filled the place of the anonymous in history because information on their activities is relatively inaccessible. One reason often cited for the appeal of Calvinism to upper-class women is that they alone had the leisure to read Scripture and the education to do so. In fact, Calvinism appealed most to artisans, and this appeal encompassed women as well as men, since middle-class women engaged in a wide variety of economic activities in urban centers. Rather than stagnating in a boring and futile existence within their homes, which, it has been charged, made them susceptible to any new doctrines that came their way, they worked in the shops, disciplined apprentices, and even ran the businesses themselves if widowed. Further down the social scale, they might be directly employed themselves, especially in the textile, clothing, or leather trades, or running inns and taverns. These women were excluded, with the noblewomen, from the highest levels of theological decision making within the Calvinist movement. However, they were encouraged to participate in ways which they had not been able to as Catholics. They could not become pastors or prophets — as the Anabaptist women might — but they took part fully in services conducted in the vernacular. Middle-class women could share in direct religious and political action linked with their occupational roles. For example, Elisabeth van den Kerck, a widow, was executed for her role in the Utrecht uprisings of 1566. She owned a tavern that provided the Calvinist gentlemen of the confederation of the nobility with a safe meeting place and was also charged with having aided and housed the image breakers. She was executed as much for political transgressions as for religious.[20]

In France and the Netherlands, the religious struggle was entangled with political struggle. In Italy and England the situation was markedly different. Local Italian rulers sided almost exclusively with the Catholic Church and their subjects took their cue from them. From its inception, also, the Italian Reformation differed from other Protestant movements. It borrowed much from the reforms of the humanists, such as Erasmus, and encouraged the reading of the classics, such as Cicero. A strong mystical element was present as well, however, so that followers of the movement were urged to contemplate Christ directly and seek as their goal mystical union with Christ himself. Vittoria Colonna, one of the noblewomen educated in the humanist tradition advocated by Erasmus, wrote that one must rise to God "on wings of faith and love. . . . They lift the soul above the mortal view. By true humility we reach the light. And know the sacred writings to be true. Read little, then, and believe the more." [21] The emphasis here is on Neo-Platonic ideals — that one must be educated but then also believe and take the leap beyond reason into mysticism. The constant emphasis on the pragmatic and the practical that is evident in Germany, Switzerland, and northern Europe as well, is here absent. After the Catholic Reformation in Italy, reforming clerical orders and revivalist preachers who originated within the church itself helped stifle these earlier traditions. The final blow to the Italian Reformation as such came with the establishment of the Roman Inquisition in 1542. After that time, the most timid expression of religious dissent could be squelched.

The Italian Reformation appears to have received direct impetus from noblewomen, who were important inspirationally in an elitist circle. In this respect, the Italian Reformation had more in common with Renaissance activities than with those of the various reformations across the Alps. After 1542, these noblewomen were effectively silenced when their views were condemned as heretical. Some, such as Isabella Bresegna, who died in Switzerland, chose exile as preferable to silence. Particularly interesting was Renée de France. Daughter of Louis XII of France, she was unable to assume the French throne because of her sex, and she became a political and religious pawn through her marriage to Ercole d'Este, Duke of Ferrara. Influenced by Marguerite of Navarre and the Christian humanists, she sympathized with the doctrines of reform and sheltered many French exiles during the 1530s. Her conversion to orthodox Catholicism, after the coming of the Inquisition, seems to have been feigned, with her primary goal that of regaining her own autonomy. Although she sympathized with Calvin's ideas, and corresponded with him, she could not take an open stand in favor of the reformed faith. She did not join that small minority in Italy who became wholehearted disciples of Calvinism, willing to sacrifice everything for their religion. The vast majority of those who supported reform supported the pope and never advocated any schism with the Roman Catholic Church. Renée's life exemplifies the difficulties inherent in adopting any reformist religious position in Italy. In any event, without hope of converting the Italian princes, politics did not become enmeshed in the Italian Reformation.[22]

In England the political situation differed again from that on the continent. The violent shifts and turns in religious policy during the sixteenth century in England were initiated by king or queen, and the people lived with them or chafed under them restively, but the nation was not torn by violent civil war in the sixteenth century. When Henry VIII came to the throne of England in 1509, he was an orthodox Catholic who recognized the pope as head of the church. Before he died in 1547, he declared himself head of the church, abolished monasticism, rejected the supremacy of the pope, and made significant liturgical changes. During the reign of his son, Edward VI, the two protectors Somerset and Northumberland brought a more distinctly Protestant identification to the English church. When Edward died in 1553, Henry's devoutly Catholic daughter, Mary Tudor, attempted to reestablish Catholicism in England. This might have been accomplished had she not died only five years later, for the vast majority of the English had not accepted the more radical forms of Protestantism that had appeared during Edward's reign. It remained for Henry's second daughter, Elizabeth I, to restore the Edwardian establishment (many of whose members had fled into exile during Mary's rule) and consolidate the position of what became known as the Anglican Church, or Church of England. In its main outlines this compromise religion was construed as broadly Catholic, so that the majority of English people might be incorporated into it with minimal difficulty. After about 1570 a distinction began to appear between "Catholic" and "Roman Catholic" for the first time. At about this time Puritanism became identifiable as a movement within the Anglican Church, connoting a desire to reform the church along more strictly Calvinist lines.

Throughout this period, religious faith was persecuted most often when it represented a challenge to political authority. The challenge was put directly by Thomas More to Henry VIII, and More was executed for his refusal to accept Henry's supremacy over that of the pope. Thus, he said that he died "the king's good servant but God's first." The question of which allegiance came first was a difficult one to answer, but answering it did not call forth systematic persecution until the reign of Mary Tudor, from 1553 to 1558. By this time a sizable minority of English had converted to Protestantism, and Mary's determination to stamp out this Protestant scourge resulted in the exile of hundreds of Protestants and the burning of close to 300 of their number at Smithfield.

Those Protestants who fled to the continent established communities of English refugees at Strasbourg, Frankfurt, Emden, Zurich, and Geneva, all places where the Reformation was strong and they would have certain refuge. The exiles were financed either by independent means or by a body of sustainers — chiefly, rich London merchants.

Such refugees fit into life around them with relative ease and were often afforded privileges as citizens of these towns when such a rank was commensurate with their status back in England. Of those who were socially and politically prominent we know quite a bit. Such a lady was Catherine Willoughby, Duchess of Suffolk. During the 1530s Catherine had been persuaded by the preacher Hugh Latimer to a more radical variety of Protestantism than Henry VIII's Anglo-Catholicism. She wished to see images and relics removed from churches, shrines destroyed, an end to pilgrimages, the reformation of the clergy, and Scripture read and heard in church in English rather than Latin. When Martin Bucer came to England in 1549, he was befriended by Catherine and taught her two sons at Cambridge. She attended many of his lectures as well. It was she who gave him a cow and calf that he might have fresh milk and nursed him when he fell sick until his wife Wibrandis arrived in England. After Bucer's death she helped Wibrandis move her family back to Switzerland. Upon the accession of Mary Tudor, Stephen Gardiner, onetime Bishop of Winchester who had been imprisoned by Edward VI, became lord chancellor. Catherine realized that her support of the Protestant cause and her outspoken hostility to Gardiner endangered her safety. She made her escape at the beginning of 1555, and with her husband and a retinue of servants, eventually made her way to Poland, where they remained until the death of Mary. The family returned to England in 1559, where Catherine became a notable proponent of Puritanism until her death.[23]

Such copious information can be obtained in Catherine's case because she was a prominent figure. We can only guess as to the number of middle-class women who were among the exiles, for the only study that surveys the Marian exiles in their entirety lists women indirectly, under their husbands or sons.[24] They certainly comprised at least one-fourth of the total, and probably more. Mrs. Jane Wilkinson, a widow, fled to Strasbourg at the urging of her friend Archbishop Cranmer in 1556. Alice Agar, a widow of Colchester, settled with her children in Geneva in 1557 and married a fellow exile that same year. These people were all reasonably affluent. Not so fortunate were those who remained in England. One of these was John Warne, an upholsterer, who was burned at Smithfield as a relapsed heretic in 1555, with friends and companions such as his wife Elizabeth following him in 1556. Margaret Polley, burned in 1555, affirmed that the "bread and wine were symbols of the Body and Blood of Christ," but "not as his body really and substantially." She was informed by the bishop of Rochester, who was interrogating her that she "was a silly woman, knew not what she said, and that it was the duty of every Christian to believe as the mother-church hath taught and doth teach." In 1556 Katherine Hut and Joan Horns were executed at Smithfield. Katherine said that Christ's true body and blood were not in the sacrament of the altar, which was a "dumb god, made with men's hands." "If you can make your god shed blood or show any condition of a true, lively body, then I will believe you," said Joan Horns. This denial of transubstantiation was typical of the beliefs of those executed during this period, and is lineally descended from the pragmatic views of the Lollards.[25]

After 1558–1559, when Elizabeth I consolidated the Reformation's achievements into the Anglican compromise, her subjects could worship in a variety of ways as long as their predilections did not run to treason, that is, support of Catholic Spain. Elizabeth finally ordered the execution of Mary Stuart, who had been exiled in England after Knox's revolution in Scotland, not because she was a Catholic but because she appeared as the focus of political discontent. Obedience to the king's constituted authority remained the major issue and was the foundation of Anglicanism to Elizabeth just as it had been to Henry VIII. Mindful of this important boundary, Catholic and Protestant women could worship, and if Roman Catholicism, or recusancy as it became known, was stifled by the government, it was not openly persecuted. Within the sphere of religious activity, since political activity was closed to them, women of the gentry and nobility in England played the same roles as did their counterparts on the continent. They set a religious example that accounted for many conversions and encouraged the religion. Catholic women such as Dorothy Lawson supported and sheltered priests, particularly Jesuits, while Puritan women such as Catherine of Suffolk and Frances, Countess of Sussex, supported ministers and established seminaries for the spread of the reformed faith. They influenced their children to take up a religious vocation, as did the Catholics, or to choose a mate of the proper religion.[26]

The rise of new religious orders and convents was one Catholic response to the Reformation. What can be inferred from the establishment of such institutions, as contrasted with the dissolution of monasteries and convents earlier in the sixteenth century? There were admittedly many poorly run convents (and monasteries) before the Reformation. Where spiritual goals had fallen from sight, the nunneries had disappeared easily. In other areas, such as Sweden, the nuns were simply pensioned off. They accepted this situation and, as a result, were not directly persecuted.

Occasionally a small group of nuns remained together after the dissolution of their convent. A group of five women from Kirklees in Yorkshire lived with their former prioress at Mirfield on their consolidated income of twenty pounds. Such an arrangement usually lasted only the duration of the nuns' lives. Marriage for the ex-religious was common, with statistics from Lincolnshire showing that approximately 18 of 61 nuns (29.5 percent) married, compared with 28 out of 108 religious and chantry priests (25.9 percent). This does not seem surprising, since most of these women had few other options, and apparently this was an acceptable procedure for ex-priests as well.[27]

In Germany the early converts to Lutheranism, such as Katherine von Bora, had left the convent voluntarily. Later, many nunneries were closed down against the wishes of the nuns. In Strasbourg, there had been a total of eight nunneries at the end of the fifteenth century. Even after the nuns were obliged to leave their cloisters by edict of the town council, their cause triumphed because their relatives prevailed upon the councilors to reopen the convents. Two of these, St. Margaret's and St. Nicholas's maintained their Catholic services, despite the arrival of such men as Bucer to preach to them. They heard him out in silence but refused to change their traditional service. Here was one instance where the nuns refused to submit and triumphed. Although their affairs were managed by the town council, they maintained their religious life intact.[28] This option, then, continued to remain open for upper-class and wealthy Catholic women in certain areas. It was no longer available for Protestant women.

For Protestant women, marriage was the acceptable option. The married Protestant woman controlled her own destiny within the limits of her household, just as the nun might within the confines of her convent. What the Protestants had done was shift the status of the wife within the family. This became most apparent in the writings of Puritan theologians, although we have already seen that marriage was dignified from the earliest days of Protestantism because of the new attitudes toward celibacy and sexuality the reformers expressed. Various Puritan theologians, already writing systematically on the subject of marriage during the reign of Elizabeth I, certainly viewed the wife as subordinate to the husband. The marriage relationship itself, however, was to be one of mutual aid, comfort, and sustaining companionship. Other treatises refer to the single essential division in the family as between the "governors" (which included husband and wife jointly) and "those that must be ruled" (children and servants). English Protestant women in particular had a reputation for living with great freedom within marriage. They were encouraged to be literate so that they might read the word of God for themselves and to take on much of the responsibility for teaching it to their children.

The sixteenth century marks the transition from medieval to modern world, and the Reformation era encompasses this period of transit with its mix of both worlds. We have already seen that in the localized, decentralized society of the feudal Middle Ages, women had greater opportunities within the family and community. During the sixteenth century, feudal society disappeared as the change to the modern states of princes advanced. The ensuing displacement of women was not necessarily a result of the Reformation. What does seem significant about the Reformation era, specifically, is that it was a period of upheaval that allowed — as do all such periods in history — women's roles to be less sharply defined or to be defined under the rubric of religious or political action rather than women's roles themselves. Katherine Zell was not concerned with the equality of women per se, but rather with the equality of mankind. In fact, the equality of women became for a time a corollary of the equality of mankind during the Reformation era, when society underwent radical religious change within a relatively short period and the scope of women's activities was temporarily broadened. As the sixteenth century drew to a close, the Reformation succeeded in some parts of Europe, such as areas in Germany and the Netherlands. In other areas, such as France, it failed.

In either case, what had been an open-ended situation for women became one of increasing rigidity. The upheaval was followed by a time of retrenchment, when the progressive elements from the standpoint of women's possibilities were expunged from these movements. One example of this conservative reaction regarded divorce. During the early Reformation, progressives had wished to grant divorce for adultery, desertion, continued absence, and even extreme incompatibility. By the end of the century, the rule in England was to allow remarriage only by a special act of Parliament for each case.[29] What the Reformation era witnessed was the changing delineation of women's roles. As this period drew to a close, women's roles became defined increasingly by sex — to the detriment of all women — rather than by class.

Notes

1. Natalie Z. Davis, "City Women and Religious Change in Sixteenth-Century France," *A Sampler of Women's Studies,* ed. Dorothy McGuigan, University of Michigan Center for Continuing Education of Women, Ann Arbor, 1973, pp. 23–25.
2. R. W. Southern, *Western Society and the Church in the Middle Ages,* Penguin Books, Middlesex, England, 1970, pp. 309–318; R. R. Post, *The Modern Devotion,* Leiden, 1968, esp. chaps. 5–6.
3. A. G. Dickens, *The English Reformation,* Schocken Books, New York, 1964, chap. 2.
4. John Thomson, *The Later Lollards,* Oxford University Press, Oxford, 1965, pp. 77, 106, 108–114, 123–128.
5. Desiderius Erasmus, *The Paraclesis,* John C. Olin, *Desiderius Erasmus: Christian Humanism and the Reformation,* Harper & Row, New York, 1965, pp. 96–97; Thomas More, letter to William Gunnel, quoted in Ruth Kelso, *Doctrine for the Lady of the Renaissance,* University of Illinois Press, Urbana, 1956, p. 62.
6. James K. McConica, *English Humanists and Reformation Politics,* Clarendon Press, Oxford, 1965, chap. 7; William Haugaard, "Katherine Parr: The Religious Convictions of a Renaissance Queen," *Renaissance Quarterly,* XXII, 4 (1969), 346–359; Pierre Jourda, *Marguerite d'Angouleme,* 2 vols., Paris, 1930; Nancy L. Roelker, "The Role of Noblewomen in the French Reformation," *Archiv für Reformationsgeschichte,* 63 (1972), 172–174; H. A. Enno van Gelder, *The Two Reformations in the Sixteenth Century,* The Hague, 1964, pp. 260–266; Henry Heller, "Marguerite of Navarre and the Reformers of Meaux," *Bibliothèque d'humanisme et Renaissance* (Summer 1970), 271–310.
7. Miriam U. Chrisman, "Women and the Reformation in Strasbourg, 1490–1530," *Archiv für Reformationsgeschichte,* 63 (1972), 143, 150; R. R. Post, *Kerkelijke verhoudingen in Nederland voor de Reformatie van ± 1500 tot ± 1580,* Utrecht, 1954, p. 131; Robert M. Kingdon, "The Control of Morals in Calvin's

Geneva," *The Social History of the Reformation,* eds. Lawrence P. Buck and Jonathan W. Zophy, Ohio State University Press, Columbus, 1972, pp. 4–5.

8. Kingdon, "The Control of Morals," pp. 5–6, 12; Philip E. Hughes, ed. and trans., *The Register of the Company of Pastors of Geneva in the Time of Calvin,* Eerdmans, Grand Rapids, Mich., 1966, pp. 58–59, 72–78.

9. Martin Luther, *Table Talk or Familiar Discourses,* trans. William Hazlitt, London, 1848, p. 299; *Selections from recently published sources of the Table Talk,* ed. and trans. Preserved Smith and Herbert Gallinger, Boston, 1915, pp. 45–46, 59.

10. Roland Bainton, *Women of the Reformation,* Augsburg Publishing House, Minneapolis, 1971, chaps. 1, 3, 4; Chrisman, "Women and the Reformation," pp. 152, 156–157.

11. Bainton, *Women of the Reformation,* chap. 4; Constantin Hopf, *Martin Bucer and the English Reformation,* Oxford, 1946.

12. Chrisman, "Women and the Reformation in Strasbourg," pp. 160–61; George H. Williams, *The Radical Reformation,* Westminster Press, Philadelphia, 1962, chap. 20.

13. Norman Cohn, *The Pursuit of the Millennium,* Secker & Warburg, London, 1957.

14. Originally collected in the seventeenth century and published in Thieleman van Braght, *The Bloody Theater or the Martyrs' Mirror,* Scottsdale, Pa., 1951, quoted in Hans J. Hillerbrand, ed., *The Protestant Reformation,* New York, 1968, pp. 147–152.

15. Quoted in John T. McNeill, *The History and Character of Calvinism,* Oxford University Press, New York, 1954, p. 178.

16. John Knox, *The Blast of the Trumpet Against the Monstrous Regiment of Women,* 1558; Patrick Collinson, "The Role of Women in the English Reformation, Illustrated by the Life and Friendships of Anne Locke," *Studies in Church History,* vol. 2, 1965, pp. 258–272; Lu Emily Pearson, *Elizabethans at Home,* Stanford University Press, Stanford, 1957, pp. 285–286.

17. Nancy L. Roelker, "The Appeal of Calvinism to French Noblewomen in the Sixteenth Century," *The Journal of Interdisciplinary History,* II (Spring 1972), 391–418; Roelker, "The Role of Noblewomen," pp. 192–193. I have utilized only a few examples from Roelker's studies, which examine this entire group of women over three generations.

18. H. A. Enno van Gelder, "Bailleul, Bronkhorst, Brederode," *Van Beeldenstorm tot Pacificatie,* Agon Elsevier, Amsterdam, 1964, pp. 49–50, 63, 65. Originally published in *De Gids,* jg. C, 1936, pp. 204–220, 348–375. All translations from the Dutch and French are my own.

19. For the terms of the sentence against her, see J. Marcus, *Sententien en Indagingen van den Hertog van Alba, Uitgesproken en Geslagen in zynen Bloedtraedt,* Amsterdam, 1735, pp. 465–469.

20. Ibid., pp. 325, 334–335.

21. Bainton, *Women of the Reformation,* chap. 12.

22. Charmarie Jenkins-Blaisdell, "Renée de France Between Reform and Counter-Reform," *Archiv für Reformationsgeschichte,* 63 (1972), 196–225; Bainton, *Women of the Reformation,* chap. 14.

23. Evelyn Read, *My Lady Suffolk: A Portrait of Catherine Willoughby, Duchess of Suffolk,* Knopf, New York, 1963; Hopf, *Martin Bucer,* pp. 14, 22–23.

24. Christina H. Garrett, *The Marian Exiles, 1553–1559: A Study in the Origins of Elizabethan Puritanism,* Cambridge University Press, Cambridge, 1938.

25. James E. Oxley, *The Reformation in Essex to the Death of Mary,* Manchester, 1965, pp. 194–196, 218, 223–224.

26. Sister Joseph Damien Hanlon, "These Be But Women," *From the Renaissance to the Counter-Reformation,* ed. Charles H. Carter, Random House, New York, 1965; Lawrence Stone, *The Crisis of the Aristocracy 1558–1641,* Oxford University Press, Oxford, 1965, pp. 738–739; Pearson, *Elizabethans at Home,* pp. 117–119.

27. Dom David Knowles, *The Religious Orders in England,* vol. 3: *The Tudor Age,* Cambridge University Press, Cambridge, 1959, pp. 75, n.3, 169–170, 412–413.

28. Chrisman, "Women and the Reformation," pp. 163–166.

29. Marshall M. Knappen, *Tudor Puritanism,* University of Chicago Press, Chicago, 1939; Levin L. Schücking, *The Puritan Family: A Social Study from the Literary Sources,* Schocken Books, New York, 1970.

Suggestions for Further Reading

Bainton, Roland. *Women of the Reformation in Germany and Italy.* Augsburg Publishing House, Minneapolis, 1971.

———. *Women of the Reformation in France and England.* Augsburg Publishing House, Minneapolis, 1973.

Biéler, André. *L'homme et la femme dans la morale calviniste. La doctrine reformée sur l'amour, le marriage, le célibat, le divorce, l'adultère et la prostitution, considerée dans son cadre historique.* Geneva, 1963.

Bolton, Brenda M. "Mulieres Sanctae." In Ecclesiastical History Society, London, *Sanctity and Secularity: The Church and the World,* ed. Derek Baker. Blackwell, Oxford, 1973. Vol. 10 in Studies in Church History.

Calvin, Jean. *Institutes of the Christian Religion,* ed. John T. McNeill, trans. Ford L. Battles. Westminster Press, Philadelphia, 1960. Vols. 20 and 21 in the Library of Christian Classics.

Chrisman, Miriam U. *Strasbourg and the Reform.* Yale University Press, New Haven, 1967.

———. "Women and the Reformation in Strasbourg, 1490–1530." *Archiv für Reformationsgeschichte,* 63 (1972).

Cohn, Norman. *The Pursuit of the Millennium.* Secker & Warburg, London, 1957.

Collinson, Patrick. "The Role of Women in the English Reformation, Illustrated by the Life and Friendships of Anne Locke." In Ecclesiastical History Society, London, Studies in Church History, vol. 2, 1965.

Davis, Natalie Z. "City Women and Religious Change in Sixteenth-Century France." *A Sampler of Women's Studies,* ed. Dorothy McGuigan. University of Michigan Center for Continuing Education of Women, Ann Arbor, 1973.

Erasmus, Desiderius. *Christian Humanism and the Reformation: Selected Writings,* ed. and trans. John C. Olin. Harper & Row, New York, 1965.

———. *The Colloquies of Erasmus,* trans. Craig R. Thompson. University of Chicago Press, Chicago, 1965.

Foxe, John. *Acts and Monuments.* London, 1631. Modern reprint published by AMS Press, New York, 1965.

Garrett, Christina H. *The Marian Exiles, 1553–1559: A Study in the Origins of Elizabethan Puritanism.* Cambridge University Press, Cambridge, 1938.

George, Charles, and Katherine George. *The Protestant Mind of the English Reformation, 1570–1640.* Princeton University Press, Princeton, 1961.

Goff, Cecilie. *A Woman of the Tudor Age: Katherine Willoughby, Duchess of Suffolk.* London, 1930.

Hanlon, Sister Joseph Damien. "These Be But Women." *From the Renaissance to the Counter-Reformation,* ed. Charles H. Carter. Random House, New York, 1965.

Haugaard, William. "Katherine Parr: The Religious Convictions of a Renaissance Queen." *Renaissance Quarterly,* XXII, 4 (1969).

Hillerbrand, Hans J., ed. *The Protestant Reformation.* Harper & Row, New York, 1969.

Hughes, Philip E., ed. and trans. *The Register of the Company of Pastors of Geneva in the Time of Calvin.* Eerdmans, Grand Rapids, Mich., 1966.

Jenkins-Blaisdell, Charmarie. "Renée de France Between Reform and Counter-Reform." *Archiv für Reformationsgeschichte,* 63 (1972).

Kelso, Ruth. *Doctrine for the Lady of the Renaissance.* University of Illinois Press, Urbana, 1956.

Kingdon, Robert M. "The Control of Morals in Calvin's Geneva." *The Social History of the Reformation,* eds. Lawrence Buck and Jonathan Zophy. Ohio State University Press, Columbus, 1972.

Luther, Martin. *Table Talk,* ed. and trans. T. G. Tappert. Muhlenberg Press, Philadelphia, 1959. Vol. 54 of Luther's *Works.*

———. *Conversations with Luther,* ed. and trans. Preserved Smith and H. P. Gallinger. Boston, 1915.

———. *Martin Luther: Selections from His Writings,* ed. John Dillenberger. Doubleday, Garden City, N.Y., 1961.

McConica, James. *English Humanists and Reformation Politics under Henry VIII and Edward VI.* Clarendon Press, Oxford, 1965.

Mattingly, Garrett. *Catherine of Aragon.* Random House, New York, 1941.

Parker, T. H. L., ed. *English Reformers.* Westminster Press, Philadelphia, 1966. Vol. 26 of Library of Christian Classics, includes writings of William Tyndale and Hugh Latimer.

Pearson, Lu Emily. *Elizabethans at Home.* Stanford University Press, Stanford, 1957.

Power, Eileen. *Medieval English Nunneries, 1275–1535.* Cambridge University Press, Cambridge, 1922.

Read, Evelyn. *My Lady Suffolk: A Portrait of Catherine Willoughby, Duchess of Suffolk,* Knopf, New York, 1963.

Reuther, Rosemary Radford. *Religion and Sexism: Images of Women in the Jewish and Christian Traditions.* Simon & Schuster, New York, 1974.

Roelker, Nancy L. "The Appeal of Calvinism to French Noblewomen in the Sixteenth Century." *The Journal of Interdisciplinary History,* II (Spring 1972).

———. "The Role of Noblewomen in the French Reformation." *Archiv für Reformationsgeschichte,* 63 (1972).

———. *Queen of Navarre: Jeanne d'Albret.* Belknap Press, Cambridge, Mass., 1968.

Southern, Richard W. *Western Society and the Church in the Middle Ages.* Penguin Books, Middlesex, England, 1970.

Thomson, John. *The Later Lollards, 1414–1520.* Oxford University Press, London, 1965.

Trimble, William R. *The Catholic Laity in Elizabethan England.* Belknap Press, Cambridge, Mass., 1964.

Williams, George H. *The Radical Reformation.* Westminster Press, Philadelphia, 1962.

Woodward, William H. *Desiderius Erasmus Concerning the Aim and Method of Education.* Cambridge University Press, Cambridge, 1904.

8

Toward a New Lifestyle: Women in Preindustrial Capitalism

Richard T. Vann

Changes in women's roles during the Reformation had been largely unintended and impermanent. But industrialization profoundly transformed the lives of all people in western Europe during the following three centuries. Richard T. Vann notes that major changes already appeared prior to the period historians usually consider as the Industrial Revolution. He asks two vital questions: How can we discover what the quality of life was for ordinary people, and how can we evaluate that information once we gather it? Vann investigates women's active role in changing patterns of sexual behavior, demographic trends, new attitudes toward childrearing, early forms of birth control, and participation in production. Finally, he observes that women began to find a public voice, if in a limited context.

Men and women working together in textile production in the eighteenth century, a plate from the great *Encyclopédie,* edited by Diderot and d'Alembert.

When women began to write and publish books at the end of the Renaissance, one way they countered the misogynist tone of so many earlier writers was by compiling lists of the eminent women of antiquity. They celebrated women notable for feats of war and statecraft, like Cleopatra and Semiramis; or, alternatively, heroic in their chastity, like Susannah or Lucretia. The epoch just beginning in the sixteenth century was to be equally rich in celebrated women. Elizabeth the Great of England comes immediately to mind, along with her contemporary, the queen of France, Catherine de Médicis. St. Theresa of Avila was as remarkable for her administrative skill as for her devotions and spiritual writings. But it is not our purpose in this chapter to describe these famous women. Instead of a history conceived as the *Lives of Illustrious Women,* we shall focus attention on the masses of ordinary women living their everyday lives in Europe and the European colonies in North America during the period from the Reformation of the sixteenth century to the Industrial Revolution, which began in England toward the end of the eighteenth century. This necessarily involves us in a "history of the inarticulate"; for most women of the time could not read or write, and even the few journals, account books, and letters the literate women left do not bulk large when compared to the archives of political history. Yet, fortunately, we can supplement the sparse literary record with a good deal of statistical evidence about the way women lived before the development of industrial capitalism.

Juliet Mitchell in her book *Women's Estate* has provided us with a useful framework for analyzing the status and lifestyles of women. She distinguishes four areas of women's life and work: reproduction, production, socialization, and sexuality. The four are, of course, intimately interrelated. For example, in the process of socialization, women impart the values that will do much to govern their children's subsequent behavior as producers and reproducers. It might happen that a breakthrough toward liberation of one area would thus have a liberating effect on the others; but it also might turn out that advances in one area would be compensated for by increased repression in others. We must, therefore, not only examine each area in turn but also the relationships among them.

Reproduction

"There is no wealth but life," as John Ruskin said; and the length of life itself is the most basic sign of welfare and status. During by far the greatest part of human history, women have been relatively deprived of life. Fewer girl babies are born (the ratio of about 100 to every 105 boys seems constant); and for millennia females had a lower life expectancy than males. There are several possible explanations for this. They may simply have had less to eat than men. Childbirth, too, was hazardous, and there were few medical techniques for alleviating its perils; indeed, up to the end of the nineteenth century physicians probably did more harm than good to their patients. Today, women can expect to live several years longer than men. This is because they are less vulnerable to the degenerative diseases of old age, especially cancer and disorders of the circulatory system. In earlier times, both sexes had life expectancies at birth of less than thirty years, and even someone who lived to age thirty would scarcely live much beyond forty. So, as the life expectancies of both men and women increased, that of women lengthened more, since they were now living to the age when their greater resistance to the degenerative diseases could come into play.

We do not know exactly when the life expectancy of women first began to exceed that of men, but we can be reasonably sure that during these 300 years in preindustrial Europe women were beginning to outlive men. People alive at the time certainly believed this, and the belief is supported by the statistics we can recreate. In the mid-seventeenth century life expectancy of the sexes was about equal; by the late eighteenth century women had taken the lead, which they have never relinquished.

For some middle-class women, outliving men created the opportunity for virtually the only independent position available to them in the secular world — widowhood. Of course, there must have been much heartbreak behind the longevity figures. Widows were not only bereft of their lifetime companions but also were plunged into poverty through the loss of their husbands' earnings. Widows, however, were virtually the only women who had the possibility of economic self-sufficiency and who were free of a man's domestic supervision. Only widows could draw up wills, since they typically had been declared the executrices of their husbands' estates. A widow could also make her own decision about whom to marry with relative freedom from family pressure. This is demonstrated by the fact that the large literature advising people what qualities they ought to look for in a future spouse addressed itself to men and widows but not to unmarried women. Thus, given the patriarchal nature of preindustrial Europe, a demographic situation that produced many widows was comparatively favorable to the position of women. No wife could attain the social freedom available to some widows.

In theory, and to a great extent in practice also, marriage was the only career available to a woman throughout this period. The one socially acceptable alternative — for Catholics only — was the convent. But there was a considerable difference among the various parts of Europe in the ages at which women married and in the proportion of women who married. Roughly speaking, from the sixteenth century onward, a line on the map of Europe from Trieste, at the head of the Adriatic, to St. Petersburg (now Leningrad) would divide Europe into sharply contrasting regions in this respect. North and west of this line the age of marriage for women was relatively late. On the average, women married for the first time in their mid-twenties and quite a few women never married at all. South and east of this line the average age at first marriage for women was substantially lower. Most women were already married by the age of twenty, and celibacy for women was virtually unknown. How did it affect the ordinary woman's life to marry relatively late or not at all? Opportunities for unmarried women to work were drastically limited, as we shall see, and most of the writers of the time held up the "old maid" to scorn, just as they urged the widow to a quick remarriage. But we must always remember that virtually all these writers were men, and in all likelihood they felt to some degree threatened by the spectacle of women without their "natural" lords, their fathers or husbands. The same line between Trieste and St. Petersburg that separates the Europe of late marriages and high celibacy from that of all but universal and early marriage also serves as a rough boundary between advanced and backward parts of Europe during this period. All the great states and kingdoms — Austria, England, France, the Netherlands, Prussia, Spain, and Sweden — were in the zone of late marriage and high celibacy. Let us see how these demographic facts were related to the larger economy.

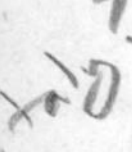

There seems little doubt that the women (and men) of western Europe were better off, because serfdom had largely disappeared, industry was more advanced, and the standard of living was higher. One reason for this economic development was directly related to the relatively late age at first marriage. For maximum productivity, the most suitable population is one that has the largest proportion of people of the age that can do full-time work, with the smallest possible number of people who are too young or too old to work. If women marry early, they not only deprive society of their labor during their early twenties, when they are most likely to become pregnant, they also produce a relatively high number of infants who require support. The nothern and western European fertility pattern maximized the number of productive workers in society. This was done without any state policy to encourage it, and there is little to suggest that women had much say in the decision to delay their own marriages. It seems most likely that inheritance customs and the necessity of providing dowries for daughters who married operated to delay marriages and to prevent some women from marrying at all. However, daughters were not entirely without influence. If they wished to marry for love, they were more likely to marry early than late — thus departing from the demographic norm.

Women shared along with men in the economic advantages that this demographic pattern made possible. In addition, it seems likely that a higher age at marriage for women reduced the submissiveness with which the bride entered her marriage, especially when — as not infrequently happened — she was older than her husband. Sometimes unmarried women were saving and raising their own dowries, as in Norwegian peasant society and also in parts of England, where women tended to marry men two or three years their junior. It was the savings the women could build up from their earnings that enabled the couple to marry and take a cottage. Something like this was still done in traditional Irish society in the twentieth century, as women left for New York or Boston to work as domestic servants, saved up enough money for their "fortune" or dowry, and then returned to marry a farmer.

Related to this pattern of late marriages was another even more significant development in the history of women — the systematic control of human fertility. In several of the parishes that have been thoroughly investigated, we find that ordinary people in sixteenth- and seventeenth-century France and England tended to have children very quickly after marriage. Often the bride was already pregnant at marriage. But in some places, particularly in the late seventeenth century, after the birth of the third or fourth child, births became less frequent. This appears to have been a matter of deliberate choice and not only the result of women's aging. Figure 8–1 shows that women of the same age who had recently married, and thus were starting their families, consistently bore more children than those who had been married for several years and already had given birth to two or three children. The explanations for this are still necessarily tentative. Infanticide and induced abortions were practiced in classical Greece and Rome and in some primitive cultures as well. However, literary evidence (which is scanty) suggests that in preindustrial Europe families limited their size mostly through contraception. Since no contraceptive devices existed before the mid-nineteenth century, the most likely explanation is that contraception was effected through the practice of the male's withdrawal before orgasm (coitus interruptus) or that couples engaged in sexual intercourse less frequently after several years of marriage. The complex relation between contraception and sexuality will be discussed in the next section; but even if it had had no effect on the expression of sexuality, the advent of family limitation alone was epoch-making because it freed women from a life largely devoted to continual childbearing.

FIGURE 8–1

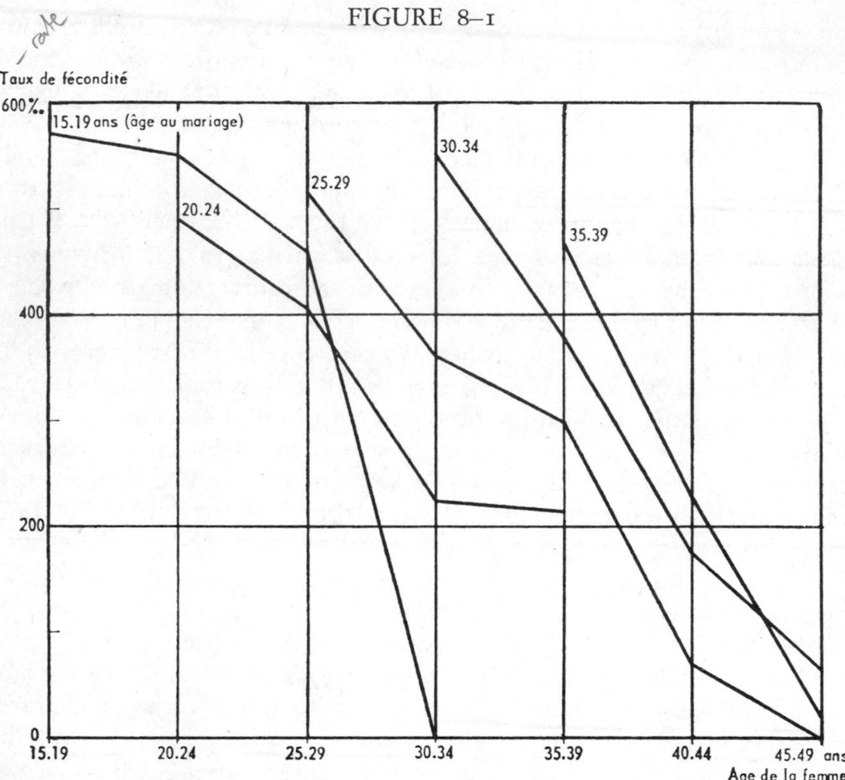

Women's fertility, by age, in a parish where family limitation is being practiced (Châtillon-sur-Seine, near Paris, from 1772 to 1784). The vertical axis is the fecundity rate and the horizontal the age of the woman. Only women who remained married through the age of 45 are included. At every age except 20–24, women of the same age who have just married have markedly higher fertility than those married five, ten, or fifteen years earlier. (Reprinted, by permission, from Antoinette Chamoux and Cécile Dauphin, "La contraception avant la Révolution française," *Annales: Economies, Sociétés, Civilisations,* 24, no. 3, 672.)

Sexuality

One indicator of the general status of women is the amount of social freedom allowed for the expression of female sexuality. If one turns to the official prescribers of morality during this period — the clergy — women were supposed to have little latitude indeed. Puritan divines, and Catholics in the Pauline tradition, excoriated the female sex as the defective portion of humanity through whom the human race was infected with sin. Such writers particularly dreaded women's sexuality and the havoc it might wreak on male virtue (for there was as yet no notion that women were asexual beings). The physiological theories of the Middle Ages, which still prevailed in modified form, held that women were more capable of sexual pleasure than men. Men were advised to exercise precautions lest the libidinous nature of women break forth. When one looks at the books that stipulate ideal conduct for men and women, the overwhelming place of chastity in the female scheme of virtues is striking. It might almost be said to have been a female virtue, in that it was seldom mentioned as an ideal for males. Chastity demanded a woman's virginity until marriage and fidelity to her husband after marriage. Once she married, it was considered her husband's responsibility to ensure his wife's faithfulness by seeing that her libidinous urgings were never aroused. Thus, the marriage manuals of preindustrial Europe gave advice exactly the reverse of what such books counsel today. They admonished the husband not to arouse his wife to any expectation of sexual pleasure. At best, the couple were told that they might experience some pleasure, so long as it was moderate — like the light supper that a well-fed person might take, as one of them puts it.

Though this repressive attitude toward sexuality is often attributed to Puritanism, it is in fact found in the writings of Catholics as well as Protestants, laymen and clergy alike, from all over Europe, and before Puritanism was ever heard of. Rather than arising only from Puritanism, men's austere attitude toward sexual self-expression, especially by women, probably resulted from a general impulse toward greater rigor and discipline that we shall also see in connection with education and socialization.

Such an attitude is also reflected in the customs surrounding marriage. The major function of marriage remained unaltered — to cement an alliance between families and transmit family property. This process is familiar in the dynastic politics of the period, when the various royal families of Europe sought to extend their territories and influence through the arrangements of favorable marriage contracts. This same concern motivated noble fathers and fathers from the high bourgeoisie, who were perhaps even more preoccupied with family marriage arrangements. Both fathers and husbands insisted on female chastity to ensure that all heirs would be the legitimate offspring of their respective families. Moreover, parents who calculated how many children they wished to support, and practiced coitus interruptus, cannot have made sexual pleasure the goal for themselves. This also reinforced the belief that women should not be tempted to sexual pleasure. Yet, at the same time, this kind of contraception severed the connection theologians tried to maintain between sexual intercourse and procreation, and therefore did allow the enjoyment of sex for its own sake. For this reason, moralists of the times denounced coitus interruptus as "unnatural."

We can see the forces affecting the expression or repression of female sexuality in a better light if we turn from the moral exhortations of the time to actual practice, insofar as we can infer it from the rising rates for illegitimate births and premarital pregnancies. Here the evidence is still scanty, but it seems that there was widespread premarital sexual activity, at least in the English-speaking world. In eighteenth-century England from one-third to one-half of the brides who were capable of having children were already pregnant when they married. In the early seventeenth century prenuptial pregnancy was perhaps half what it became in the late eighteenth. (The late-eighteenth-century rate, incidentally, was about twice the rate in the same rural areas in 1938.) The rate of illegitimate births and prenuptial pregnancies was also high in Norway. It seems to have been consistently lower in Scotland and in France, although some increase in prenuptial pregnancies was noted there too.

It may be that these high rates of prenuptial pregnancy resulted in part from an understanding in peasant societies that it was permissible for betrothed couples to have sexual relations without waiting for the wedding ceremony. Given their knowledge of contraceptive techniques, there probably was even more premarital sexual intercourse than resulted in bridal pregnancy.

The fact that the ideals presented in sermons and conduct books, which presumably were reinforced in the confessional and by pastoral precept (if not always example), contrast so sharply with the actual practice of peasant societies suggests that lower-class women gained some sexual freedom, at least before marriage. After marriage, such freedom was chiefly indulged in by members of the aristocracy among whom adultery was common. The ideal of chastity seems to be part of a cluster of ideals — such as sobriety, hard work, and thriftiness — which the upper classes urged upon the lower. Not coincidentally, these were the desiderata of a docile and productive laboring force.

Production

The place of women in the productive order before the Industrial Revolution has been the subject of no little romanticization. Perhaps some of this can be detected in such evidence as the charming domestic scene shown at the beginning of this chapter, which the great French *Encyclopedia* of the eighteenth century used to illustrate the technology of weaving. In domestic industry in its ideal form, every member of the family contributes something toward the production of the finished article. While the father weaves, assisted by his older sons, the mother attends to the spinning.

Her daughter helps prepare the wool for the spinning wheel, while the youngest children make the thread up into a skein. Such collaboration certainly represents the ideals of the time, which mostly means what the rich thought was the most desirable state for the laboring poor. No one had any doubt that children were better off employed. Daniel Defoe exults whenever he finds child labor, and commends one town because even the four- and five-year-olds were at work all day, bringing in their few coppers a week for their families. Similarly, working-class women expected to work for wages whenever they had the opportunity. Even upper-class women lived busy and productive lives; the idea that women whose husbands could afford it should be ladies of leisure was just coming into fashion among the nobility and the richest mercantile families in the seventeenth century.

Women and children were expected to work because most of Europe still lived uncomfortably close to the starvation line. Disastrous famines broke out in France during the glorious reign of Louis XIV, and they were common throughout Germany during the Thirty Years' War and its aftermath. Though few people were recorded as actually dying of starvation, many were so weakened by malnutrition that they fell victim to diseases a well-nourished person could have thrown off. Such conditions allowed few to remain idle by choice. Yet, there was constant underemployment, and in periods of economic crisis industrial workers lost their jobs. Anyone who could work most of the time counted himself or herself fortunate.

Most people were engaged primarily in the production of food, and the farm housewife probably worked even harder than her husband, who had at least some seasonal respite from working the fields. There was little that she did not do in the fields herself: reaping, threshing, collecting and spreading dung, and even plowing were all tasks that women performed. Peasant women were considered neither weak nor delicate. Ralph Josselin, a well-to-do seventeenth-century English clergyman who probably counted himself one of the gentry, notes incidentally in his diary that he and his wife uprooted a dangerously rotten tree on their farm. They both narrowly escaped injury as the tree fell. In addition to participating in general agricultural chores, almost everywhere women took care of the gardening, dairying, and poultry, and traditionally kept for their own the cash that came in for these products.

Women also did much of what contemporaries called housewifery. We must understand what this term meant if we are to grasp what most women's life was like. Most of what we know of housewifery comes from the theoretical treatises that men wrote about it; women, so far as we know, never wrote on this subject, nor indeed could they have found any time to do so if they did all the prodigious work that the men's treatises prescribed for them. The sort of value that men set on good housewifery can be seen in the will written by a seventeenth-century English yeoman.

In it he made his wife his executrix, as did most men who left wills. He says he is "well assured she may take the executorship upon her, having sufficient to pay my legacies with a competent portion for her plentiful maintenance, as in conscience I am bound to do, she having always carried herself as a very loving and dutiful wife to me, being a special means by her good housewifery, painfulness, and diligent walking in her calling to raise that estate the Lord hath blessed us withall."

Housewifery went well beyond what a modern woman generally means by "occupation: housewife." A farm of any size resembled a small multipurpose factory, for most things in common use were made on the property rather than bought. It had its labor force — the children of the family and, in richer farming areas of Europe (perhaps one household in three) servants.[1] The housewife supervised all their activities. If necessary, she disciplined both servants and children. (Samuel Pepys's wife, for example, frequently took the back of her hand to her maidservants.) She had to get up herself at dawn to make sure that none of the children or servants lay abed (only the sluggard would still be asleep by 4:30 A.M. of a summer's day). She saw to it that the soap was boiled and the candles molded, and she was likely herself to concoct medications from herbs grown in her kitchen garden. Since most foods underwent all the stages of their preparation in the household, it was much more common to bake bread than to buy loaves already baked. In northern Europe the housewife also supervised the brewing of beer in the domestic malthouse. Each household made its own butter and cheeses and preserved its own food. Meat had to be smoked or salted when there was not enough fodder to keep animals alive through the winter. When fruit trees, bushes, and vines were bearing, women made jellies and conserves. In addition to these seasonal tasks women, of course, cooked the daily meals, did the washing, produced the cloth for the household's own use, and sewed the family's clothing. Responsibilities of this kind remained a part of housewifery well after the beginning of the Industrial Revolution. As late as the middle of the nineteenth century, writers urged housewives who had moved into suburban villas around the great cities to put the attached grounds to good use by keeping a cow, a pig, and some hens for the delights of fresh cream and eggs.

As if these duties were not enough, wives whose husbands did not have enough land to support the family fully worked at supplementary employments. The most common combination was weaving and farming, with the wife and other women workers taking responsibility for the spinning of thread to be worked up in the loom. Many of the male hand-loom weavers who put up such a tenacious, if doomed, resistance to the power looms of the early nineteenth century were enabled to do so by their possession of some land and the fact that their wives and daughters added to their earnings by participating in these side employments.

The wife of an artisan or small shopkeeper also shared substantially in the world of work, though her participation was circumscribed by her position in the family and she could seldom enter a trade except as her husband's assistant or widow. In medieval Europe, women usually had been admitted to the craft guilds and, as guild members, could enter contracts and were responsible for their own debts. The guilds were now in decay, and the newer forms of commercial organization were almost entirely male dominated. Since men in all trades objected to competition from lower-paid women, it is not surprising that they tried to confine them to the least lucrative work. Throughout this period men were invading trades traditionally exercised by women, just as they had already ousted them from work such as wholesale brewing. The *cahiers* drawn up for presentation to the French Estates General in 1789 complain of the incursion of men into dressmaking and hairdressing. In England men — "male midwives," as they rather oddly called themselves — even began to displace women from delivering babies. A good deal of the practice of medicine remained, however, in women's hands. The use of herbal medicines was widespread and was generally carried on by women, whose recipes were the chief prescriptions of the time. This folk medicine flourished alongside the more learned, though probably no more efficacious, medicine practiced in the larger towns by physicians and, much lower on the social scale, by barber/surgeons — all of whom were men.[2] Even sophisticated people often preferred to consult a herbalist, who was, quite often, a white witch. But it is not clear that any woman could make a living practicing this sort of medicine. It seems instead to have been a side employment.

There was, of course, always unskilled labor for women. They were employed as mowers, reapers, and sheepshearers — drawing less than half the wages paid men doing the same kind of work. Most unmarried women were employed as maidservants, placing themselves under the discipline of another household and working for scanty wages, though food, lodging, and sometimes clothing as well were supplied.

With respect to employment, the middle-class woman was in some ways at a disadvantage compared to the working-class one. There was little paid work she could do other than manual labor, which was incompatible with her middle-class rank. There were very few secretaries, and all of them were men, as were most teachers. The middle-class woman who was waiting to be married had virtually nothing else to do except be a governess of another person's children or a lady-in-waiting to a gentlewoman. Both of these were in fact only the most prestigious kinds of domestic service.

Increasingly, the most common type of wage labor for women was the manufacture of textiles. Before the Industrial Revolution it was the drapers or clothiers — all men — who traded the finished cloth. They gave the raw materials — packs of wool — to domestic weavers, from whom they picked up the finished cloth. Weaving and wool combing, stages in the production of worsted cloth, were done almost entirely by men. It was sometimes said that women could not operate the looms because it was beyond their physical strength. Likewise, they purportedly were also incapable of pushing the heated combs through the pelt in the hot and smoky quarters of the wool comber. However, women did jobs just as physically taxing in other parts of the economy. The assignment of work by sex seems instead to be a feature of the increasing specialization of labor in one of the most technologically advanced sectors of the economy. Women's particular task was the less-well-paid job of preparing the yarn for the loom — work so identified with women that the Wife of Bath listed spinning along with tears and deceit as God's particular gifts to womankind, and the English word for an unmarried woman came to be "spinster." It is often said that cottage industry of this sort was free of the evils for the working class that attended the Industrial Revolution. This is hard to establish if one looks purely at the economic facts, for factory workers probably had a higher real income than people in cottage industries, and hours of work were probably just as long in the domestic workshop as in the factory. Child labor, as we have seen, was no invention of the Industrial Revolution; indeed, it was curtailed only after the earliest stages of industrialization. Yet there is no doubt that many workers, both male and female, made heroic efforts to continue in domestic industry even when it meant pitting their unaided hands and muscles against power-driven machinery that could produce ten times as much. This preference is impossible to understand if one looks simply at the apparent rise in the standard of living of factory workers. The explanation seems to lie in the way that household work coordinated with other aspects of life.

Early factory workers, most of them country folk accustomed to the rhythms of an agricultural life, had to keep pace with the rapid and monotonous tempo of the machines. Discipline was severe: punctuality and neatness were particularly demanded. Whereas — to borrow a distinction made by Karl Marx — the workers had once at least owned their own tools, even though they did not own the raw materials they worked up, now they owned neither tools nor raw material, and thus were totally subject to regulation of their time by their employers.

It is hard to tell whether women felt the shock of these changes more than men. In general, their lot under preindustrial capitalism was a constant round of hard and ill-compensated toil. Yet the framework of cottage industry was favorable to the integration of various female roles, especially those of production and socialization, whereas the development of industrial capitalism led to a much greater division or specialization of labor than had ever been known before, and thus to a splitting apart of these roles. It became increasingly difficult for ordinary women both to work and to perform most of the functions of housewifery and motherhood. The older style of integration of roles persisted on the family farms (one reason for their idealization) and among women who could afford servants but quickly died out in the urban working class.

This process was symbolized in the very language of factory owners. With little thought for the wholeness of men and women, they simply referred to their workers as "hands." Some women may have been only too delighted to leave the home and go out to work; but for most, despite the long hours, low wages, and difficult working conditions, domestic industry seemed preferable to going out to the factory. Yet the economic strength of the latter was overwhelming and virtually all cottage workshops were shortly put out of business. If the advantages of division of labor and economic productivity were to be turned to women's advantage, the struggle to do so would be a long one, and it is yet to be won.

Socialization

Adults have always inculcated the ideals of the culture in their children and passed on to them the skills needed for work and for adaptation to the existing political and social structure. In all societies, some of this conscious and unconscious teaching has been done distinctively by women. But no culture has considered this acculturation such a monumental task, nor entrusted it so completely to women, as our own. The first steps in this process were taken during the period of preindustrial capitalism.

Broadly speaking, the attitude of medieval parents toward child raising differed from our own because "childhood" was not recognized as an epoch in life. Children in medieval paintings are depicted simply as adults on a miniature scale, and this aptly represents their view of children. After the period of gross physical dependency was over and the child could feed and dress himself or herself, he or she was treated as a miniature adult. There was no conception of childlike innocence; adults had no inhibitions about playing with their children's genitals or telling bawdy jokes in their presence. No games or stories were reserved for children; Louis XIII of France, who grew up in the early seventeenth century, played golf and tennis as a child, while the adults around him did not feel silly playing with hoops. Children's literature was not a segregated genre; Colbert, the chief minister of Louis XIV, used to divert himself when the office routine became too tedious by having some of the original Mother Goose stories read to him.

Just as women were able to work without giving up all influence as mothers in the conditions of preindustrial capitalism, so men were able to take a larger part in the socialization of their children than is possible when work routines require that they be on their employers' premises most of the time. But neither the mother nor the father had nearly as much responsibility for socialization of the children as seems natural to us; siblings and relatives had rather more, and much was learned from simply hanging around other adults and children (and later from work and apprenticeship). A sharp contrast between our own society and that of this period requires emphasis. We expect the schools to do a good deal of the work of socialization; this is one of the reasons why, through compulsory school-attendance laws, we conscript all persons between the ages of six and sixteen into them. But in their origins, in the Middle Ages, schools were not particularly expected to form the character of their pupils. Children attended school chiefly to learn a trade. Reading and knowledge of theology and canon law qualified one not only for the priesthood but for the highest positions in the service of the king. In preindustrial Europe the ways to rise dramatically in the social order and make a great deal of money were to marry into wealth or to have a successful career in high political office, for which training in canon law (or, in England, common law) was normally required.

Because they concentrated so completely on imparting bodies of knowledge by rote memorization, the pedagogical practices of medieval and early modern schools seem somewhat strange. Children of all ages were mingled together in the same classes, and classes could be repeated or taken in a different order, so that a child of six might find himself sitting next to a lad of sixteen. Since most formal education was in the hands of the church, it was mostly done by men. Although there were a few nunneries where young girls of the upper class could be sent for instruction, from the late Middle Ages the majority of teachers and pupils alike were males. Beyond the elementary schools, education was a male monopoly.

During the sixteenth and seventeenth centuries some changes may be detected in attitudes toward socialization that left the mother in a situation of ambiguous demands and unresolved dilemmas. These dilemmas began with childbirth. The act of giving birth itself was highly valued in early modern society. With women of exalted rank, it was turned into a public occasion; the mother of Louis XIII held court and conversed with her visitors while she was actually in labor. Even in villages several women usually attended the delivery. Once the child had been brought into the world, its further nurture seems to have been regarded as a disagreeable duty. Those who were rich enough or who were forced by economic circumstance to work discharged this duty by finding a wet nurse. Sometimes the wet nurse (usually a peasant woman who was already suckling a child of her own) would be brought into the household; or else the child would be sent into the country to the wet nurse's home. Either way the maternal bonds were loosened. The rich mother, freed from a long period of nursing, obviously had more time for other pursuits and also ran less risk of losing her figure. She hardly saw her child even if the wet nurse had been brought into the household. The wet nurse, since she was being paid for her milk, owed it to her employers to deprive her own child if necessary rather than the one she was being paid to nurse. There were few alternatives to the wet nurse before the development of the rubber nipple in the middle of the nineteenth century. Sometimes in the early modern period when there was no woman with a reliable supply of milk available, medical authorities recommended that the baby suckle a farm animal. There were also ways of feeding babies pap, a concoction of flour and water that was given on the finger or from the finger of a glove with a small hole cut in it. But babies seldom thrived, or even survived, without a regular supply of breast milk.

We are more concerned here with the psychological than the nutritional consequences of wet nursing. The habit of contracting out this function clearly fits the pattern of a diffuse responsibility for socialization. But in the seventeenth and eighteenth centuries, moralists began increasingly to recommend that mothers should nurse their own infants. They accused women who did not of selfish frivolity. Some claimed that virtues were actually transmitted with the milk, and that children put out to nurse to lower-class women would acquire their base dispositions. Others advanced arguments about the dangers to health in putting children out to nurse. By the time that Rousseau, toward the end of the eighteenth century, made his famous plea for mothers to nurse their own children, most were willing to take up this responsibility. And as the nurture of the child in its earliest period was increasingly secured to the biological mother, so the way was opened for her to take greater responsibility in other areas of socialization.

What society was coming to expect can be seen most clearly in the schools. Medieval schoolboys — including university students — had been notoriously unruly; but at the beginning of the Renaissance a reaction against such free and easy ways set in. Schools and colleges were reformed to emphasize a more vigilant guarding of the morals and behavior of the students. Corporal punishment was freely used; even at Oxford tutors sometimes whipped the undergraduates. This belief that children needed more rigorous discipline antedates the Reformation; indeed, a belief that authority was lax as well as unfair seems to have been prevalent in the Europe where John Calvin and Ignatius Loyola were growing up, and a desire for a more stringent and godly order of things can be seen in the Catholic Reformation just as much as in the Protestant one. In fact, the Jesuits, who soon extended their influence into most of the schools of Catholic Europe, made a particular point of forming the morals of the schoolchildren, and sometimes regarded the schools as the necessary remedy for the coddling and old-fashioned methods of parents and governesses.

Discipline of this kind was overwhelmingly exercised by males over males. But in the home, too, parents were exhorted to break the wills of their stubborn children. In this new dispensation mothers were placed in a somewhat ambivalent position. To judge from the books of advice on childrearing and from the few autobiographies that have survived, the mother was never the ultimate judge of the children, but she was assumed to be in more intimate touch with them, and she could also mingle severity with gentleness, whereas the father dare not err on the side of leniency. Since the advice of the experts was so heavily inclined to harsh discipline and frequent beatings, the mother risked a double-bind situation from any intervention in discipline. She was supposed to temper the father's severity, and yet if she did so, any subsequent misconduct by the children could be attributed to excessive leniency on her part. In this respect the comparatively greater participation by men in the socialization process was not an unmixed blessing to their wives!

One area that was unambiguously assigned to the mother was the education of her daughters. At about age seven, a male child passed forever "out of the hands of women." The development of girls, however, was less clear-cut. In the seventeenth century, especially in France, a lively debate broke out on the question of whether and where women should be educated. Although there were few who argued outright for female ignorance, many felt that the place for girls to learn was the home rather than the school. Even in the eighteenth century, Voltaire, for example, believed that the education of women should be carefully attuned to their individual differences, to which a mother would be much more sensitive. Schools were unsuitable for girls because all the pupils were taught the same things and subjected to the same unvarying routines. Attitudes such as this even defeated one plan to endow a college for women in England; the proposed headmistress declared that women learned best not in a formal school setting, but "in a family way of discourse."

If she undertook to educate her daughters, the mother bore the full weight of the demand that she teach them modesty, chastity, good housewifery, and all the other virtues recognized as crowning the female character. Sometimes, contemporaries recognized, the mother might be carried away into leniency by her love of her daughters, and it might be advisable for a governess, ideally of the crusty Scottish sort, to undertake the instruction and discipline. But in general, by the time the debate petered out in the mid-eighteenth century, the tendency was to exalt motherhood and deprecate the sharing-out of maternal tasks to other women. In education, as in breast feeding, mothering received new social importance.

This was all very well for the middle-class mother who might by the eighteenth century be getting some leisure time she could devote to the education of her daughters. For the working-class mother, a combination of mothering and productive work would be much less difficult to achieve in domestic industry than in factories; as we have seen, this is undoubtedly one of the reasons for the perseverance of the former. In weaving and spinning, especially, it was possible to combine socialization with wage earning, for there were stretches of time in which the parents could instruct and even catechize their children. Contemporaries thought such hours might be spent reading aloud or singing together; a popular work called *Weaving Spiritualized* recommended the chanting of psalms and reading the Bible. One of the reasons why the very young were recommended to work was that they would be under their parents' direct supervision and have no opportunity to ramble around the village and get into mischief.

When the full impact of the Industrial Revolution destroyed the possibility for husband and wife to work together and still teach and supervise their children, some alternative form of child care had to be worked out. The eventual answer, of course, was compulsory schooling, but this did not arrive in England until the latter part of the nineteenth century — and even then did not provide for children younger than six. When the father had to work away from home, the mother was encouraged to remain at home; if she did not withdraw from the world of work, she — like the father — would partially have to surrender her role in socialization. For most women, the choice had to be made in favor of socialization, both because of social pressure to regard motherhood as a full-time occupation and because they were being excluded from various fields of employment.

Women Find a Public Voice

We have briefly surveyed the situation of women under preindustrial capitalism, but we have not yet told quite the whole story. During the period from the sixteenth to the eighteenth centuries women slowly and hesistatingly found a public voice. It was not nearly so strong as it came to be in the nineteenth century, and feminism as a movement did not exist. Yet by the end of the eighteenth century Mary Wollstonecraft had produced, in *The Rights of Woman,* the first thoroughgoing vindication of women in the political and economic sphere to be written by a woman. The discussion of literature and public affairs in the salon society of the Enlightenment over which women presided could no longer be mocked as *précieuse* affectation, as it had been a century earlier. The writing of books by women was no longer a curiosity (even if they still sometimes had to sign men's names to them), and in Jane Austen, Europe had produced a writer whose greatness was undisputed. What in the previous centuries had made this attainment of a public voice possible?

In the realm of public authority, women occupied a curiously mixed position. The long regime of feudal law was not yet over, and a woman might succeed to many positions after the death of her husband or father. She could be a queen regent or even reigning queen. She could be a lord of the manor, hold manorial court, and perform feudal services. There were even local elective offices a woman might hold: churchwarden, for example, an onerous position with considerable responsibilities for the relief of the poor. Before the nineteenth century a few women in England even had the right to vote, if they qualified in other ways. The idea that women might be generally admitted to political rights, however, was barely beginning to be heard from such radicals as Condorcet at the end of the eighteenth century.

It was entirely unknown in the seventeenth century, where the chief revolutionary struggle, that of the English Parliament against the power of Charles I, mobilized women to only a limited degree. On some occasions delegations of women lobbied in the House of Commons. These seem mostly to have been wives of merchants or landowners, and they either presented private grievances of their own (asking for the restoration of land that had been sequestered, for example) or supported a general political aim that had been formulated by men. At no time did they speak for themselves as women — only as friends of peace, supporters of the established church, or Quakers. Individual women performed courageously in the English civil war and in the contemporary wars of the Fronde in France; Lady Brilliana Harley defended Brampton Castle against the Royalists for six weeks, and a woman commanded troops in the field in the Fronde. But these were again examples of the responsibilities that a still half-feudal political order might throw on some women. It is significant that the only radical mass movement in the English Revolution, that of so-called Levellers, did not include women in their political program. They advocated the vote for all male heads of household — who made up less than one-fifth of the total population — but gave no consideration at all to the vote for women.

Nevertheless, even though they did not yet speak for themselves as women, the fact that even a few women spoke at all is important. And though they shared to only a limited degree in the political ferment of seventeenth-century England, women were thoroughly caught up in the concomitant religious stirrings. It was here, among the Puritan sects, that they first achieved the freedom to speak regularly in public. Women sometimes preached in Congregationalist and Baptist meetings and also made up a considerable majority of the membership in these groups. Since the prerequisite for membership in such churches was to be in a state of salvation, women might even be members when their husbands or sons were not judged to have achieved a sufficient state of sanctification. In fact, women sometimes voted on whether or not to admit their husbands to membership.

It was, however, only among the Quakers that the women achieved something like full parity with men. Against the opposition of some of the male Quakers, George Fox championed the establishment all over England of separate women's meetings for church business, attended, financed, and administered entirely by women. Women also shared in the hazards of traveling around the country preaching the Quaker message. "Must not the Spirit of Christ, or the same that is begotten of God in the female, as well as in the male . . . speak?" demanded two such dauntless women, Katharine Evans and Sarah Chevers, who undertook to preach Quakerism in Alexandria and other parts of the Ottoman Empire. Both had husbands and children at home, but they nevertheless set forth from London to Plymouth and thence to Livorno. Unfortunately for them, the ship they had hoped to take to Cyprus put into Malta on the way, and they were captured and imprisoned by the Holy Inquisition. For more than three years they were detained there, alternately threatened with being burned as witches and heretics and tempted with money and food. Both held firm in their convictions, resisting their captors by prolonged fasting — a prototype of the suffragists' hunger strikes. (Even this treatment, it must be said, was gentle compared to that meted out by the Puritans in Massachusetts Bay, who in 1659 hanged Mary Dyer and two male Quakers on Boston Common for returning to preach after being once deported.) Much of the leadership for women's causes in the nineteenth century came from such Quakers as Susan B. Anthony, the Grimké sisters, and Lucretia Mott. They stand in a line of descent from such women as Katharine Evans and Sarah Chevers.

It would be wrong to forget the antifeminist views of the main body of Protestants. The Reformers severely attacked the cult of the Blessed Virgin Mary, Queen of Heaven, and showed themselves scarcely less hostile to the "monstrous regiment of women" on earth — as John Knox demonstrated in his assault on Mary, Queen of Scots. Madonnas virtually disappeared from the Church of England because, as one theologian put it, it was objectionable to see the Son of God under the domination of a woman. They objected to the practice of midwives' baptizing infants because this sort of ecclesiastical function should be exercised by men only.

Furthermore, the mainstream of Protestant piety could see women only as mothers in the home. The Reformers justified the suppression of nunneries because these provided women with the temptation to live a life of idleness. They also disapproved of women having the sort of spiritual and administrative responsibilities that the great abbesses had exercised. Their attack on the ideal of celibacy is important in this context; by denying celibacy to the religiously intense woman they confined her to marriage and motherhood. At the same time, Protestant divines increasingly emphasized that the family itself was a religious agency, thus adding the influence of the church to the voices urging parents to give greater care to the socialization of their children.

Yet when all this has been said, it remains true that women enjoyed considerably more legal rights and social freedom in those countries most influenced by the Protestant Reformation, especially in its Calvinist version. This can be seen by comparing the United States, England, the Netherlands, or the Scandinavian countries with France, let alone Spain or Italy. This suggests, first of all, that the high ideal of womanhood entertained in Catholic countries was not incompatible with consistently oppressive treatment of women. Despite the claims of Robert Graves and his admirers, women can be worshiped as goddesses and still be treated nearly as slaves (a syndrome that has received the unlovely name of "pedestalization"). Second, Protestantism may have been more important for its unintended consequences than its professed ideals. As we have seen, more orthodox Protestants were horrified by radical Quakerism. They would no doubt have been equally scandalized by the pervasive secularization of society that set in shortly after the religious wars of the early seventeenth century — wars that did much to discredit religion generally. Yet the growth of mercantile wealth contributed greatly to the development of a secular outlook on life most pronounced in the urban centers of the Protestant world, where the new voices of women were most to be heard.

Conclusion

There are very few straight lines of development in history, and certainly an enormously complex history like that of women cannot be told as a simple story of progress. Nevertheless, it may be useful by way of conclusion to contrast the position of ordinary women at the beginning of the sixteenth century with that at the beginning of the nineteenth century. In the generation when the Reformation began, almost all women were totally involved in the world of production, and all married women, so far as we know, were totally involved in the world of reproduction as well, for they had no conscious control over their fertility. Socialization was relatively less the concern of mothers as it was a shared responsibility by fathers and mothers together, substantially assisted by other relatives and the community at large.

Social change during the subsequent three centuries was slow and uneven. Nevertheless, it does seem clear that women partially withdrew from the world of work from the seventeenth century onward. Rich women were increasingly being kept in idleness, perhaps because their husbands valued them as objects of conspicuous consumption while working-class women were confronted by a growing tendency for men to organize trades so as to exclude them from the better-paying jobs, even before the onset of the factories posed to both men and married women the choice of work *or* staying at home. Although old-fashioned housewifery lingered on, especially on the larger farms and estates, more and more articles could be manufactured more cheaply than they could be made at home, and thus the housewife was coming to some degree to be technologically unemployed.

Patterns of reproduction and sexuality were such as to enhance economic growth. Because of late marriage and high celibacy, the population had an unusually high percentage of workers. In general, women tended to outlive men, which meant that there was a fairly large number of widows together with women who never married. Within some marriages, family limitation was practiced. The moralists' repressive attitude toward sexual self-expression made it possible to introduce such pleasure-denying techniques as coitus interruptus. Yet many brides were pregnant at the time of their marriages, indicating that ordinary people indulged freely in sexual intercourse, though we cannot know how much they enjoyed it.

The practice of socialization by father, relatives, and fellow villagers as well as by mother was well suited to an organization of production in which both men and women worked together at home and to an acceptance of however many children might be born, as though fertility were simply an expression of God's will or a part of the laws of nature. But the era of the Reformation was an era of rising expectations for the way that children were to be brought up; both Protestants and Catholics shared an impulse toward greater discipline of life and education. Protestants, with their opposition to the celibate clergy and religious orders, put a great deal of confidence in the family as the place where the character of children should be formed. Whereas couples who could afford it had formerly put children out to wet-nurse, and subsequently entrusted their education to servants, the opinion was growing that the mother should nurse her child herself. At the same time that the Protestants were urging parents to make the home a little church and the moralists were urging mothers to take on more of the responsibilities for the nurture of their children, developments in the economy, as we have seen, were tending to force women out of their former roles in production. What seems to have been happening, in short, was that the career of mother was slowly being invented. It may even have been the case that the practice of family limitation had something to do with a growing feeling that parents would be able to give more care and resources to a smaller number of children, and thus the new feelings about socialization may have been reflected in this pattern of reproduction.

Yet if the increasing division of labor was tending to specialize women as mothers, with relatively lesser contributions to production, the demographic tendency, with its relatively high numbers of spinsters and widows, was to deny a considerable number of women the possibility of this role. Nor were women as willing to content themselves with a silent acceptance of such confinement; a distinctive female voice was coming to be heard in the Quaker ministers' gallery, in the aristocratic Frenchwoman's salon, and even now and then in the streets. Though their problems were different, modern women owe the distant beginnings of their own movement for liberation to their grandmothers of ten generations ago.

Notes

1. This specifically does not apply to the North American colonies, where domestic servants seem to have been relatively rare. Of course, in the southern and mid-Atlantic states housewives on the larger holdings had to cope with the management of household slaves.
2. This older pattern of folk medicine practiced largely by women persisted in eastern Europe, which in part accounts for the well-known predominance of women in Soviet medical practice today. Although the Soviet women doctors do receive extensive professional training, one main reason why the great majority of Soviet doctors are women is that women were never driven out of medical practice (or reduced to the ancillary role of nurses) by the sort of professionalization of medicine that has been carried out in the last hundred years in the United States and western Europe.

Suggestions for Further Reading

Ariès, Philippe. *L'Enfant et la vie familiale sous l'Ancien Régime.* New edition, Paris, 1973. English translation of the 1960 edition: *Centuries of Childhood.* London, 1962.

———. *Histoire des populations françaises et de leurs attitudes devant la vie depuis le XVIIIe siècle.* Paris, 1948.

Ascoli, Georges. "L'histoire des idées féministes en France du XVIe siècle à la Révolution." *Revue de Synthèse Historique,* 13 (1906), 25–57, 161–184.

Baumal, Francis. *Le Féminisme au temps de Molière.* Paris, n.d.

Beard, Mary R. *Woman as Force in History.* New York, 1946.

de Beauvoir, Simone. *Le Deuxième sexe.* 2 vols. Paris, 1949. English translation: *The Second Sex.* New York, 1953.

Benton, John F. "Clio and Venus: An Historical View of Medieval Love." *The Meaning of Courtly Love,* ed. F. X. Newman. Albany, 1968, pp. 19–42.

Bergues, Hélène, et al. *La Prévention des naissances dans la famille.* Paris, 1960.

Camden, Carroll. *The Elizabethan Woman.* Houston, 1952.

Chamoux, Antoinette, and Cécile Dauphin. "La contraception avant la Révolution française: l'exemple de Châtillon-sur-Seine." *Annales: Economies, Sociétés, Civilisations* (May–June 1969), 662–684.

Clark, Alice. *Working Life of Women in the Seventeenth Century.* London, 1919.

Demos, John. "Families in Colonial Bristol, Rhode Island: An Exercise in Historical Demography." *William and Mary Quarterly,* 25, 3rd ser. (1968), 40–57.

———. *A Little Commonwealth: Family Life in Plymouth Colony.* Oxford, 1970.

Douglas, Mary. "Population Control in Primitive Groups." *British Journal of Sociology,* 17 (1966), 263–273.

Drake, Michael. *Population and Society in Norway, 1735–1865.* Cambridge, 1969.

Fussell, G. E., and K. R. Fussell. *The English Countrywoman: A Farmhouse Social History, 1500–1900.* London, 1953.

Gautier, Etienne, and Louis Henry. *La Population de Crulai, paroisse normande.* Paris, 1958.

Godfrey, Elizabeth [Jessie Bedford]. *Home Life under the Stuarts, 1603–1649.* London, 1925.

Goubert, Pierre. *Beauvais et le Beauvaisis de 1600 à 1730.* Paris, 1960.

Greven, Philip. *Four Generations: Population, Land, and Family in Colonial Andover, Massachusetts.* Ithaca, 1970.

Hair, P. E. H. "Bridal Pregnancy in Rural England in Earlier Centuries," *Population Studies,* 20 (1966), 233–243.

Hajnal, J. "European Marriage Patterns in Perspective." *Population in History,* ed. D. V. Glass and D. E. C. Eversley. London, 1965, pp. 101–143.

Hecht, J. Jean. *The Domestic Servant Class in Eighteenth-Century England.* London, 1956.

Hill, Georgiana. *Women in English Life from Medieval to Modern Times.* 2 vols. London, 1896.

Hole, Christina. *English Home-Life 1500 to 1800.* London, 1947.

Hopkins, Keith. "Contraception in the Roman Empire." *Comparative Studies in Society and History,* 8 (1965), 124–151.

Hunt, David. *Parents and Children in History: The Psychology of Family Life in Early Modern France.* New York, 1970.

Kelso, Ruth. *Doctrine for the Lady of the Renaissance.* Urbana, 1956.

Laslett, Peter. *The World We Have Lost.* London, 1965.

———, ed. *Family and Household in Past Time.* Cambridge, 1972.

Luppé, Comte de. *Les jeunes filles à la fin du XVIIIe siècle.* Paris, 1925.

Macfarlane, Alan. *The Family Life of Ralph Josselin, a Seventeenth-Century Clergyman.* Cambridge, 1970.

Mitchell, Juliet. *Women's Estate.* London, 1971.

Powell, Chilton L. *English Domestic Relations, 1487–1653.* New York, 1917.

Power, Eileen. "The Position of Women." *The Legacy of the Middle Ages,* ed. C. G. Crump and E. F. Jacob. Oxford, 1926.

Racz, Elizabeth. "The Women's Rights Movement in the French Revolution." *Science and Society,* 16 (1952), 151–174.

Rogers, Katherine. *The Troublesome Helpmate: A History of Misogyny in Literature.* Seattle, 1966.

A Short Relation of Some of the Cruel Sufferings (For the Truths Sake) of Katharine Evans and Sarah Chevers, in the Inquisition in the Isle of Malta. London, 1662.

Smelser, Neil J. *Social Change in the Industrial Revolution.* Chicago, 1959.

Snyders, Georges. *La Pédagogie en France au XVIIe et XVIIIe siècles.* Paris, 1965.

Thirsk, Joan, ed. *The Agrarian History of England and Wales.* Vol. 4: *1500–1640.* Cambridge, 1967.

Thomas Keith. "Women and the Civil War Sects." *Past and Present,* 13 (1958), 42–62.

Thompson, E. P. *The Making of the English Working Class.* London, 1963.

Thompson, Roger. *Women in Stuart England and America: A Comparative Study.* London, 1974.

Vann, Richard T. *The Social Development of English Quakerism, 1655–1755.* Cambridge, Mass., 1969.

Wrigley, E. A. "Family Limitation in Pre-Industrial England." *Economic History Review,* 19, 2nd ser. (1966), 82–109.

———. *Population and History.* London, 1969.

9

Women in the Age of Light

Abby R. Kleinbaum

Intellectual and political movements affected women far less than the kind of social change described in the previous essay. The Enlightenment, like the Renaissance, was a cultural event that aimed to liberate the human spirit. However, like the French Revolution it helped to shape, the Enlightenment not only failed to improve women's lot but worsened it in some ways. Abby Kleinbaum notes the hypocrisy of the eighteenth-century philosophes, *who either overlooked the question of women's equality in their general criticism of society or attacked aristocratic women, whose relative freedom symbolized the immorality of their entire class. In reaction, the philosophes wanted to see bourgeois women more carefully controlled, at least through education. They disagreed about the way in which natural law accounted for inequality between the sexes, some arguing for a biological explanation, others for socially conditioned but necessary subordination of women.*

The chief spokesman for the restive middle class, which triumphed in the French Revolution, was Jean Jacques Rousseau. He glorified the nuclear family and the nurturing female confined to it, an ideal we have come to recognize as typical of bourgeois anxiety about legitimate heirs. Robespierre and Napoleon later enforced this vision through legislation. Only a few premature voices, like those of Wollstonecraft and Condorcet, extended the rhetoric of "Liberty, Equality, and Fraternity" to include women.

La Bonne Mère (The Good Mother), etched proof by Laurent Cars, after Greuze. With one child dozing at her breast, another in a chair, and a third tooting a horn over her shoulder, this tranquil and contented mother illustrates the emerging Enlightenment ideal of domesticity. (The Metropolitan Museum of Art, The Elisha Whittelsey Fund, 1959)

If enlightened centuries are not less corrupt than the others, it is because the light therein is too unevenly spread. The great defect in this philosophical century is in its not being more so. . . .

JEAN LE ROND D'ALEMBERT[1]

That women are intellectually inferior to men, and inherently emotional, irrational, and incapable of contributing to the political process or to the great works of civilization, that their sexuality is dangerous, and that they are deceitful and treacherous — these are very old ideas. They have been voiced in faint or resounding chorus throughout historical time. The Enlightenment, the intellectual movement that dominated Europe and America for the first three-quarters of the eighteenth century, might have attacked these ideas on two fronts. First, the *philosophes,* the thinkers of the Enlightenment, claimed to be unimpressed by the age or pedigree of an idea. Only critical examination could test the validity of a concept. Inspired by the scientific revolution of the seventeenth century, the philosophes saw Newton and Newtonian science as models worthy of their emulation. If Newton, in rejecting authority and relying on the strength of his own reason and the data of his experiments, could explain the mechanism of heaven and earth in three simple mathematical laws, then scientific reasoning offered infinite possibilities for the reform of the social sciences. The state, the economy, education, the very structure of society itself should now be analyzed and scrutinized, and outmoded ideas and prejudices must yield to the test of criticism. Second, the philosophes' declared hostility to Christianity could have permitted them at least to reexamine traditional ideas about women. Although the church did not invent misogyny, it was the Christianity of St. Paul and the early church fathers that helped to institutionalize female oppression by approving of sex only for the purposes of procreation. They declared women unworthy of preaching and admonished them to obey God and their spouse, created in His image. Enlightenment thinkers blamed the church more than any other institution for obstructing reason and progress through its perpetuation of myth, ritual, and tradition. The philosophes almost unanimously declared that to be a priest, monk, or nun was to be a social parasite, and that celibacy, actual or avowed, did not increase one's human worth.

But the philosophes' light was dim and imperfectly transmitted. Thus, a study of the ideas of the major theorists of the century reveals no trend toward opportunity and freedom for women.

The philosophes were not themselves revolutionaries; they saw themselves as observers and critics. The truth, once exposed, was often left to create its own program. Typical of this stance was the discussion of women in the great intellectual work of mid-century, the *Encyclopédie.* The Chevalier de Jaucourt signed one of the four articles on women — "*Femme* (*droit nat.*)" — "Woman (natural law)." [2] The questions Jaucourt raised were central to the primary intellectual problem of the Enlightenment: what is the nature of humanity? What characteristics and qualities of our existence stem from our nature, and thus from unchanging natural law? Which aspects of our lives result from the caprice of custom, and hence from man-made positive law? Jaucourt, when he placed the question of the authority of the male in marriage in this context, readily concluded that male dominance is the result of civil law and not of nature. His argument was threefold. First, reason points to the natural equality of all humanity. Second, the husband does not necessarily have more bodily strength, or wisdom, or intelligence than his wife. And finally, he reminded his religious readers that even the Bible supports the obedience of women on the grounds of positive law — for God established the authority of Adam over Eve as part of Eve's punishment. From this, Jaucourt concluded that prior to the Fall, a natural equality must have reigned between the sexes. Thus, marriage is a purely contractual agreement; it is up to both partners involved to determine the terms of the contract. Ordinarily, men are more capable, he argued, in governing affairs, and so civil law gives them precedence; but there is no reason to believe that in certain instances (as when a queen marries below her rank and authority) a different kind of contract cannot be made. Jaucourt never examined the possibility of revising the marriage contract on a larger scale or of eliminating the question of authority in marriage altogether.

Several prominent philosophes pursued Jaucourt's train of thought, arguing the equality of women from the vantage point of natural law theory. Voltaire, the most notable of this group, was a declared enemy of the church and an adoring friend of Madame du Châtelet, one of the most gifted women of the century. He was a brilliant publicist and had he chosen to make the status of women an issue, it might have burned on everyone's minds. But he never viewed the plight of women as a critical issue worthy of his full energy and genius. There are occasional references to the talents of women in his works (preface to *Alzaire,* 1730) and to legal injustices that existed against them ("Adultery" in the *Philosophical Dictionary,* 1764). But this was scant notice indeed from the most prolific pen of the century.

Montesquieu, by contrast, not only adhered to the natural law theory of equality but also displayed a sensitive understanding and recognition of women's sexuality. In his *Persian Letters*[3] of 1721, he pretended that some Persian gentlemen lodged with him and showed him correspondence they received from their eunuchs and from the chief wives in their harems back home. Actually, Montesquieu used the confinement of women in a seraglio as a metaphor for the enchainment of humanity under a despotism. The yearning of the women in the harem for liberty and sexual expression is symbolic of the yearning of all humanity for freedom. In this context, he showed that despotism is hollow and corrupt; when the Persians go to Paris, their little societies fall apart. The women rebel and fight with the eunuchs, the eunuchs fight with each other. Montesquieu closed his *Persian Letters* with a letter from Roxanne, the favorite wife of the Persian Usbek (letter 161). She will now tell him, she writes, why she never appeared to share the passion he showed for her. It is because she always hated him, and the menial signs of worship he expected her to display. His love would never have been sufficient to make her life worth living; she deceived him all the time that he kept her in the harem, and she is now taking poison to deny him the final tyranny of punishment. Yet Montesquieu did not go beyond this to challenge the authority of the male in marriage. In his great work on government and society, *The Spirit of the Laws,*[4] Books 7 and 8, he related the virtue and probity of women to the strength of republican governments. When women become licentious, when they refuse to obey their husbands, their behavior foretells the decline of a republic. His only statement on female rights is in Book 16, where he argued that the laws of each nation should allow women and men equal rights to initiate divorce proceedings.

The work of Antoine Thomas (*An Account of the Character, the Manners, and the Understanding of Women,* 1772),[5] while not following the natural law theory of equality, does have some insights into the status and life experience of women. Thomas's book is commonly known only through the well-known philosophe Diderot's attack upon it, as if its only distinction was to be the occasion for Diderot's essay "On Women" (1772).[6] In many ways, however, Thomas's work is more perceptive than Diderot's, especially in his attempt to find patterns and themes in the history of women. Thomas noted that the oppression of women is a very complex phenomenon — since women typically have been oppressed and adored at the same time. He argued that the men of classical Greece were especially cruel; in wishing to preserve the beauty and purity of their wives, they cloistered them in their homes and denied them the awards of public esteem. The Athenian orator and leader Pericles declared that to live unnoticed, to receive neither praise nor blame, is the greatest glory of a woman. Since knowledge and understanding can only develop in the context of social interaction, Thomas argued, these practices effectively excluded the women of classical Greece from the world of ideas. Understandably, the Greek men favored the company of courtesans, whose minds were not stunted by isolation from society. A major point in Thomas's work was his notion that the status and comportment of women is, at least in part, the result of socialization. In warlike societies, women lived in tents and fought in armies; in Renaissance Italy, he said, women were philosophers, scholars, and teachers.

Thomas believed, however, that most women are not the intellectual equals of men; that their minds are "more pleasing than strong." [7] He expressed particular concern about the liberty and infidelities of the women of contemporary Parisian society, and the fact that the genuine sentiment of love had degenerated, he argued, into a cruel and unfeeling game of seduction. He blamed these brief and often hostile sexual encounters on the impulse to gallantry. Since the twelfth century, this tradition of illicit and adoring courtly love had become severed from Christian chivalry. Stripped of honesty, nobility, fidelity, and trust, gallantry appeared naked as "a vile sentiment." [8] Thomas proposed that the sexes return to their original natures which, he said, they had reversed. Men should stop trying to please, and women should cease attempts to dominate. Women should stay home, obey their husbands, bear children, nurse their own babies, and abandon the amusements of society.

Was it this conclusion that provoked Diderot's sharp attack in his essay "On Women"? Not at all. Diderot's main point of contention was what he considered to be Thomas's lack of sensitivity. Thomas failed to evoke the tragedy of women; his account was lacking in both pity and terror. "When we write of women, we must dip our pen in the rainbow, and throw upon the paper the dust of butterflies' wings." [9] For Diderot, woman was a poignant and seductive "other," oppressed not only by nature but also by civil law, which treated her like an imbecile child and permitted men to commit outrages against her with impunity. If Diderot could be the legislator, the tyranny of the law would end — but the tyranny of nature was forever. Diderot considered the female capacity for sexual pleasure to be far inferior to that of the male; many women die without ever having achieved orgasm. The height of sexual pleasure, which "never fails when we [men] call for it" is for women "less prompt and certain." [10] Woman has a more "mobile soul" and more "delicate organs" than man; she is in fact dominated by her uterus, "an organ, subject to terrible spasms, which rules her and rouses up in her phantoms of every sort." [11] Her strength is weakened and her life imperiled by pregnancy. Old age leaves her alone, unlovely, bad tempered and bored, fleeing into the arms of religion.

But did Diderot really want to improve the lot of women? In his primitive utopia, "Supplement to Bougainville's Voyage" (written in 1772), he envisioned a community of wives and daughters. The young girls signaled their readiness to participate in adult society by becoming "pale and listless." [12] But even in his paradise, there was no free expression of sexuality.

Diderot envisioned his men and women of nature indulging in sex only for purposes of procreation. In another instance, Diderot actually had the opportunity to serve as legislator. He drew up a plan for Catherine the Great for the establishment of a university in Russia. Here he suggested that the students and professors be male and that the professors' wives should not be allowed on campus, as the mingling of the sexes would have a "bad moral effect." [13]

Even less sympathetic than Thomas and Diderot were a large group of Enlightenment thinkers who explicitly denied, on grounds of law or nature, the equality of men and women. The presence of four articles on women in the *Encyclopédie* clearly indicates the ambivalence of Enlightenment ideas on the subject. As we have seen, one article, "*Femme* (*droit nat.*)" by Jaucourt, upheld the natural equality of the sexes. Another, "*Femme* (*morale*)" by M. Desmahis,[14] presented the opposing view. For Desmahis, there were important differences in the nature of men and women, and in his comparison, women did not fare very well. Not only are they inferior in physical strength but also in understanding; they are timid and dissembling, weak in commitment to virtue and strong only in their pursuit of vice. Desmahis upheld a double standard; what is praiseworthy in men (force, majesty, courage, and reason), he considered deformity in women. Women should not be educated in convents, which, he contended, ill prepare them for their domestic role in society. After a lengthy description of the women of society as vain and mindless coquettes, he turned his attention to the only women who were worthy of praise — the wives and mothers who ignore society and whose glory it is to be in turn ignored.

Thus, Desmahis, and later Rousseau and Holbach held up for emulation the values of classical Athens. The thinkers of this age also developed sociology, anthropology, and psychology to elucidate their understanding of history and the human condition. They were well aware of the fact that the life experience of the lady in classical Athens was profoundly different from that of her spouse. Enlightenment thinkers who praised the Athenians sincerely believed that men and women should lead separate and unequal lives. Alongside the argument for female equality, based on natural law, there existed a second, even stronger trend in Enlightenment thought, which stressed the sexual differences and the appropriateness of an exclusively domestic role for women.

Ironically, this idealization of the family and of motherhood seemed to contemporaries more modern and forward looking than the apparent independence of the upper-class woman. In fact, it was more modern since it reflected the coming of age of the bourgeoisie and the triumph of its values. The free woman, as the eighteenth century had known her, had few outlets for creative expression. She was aristocratic, wealthy, and may very well have been the vain coquette that moralists frowned upon. The upper-class Frenchwoman often found herself in a union arranged by her parents and based on financial transactions. Marriage signified a sharing of names and fortunes but not of love and affection. Her sexual needs were frequently pursued elsewhere. In railing at her, critics were not just defending standards of virtue. They were expressing their utter exasperation with the society that produced her, a society wherein birth determined the parameters of one's existence — a society that was worn out and that received its final death blow with the storming of the Bastille. From its ashes rose the society of wealth, the bourgeois society, which could see a free female spirit only as decadent or, worse, counterrevolutionary.

The thinker who gave the clearest expression to the values of the middle class was the most gifted and complex of all the philosophes, Jean Jacques Rousseau. His love of nature, his egotism and emotionalism have led some scholars to classify Rousseau as a Romantic rather than an Enlightenment figure. Yet Rousseau and the philosophes focused their attention on the same basic problems. Although the solutions Rousseau suggested were sometimes at variance with the beliefs and values of his contemporaries, and even with his own behavior and comportment, his importance stems from the fact that his ideas played a central role in Enlightenment dialogue. He led a life plagued by fears, anxieties, and suspicions, and he lashed out at supporters and detractors alike with accusations of malice and betrayal. Although much of his weeping and ranting must be explained in terms of his own personality, Rousseau did face a very real dilemma. He often found himself relying on an aristocratic benefactor for his support while writing works that attacked the political, moral, and social structure of the establishment. He claimed to be uncomfortable in the Paris salons. At least some of this uneasiness must have stemmed from the realization that his ideas did not belong in these drawing rooms of the old social order.

The very idea of a salon seemed to Rousseau to be "unnatural" for both men and women. While the women sit quietly, the men restlessly walk about, demonstrating "that they are under confinement." The French "are the only people in the world where the men *stand* at the theatre, as if they went into the pit to relieve themselves of the fatigue of having been sitting all day in a drawing room." [15] The typical salon society was not one of women relating freely and openly to men but rather of women presiding over an extremely controlled performance where men exchanged views. But even so, Rousseau had little use for the charms and artifices of the hostesses who guided the evening through its expected course of courteous and often disingenuous exchange. He wrote that he "would a thousand times rather have a homely girl, simply brought up, than a learned lady and a wit who would make a literary circle of my house and install herself as its president. A female wit is a scourge to her husband, her children, her friends, her servants, to everybody." [16] What did Rousseau see as the proper function of the female sex?

The first discussion of the status and role of women Rousseau published appeared in his letter to d'Alembert concerning the theater[17] in 1759, in which he responded to the article "Geneva," which d'Alembert wrote for the *Encyclopédie*. Rousseau was fiercely proud of his citizenship in this tiny Calvinist, theocratic republic, which he tended to view, rather unhistorically, as a modern incarnation of the virtues of classical Greek society. Although d'Alembert's article had been generally favorable, it included the suggestion that the life in this city would be greatly enhanced by the introduction of a theater — a notion that infuriated Rousseau. Rousseau's main argument against the theater was that most plays deal with love, "the empire of the fair," [18] and hence represent an inversion of the real order of things. In truth, women are not rulers but are created to be ruled and to lead lives exclusively concerned with the care of the home and of the family. Rousseau admitted that the "new philosophy" [19] tended to pin the difference between the sexes on the prejudices enforced by laws and education, but he took strong exception to this view. Female shyness and modesty stem from nature: woman was designed, said Rousseau, "so that she would submit to men." [20]

Rousseau not only believed women to be naturally inferior and submissive but also put great emphasis on the notion that the sexes should be separated. It is the plan of nature, he claimed, for the sexes to have "different inclinations"; the purpose of this plan being that they "may live apart, each after their own manner." [21] The classical Greeks were correct in the cloistering of women, their determination clearly to separate the work of men and women, and their refusal even to dine with their wives. This consummate wisdom assured the Greeks a degree of domestic tranquillity hardly to be found in Rousseau's time.

He objected to the presence of a theater in Geneva not only because of the content of the plays that would be performed but also because the very existence of the institution would serve to tempt women to venture out of their homes. This opportunity to appear in public would cause women, whom Rousseau believed to be vain and narcissistic, to abandon their domestic responsibilities entirely and to be concerned only with the acquisition of finery and with self-adornment. Competition among women to appear the most elegantly dressed would lead directly to the moral and financial ruin of the family. When the mistress of the house goes wandering, "her house is like a lifeless body which is soon corrupted; she herself loses her chief lustre." [22]

Rousseau believed that it was inappropriate for women to share and participate in society outside the home. "If she is married, what business has she among men?" he asked, and if she is single, "why does she run the risk, by her indecent deportment, of shocking the man who would be inclined to make her his wife?" [23] Rousseau believed that women had no ability to contribute to the art and work of civilization, apart from their domestic roles. They lacked the intellectual ability of men, and although some women could acquire a smattering of knowledge in science, literature, and the like, books by women artists would forever lack the fire of true genius.

D'Alembert countered Rousseau's criticism with an argument that appeared, at first glance, to be remarkably sympathetic to women ("Lettre à J. J. Rousseau"). If no honest and virtuous woman can be found, he wrote, then the fault lay with a society that enslaved and degraded women by chaining their minds and spirits. It was a society that addressed them in a trite and frivolous jargon, humiliating both to them and to the men who employed it. It is not weakness of body that hinders genius and wisdom but lack of education. Since women are not exempt, d'Alembert argued, from the trials and tribulations of life, why should they be excluded from that cultivation of the mind and talent that makes life worth living? Reason, humanity, and justice argue for the education of women. D'Alembert made an impassioned plea to philosophes all over the world to end a barbarous custom and to point the way to others by "giving your daughters the same education as your other children." [24]

His hypothesis was based upon his faith in what women might become rather than on what they were in his own day. The force of his argument was that women should be accorded equality of opportunity (except for military pursuits) and that this equality between the sexes should be bolstered by equal education. Until such conditions exist in society, no one ought to criticize women for ignorance and coquetry.

But d'Alembert's convictions were not so strong and well thought out as to prevent him from stumbling into self-contradiction. Shortly after he penned his reply to Rousseau's attack on his article "Geneva," he wrote a note on Rousseau's newly published work on education, *Emile* (1762). This time, he had words of praise for Rousseau; all that he wrote on the education of women was "true, well thought out, and eminently practical." [25] Of course, as later critics were to demonstrate, Rousseau's *Emile* did not suggest that boys and girls receive the same education. His plans for the two sexes were profoundly different.

Emile was one of Rousseau's major works and, in a sense, it was a companion piece to his great work on political theory, *Contrat social* (*The Social Contract*), which also appeared in 1762. In both works, the central issue was the problem of human freedom. In *The Social Contract,* Rousseau asked: How can we belong to the state and still be free? He turned to the Greek idea of liberty, often closely paraphrasing Aristotle's *Politics*: Liberty is not absence of law and restraint, but rather freedom is obedience to self-imposed laws. There is no conflict between freedom and the demands of society, as long as citizens freely choose to do that which is in fact their duty.

Rousseau saw members of contemporary society, especially French society, as incapable of exercising the kind of liberty necessary for making his social contract viable. Corrupted by evil institutions and by a system of education that was deficient, competitive, and degrading, they were unable to see beyond their own particular wills to a vision of the general good. One way to solve this dilemma was totally to reform education. Hence, in *Emile,* Rousseau confronted the problem of how to raise a man who is capable of freedom.

Rousseau presented his ideas in the context of a fictitious biography. To remove the influence of corrupt social institutions (since laws help to mold citizens and bad laws make bad men), Emile is raised in the countryside by a tutor. Free from the arbitrary or irrational will of others, he learns from his own experience. His knowledge proceeds from his own interests, which the tutor helps to stimulate and develop. He is not spoiled, but when punished, he is made clearly to understand that his actions have violated his own interest or threatened his well being. Emile's education produces a young man who is hardly a walking encyclopedia, but one who has a degree of wisdom and who will be sought after as a judge. Emile will have no conflict between interest and duty — in short, he grows up to be the very model citizen for a society based upon *The Social Contract.*

That Emile is a male child was no accident or random choice. Rousseau saw political society as the proper and exclusive domain of men; his major goal, therefore, was to design an education for these future male citizens. Since they must propagate, Rousseau could not wholly ignore the problem of training the wives and mothers of citizens. Hence, Book 5 of *Emile* introduces the reader to Emile's eventual wife; it is entitled, "Sophie, or Woman."

It is interesting and significant that while classical Sparta was the Greek city-state Rousseau held up for emulation in *The Social Contract,* when it came to his discussion of the education and role of women, his model was Athens. Aside from the fact that Spartan men and women saw each other infrequently, he found little to admire in the comportment of Spartan women. Many of the ancients, among them Aristotle and Xenophon, criticized the Spartans for giving women too much freedom. Rousseau much preferred the weak, delicate, and confined women of Athens. Although Rousseau was silent on the homosexual component of Athenian social life, his clear admiration of other aspects of Athenian society led him to make some novel proposals for the rearing of young girls. But the changes and reforms he suggested in outlining the education of Sophie fall far short of making her education the equivalent of Emile's.

Rousseau has Sophie raised and schooled at home, rather than in the convent. Like the girls of classical Athens, she is taught by her mother. She wears no stays, corsets, or wigs, but rather comfortable clothing suitable for running about, dancing, and playing. She receives no religious education and her inquiries about God are answered with "your husband will teach you when you are grown." [26] Her mother teaches her that women are made for the delight of men, and that the bearing of children is their proper business. She learns that motherhood is a total career and commitment in itself. There is no way she can be "a nursing mother today and a soldier tomorrow." [27] To prepare her for her role of pleasing men, her parents develop her natural vanity and teach her to dress dolls as a practice for self-adornment ("in due time she will be her own doll").[28] Her parents seldom feed her meat, the food of men, but rather indulge her natural passion for "milk, sweets, and pastry," [29] the diet of Athenian women. Sophie's mind and reason are cultivated, but through an emphasis on practical and applied studies rather than on abstract and speculative sciences, whose principles and axioms are beyond her grasp. Her mind is "pleasing" and "thorough," but not "brilliant" or "deep." [30] During her courtship with Emile, he tries to teach her what he knows about mathematics, the sciences, and philosophy. She listens intently and understands him; but (alas) forgets all shortly thereafter.

When their love deepens and they eagerly anticipate the joys of marriage, the tutor intervenes. He whisks Emile away, telling him that he must not marry until he had seen the world, and that if his love is true it will not suffer from his going abroad for two years. As for Sophie, how is she to pass the time? Rousseau provides no program of travel or intellectual stimulation to enhance and develop her human potential. Her lot is just to live in hope, to extend her childhood, and anxiously to await Emile's safe and loving return.

Her subordination continues into marriage. After her wedding night, Sophie passes the first day of her married life "in the arms of her tender mother," something Rousseau presented as perfectly natural and appropriate ("a pleasant resting place, after a night in the arms of her husband").[31] The newlyweds have no privacy — every detail of their relationship is known to those around them. When, one night, Sophie refuses to sleep with Emile ("that haughty lady made haste to assert her right"),[32] the tutor mediates their dispute, whereupon she blushes and demonstrates her contrition to all.

Women's submission to perpetual adult authority was also emphasized by Rousseau in his romantic novel, *Julie, ou La Nouvelle Héloise.*[33] Published in 1761, the story unfolds through the format of a correspondence between the major characters. Julie, the good and beautiful daughter of an aristocratic family, is hopelessly in love with her handsome, wise, and virtuous tutor, who is not of noble birth. So great is their love that it leads to an affair, even though there is little hope for future marriage. The lover maintains that the bond of love should be the only one they observe — that they should elope. But Julie, with endless tears and weeping, cannot contemplate this heinous violation of parental trust and family duty. She tells him, "I am determined never to be your wife without the consent of my father, but I will never marry another without your consent" (letter 76).

When Julie's father learns of the tutor's love for her (but *not* of their affair), he goes into a rage, cursing his wife for allowing a commoner to enter their home and defaming the young man. When Julie protests, he beats her "without mercy" (letter 63). Her mother attempts to shield her from some of the blows and is brutally beaten herself. Finally, Julie falls to the floor, striking a piece of furniture, and suffering bruises and a bloody nose. Her father shows some concern, but remains silent. After dinner, he makes his amends by drawing his daughter, whom he has so recently brutalized, to his lap. The reader is left to ponder the picture of a twenty-year-old woman perched on the lap of her seventy-year-old father. Julie is so touched, she lays her face close to his cheek, which she bathes in kisses and tears. This scene of domestic tenderness causes the mother to run over to them, and the three happily embrace. Julie writes that were it not for the gnawing guilt over her loss of innocence, this would have been "the most delightful moment" of her life.

Both Julie and her father plead with the tutor to release her from the vows she had made to him. Once freed, Julie is promptly married off to an old military friend of her father's. Judging from the age of the latter, the groom could hardly have been less than fifty. This vast age difference between the bride and the groom is, once more, reminiscent of what was considered to be the perfect upper-class Athenian marriage. This resemblance was not incidental; judging from Rousseau's description of the household and even from his choice of language, it is quite clear that he intended precisely this comparison.

The still adoring tutor visits Julie a few years after her marriage and is astounded and enraptured by the vision of her as a mother: "What a lovely sight! What bitter regrets! I found myself distracted with grief and transported with joy" (letter 125). He very quickly perceives that their affair could never resume again and that henceforth their relationship must be on an entirely different basis from what existed in the past. He stays on to become a friend of the family and the eventual tutor of her sons. In a brief moment alone together, Julie confesses that for all the joys and satisfactions she has derived from her lovely and precious household, the ecstasy of true happiness has eluded her. He, in turn, reveals to her that he has carved her name in stone, that she is the only true love of his life, that he will never know another. They weep briefly together but quickly recover their composure.

The highlight of the tutor's stay is his invitation to one of the Sunday night gatherings Julie holds for the ladies (herself and her cousin) and the female servants, in what Rousseau calls the "*gynaeceum,* or women's apartment" (letter 142). Here the women sing and dance, eating lovely cream cakes and other foods "such as suit the taste of women and children" (letter 129). Julie serves no wine, and is, in her own habits, virtually a vegetarian. As a member of the fair sex, she adores milk and sugar, which are "symbols of innocence and sweetness." (She has become rather plump since last seen by her true love, but this only increases his ardor.) Their chaste mutual longing ends only when Julie meets an early and tragic death from an illness contracted during one of her final expressions of perfect motherhood: she had plunged into icy waters to rescue her drowning child.

Rousseau himself seems to waver between two mutually exclusive ideas: that the home is precious to all, and that men and women should have entirely separate pursuits. He never resolves this contradiction. The Greeks would have been puzzled by his emotional treatment of the gynaeceum, which some have seen as the most "modern" element in Rousseau. The Greeks admired a pure wife, a well-ordered house, and carefully brought-up children but never would have been transported to tears and ecstasy by the sight of a chaste mother and child, nor hungered for her milk and sugar. Rousseau's sentimental admiration of the household, however, did not alter the fact that the ideal woman was excluded from the world outside of the home.

Rousseau was not Julie's only muse. The Baron d'Holbach, coming from very different social and economic circumstances, gave a complete endorsement to Rousseau's values in his *Système social* (*Social System*) (1770).[34] From his high praise of the virtues of middle-class marriage, to his lauding of girls well educated at home by their mothers, to his criticism of libertinism, to his critique of the theater as damaging to female sensibilities, he painted the topography of the new world — its elevated morality and its shrunken women.

Why did the liberal thinkers of the Enlightenment choose to exclude women from their visions of the realm of political action? Perhaps it is in part because they understood freedom in the classical Greek sense of active participation of a citizen in a polis. The society of a polis was dominated by the bourgeois patriarchal family, with its need for the orderly transmission of property through legitimate heirs. Rousseau clearly recognized this problem when he pitied "the unhappy father who, when he clasps his child to his breast, is haunted by the suspicion that this is the child of another, the badge of his dishonour, a thief who is robbing his own children of their inheritance."[35] He concluded, "It is not enough that a wife should be faithful; her husband, along with his friends and neighbours, must believe in her fidelity."[36] She must follow the example of those Greek women who, once married, "disappeared from public life; within the four walls of their home they devoted themselves to the care of their household and family."[37]

Only in a slightly later generation, during the French Revolution, do we find voices of lasting interest speaking for female equality, the Marquis de Condorcet and Mary Wollstonecraft. Both based their ideas on a very similar foundation — a logical continuation of the argument from natural law.

Mary Wollstonecraft penned her *Vindication of the Rights of Woman*[38] in 1792. She was a woman who fought poverty and numerous family obligations to become self-sustaining as a writer and a voice in late-eighteenth-century radical political theory. Her publisher was Joseph Johnson, who also published her friends Tom Paine, Joseph Priestley, and William Godwin (later her husband). In spite of friends who supported her and encouraged her, her life involved many years of difficulty and unhappiness. Her death in 1797 from complications following the birth of her daughter (the future wife of the poet Shelley and the author of *Frankenstein*) brought an early end to her union with Godwin, which had promised to be a happy marriage between peers.

Wollstonecraft's argument centered on two key points. First, she reasoned, if women fail to become men's equals, the progress of human knowledge and virtue will be halted. Second, if women were to contribute to the process of civilization, their education must prepare them for this task. Wollstonecraft shared Rousseau's contempt for the vanity, frivolity, and immodesty of aristocratic women. She made a point of noting that she was not addressing herself to ladies but to women of the middle class. She bemoaned the fact that women believed the only way to establish themselves in the world was by marriage and that their education prepared them poorly even for this status. "They dress, they paint, and nickname God's creatures." Women's activities were more "fit for the seraglio" than the home.[39] She agreed with Rousseau that virtue and independence are traits that result from a perfect education. "This was Rousseau's opinion respecting men; I extend it to women,"[40] she wrote, thus underscoring her major quarrel with him. Rousseau proposed to enhance women's virtue without enhancing their wisdom. Wollstonecraft saw that Rousseau's suggested reforms for female education would serve only to change the frivolous coquette into the obedient wife, equally as mindless in her new role as she was in her former one. The education of women must not just be changed — it must be made equal and identical to the education of men. Real virtue stems from knowledge, and unless women have the *same* access to knowledge as men, they will be unable to realize their potential contribution to civilization.

Her reforms were designed not to free women from the burdens of the nuclear family but rather to strengthen the family. Only the woman who has received an excellent education and who has fully developed her intellectual potential could, she argued, properly fulfill the roles of wife and mother. In spite of the unconventional nature of her own lifestyle, she never questioned the intrinsic value of marriage or of motherhood.

Although Wollstonecraft supported social and political change, based on the principles of natural right and human equality, she did not envision a fundamental restructuring of the fabric of society. Condorcet, while also hoping for change based on the foundation of his contemporary society, had a vision of a future world in which the fruits of science, education, a universal language, and social, economic, and sexual equality would raise all of humanity to a new infinitely higher level of existence.

Condorcet began his career as a geometer, and briefly held a post in the Royal Office of the Mint under the ministry of Turgot. After years of friendship with Mme. Suard (who had the admiration of several philosophes), he married Sophie de Grouchy. She was a young aristocrat and a scholar in her own right, and her republican politics and views on women's rights served to radicalize her husband. Originally associated with the Physiocrats and their doctrines, Condorcet, in his first political works, limited the rights of citizenship to property holders only. These works, *Letters of a Citizen of New Haven to a Citizen of Virginia* (1787), *Essay on the Structure and Function of the Provincial Assemblies* (1788), and *On the Admission of Women to the Rights of Citizenship* (1790),[41] were noteworthy for his insistence that women, insofar as they were property holders, should also have the right to vote and to hold office. He pointed to the irony of custom and habit making the idea of a female ruler acceptable but excluding even the notion of a female citizen.

In his *Letters* he examined the arguments most often advanced against the extension of rights to women. Most women do not have the physical strength of men, although, Condorcet noted, some women are as strong as some men. Women should not serve in the military, and they are, on occasion, confined by childbirth. According to Voltaire, they appear to lack the spark of creative genius sometimes present in men. Condorcet agreed, but thought the lack of creative fire might be due to suffocation by faulty education, society, and manners. Condorcet found none of these arguments sufficient to justify denying women the rights of citizenship, especially since potential male citizens were never tested for their health, strength, or creativity.

A monarchist at the outbreak of the Revolution, Condorcet eventually became a supporter of the republican Girondist government and helped to frame its constitution in 1793. At this time he changed his ideas on property being the basis for the right of suffrage and argued for universal suffrage grounded on the existence of a shared common reason. However, he apparently acquiesced to the views of his colleagues and agreed to universal *male* suffrage, until such time as an improved system of education for women would prepare them for the vote. Similarly, his *Report on Public Instruction* (1792) survives as part of his plan for free public education, but there are no known copies of the special report on the education of women he promised to write. The documents convey the appearance that under the pressure of events, Condorcet sacrificed his allegiance to female emancipation.

When the Revolution moved further to the left, with the Jacobin party ousting the Girondins from power, Condorcet's former association with the Old Regime branded him as an enemy of the state. Hiding from the Reign of Terror (he was captured, but his death in 1794 was probably a suicide), he wrote his *Outline of the History of Human Progress*,[42] describing ten stages of progress leading to the perfection of humanity. In Book 10, he discussed the highest level of perfection, stressing that it could not be achieved without universal education and full equality of the sexes.

Since Condorcet's last work is indeed only an outline, it is difficult to gauge the breadth of his vision of the future, or even of his feminist insight. Like Wollstonecraft, he believed that the family should continue to be the basic unit of society. Both thinkers maintained that all of humanity had yet to reap the fruits that conjugal life between equals could yield. They saw the family as a social unit, still in the process of development and capable of achieving an almost infinite improvement.

Wollstonecraft and Condorcet had in common tragic and premature deaths, and their ideas appear to have suffered a similar fate. Although the essential points in their arguments for female rights can be traced to the dialogue of the eighteenth century and were echoed in a few of the pamphlets penned during the French Revolution, their ideas cannot be characterized as typical of that time. In the Age of Light, the problem of opportunity and freedom for women was, even for the most brilliant and dazzling of minds, a blind spot. It was Rousseau, in spite of his claims of aloneness and persecution, who shaped the legacy of Enlightenment ideas on women: that marriage and motherhood were both the destiny and the worth of their lives. The Enlightenment emerges as another great age marked off by conventional methods of historical periodization in which man improved his understanding of nature and society and broadened his participation in the political process, while denying women an increment in opportunity and in freedom.

Notes

1. Jean Le Rond d'Alembert, "Lettre à J. J. Rousseau," *Oeuvres philosophiques, historiques, et littéraires,* vol. 5, Jean-François Bastien, Paris, 1805, pp. 351–352.
2. *Encyclopédie, ou Dictionnaire raisonné des sciences, des arts et des métiers,* vol. 6, ed. Denis Diderot and Jean Le Rond d'Alembert, Briasson, David, Le Breton, & Durand, Paris, pp. 471–472.
3. Charles de Secondat, Baron de Montesquieu, *Persian Letters,* trans. C. J. Betts, Penguin Books, Middlesex, England, 1973.
4. Charles de Secondat, Baron de Montesquieu, *The Spirit of the Laws,* 2 vols., trans. Thomas Nugent, Colonial Press, London and New York, 1900.
5. Antoine Thomas, *An Account of the Character, the Manners, and the Understanding of Women, in Different Ages, and Different Parts of the World,* trans. Mrs. Kindersley, J. Dodsley, London, 1800.

6. Denis Diderot, "On Women," *Dialogues,* trans. Francis Birrell, George Routledge & Sons, London, 1827, pp. 185–196.
7. Thomas, *An Account,* pp. 124–125.
8. Ibid., p. 195.
9. Diderot, "On Women," p. 194.
10. Ibid., p. 186.
11. Ibid., pp. 190–191.
12. Denis Diderot, "Supplement to Bougainville's Voyage," *Dialogues,* pp. 111–158, 136.
13. Denis Diderot, "Plan of a University for the Russian Government," *French Liberalism and Education in the 18th Century,* ed. and trans. François de la Fontainerie, McGraw Hill, New York and London, 1932, p. 304.
14. *Encyclopédie,* vol. 6, pp. 472–474.
15. Jean Jacques Rousseau, *Eloisa: A Series of Original Letters Translated from the French,* 3 vols., trans. anon., John Harding, London, 1810, letter 129. All my citations are to the letters in this edition.
16. Jean Jacques Rousseau, *Emile,* trans. Barbara Foxley, Everyman's Library, Dent, London, 1911, reprinted 1963, p. 371.
17. *A Letter from M. Rousseau, of Geneva, to M. d'Alembert of Paris, Concerning the Effects of Theatrical Entertainments on the Manners of Mankind,* trans. anon., J. Nourse, London, 1759.
18. Ibid., p. 57.
19. Ibid., p. 108.
20. Ibid., p. 112.
21. Ibid., p. 144.
22. Ibid., p. 115.
23. Ibid., pp. 115–116.
24. D'Alembert, "Lettre," p. 353.
25. D'Alembert, "Jugement sur *Emile,*" *Oeuvres,* vol. 5, p. 380.
26. Rousseau, *Emile,* p. 354.
27. Ibid., p. 325.
28. Ibid., p. 331.
29. Ibid., p. 358.
30. Ibid.
31. Ibid., p. 442.
32. Ibid.
33. All citations will be from the English *Eloisa.*
34. Paul Heinrich Dietrich, Baron von Holbach, *Système social, ou Principes naturels de la morale et de la politique,* 3 vols. in one, n.p., London, 1773. See especially vol. 3, chap. 10, "Des Femmes," pp. 123–136.
35. Rousseau, *Emile,* p. 325.
36. Ibid.

37. Ibid., p. 330.

38. Mary Wollstonecraft, *A Vindication of the Rights of Woman,* ed. Charles Hagelman, Jr., Norton, New York, 1967.

39. Ibid., p. 35.

40. Ibid., p. 52.

41. Marie Jean Antoine Nicolas, Marquis de Condorcet, *Oeuvres complètes,* 18 vols., Nieweg, Brunswick & Henrichs, Paris, 1804. The full French text of the *Letters* is in vol. 12, and the *Essay . . . on Provincial Assemblies* is in vol. 13. There is a rare English ed. of the third work, Dr. Alice Drysdale Vickery, trans., *The First Essay on the Political Rights of Women: A Translation of Condorcet's "Sur l'Admission des femmes au droit de Cité," from his Collected Writings, 1789,* Letchworth Garden Press, 1912.

42. Condorcet, *Oeuvres complètes,* vol. 8.

Suggestions for Further Reading

Condorcet, Marie Jean Antoine Nicolas, Marquis de. *Oeuvres complètes.* Nieweg, Brunswick & Henrichs, Paris, 1804.
Vol. 8: *Esquisse d'un tableau historique des progrès de l'esprit humain.*
Vol. 12: *Lettres d'un bourgeois de Newhaven à un citoyen de Virginie.*
Vol. 13: *Essai sur la constitution et les fonctions des assemblies provinciales.*

———. *The First Essay on the Political Rights of Women: A Translation of Condorcet's "Sur l'Admission des femmes au droit de Cité," from his Collected Writings, 1789,* trans. Dr. Alice Drysdale Vickery. Letchworth Garden Press, 1912.

Diderot, Denis. "On Women." *Dialogues,* trans. Francis Birrell. George Routledge & Sons, London, 1827, pp. 185–196.

———. "Supplement to Bougainville's Voyage." *Dialogues,* pp. 111–158.

Montesquieu, Charles de Secondat, Baron de. *Persian Letters,* trans. C. J. Betts. Penguin Books, Middlesex, England, 1973.

Rousseau, Jean Jacques. *Emile,* trans. Barbara Foxley. Everyman's Library, Dent, London, 1911. Reprinted 1963.

———. *Eloisa: A Series of Original Letters Translated from the French,* 3 vols., trans. anon. John Harding, London, 1810.

———. *A Letter of M. Rousseau, of Geneva, to M. d'Alembert of Paris, Concerning the Effects of Theatrical Entertainments on the Manners of Mankind,* trans. anon. J. Nourse, London, 1759.

Thomas, Antoine. *An Account of the Character, the Manners, and the Understanding of Women, in Different Ages, and Different Parts of the World,* trans. Mrs. Kindersley. J. Dodsley, London, 1800.

Wollstonecraft, Mary. *A Vindication of the Rights of Woman,* ed. Charles Hagelman, Jr. Norton, New York, 1967.

10

Loaves and Liberty: Women in the French Revolution

Ruth Graham

The French Revolution was fought in the name of human freedom, but it overturned aristocratic privilege only to ensconce the bourgeoisie. Hence, while women were drawn to its ideals, their political activity was ultimately suppressed. Ruth Graham describes women's participation in the various stages of the Revolution, from bread riots, through club activities, to battlefield action. She notes the gains they made in revolutionary civil law and the first stirrings of a feminist consciousness in declarations of women's rights and in the formation of separate women's clubs. Mainly, however, women's political response was informed by their class interest, mirrored class divisions, and failed to evolve a distinct feminist program. Military reverses in the revolutionary wars and internal divisiveness caused the government to subdue women's independent political activity and emphasize family cohesion instead. Working-class women were still exposed, with their families, to a hungry and precarious existence. Under Napoleon, women lost the civil rights gained during the Revolution. As other essays in this volume indicate, politics alone did not end women's inequality.

A woman of the Revolution, as portrayed by Jacques Louis David. (Musée des Beaux-Arts, Lyon)

The French Revolution was fought in the name of a stirring slogan: Liberty, Equality, Fraternity. Many classes flocked to its banners: bankers and merchants chafing against the privileges of the aristocracy and its stranglehold on politics; peasants hungry for land and struggling to cast off seigniorial dues; and the wage-earning poor of the cities fighting for daily food. Each class included, of course, women, most of whom did not see themselves distinct from their class. They marched for bread and a constitution alongside their men, sometimes even taking the initiative. A tiny few achieved, at least for a little time, a dim awareness of a separate consciousness.

We first hear women's voice in the *cahiers,* the list of grievances that heralded the French Revolution. Here we find demands for legal equality, for equal education, for reform of the marriage laws, for protection of female trades from male incursions, and even for political representation. We see women joining and sometimes leading the tide of protest as the Revolution gained momentum. We see them forming their own political clubs and writing their own newspapers, learning politics as they went along and demanding the right to participate. We see them fighting for the right to fight, to bear arms against the foreign foe. We also see them in familiar supportive roles on the home front. All in all, the French Revolution mobilized the highest level of organized female activity in its time. Some of it was traditional: bread riots are as old as the poor, and women have always cared for fallen soldiers. But some of it was new: club activity, political assemblies, and journalism on behalf of women's rights established new options.

What we know of these revolutionary women is more often legend than fact. We must put aside the bloodthirsty image of Mme. Defarge in Charles Dickens's *A Tale of Two Cities,* who swears vengeance for the oppression of her people while knitting at the guillotine, happy at the sight of blood spurting from aristocrats' necks and who wields her ax when leading the mob, later dancing the *carmagnole* in triumph. In contrast to

Mme. Defarge, Dickens's heroine, Lucie, is so helpless that she needs an Englishman who worked for a bank to rescue her.

Mme. Defarge was pure fiction — the creation of an anti-revolutionary reformer writing over a half a century after the event. But the 6,000 women who marched to Versailles on October 5, 1789, were real. Market women, wage earners, wives of artisans, craftswomen, small businesswomen, and women from the middle class were on the march in support of the Revolution. We can see this clearly in the women's unofficial cahiers, or notebooks of grievances, which appeared earlier in 1789. They were unofficial because women were neither represented nor seated in the Estates General, the assembly of the clergy, nobility, and commoners, which met for the first time in 175 years in May of 1789 at Versailles. Resorting to their time-honored right to petition for aid, women addressed their cahiers to the king and to the Estates General.

Most of the women's cahiers expressed the wishes of the educated middle classes and even of some noblewomen, since illiterate women of the poorer classes could not write. On the eve of the Revolution, primary schools for girls, scattered unevenly throughout France, were church connected and mostly limited to teaching religious duties and housewifely skills. They had taught only 27 percent of the women to sign their names on the marriage registers, compared to 48 percent of the men. But in Paris the literacy rate for women was much greater than in rural areas. Wage earning Parisian women later testified that they attended demonstrations after they had read announcements about them in the newspapers.

There were some poorer women's pamphlets, however; the most interesting one was that of the illiterate market women of Paris, who dictated it to a scribe in colorful colloquial French. They complained of the harsh conditions of their trade, the cruel winds in the open market, the rapacious tax collectors at the city's gates. They wanted to punish grain speculators for starving poor people. As mothers of families, they cried out against the overcrowding in the city hospitals, where four lay dying in the same bed and children contracted diseases. They expressed contempt for bishops who lived in luxury but compassion for poor priests who, they thought, should marry because they were "flesh and bones like ourselves." Anticlerical but not irreligious, the market women promised to light candles in church for the success of the Estates General. And though they found fault with the king's ministers, they loved the good king, believing he cared about the misery of the poor.

Most of the cahiers, however, were written by middle-class women, influenced by Rousseau's views on education and the family. They demanded laws acknowledging the importance of women to the family and to the moral fabric of society. Some of these pamphlets expressed the more advanced views of the Marquis de Condorcet, who in 1787 protested the unequal laws for men and women and urged better education to prepare women for equality. They also called for voting by head and not by separate order in the Estates General and for a constitution that would put an end to privileges. They denounced male midwifery (in the interest of female modesty). In return, they offered not to intrude on traditionally masculine occupations.

Marriage did not offer women sufficient protection. Some complained in these pamphlets that husbands dissipated their dowries and then abandoned their wives. Other women asked for laws to protect them from husbands' abuse and to gain some control over family property and their children. They wrote that women were man's natural companion, not his slaves. Although disenchanted with their husbands, they considered marriage a desirable institution. Men, they wrote, should be obliged to marry women from families too poor to afford dowries. Bachelors were social parasites who should pay double in taxes and be denied positions in favor of fathers of families. Motherhood was extolled because, they believed, a growing population insured the nation's prosperity. The pamphlets demanded that society protect women by providing them with suitable employment to keep them from prostitution. The pamphlets strongly condemned prostitution (as did many official cahiers, notably that of the Third Estate of Paris).

Women wanted a better education in order to find decent work, but they argued more often that girls needed education to become better mothers and to teach their children. Some women asked the king to establish free schools for girls. One woman writer reproached men for neglecting women's education in order to prevent women from realizing their talents. Another woman demurely denied that her purpose in learning was to usurp the authority of men. An alternative to marriage, the convent, was held in disrepute. Some women asked that girls forced to enter convents now be given their freedom, but one ex-nun added that those who wished should be allowed to remain in religious communities. Clearly, options for women without husbands or vocations in secular life were not promising.

Optimism permeated these women's cahiers as they joined in the effort to abolish the abuses of the Old Regime. The Estates General met at Versailles in May 1789; in June, the Third Estate formed the National Assembly to express the will of the nation. On July 14, the Parisians stormed the Bastille to foil a counterrevolutionary plot of the royal court to starve the city into submission. In the countryside, peasants and the landless poor burned the property of the privileged orders. Throughout France, the middle class organized citizens' militias, the National Guards, to enforce the laws of the National Assembly. France awaited a new constitution based on liberty and equality and security from oppression. Women expected much from the Revolution, although the Declaration of the Rights of Man and of the Citizen, which the National Assembly decreed on August 26, 1789, did not explicitly extend to them these rights.

But it was economic rather than political demands that sparked the first important women's protest. When on October 5, the market women learned there was no bread in Paris, they led 6,000 women to Versailles to see the king. A few hours later the National Guards followed, under the command of the Marquis de Lafayette, who had orders from the municipal government to prevent a counterrevolution by bringing the king to Paris. The women arrived toward evening, tired but exhilarated by their more than twelve-mile march. A women's delegation entered the National Assembly to petition for a fixed price for bread. Other bedraggled women sat down next to the deputies, who were startled to see them bearing knives and sticks. The women cried, "Down with the clergy!" to the ecclesiastical deputies, who were at that time resisting the confiscation of church property. Meanwhile, the king received a deputation of six women, including a very articulate young flower girl. Although he promised to provide Paris with bread, the women who waited outside were not satisfied; they wanted proof of his good intentions.

Early the following morning, a crowd of women and a few men entered the palace door leading to the queen's chambers, where they clashed with the king's guards. After Lafayette persuaded the king and the royal family to appear with him on the balcony in order to calm the crowd, the king agreed to return to Paris with the royal family. On the march back to Paris, some women rode astride the cannon of the National Guards while some distributed the national tricolor cockade of red, white, and blue ribbons to spectators. Triumphantly, they escorted the royal family, referring to them as "the baker, the baker's wife, and the baker's little boy." Historians describe these women as good-natured and apolitical, wanting only bread, but the women's march coordinated well with the strategy of the members of the National Assembly, who forced the king to sanction the Declaration of Rights.

Our rather unreliable information about the women in the march on Versailles comes from a police inquiry in the spring of 1790. Renée or Reine-Louise Audu (called Queen of the Markets), asked the king at Versailles on October 5 to sanction the Declaration of Rights. Six months later, she testified at the police inquiry, which accused her of having urged women to march to Versailles. Her lawyer claimed in her behalf that she had led a contingent of 800 women in perfect order. Reine Audu was sentenced to almost a year in prison.

Another woman, a former *demi-mondaine,* Théroigne de Méricourt, supposedly appeared on October 5 at Versailles dressed as an Amazon or female soldier. More likely, Théroigne had come to Versailles on October 5 to sit in the galleries and listen to the deputies who attended her salon at Paris. Legend has it that she mixed with the royal regiments that day to distribute money and win them over. Other, more prosperous women also considered themselves patriots and supported the Revolution. Since September, when the king's minister, Jacques Necker, asked for personal sacrifices to avert national bankruptcy, these women appeared at the National Assembly to offer their jewels and valuables.

Along with respectable matrons, actresses and singers appeared. Though considered immoral by the prejudices of the Old Regime, many of these women were hard working, and admired for their talent. One of them, Olympe de Gouges, a playwright, urged women to emulate the women of ancient Rome by making sacrifices to support their patriotic husbands and fathers. The daughter of humble parents, although she hinted at a noble, illegitimate birth, de Gouges had written about thirty plays by 1789. Most of them remained on paper because she quarreled with acting companies, but one play condemning slavery was produced in 1789 at the Théâtre Français. That year she also wrote patriotic tracts hailing the Revolution, praising Necker, Lafayette, the Duke of Orléans, and the king.

On July 14, 1790, in Paris and throughout France, women paraded at festivals of the federation of the National Guards to celebrate the first anniversary of the fall of the Bastille. Detachments of women marched, some carrying arms as auxiliaries of the National Guards, and they took the civic oath at the public altar to live or die for their country. Political clubs and women's newspapers had prepared them for this role. Hardly political at first, with their interests in fashions and marriages, the newspapers' viewpoints had shifted with revolutionary events. In 1790 women's newspapers were advocating better education and the right of women to serve on juries and to participate in primary electoral assemblies. They published statements from women's clubs calling for reform of the marriage laws and the right of divorce. Louise Kéralio, a well-known journalist and a member of the Academy of Arras, ran a political newspaper with her husband, François Robert, a professor of law and later a member of the National Convention, which declared France a republic. Together they participated in the Fraternal Society for Both Sexes, which met in the library of the Jacobin Club in Paris. The purpose of this society was to educate men and women in the neighborhood to support the policies of the radical Jacobins. Although women attended Jacobin society meetings, and upon occasion addressed the members (as Louise Kéralio did), they sat in a separate section and did not have the right to vote. In February 1790, Théroigne de Méricourt addressed the more radical Cordeliers Club, and though they applauded her, they refused to admit her as a member.

Other fraternal societies for both sexes, which in practice became women's clubs, met in Paris, while outside of the city hundreds of clubs were formed exclusively for women. Somewhat different was the educational Social Circle, sponsored in Paris by the Friends of Truth which, under the influence of Condorcet and others, advocated women's rights. On November 26, 1790, a Dutchwoman, Etta Palm d'Aelders, congratulated this society for admitting women. She criticized discriminatory laws and advocated the same education for both sexes. Mme. d'Aelders's address was well received, but enemies of the Friends of Truth ridiculed the club for listening to a female orator. In 1791 she attempted to found a federation of women's clubs affiliated with the Friends of Truth, but without much success.

In the political crisis that followed the king's failure to escape from France in June 1791, and the subsequent threat of foreign intervention, the National Assembly spent little time considering the rights of women. The republican Louise Kéralio organized a demonstration on July 17 at the Champs-de-Mars against the monarchy; many women were among the demonstrators when Lafayette gave orders to the National Guards to fire on them.

In September 1791, when the king took the oath to support the new constitution, at least one woman expressed disappointment that the new constitution did not recognize women's rights. Olympe de Gouges published the Declaration of the Rights of Woman and of the Citizen, which closely paralleled the seventeen articles in the Declaration of the Rights of Man and of the Citizen. She dedicated the women's declaration to the queen — an odd dedication, since the public blamed Marie Antoinette for the king's attempted flight. She contended that since women had the right to mount the scaffold, they also deserved the right to mount the political platform — an argument that was prophetic in her case. The articles of the women's declaration proposed freedom of thought for women, government employment for women, and equal rights to property. In the section following the declaration she asked for better education for women and also reform of the marriage laws. She added what she called a "social contract," a marriage contract that would state that the husband and wife would be united during their lives for the duration of their affections and their fortunes would be held in common. If they separated, their property would be reserved for their children, or illegitimate children if designated. All children had the right to take the names of the mothers and fathers who avowed them.

It took several revolutionary crises for France to give women some of the rights enunciated in Olympe de Gouges's declaration. After April 20, 1792, when France declared war on Prussia and Austria, the government praised women's significant contribution to the war effort. Even before the outbreak of war, delegations of women asked the Legislative Assembly for the right to take up arms. In March 1792 a young wage earner, Pauline Léon, presented a petition signed by over 300 female citizens of the fraternal society of her section in Paris. Disclaiming any intention of abandoning their families, they requested the right to defend themselves from the enemy and permission to assemble on Sundays to exercise with arms. A few days later, Théroigne de Méricourt petitioned to form a women's legion. On April 1, 1792, Etta Palm d'Aelders led a woman's delegation to the Assembly to ask for civil and military positions. And on July 14, 1792, anniversary of the fall of the Bastille, Olympe de Gouges paraded at the head of a group of armed women.

When the enemy advanced into France with little resistance from the garrisons, the king was suspected of treachery. On August 10, 1792, women fought in the insurrection at the palace of the Tuileries that overthrew the monarchy. The newly formed Paris Commune had organized the insurrection and allowed women to be members of popular assemblies in the sections. On August 10, Théroigne de Méricourt was at the Tuileries dressed in a flamboyant uniform; also Reine Audu, released from her year in prison for her part in the march on Versailles; present also were Pauline Léon and her coworker, Claire (Rose) Lacombe, an actress from the provinces who was now active in popular societies.

After the monarchy fell, the National Convention declared France a republic on September 22, 1792. French armies stopped the advancing Prussian and Austrian soldiers in the Netherlands in November at the battle of Jemappes. In December 1792 the National Convention tried the king for treason, and on January 21, 1793, executed him. By the spring of 1793 the French Republic was fighting a coalition of five countries. Waging an all-out war, the government encouraged Frenchwomen to aid their country. Women rolled bandages at hospitals; *tricoteuses,* or knitters, sat at public meetings making shirts, stockings, vests, trousers, hats, and gloves for their men in the army. These women doing war work provided the model for Dickens's Mme. Defarge.

When women volunteered to serve in the army, the Convention recognized their value to morale. Separate women's legions, however, were never sanctioned. Municipal authorities responsible for the requisition of soldiers issued uniforms and military equipment to some women, who fought alongside their husbands, fathers, or brothers. Other women disguised themselves as men and their bravery called attention to their sex. The Fernig sisters, teenaged daughters of a commander of the National Guards in northeastern France, joined a nearby army camp. General Dumouriez made them his aides and the National Convention rewarded them after they fought in Belgium at the battle of Jémappes. Other young women in their teens, wives of soldiers, and mothers of many children were cited and rewarded by the Convention for their bravery and — significantly — for their irreproachable morals. However, in the spring of 1793, after Dumouriez defected to the advancing enemy, and the republic was fighting for survival, the Convention now complained that too many women accompanying the French troops weakened morale and wasted equipment. On April 30, 1793, the Convention ordered women sent home who performed no useful service to the army, including those married to soldiers. Although Article 11 of this decree also expelled women who actively served in the armies, it was not strictly enforced. Women continued to fight alongside men during the French revolutionary wars.

The republic showed its appreciation of women by passing laws to give them civil rights. In September 1792, as the government moved toward secularization, marriage became a civil contract. A decree granted the right of divorce, entrusting children of the dissolved marriage to the mother if they were girls and to the father if they were boys older than seven, unless the parents agreed to other arrangements. By 1793 wives had gained the right to share family property and girls inherited equally with boys. Children born out of wedlock won equal rights to the inheritance of their parents who acknowledged them. The Convention passed two laws in 1794 and 1795 providing free and compulsory primary schools for both girls and boys, but each primary school had separate divisions for boys and girls with teachers of their own sex. Although the turmoil of the Revolution prevented the implementation of this education, in the nineteenth century primary schools were founded along these lines.

The issue of political rights for women met more resistance. Since the leaders of the Revolution pursued goals they considered to be rights of nature, and since they viewed woman as man's natural companion, those women in opposition to their policies were termed "unnatural." The men in power feared that women in politics would be manipulated by counterrevolutionaries or by opposing factions. In fact, in some rural areas, religious women had defended counterrevolutionary priests who had refused to take oaths of loyalty to the government. When civil war broke out in northwest France in March 1793 in opposition to the republican levy of troops, large groups of women fought with men in the name of their old religion and the king.

In Paris, distrust grew of *all* politically active women during the struggle between the more conservative faction, the Girondins (named for the deputies from the department near Bordeaux), and the more radical Jacobins, or men of the Mountain (so named because they sat on the high seats in the National Convention). The Girondins, who controlled the ministry, were suspicious of the women of Paris, who in February 1793 demonstrated against high prices and the scarcity of bread. These women, who listened to the *enragé,* or ultrarevolutionary, priest Jacques Roux and journalist Théophile Leclerc, seized merchandise and forced its sale at fixed prices. Also, women in the popular societies censured the Girondin ministry's conduct of the war after the treason of General Dumouriez. The men of the Girondin faction suspected women activists of helping the *sans-culottes* (revolutionary artisans and small businessmen) plan an insurrection that would give the Jacobins control of the Convention.

But the Jacobins also thought women should not meddle in politics. Jean Paul Marat, the journalist most loved by the sans-culottes, and a Jacobin deputy, accused Mme. Roland, the wife of the Girondin minister of the interior, of being the real power behind her husband. Mme. Roland had always denied such a role for herself, although she exerted much influence on the ministers who met at her home. In her memoirs, written later that year when she was in prison, Mme. Roland revealed herself as a disciple of Rousseau. Women, she wrote, ruled through the hearts of men, who alone had the talent and force for politics. Mme. Roland had used considerable talent and force in editing her husband's speeches, and she kept secret the fact that she had written his June 1792 letter of protest to the king. Once a friend of Louise Kéralio, she now despised her for her activism among the Jacobins. Mme. Roland also despised the sans-culottes women, who in May 1793 swarmed the Convention calling for the fall of her husband's ministry and the expulsion of the Girondins.

On May 10, 1793, a club exclusively for women, the *Femmes républicaines révolutionnaires,* or Republican Revolutionary Women, met in the library of the Jacobin Club. This action aroused the suspicion of many men. On May 25 Girondin deputy Isnard warned that women planned to gain control of the galleries of the Convention to set off an insurrection. On that day some women at the Convention attacked and publicly whipped Théroigne de Méricourt because of her allegiance to the Girondin deputies.

On May 31 and June 2, thousands of armed Parisians succeeded in purging the Convention of Girondin leaders. The Jacobins knew they owed their power to the sans-culottes, but they distrusted the politically active women among them. Those women who were anti-Jacobin were harshly treated. Etta Palm, who had left France in the beginning of 1793 to serve on a mission to her native Netherlands, was later arrested as a royalist agent of that country. By mid-1793 both Olympe de Gouges and Théroigne de Méricourt were in disgrace. Théroigne disappeared from public life after the humiliation of her whipping. Olympe de Gouges made no secret of her opposition to the June 2 insurrection. Although her royalist sympathies had been obvious since December 1792, when she had rashly offered her services to defend the king while he was on trial for treason, she pretended in 1793 to be a true republican. On June 4 she published her *Political Testament,* in which she called Robespierre and Marat monsters. She was arrested a few weeks later, after she advocated an uprising throughout France to put down the Jacobins in the Convention. Anticipating martyrdom, she had willed her heart, in the *Political Testament,* to her country, her probity to men (who needed it, she said), and her spirit and soul to women. She was guillotined (after a postponement for a false pregnancy) in November 1793, shortly after the queen and Mme. Roland.

On July 13, 1793, Charlotte Corday, a young supporter of the Girondin cause, assassinated Marat in revenge for the purging of the Girondins and the crushing of their uprisings. Revulsion for Corday's crime, viewed as particularly heinous because she was a woman, set off a reaction against women in politics. Newspapers demanded the guillotine for the queen as a monster who not only committed crimes against France but was an unnatural mother. The reaction against counterrevolutionary women threatened even the women among the sans-culottes who showed political initiative. True, Pauline Léon was well received by the Jacobin society on August 15, when she led a deputation of Republican Revolutionary Women to ask for affiliation and contributions to a monument in Marat's honor. But the Jacobins feared that these women were tools of extremists who incited them to riot for bread. After some friction with the women of the Jacobin fraternal society, who echoed Jacobin policies and hesitated to call for price controls, the Republican Revolutionary Women moved to the charnel house of Saint-Eustache.

On August 26, the Republican Revolutionary Women called for the arrest and trial of counterrevolutionary suspects. These women supported the Terror: legal machinery to punish the selfish rich as foreign agents who cared nothing for poor people's suffering. In the autumn of 1793 Claire Lacombe led the Republican Revolutionary Women to petition the Convention for price controls.

Soon, every political group struggling for power within the National Convention denounced the Republican Revolutionary Women as counterrevolutionary. Even a strong advocate of women's rights, François Chabot, turned against them. Earlier in 1793 he had proposed a plan for a constitution that granted married women who were mothers the right to serve on juries and also to elect local officials, although it denied female citizens the right to preside over electoral assemblies. In September, Chabot served on a commission to fix prices by means of the proposed Law of the Maximum. Yet he became a fierce opponent of the Republican Revolutionary Women. Why? The explanation could lie in prevalent male attitudes toward the "unnaturalness" of women in politics or fears of their manipulation by counterrevolutionary factions. But Chabot was also in trouble. He was accused in September by the sans-culottes press of financial corruption. Shortly thereafter, he planned to marry a rich foreigner, a step that he knew would displease Jacobins. To prove that his reputed weakness for women could not corrupt him, Chabot attacked the Republican Revolutionary Women on September 16 at the Jacobin Club. A quarrel within the women's club provided Chabot with an excuse to attack Lacombe, its president. He accused her of having asked him, when he was a member of the Committee of General Security, to free an alleged counterrevolutionary. Members of the Jacobin society prevented Lacombe from answering Chabot at the meeting and called for her arrest.

Instead of being intimidated, the Republican Revolutionary Women two days later petitioned the Paris Commune to arrest *émigrés'* wives who remained in Paris and to transfer prostitutes to national homes, where they would learn useful work and listen to patriotic talks. These proposals did not please Pierre Gaspard Chaumette, the public prosecutor of the Commune, who had taken an aggressive stand against priests and prostitutes, both of whom he believed to be conspiring for the counterrevolution. Moreover, the Republican Revolutionary Women annoyed Chaumette by patrolling the streets to report food hoarding and by forcing women to wear the national cockade.

On September 21 the Convention responded to petitions from these women by decreeing that all women must wear the national cockade. And on September 29, under pressure from sans-culottes and revolutionary women, the Convention passed the Law of the Maximum, which regulated prices on forty commodities. However, the market women, who had rallied to support the Revolution during 1789, now opposed the Maximum, which made business difficult for small dealers. When Lacombe appeared at the Commune to call for inspection of homes and businesses to detect evasions of the Maximum, she made enemies of the market women. Nor was the Commune well disposed toward the Republican Revolutionary Women. Some of them patrolling the streets wore trousers with pistols in their belts; they wore not only the national cockade but the *bonnet rouge,* or red cap of liberty worn by male sans-culottes as a symbol from ancient times of freedom from slavery. The market women complained that the Republican Revolutionaries wished to impose male clothing on them as well as the cockade. In October 28, 1793, the market women beat up women who appeared on the street wearing the red caps and then complained to the Convention that the Republican Revolutionaries forced them to wear men's hats. They insisted in the name of liberty that they be allowed to wear what they pleased. The Convention applauded, and repealed the law requiring women to wear the national cockade. One deputy, Fabre d'Eglantine, an opponent of the Maximum, blamed the Republican Revolutionary Women for causing trouble and accused them of wearing pistols in order to lead troops of women to get bread by force. Fabre (executed a few months later with Chabot for corruption) claimed these women were immoral because few of them lived with their families. The Committee of General Security declared that any brawl over the bonnet rouge was a counterrevolutionary plot. On October 30, the Jacobin deputy Amar, speaking in the Convention for this committee, questioned whether women should exercise political rights at all. Women, said Amar, did not have the moral and physical strength for politics because nature destined them for functions within the family. The Convention then decreed the suppression of all women's clubs.

The Republican Revolutionary Women did not recover from this blow, although some members continued to be active in local popular societies. However, after Robespierre put an end to all opposing factions in the spring of 1794, the Convention prohibited women's admission to popular assemblies. That Robespierre hated politically active women we know from his private papers, found after his execution in July 1794. According to him, the Republican Revolutionary Women cried famine to spread despair and turn people to counterrevolution. These women were unnatural, thought Robespierre, because to them female modesty was only a prejudice, and they wanted men to make room for women in the legislature and on the platform of political assemblies. Robespierre called these women "sterile as vice," presumably because he thought they were not wives or mothers (which was not true), and he concluded that they revenged their unnatural state by slandering the representatives of the people. Although Robespierre did honor the women of the October Days of 1789 and those who bravely helped repulse the foreign invaders, he reserved most of his praise for women who bore children and sacrificed their sons and husbands for the republic.

Perhaps this shudder of distaste for female activists can be blamed on the ideas of Rousseau, which influenced Robespierre and his generation of revolutionaries. Again and again at patriotic festivals the Jacobins idealized a Rousseauean heroine. Some Jacobins at first worshiped a Goddess of Liberty, who was created in November 1793 at the very time and by some of the very men who were censuring the Republican Revolutionary Women. After the bishop of Paris appeared at the Convention to renounce his ecclesiastical post, the Commune closed the cathedral of Notre Dame and three days later consecrated it as the temple of Reason. During the ceremony a woman dressed in classical robes emerged from a replica of a Greek temple dedicated to Philosophy while citizens sang hymns to liberty in her honor. Two rows of girls dressed in white, crowned with oak leaves and bearing flowers, bowed before the altar, where burned the torch of Truth, as they ascended a platform, the "holy mountain." Revolutionary newspapers reported the goddess to be beautiful and a more fitting tribute to nature than an inanimate statue. Who played the role of the Goddess of Liberty of the cult of Reason? We cannot be certain but she may have been a member of the Opéra. Frequent festivals in Paris probably drew on the acting talent of the Opéra, which had undergone a revolutionary change in moral and social outlook. In the departments outside Paris, those chosen to represent the goddess were selected from the respectable daughters of middle-class Jacobin families.

The Jacobins, however, soon repudiated the cult of Reason and its Goddess of Liberty. Robespierre, in particular, did not approve of the cult, which to him smacked of the aristocratic Voltairean Enlightenment, as distinct from Rousseau's religion of civic virtue. Politically he thought the cult of Reason unwise, as it offended many good Catholics, who thought the Goddess of Liberty parodied the suffering Virgin mother. On November 21, 1793, at the Jacobin Club he denounced the cult of Reason as atheistic. Within a few days the Convention reaffirmed the principle of freedom of religion and forced the Commune to reopen a number of churches for Christmas worship.

Although the deification of women as goddesses of liberty disappeared, women continued to be honored in patriotic festivals and processions for their virtue, patriotism, and strength. On December 28 the Commune decreed that the women of the October Days would march in public ceremonies carrying banners: "Thus they drive the vile tyrant like a prey before them!" In Bourg-en-Bresse on January 10, 1794, in a festival in honor of the movement to abolish slavery, a white woman driven in a cart gave milk to a black child while a black woman nursed a white child. Everywhere the Rousseauean ideal of pregnant and nursing women personified the regeneration of France.

On May 7, 1794, Robespierre proposed the establishment of a civic religion in honor of the Supreme Being. In his discourse at the festival for the Supreme Being on June 8 he conceived of the deity not as the Christian God but as a supernatural force who blessed republican liberty and guided the Republic of Virtue. This impersonal Supreme Being, masculine in concept, had no need of a goddess, but festivals in its honor stressed familial cohesion. Thousands of women took part, emulating the ancient Greeks of Sparta in their religious processions by marching in separate detachments subdivided into groups according to familial functions and singing the appropriate songs for each group. Women had sacrificed for the republic and in return the Jacobins honored the importance of women *within the family* in revolutionary France. Gone were the Amazons, the activists, the petitioners for women's rights, the clubs of revolutionary women.

After Robespierre's downfall on July 27, 1794, the Convention ended the Reign of Terror. Price controls stopped. The prisons released counterrevolutionary suspects, including priests. The moderates closed the Jacobin Club and then drafted conservative laws to replace the democratic constitution of 1793. The end of the Terror also brought a reaction against revolutionary puritanism. In Paris a new group of women, the wives and mistresses of those who profited from the victories of French armies, displayed their new riches with insolence, while others went hungry again in the spring of 1795. After the repeal of the Maximum, when peasants refused to provide Paris with food in retaliation for the devaluation of paper money, the poor women of Paris watched with alarm the rise of prices in the open market. Their children starved; families unable to bear their hunger jumped into the Seine. The police reported that women waiting in bread lines to receive their daily ration urged men to organize another uprising.

Seemingly little had been gained for the poor, the wage earners, the artisans, and craftsmen. From police records we learn of the hardships they suffered in January and February 1795, when the government closed the arms workshops. In March, the police reported that women rioted for bread and sent deputations to the National Convention to protest. These women accused their men of cowardice for taking no action, and they organized marches to the Convention, which were dispersed by the National Guards. On April 1, after the bread ration was reduced and in some sections not distributed, men and women burst into the Convention demanding bread. But they had neither leaders nor plans and were again dispersed. The Convention did little to increase the amount of rationed bread, despite daily reports of starvation and suicide.

In the days that followed, women continued their protests at bread lines and illegal assemblies in various parts of the city. The daily ration of bread fell from six to four ounces to two ounces. Some women even refused to accept the reduced bread ration. Early in the morning of May 20, the women called the men out from work and forced shops to close; they assembled in the streets and convinced other women to march with them; they beat drums to call men to arms. At two o'clock in the afternoon, women with children among them, followed by armed detachments of sans-culottes, surged into the halls of the Convention. The women wore signs: "Bread and the Constitution of 1793!" on their bonnets and blouses.

The Convention listened to their demands after the insurgents killed a deputy who had resisted their entry. A few Jacobin deputies supported them. The insurrectionaries thought they had won a victory, but while they made speeches, the Convention called out armed forces to expel them. The following day the sans-culottes marched again on the Convention, this time with many more thousands of armed men and women. The forces of the Convention went over to their side. Instead of firing, the insurrectionaries negotiated for "Bread and the Constitution of 1793!" and withdrew with promises. The next day the Convention called out the regular army to surround the rebellious neighborhood of Saint-Antoine and starve it into submission. Despite the attempts of women and men from other sections to relieve Saint-Antoine, it surrendered and suffered terrible repression. On May 23, 1795, the Convention decreed that women were disturbers of the peace and they must remain in their homes; gatherings of more than five women would be dispersed by force.

It would be wrong to assume that because women had come into the Revolution in 1789 asking for bread and liberty and had come out in 1795 with starvation and restriction of their movements, they had gained nothing. They won laws protecting their rights in marriage, property, and education. True, women were denied political rights in the French Revolution (as were the majority of men when the Convention scrapped the democratic constitution of 1793) but nowhere else at the time did women share political rights with men.

Although women were a cohesive group during the Revolution, they responded mainly to the needs of their class and were never an autonomous force. The ideology of the revolutionary authorities who distrusted women's political movements derived seemingly from Rousseau, but actually from the facts of their lives: France's small-scale, home-based economy needed middle- and working-class women to contribute their special skills and labor to their families. Women were not yet a large, independent group in the working class.

In the early days of the French Revolution, women from the middle classes (as can be seen from cahiers written by them) welcomed the restoration of their natural rights as wives and mothers to participate in society as men's "natural companions." Women of the urban poor — wage earners, artisans of women's crafts, owners of small enterprises, such as the market women — agitated for bread rather than for women's rights. There is, however, evidence that "respectable" middle-class women joined them. Although these movements crossed class lines, which were perhaps not rigidly fixed, they did not cross sex lines. When men participated, as they did in the October Days of 1789, they came as armed escorts or separate detachments.

As the Revolution entered its more radical phase, as economic crisis followed war and civil strife, the polarization between the rich and the poor sharpened the older struggle between aristocrat and patriot. During the last days of the National Convention, the women who surged into the hall crying "Bread and the Constitution of 1793!" truly represented the poor, whom the upper classes and their women now feared. The bread riots belonged to the women of the poor, who incited their men to insurrection, but the insurrection belonged to both of them, the sans-culottes and their women.

Yet, the Revolution had called upon women to make great sacrifices and they did; in consequence, women became a revolutionary force unprecedented in history. The men in power feared women who challenged the Revolution's failure to guarantee bread for the poor. So feared were the women of the French Revolution that they became legendary — they became Mme. Defarge later to those who feared revolution itself.

A new elite of the upper middle class, men of wealth and talent, rose to power in the four years of the Directory following the dissolution in 1795 of the National Convention. Their women had no political rights but emerged as influential ladies of the salon, such as the brilliant writer Mme. de Staël, and Mme. Tallien, former wife of an aristocrat and now derisively called "Our Lady of Thermidor," as a symbol of the reaction. One of these ladies, Josephine de Beauharnais, the widow of a general, became the mistress of one of the Directors before she married the young Napoleon Bonaparte, who soon afterward became general of the armies in Italy.

Outside of Paris, away from the glamour of these women, middle-class morality prevailed. Napoleon subscribed to this morality. When he became emperor in 1804, he wrote laws into his code to strengthen the authority of the husband and father of the family as a safeguard for private property. Women lost whatever rights they had gained in the Revolution, for now they had to obey their husbands unconditionally. Napoleon left women the right to divorce (for Napoleon to use against Josephine when she failed to provide him an heir), but this right was taken from them after 1815 by the restoration of the Bourbon monarchy.

What could not be taken from women was their memory of victories during the French Revolution: their march to Versailles in the October Days, their petitions to the legislature, their club meetings, their processions, their insurrections. Their defeats served as lessons for next time. "We are simple women," a woman was reported to have said at a club meeting in the days of the uprising of the Paris Commune in May 1871, nearly a century later, "but not made of weaker stuff than our grandmothers of '93. Let us not cause their shades to blush for us, but be up and doing, as they would be were they living now."

Suggestions for Further Reading

Abray, Jane. "Feminism in the French Revolution." *American Historical Review,* 80 (1975).

Hufton, Owen. "Women in Revolution, 1789–1796." *Past and Present,* 53 (1971).

Lytle, Scott. "The Second Sex (September, 1793)." *Journal of Modern History,* 27 (1955).

May, Gita. *Madame Roland and the Age of Revolution.* Columbia University Press, New York and London, 1970.

Racz, Elizabeth. "The Women's Rights Movement in the French Revolution." *Science and Society,* 16 (1951–1952).

Rudé, George. *The Crowd in the French Revolution.* Clarendon Press, Oxford, 1967.

Stephens, Winifred. *Women of the French Revolution.* Chapman & Hall, London, 1922.

Williams, David. "The Politics of Feminism in the French Enlightenment." *The Varied Pattern: Studies in the Eighteenth Century.* Toronto, 1971.

Wollstonecraft, Mary. *Vindication of the Rights of Woman* (1792). W. W. Norton, New York, 1967.

Recent Works in French

Cerati, Marie. *Le club des citoyennes républicaines révolutionnaires.* Éditions Sociales, Paris, 1966.

Collins, Marie, and Sylvie Weil Sayre. *Les Femmes en France.* Charles Scribner's Sons, New York, 1974.

Duhet, Paule-Marie. *Les femmes et la Révolution, 1789–1794.* Collection Archives Julliard, Paris, 1971.

Sullerot, Evelyne. *Histoire de la presse féminine des origines à 1848.* A. Colin, Paris, 1966.

11

Working-Class Women During the Industrial Revolution, 1780–1914

Mary Lynn McDougall

The foregoing essays force us to the conclusion that the major political upheavals that fill so many pages in standard historical surveys have had only a temporary impact on the lives of women. Far more important have been transformations in social structure, such as the transition from aristocratic to middle-class rule in the ancient polities or from feudal to bourgeois rule in early modern Europe. Undoubtedly, the greatest of these changes has been the Industrial Revolution. Conventional histories assume that the emergent technological and social transformations of industrialization allowed women increasing access to economic activity. The essays in this volume by Mary Lynn McDougall, Theresa McBride, and Renate Bridenthal arrive at quite a different conclusion. McDougall draws a composite portrait of the life of the working-class woman. Rather than claiming that the Industrial Revolution affected all working-class women equally, she points to the unevenness of its impact on women's work. She analyzes changes in the type of work women did and when in their life cycles they did it. Were these changes beneficial for women relative to men? Richard T. Vann has optimistically noted an increase in longevity and some control over fertility just before industrialization, but McDougall points out the appalling toll in women's lives the exploitation of their labor took. Also, while single women may have enjoyed some new opportunities for economic self-sufficiency, married women experienced a drastic curtailment of theirs, introducing a curious reversal of adult and adolescent status. On the balance, this author concludes that the Industrial Revolution exerted a smaller and more negative impact on women's lives than conventional interpretations assert.

Carding, Drawing, and Roving, operations in the manufacture of cotton. (From Edward Baines, *History of the Cotton Manufacture in Great Britain,* intro. by W. H. Chaloner, Kelley, New Jersey, 1966; reprinted from the 1835 edition)

In 1837 a French economist used the term "revolution" to describe the transformation of certain English industries since the 1780s, thereby suggesting that these economic changes rivaled the more political French Revolution in their impact and import. Historians went further and gave the label "Industrial Revolution" to the substitution of steam-powered machinery for human skill and work, the changeover from an artisanal and domestic system to a factory system of production, and the unprecedented rise in productivity that resulted. Both contemporaries and historians believed that the economic transformation caused profound social upheaval, particularly among workers, including women workers.

During the Industrial Revolution, conservatives and social reformers expressed grave concern about the employment of women in factories. Women working outside the home, minding large and complicated machinery, and earning their own living ran counter to the prevailing middle-class ideal of women as domestic, delicate, and dependent upon the support of a father or husband. As one commentator put it: "A woman, become a worker, is no longer a woman." Women whose work kept them away from home as many as sixteen hours a day, five and a half or six days a week, threatened two highly sanctified institutions: the patriarchal family and the home. "What remains of the poor person's home if it is abandoned by she who is both its servant and its mistress?" Lastly, constant, excessive work by young women imperiled the health of infants and thus "the integrity of the race." [1]

Some contemporaries did favor women in the factories. Industrialists and advocates of the factory system pointed out that machinery made work easier and that, in the early stages of industrialization, women often worked with their children, under the supervision of their husbands and fathers. In the second half of the nineteenth century, after attempts to exclude women from some factories and reduce the number of hours they could work in others, feminists argued women's need, desire, and ability to work anywhere, as long as men, for equal wages. By the end of the century, a few Englishwomen reported that they preferred factory to workshop or domestic work, paid or unpaid, liked the companionship of their colleagues, and enjoyed the independence derived from earning their living (though the majority of factory women interviewed said that they worked because of economic need).[2]

In the twentieth century, as most of western Europe moved beyond the stage of industrialization, the debate about women in the factory receded but did not disappear. Historians with a pessimistic view of the Industrial Revolution emphasized the large number of women forced to do monotonous yet intense and fatiguing labor, leave their children with ignorant, venal nurses, and neglect their homes. Historians with an optimistic view noted that women had long done unpleasant work, that factories relieved them of many boring domestic tasks, that they opened up fields of endeavor outside the home, and that they increased women's independence by paying individual as opposed to family wages. Recently, quantitative historians have undermined the assumptions that industrialization brought a significant proportion of women employment outside the home or a meaningful increase in independence.[3]

Obviously, the Industrial Revolution's impact on working women is controversial. Yet the controversy can be minimized by moving beyond grand generalizations about the Industrial Revolution to the precise, often contradictory, ways it affected working women, and by using statistical sources and, wherever possible, the admittedly scarce testimony of working women. We will study working-class women in nineteenth- and early twentieth-century England and France. Two basic questions will be addressed: How did the work experience change for lower-class women, as compared with lower-class men? What influence did women's work have on their lives and on the working-class family?

The Work Experience

One generalization about the Industrial Revolution claims it removed labor from the family workshop and relocated it in the factory. Since women had presumably been restricted to the family workshop, and since the first branch of industry transformed was a "feminine" one, spinning, the relocation is considered liberating for women. Like other generalizations, this one contains a truth in exaggerated form. It calls for qualifications. Long before the first factory (probably Arkwright's cotton mill, 1780) some women worked part of their lives away from home, in small workshops. Milliners and dressmakers regularly did this. In France, orphan girls spent many years spinning or sewing in convent workshops. Orders of nuns operated these workshops as charities, to teach indigent girls trades.

Furthermore, industrialization did not shift all work to factories. Modernization in one branch of an industry could cause expansion in more traditional branches of the same industry. As cotton spinning became a factory occupation and thread output rose in early nineteenth-century England, the number of cotton hand-loom weavers increased. Even when steam-powered cotton looms and weaving factories entered the field (beginning about 1830) many hand-loom weavers held out by lowering their rates. Of course, they could not continue indefinitely: by the 1860s, few cotton hand-loom weavers remained in England. Similarly, modernization in one industry could spur on more traditional industries in the same industrial sector. The threat of abundant, inexpensive cotton goods galvanized the silk industry. Because of the fragility and costliness of silk thread, merchant-manufacturers could not adopt the power loom until thread and loom had been improved, late in the nineteenth century. Until then, the merchant-manufacturers of Lyon reduced costs by producing simpler fabrics and employing cheaper labor: peasants and women. Most peasants and women wove in their homes, but thousands of girls and young women wove in the convent or charitable workshops that sprang up around Lyon and all over southern France. Finally, the growth of a wealthy middle class resulted in rising demand for consumer goods, such as clothing, which were still made in workshops or homes.[4]

A second commonplace about the Industrial Revolution is that by harnessing inanimate sources of power — steam and electricity — it reduced the premium on brute strength that had allowed masculine monopolies in certain trades. In the long run, industrialization has opened up trades previously closed to women. In the short run, however, complications arose. Although the first cotton mills did employ girls, most mills laid them off when they became adults. Later, as spinning machines — the jenny, then the mule — increased in size, men took charge of them, aided by children. Thus, industrialization first affected women by displacing them in a traditionally "feminine" branch of industry! Women returned to the mill, in auxiliary positions, after the factory acts forbade the employment of children. Conversely, women flowed into cotton weaving, considered the "masculine" branch of the industry because it required more strength and, in some cases, skill before the power loom spread. Women deprived of their traditional occupation, spinning, moved into an expanding field and learned the old techniques (though they specialized in lighter, unskilled work). To be sure, when the power loom took over, more women became weavers. The original factory masters actually preferred women because men were "more difficult to manage" and demanded higher wages.

Industrialization can also be credited with simplifying many work processes, thereby minimizing the skill required and ending men's monopoly on skilled trades. Once the work could be learned without a long apprenticeship, usually restricted to men, women could take up the now-semiskilled trade. Even so, there were impediments. Skilled men formed craft unions, and these unions fought long and hard to keep women out of their trades (hoping to keep wages high). In addition, some industrial technology developed to the point where it demanded technical training. This excluded women, at least until industry sorely needed them. Only the onset of World War I enabled women to enter many skilled trades in any significant numbers.

Today even the most convinced pessimist would not argue, as some earlier authors did, that the Industrial Revolution changed work from a pleasant, wholesome family activity into a harsh and utterly demoralizing drudgery. Before industrialization, most women did monotonous and repetitious work such as spinning, tatting, or setting up looms. Other women did heavy labor, like hauling coal for their fathers or husbands. While these women could take breaks, they could not stop at will. If they spun or tatted, they worked when they had enough light, and when they could get orders. Though spinning rates occasionally rose to high levels, more often low rates required long hours of work to earn a reasonable living. If women did preparatory or auxiliary jobs for their fathers or husbands, they geared their work to the men's. And the men, like the women, usually had no alternative but working long hours. Moreover, when women took breaks from this form of labor, they generally turned to other labors, notably housekeeping and child care. Industrialization did not alter some aspects of women's work. Factory labor was also monotonous and repetitious; factory women frequently did preparatory and auxiliary work; they worked long days and still did housework.

Yet, factories did produce changes, negative and positive. Factory work was more regulated and regimented. Workers no longer set the pace; they adopted the steady pulse of the machine. Initially, industrialists had to struggle to instill in their workers the then novel idea that work began and ended at precise times (ergo, the factory bell). They posted exhaustive lists of rules and imposed penalties, mainly fines, for infractions. Labor historians have seen the rules and penalties as signs that workmen rebelled against the regimentation of factory life. But rules and fines also applied to factories where women predominated, and the numerous comments on impudent "mill girls" suggest that they too rebelled. Even the large charitable workshops established strict, conventlike regulations and enforced them with punishments.[5]

Another negative feature of early factory work derived from masculine supervision. No doubt contemporary social reformers, shocked by the very thought of women being supervised by men who were not relatives, overemphasized the comparative evils of the system. Fathers and husbands who doubled as overseers inflicted some of the beatings in early factories, as they had long done in workshops. Women in the putting-out system had tolerated advances from men crucial to their economic well being, since they had acted as their husbands' intermediaries to the merchant-manufacturer who "employed" them. Nevertheless, these evils increased in factories. Not only immediate overseers — who might not be relatives — but foremen and owners exerted authority over factory women. Some early overseers and foremen, and even a few masters, abused their authority by "seducing" their female "hands." At least one operator of a "charitable workshop" tried raping the young women in his care.[6]

Factories accentuated other unhealthy working conditions. Most workshops had been and continued to be stuffy, crowded, and unclean; until the late nineteenth century, most factory buildings were poorly ventilated, jammed with noisy machinery, and lacking in basic sanitary facilities. Certain kinds of spinners had always worked in extremely hot and humid rooms; in nineteenth-century mills, linen spinners dressed in loose, scanty shifts stood in steaming 120- to 140-degree temperatures as many as fourteen hours per day. Other workers in spinning and trades such as metal polishing had long breathed air polluted with minute particles of fiber or metal, including lead; nineteenth-century mills produced even denser atmospheres by gathering many fast-moving machines in one confined area. No wonder, then, that in the English mill town Oldham, in the early 1850s, the deaths from tuberculosis were double the national average, and among women of twenty-five to thirty-five, triple the average. Factories also threatened life and limb by exposing many people, including children, to large, complex machinery devoid of safety devices. Every year in the early 1850s fifteen out of every 1,000 mill workers in Oldham died, lost fingers or limbs, or suffered lacerations in factory accidents.[7]

In time, factories improved, thanks to the efforts of paternalistic employers, factory workers, and outsiders. At first, when mills located on streams in small villages, employers like Arkwright provided housing and services to attract workers. (Others dealt with the labor shortage by exploiting pauper children.) When the use of steam engines dictated an urban setting, with a plentiful labor supply, few industrialists did anything for their workers. Even then, though, Alsatian cloth manufacturers built housing, educational, and child-care facilities for their workers. Still, until the 1850s and 1860s the actual work experience did not improve. Then some English industrialists, called the "new model" employers, ameliorated work conditions out of confidence in the booming economy and awareness of a new theory that better work conditions would raise productivity. For their part, workers became familiar with factory routine, which contributed to the declining ferocity of factory discipline. Trade unions added to their interest in wages a new concern about work hours and conditions. Since women unionized only slowly, they made little input into the improvement in factory life until the twentieth century.

Outsiders used public opinion to influence women's and children's labor. Beginning in the 1830s, doctors, early social scientists, and the social novelists "discovered" the factory workers and publicized their plight. Novels like Charles Dickens's *Hard Times* and Emile Zola's *Germinal* movingly condemned the regimentation and strain of work in factories or mines. In England, Mrs. Gaskell and Mrs. Tonna specifically exposed the wretched situation of women workers. These exposés created an adverse public image of industrialists and sympathy for workers; this climate of opinion encouraged change. The "new model" employers wanted to improve their image. Distrust of industrialists and sympathy for workers motivated conservative, radical, and socialist politicians to press for state intervention.

The state proved to be the most effective agent in establishing and maintaining minimal standards for women's and children's work. As early as 1802 the English Parliament passed the first Factory Act, designed to control working conditions of pauper children. In 1833, a more comprehensive and enforceable Factory Act extended the controls to all mill children and instituted a system of factory inspection. A series of acts ensued; they eventually covered all children and provided for inspection of most worksites. France followed suit, beginning in 1841. Next came legislation for women, starting in England in 1844 and in France in 1874. This body of legislation gradually encompassed many aspects of women's work: it established a limit first of twelve, then of eleven and, in some cases, of ten hours work per day; it prohibited most work at night, on Saturday afternoons, and in particularly dangerous places, such as underground mines; it set basic health and safety standards; and it forbade the rehiring of new mothers within four weeks of giving birth. From the 1890s the authorities appointed women factory inspectors. Thereafter more women reported grievances — and received some relief.[8]

This legislation had some pernicious side effects. Proponents of the legislation postulated women's inferior physical strength and moral fiber, one of their more outrageous arguments being that girls should not work in intense heat because heat aroused passions they could not control! Proponents assumed that women belonged in the home and, like children, required protection. The legislation also discriminated in very practical ways. Many factory women and feminists protested that shorter hours meant smaller earnings or even loss of employment. Since industrialists wanted their expensive plants operating as long as possible, they often fired women after laws prohibited them from working as long as men. Some women disliked the laws that excluded them from dangerous places, thereby depriving them of their traditional work and sometimes of the only work available in their area. Lastly, many laws left loopholes. For example, early legislation limiting hours did not impose set times for beginning and ending work. Consequently, factories could avoid the shorter work day by using a relay system. Women worked in teams, on split shifts, so the factory could operate fourteen or sixteen hours. Women often had to spend the periods between shifts at the factory, cleaning machinery or workrooms. As the shorter day became a reality, factory work intensified: workers watched more machines; the machines moved faster. Health standards were frequently illusory. Maternity legislation did not insist on proof of date of birth, so new mothers who needed money simply lied about the date and returned to work early.[9]

Despite its drawbacks, protective legislation did help women. Instead of starting work at age six or seven, girls began at eight, ten, twelve, and, by the twentieth century, thirteen or fourteen. They received more education. Shorter days gave women more leisure time. In the second half of the nineteenth century, wages generally rose and compensated for the pay loss from shorter hours. The incidence of occupational diseases and deformities declined. These very real gains take precedence over the laws' defects and discriminatory aspects, especially since legislators ultimately strengthened and extended them to men. Even before the laws applied to men, they benefited men. Where men and women worked together, shorter hours for one eventually meant shorter hours for the other, and both sexes shared better health conditions. By the 1890s — and the growth of socialist movements — the English and French governments began to intervene in favor of workers regardless of their sex.[10]

The factory system had more direct advantages for women. Factory work was not as seasonal as most other kinds of work. Because an industrialist invested in expensive machinery and plant, he had fixed costs (rent or taxes, maintenance) and therefore rarely closed down operations, even in hard times. Since a merchant-manufacturer who put out work did not own the means of production, he could cease putting out work every slack season without great loss. As a result, factory workers worked while artisanal and domestic workers were unemployed or underemployed, sometimes two or three or even six months per year. This had a special impact on women, whose work in factories often carried their families through the slack season in their husbands' trades.

Another positive feature of factory work for unskilled or semiskilled women — most women — was higher earnings. In addition to higher yearly incomes from working year-round, most factory women received higher daily wages than other unskilled or semiskilled women. In the 1830s, in the French cotton city of Lille, women in spinning mills received between 75 centimes and 1 franc 75 centimes per day whereas lace makers working in their homes earned between 60 centimes and 1 franc 25 centimes for an equally long day. At the end of our period, 1914, a sample of working wives in the English cotton city of Manchester found that those in the cotton factories had average weekly wages more than twice as high as those who hemmed handkerchiefs in their homes. Finally, while the remuneration for most work rose in the course of the Industrial Revolution, factory wages fluctuated less than artisanal or domestic rates, which frequently sustained steep declines.[11]

In spite of the advantages of factory wages, women workers remained underpaid. Though the average wage rose slightly more for women than for men, at the end of the nineteenth century the average wage for women was still less than half that of men. Part of the explanation lies in different professional profiles: more men worked in skilled trades, with higher remuneration. However, differences also existed within the same trade. In the 1830s men in the Lille spinning mills earned from 2 francs 50 centimes to 3 francs per day. They began at a higher rate than women could ever achieve because they managed the huge "mule" machines, while the women helped them or handled the smaller "throstle" machines. This distinction between the principal and the auxiliary operative, and between large and small machine operatives, applied in many industries to the detriment of women.[12]

More important than the sex-based wage differential, at least to the women involved, was the sheer inadequacy of their income. In the Paris of 1860 — a city of artisans and domestic workers — no fewer than 17,000, or 17 percent, of the working women earned less than or only 1 franc 25 centimes per day. A woman could not properly feed and house herself, let alone children, on this amount. In the same year, the Paris welfare bureau assisted 22,777 single and 35,432 married women. Of course, many other people, including men, lived in poverty without any official relief, especially in England, where the poor law policy discouraged people from seeking relief. Even in two cotton towns, Oldham and Preston, in two good years, 1849 and 1851, about 20 percent of the population lived in primary poverty, that is, their income kept them at or below the level of subsistence. Others suffered from secondary poverty, or from the inability to manage their income well enough to keep themselves above the level of subsistence.[13]

To this point we have only suggested some reasons for women's low wages: few underwent formal training, so few became skilled; unions restricted the number of women in the better-paying semiskilled jobs; women did auxiliary work. Rationalizing these practices was an assumption that women needed less because they did not have as many needs or responsibilities. Not only did this ignore the single, deserted, or widowed mother, it overlooked the wife who worked because her husband was ill, unemployed, or underpaid. In a working-class section of London, in the 1880s, 11,750 women headed families (154,674 men headed the other families). Only if a wife worked to fill a deficit between her husband's earnings and the family expenses could she accept less than she needed for her subsistence. This motive for accepting less has been overemphasized. The real explanation for low wages lies in lack of skill and organization. A large pool of unskilled, unorganized labor must compete for jobs and take low pay. Unskilled workers, who are easily replaced, can be afraid of unionizing. Those dispersed into many workshops and homes have trouble even getting together. Nineteenth-century women faced all these barriers and more: they had no tradition of sociability or solidarity outside the home; they could not meet where early unions met, in bars; wives and mothers had little time for meetings or money for dues. The hostility toward women workers in many men's unions added to their difficulties. It is hardly surprising that unskilled women unionized slowly.[14]

Some courageous women overcame their isolation and alienation by forming unions. Women in "feminine" trades changing over to factories organized first. As soon as 1788, the hand spinsters of Leicester, England, had an informal sisterhood that fomented an early form of industrial protest, the destruction of spinning machines. Subsequently, women joined the predominantly male Manchester spinners' union, and in 1818, some women participated in their strike. Shortly afterward, the union ousted all women because some failed to abide by union rules! Spinning unions remained closed to women until the end of the century. In France, the Lyonnais silk spinsters organized and struck in 1848 and 1869, and in the latter year, adhered to the Workingmen's Association (later called the First International) en masse. Women in industries with a high proportion of women organized next. From the 1870s, they formed unions, joined mixed — male and female — unions, and established ties with one another. In England, the feminist-inspired Women's Trade Union League (1874–1921) helped found over thirty women's unions and initiated contact with the Trade Union Congress. Although many of the league's original unions floundered, women breached the wall men had raised around unionism. By 1907, over 15 percent of all British unions — 182 of 1,173 unions — admitted women. By 1914, the 357,956 women unionists represented about 6.5 percent of all women workers. Nothing like the league appeared in France, though individual feminists aided women organizing or breaking into particular syndicates. Delegates from women's and mixed syndicates attended syndical congresses and participated in the frequent, usually unfriendly, discussions about women. Here, too, they made a modest breakthrough: by 1911, 101,049 or 1.3 percent of all French women workers belonged to syndicates. They constituted 10 percent of all French syndicalists.[15]

To complete the inquiry into the influence of the Industrial Revolution on women's work we must look at workshop and home labor. Factories undermined artisanal and home work, which could not produce as rapidly or cheaply. Workers threatened by machines could — and some did — enter the factory. However, many refused as long as they could, though this meant lowering rates for their work or learning another trade still organized on artisanal or domestic lines. These solutions were problematical.

Lowered rates required longer hours for the same and often less money. An influx into an unskilled trade resulted in overcrowding, fierce competition, still lower rates, and longer hours. Large firms subcontracted with middlemen, who crammed dozens of workers into tiny garret workshops or hired hundreds of domestic workers. The subcontractors worked both groups sixteen, eighteen, and occasionally twenty hours per day in the busy season, then laid them off or gave them half-time work in the slack season. When this happened, the trade ceased to be considered "honorable" and became "sweated." This occurred in hand-loom weaving and many other trades, including tailoring and dressmaking, which became the notoriously sweated garment industry.

Women were especially vulnerable to this development. While men stayed in their old trades from pride, many women remained from lack of choice. Since a family lived near the head of the household's job, a wife could only do work available in that area — though women regularly walked farther than their husbands to their jobs. Some women who could have worked in factories did not because of the strong prejudice against women in factories, shared by many working-class women and men. Some women could not get factory jobs because some industrialists did not hire married women, usually on the mistaken grounds of their supposed unreliability. Other wives and mothers did not work outside the home because they or their husbands believed that they belonged at home. All these factors pushed women, particularly wives and mothers, into home work. While the overall number of domestic workers declined in the process of industrialization, mainly men gave it up, leaving behind a preponderance of women. At the same time, the major kind of work done in the home shifted from spinning and weaving to sewing.[16]

The general public learned about the drastic changes in workshop and domestic labor the same way they learned about factory work: through novels, newspapers, and government reports. Many novelists wrote about pitiful dressmakers. *Punch* published an evocative poem by Thomas Hood called "The Song of the Shirt." One stanza went:

With fingers weary and worn,
With eyelids heavy and red,
A woman sat, in unwomanly rags,
Plying her needle and thread —
Stitch! Stitch! Stitch!

The *Morning Chronicle* ran a series of articles by Henry Mayhew describing the horrors of slopwork (plain sewing, usually of shirts). Artists painted pathetic scenes of seamstresses bent over their work, straining to see in poor light. Prominent social reformers sponsored a Needlewomen's Benevolent Association. Royal commissions investigated sweated industries; parliamentarians introduced regulatory bills. None of these efforts succeeded until 1909, when legislation imposed a minimum wage on sweated industries. The French mounted a similar campaign but did not get the all-important legal minimum wage. Without a minimum wage, maximum working hours cannot be enforced, since workers who do not earn enough in the allotted hours must work longer, and no amount of policing can cover all the small workshops and homes.[17]

In sum, women's work changed in many different ways. But how many women did these changes affect? Despite the absence of accurate statistics before the census of 1851, British economic historians assume a high rate of female participation in the labor force before the Industrial Revolution. By comparison, the census of 1851 indicates a surprisingly low rate of participation. That year approximately 2.8 million or just over one-quarter of all British women were employed. Though the number of women working for wages reached 5.4 million in 1911, the proportion remained substantially the same. The French figures reveal a different trend. There the proportion rose from less than one-quarter in 1856 to over one-third in 1911 (the actual numbers of women workers were 4.4 and 7.7 million, respectively). Different methods of collecting data on labor do not fully explain the divergence. One explanation may be that England industrialized more completely, while France combined development of factory-based industries with expansion of its more traditional industries. Certainly, the highly industrialized areas of France often employed a smaller proportion of women than the areas dominated by putting-out or domestic industries. France's slower rate of population growth may also account for its greater reliance on female labor. Whatever the explanation for the different trends, both sets of figures suggest that the process of industrialization added to women's opportunities for gainful employment, but not as much as one might expect.

An occupational breakdown of women workers indicates little diversification. In both countries the majority of women workers concentrated in a few occupations, which they dominated numerically. Women had taken up the same occupations, each of which had affinities to housework, before industrialization. Factories had not transformed two of the three major occupations, though sweating had changed one of the two nonfactory occupations. The figures startle. As late as 1911 over 70 percent of English working women were either domestic servants (35 percent of all working women), textile workers (19.5 percent of women workers), or garment workers (15.6 percent of women workers). In 1896, 59 percent of France's nonagricultural women workers had similar employments, with most in the garment industry (26 percent) and least in textiles (14 percent). Analysis of all French industrial sectors reveals that the three cited above were dominated by women. Women comprised over 87 percent of French clothing workers, 77 percent of French domestic servants and 51 percent of French textile workers.[18]

These statistics suggest that the Industrial Revolution had a limited impact on most women's work. Although it created more paying jobs for women, it did not offer the majority paid employment; while it opened up a few "masculine" trades like weaving, it restricted most women to sexually segregated industries; and if it drew a minority of women into factories (where they were better paid and worked shorter hours), it drew as many into sweated trades.

Other statistics show that the Industrial Revolution did have an influence on when and why women worked. In 1911, no less than 69 percent of all single Englishwomen worked, compared with a mere 9.6 percent of married women. Fifteen years earlier, the French figures had been 52 percent of single women and 38 percent of married women. It would seem that the further industrialization advanced, the greater the tendency for women to work only if and when single. Examination of the age and marital status of women employed in the textile industry, which was most transformed by machines and factories, confirms this tendency. Every source on the English cotton mills agrees on the youthfulness of the female operatives. The majority were between sixteen and twenty-one years old. Census data for the English cotton district, Lancashire, between 1841 and 1911, prove that 70 to 75 percent of the female cotton operatives were single. Clearly, most "mill girls" left the factory after marriage. Only a few returned to work: a sample from Preston in the early 1850s found that 26 percent of wives living with their husbands worked, but despite a shortage of alternative occupations, over a third of the working wives shunned factory jobs.[19]

Working-Class Women and the Family

The pattern of women working, particularly in factories, when young and single, then quitting or turning to putting-out work when married implies some alterations in women's working lives. It meant that women often received their highest wages when young and single, and reversed the old pattern whereby many women did their most rewarding work when married, as mistress of the family workshop. From these reversals, other changes have been deduced: in working women's life cycle, in their relationship to their parents, in their attitude toward and experience of marriage, childbearing and childrearing, and thus in the working-class family.

Contemporaries deduced that single working women who earned good money must be impudent and immoral; their earnings encouraged early, bad marriages or illicit relationships with parasitical men; their youthful work prevented them from learning to be good housewives and mothers and predisposed them to work after marriage and motherhood — by definition bad. Historians and sociologists criticize less; but they too correlate alterations in women's work experience both with alterations in their life cycle and with the breakdown of the working-class family. A sketch of the lives of typical working women should temper the criticism — and the correlations.[20]

Until the end of the nineteenth century, most working-class girls had short childhoods. Their play-filled days might end as early as the age of four if their parents worked at home and needed their assistance for such simple tasks as winding thread. As women took over putting-out or domestic work, they probably asked for assistance from and thereby taught their daughters more often than their sons. In addition, mothers had daughters aged seven to ten mind younger children and do housework while mothers worked. "Extra" daughters performed the same functions for neighbors. Equally young girls entered factories (until 1833 and 1841) or workshops (until the 1870s and 1880s). Only the adoption of free compulsory education, beginning in the 1870s, succeeded in raising the age for starting work to twelve or thirteen. Even then, girls helped out after school.

Children, especially girls, must have felt closer to their mothers than their fathers. Children saw more of their mothers, because mothers spent more time at home and in the neighborhood. This also applied to most mothers working outside the home, since most of these mothers spent what leisure time they had at home, while most working-class fathers habituated pubs or cafés. When fathers came home, for example at mealtimes, many set themselves apart, either physically by dining alone, before the children ate, or psychologically by eating different — and better — food. Though many fathers joined their families for Sunday walks or special occasions, particularly in France, most remained rather removed from their children. They demanded and usually received respectful obedience. Unfortunately, respect often gave way to fear, as many working-class men drank excessively, then would berate or beat their wives and children. Mistreatment not only alienated children from their fathers; it could strengthen affective bonds between the aggrieved parties, mother and children. Generally, fathers' distance from and abuse of their children more than counterbalanced the working-class mothers', whose exhaustion and irritability made their children's lives difficult.

The formal education given most working-class girls had little lasting impact on their lives. Before the free public schools initiated in the 1880s and 1890s, most workers' children attended church- or charity-sponsored schools; a minority participated in factory classes provided by paternalistic employers or required by protective legislation. Most of these schools, especially the secondary and technical ones, catered to boys and men. The few girls' schools that existed offered as much instruction in the fourth

"R," religion, as in the other three "R's." Even institutions that trained poor girls and women for more highly paid occupations were encumbered by heavy moral overtones. Yet basic literacy improved so that by the second half of the nineteenth century a market for popular women's literature developed. Unhappily, though understandably, most of this literature was escapist and/or sensationalist, albeit moralistic. Once public schools opened, more girls attended schools, and schools put more emphasis on practical subjects. But girls still received very little technical training and very inadequate instruction in home economics. A few of the more fortunate girls used their education as a steppingstone to more "respectable" positions as shop clerks; the majority found little application for their "learning."[21]

When girls began work, they did not protest or complain. Working-class cultures expected children, particularly adolescents, to work and contribute to the family income (some saw this as compensating parents for the expense of raising children). Children accepted this. In fact, many girls prided themselves on working and helping their families financially; it made them feel important. Moreover, work could have attractions: one could meet people and make friends at work. Workers talked and sang in many workshops — though rarely in factories; they ate two meals a day together; friends walked to and from work arm in arm.

The custom of living at home until marriage further eased the transition to work. In the Preston sample mentioned previously, about three-quarters of the girls and young women aged fifteen to twenty-four who had parents alive lived with their parents. (About 15 percent of the people in this age group had lost both parents. Many of them lived with relatives.) Impressionistic accounts confirm that the custom of living at home persisted into the twentieth century. These accounts also affirm that young workers paid their parents most of their wages for room and board. Such information indicates that young workers had a long adolescence and that they rarely rebelled against their parents in any significant way. Obviously, contemporary fears that young women working away from home for wages would become too independent and thereby undermine parental authority and the family were grossly exaggerated. Similarly, sociologists and historians who have based their claims about increased independence for young women and the destruction of the working-class family on contemporary reactions have been misled.[22]

It is true that working-class parents did not supervise their children with the same care as contemporary middle-class parents. Workers lived in cramped quarters: poor families might crowd into one or two rooms; more fortunate families might have four or five rooms. Under these circumstances, everyone spent a lot of time outside. Groups of adolescents wandered around the streets until ten or eleven at night; young couples went "walking out" night after night. Proper middle-class people disapproved of these practices because they believed unchaperoned adolescents would get into trouble. They failed to understand that the groups did little damage and the couples were courting in the only way they could, given the lack of privacy at home and their impecunious state.

The clothing worn by some young working women, and the entertainments some enjoyed, also offended middle-class observers. Young seamstresses tried to dress fashionably; some factory women wore colorful and/or revealing clothes, though the majority wore dull-colored shifts and shawls. To contemporaries, the seamstresses' clothing seemed inappropriate, the factory women's indecent. In retrospect, their mode of dress seems to have been a way of expressing themselves and brightening a rather tedious existence. Other ways of relieving the tedium included drinking or dancing. Although few young women drank, and those who attended public dances were not necessarily "loose," contemporaries constantly censured these activities. They overlooked the lack of alternative forms of entertainment. Some charitable ladies did notice the need for "wholesome" activities. They established and operated working girls' clubs, where young women could visit one another indoors, "improve" themselves through courses, and even dance under "proper" supervision. Not surprisingly, the moralizing tone and propriety discouraged all but the "more refined" young workers.[23]

Behind the excessively critical attitude toward drinking and dancing lay concern about sexual encounters and illegitimacy. Young workers participated in premarital sex; high illegitimacy rates prevailed in working-class communities growing through immigration from the countryside; and many working-class communities did not ostracize unmarried mothers. These facts should be seen in perspective. Most of the sexual encounters between single workers were premarital in the strictest sense, that is, the two partners intended to marry. This pattern of behavior had long been common in the countryside, where most workers came from. Furthermore, most young women who conceived out of wedlock had their reputation cleared and their child-to-be legitimized by marriage before giving birth. This too was an urban extension of a rural tradition. However, more urban men did not marry the women they impregnated because in cities they could more easily abandon women or live with them without benefit of marriage. It is in this context that we ought to evaluate the working-class acceptance of unmarried mothers and illegitimacy that bourgeois contemporaries saw as moral laxity.[24]

Two other practices frowned upon by moralizers, common-law marriages and prostitution, must also be viewed in perspective. Some working-class women lived with men they did not marry, usually for long periods of time. Often the couple could not afford a wedding ceremony; sometimes one partner could not divorce a previous spouse. Whatever the reasons for not marrying, these unions were stable. Fathers often legally recognized the children born of such unions. This hardly constituted an irresponsible arrangement — as one "respectable" observer admitted. A few women did live with one man after another. Contemporaries frequently confused these women with prostitutes, which accounts for some of the inflated estimates of the number of prostitutes. Their assumption that women entered such relationships out of economic considerations had some foundation: most women, especially mothers, needed a man for financial support. One student of working-class life, a woman, mentioned another motive for serial monogamy: women unfettered by marital bonds felt they could leave drunken, abusive men and form more satisfying relationships.

Other women did engage in prostitution. Some women living alone or with a child they had to support earned so little at work that they regularly supplemented their income by soliciting after work. Contemporaries thought that factory women and dressmakers were particularly prone to this kind of occasional prostitution. The factory women's (relatively) high wages militate against their inclusion, but slopworkers, with their minimal income, were likely candidates. Nonfactory workers certainly engaged in more seasonal prostitution since they suffered more seasonal unemployment. Women forced to solicit temporarily might be forgiven by the community and rehabilitated by marriage. Those who took up prostitution as a profession met with less understanding, even if they married and lived respectable lives. But very few working women became professional prostitutes.[25]

Most working women married in their early or mid-twenties. In England, city women married younger than their country cousins: in 1884 the average age at first marriage was twenty-three for women in textiles, almost twenty-four for women doing common labor or artisanal work, and almost twenty-seven for farm women. French working women, who usually wed at twenty-five or twenty-six, waited longer than their English counterparts and than some French peasant women. While the English statistics cited above confirm contemporaneous observations about factory women marrying younger, other English statistics and the French figures suggest that women who could work at home married youngest. Perhaps city women married earlier because they could compile a "trousseau" of the necessary household goods sooner than rural women. Domestic workers probably married earliest because most workmen wanted their wives to work, if they had to work, at home. Two reasons for young marriages ignored by critics of factory women and their husbands were high wages for young work*men,* and urban rejection of the rural tradition of waiting to inherit a farm or cottage. These reasons undermine complaints about factory women's high wages attracting parasitical men and thereby fostering bad marriages.[26]

After their wedding — a church or civil ceremony, sometimes followed by a dinner — most young couples moved to their new home. They stayed near their parents or, failing that, some relative. Parents, and particularly mothers, helped obtain scarce apartments and credit, as well as providing a meal now and then. Kin networks also eased the establishment of a new household. A minority of young couples — 10 to 21 percent of Preston's childless, working-class couples — remained in one of their parents' homes. They left when they could find or afford a place of their own, or when the babies started arriving and the parents' home became unbearably crowded — only 1 percent of Preston couples with four children stayed with kin. Propinquity and coresidence reveal the usefulness of the extended family and refute the commonplace about its destruction by industrialization.[27]

Many brides continued working, even outside the home, "to build the household" (acquire furniture, etc.). Those who held good jobs kept them because they liked their work and wages. Most of these wives quit or took leave when they became noticeably pregnant, which happened quickly due to ignorance about birth control. The poorest worked until confinement, and almost immediately afterward, even if the infant lived. A few women with good jobs returned to work some months after giving birth. A second live birth finished most mothers' outside employment, though some still worked for wages in their home. Only the very poorest worked through many pregnancies and births. Not until they had children working could these women retire. Some women who had stayed home, raising children, returned to outside work when their husbands lost their jobs, died, or abandoned them. Others waited until an older daughter could care for the younger children and then went back.

Throughout their married life, most working-class women subordinated themselves to their husbands. They served their husbands the best food and often the only meat. They bought their husbands better clothes. Many English and some French wives never knew exactly what their husbands earned; they merely received a household allowance. Wives stayed home while their husbands went out, night after night. Wives tolerated brutal husbands stoically. Why this subservience? The answer lies in part in the husband's role as principal breadwinner. As breadwinner, he had to be properly fed or else everyone in the family might suffer. He needed appropriate work clothes, especially if he worked outdoors. The answer also lies in the persistence of traditional women's roles: they stayed home, did not go to pubs, and did not leave their husbands, even for good cause. Working men and women rejected the traditional woman's role slowly because it continued to be necessary, important, and even rewarding. Considering the lower wage scales for women and the drain on their physical resources from recurring pregnancies, staying at home seemed to be the obvious choice for most. Without adequate child-care facilities, women had to take responsibility for child care, at least until their oldest daughter could help them. Where economic survival was so very precarious, a good housewife could make the difference between well being and indigence. A good housewife was appreciated, not only by her family but by her community. And her community's opinion mattered, since housewives' main form of recreation was chatting with the neighbors.

Moreover, this harsh picture of abject submission to husbands and a role should be softened. Women who worked because their husbands had lost their health and/or their jobs became the principal breadwinners. Then they ate and dressed better. Unemployed men and husbands of sickly or very pregnant women often took over child care and housework. (Since men also had a narrowly defined sex role, they did not let anyone know they were doing such work. To avoid being called a "mop rag" or "diddy man," husbands in one Lancashire slum shut the doors and covered the windows before helping their wives.) Most wives deduced approximately what their husbands earned; some received and disbursed all their husbands' earnings, giving them "pocket money" for tobacco or liquor. Many wives chased their husbands from the pub on paydays so that the week's wages would not be entirely dissipated. A few joined their husbands, or more likely other women, in the pub. Wives often held their own in family arguments, though rarely in family fights.[28]

The suggestion that working-class wives were good household managers must be modified. True, many excelled in stretching a tiny budget. But they found it difficult if not impossible to provide good food and a clean environment. They could not buy food in large, economical quantities because they could not afford or store it. Since they lacked cooking facilities and culinary skills, they relied on prepared foods. They seldom found fresh, unadulterated food, and could purchase meat only for special occasions. Furthermore, lower-class women knew little about hygiene or health until the end of the nineteenth century. Even when they did know, they faced problems: lack of water, lack of fuel, lack of space, etc.

Unhappily, some working-class women were deficient mothers. If they worked outside the home, they left infants as young as ten days with paid nurses; they breast-fed infants as few as three times a day and weaned them as soon as possible; they and the nurses stifled infants' hungry cries with patent medicines laced with narcotics, one of which bore the name Atkins Royal Infant Preservative! While mothers worked, nurses fed infants a mixture of crumbled bread and watered-down milk. Even mothers who stayed home bought little milk for their children and fed them adult food. (This may have been a blessing in disguise: until the twentieth century, milk was unpasteurized and contaminated, not least of all by the preservative formaldehyde.) Partly as a result, infant and childhood mortality remained high among working-class offspring long after it began to drop among middle-class offspring. In the 1870s, a sample of working mothers in an English cotton town, Bradford, found that they lost 68.8 percent of their children. Even in the twentieth century, mothers working in the smaller London trades lost 55.5 percent of their children.[29]

Before condemning working-class mothers for these gruesome statistics, contemporaries might have delved into the incidence of and reasons for neglect. Few mothers with young children worked, and most of those who did, worked at home (e.g., sewing). Most mothers worked to keep their family from falling into desperate poverty. In the early Industrial Revolution, factory and workshop women brought their children to work. When they lost that option, working mothers tried to get a responsible relative, preferably a grandmother, to mind their children in their own (the mother's) home. Only if this was impossible did mothers take their children out to be minded. Very few children could be accommodated at the nurseries supported by concerned industrialists or city governments in France, and partially funded by charities in England. Even when mothers had access to nurseries, many hired nurses because they knew the nurses personally. Their decision reflected ignorance of the better conditions in the nurseries, not lack of concern. Indeed, ignorance and poverty account for many mothers' "faults." Mothers knew little about infant diets before the end of the nineteenth century. High milk prices restricted the amount of milk mothers could buy; baby foods, when they appeared in the 1860s, were prohibitively expensive.

For all the contemporaneous criticisms of working-class women, for all the dire predictions about the disintegration of the family, most women lived decent lives, and the family survived. The experience of working for individual wages, both before and after marriage, did not materially increase single or married women's independence from the family, since they plowed most of their wages back into the family. From our perspective, the withdrawal of most married women from paid labor at a time when the work ethic was being instilled constitutes a serious reversal in the position of married women. But to most nineteenth-century working women, it meant a release from ceaseless, ill-paid labor, and a step up in status. Few of them saw their work as self-fulfilling or liberating. The whole society told them to be good wives and mothers, so it is not surprising that most of them tried, not always successfully, to be good wives and mothers.

Answering our two central questions — how did the Industrial Revolution change women's work and what effect did the change have on women's lives and families — has not been simple. The one generalization we can safely make is that the powerfully corrosive and creative force of industrialization had surprisingly little impact on most women's work and lives. Fundamental change in the mode of production created more outside employment, but only for a minority, or more correctly, for young women. Technical progress opened up very few "masculine" trades to women. Women's wages rose, though not to the level of men's wages. These modifications, in turn, allowed greater independence and choice — for a minority of young women. More important, the removal of most married women from the labor force brought a decline in the position of married women. Thus, ironically, the Industrial Revolution's most revolutionary influence on working-class women was a negative one.

Notes

1. Jules Simon, *L'Ouvrière,* Hachette, Paris, 1861, p. vi, and Paul Foucart, *De la Fonction industrielle des femmes,* Revue Occidentale, Paris, 1882, pp. 31–32, 35.

2. For working women's attitudes toward their work, see Clementina Black, *Married Women's Work,* G. Bell & Sons, London, 1915, passim, and E. Cadbury, M. C. Matheson, and G. Shann, *Women's Work and Wages,* University of Chicago Press, Chicago, 1907, pp. 113–116.

3. For example, Margaret Hewitt, *Wives and Mothers in Victorian Industry,* Rockliffe, London, 1958; Wanda T. Neff, *Victorian Working Women,* Allen & Unwin, London, 1929; Ivy Pinchbeck, *Women Workers and the Industrial Revolution, 1750–1850,* Kelley, New York, 1969; Joan Scott and Louise Tilly, "Women's Work and the Family in Nineteenth Century Europe," *Comparative Studies in Society and History,* 17, no. 1 (1975), 36–64.

4. Mary Lynn McDougall, "After the Insurrections: The Workers' Movement in Lyon, 1834–1852," Ph.D. dissertation, Columbia University, 1974, pp. 46–54; Laura Strumingher, "Les Canutes: Women Workers in the Lyonnais Silk Industry, 1835–1848," Ph.D. dissertation, University of Rochester, 1974, pp. 6–12.

5. On work discipline, see S. Pollard, "Factory Discipline in the Industrial Revolution," *Economic History Review,* 16 (1963), and E. P. Thompson, "Time, Work Discipline, and Industrial Capitalism," *Past and Present,* 38 (1967). On predominantly female factories, see Cadbury et al., *Women's Work,* pp. 200–201, 205, and Georges Duveau, *La Vie ouvrière en France sous le Second Empire,* 7th ed., Gallimard, Paris, 1946, p. 289. On convent workshops, see M. R. L. Reybaud, *Études sur le régime des manufactures: Condition des ouvriers en soie,* n.p., n.p., 1859, pp. 197–199 and Appendix A.

6. There is understandably little solid evidence on seductions, but see Friedrich Engels, *The Condition of the Working Class in England,* trans. W. H. Chaloner and W. O. Henderson, Basil Blackwell, Oxford, 1958, pp. 166–168, and the defense of Engels's statements by E. J. Hobsbawm, "History and the Dark Satanic Mills," *Labouring Men,* Anchor, Garden City, N.Y., 1964, p. 133. For France, see Duveau, *La Vie,* pp. 290, 301; McDougall, "After the Insurrections," p. 146; and Strumingher, "Les Canutes," p. 38.

7. The statistics derive from John Foster, *Class Struggle and the Industrial Revolution: Early Industrial Capitalism in Three English Towns,* Weidenfeld & Nicolson, London, 1974, pp. 91–92.

8. B. L. Hutchins and A. Harrison, *A History of Factory Legislation,* King & Son, London, 1911; B. L. Hutchins, *Labour Laws for Women in France*, The Women's Industrial Council, London, 1907; Adelaide M. Anderson, *Women in the Factory: An Administrative Adventure,* Dutton, New York, 1922.

9. The heat argument is found in Peter Gaskell, *The Manufacturing Population of England,* Baldwin & Craddock, London, 1833, pp. 68–74. For critiques of the legislation, see Hutchins and Harrison, *History of Factory Legislation,* pp. 173–199; Hutchins, *Labour Laws,* pp. 3–4; Cadbury et al., *Women's Work,* pp. 59, 64–66; Hewitt, *Wives and Mothers,* pp. 25, 28; and Neff, *Victorian,* pp. 67–68, 108. An interesting contemporary critique is Harriet Martineau, *The Factory Controversy: A Warning Against Meddling Legislation,* n.p., Manchester, 1855.

10. Hutchins and Harrison, *History of Factory Legislation,* pp. 251–257; Hutchins,

Labour Laws, pp. 7–8, 11; and B. L. Hutchins, *Women's Wages in England in the Nineteenth Century,* The Women's Industrial Council, London, 1906, pp. 5–7.

11. Figures drawn from M. Villermé, *Tableau de l'état physique et moral des ouvriers employés dans les manufactures de coton, de laine et de soie,* Renouard, Paris, 1840, p. 93; and Black, *Married,* p. 165.

12. Figures from Villermé, *Tableau de l'état,* p. 93. Data on average wages in Madelaine Guilbert, *Les Femmes et l'organisation syndicale avant 1914,* Centre National de la Recherche Scientifique, Paris, 1966, p. 18. Further information on wage differentials in A. Audiganne, *Les Populations ouvrières et les industries de la France,* Franklin, New York, 1970, pp. 304–305 (vol. 1) and 190–191 (vol. 2); Black, *Married,* p. 130; and Ivy Pinchbeck, *Women Workers,* pp. 190–194.

13. Figures from Duveau, *La Vie,* p. 327; Paul Leroy-Beaulieu, "Le Travail des femmes dans la petite industrie," *Revue des Deux Mondes,* 99 (1872), p. 335; Foster, *Class Struggle,* p. 96; and Michael Anderson, *Family Structure in Nineteenth-Century Lancashire,* Cambridge University Press, Cambridge, 1971, p. 31.

14. Figures from Charles Booth, *Life and Labour of the People in London,* First Series, I, Macmillan, London, 1902, p. 34.

15. Katherine G. Busbey, "Women's Trade Union Movement in Great Britain," *Bulletin of the Bureau of Labor,* 83, Government Printing Office, Washington, 1909, p. 20; Barbara Drake, *Women in Trade Unions,* Allen & Unwin, London, n.d., Table A; T. Deldyke, H. Gelders, and J. M. Limbor, *The Working Population and Its Structure,* Editions de l'Institut de Sociologie de l'Université Libre de Bruxelles, Brussels, 1968, pp. 29–30; Guilbert, *Les Femmes,* pp. 28–29.

16. Audiganne, *Les Populations,* vol. 2, p. 101; Black, *Married,* passim; Cadbury et al., *Women's Work,* passim; Madelaine Guilbert and V. Isambert-Jamati, *Travail féminin et travail à domicile,* Centre National de la Recherche Scientifique, Paris, 1956, pp. 9–17; Simon, *L'Ouvrière,* pp. 125–256; and *The Women's Union Journal,* 16 (1877), 27.

17. On campaigns for dressmakers, see Neff, pp. 116–146; Paul Gonnard, *La Femme dans l'industrie,* Libraire Armand Colin, Paris, 1906, pp. 243–260; Guilbert and Isambert-Jamati, *Travail,* pp. 27–30. On the minimum wage, consult *The Case for and against a Legal Minimum Wage for Sweated Workers,* The Women's Industrial Council, London, 1909.

18. Deldyke et al., *Working Population,* pp. 29–30, 169, 185; Gonnard, *La Femme,* pp. 45–48; Guilbert, *Les Femmes,* pp. 13–14; B. L. Hutchins, *Women in Modern Industry,* Bell & Sons, London, 1915, p. 84; Scott and Tilly, "Women's Work," pp. 37–39.

19. M. Anderson, *Family Structure,* p. 71; Deldyke et al., *Working Population,* pp. 169, 185; Hewitt, *Wives and Mothers,* pp. 15–17; Pinchbeck, *Women Workers,* p. 197; Scott and Tilly, "Women's Work," p. 40.

20. The sketch is based on biographical data scattered through most of the sources previously cited, and particularly in M. Anderson, Audiganne, Black, Cadbury, Duveau, Hewitt, Simon, and Villermé. In addition, I used biographical and autobiographical data in *Annals of Labor: Autobiographies of British Working Class People 1820–1920,* ed. John Burnett, Indiana University Press, Blooming-

ton, 1974; Lady Bell, *At the Works,* Arnold, London, 1907; Ernst Duckeshoff, *How the English Workman Lives,* King & Son, London, 1899; Frederic Le Play, *Les Ouvriers européens,* 2nd ed., Mame & Fils, Tours, 1878, vols. 3, 5, and 7; Robert Roberts, *The Classic Slum,* Manchester University Press, Manchester, 1971; *Working Days, Being the Personal Records of Sixteen Working Men and Women,* ed. M. A. Pollock, Cape, London, 1926.

21. J. F. C. Harrison, *Learning and Living, 1790–1960,* Routledge & Kegan Paul, London, 1961; Richard Hoggart, *The Uses of Literacy,* Essential Books, Fair Lawn, N.J., 1957.
22. M. Anderson, *Family Structure,* p. 54.
23. Maude Stanley, *Clubs for Working Girls,* Macmillan, London, 1890.
24. For statistics on illegitimacy, see E. Shorter, "Illegitimacy, Sexual Revolution, and Social Change in Modern Europe," *The Family in History,* eds. T. K. Rabb and R. I. Rotberg, Harper & Row, New York, 1971, pp. 77–84. For a better interpretation of the statistics, see Scott and Tilly, "Women's Work," pp. 55–56.
25. William Acton, *Prostitution,* ed. P. Fryer, London, 1968, and J. and D. Walkowitz, " 'We are not beasts of the field': Prostitution and the Poor in Plymouth and Southampton under the Contagious Diseases Acts," *Feminist Studies,* I (1973).
26. H. J. Habakkuk, *Population Growth and Economic Development Since 1750,* Leicester University Press, Leicester, 1972, pp. 43–44; Hewitt, *Wives and Mothers,* pp. 40–45; Etienne van de Walle, *The Female Population of France in the Nineteenth Century,* Princeton University Press, Princeton, 1974; and Villermé, *Tableau de l'état,* pp. 51, 69, 113, 190.
27. M. Anderson, *Family Structure,* pp. 51, 56–67.
28. On the allocation of money within the family, see Laura Oren, "The Welfare of Women in Laboring Families: England, 1860–1950," *Feminist Studies,* I (1973).
29. Hewitt, *Wives and Mothers,* p. 109, and Black, *Married,* pp. 276–280.

Suggestions for Further Reading

Anderson, M. *Family Structure in Nineteenth-Century Lancashire.* Cambridge University Press, Cambridge, 1971.

Black, C. *Married Women's Work.* G. Bell & Sons, London, 1915.

Burnett, J., ed. *Annals of Labor: Autobiographies of British Working Class People 1820–1920,* Indiana University Press, Bloomington, 1974.

Busbey, K. G. "Women's Trade Union Movement in Great Britain." *Bulletin of the Bureau of Labor,* 83, Government Printing Office, Washington, 1909.

Cadbury, E.; M. C. Matheson; and G. Shann. *Women's Work and Wages.* University of Chicago Press, Chicago, 1907.

Clark, A. *Working Life of Women in the Seventeenth Century.* Harcourt, Brace & Howe, New York, 1920.

Clark, F. *The Position of Women in Contemporary France.* King & Son, London, 1937.

Collier, F. *The Family Economy of the Working Class in the Cotton Industry, 1784–1833.* Manchester University Press, Manchester, 1964.

Drake, B. *Women in Trade Unions.* Allen & Unwin, London, n.d.

Duveau, G. *La Vie ouvrière en France sous le Second Empire.* 7th ed. Gallimard, Paris, 1946.

Engels, F. *The Condition of the Working Class in England,* trans. W. H. Chaloner and W. O. Henderson. Basil Blackwell, Oxford, 1958.

Foster, J. *Class Struggle and the Industrial Revolution: Early Industrial Capitalism in Three English Towns.* Weidenfeld & Nicolson, London, 1974.

Gaskell, P. *The Manufacturing Population of England.* Baldwin & Craddock, London, 1833.

Guilbert, M. *Les Femmes et l'organisation syndicale avant 1914.* Centre National de la Recherche Scientifique, Paris, 1966.

Guilbert, M., and V. Isambert-Jamati. *Travail féminin et travail à domicile.* Centre National de la Recherche Scientifique, Paris, 1956.

Gross, E. "Plus ça change . . .? The Sexual Structure of Occupations Over Time." *Social Problems,* 16 (1968).

Hewitt, M. *Wives and Mothers in Victorian Industry.* Rockliff, London, 1958.

Hobsbawm, E. J. *Labouring Men.* Anchor, Garden City, N.Y., 1964.

Hoggart, R. *The Uses of Literacy.* Essential Books, Fair Lawn, N.J., 1957.

Hutchins, B. L. *Women in Modern Industry.* Bell & Sons, London, 1915.

Kemp, T. *Economic Forces in French History.* Dobson, London, 1971.

Neff, W. *Victorian Working Women.* Allen & Unwin, London, 1929.

Oren, L. "The Welfare of Women in Laboring Families: England, 1860–1950." *Feminist Studies,* I (1973).

Pinchbeck, I. *Women Workers and the Industrial Revolution: 1750–1850.* Kelley, New York, 1969.

Richards, E. "Women in the British Economy Since About 1700: An Interpretation." *History,* 59 (1974).

Roberts, R. *The Classic Slum.* Manchester University Press, Manchester, 1971.

Scott, J., and L. Tilly. "Women's Work and the Family in Nineteenth Century Europe." *Comparative Studies in Society and History,* 17 (1975).

Stearns, P. "Working Class Women in Britain, 1890–1914." *Suffer and Be Still: Women in the Victorian Age,* ed. M. Vicinus. Indiana University Press, Bloomington, 1972.

Thompson, E. P. *The Making of the English Working Class.* Vintage, New York, 1963.

Ure, A. *The Philosophy of Manufactures.* Franklin, New York, 1969.

12

The Long Road Home: Women's Work and Industrialization

Theresa M. McBride

Theresa McBride also disputes the notion that industrialization immediately transformed all women's lives. Rather, she proposes that the process of industrialization must be analyzed in a chronological framework, as does Renate Bridenthal in a later essay. McBride examines the early stages of this process and concludes that, despite several liabilities, industrialization as a whole improved the lot of women, both as workers and as mothers. She notes that, contrary to earlier assumptions, family life did not immediately disintegrate, so women were not set adrift in an alien urban environment. Furthermore, most new jobs for women were in traditionally "feminine" fields: agriculture, textiles, and domestic service. Of these, the last was the most rapidly expanding. As servants, young women had some advantages: they could remain in a family environment, save money for their dowries, defer marriage until they were more mature, and choose a husband wisely. After marriage, women's participation in the economy did not stop, as McDougall asserts, but continued in other ways, though the census may not have counted these women as being employed.

The Laundresses by Marie Marc Antoine Bilcoq (1755–1838). (Worcester Art Museum, Worcester, Massachusetts)

Industrialization is an irreversible and seemingly inevitable process. Whether beneficial or disastrous, the changes wrought by industrialization represent the most profound changes in the nature of daily life since the establishment of stable agricultural societies. Yet the ordinary people most affected by industrialization have left few records of their reactions and, consequently, there remain many unanswered questions about its effects. In particular, one group that has been little considered in the written histories of industrialization until very recently is women. In spite of some historians' assumption that to write about the history of men includes the history of women, women experience historical processes differently. Women differ from men both biologically and in the roles they have played throughout history; industrialization affected them uniquely, just as their participation in the industrial process was distinctive. Hence, this chapter consists of an explanation of women's special roles during this period and encompasses an examination of a wide variety of women's experiences during industrialization.

Since industrialization consisted most basically of a change in the structure of work, the first questions we will attempt to answer relate to women as workers: the types of work they performed, their attitudes toward work, and their participation in industrial protests. Second, we must examine the female role in a more general context. How did industrialization alter women's status and function in the family structure? Finally, we must evaluate the advantages and disadvantages of industrialization as women experienced them, as workers, as wives, as mothers.

Women have always worked. The Industrial Revolution did not usher in a new phase in the employment of women in that sense. But the nineteenth century did "discover" the woman worker as an object of pity, and the Victorian social conscience was aroused as never before by the plight of working women and children.[1] Because women's work in the preindustrial world had been home based and largely seasonal, work had not seriously interfered with women's responsibilities in child care and household duties.

But industrialization required that workers perform their jobs away from their homes, and the industrial process could not tolerate an erratic work force. Thus, industrialization exacerbated the problems of a working mother and made her plight more visible, even though the fact of her work was scarcely new.

The crucial factor in women's work experience involves her duality of roles. In addition to her primary biological and social role as wife and mother, the woman in preindustrial and early industrial societies made a vital contribution to the family's total earnings. In the nineteenth century, as a general estimate, more than two-thirds of all single women worked and between one-quarter and one-half of married women were employed, depending on the geographical area. Most women worked for several years before marriage, which occurred for the average western European woman at about the age of twenty-four.[2] The average female life cycle then included a long period of childbearing and childrearing, generally shortened only by sterility or by death. Most women worked sporadically during this period in agriculture or in the various kinds of domestic manufacturing. But industrialization introduced a conflict between the two female roles by separating the place of work from the home, and thus initiated the eventual decline of women's work opportunities and the virtual disappearance of married women from the work force until the very recent past.[3]

Women in the preindustrial era were mainly employed in agriculture, domestic manufacturing, and household service. Preindustrial society also emphasized the "family economy," i.e., the determination of family subsistence by the contributions of all family members capable of earning. Paradoxically, women were often underemployed because of their extensive familial obligations, which caused them to work only sporadically or seasonally and close to home.

Industrialization affected women most profoundly through the separation of work and home. Facing a conflict between their family obligations and their ability to earn money, women ultimately altered their occupational choices, experienced a fundamental reformulation of their attitudes about work, and gradually developed a characteristically female work pattern. This evolution of the structure of women's work and feminine attitudes about work can be divided into three phases. The first phase from the 1760s to about 1880; the second from the 1880s through the 1940s; and the third, the postwar period. This division of the process into phases should not be interpreted to mean that women's employment underwent a radical change in the 1880s or again in the 1940s. One could view the whole of phases one and two as a unified period of gradual adjustment to industrialization. Indeed, it is not the particular years that are important in this process but the stages of development, which must be adjusted to fit different national patterns.[4] This essay will concentrate almost exclusively upon phase one with some analysis of the transition to phase two, but it is important to understand how these two phases contributed to permanent changes in women's working lives.

The first phase consisted of the persistence of artisanal production, of the expansion of domestic manufacturing (piecework done by workers in their own homes), and of the rapid development of the textile industry, particularly the cotton industry. This first phase was a transitional period of employment for both single and married women in domestic production and the early textile mills, in domestic service, and agriculture. But in the long run, women's employment opportunities began to decline and become associated with the stagnating textile industry, along with domestic manufacturing, agriculture, and domestic service, which had all begun to contract by phase two. In the second phase, from the 1880s until after World War II, the structure of industry changed toward heavy industries like mining, metallurgy, and machines, and this meant a significant decrease in married women's work.

Indeed, the most significant change in women's work to emerge from industrialization was the notion that women should retire from work when they married. This idea arose partially from the assumption that the male wage alone should be sufficient to support a family. But it also reflected a kind of resolution of the conflict introduced by industrialization between the married woman's two roles since, in effect, it reduced her to a single primary role. Combined with some redistribution of the female work force, this decline in married women's work and the contingent pattern of a merely temporary work experience represented the most typical aspect of phase two.

The third and contemporary phase constitutes the eventual outcome of this long process of adjustment and marks a radical break with preindustrial and early industrial work patterns for both married and single women. Only in the recent past have women begun to reenter the labor force in a diversity of occupations and in significant numbers with the prospect that this may signify a permanent trend.[5] How soon this may result in a change of attitudes about the permanency of work in the female life cycle or about the kinds of jobs preferred by women we cannot yet predict.

Historians often search for the most pervasive changes in lifestyles in the sectors of the economy that were modernizing rapidly during industrialization, but this search will be fruitless for those interested in the ways in which most women experienced industrialization. Most women in the early industrial period continued to be employed in their traditional occupations: in agriculture, in domestic service, in domestic manufacturing, and in commercial distribution. In England, more rapid urbanization and the decline of agriculture forced some women into new roles much earlier — by the middle of the nineteenth century. But in France and throughout Europe, agriculture remained the most important employer of women until the post-1880 period, and women clung to other traditional occupations like domestic service until late in the century.[6]

Additionally, the continental countries preserved the tradition of employing women in domestic manufacturing much longer because the home workers were not so heavily concentrated in cotton-cloth production, which declined early in the nineteenth century leaving many British home workers unemployed. But even in England, the factories absorbed only a minority of women in the nineteenth century. In England in 1841 female factory operatives numbered only 8,879.[7] Obviously, this was not the typical form of female employment. Thus, while one often cites the English example as the key to industrialization, the French experience was more typical of the evolution of female work roles in the West.

Women's employment in the first phase of industrialization continued to be concentrated in four major categories: agriculture, domestic manufacturing, retail distribution, and domestic service. In France in 1866 nearly 2,000,000 women were still employed in agriculture, compared with about 1,000,000 in all aspects of manufacturing (both factory work and domestic production).[8] Female employment in agriculture remained high throughout Europe wherever the pattern of small farms was customary, but women also were increasingly employed as day laborers in large-scale agriculture, particularly in the expanding wine industry and in the growing of beets for sugar and alcohol. Women involved in wine growing participated in a culture that was almost urban, for the wine growers lived in large villages and their lives were influenced by the market economy much more than the average peasant's.[9] Large-scale agriculture thus involved women in a partly urban and modernized culture. Though a traditional occupation for women, agriculture thus remained a significant employment option that could provide women with experiences that had considerable consequences for their modernization.

Wine growing was one method of supplementing the average income of an agricultural family, but domestic manufacturing was another. When wine growing proved unprofitable, or in those areas that could not accommodate viniculture, the women turned to lace making or spinning or silk weaving. Throughout the early industrial period, women workers dominated the domestic labor force; they represented three-quarters of this group in France in 1866. Like the preindustrial textile family, the early industrial family was an economic unit. The father worked as a weaver (work considered too difficult and too dangerous for a woman) and apprenticed his older sons to his trade, while the mother, assisted by younger children, did the spinning, combing, and carding. In the early textile mills in England, this configuration remained relatively unchanged at first, since the family could be hired to work as a team in the factory.[10] Or, as a variation of this arrangement, the father and sons would be hired as weavers to work in the mill, while the mother and daughters continued to work at spinning in their cottages. In this way, both domestic production and factory work expanded during the first phase of industrialization.

The textile industry provides us with a classic example of the way in which industrialization disproportionately and temporarily increased certain jobs that became almost exclusively female. Even though most women were employed elsewhere, female labor was vital to the early factories, where women and children constituted 40 percent of the total labor force. Women were paid about half as much as adult male workers, so that single women who were helping to support their families or women whose husbands also worked in the factories were the most likely to take up this kind of work. But women benefited both from the proliferation of the factories and the rising level of domestic manufacturing.

Since domestic manufacturing was scarcely new to women, and factory work involved only a small minority, many of the traditional aspects of women's work experience persisted. Industrialization did not immediately disrupt the pattern of the family working together as a unit of production. Clearly, the family economy, to which all members contributed their earnings, remained as strong as ever, and women, whether as wives or daughters, continued to assume a major part of the family's economic responsibilities.[11]

But it would be inaccurate to overemphasize the traditionalism that this kind of work perpetuated. Both the single and the married women employed in textile production were exposed to novel circumstances and experiences. Increasing contacts with intermediaries and with the market must have enhanced their market sense. Because they could contribute on a more regular basis to the family income, they often gained more status in family decisions. Women had always played an important role in western European families by managing the family budget, and their economic decisions assumed greater importance as the family's income rose above the level of subsistence.[12] It was women's desires for small consumer goods like metal pins and buttons that expanded the domestic market for such products and in turn created more work for the women who produced them.[13] Thus, new experiences and new attitudes emerged within the context of traditional roles and occupations.

While single women in this period could seek work as domestic servants and in the factories, married women tended to be employed in agriculture, domestic manufacturing, or in part-time or casual employment often associated with retailing. Married women commonly worked in food shops or beer houses or bars or helped to run small shops or inns. In the industrialized area of Lancashire, England, in the mid-nineteenth century 26 percent of the wives living with their husbands were recorded in the census as gainfully employed on a regular basis.[14] About one-third of these worked in the nonfactory occupations described here. Those who were employed, particularly in the factories, were primarily the youngest wives, who had few or no children to care for. Many other wives, who were not recorded in the census as employed, supplemented the family income by taking in lodgers or doing some cleaning part time or taking in laundry. Thus, retailing occupations and other service jobs remained a consistent employment option for married women throughout phase one.

But the largest employer of women in the nineteenth century, and the dominant employment option for single women after agriculture, was domestic service. In the nineteenth century, domestic service employed more women than all types of manufacturing put together.[15] The size of the domestic servant class rose rapidly in phase one, then remained stable during phase two, and declined in total numbers only at the end of phase two during World War II. During the first phase of industrialization, about one in every three women in Europe was a servant at some time in her life.

Domestic service comprised an amorphous occupational group in the nineteenth century; it included workers as diverse as some dairymaids and some silk weavers, for the crucial distinction was not the kind of work performed but rather the fact that the worker lived in her employer's household and received her board as compensation for her labor. In the countryside, daughters of tenant farmers traditionally took up employment as servants in neighboring farms. With industrialization, positions in household service multiplied as the urban middle classes grew in numbers and wealth.

Domestic service in the industrial age frequently involved long-distance migration in search of positions in the cities. In spite of the traditional interpretation of labor migration, which assumed that women tended to travel much shorter distances than men in search of work, domestics' migration was uniquely adventurous.[16] Female domestic servants were considerably more mobile than either females who went to work in factories or males in general. Most servants in the nineteenth century came from rural backgrounds, but few worked in the same areas in which they had been born. Consequently, even though domestic service was a traditional occupation for women, it increased the potential for the weakening of family ties and for the diluting of time-honored values.

The highly traditional character of domestic service and the accessibility of positions in service explain much of the popularity of household service. But service also offered some distinct advantages over other kinds of work. Domestic service preserved the familial context of work even though it took the young woman out of her own home. The young woman left parental control and protection only to become subordinated to an employer. In fact, the contract for a young servant's services could be arranged between her parents and her employer without her participation, though older, more experienced servants generally found their positions on their own. In spite of low monetary wages, servants were better off than other kinds of workers because of the compensation of room and board. And their contacts with wealthy middle- and upper-class families were often lucrative for loyal servants: Juliette Sauget's memoirs of service in the period just before World War I recall an employer who wanted to send her to cooking school so that she could qualify for a better job. An occasional servant even received an annual income for life by the death bequest of a grateful employer.

Servants had a reputation for saving, and they constituted the overwhelming majority of depositors in nineteenth-century savings banks. Servants also frequently retained close links with the families they had left behind in the countryside. Many a servant sent all or part of her wages to her parents, suggesting that many young women continued to think of the family as an economic unit. But more individualistic motivations were also evident as servants accumulated dowries so that they could enhance their marriage prospects or sought to use their savings to start a career, for example through apprenticeship to a dressmaker. Gradually, but almost visibly, young women's aspirations became less family oriented.

Though it constituted no clear break with tradition, domestic service involved several new features in the period of early industrialization. Household service became more highly urbanized than ever before. It no longer consisted simply of sending one's daughter to work in a wealthier peasant's house or in the home of the local gentry. As young women moved farther from their parental homes, family ties weakened. Daughters living away from their parents, for example, gained considerably more control over the timing of their own marriages and the choice of their spouses.[17] For most servants, their first positions in service represented their initial encounter with the city and with urban life, and thus the experience became a period of acculturation to urban life and to middle-class values.

The experience of servanthood even more than other kinds of work was individualized and defined by the personal relationship of the servant and her employer, but some of its aspects can be generalized. Servanthood was merely a temporary stage in life; no more than one servant in ten remained a servant throughout her life. Once the servant had settled into the city and accumulated some savings, she generally found herself a husband or another job. Servants were nearly always young and single: in England, 40 percent of the female servants were under twenty; in France, 40 percent under twenty-five. Live-in domestic service almost required celibacy, since the work days were long (sixteen to eighteen hours) and there were few days off to spend with one's family. This experience of servanthood, then, often coincided with an important transition in an individual's life.

Middle-class employers apparently tried to mold their young servants to accept the middle-class values of cleanliness, sobriety, self-discipline, and respect for authority. But many despaired of ever accomplishing this task. In the process, however, servants were inevitably exposed to some basic training (servants were more literate on the average than the other members of their rural-born cohort) and to the middle-class emphasis on individual mobility through planning, education, and saving. Some servants clearly learned their lessons well. But the heavy-handed stress on total obedience and subservience to the employer's whims could also be devastating. Some servants probably internalized the feelings of inferiority.[18] In fact, a substantial segment of the servant class was unable to cope with the demeaning aspects of service and with the liberation from rural constraints. These individuals entered the ranks of the disreputable poor through the birth of an illegitimate child, through involvement in theft or other crimes, or because of drunkenness. In many cases, the employer class was directly involved in the servant's deterioration; one of the most common motivations listed by Parisian prostitutes in the 1830s for taking up their occupation was a prior seduction by their employer. Ex–domestic servants comprised the largest group of prostitutes. Thus, the employer's paternal authority could be used to destroy an individual as well as to constructively shape her character. Much depended upon the individual employer and the particular servant. Some servants, like a kitchenmaid named Jean Rennie, became defiant in the face of an employer's belittling tactics. When Rennie found a coin placed under a rug to test her honesty, she glued the coin to the floor. She was never tested again.

This period of acculturation, then, had divergent impacts on different individuals. The qualities of cleanliness, obedience, and diligence were prized in a wife, so domestic service had a traditional reputation as a better preparation for marriage than other kinds of work. The docile servant was expected to make a docile wife. Other servants' aspirations evolved toward more individualistic goals of self-satisfaction and self-improvement. Most servants changed positions as often as every year either to escape an unpleasant job or to improve their prospects or simply to avoid boredom. Because of the enormous demand for domestic labor, this spirit of independence (which the middle class termed disloyalty) was frequently rewarded by an improvement in wages or working conditions.

Most important, women's experience as domestic servants in phase one established two characteristic trends. First, service was viewed as a useful preparation for later life, but required no lifetime commitment. It should be remembered that since women had always worked, the presumption that formal employment should terminate at marriage was novel. The full consequences of this attitude will be examined more completely later, but the link between this new assumption and the experience of servants is pertinent here. Unlike either agriculture or domestic manufacturing, both service and factory work conflicted too strongly with women's responsibilities as mothers to be continued after marriage and the birth of children. Single women predominated in both domestic service and factory work. But servanthood much more than factory work set the tone for women's work patterns in the industrial era simply because servanthood was the most pervasive shared experience of lower-class women in the nineteenth century and far outweighed factory work in its impact upon a wide number of women.

Second, the preference of women for domestic service over industrial work suggests that women's dispersion throughout the economy had much to do with their own attitudes about work. Women disliked factory work because it was too impersonal and likely to involve them with bad companions. They preferred service because it offered them a substitute home, though many recognized that service positions were more remunerative than other jobs. This desire for a personal relationship with their employers was not new to women, but neither was it a customary response that dwindled in the industrial context. The desire for a personal relationship in work has remained deeply ingrained in women's approach to occupational choice, and this attitude became firmly established in the early industrial period with the concentration of women in service occupations.

Related to women's attitudes about work in the industrial age is the comparatively low level of women's participation in protest. Because work for women comprised only a temporary stage, they did not feel the same stake in improving their economic position by striking as did male workers. The interruption of work and consequent loss of pay might have seemed an unwanted hindrance to their future plans. Thus, women workers had a low incidence of industrial protests on their own behalf. Nevertheless, women were not absent from industrial protest. In an important strike in 1900 in the Breton town of Fougères, the striking shoemakers had the full support of their wives and daughters, who blocked the roads into the town with their bodies to prevent the arrival of strikebreakers and troops.[19] Women often strongly and violently supported male strikers because these protests related to their own welfare as wives and daughters. But this kind of participation and support underlined women's traditional role as consumers rather than breadwinners.

In summary, women's work experience in phase one of industrialization consisted of some persistence of traditional patterns and of considerable change. The expanding sectors of domestic service, domestic manufacturing, and even certain types of factory work had all begun to decline by the 1880s, destroying the temporarily advantageous situation of women workers. But phase one did not consist simply of an interim of adjustment; instead, it represented a crucial transition, particularly in the formation of a modern work pattern for women. The idea of employment as a temporary stage in a woman's life spread. Women began to develop more individualistic aspirations. And women seemed to exercise some occupational choice as the traditional sectors expanded and new possibilities arose. This choice indicated a clear preference for a personal relationship with an employer. The attitudes thus firmly established by the end of phase one set the pattern for women's work in phase two and many of them pervade modern women's feelings about work.

By the beginning of phase two the fundamental attitudes about work had already been formulated, and the redistribution of women throughout the labor force was already well under way. The decay of family-centered agriculture meant the loss of an important source of female employment, particularly for married women, a process that had begun in phase one if not before. More recently, large-scale agriculture, and specifically viniculture, had suffered a profound crisis with the economic depression of the 1870s and a consistent problem (after 1870) of overproduction. Most types of domestic manufacturing were also on the wane by phase two, replaced by mechanized processes. In France, some of the unemployed domestic textile workers found employment as seamstresses because the garment industry retained its small scale and its outwork system until very late. In England, where the decline of both agriculture and domestic manufacturing had been evident much earlier, some of the surplus female labor had been absorbed into domestic service. But by 1880 the domestic servant class had leveled off and began to decline relative to the total labor force.

The decline of domestic service signifies broader attitudinal changes that coincided with the transition from phase one to phase two. The middle-class housewife was no longer so willing or even financially able to invite a stranger into her home to assist in the household work. The middle-class lifestyle, growing ever more inclusive, became increasingly privatized and demanded greater concentration than ever before by the wife and mother on domestic concerns. The sometimes obstreperous, disorderly, and disrespectful servant became too much of a burden, and so was dispensed with in the middle-class household. Servants themselves, unwilling to be subject to the capricious demands of employers and to the demeaning requirements of service, sought employment in other sectors, which offered them more freedom. Urbanization and the spread of primary education also undermined the usefulness of domestic service as a rural-urban link, or even as a period of training before marriage.

For single women, phase two meant new opportunities emerging about the turn of the twentieth century, especially in the tertiary (or service) sector. This sector became increasingly feminized as it expanded, providing numerous jobs for single women in clerical work, and as teachers, nurses, and retail clerks. These new work options soon became characteristic female occupations, but they did not provide a considerable source of employment for women until the third phase of industrialization. Part of the reason that employment in the clerical and service areas became identified with women lay in the fact that women continued to take jobs that, like domestic service, provided a personal relationship with an employer or at least greater contact with people. This aspect of work remained important to women even after other types of work had been removed from the family context.

The diversification of single women's employment alternatives resulted less from changes in employer policies, feminist agitation, or active opposition from male workers in the older industries than from the changing structure and maturation of industry. Agricultural depression and the stagnation of the textile industry, as we have already mentioned, eliminated much of the temporary work married women had performed in or near their homes and caused single women to move into the tertiary sector. The evolution of large retail outlets in phase two further threatened the small retail shops and family-run businesses, curtailing a consistent source of employment for a minority of married women. Hence, the expansion of single women's employment options was inversely proportional to the decline of married women's status in the labor market.

Again, the evolution of domestic service in phase two is suggestive of a more general pattern. The decline in live-in servants that resulted when younger single women took up other kinds of employment made available greater employment for part-time cleaning women. Virtually the only kind of part-time work available to unskilled older women in the post-1880 period was employment as a daily worker or charwoman, and older women eagerly sought out jobs as poorly paid chars.[20] Thus, while single women were very gradually achieving somewhat more independence and even limited professionalism in their employment, married women's work was declining in numbers of women employed and was increasingly confined to the lowest-status, least-skilled, and poorest-paid jobs.

In phase two, then, married women faced vastly reduced options. Married women continued, as in phase one, to work during periods of a husband's illness or unemployment or when advancing age curtailed or eliminated the husband's income. These "critical life situations" were clustered in the decades of the 1870s and 1890s because of a series of economic crises, but they could occur in individual families at any time, particularly as the couple grew older. Married women's work thus became less a natural phase in a woman's life and was dictated increasingly by the adequacy of her husband's income and by the occurrence of family crises. But married women found fewer opportunities to work even when family hardship forced them to do so.

When the evolution of technology and industrial organization limited women's productive role, they also helped to shape the cultural attitudes that would restrict a woman's activities to the home as never before. The industrial period brought a complex change in the attitudes about children that had a profound impact upon the role of women as mothers. Paradoxically, the new importance attached to the role of the mother came at a time when the reduction in family size also lightened the burden of child-rearing. Not only were women bearing fewer children but these children were being taken out of the home much earlier by the spread of public education. Ironically, society ascribed greater importance to the role of the mother precisely at a time when her function was being undermined or at least significantly altered by the evolution of social institutions.

The impart of industrialization has involved a three-stage process in which the third stage is only beginning. The first stage represented a century-long transition, characterized by a merely temporary increase in women's employment levels and limited reassignment of women in the labor force. But in this first phase, the young women who went to work as domestic servants or factory workers or did piecework at home acquired a particular set of attitudes about work. The modern and typically female work pattern of a short period of employment before marriage reinforced the general attitude that women should not work after marriage but should confine their activities to their maternal responsibilities. Women exercised their preference for social contact or a personal quality in their jobs and consistently entered occupations as facilitators or providers of services. Phase two had little effect on the attitudes already set in phase one, but the maturation of industry channeled many more single women into the modernizing sectors as traditional occupations declined. The major impact of phase two was the irreconcilable polarization of the dual functions of women, confining women to a limited and decidedly inferior position in the work force.

It is clear in retrospect that women's decline in the labor force during industrialization was merely a temporary phase. Indeed, although phase three lies outside the limits of this essay, current trends suggest that much more permanent and revolutionary changes are now under way in women's employment options and the female commitment to work. Women's return "home" during industrialization is ending as women and men set off on another road toward an undetermined goal.

Notes

1. Wanda F. Neff, *Victorian Working Women,* London, 1929, p. 1.
2. J. Hajnal, "European Marriage Patterns in Perspective," *Population in History,* eds. D. V. Glass and D. E. C. Eversley, London, 1965, pp. 101–143.
3. Alice Clark, *The Working Life of Women in the Seventeenth Century,* London, 1919, dates the decline in married women's work from a much earlier period; Leonore Davidoff, "The Employment of Married Women in England, 1850–1950," M.A. thesis, University of London, 1955–1956; Margaret Hewitt, *Wives and Mothers in Victorian Industry,* London, 1958.

4. Eric Richards, "Women in the British Economy Since About 1700: An Interpretation," *History,* LIX (October 1974), 337–357, provides a conceptualization from the English perspective.

5. See, for example, Catherine Bodard Silver, "Salon, Foyer, Bureau: Women and the Professions in France," *Clio's Consciousness Raised,* eds. Lois Banner and Mary Hartman, New York, 1974, pp. 72–85, and Neal A. Ferguson, "Women's Work: Employment Opportunities and Economic Roles, 1918–1939," *Albion,* VII (Spring 1975), 55–68.

6. Patricia Branca, "A New Perspective on Women's Work: A Comparative Typology," *Journal of Social History,* IX (December 1975), presents an important new conceptualization of women's work history with a European focus.

7. *Census of England and Wales,* 1841.

8. *Statistique générale de la France,* 1866.

9. Theodore Zeldin, *France, 1848–1945,* vol. 1: *Ambition, Love, and Politics,* Oxford, 1973, p. 165.

10. Neil Smelser, *Social Change in the Industrial Revolution,* London, 1960, especially pp. 225–264.

11. Joan Scott and Louise Tilly, "Women's Work and the Family in Nineteenth-Century Europe," *Comparative Studies in Society and History,* XVII (1975), argue that women's work experience reflects more traditionalism than change.

12. But this pattern of increased responsibility in determining the family budget may not be true in phase two, when working men tended to keep a larger proportion of their wages before turning over household money to their wives. See Peter N. Stearns, "Working Class Women in Britain, 1890–1914," *Suffer and Be Still,* ed. Martha Vicinus, Bloomington, 1972, pp. 100–120.

13. Neil McKendrick, "Home Demand and Economic Growth: A New View of the Role of Women and Children in the Industrial Revolution," *Historical Perspectives: Studies in English Thought and Society in Honor of J. H. Plumb,* London, 1974, pp. 152–210.

14. Michael Anderson, *Family Structure in Nineteenth-Century Lancashire,* Cambridge, 1971, p. 71.

15. For a much fuller discussion of domestic service in the nineteenth century, see Theresa M. McBride, *The Domestic Revolution: The Modernization of Household Service in England and France, 1820–1920,* London, 1976.

16. The classic interpretation of labor migration is that of Arthur Redford, *Labor Migration in England, 1800–1850,* rev. ed., New York, 1968, see p. 183.

17. The research of Vivien Elliott, Research Fellow, Radcliffe Institute, on earlier marriage patterns in England suggests that the important variable in determining how much freedom women had in choosing their own spouses was whether or not they lived at home with their fathers, for this determined how much paternal authority was exercised.

18. Leonore Davidoff, "Mastered for Life: Servant and Wife in Victorian and Edwardian England," *Journal of Social History,* VII (June 1974), 406–428.

19. This incident is taken from the research of Allan Binstock, "The Shoemakers of Fougères," Ph.D. dissertation, University of Wisconsin, 1975.

20. F. Zweig, *Women's Life and Labour,* London, 1952, p. 140; see also McBride, *The Domestic Revolution.*

Suggestions for Further Reading

Boserup, Ester. *Women's Role in Economic Development.* London, 1970.

Branca, Patricia. "A New Perspective on Women's Work: A Comparative Typology." *Journal of Social History,* IX (Winter 1975), 129–153.

Hewitt, Margaret. *Wives and Mothers in Victorian Industry.* London, 1958.

McBride, Theresa. *The Domestic Revolution: The Modernization of Household Service in England and France 1820–1920.* London, 1976.

McKendrick, Neil. "Home Demand and Economic Growth: A New View of the Role of Women and Children in the Industrial Revolution." *Historical Perspectives: Studies in English Thought and Society in Honor of J. H. Plumb.* London, 1974.

Pinchbeck, Ivy. *Women Workers in the Industrial Revolution.* London, 1931.

Richards, Eric. "Women in the British Economy Since About 1700: An Interpretation." *History,* LIX (October 1974), 337–357.

Scott, Joan, and Louise Tilly. "Women's Work and the Family in Nineteenth-Century Europe." *The Family in History,* ed. Charles Rosenberg. New York, 1975.

Stearns, Peter N. "Working-Class Women in Britain, 1890–1914." *Suffer and Be Still,* ed. Martha Vicinus. Bloomington, 1972.

13

Angels in the Devil's Workshop: Leisured and Charitable Women in Nineteenth-Century England and France

Barbara Corrado Pope

As indicated in the preceding essays, it would be misleading to assume that industrialization made its greatest impact on women who labored in the factories. Equally important was its effect on middle-class wives who remained in their homes while their husbands sallied forth into the world of business, politics, bureaucracy, and the professions. Barbara Corrado Pope portrays the dilemma faced by these women who were freed from the necessity of contributing to the family economy. Not only did a life of leisure conflict with the middle-class work ethic, but it was psychologically oppressive as well. The Victorian ideal of womanhood epitomized the traditional image of woman's superior virtue and guaranteed her subjection to the family and her husband. Inferior female education further reinforced cultural and legal strictures against women's participation in the public sphere. But after several generations of "true womanhood," many energetic women developed psychological survival skills to compensate for the limitations on them. Englishwomen applied their moral beliefs to the reform of all aspects of late-nineteenth-century society. In France, where such work had long been the monopoly of the church, the salon tradition provided many women with a cultural sphere in which they could act. Thus, without invading "masculine" occupations, women began to challenge the stereotype of the passive Victorian lady. They used their leisure to go to work.

OVERDOING IT

"What? Going already? And in Mackintoshes? Surely you are not going to walk!"

"Oh, dear no! Lord Archibald is going to take us to a dear little slum he's found out near the Minories — such a fearful place! Fourteen poor things sleeping in one bed and no window! — and the Mackintoshes are to keep out infection, you know, and hide one's diamonds, and all that!"

The December 22, 1883, issue of *Punch* satirizes a Lady Bountiful.

An Idle Brain is the Devil's Workshop.
ANONYMOUS

The Devil soon finds work for Idle Hands.
ANONYMOUS

If the devil had been alive and well in nineteenth-century France and England, idle hands and brains would by no means have been his most potent weapons. All around he would have seen more fruitful fields for his labors. Rapidly expanding industrial and commercial enterprises offered vast opportunities to infect bourgeois men with avarice and materialism, to make them ruthless competitors and heartless exploiters of their employees. Cities grew apace; and the squalor of abject poverty that greeted the job seekers who flocked to urban centers led to every kind of crime and indecency. Indeed, France and England were filled with people frantically pursuing what they considered the necessities of life. Businessmen struggled to stave off financial ruin; professional men and bureaucrats strove to find and maintain a position. The vast majority of the populace, both male and female, worked long, hard hours on farms, in shops and factories, and in wealthy homes as servants. The unemployed and underemployed new city dwellers engaged in any activity that would assure them shelter and the next meal, efforts that earned them the label "the dangerous classes." Only a select portion of the population would have had time to suffer the afflictions of idleness. Increasingly, these afflictions fell upon middle-class women.

At first glance it seems ironic that middle-class men, who extolled the virtues of hard and productive work, tried so much to make their wives and daughters leisured. Yet this is exactly what they did. As we shall see, the Industrial Revolution freed many middle-class women from the need to work in shop or home. Most men of their class saw this female disengagement from domestic and business employment as a social necessity, as the imperative symbol of increasing economic and political power. In the eighteenth century leisure had been an attribute of class — of the aristocracy and those members of the upper middle or bourgeois class who could afford to imitate aristocratic lifestyles. "To live nobly" meant being leisured, being free to pursue pleasurable, sociable, cultural, and intellectual activity. Since middle-class men engaged in finance, commerce, industry, civil service, and the professions, they themselves could not rise above the grubby process of moneymaking. They could and did remove their women from employment and encouraged them to be as beautiful, as delicate, and as cultured as money, good fortune, and application allowed.

Despite the desirability of female leisure as a status symbol, the moral difficulty remained. To industrious men much of what the aristocracy did with its leisure seemed frivolous and morally dangerous — the devil's work for idle hands and brains. How, then, were their women to use this freedom, which their new standing required? In the nineteenth century the solution to this problem rang out with resounding clarity: by being better wives, better mothers, and morally superior beings. This answer was rooted in Christian, and particularly Protestant, tradition but came into full flower only after the experiences of the French and Industrial revolutions. It culminated in the cult of domesticity, according to which the home became a sanctuary and woman its guardian angel. This cult dominated thinking about women in England, on the continent, and in America, and helped to make the gulf between the male sphere of work and politics and the female sphere of society and the home wider than ever before. We will see what it meant in France and England by following women's careers from their teens to their marriages and, for many, to reforming matronhood.

In each country the bourgeoisie and its ideal of the family triumphed during the nineteenth century. Yet each had a different tradition, religion, and rate of industrial development. These differences will help illustrate how one ideal of women fit into two cultural patterns. By examining memoirs, educational manuals, books on morality, and advice to women, we will see that at the beginning of the century moralists and teachers urged French and English women to confine themselves to their duties in the home. At mid-century, finding this role too narrow, many women sought to expand their supposed moral influence outside the family circle. They took their role as angels quite seriously. When they stepped out of the home and slammed the door on the devil's workshop of idleness, they set forth, protected by the moral superiority in which domestic idealism had cloaked them, to do good in more dangerous wellsprings of evil like army hospitals, city slums, prisons and poorhouses, and even prostitutes' haunts.

Today the term "family" evokes a very specific image: the single household of parents and children united, ideally at least, by mutual respect and affection. Mother and father are supposed to play very different roles, the man that of the primary breadwinner and the woman that of the spiritual and emotional center of the home. In the eighteenth century the word "family" had several meanings, corresponding to its form in various classes of society. Our image of the nuclear family is the product of a long development that took place among the bourgeoisie. Even before the French and Industrial revolutions, which completed this process, contemporaries noted the unique middle-class stress on the emotional and moral values of family life. Other characteristics marked this social stratum as well: the tendency to divide property more equally among the children; the affectionate relationship between husband and wife, who often worked together; and the insistence on female marital fidelity, which derived from the male fear of leaving family property to another man's progeny. To the aristocracy, by contrast, family meant the extended family, including perhaps several households of grandparents, cousins, aunts, and uncles, bound by considerations of property, prestige, and title. The prevalence of primogeniture gave the eldest son the lion's share of the patrimony. In the interest of aggrandizing or keeping landed property intact, girls might not be sufficiently dowered to marry (and in France they might have to enter a convent); and boys might be forced to take up a career in church or army. Thus, two distinct family ideologies existed in the eighteenth century; and each entailed different role expectations for women. Before the French Revolution, most upwardly mobile people aspired to "live nobly." In the nineteenth century, the choices seemed to narrow, and the bourgeois way of life became dominant. A glance at aristocratic family life and the nineteenth-century view of it and its morality explains this reversal.

Typically in the eighteenth century an aristocratic woman was married off by the age of twenty to the man who best suited the property, power, and status ambitions of her family line. To fulfill her marital role she had only to produce an heir, not to nurture or educate him. This she left to a succession of hirelings. Often, if the husband allowed, she had a certain sexual liberty, a kind of compensation for loveless marriage. For the rest, she spent most of her time either in the country during the warm seasons or in the capital during the winter, creating a life of sweet sociability. She used her leisure to arrange suppers and balls, private theaters and concerts, promenades and hunts. In France, the most intellectual and ambitious of these women hosted salons, where they used their much recognized and admired conversational skills to facilitate and direct discussions about art, religion, philosophy, and politics. The most important figures of the Enlightenment — foreigners as well as French men and women — first articulated their views or read parts of their works on these occasions. The brilliant and witty critique of church and state gave the salons political as well as cultural significance. Especially in France, aristocratic men and women shared responsibility for and enjoyment of leisured activities. If parents wished to participate in the education of their children, either the mother or the father or both gave them lessons. Neither leisure nor the socialization of children had yet become exclusively women's domain. The men of the English aristocracy played a leading role in political life, both in London and in their local districts. The French nobility by and large had lost this vital function. More leisured, more theatrical in its display of the aristocratic virtues of gallantry, magnanimity, refinement, and wit, the French nobility also became increasingly vulnerable to criticism.

The most famous and influential critic of aristocratic life was Jean Jacques Rousseau. He declared French urbane society to be artificial and immoral. Rousseau seemed particularly annoyed at the freedom and domination of women in the salon setting and wanted to confine them to their domestic role. Despite his irascible attitude toward them, many noblewomen found his exaltation of emotions most attractive. They appreciated his books and those of his equally sentimental contemporaries, who also glorified conjugal love and motherhood. Breast-feeding, which Rousseau extolled, became a kind of fad among upper-class women, who formerly would have sent their children out to a wet nurse. The Comtesse de Boigne reports in her memoirs that her mother received a great deal of homage and attention at the court of Marie Antoinette because she chose to fulfill this maternal function. Such adherence to sensibility was superficial, however, and did not go beyond such gestures. It took two revolutions to realize Rousseau's ideals.

The French Revolution traumatized the upper classes. They witnessed what they considered a terrible upheaval in the "natural" (i.e., class) order. Europeans stood aghast at the spectacle of a powerful monarch beheaded, a great aristocracy persecuted and exiled, and the poor of Paris dancing in the streets and even seeming to rule. Such a dizzying turnabout of fortune demanded explanation. Where counterrevolution reigned — and that was almost everywhere in the early part of the nineteenth century — that explanation came in the form of a moral judgment of the past. Mme. de La Tour du Pin tells in her memoirs how she grew up before the Revolution among "the scandalous examples of Parisian society" without the aid of a religious or moral education. "The older I grow," she wrote in the 1830s,

> the more sure I become that the Revolution of 1789 was only the inevitable consequence and, I might almost say, the just punishment of the vices of the upper classes. Vices carried to such excess that if people had not been stricken with a mortal blindness, they must have seen that they would inevitably be consumed by the very fire they themselves were lighting.[1]

Throughout the century conservative writers concurred with this opinion. "The 18th century with all its corruption, its scandal, its irreligion, weighs still upon us with all the weight of a Satanic inheritance," declared the French Archbishop Dupanloup in *Studious Women* (1867). "Like original sin," he continued, "its faults have been bathed in blood, and this is the history of all great aberrations."

One logical, if not very enlightened, conclusion of this conservative analysis was that the lessons to be learned from the Revolution had little to do with social or political rights, as radicals claimed. Rather, they were simple lessons about conventional, bourgeois morality: The poor had revolted because their betters had set a bad example. The aristocracy had acted *frivolously.* It had ignored or disdained the virtues of good family life, religious practice, sexual morality, and honest labor. One possible solution to the problem of controlling the lower classes, then, was to set a good example, to act *seriously,* and demonstrably to live by high moral standards. The French aristocracy's (and Mme. de La Tour du Pin's) espousal of Catholicism after the Revolution was partly due to this analysis. In England, at the same time, Evangelicalism waged and won a successful war against the convivial excesses of drink, sexual liberty, and religious indifference.

The fear of revolution also brought about a reexamination of women's role in society. Aristocratic women became scapegoats. The ladies at the court were blamed for all the intrigues that had blocked reform, the *salonières* for the debilitating mockery of church and king that had taken place in their drawing rooms. Scores of books written in nineteenth-century France called upon women to give up their former sway over society and to retreat into their homes. Even the English feminist Mary Wollstonecraft, in her *Vindication of the Rights of Woman* (1792), urged that most women should be educated so that they could become better wives and mothers, revealing a profoundly middle-class bias. Duty became just about the favorite word of the morally earnest nineteenth century. Where the activities of sweet sociability, such as the salons, still existed, political timidity and a new prudery veiled their brilliance and muffled their gaiety.

The family that Rousseau had idealized came much closer to the eighteenth-century bourgeois form than to the aristocratic. A middle-class woman's life differed greatly from that of her aristocratic counterpart for both emotional and economic reasons. In the closer-knit bourgeois family, a daughter could expect to have more say in the choice of her husband, a wife could expect more affection from her mate, a mother could expect to spend much more time rearing her children. Unless she came from or moved into a very wealthy family, she could also expect to work. Traditionally, she kept the accounts. In the retailing class she also served the customers. Among the petit bourgeois and artisan classes, her duties might include the practice of a craft, supervision of employees, and providing meals and lodging for apprentices. The women of the "industrious classes" clearly kept very busy.

The Industrial Revolution drastically reduced women's role in commerce and manufacturing. The very tendency of industrialization and increasing capitalization toward largeness and joint stock rather than family business meant the separation of shop and craft from the home. Of course, no natural law decreed that when the business moved women should remain behind. The aspiration for genteel status and the domestic ideal partially explains the female retreat from moneymaking. This retreat, like industrialization itself, was an uneven one. The cases of England and France differ greatly, for example. By mid-century most English middle-class women had relinquished their involvement in trade and lost their knowledge of business and the professions. In France, which was less industrially advanced and the classical land of family-owned businesses, this did not occur. The wives of some provincial manufacturers retained their bookkeeping functions late into the nineteenth century. Even today many small cafés, restaurants, and shops, are run by a husband and wife team. Yet most prosperous English and French storekeepers, who still relied on their wives' skills, had a different future in mind for their daughters. In the family rooms above or behind the shop these girls learned painting, the pianoforte, and foreign languages in the hopes of making a good enough match to enter a leisured existence. The sons of the same families learned accounting, law, medicine, or any number of professional skills that allowed them to enlarge or escape from the family business. By and large, as enterprises grew, women went up the social hierarchy and out of the business. In their homes, the middle classes used much of their new wealth to hire more and more servants, some with very specialized skills. This, too, gave women the possibility for more leisure.

Separation of shop and home also meant the separation of men and women and a polarization of familial roles. Woman alone became the socializer of children, because she alone spent her days with them. Men became increasingly involved in getting ahead in business, the professions, and the new state bureaucracies. Perceptions about the new industrial society reinforced this polarization of roles. The new factory towns and their squalor, the growing problems of crime and urban poverty, the competition for profits and position, and the possibility of financial ruin characterized the world outside, the man's world. The comfortable and secure middle-class home, woman's sphere, came to represent an escape from an ugly and threatening society. It followed that women should have all those qualities that could not be found in the world outside, such as gentleness and piety, submissiveness and fragility, chasteness and devotion. Thus, the middle class created an ideal of womanhood that best suited its economic and emotional needs: the sympathetic companion to her husband, the teacher and moral exemplar to her children, and the kind mistress to her servants. Her major duty was, according to one English preacher, to create a home that would be a "bright, serene, restful, joyful nook of heaven in an unheavenly world," and as Sarah Stickney Ellis, in *The Mothers of England: Their Influence and Responsibility* (1844), admonished her,

> to guard against any weakening of the bounds of family affection — to see that the fountain of love is kept fresh, pure and perpetually flowing . . . for without this, the pilgrimage of life will have neither flowers to enliven, verdure to refresh, nor fruits to sustain the traveller on his way.

This is the ideology of domesticity, the notion that the home should be the source and repository of all affections and virtues and woman its guardian angel. Its major precept is that women are or can be morally superior and that they will use their particular moral qualities to imbue every member of their household with virtue and, through their family circle, to bring about the betterment of the world. Ironically, the idea of female *moral superiority* rested upon the rather shaky base of other commonplaces about women that assumed their *inferiority,* like their physical and intellectual weakness, their susceptibility and flightiness, and their passivity. Clearly, in order to maintain their special goodness, women needed male protection. In the very popular *Women of England: Their Social Duties and Domestic Habits* (1839), Mrs. Ellis depicted the emotional function of the middle-class female in the industrial world. She thoroughly accepted the notion of male superiority in most things and particularly admired the men of her own class. However, she knew they often faltered morally and sympathetically attributed these failings to the fact that they had to do daily battle in the jungle of politics and business. She urged the women of England to take pity on them:

> How often has a man returned to his home with a mind confused by many voices, which in the mart, the exchange or the public assembly have addressed themselves to his inborn selfishness, or his worldy pride; and while his integrity was shaken, and his resolution gave way beneath the pressure of apparent necessity, or the insidious pretences of expediency, he has stood corrected before the clear eye of woman, as it looked directly to the naked truth, and detected the lurking evil of the specious act he was about to commit. Nay, so potent may have become this secret influence, that he may have borne it about with him like a kind of second conscience, for mental reference, and spiritual counsel, in moments of trial; and when the snares of the world were around him and temptations from within and without have bribed over the witness in his bosom, he has thought of the humble monitress who sat alone, guarding the fireside comforts of his distant home; and the remembrance of her character, clothed in moral beauty, has scattered the clouds before his mental vision, and sent him back to the beloved home a wiser and better man.

This lovely portrait of the calm, unharried wife and the handsome hearth implied a certain wealth and financial stability and had great appeal to the striving middle-class men. Thus were angels made in men's minds and, seemingly, by men's labor. Actually, *women* undertook the major part of the task of making angels by educating girls, either in the home with the help of a governess or masters or as teachers at boarding and day schools.

Middle- and upper-class families usually sent their sons to school to obtain either a liberal classical education (including Latin and Greek) or professional training or both. Boys left home by the age of ten because their parents believed that by that time they had gained sufficient moral understanding from their mother but now should be separated from her soft influence in order to become men capable of dealing with the tough heterogeneous world. Most writers on educational subjects preferred home education for daughters because, they reasoned, girls could only benefit from prolonged contact with their mothers and did not need to, and perhaps should not, know about the world outside. However, many mothers could not or did not want personally to supervise their daughters' education. Thus, boarding schools proliferated in France and England during the first part of the century. What a girl learned, whether at home or school, can be conveniently divided into three categories: academic subjects; those arts needed to make her appear "accomplished" and to help her capture a husband; and, finally, that which everyone said female education should be all about — morality, religion, and women's duties. With one exception, no one attempted to train women to do anything that would help them earn their living. The exception was teaching, which required no specific training, since governesses and teachers, like mothers, only had to pass on what they knew.

Under the heading of academic subjects the following were taught and imbibed by rote in small, variable doses: reading, writing, grammar, spelling, and arithmetic; some geography and astronomy; ancient, national, and Bible history; literature and a bit of the natural sciences. Usually much more time and expense went toward the inculcation of the so-called female accomplishments. In this category we find foreign languages (French for the English and English for the French), piano, voice, the harp, drawing, reading aloud, flower arranging, fancy needlework, dancing ("to improve posture and carriage"), and, in some very select French schools, conversation. Finally came duty and morality, which included religious practice (like attendance at Sunday services, prayers at meals and bedtimes, Bible reading), domestic economy, sewing and knitting (often done for the poor of the neighborhood), and some practice in housewifery and mothering, like making one's own bed, checking the linens, and tutoring the younger children in the school or at home. The meaning of domestic economy was rather vague. Women were supposed to know how to administer a house with servants and to keep within a budget suitable to their station. In the nineteenth century the economics of home management included such tasks as hiring, directing, and supervising the domestics; knowing how and when to preserve food and do the yearly cleaning chores; making an annual inventory of linens, silver, and dishes; and being economical without any appearance of stinginess.

Moralists and pedagogues constantly complained that parents, governesses, and teachers stressed the accomplishments at the expense of rudimentary academic subjects, economics, and moral training. The report of government inspectors in Paris and the personal experiences of women who attended these schools verify the validity of these complaints. The three *dames-inspectrices* who visited Parisian lay schools during 1844–1845 lauded the fact that all headmistresses either taught religion or sent their girls to the local parish for instruction, religion being the one aspect of women's training upon which the municipal government insisted. However, the inspectors also found the presentation of all other essential subjects to be extremely uneven. Some schools had no Bible history. Many did not competently teach reading and writing, although they hired visiting male professors to lecture on literature and the natural sciences to illiterate students. This happened, the report explained, because male professors had more prestige than women and their presence enhanced the reputation of a school. Although the three women inspectors did not mention domestic economy specifically, we can assume that teachers gave this prosaic subject rather short shrift because many of the students did not even know the legal weights and measures and could not do simple arithmetic. Sewing, dancing, and the piano appeared on every curriculum. The inspectors blamed this haphazard education on doting relatives more than on the underpaid and overworked teachers. Parents, they said, wanted to see their daughters indulged and become "cultured." With this in mind, the report condemned the universal passion for the piano. "If one judged by the considered number of pupils of all ages and conditions who receive lessons," the inspectors wrote, "the study of the piano would seem to be the very basis of education and instruction in the eyes of families." [2]

The Duchess d'Agoult, who at the age of sixteen entered the best and most aristocratic Parisian school in the 1820s, recalls in her memoirs the shock she felt at discovering that her comrades in the senior class could not spell. Worse, the good sisters who ran the school showed so much disdain for the needs of the flesh that the standards of hygiene, diet, and cleanliness were extremely poor. The biggest event of the week occurred every Thursday afternoon, when relatives and friends visited the school's salon. There, under the supervision of the nuns, the brightest and prettiest girls "shone" for their guests by displaying their accomplishments and their skills of conversation. What made these days particularly thrilling to the students, however, was not the chance it gave them to act grown up, but the fact that relatives usually brought them bonbons, which the hungry, undernourished girls hoarded and traded.

A decade later, Frances Power Cobbe, a young lady from Ireland, attended one of England's finest girls' schools at Brighton, where, she recalls in her memoirs, "Everything was taught us in the inverse ratio of its true importance. At the bottom of the scale were Morals and Religion, and at the top were Music and Dancing; miserably poor music, too. . . ." She considered the instrumental, dance, and deportment lessons a waste of precious time and money and longed for lessons in Greek and Latin, or at least good, plain English. Instead, "French, Italian and German were chattered all day long, our tongues being only set at liberty at six o'clock to speak English." Even at that, she concluded, the languages the teachers and the pupils spoke had little resemblance to what German, Italian, and French really sounded like. A degrading disciplinary system complemented this inadequate instruction. Cobbe reports seeing at one of the weekly punishment sessions, girls, old enough to be married, forced to sit in a corner all night in full evening dress, because they had been impertinent or had failed to do their homework.

Nothing in the formal education of either Frances Power Cobbe or the Duchess d'Agoult prepared them for their later lives. D'Agoult wrote history, novels, and political and philosophical essays under the pseudonym Daniel Stern and hosted one of the few politically important salons of the nineteenth century. Cobbe became a philanthropist, writer, feminist, and campaigning antivivisectionist. Both got their real education in the most haphazard fashion, from relatives and governesses, but mostly through their own intellectual drive. Both led independent lives only as a result of unexpected circumstances. Forced into a marriage of convenience, d'Agoult felt unfulfilled, despite her beauty, her social successes, and motherhood. In 1833 she ran away to Italy with the pianist and composer Franz Liszt. When she returned, the aristocratic world shut her out. She gave up her high position, rejecting also its conservatism and Catholicism. Cobbe never married and devoted her young womanhood to looking after her father's Irish estate. She was "declassed" at his death, for her brother took over the house and *his* wife became its mistress. She returned to England, where she began her long philanthropic career by teaching in a girls' reformatory. Like most famous women of their century, d'Agoult and Cobbe *made* their place, just as they had *made* their education.

If female education did not serve women who wanted or had to lead an independent life, neither did it fully please those moralists and writers who wanted to see women trained to become home-bound angels. The reason for this is quite simple: The major goal of parents and educators was to make it possible for a girl to attract a husband. This is not to say that parents did not care whether or not their daughters had strong moral character or the ability to become good, efficient home managers. Parents just did not believe in putting the cart before the horse. If the virtues of womanhood flowered best in the vocation of wife and mother, then young women first of all had to be in a position to realize these virtues. That position was a good marriage; the competition to make one was fierce, and, therefore, the more demonstrable talents got priority.

The term "marriage market" is a much better evocation of nineteenth- than twentieth-century social practice. Some, especially the early French socialists, even labeled it the slave market, for the way to be married was to be displayed and, if one came from an important and wealthy family, to be contracted for. Conversation represented one mode of display, dancing another; hence the family gatherings, the parties, the balls, and, in France, the salons. Young ladies usually also demonstrated their talents by singing, playing instrumental solos, accompanying dancers and singers at the keyboard, and partaking in dramatic readings. All this, of course, occurred under the vigilant eyes of mother or some other suitable female relative. This type of maneuvering seemed to please the young men of the day because it allowed them to measure the potential brides against their own romantic notions of what these angels should be like. Besides, until the advent of mass culture, such performances represented an important form of entertainment. It need hardly be added that insofar as family budget could stretch and the young woman could shrink — into corsets, tiny shoes, and other paraphernalia of fashionable conformity — mother and daughter carefully fostered the romantic image.

Financial considerations still mattered a great deal, the rule of thumb being that the more wealth and prestige the family had, the more weight it gave to wealth and prestige in marrying off a daughter. In France, practically all upper- and middle-class families drew up marriage contracts, although their use declined in the course of the nineteenth century. In England, usually only upper-class families utilized contracts. Such arrangements most often protected the *family* of the bride from her husband's mismanagement of dowry or inheritance. However, in a few cases, the young woman herself had some financial control. The bourgeois notion of equitable distribution of property among all the children had been written into the Napoleonic Code. This gave a Frenchwoman the right to sue her own family for her fair portion of the patrimony. Once married, she could protect her dowry from her husband's creditors by moving for a separation of their estates. An Englishwoman, too, could take some measures against a husband's complete squandering of her property. This, of course, entailed knowledge of the law, which many women did not have.

The French and English liked to point to basic distinctions in their marrying practices. One of the most common observations was that the more sheltered and carefully chaperoned French *demoiselle* had to accede to family and financial considerations in marriage, while the English miss, being more accustomed to social exchange between contemporaries of both sexes, had more freedom to choose her life's partner. This stereotype is correct only in the most limited sense, for most young people married within a narrowly defined social group. Few families of either nation really forced their daughters to marry someone against their will. Rather, most young women had already internalized a system of values that shaped their wills.

That marriage was imperative was the chief tenet of this system, for bourgeois society made no place for the single woman. Accordingly, young women tended to agree with their families that one settled for a reasonable match and did not hold out for an ideal relationship or a romantic attachment. Further, parents and daughters were in accord about the qualities a prospective husband must have: He should come from a similar religious and social background, be "solid," present a decent appearance, and, most important, either have a sufficient inheritance or show enough promise to guarantee financial security.

In order to be chosen by a suitable man, a young woman had to adapt herself to society's ideal of womanhood, to be passive and innocent, cultured and submissive. The pressures to conform, at least outwardly, continued in marriage. Many forces in society fostered adaption to a narrow role. Education, as we have seen, may not have thoroughly prepared women for marriage and motherhood, but by not preparing them for anything else, it made independence almost impossible. So did the law, which particularly oppressed married women. They were treated either as civilly nonexistent for most of the century (in English common law) or as minors (according to the Napoleonic Code). They had no political rights, almost no economic power, and little judicial recourse in case of maltreatment or the infidelity of their husbands. Also, by the time a woman married, expectations about female behavior had been communicated to her through religion, popular novels, the courtship system and, most important, the family. Now her husband would second these expectations. If she still did not know how to go about becoming the angel of the house, as the poet Patmore put it, there was an abundance of literature, reaching a peak of production in the 1830s and 1840s, to guide her.

In England the most popular adviser was Sarah Ellis, who not only produced *The Mothers of England* and *The Women of England,* but also *The Daughters of England* and *The Wives of England, all* in multiple editions. She wrote for her own class, for those women of England who

> belong to that great mass of the population of England which is connected with trade and manufactures, as well as to the wives and daughters of professional men of limited incomes; or, in order to make the application more direct, to that portion of it who are restricted to the services of from one to four domestics, — who, on the one hand, enjoy the advantages of liberal education, and, on the other, have no pretension to family rank.

Thus she aptly distinguished the women of the middle ranks of society, where the domestic ideal flourished, from those who were above or below on the social scale. Proud of her class, she wrote to impress upon her readers that they should not strive to become ladies, to take on the sickliness, the incompetence, and the bored and listless airs she identified with that designation.

Restricted by the biases of her own social milieu, Mrs. Ellis judged the women of the upper class unfairly, for they did have important functions to perform. Ladies belonged to the top stratum of the social hierarchy, which still-powerful aristocrats now shared with the bourgeois leaders of finance, commerce, manufacture, the law, and politics. Like middle-class women, they had to keep up the appearances, including their own toilet and the presentation of home and family, that produced the subtle distinctions in socioeconomic rankings. Unlike other women, they spent much of their time arranging the great social events of the "best circles." Especially in England, where men's clubs became popular, the orchestration of other leisured activity fell more and more into women's domain. We should not, like Mrs. Ellis, discount this enterprise as useless. The Frenchwoman's salon and the Englishwoman's dinners provided meeting places for the men of politics, business, and the professions and for anyone who could best effect family success. The right occasion brought off with aplomb by the proper wife enhanced the prestige of her husband, made certain social contacts possible for their sons, and served as a suitable showcase for marriageable daughters. Mrs. Ellis was correct in one respect, though. Some of the wives and many of the unmarried daughters of the upper class came close to being merely ornaments — beautiful and delicate symbols of their husbands' and fathers' prosperity — who spent their time visiting, reading light novels, arranging flowers, and embroidering.

The good middle-class woman left gross physical tasks to her servants, not because of the demands of social engagements but in order to give her attention to the moral development of her family. She could now give each of her children the benefits of the sympathetic understanding and sensibility supposedly natural to women. Above all, she could be there, in the home, prepared to deal with all those major housekeeping decisions and minor trifles that made real comfort possible, and ever ready to meet the emotional demands of her entourage. Mrs. Ellis counseled the women of England to rise early every morning and not to ask themselves "What shall I do to gratify myself — to be admired — or to vary the tenor of my existence?" but to seek to correct yesterday's lapses of kindness and consideration by helping every member of the family. According to Mrs. Ellis, the good wife should say to herself:

> I will meet the family with a consciousness that, being the least engaged of any member of it, I am consequently the most at liberty to devote myself to the general good of the whole, by cultivating cheerful conversation, adapting myself to the prevailing tone of feeling and leading those who are less happy to think and speak of what will make them more so.

Among her daily tasks might be waking and washing the children, checking the menu and shopping list with the cook, supervising cleaning chores and giving out supplies to servants, going over clothing for needed sewing repairs, giving lessons, caring for the sick of the household, and making and receiving visits.

There is nothing in this of hard labor or drudgery, for Mrs. Ellis had only contempt for those graceless souls who "of their own free choice, employ their lives in the constant bustle of providing for mere appetite."

> It can never be said that the atmosphere of the kitchen is an element in which a refined and intellectual woman ought to live; though the department itself is one which no sensible woman should think it a degradation to overlook. But instead of maintaining a general oversight and arrangement of such affairs, some well-intentioned women plunge head, heart and hand into the vortex of culinary operations, thinking, feeling, and doing what would be more appropriately left to their servants.

Obviously, the woman who lived by the precepts of the cult of domesticity had to keep a very delicate balance. She must be cultured enough to teach her children, sing and play songs for them, and distract the weary master of the home. Yet she must not pretend to be too good for homemaking. Above all, she must dedicate herself to the happiness of those around her — especially her husband — and be the calm at the center of the storm of modern life.

In France, the authors of the literature of domesticity described the ideal woman in much the same way, except that they stressed, in accord with the salon tradition, her role as a purveyor of culture and learning. Most of the writing came from the "ladies" themselves, women who would have thought of themselves as aristocrats or their allies. Their mood, however, was not one of class chauvinism, but of postrevolutionary contrition. In at least a score of books with titles like *The Life of Woman, The Education of Women,* and *The Influence of Women,* they called upon their readers to turn away from the sway they had held over high society before 1789 and to exert, instead, a new moral influence through their natural roles as wives, mothers, and agents of charity. Two writers whose fame endured throughout the century demonstrate this aristocratic identification: Mme. Campan, a former lady in waiting to Marie Antoinette, and the Countess de Rémusat, who had served at the court of Empress Josephine. The Countess Maisonneuve, however, is the woman who best illustrates the effect of the Revolution on the old high aristocracy. Before 1789, as the daughter of an old, important family, she entered a convent by choice in order to become a scholar. She hoped to spend her life in obscurity studying the classics and writing. During the Revolution she and her family went into exile. She had to support them by the only means she had, fancy embroidery. Upon her return to France she became a schoolmistress and the mentor of middle-class housewives. She did this not only because all convents for scholarly women had been closed but also because she felt her own experiences had taught her the values of the down-to-earth domestic existence. Having suffered during the Revolution from a lack of practical education, she gave training in the economics and skills of homemaking the highest priority in her school. "Society," she wrote in *An Essay on the Instruction of Women* (1801),

> which requires from each man an homage proportioned to the gifts which he has received from nature, seems to demand from women only a fairly uniform tribute . . . that she is amiable and useful in her home.

For the sentiments expressed in this thin volume, Mme. Maisonneuve received the homage of Emperor Napoleon and Pope Pius VII.

The distinguishing feature of the French literature of domesticity is its emphasis on the mother-teacher. England also had its advocates of home instruction, but their number was much greater in France where "maternal education" became the keystone of domestic ideology. "Maternal education" implied three functions. The first pointed to the mother of a family as quite naturally the one who by example and prescription should teach her children about morality and religion. Through her children the mother-teacher could hope to influence all of society. Sons, of course, set forth from the home to have a direct effect on the world; daughters could only hope to duplicate the role of their mother. Second, writers used the term maternal education to mean that a mother should give instruction in the elementary subjects of reading, writing, and arithmetic to her very young children. The final definition entailed a mother's keeping her girls at home until they married, training them in morality and religion, the domestic arts and economy, and hiring tutors to teach them academic subjects and the arts. This fitted in with the Latin-Catholic attitude that young women should be sheltered and that the best person to protect a girl was her mother. Unlike Protestant England and America, the French never disregarded or discounted female sexuality. This recognition of female desires hints at another, unstated advantage of maternal education: It gave women something *to do*. French novelists and moralists referred constantly to the problem of *ennui,* or boredom, among middle- and upper-class women. Suffering from ennui led to sin as surely as idle brains and hands. If women, however, became devoted mother-teachers they would not be bored and tempted into sexual adventures. The literature on maternal education in France did have some discernible effects. The French bourgeoisie never developed the nanny system, which characterized the homes of the upper middle classes of high Victorian England. As late as 1950 some bourgeois mothers still "made it a point to give their children the equivalent of an elementary education." [3]

But we will never know how many women succeeded in becoming mother-teachers, just as we will never know how many women became domestic angels. We do know that the cult of domesticity was compelling, because it still affects thinking about women today. From the middle classes the cult first spread to the upper class, where its greatest effect was the idealization of women as more delicate, more religious, more sensitive than men. No one ever idealized lower-class women, but the assertion grew (often in the face of cruel and contradictory realities) that women should not be wage earners, that they ought to stay in the home for the moral benefit of their children, and that they should become good housekeepers and cooks. Working-class husbands began demanding more and better homemaking skills from their wives by the last quarter of the nineteenth century in England (although not yet in France).[4] Just as in the middle classes, the separation of home and work fostered these attitudes. But so did the dominant society, which exerted pressures to conform, often through the agency of upper- and middle-class female charity workers. Even among the middle classes, the ability and desire to conform varied. The women at the bottom of Mrs. Ellis's ranking, for example, might have had very little time for culture and calm; throughout most of the century, hot running water, refrigeration, and ready-made clothing did not exist, so lower-middle-class women with families to care for and only one servant to help had plenty to do. Others did not have enough to do. Rich middle-class women with housekeepers and several servants could finish the daily routine tasks in a few hours. Beyond the question of economics and social rankings, many women could not fit themselves into the narrowly prescribed role. Some rebelled, like the Duchess d'Agoult, the French novelist Georges Sand, and the English feminists. Some reacted by being prone to nerves and hysteria. Others simply subverted the ideal merely by doing the things they were not supposed to do: Flaubert's adulterous Emma Bovary exemplifies the ill effects of ennui.

The easiest and most acceptable way of dealing with the narrow domestic role, however, was to expand it. After mid-century hundreds of thousands of women left the retreat of the home to serve as examples of superior moral values to benighted souls beyond their family circle. They became charity workers, the angels of the slums, hospitals, and workhouses. So many women flung themselves into this new mission that some writers, like John Stuart Mill in *The Subjection of Women* (1869), condescendingly labeled it a modern addiction. However, no one condescended to the great woman leaders of the philanthropic movement, who were universally considered the best of their sex, the true angels. Not surprisingly, the women who made the real innovations in charity work stand out markedly from the rest. They were *not* angelic, nor were they fashionable or submissive, nor could they always care about the happiness of *everyone* around them. No one illustrates this better than the most remarkable benefactor of them all, Florence Nightingale.

With the exception of her queen, Victoria, Nightingale was the most famous woman of her century and undoubtedly the most adored and praised. The praise and the legend stem from a single incident in her long life of service to England and to health care, her nursing work at the front during the Crimean War. It is difficult for us to imagine how revolutionary this was. Before Florence Nightingale made nursing a real profession with a set of prerequisite qualifications and ethical standards, hospitals employed and received only the very poor, who usually went there to die. Since the abolition of religious orders during the Reformation in England, nursing had become an occupation for drunken and fallen women, because no one else would take up such dangerous, distasteful, and filthy work. (By contrast, in Catholic France the Sisters of Charity, a nursing order, served the hospitalized.) Conditions in the makeshift hospitals at the front, filled to overflowing with wounded and disease-ridden soldiers, were, if anything, even more appalling than in civilian institutions. Florence Nightingale led a corps of nurses that she herself had trained to the front in 1854. After returning to England, she spent a half-century, much of it as a semi-invalid, writing and researching in order to improve hospital and health conditions in England, in the army, and in the empire. She tried to influence government policy through Sidney Herbert, a Cabinet member, who faithfully acted as her intermediary until his death.

Before the Crimean War her position in society had been that of an unmarried daughter of an upper-class British family. In the tradition of a gentlewoman she had cared for the poor near her family's estate. She grew to hate this "Lady Bountiful" role, however, because of her increasing awareness that she did not know how to help the poor and sick. At the age of twenty-five, she announced her plan to become a nurse. This so horrified her mother and elder sister, Parthe, that they cried, cajoled, and obstructed Florence from training for and practicing her vocation for nine years. They liked their life, their family, and social obligations, and could not understand why Florence did not. They accepted the duties of caring for the poor sick of the neighborhood and could not understand why Florence should be so impatient with their well-meaning efforts. This "lack of charity" in one whom everyone admired as good and pious exasperated the thoroughly conventional Parthe, who wrote a perceptive, if rather petulant, letter to a friend in 1853 about her sister.

> These eternal poor have been left to the mercies of Mamma and me, both very unwell and whose talkey talkey broth and pudding she holds in very great contempt. . . . I believe she has little or none of what is called charity or philanthropy, she is ambitious — very and would like well enough to regenerate the world with a great *coup de main* or some fine institution, which is a very different thing.[5]

For her part, the Lady Bountifuls like her mother and sister thoroughly exasperated Florence. Unlike Parthe, she did not look forward to marriage, to filling up, as she put it, the subordinate part of a husband's vocation. She wanted her own serious work. But in her position this seemed impossible. Florence Nightingale discovered the supreme irony of being a leisured woman: she had no time to develop herself.

This is the theme of an essay she wrote in 1852. "Cassandra" is Nightingale's long cry of desperation against her leisured upper-class life. Its bitterness against some of the sacrosanct ideas of Victorian society is enormous. She particularly disdained the dictum, propounded by Mrs. Ellis, that women must be there simply to make the lives of others more pleasant. She wrote:

> Women are never supposed to have any occupation of sufficient importance not to be interrupted . . . and women themselves accepted this, have written books to support it and have trained themselves so as to consider whatever they do as *not* of such value to the world or to others, but that they can throw it up at the first "claim of social life." They have accustomed themselves to consider intellectual occupation as merely selfish amusement, which it is their "duty" to give up for every trifler more selfish than they.[6]

The author of this mental and physical enslavement, she continued, is the family, which

> uses people, *not* for what they are, nor for what they are intended to be, but for what it wants them for — its own uses. It thinks of them not as what God has made them, but as something which it has arranged that they shall be. If it wants someone to sit in the drawing room, *that* someone is supplied by the family, though that member may be destined for science, or for education or for active superintendence by God, i.e., by the gifts within.

That member of the family so conveniently seated in the drawing room is, of course, always female. One of the reasons women love novels so much, Nightingale continued, is because "the heroine has *generally* no family ties (almost *invariably* no mother), or, if she has, these do not interfere with her entire independence."

For her the home was a prison where passionate women (who did exist, she insisted) hide a sickening burden of unused energy under calm exteriors and where they dream dreams that cannot be fulfilled. The life of visits, of mending worsted stockings, of going out for drives in the afternoon, of reading aloud, of "keeping up" in order to make conversation, of ignorant "poor peopling" is shadowed by fantasies of romance and high-minded ambition, fantasies that are dangerous because they are addictive. Nightingale knew this only too well, for she had been a daydreamer since the age of sixteen, and in her twenties she feared for her sanity because she began to lose her sense of reality. In "Cassandra" she tells of her struggle against escapism and assumes that she shared this particular battle with other passionate women.

> We fast mentally, scourge ourselves morally, use the intellectual hairshirt, in order to subdue that perpetual day-dreaming, which is so dangerous. We resolve "this day I will be free of it"; twice a day with prayer and written record of the times when we have indulged in it, we endeavor to combat it.[7]

The only solution for her was to find an interest, a mission. Being very religious she turned to God. He spoke to her, He whose law is above that of mere convention, and told her to work for mankind.

Not all the other remarkable women of philanthropy had the sense of direct communication with God that inspired Nightingale, but they all had a sense of mission strong enough for them to break with the conventional view of their sex. Most of them, like Nightingale, remained unmarried; and many came from the middle class rather than the upper class. Mary Carpenter, Louisa Twining, and Octavia Hill are three of the most famous of these passionate middle-class women, who found, respectively, new ways of dealing with the problems of juvenile delinquency, the poorhouse, and urban housing. In the process, like Nightingale, they opened up new professions for women.

Mary Carpenter began teaching at a ragged school (a privately financed institution for slum or "ragged" children) in Bristol in 1846 at the age of thirty-nine. She developed a deep love for and commitment to the toughest of her rambunctious charges. In 1851 she wrote *Reformatory Schools for the Children of the Perishing and Dangerous Classes and for Juvenile Offenders,* in which she asserted that juvenile delinquents should be treated differently from adult criminals and called for the extension of the ragged school system and the establishment of vocational schools and reformatories. Before the publication of this book the penal system of England allowed for no special means of treating the young. For the rest of her life Carpenter worked with government committees and national organizations to implement her proposals and headed several institutions herself. Frances Power Cobbe, in fact, began her career in philanthropy at Carpenter's Red Lodge Girls' Reformatory. Cobbe admired the enthusiastic and charismatic Carpenter but soon left the institution. She did not agree with Mary's assurances that "anything whatever which could pass from my thoughts" to the young girls "would be a benefit." Cobbe, like Nightingale, already sensed that in order to truly help the poor and disadvantaged one needed certain training, knowledge, and skills.

Unlike Cobbe, Nightingale, or Carpenter, Louisa Twining had not set out to be a full-fledged philanthropist, and yet she became the leader of women's efforts to reform the poorhouse, that dreaded domicile for England's indigent. She had hoped only to "do good" in the most genteel manner, by reading aloud to an elderly friend. In 1852 the friend entered the poorhouse and when Twining visited her there, she was so shocked by the conditions she encountered that she felt compelled to stay and do more. The old, the sick, the criminal, the demented, and children shared a thoroughly filthy and unhealthy environment that fostered lethargy rather than physical and moral rehabilitation. Within the year she had convinced the local poorhouse board to admit women visitors as inspectors and advisers, arguing successfully that women, as managers of the home, had the skills to reform such institutions. Her struggle led to a national organization of poorhouse visitors, generally improved conditions, and separate provisions for the care of the sick and aged. In 1875, by an act of Parliament, women began receiving official positions as poorhouse guardians, partly as a result of Twining's work.

Octavia Hill came to philanthropy almost by birth: her grandfather, Dr. Southwood Smith, had been a pioneer in the public health movement; and she began teaching in ragged schools at the age of fourteen. During the course of her work in the London slums, she visited the homes of some of her pupils. Because their living conditions were so wretched and because she strongly believed in the importance of environmental influences, she became urgently involved with the problems of housing for the indigent poor. Others had built "model housing" for the model poor — those who had regular jobs and the proper self-help attitudes. She wanted to help those whom others considered hopeless. When her friend John Ruskin came into an inheritance and asked her how he could best help the poor, she proposed renovating buildings for the unemployed, the drunk, and the rowdy. She started with three large old houses at Paradise Place in the Marylebone district of London and continued her work in such privately funded housing into the 1890s. By that time people looked upon her as the expert on working-class housing. Crucial to the "Hill system" was her corps of rent collectors. This group of young ladies visited the tenants weekly, developing relationships with them in order to find out how best to help them attain independence and self-respect. Hill closely controlled the activities of these volunteers. Those who succeeded according to her standards — always too few — were virtually social caseworkers as we know them today.

We could add many Englishwomen to the roll call of pioneering philanthropists; and certainly no global list would be complete without the American Jane Addams. Yet there are no Frenchwomen who really stand out as leaders and innovators. Why? The most important determinant was the existence of a revitalized Catholic Church. The church had always taken a leading role in philanthropy and continued this involvement with renewed vigor in the nineteenth century. Being a national, tightly structured, hierarchical institution, it provided a tradition for female charity work that tended to stymie initiative. By contrast, in Protestant England and America, women usually carried out their work on a local and private basis. Lay workers in France often called themselves the *dames de charité,* recalling the seventeenth-century work of St. Vincent de Paul. His organization for sending upper-class women to visit and care for the poor had been innovative in the 1600s but allowed for little change or movement toward professionalization in the nineteenth century.

Further, for those who wanted to devote their entire lives to helping others, the church still provided a religious vocation. In France, as many as 150,000 women entered the convent in the last fifty years of the century. Nuns, like the dames de charité, most often did good according to *old* plans, while Nightingale, Cobbe, Carpenter, Twining, and Hill became philanthropists and pioneers of *new* policies. In fact, the church often had a sort of monopoly over certain aspects of charity and intentionally blocked some innovations and professionalization. It took quite a struggle, for example, to introduce secularly trained nurses into French state hospitals. Where Catholicism did not dominate philanthropy, municipalities often did, for the government traditionally intervened in charity work in France. Needless to say, men commanded the power structures of both church and state institutions.

One final cultural difference may explain women's lesser role in France — the continuing salon tradition. The salon provided upper-class Frenchwomen with a prestigious role that did not exist in England. The attraction it held for two young English tourists illustrates this point. On her first visit to Paris, Florence Nightingale became a lifelong friend of Mary Clarke, an English expatriate who hosted a salon. Nightingale particularly appreciated the freedom of intellectual exchange between adults of both sexes that took place in Clarke's drawing room. She probably did not desire this role for herself, however, because of her sense of religious mission. The other tourist, feminist Emmeline Pankhurst, definitely would have preferred to settle in France and pursue the life of sociability. Her career, because of her family's wishes to keep her at home, followed a more English pattern: marriage, children, and reforming matronhood.

Even so, France produced more secular charitable women in the latter half of the century than ever before. Just as in England, the newly leisured middle-class woman began to partake in what had once been an upper-class privilege. Previously, the very wealthy had given money through endowments or, more haphazardly, through simple alms giving. This meant that the highborn threw coins at their pleasure to supplicants at the church door and on the street or carried gifts and provisions to their favorite poor in the neighborhood. The nursing of Parthe Nightingale and her mother represents the survival of this earlier tradition. But this would no longer do. It took a more concerted and unified effort to deal with the new urban poverty of the industrialized age. In the absence of any real movement toward social or economic equality on the part of the upper and middle classes, they still saw charity work — but now, charity work *properly done* — as the solution to the "social problem." Women offered a wealth of unused energy for this endeavor, and the charity organization offered a way in which effectively to channel this female capability. Such organizations usually started in a single location. If successful, other philanthropists often imitated and linked them into regional and national groupings. Because charity organizations involved group rather than individual efforts, it did not take a great commitment of time or money to be a charity worker. This made it possible for more and more middle-class women to join their wealthier and more leisured upper-class counterparts in philanthropy.

What did the charity organizations and the women who worked in them do? Almost everything. The "friendly visitor" was the most ubiquitous member. She went to the poor, gave advice and consolation, asked questions, wrote reports, made recommendations, and carried out the decisions of her organization. The rent collectors of the Hill system became the best trained "friendly visitors" in England. Women also typically took up fund raising: planning and selling tickets for balls and theatrical events, donating time and needlework to charity bazaars, and soliciting money on the street and in churches.

In France, one of the oldest and most artistocratic organizations was the Society for Maternal Charity. It aided poor, pregnant women by giving food, equipment, and medical care to those who could prove themselves to be legally married and sufficiently poverty-stricken. The follow-up work of this group included special allowances for women who chose to breast-feed their own children, a way of bringing Rousseau's recommendations to the poor. Middle-class women of the St. Regis Society located common-law marriages in the slums and arranged state and church ceremonies to legalize and sanctify them. Older women and their teenaged daughters founded schools for poor girls and clubs for young working women. Respected matrons taught practical sewing and moral lessons to prostitutes "taking the cure" at state hospitals. The most innovative and enduring aspect of female charity work in France was the foundation of the *crèche,* a nursery for the infants and preschool children of working mothers. By the end of the nineteenth century thousands of crèches existed throughout the country. Typically, Catholic nuns staffed at least half of them. But the charity organization only came into "full, indeed rankly luxuriant bloom" in England, where by 1898 an estimated 500,000 female volunteers engaged in countless beneficent activities: rescue organizations for fallen women, ragged schools, district nurse associations, mothers' clubs in the slums, fresh air camps for the poor city children, and homes for various needy people — orphans, the blind, the deaf and dumb, the aged, unemployed governesses and, even, a Home of Rest for Horses, founded in 1886 by Miss Anna

Lindo for "old favourites, the property of poor persons," where 600 animals had "received the comforts of Home" by 1898.[8]

Despite the fact that women kept philanthropy going, their participation was often harshly criticized. Charles Dickens and Mrs. Ellis preached that charity began at home and should stay there. Both Balzac and Flaubert depicted female hypocrites who displayed their goodness by visiting the poor. These four authors charged that some middle-class women did philanthropic work because it tended to put them in the right circles and presented an excuse to leave home and demonstrate their genteel sensibilities to a large audience. Indeed, as Miss Lindo's home illustrates, the line between charity, silliness, and self-gratification could be very thin. Fund raising often became a fashionable activity that easily lent itself to being done "prettily." A more serious charge than self-gratification or frivolity — and one more often voiced in high places — was that women, because they had so much natural sensibility and so little talent for abstraction, actually did more harm than good! Critics as diverse as John Stuart Mill, Octavia Hill, and Florence Nightingale contended that women only perceived the individual case and missed the general principle; that they were unscientific, unprofessional, undisciplined, and, worst of all, pauperizers. Pauperization — the encouragement of sloth among the poor by indiscriminate giving — was the great bugaboo of the educated, "scientific" philanthropists. The new philanthropists believed that being poor denoted a certain lack of morality and that being overkind involved a certain lack of judgment.

The critics judged charitable women too harshly and probably wrongly. Much charity work took real courage and devotion and cannot be categorized as either fashionable or frivolous. The many young women who taught at the early ragged schools, for example, certainly needed daring and fortitude to face down unruly and taunting students. More important, there is no evidence that female volunteers feared encouraging pauperization less than their male counterparts. Indeed, from their writings we can see that they accepted the dominant view that one could best help the poor by instilling in them the proper attitudes about work, drink, and family life. Accordingly, the friendly visitors often carried the lessons of domesticity to poor women, that is, advice on how to be a good wife and mother. Members of the French Maternal Charity and St. Regis societies tried to promote good family life. In England, the Bible societies and Mother's Missions performed the same function, perhaps more subtly. These organizations sought to reach all the poor through the mother, by instructing her in the habits of frugality and cleanliness. A model mission illustrates how the volunteers did this. In 1858 the *English Woman's Journal* described an evening meeting of the Mother's Mission at Pear Street and Duck Lane Ragged School in London. The sessions began with ten minutes of hymns, Bible reading, and prayers; then the lady charity workers distributed sewing to the poor mothers, who worked while the ladies read pious literature aloud; attendance was taken and the meeting ended with more songs and prayers. Each week the slum dwellers brought in a few pennies to pay for the cloth. The poor had permission to take the garments home only after they were completely finished. The ladies proudly reported that the women who had been attending the meetings for some time appeared in clean clothes and not in rags as before.

In both England and France upper- and middle-class women fostered the principle of self-help by making it possible for lower-class girls to become good servants and dressmakers. In 1875 a London group founded the most famous of these organizations, the Metropolitan Association for Befriending Young Servants, to follow up Twining's reform work. Fashionable women provided residences, training, job recommendations, and mothering to girls who had lived in the poorhouse most of their lives. The ladies visited employers to see how the girls were getting on, arranged for further instruction if necessary, and entertained the girls on holidays. In 1898, 1,100 volunteers worked in 32 district branches of the MABYS, which reported a 90 percent success rate among its 13,000 or so young clients. None of these ladies, of course, questioned the justice of assuring the other women of their own class the services of docile and well-trained domestics and seamstresses.

But we can see, as their critics did not, that the female charity worker served her society — at least the most conservative elements in it — very well by teaching the poor how best to survive *within* their lower-class standing. Women probably succeeded in reaching more people than the men of their class because the poor did not identify them so conclusively with political power or economic exploitation. The volunteers thought of themselves not so much as purveyors of the dominant value system but as peacemakers. Fully aware of the class hatreds and the conditions that bred mutual distrust, they put themselves in the middle, mediating — often through mothers, girls, and children — between the men of the lower and their own class. Indeed, the role of the angel on the outside was very much like her role in the home: to conciliate, to make people happy, to exemplify the moral standards of her society. The seventh stanza of Mrs. Alexander's poem "The Work of Woman's Hand" expresses succinctly both woman's fear of pauperizing and her belief in individual kindness as a means of conciliation between hostile forces:

> Not alms profuse at random thrown
> Not class 'gainst class her lip would teach
> But brave self-help, sweet mercy shown
> And free dependence each on each.

Another lady charity worker tells us how one can reach the poor through their children. Wrote a Mrs. Molesworth about the opening of the fresh air camps in the 1890s:

> I believe that one of the most distinctly happy effects of the kind of benevolent effort which we are considering is that it bring home so plainly to the children the fact that among their superiors in the social scale, above all among "ladies," there are those that *do care for them.* The drawing closer together of the classes, and inspiring the poor with confidence in the sympathy of the rich are among the greatest goods that can be done for both. And towards children it comes so easily to be friendly and affectionate. . . . A rather grimy little mouth held up to "kiss the lady" may not be precisely tempting, but it is irresistible; Tommy's "my eye, ain't it jolly" if not exactly a graceful and elegant acknowledgement of his slice of Xmas pudding comes from the heart and goes to yours. And when two hearts meet is not half — or all — the battle won? [9]

But the battleground was shifting — both for the poor and for women. The welfare state and the professionalization of services transformed the duty of voluntary charity into paid social work, although this transformation did not always alter the patronizing and accusatory attitudes of the rich toward the poor. Many middle-class women entered the so-called helping professions of teaching, social work, and nursing. As the institutions of education and social services grew and became more powerful, however, men usually obtained the executive positions in them. Thus, women became subordinate in the work they in large part had initiated. Just as important for middle-class women, these preferred occupations still carried the taint — or, perhaps better, the glow — of nineteenth-century ideas. Even today there are those who claim that if a woman wants a role outside the home it must be one that supposedly comes "naturally" to her, that employs her talents for mothering and consolation. The role of the angel, with its special qualities, privileges, and very real limitations, has been very difficult to give up in the industrial society that created it.

Notes

1. *Memoirs of Madame de La Tour du Pin,* trans. Felice Harcourt, McCall, New York, 1971, p. 27.
2. David-Eugene Lévi-Alvarès, "Education secondaire et supérieure des jeunes filles. Quelques observations sur les examens et le nouveau programme de l'Hôtel-de-Ville, pour l'obtention des diplômes de maîtresses de pension et d'institution . . . d'après les inspections des Dames déléguées pendant l'année scolaire 1844–1845," Paris, 1845.

3. Jesse Pitts, "Continuity and Change in Bourgeois France," *In Search of France,* ed. Stanley Hoffman, Harper & Row, New York, 1965, p. 255.
4. Peter Stearns, "Working Class Women in Britain, 1890–1914," *Suffer and Be Still,* ed. Martha Vicinus, Indiana University Press, Bloomington, 1972.
5. Quoted in Cecil Woodham-Smith, *Florence Nightingale, 1820–1910,* Constable, London, 1950, p. 107.
6. The essay "Cassandra" can be found in Ray Strachey's *The Cause,* reprint, Kennikat Press, Port Washington, N.Y., 1969, pp. 395–418. This quote is from p. 401.
7. Ibid., p. 397.
8. This phrase is David Owen's in his *English Philanthropy, 1660–1960,* Harvard University Press, Cambridge, 1962. The estimate comes from Louisa Hubbard's article "Statistics of Women's Work," *Woman's Mission: A Series of Congress Papers on the Philanthropic Work of Women by Eminent Writers,* ed. Angela Burdett-Coutts, Sampson Low, London, 1893.
9. Burdett-Coutts, *Woman's Mission,* pp. 2, 17.

Suggestions for Further Reading

Unfortunately, there are no good secondary works in English on upper- and middle-class women, charity work, or the salon in nineteenth-century France. The interested reader will learn a great deal about the leisured woman by reading the novels of Balzac, Stendhal, and Flaubert.

Victorian women, on the other hand, have been the subject of many good studies. Some of the most important and more recent are:

Banks, J. A. *Prosperity and Parenthood: A Study of Family Planning among the Victorian Middle Classes.* Humanities Press, London, 1954.

Banks, J. A., and Olive Banks. *Feminism and Family Planning in Victorian England.* Schocken Books, New York, 1972.

Davidoff, Leonore. *The Best Circles: Women and Society in Victorian England.* Rowman and Littlefield, Totowa, N.J., 1973.

Vicinus, Martha, ed. *Suffer and Be Still: Women in the Victorian Age.* Indiana University Press, Bloomington, 1972.

Welter, Barbara. "The Cult of True Womanhood: 1820–1860." *American Quarterly,* XVIII: 2, part 1 (1966), 151–174.

Women's domestic and charitable work has also received considerable attention. Two important primary sources are:

Beeton, Isabella. *Beeton's Book of Household Management.* Farrar, Straus, & Giroux, New York, 1975.

Burdett-Coutts, Angela, ed. *Woman's Mission: A Series of Congress Papers on the Philanthropic Work of Women by Eminent Writers.* Samson Low, London, 1893.

The following are very useful secondary sources on women's charity work:

Heasman, Kathleen. *Evangelicals in Action: An Appraisal of Their Social Work in the Victorian Era.* Geoffrey Bles, London, 1962.

Owen, David. *English Philanthropy, 1660–1960.* Harvard University Press, Cambridge, 1962.

Young, A. F., and E. T. Ashton. *British Social Work in the 19th Century.* Humanities Press, London, 1956.

14

The International Sisterhood

Edith F. Hurwitz

Although, as Barbara Pope's essay showed, large numbers of women worked for charitable and philanthropic causes, many became frustrated with that alternative. By working for the welfare of the poor and outcast and socializing them to their own values, middle-class women became increasingly aware of their own legal and social subordination. During the last third of the nineteenth century, hundreds and even thousands of women from all European nations turned their backs on the male-dominated politics of their respective homelands and formed an international sisterhood. They by-passed national and regional strictures against their cause and convened international conferences, edited hundreds of newsletters, corresponded with one another, and passed resolutions they believed would enhance their power. Naturally, the sisterhood was frequently rent by disagreements. Which was to be more important in nations without universal suffrage, middle-class women's suffrage or universal adult suffrage? What would improve the lot of women most — educational reform, legal change, a more enlightened birth-control policy, a crackdown on prostitution? Or was it more essential first to change basic social attitudes toward women, the family, and sexuality? Ought women to aspire to be the same as men or to carve out their own feminine areas of influence? As we look back with the benefit of hindsight, we must ask if the international sisterhood did exert a direct impact on national politics. What, ultimately, was the result of this first wave of feminism?

Carrie Chapman Catt (1859–1947). As founder and first president (1904–1923) of the International Woman Suffrage Alliance, she brought together European and American women who shared a political cause. (The Bettmann Archive)

As women organized for reform in the arena of national politics, they concluded that some of the problems they sought to overcome had to be attacked on an international level. Slavery, for example, depended upon international trade, as well as exploitation within national boundaries. So, if early women reformers had ventured into the devil's workshop, in later generations they moved ambitiously into a larger arena of evil. Since they had encountered great obstacles at the national level, they reached out to one another and formed an international sisterhood to overcome the opposition they met in their homelands.

The internationalization of the women's movement reveals the mutual dependence and trust that bourgeois women felt toward each other. A common empathy and purpose swept over oceans and erased cultural and political conditions that might otherwise have created obstacles toward unity. This could be accomplished because of the purposeful way in which American women worked to form international organizations. European women readily followed their leadership, admiring their drive and determination. America was a democracy and new ideas were more easily transmitted. Consequently they believed American women possessed the most innovative perspective.

When Madame Hubertine Auclert of France agreed to become a member of the proposed international organization, she wrote Susan B. Anthony in 1884 explaining how far France had strayed from the ideal of liberty and freedom. As France had once supported the American Revolution, now American women must support the emancipation effort of French women.

> We call upon you to come to our aid, as your countrymen, a century ago besought France to help them escape the subjection of England. Will you not come to our help as Lafayette and his legion flew to yours? [1]

The international sisterhood went through several stages. The first tentative contacts in the 1880s derived from the disappointing failure of American and English women to be accepted equally in the abolitionist struggle. Despite their fervent opposition to slavery, women's voices did not count as much as their male colleagues' voices. Resentful and frustrated, many abolitionist women turned their attention to their own second-class status. While they all agreed that women ought to be equal, major disagreements broke out over how that goal could be achieved.

The first organization that emerged, the International Council of Women, included two major points of view, social feminism and political feminism. The former concerned itself with general issues pertaining to women's disabilities and legal reform, such as temperance, higher education for women, career opportunities, and charitable work. The latter focused on attainment of the vote as being the key to progress in all other areas. Political feminists established their own separate organization, the International Woman Suffrage Alliance, soon after the turn of the century. With the achievement of suffrage in many countries after World War I, they expanded their interests. Both major international groups worked to influence the League of Nations, not only on matters pertaining to women's rights but on the vital issue of peace.

But lobbying in a larger arena of power did not itself bring women more rights. The international women's organizations worked tirelessly until communications were cut — this time by World War II. The limits of world sisterhood and of the class ideology of liberalism on which it was based became obvious. However, the ideas proclaimed by the international sisterhood left a lasting impression beyond the organization's actual achievements.

The Formation of the International Council of Women

During the middle of the nineteenth century, European and American women failed in their agitation to gain national suffrage, although some progress was made in related areas. In Britain, for example, unmarried propertied women received the municipal franchise and all women gained the right to stand for election to school boards and poor law boards of guardians. In 1882 a Married Women's Property Act gave married women the right to own property independent of their husbands.

On the question of national suffrage, little progress had been made in Europe, either. Municipal suffrage had been given to unmarried propertied women in Sweden in 1862 and to all propertied women in Finland in 1872. Women could also vote for local school boards in both countries. By contrast, Danish women had no franchise and women in Norway had the school board vote only. American women met similar failures and fewer successes. Two states, Wyoming and Utah, granted women suffrage; other states had school board suffrage, and three-quarters of the states had passed married women's property acts. Suffrage societies existed in all the Scandinavian countries as they did in the Anglo-American nations and Canada, Australia, and New Zealand in the British Empire. Neither Germany, Italy, Russia, Holland, nor Austro-Hungary had broadly based women's federations until the 1890s.

Elizabeth Cady Stanton and Susan B. Anthony, founders of the woman's rights movement in America in 1848, visited Great Britain in 1883. They proposed to their old friends from antislavery times and many younger ones that an international suffrage association be formed. All thought it a good idea. Though progress had been made in many areas, this issue remained totally unresolved. Universal male suffrage, even for the illiterate, passed in England in the election reform bills of 1868 and 1884, while in America suffrage, without a literacy requirement, had been extended to all men, including working-class immigrants and emancipated slaves. Yet in both nations, middle-class educated women had been rebuffed by middle-class men in their demands for equality. A common adversary and a common feeling of disappointment linked the British and American women together.

After Stanton and Anthony visited Britain, they and their younger colleagues on the Executive Committee of the National American Women Suffrage Association (NAWSA) set out to organize the first meeting of the new international group. One of the younger women, a college graduate, teacher, and chairwoman of the Executive Committee of the NAWSA, May Wright Sewall, convinced Anthony and Stanton that it would be better not to form an international group devoted solely to the suffrage at that time. As a member of the Association of Collegiate Alumnae she came into contact with other women activists. Wishing to attract them to the group, she believed that the unity of all women's organizations remained the first priority. From this would follow the attainment of all reform goals, suffrage included. "Organizations of women" Sewall believed, "tell the story of the apprenticeship of women in getting knowledge of the use of their own powers and resources."

Women reformers in those years fell into two categories, those with purely political goals and those with purely social goals. Exclusion from the vote symbolized to the political reformer the second-class citizenship of women. The social reformers promoted temperance, higher education for women, charitable work, women's self-development, and more career opportunities in professions such as law and medicine. They judged the political goal alone to be too narrow.

Sewall believed that an international organization could surmount these domestic differences and on that basis developed the organizing principle behind the new group. Her idea was to bring all women's groups together nationally as a prelude to forming an international organization. The new organization would unite established church groups, temperance groups, child welfare groups, and professional organizations to create a national council of women. The national council would then elect delegates to an international council. Delegates from the national councils would sit on an international executive board, which would make major policy decisions. The entire affiliated international membership would meet for a large conference every five years. Unity on the national level was to be achieved by the selection of council delegates and on the international level through the policy making of the elected representatives. Sewall's ideas became reality at the founding convention of 1888. At this conference, held in Washington, D.C., sixty American and eight European delegates discussed the goals of the new organization, the International Council of Women (ICW), with "unanimity, good will, and enthusiasm."

Consensus was accorded top priority. To maintain unity, the council avoided taking a public stance on any issue that divided the membership. Instead, it provided a neutral arena where deeply felt beliefs could be debated. These women believed that the universe must be a moral one, and in those times both men and women shared the view that women more than men could apply moral principles in their daily life. Women's very exclusion from public life enabled them to be more righteous. Hence, when women entered public life through their organizations, they brought this ideal with them.

This same purity of purpose informed the ICW's drive for a new morality in politics. Julia Ward Howe, author of "The Battle Hymn of the Republic" and veteran of antislavery and suffrage activity, told the 1888 convention:

> The business world is full of organized robbery. The political world is full of organized injustice. The religious world is organized to uphold inspiration and intolerance. The military world is the stronghold of wholesale murder and spoilation. Who will organize a brave and patriotic resistance to all these evils? Can we women with white hair go peacefully to our graves leaving the young generation bound hand and foot in the slavery of evil institutions? I hope that from this council a new influence will go out. . . .[2]

In her closing remarks to the convention, Stanton proclaimed that women would create an internationalism that would override all other ideologies of the day.

> In every country we see the wisest statesmen at their wits end vainly trying to meet the puzzling questions of the hour; in Russia, it is Nihilism; in Germany, Socialism; in France, Communism; in England, Home Rule for Ireland and the Disestablishment of the Church; and in America, land, labor, taxes, tariffs, temperance, and woman suffrage. Where shall we look for the new power by which the race can be lifted up and the human mind made capable of coping with the daily-increasing complications of a new civilization? [3]

Stanton believed that women could find the solutions for those problems. She and her followers hoped that the supportive role women played in the home could now benefit society as a whole. Mme. St. Croix, a French delegate, saw women coming together in their organizations as a way of utilizing the "motherheart of the world" to achieve moral betterment. Custom, tradition, and habit had kept women from participating in national and local government, higher education, and equality of opportunity in the professions and for work and wages. However, these cultural conditions could be altered if male society could be convinced that reforms would bring beneficial results to the entire social order. The founders of the ICW cultivated the hope that the prejudices against them would dissolve once their altruism became better understood. Who could deny them equality, they confidently maintained, if all benefited from this change? Indeed, the interests of these women, as reflected in the papers they gave at the founding meeting, showed their deep concern for a calling higher than just their own advancement. They discussed their activities and work in philanthropy, temperance, industry, the professions; legal and political struggles, social purity, prison reform, hospital work, missionary work, industrial work; and the advancement in the education of women at primary, secondary, and university levels.

The founding meeting concluded with a plan for action designed to end the oppression of women. Women demanded access to higher education and professional training, equal wages for equal work, and an identical standard of "personal purity and morality for men and women." The last goal opposed the acceptance of prostitution as a necessary evil. Charged with these goals, the delegates returned home to organize their national councils.

Sewall, as president, tirelessly toured the continent and carried on an extensive correspondence to reach even more European women. Her work came to fruition at the 1899 meeting of the ICW, held in London. National councils had been formed in the United States, Canada, Germany, Sweden, Great Britain, Ireland, New South Wales, Denmark, Holland, New Zealand, and Tasmania. Other delegates came from Italy, Austria, Russia, Switzerland, Norway, Cape Colony, and Victoria, as their councils had nearly completed their organizing work. Observers came from France, Belgium, China, Persia, India, Argentina, Iceland, and Palestine. The costs of the conference were met by donors, with American women contributing the most money, the British the second most, and the Germans the third. Five thousand women attended the sessions. The eleven affiliated councils had memberships of 6,000,000. This, to the organizers of the ICW, represented their collective will internationally.

For most of that London convention unanimity of purpose prevailed. But the suffrage question provoked a decided difference of opinion. A lengthy session on the political enfranchisement of women was scheduled.

Participants included Millicent Garrett Fawcett, British suffragist leader, Marie Stritt, President of the German National Council of Women, and Susan B. Anthony. Antisuffragist women, supported by the council executive board, demanded the right to speak. When the organizers of the session refused, the council refused to sponsor the session. Only under the independent sponsorship of the Union of Women's Suffrage Societies of Great Britain did it take place. The council adhered strictly to its original goal of neutrality and refused to compromise on the ideal of the organization to represent all women.

American women dominated the leadership of the ICW until 1904. Then Lady Ishbel Aberdeen of Great Britain became the organization's president and served until 1936. Born in Scotland in 1857, she got her education through tutors and the salons of her family's social circle like most of the noble European women of her generation. The particular political tradition that she came from is characteristic of many British feminists. For example, Millicent Garrett Fawcett, President of the Union of Women's Suffrage Societies of Great Britain, came from a family identified with the Liberal party and married a Liberal member of Parliament. So did the militant suffragette Emmeline Pankhurst, whose husband Henry also played a role in the Liberal party. Other council participants from Britain included Mrs. Ashton Dilke and Mrs. Charles McLaren, who had husbands with careers in the Liberal party. Lady Aberdeen's husband, John Gordon Campbell, the seventh Earl of Aberdeen, whom she married in 1877, served the Liberal party in the diplomatic service. Exposed to foreign travel and accustomed to mixing with a variety of peoples, Lady Aberdeen, after meeting with American women at the Chicago World's Fair/Columbian Exposition in 1893, became their choice for the presidency.

Like her counterparts in the council, Lady Aberdeen had many years of experience in organizing women for social purposes. With the support of her husband she had founded Onward and Upward, an association for the recreational and educational development of young girls. In Canada she had organized the Victorian Order of Nurses, a nationwide health service. When her husband served in Ireland as governor general, she organized the Women's National Health Association, which crusaded against infant mortality and tuberculosis and pioneered in preventive hygiene and public health education. Lady Aberdeen had also served as a member of the executive board of the association of women connected with the Liberal party. She became the second president of the National Women's Liberal Federation, succeeding Catherine Gladstone, wife of William Gladstone, the Liberal party's prime minister. She resigned the presidency in 1894 when her husband took up his diplomatic appointment in Canada. After resuming the presidency of the ICW, she served in that office until 1936. Because Lady Aberdeen had participated in both political and social feminist organizations, she was capable of bringing together all the diverse groups that were affiliates of the council.

Baroness Alexandra Van Grippenberg of Finland was another early leader. An exact contemporary of Lady Aberdeen, her life began in Jurjijoki, Finland, in 1857. Her background also included political activism, for her father worked for Finnish nationalism and as a member of the Diet. Yet, unlike Lady Aberdeen, who dedicated herself solely to public service, Baroness Van Grippenberg had a literary career. She authored several novels, edited a children's magazine, and pursued journalism. After the founding of the ICW Baroness Van Grippenberg became the founding president of the Finnish Women's Association and treasurer of the ICW from 1893 to 1899; after that she became its honorary vice president. After 1888 she focused all her reform efforts on political goals. When Finnish women received the vote in 1905 she served in the Diet from 1907 to 1908. Shortly before her death in 1913, Baroness Van Grippenberg was nominated to the presidency of the ICW.

Under the leadership of Lady Aberdeen, Baroness Van Grippenberg, and others like them, the council remained dedicated to the exchange of information to further the understanding of women and reform. It supported suffrage along with a variety of other causes. Service to society as justification for changes in women's status broadened to include programs for not only the general welfare of women and children but for natural conservation and international peace. The ICW kept track of women's progress in the areas of legal and educational reform through more than a dozen standing committees whose members met independently and in conjunction with international meetings at five-year intervals. Executive meetings determined council policy during the four years that separated the large international meetings. All this activity required an elaborate organizational structure, but these upper-class women had the time and money to fulfill their responsibilities as committeewomen, council executives, and conference participants.

The International Woman Suffrage Alliance

The development of a second organization, the International Woman Suffrage Alliance (later to become the International Alliance of Women, or IAW) in 1902, proves how controversial an issue suffrage remained even for women themselves. Even though the ICW supported that goal among many others, politically oriented women believed that they needed their own forum to exchange ideas and plan strategy. Government participation had for so long been narrowly defined as a masculine activity that many women tended to accept rather than challenge the concept. The state perpetrated war, destruction, and corruption. Many women felt perfectly content to limit their emancipation to all areas of modern life except the government because they feared a corruption of their morals. Thus, in both America and Great Britain, antisuffrage associations had been formed.

Despite the heavy opposition from both males and females, the national suffrage debate had been before the public for close to half a century. By 1912 some victories had been won in Wyoming, California, Oregon, Colorado, Utah, Idaho, and the Alaska Territory as well as in Australia and the Isle of Man. Married women as well as single women had acquired municipal suffrage in Great Britain. After 1900 an ever-increasing number of European women dedicated themselves to acquiring the vote. For them it represented the ultimate in women's reforms. In the United States, Great Britain, Australia, Norway, Sweden, and Holland women formed organizations devoted exclusively to acquiring national suffrage.

The organizer and founder of the IAW, Carrie Chapman Catt, came to the fore of the leadership of the American movement as a protégé of Susan B. Anthony. Remembering their earlier efforts to form such an organization, Anthony encouraged Catt. For Catt, national suffrage provided "the dynamite and steam derricks with which we build institutions." A brilliant organizer and administrator, she held the presidency of NAWSA from 1901 to 1904. She viewed the American struggle as part of an evolutionary development that would bring greater political freedom to women everywhere. The impact of its success or failure was not limited to American national boundaries. Therefore, Catt invited representatives from several nations to attend NAWSA's 1902 national convention to make plans for the new organization.

Both general principles and specific purposes came out of the organizational meeting of 1902. Cooperation and dependence between the sexes made "the repression of the rights and liberty of one sex" an inevitable "injury to the other and hence the whole race" — a statement that paraphrased the language of the Declaration of Independence. The women believed that so far its proclamation of the principle of liberty and justice for all had been applied only to men. Now they demanded these rights for women as well.

IAW became a separate entity at the 1904 meeting of the ICW. It did for suffrage what the ICW had done for all women's organizations: provided a forum to exchange ideas and share experiences. Its stated purpose: to act as a "central bureau for the collection, exchange and dissemination of information concerning the methods of suffrage work and the general status of women in the various countries having representation on the Committee." Like the ICW, it did not wish to interfere or take sides in national controversies; hence, it took no position for or against a specific type of national suffrage. It did not demand that every nation give *all* adult males and females the vote. Rather, it demanded that women get the vote on whatever terms men got it. If in America the vote belonged to all adult men paying a certain property tax, then women paying the same taxes should have it as well. Where the property qualification for men was even narrower, only those women who could meet it should be similarly enfranchised.

In addition to fighting for suffrage and fostering unity and comradeship among women, the alliance courageously supported internationalism in an era of staunch nationalism. To Annie Furuhjelm of Finland, the alliance meant

> the equality of nations. The Great Powers and the small nations, those who can boast of bayonets and dreadnoughts, and those who have none, are on the same footing, and send the same number of delegates. Some people will probably shrug their shoulders, saying, "A woman's dream." Yes, a woman's dream, and a vision of justice and peaceful evolution. The true spirit of internationalism which pervades the meetings of the Alliance cannot be described; it must be felt.[1]

How the IAW filled a real need of political activists to have the support of an organization of their own can be illustrated by looking at the German experience. There, bourgeois women remained particularly aloof from politics because laws prohibited them from participation in political organizations. When the German National Council of Women organized in 1894, its members refused even to discuss the suffrage issue, fearing the organization would split apart. When its second president, Marie Stritt of Dresden, came out in favor of suffrage in 1899, rifts did, in fact, appear. Stritt worked from 1899 until 1902 to get the organization to adopt suffrage as its goal. Then, Catt's invitation to organize the IAW provided the stimulus for the formation of a new group, the German Association of Woman Suffrage. Its president, Dr. Anita Augsburg of Hamburg, became a first vice president of the alliance. The creation of this rival organization demonstrated the ever increasing appeal of national suffrage. Finally, the National Council accepted Stritt's advice and endorsed national suffrage as an important objective for women's reforms. After this struggle, she reminisced about "the joy of knowing that we are united in solidarity with all women of the world, who are striving and fighting for the greatest ideal of our time." Between 1904 and 1906 not only Germany but Austria, Hungary, Denmark, France, Switzerland, and New Zealand, after sending delegates to the 1904 IAW conference in Berlin and the 1906 IAW meeting in Copenhagen, formed independent suffrage groups of their own.

IAW's dedication to such a blatant political purpose caused considerable controversy. "There was even a suspicion," the president of NAWSA, Anna Howard Shaw, related, "that its purpose was to start a rival organization." Many bourgeois women felt threatened by the collective power of political women. At the 1904 meeting of the ICW, when the IAW met for the first time as an independent group, Lady Aberdeen asked Susan B. Anthony not to attend a mass meeting of the alliance. Anthony, who had looked forward to the formation of such an organization for decades, complied with Lady Aberdeen's request and remained in her hotel room during the proceedings. Once again true to the ideal of unity, Anthony, much to her unhappiness, stayed away.

However, she received the collective tribute of the ICW the following week in a mass standing ovation. Chocolate bonbons wrapped in gold paper bearing her image rested prominently on banquet tables. Despite her strong identification with the cause of suffrage, most ICW members preferred to see her as *the* woman reformer who had devoted her life to the general advancement of women.

After Susan B. Anthony's death in 1905, Carrie Chapman Catt led the international suffrage movement until 1923. The alliance met in Copenhagen in 1906, in Amsterdam in 1908, London in 1909, Stockholm in 1911, and Budapest in 1913, using these capital cities for their congresses to publicize the suffrage question throughout Europe. Despite its comradeship, unity, and homogeneity, the alliance could not agree on a united position on suffrage tactics. In Britain during those years, for example, two independent societies for acquiring suffrage existed. One sought only peaceful methods of reform and had been led since 1867 by Millicent Garrett Fawcett. The other society, formed in 1902, the Women's Social and Political Union, used extremist tactics, including smashing windows, bombings, arson, disruption of parliamentary meetings, hunger strikes, and even suicide. Its leaders, Emmeline Pankhurst and her daughters, Cristabel and Sylvia, and their followers had been jailed, gone on hunger strikes, and had created a public clamor.

Fawcett disavowed all contacts with the Social and Political Union, claiming it ruined the cause of suffrage in Britain. As vice president of the alliance, she no doubt influenced its decision to bar the union from membership, although it had a large and ever growing following in Britain. This position on extremism remained unchanged until 1913 when Catt, impressed by the heroism and nerve of the union members, changed her mind. In a lengthy exposition paper written for the June 1913 conference she analyzed the meaning of the Pankhursts' experiences. The suffrage movement, she claimed, owed the Pankhursts a great debt for arousing, through their sufferings, a worldwide discussion of the question of women's suffrage. She called Emmeline Pankhurst the John Brown of the suffrage movement, because she and her followers were willing to suffer martyrdom for their cause.

"In a state of insurrection" against the British government for its failure to make good on its promises to grant them suffrage, the Pankhursts, Catt believed, must be thought of as "civil insurrectionaries and not military prisoners." [5] Catt managed to persuade the alliance executive board to offer a special resolution supporting the Pankhursts, although more conservative members of the IAW wanted to condemn their militant methods. Though the resolution reiterated the traditional alliance position of strict neutrality on questions of strategy and tactics, it also added that since

> riot, revolution, and disorder have never been construed into an argument against man suffrage, we protest against the practice of the opponents of woman suffrage to interpret militancy employed by the minority of one country as an excuse for withholding the vote from the women of the world.[6]

While women may have disagreed about suffrage, they unanimously condemned prostitution, which represented the subjugation of all women. In 1904 the ICW adopted a special resolution on prostitution at the international meeting in Berlin:

> That considering the fact that the White Slave Traffic is a disgrace to humanity and a slur on all women, the International Council of Women is earnestly requested to take active steps to have it abolished and to keep it on the international programme until its abolition is accomplished.[7]

At the 1913 convention, Fawcett described prostitution as "the compulsory subjection of women for the pecuniary benefit of men." When suffrage was granted, or where it had already been granted, women could use their influence to change the laws dealing with the issue.

The two major concerns of middle-class international feminism before World War I were suffrage and prostitution. Both symbolized the struggle that bourgeois women had with men of their class for control and power.

The ICW and the IAW: 1920–1939

When the ICW and the IAW met for postwar conventions in 1920, the impact of the war and its effect on women's status had to be reconsidered. The war itself, with its destruction and carnage, its disruption of family life and the home, the suffering it had brought to untold numbers of European women, had a profound impact on the thinking of the leadership of both organizations.

The first standing committee of the ICW, organized in 1899, had been Peace and International Relations. May Wright Sewall chaired its proceedings. Repeatedly, this committee called for some type of international organization to preserve peace. But during World War I, it was the

IAW that provided the leadership that organized a major peace effort — a women's international conference held at The Hague. Despite harassment from governments and the press, German, British, Austro-Hungarian, and Italian women met to condemn the suffering and victimization of women in war. In contrast to the belligerency of their nations, women met as sisters offering support, sympathy, and peace proposals. The conference sent delegates from nonbelligerent nations like the United States and the Netherlands to Great Britain, Germany, and Austro-Hungary to offer personal appeals on behalf of the world's women.

The ICW became active during the Paris Peace Conference in 1919, when Lady Aberdeen led a committee representing women's organizations. She successfully lobbied for a clause in the Covenant of the League of Nations that prohibited sex discrimination in league activities. After the war, liberals of both sexes heartily endorsed the League of Nations. The chairwoman of the ICW's Committee on Peace and Arbitration, Mrs. George Cadbury, a prominent English Quaker, addressed the ICW's first convention after the war in Christiania (Oslo) with these words: "We realize that no more important work could come before us than co-operation with those statesmen in every country who are trying to perfect the machinery of the League." [8] In 1920, Mrs. Margaret Corbett-Ashby, who in 1923 replaced Carrie Chapman Catt as president, took the job of coordinating IAW's work with the league. The 1920 meeting in Geneva recognized that the league "is now part of the international political machinery affecting the whole world . . . [established] on the principles of right and justice." [9]

In 1923 the ICW sponsored a conference on "The Prevention of the Causes of War" at the British Empire Exhibition in London. All of the international women's organizations sent delegates to the conference, and many of them had speakers on the program. Most of the feminist issues proposed by the ICW before the war came up for discussion at the conference: legal equality, education, temperance, health, and international traffic in women. Unless the world could live in peace, the conference agreed, nothing else could really be reformed. Hence, the linking of all feminist reform to the peace issue.

In 1926, Millicent Garrett Fawcett, IAW's first vice president, who had championed the cause in Great Britain since 1867, spoke of the connections between feminists, the peace movement, and the League of Nations. Well into her seventies, Fawcett, who had devoted her life to the women's movement and the suffrage fight in particular, believed the league could be used as an arm of feminism. Women's suffrage supporters, she wrote in an article published in the April 1926 issue of the *International Suffrage News,* had long ago advocated an international order built around an organization like the League of Nations. Suffrage organizations comprehended its spirit and understood its methods and aims far better than those who had little sympathy with the political emancipation of women. Women's suffrage workers, in Europe as well as in the United States, now joined the associations working to promote the league. Its close relationship to the values and ideals of the women's movement could not be denied.

It had been through their national communities that both organizations' affiliates had worked before the war. Their purpose had been to use the international forum of women to strengthen their common will at home. Now, in the postwar years, the international forum could be used to focus organizational efforts on additional goals: achievement of reforms that could be implemented through the League of Nations. As both the ICW and the IAW concentrated on open discussion, exchange of information, and saturation of public opinion, the league and its agencies provided open access to channels that had great potential for promoting their programs.

The new commitment to the league did not stop either organization from pursuing its prewar goals of help and support for women's emancipation. Each organization recruited in Latin America, among the newly formed states of central Europe (Yugoslavia, Poland, Czechoslovakia, Bulgaria, Greece), and in Asia. Their success was measured by the number of additional affiliates, the IAW going from twenty-six to forty-six, the ICW from eighteen to thirty-eight. Of the European affiliates, Great Britain led with almost 2,000,000 members; Germany followed with 1,000,000; Canada with 450,000; Norway with 180,000; Switzerland, New Zealand, Denmark, Yugoslavia, Australia, and Sweden with from 30,000 to 50,000; Czechoslovakia with 27,000; while Finland, Greece, South Africa, and Ireland had among them somewhat over 40,000 members. Each nation pledged annual contributions to the ICW on the basis of its membership.

In 1920 the IAW reconsidered its function. As a result of the war, women's suffrage had been introduced in Austria, British East Africa, Canada, the Crimea, Czechoslovakia, Denmark, Estonia, Germany, Great Britain, Hungary, Iceland, Lettonia, Lithuania, Luxembourg, the Netherlands, Poland, Rhodesia, Russia, Sweden, the Ukraine, and the United States. The congress of the IAW, meeting in Geneva, resolved by an overwhelming majority to continue to work for the suffrage in nations where it had not as yet been introduced, but the membership felt that it had to expand its original purpose. So the IAW followed the example of the ICW in establishing standing committees to formulate new programs for the benefit of women. The welfare of working-class women became their newest concern. Family endowment and allowances, equal working conditions for men and women, the support and education of illegitimate children, and the nationality of married women were discussed at the 1923 Rome meeting. To publicize its broader purpose, the IAW changed its name in 1926 to the International Alliance of Women for Suffrage and Equal Citizenship. Rather than merely supporting male politicians through segregated organizations, some IAW leaders, such as the new president,

Margaret Corbett-Ashby of Great Britain, and Eleanor Rathbone, also of Great Britain, actually competed for political office themselves. Their activity in the alliance demonstrated that even though they had held political power nationally, they still believed that women's struggle needed to be projected into the international community.

Since the common concerns of both the IAW and the ICW overlapped, the heads of both organizations thought seriously about merging into one organization. The 1923 Rome congress of the IAW approved a new draft of a constitution for the combined organizations. But the merger never came about. The close ties of both groups with the League of Nations prompted them to relocate their international headquarters to Geneva. There they became part of a multiorganizational women's committee, the Joint Committee of Representative Women's Organizations, for it seemed easier to join with other organizations in this loosely structured lobbying group.

Created in 1925, this committee included the Women's International League for Peace and Freedom, the World's Women's Christian Temperance Union, the World's Young Women's Christian Association, the International Council of Nurses, the World's Union of Women for International Concord, and the International Federation of University Women. Women of these groups came to realize that in the League of Nations, as in every other area of masculine power, their combined strength could exert a most effective political influence, and many sections of the league were investigating and creating policy and programs on issues of interest to women. Besides the programs to promote world peace and abolish prostitution, there were many others, including child welfare, world health, education of youth, and the wages and working conditions of the working class.

The ratified international convention (agreement) in 1932 on nationality failed to include the major recommendations of the Joint Committee, which had demanded that women have free choice in nationality rather than being forced to follow their husbands. International law maintained that they had no independent nationality of their own; peace treaties between the allied and associated powers concluded at the end of the war reaffirmed this principle. The Joint Committee angrily protested: "Women deeply resent the writing into an international agreement of articles founded upon the theory of subjection of women. To recognize in practice this old idea is a refusal to treat a woman as citizen of her own person. . . ." [10]

The Joint Committee also failed, after strenuous efforts, to have a higher proportion of women employees and women delegates participate in league proceedings. The secretary-general's report of August 25, 1932, discussed the "Collaboration of Women in the Organization of Peace" and noted that in September of 1931 both the assembly and the council of the league passed resolutions of warm praise for the part women and their organizations had played in promoting the work of the league. Yet, the secretary-general felt that he could make no special provisions for women since, under Article 7 of the Covenant, the principle of equality had been established. Hence, women should not be given any special privileges or favored status within the league.

As in the prewar years, women, after a respectful hearing, would be politely put off, although the merits of their proposals were duly acknowledged. Yet, because of the persistence of the Joint Committee as a pressure group, women's issues constantly confronted the League of Nations. In 1935 and 1937, the assembly acted on one recommendation of the Joint Committee, the question of the legal status of women. In 1937 a memorandum from some thirty governments also suggested that the league take up the question of the legal status of women, a sensitive and controversial issue. The legal structures of each nation became targets of investigation despite some protests that each nation's legal code remained outside the scrutiny of the international organization. Nevertheless, on September 30, 1937, the assembly approved the appointment of a Committee for the Study of the Legal Status of Women to make a comprehensive survey. Conditions of employment fell within the jurisdiction of the International Labor Organization.

By 1939 women's organizations had achieved no greater influence in the league than an advisory function. Though seemingly limited, this role nonetheless had the whole organizational tradition of women behind it. Women had been ready, from the moment they organized, tirelessly to explain their position. They sought to advise and persuade through reasonable and peaceful methods. They demanded equal rights, using arguments that stressed the common social and moral concerns uniting the sexes.

Women demanded an ever greater share in the league's work because a unified international policy represented the best means of controlling national aggression and keeping the peace. Like their founders, the new generation of ICW and IAW women continued to strive to overcome the discriminatory practices against women, to expand their opportunities both nationally and internationally. On the eve of World War II, the ICW and the IAW continued to be committed to their mission of education, explanation, and justification not only for themselves but for the whole human race.

Notes

The author wishes to acknowledge with grateful thanks the strong support given to me by the Department of History, Wesleyan University, Middletown, Connecticut, while doing the research and writing of this chapter. As visiting scholar, I not only enjoyed the intellectual give-and-take with my colleagues but had the superb services of Mrs. Dorothy Hay and Mrs. Edna Haran, secretaries of the department. Mr. William Dillon of the Interlibrary Loan Department of the Olin Library at Wesleyan deserves special mention for his cheerful efforts, which were always successful in ferreting out many of the obscure reports and books used in this essay.

1. May Wright Sewall, *Genesis of the International Council of Women and the Story of Its Growth 1888–1893* (Indianapolis, n.p. 1914), p. 5.
2. International Council of Women, *Report of the International Council of Women Assembled by National Women Suffrage Association*, Washington, D.C., R. H. Darby, printer, 1888, p. 195.
3. Ibid., p. 438.
4. *International Woman's Suffrage News*, vol. 8, no. 9, May 1, 1914, p. 99.
5. Carrie Chapman Catt, "Suffrage and Militancy" (April 17, 1913), unpublished typescript, C. C. Catt Papers, Manuscripts and Archives Division, The New York Public Library; Astor, Lenox and Tilden Foundations.
6. International Alliance of Women, *Report of Seventh Congress*, Budapest, June 1913, Percy Brothers Ltd., Hotspur Press, Manchester, 1913.
7. International Council of Women, *Report of Transactions During the Third Quinquennial Term of Executive and Council* (Boston, 1909), vol. 1, p. 173.
8. International Council of Women, *Report on the Quinquennial Meeting, Christiania, Norway, 1920*, edited by the Marchioness of Aberdeen and Temair, The Rosemont Press, Aberdeen, Scotland, 1921, p. 369.
9. International Alliance of Women, *Report of Eighth Congress*, Geneva, Switzerland, June 1920, Percy Brothers Ltd., Hotspur Press, Manchester, 1920, p. 25.
10. "Nationality of Women: Observations By The Committee of Representatives of Women's International Organizations," League of Nations Publications: Legal 1932, vol. 3, p. 2.

Suggestions for Further Reading

Aberdeen and Temair, Ishbel Maria (Marjoribanks) Gordon. *Canadian Journal of Lady Aberdeen 1893–1898*, ed. John T. Saywell. Champlain Society, Toronto, 1960.

Aberdeen and Temair, Ishbel Maria (Marjoribanks), and John Campbell Gordon, 1st Marquis. *We Two: Reminiscences of Lord and Lady Aberdeen*. 2 vols. W. Collins & Sons, London, 1925.

Anthony, Katherine. *Feminism in Germany and Scandinavia*. Henry Holt, New York, 1915.

Catt, Carrie Chapman. "Suffrage and Militancy." April 17, 1913. Unpublished typescript, Carrie Chapman Catt Collection, New York Public Library.

———. "The history of the origin of the International Alliance of Women." Unpublished typescript, Carrie Chapman Catt Collection, New York Public Library.

Deutsch, Regina. *The International Woman Suffrage Alliance: Its History from 1904–1929.* N.p., London, 1929.

Earhart, Mary. *Frances Willard: From Prayers to Politics.* University of Chicago Press, Chicago, 1944.

The Finnish Woman, ed. Anni Vorpio and Juvas and Kaarina Ruohtula. W. Soderstrom, Helsinki, 1949.

Giele, Janet Zollinger. "Social Change in the Feminine Role: A Comparison of Woman's Suffrage and Woman's Temperance, 1870–1920." Ph.D. dissertation, Radcliffe College, 1961.

Gilman, Charlotte P. "The Woman Suffrage Congress in Budapest." *The Forerunner,* IV (1913), 204–205.

Grippenberg, Alexandra Van *A Half Year in the New World: Miscellaneous Sketches of Travel in the United States,* trans. and ed. Ernest J. Moyne, University of Delaware Press, Newark, Del., 1954.

Harper, Ida Husted. "Woman Suffrage Throughout the World." *North American Review,* CLXXVIII (March 1904), 367–374.

———. *The Life and Work of Susan B. Anthony.* 3 vols. Hollenbeck Press, Indianapolis, 1898, 1908.

History of Woman Suffrage, eds. Elizabeth Cady Stanton, Susan B. Anthony, and Matilda J. Gage. Vol. 7. Fowler & Wells, New York, 1881.

History of Woman Suffrage, ed. Susan B. Anthony. Vol. 4 (1883–1900), Susan B. Anthony, Rochester, 1902.

History of Woman Suffrage, ed. Ida Husted Harper. Vols. 5, 6 (1900–1920). National American Woman Suffrage Association, New York, 1922.

International Alliance of Women. *Report of Third Congress.* Copenhagen, 1906.

———. *Report of Fourth Congress.* Amsterdam, 1908.

———. *Report of Fifth Conference and First Quinquennial.* Samuel Sidders, London, 1909.

———. *Report of Sixth Conference* (Stockholm, June 12–17, 1911). London Women's Printing Society, London, 1911.

———. *Report of Seventh Congress* (Budapest, June 1913). Percy Brothers, Hotspur Press, Manchester, 1913.

———. *Report of Eighth Congress* (Geneva, June 1920). Percy Brothers, Hotspur Press, Manchester, 1920.

———. *Report of Ninth Congress* (Rome, May 1923). B. G. Teubner, Dresden, 1923.

———. *Report of Tenth Congress.* Paris, 1926.

———. *International Woman's Suffrage News, passim.*

———. *Woman Suffrage in Practice, 1913, Second Impression with Corrections and Additions,* compiled by Chrystal MacMillan, Marie Stritt, and Maria Verone. National Union of Women's Suffrage Societies, London, and National American Woman Suffrage Association, New York, 1913.

International Council of Women. *Report of the International Council of Women Assembled by National Woman Suffrage Association.* R. H. Darby, Washington, D.C., 1888.

———. *Report of Transactions of Second Quinquennial Meeting Held in London July 1899,* ed. Countess of Aberdeen. 7 vols. T. Fisher Unwin, London, 1900.

———. *Report of Transactions During the Third Quinquennial Term of Executive and Council.* Boston, 1909, vol. 1.

———. *Annual Reports of Fifth Quinquennial Period,* compiled by Dr. Alice Solomon. Schoneberg, Langenscheiatsche buchdruckerei, Berlin, 1910–1914.

———. *Report on the Quinquennial Meeting, Christiania, Norway, 1920,* ed. Marchioness of Aberdeen and Temair. Rosemont Press, Aberdeen, 1921.

———. *Biennial Report 1925–1927,* ed. Elsie M. Zimmern. N.p., London, 1927.

———. Standing Committee on Laws Concerning the Legal Position of Women. *Women's Position in the Law of Nations.* B. G. Braunsche holfbach drukereu und verlag, Karlsruke, 1912.

———. *Prevention of the Causes of War.* Tarland, Aberdeenshire, 1924.

———. *Standing Committees of the International Council of Women,* Zurich, 1957.

———. *Women in a Changing World: The Dynamic Story of the International Council of Women.* Routledge & Kegan Paul, London, 1966.

League of Nations. Collaboration of Women in the Organization of Peace. *Report by the Secretary-General.* General Publications, no. 4 (1932), pp. 3–4.

———. Nationality of Women. *Observations by the Committee of Representatives of Women's International Organizations.* Legal Publications, vol. 3 (1932), p. 2.

———. *Report of the Work of the League 1937/1938, Part I,* General Publications, no. 4 (1938), pp. 124–128.

———. International Labor Office. *The Law and Women's Work: A Contribution to the Study of the Status of Women.* Geneva, 1939.

———. Committee for the Study of the Legal Status of Women. *Report on the Progress of the Inquiry.* Legal Publications, vol. 7 (1939).

Nathan, Maude. *Once Upon a Time and Today.* G. P. Putnam, New York, 1933.

Paulson, Ross Evans. *Women's Suffrage and Prohibition.* Scott Foresman, Glenview, Ill., 1973.

Peck, Mary Gray. *Carrie Chapman Catt.* H. Wilson, New York, 1944.

Present Position of Woman Suffrage on Behalf of the International Alliance, ed. Margarete Bernhard. N.p., Berlin and London, 1929.

Ray, P. Orman. "The World-Wide Woman Suffrage Movement." *Journal of Comparative Legislation,* n.s. I (1919), 220–231.

Rover, Constance. *Women's Suffrage and Party Politics in Britain 1866–1914*. Routledge & Kegan Paul, London, 1967.

Schirmacher, Käte. *The Modern Woman's Rights Movement,* trans. Carl C. Eckhardt. Macmillan, New York, 1912.

Sewall, May Wright. *Genesis of the International Council of Women and the Story of Its Growth, 1888–1893*. N.p., Indianapolis, 1914.

Shaw, Anna Howard. *Story of a Pioneer*. Harper, New York, 1915.

Solomon, Hannah Greenbaum. *Fabric of My Life: An Autobiography of a Social Pioneer*. Block Publishers, New York, 1946.

Stanton, Elizabeth Cady. *Eighty Years or More: Reminiscences 1815–1897*. T. Fisher Unwin, London, 1898.

Strachey, Ray C. *The Cause: A Short History of the Women's Movement in Great Britain*. Kennikat Press, Port Washington, N.Y., 1969. (Originally published in London, 1928.)

Ten Years of the League of Nations, compiled by John Eppstein. Mayfair Press, London, 1929.

The Woman Question in Europe, ed. Theodore Stanton. Sampson Low, Marston, Searle & Rivington, London, 1884.

15

Women as Revolutionaries: The Case of the Russian Populists

Barbara Engel

In Russia, as elsewhere, awareness of women's oppression arose in the context of a more general critique of the old regime and a corresponding commitment to universal human rights. As liberal Russians fought for the abolition of serfdom, several intellectuals expanded their analysis into a sweeping attack on the patriarchal system, which oppressed women as well as serfs. The first women thus inspired had to struggle just for a modicum of personal autonomy, but the next generation used the small degree of independence they had acquired to get an education. At this juncture Russian feminists faced a dilemma that figures large in any discussion of political feminism. If women pursued their personal emancipation they could best achieve it in an all-female context. As Temma Kaplan notes in a later essay, this reluctance to join sexually integrated groups sprang less from hostility to men than from shyness of them, common to sexually segregated cultures. However, by the 1870s, many Russian feminists began to realize that their oppression was only part of the pervasive oppression of Czarist rule. Like women in the French Revolution and anarchist movement, discussed elsewhere in this book, Russian radical women made their feminist concerns secondary and joined male-led revolutionary movements. Barbara Engel notes that women in terrorist, populist organizations made ideal revolutionaries because they had been socialized to sacrifice. Their very selflessness drove them out of the feminine mold into more assertive conduct.

The hanging of Sofia Perovskaia and four men for the assassination of Czar Alexander II. (Culver Pictures)

On March 1, 1881, Sofia L'vovna Perovskaia led the successful plot to assassinate Alexander II, Czar of Russia, culminating two years of terrorist activity. A month later, sentenced to death by hanging, she became the first woman in Russia to receive capital punishment for a political crime. Although Perovskaia's presence on the scaffold was unique, hundreds of other women shared her commitment to the cause of social revolution in Russia. Of the 2,564 individuals arrested for political crimes between 1873 and 1879, roughly 15 percent were women; in the People's Will, the terrorist faction that arose at the end of the decade, the percentage of women rose to 30. These numbers, which would be sufficiently striking in any western European country during this period, become all the more so since women still had no access to university education in Russia, and many of the women arrested did not come from wealthy or upper-class families — indeed, a few could scarcely read or write. Yet, not only did the populist movement of the 1870s attract remarkably many women activists, but the most outstanding of these women took positions of leadership appropriate to their skill and dedication. We can best understand these women through their biographies, which illustrate their growing commitment to social change. To that evolution, the powerful feminist upsurge of the 1860s was absolutely critical. Only after women's traditional role had been questioned, after rigid social barriers had been breached, and after both men and women had become conscious of women's potential in other areas, did it become possible for them to join together in political activity as well.

Before the emancipation of the serfs in 1861, the authoritarian patterns generated by serfdom largely determined the position of women in Russian society. Serf men, themselves brutalized and powerless, took out their rage on their women and children, the only beings more helpless than they. In mid-nineteenth-century Russia, serfs made up roughly 75 percent of the population and the gentry less than 1 percent. Intermediate social groups such as merchants or petty bourgeoisie had often emerged from the peasantry or lived in close proximity to them. They differed little in their ways of living, which reflected the same brutalizing influences. The authoritarian patterns of serfdom also left their mark on those who owned serfs. Many gentry patriarchs still followed the instructions set forth in the *Domostroi,* a sixteenth-century household guide that encouraged the head of a household to enforce family discipline by administering beatings. For example, Sergei Aksakov's semiautobiographical novel, *The Family Chronicle,* depicts Stepan Bagrov, a late-eighteenth-century patriarch and by no means an evil man, who kept his wife and daughters in a state of perpetual terror. A man encouraged by tradition and able to exercise his unrestrained will in his relations with his serfs rarely exercised greater restraint in regard to his wife and children, over whom he had similar mastery in law. The authorities rarely intervened in the relationship between landlord and serf and could be trusted to remain equally uninvolved in the relations between husband and wife, father and children. The vastness of Russia's territory and the weakness of state power on the local level prevented the government from undertaking the role of policeman. Indeed, since gentry landlords acted as agents of the state, as local policemen of sorts, their authority carried over to their household. Such authority especially restricted the women of the family: while sons could eventually escape their fathers by leaving to perform state service, daughters could only marry, which meant exchanging one form of subjection for another, usually no better and occasionally worse.

Because of the intimate connection between the serf system and authoritarian family relationships, Russian intellectuals in the 1850s began to attack them both. Discussing at length the petty despotism of Russian family life in his essay "Realm of Darkness," the radical critic Nikolai Dobroliubov wrote: "The weight of despotism in this 'realm of darkness' comes down most heavily on women. . . . The way that our society is arranged, almost everywhere women have about as much value as parasites." Degradation of women, he said, is so pervasive that even the men who allow their wives some say in the household would never think that "A woman is also a person like themselves, with her own rights. Indeed, women themselves don't believe it." [1] Intellectuals called for a regeneration of Russian society: they demanded that patriarchal relations be destroyed and replaced with egalitarian ones, and that peasants and women, who had escaped the corrupting influence of patriarchal power, become active members of society and help to renew it. Women in particular, assigned special moral qualities by both religious and secular tradition, would be essential to the regeneration of society as a whole. They expected the liberation of women from the patriarchal family to bring direct and immediate benefits to everyone. In that sense, male intellectuals never viewed the "woman question" as an entirely separate issue but always as an important component of fundamental social change. Numerous articles emerged in the late 1850s, either addressed directly to the "woman question" or at least peripherally concerned with it. Writers such as Mikhail Mikhailov analyzed and discussed the oppression of women and demanded sweeping changes in their treatment: women must be given an education equal to that of men, men must cease to regard them as inferior, and the barriers to women's full participation in the life of society must be removed. He, like others, argued that women must be liberated in order to join men in the struggle for a better society.

The writings of these male intellectuals found a ready audience among women of the gentry, particularly those in the provinces. Only the wealthiest members of the gentry could afford to maintain homes in the cities, and the rest spent practically the entire year in the vast and sparsely populated countryside. There, life was usually idle and often excruciatingly dull for both men and women, but men, at least, could occupy themselves by managing their estates or serving in local government or gentry organizations. During the seemingly endless winter months, when visiting was impossible, reading became virtually the only diversion. Provincial gentlewomen eagerly read the articles on the "woman question" that appeared frequently in the most popular journals of the day, and these articles evoked a powerful response. Anna Korvin-Krukovskaia, the daughter of a wealthy provincial gentry family, put aside her fancy clothes and began to dress simply, lost interest in parties, and started to read serious scientific works shortly after she had first read a series of articles on the "woman question." Then she begged her father for permission to study in St. Petersburg. He refused it. Subsequently, however, Korvin-Krukovskaia convinced him to let her accompany her married sister abroad, where both women became active participants in the Paris Commune. Other women reacted to such treatment by joining together. Toward the end of the 1850s, women, both young and old, had begun to hold separate meetings at gatherings of the provincial gentry. They required simple dress in order to minimize social distinctions among women as much as possible. At the same time, individual women began speaking out on behalf of their sisters. In 1861, a woman named E. A. Slovtsova-Kamskaia declared: "The morally developed woman of our time suffers for every injustice borne by another woman. Feelings of envy, ambition, coquetry, the slavish desire to please men at the expense of her sisters should be alien to her. . . . Each act of kindness she performs for her sisters, she performs for herself." [2] By the early 1860s, the response of young gentlewomen had reached massive proportions.

> Whatever gentry family you inquired about at that time, you heard one and the same response: the children had fought with the parents. . . . "Their beliefs are different" — and that's all there was to it. Children, particularly girls, seemed to be possessed by an epidemic at that time — to flee from their parents' home. From the family of this or that landlord a daughter had fled.[3]

Many sought an education: between 1859 and 1861 many women even began to audit university lectures. Then Moscow University closed its doors to them. Those who wished to pursue a course of professional study or earn an advanced degree had to travel abroad. Other women sought work to support themselves. Almost all tried conscientiously to free themselves from the helpless, dependent, and decorative feminine stereotype that had molded them.

They faced formidable obstacles. The law subjected women first to their fathers, then to their husbands. Without the permission of one or the other, they could not leave home; outraged husbands or fathers occasionally resorted to the police, sending them after runaway wives and daughters. Of all the obstacles confronting women, however, economics proved the greatest. Even after the emancipation of 1861, Russia remained a pre-industrial society. The economy was predominantly manorial; most production for consumption was still carried out in the countryside, on gentry estates. Although textile factories, one of the prevalent forms of industry, did employ women, the work was extremely arduous, the hours long (thirteen to fourteen hours a day), and the premises filthy. These factories hired mainly peasant women and women of the lowest social strata. In the 1860s, despite the egalitarian ethos of that decade, no gentlewoman or woman with any education would enter them. But alternatives were few. A woman could become a governess or a *klassnaia dama*[1] — positions so limited, isolated, and dependent that only the most desperate accepted them. If sufficiently educated, a woman could be a translator, but the work often proved sporadic, and it did not pay well. Women received no professional training at this time; pedagogical courses opened only in 1866.

To meet their needs, organizations were set up by philanthropic feminists solely for the purpose of helping other women. In St. Petersburg in 1862, a group, led by the "triumvirate," as Nadezhda Stasova, Anna Filosofova, and Maria Trubnikova came to be known, formed the first organization run by women for women. They called it the Society for Inexpensive Quarters. The society was intended to provide housing primarily for a genteel clientele: widows, abandoned wives, and unmarried daughters of poor gentry or minor bureaucratic families. In short, its beneficiaries were women somewhat like their benefactors, but impoverished and usually poorly educated. Soon after they established the society, the founders realized that women needed jobs as much as housing. To meet that need, they set up a second organization, the Society for Women's Labor.

The tenets of this second organization contain a clear exposition of philanthropic feminist ideas:

1. One of the most difficult positions in our society is that of women.

2. Most occupations are closed to them, not because of their lack of ability, but because society is not accustomed to seeing women in positions that men usually occupy.
3. The results of this are very harmful for social well-being.[5]

Women's talents were wasted and they were forced to depend on men, who looked down on them as a result. These feminists believed the inequality between men and women to be economic in origin, and they sought to rectify it by providing jobs and education.

While some women shared the goals of the philanthropic feminists, they could not accept their hierarchical organization. The leaders made decisions without seriously consulting the women who lived in their houses or worked in their shops. Furthermore, the philanthropic feminists, well born and well bred, had committed themselves to working within the limits permitted by an increasingly conservative Russian government. This ensured that generations of young, politically aware women would not remain within their ranks for long. The philanthropic feminists came into conflict with these younger women at an open meeting in 1864. The conflict centered on two interrelated questions: who would be included in the list of officers for the Society for Women's Labor, and what voice would working women have in that organization? A group of women objected when six men, who did not even care about women's labor, were included on the list of officers drawn up by philanthropic feminists. The protesters demanded that at least one-half of the officers be working women: translators, typesetters, weavers, and so forth. The philanthropic feminists, fearful of losing control of their organization, responded that women workers would be unable to defend their own rights, and that society people would have to do it for them. Then, using a dubious parliamentary maneuver, they excluded the younger women from the organization altogether. As a result of such treatment, many young women turned to the left for assistance.

Guided by Chernyshevskii's novel *What Is to Be Done?,* young men were trying to assist women in their search for autonomy. The book offered a solution to obstacles confronting women by linking their individual aspirations to the broader social issues that concerned the nihilist generation. Published in 1862, the novel set the tone for radical experimentation in the early 1860s by combining solutions to the specific difficulties experienced by women with ideas for restructuring all of Russian society along socialist lines. To the problem of authoritarian families that prevented daughters from living as they chose, the novel suggested fictitious marriage — marriage solely for the purpose of liberating women from their families. Pretending to be in love, Chernyshevskii's heroine, Vera Pavlovna, convinces her mother to let her marry Dmitrii Kirsanov, a young and idealistic student. After their wedding, Vera Pavlovna lives with her new husband in nonsexual cohabitation: he never interferes with her life, and she remains free to pursue her own interests. During the 1860s and 1870s, hundreds of young women in real life followed her example, marrying young men they scarcely knew in order to break free of their families. *What Is to Be Done?* also dealt with such difficult subjects as jealousy and possessiveness, providing an example of the equality and comradeship that were expected to replace outmoded patriarchal patterns. In the new relations between the sexes, neither partner would "own" the other, and both would be free to act on their emotions. When Vera Pavlovna falls in love with her husband's best friend, her husband feigns suicide and conveniently disappears so as not to be an obstacle to his wife's true love. Vera Pavlovna marries her lover and lives as independently with him as she had with her first husband. According to Chernyshevskii, it was ultimately in the interest of both partners to allow each other total freedom. He was advocating marriage between equals to replace the coercive, possessive relations that had prevailed in the past.

While Chernyshevskii's ideas on the relations between the sexes were certainly important, it was in the realm of economics that the novel addressed itself to the most critical problem facing women in the 1860s. Traditionally, unmarried women remained at home with their parents or lived with close relatives — not always a pleasant life, but secure, and preferable to work as a lowly governess or klassnaia dama. However, the emancipation of the serfs in 1861 had been a financial disaster to numerous gentry families and many of them now found themselves unable to support their unmarried daughters, even if the latter wished to remain at home — and many did not. Young gentlewomen fled their families in droves, only to find that they could not make a living. Vera Pavlovna, Chernyshevskii's heroine, organizes a sewing workshop that not only provides employment for needy young women such as herself but also demonstrates that collective principles could work and work profitably. Instead of drawing a salary, the seamstresses, never greedy and never asking too much, take what they need from a common pool. Instead of pocketing the profits, Vera Pavlovna uses them for the benefit of the workers, or reinvests in the business, while training the seamstresses themselves to manage the operation. This arrangement turns out to be so successful that the collective workshop is expanded to include a bank and a commune that houses the seamstresses and their poor relatives.

To the generation of the early 1860s, Vera Pavlovna's workshop provided a perfect model for testing the viability of socialist relations. Immediately after the novel was published, numerous people established cooperatives based on Chernyshevskii's book. Indeed, it was used as a blueprint. The organizers of such workshops would open the book to the appropriate page, read aloud what Vera Pavlovna had done, and attempt to imitate it as closely as possible. But what had worked in the novel generally failed in reality. Women needed money to start these workshops, and thus, they were dependent from the first on wealthy individuals or radical men. The principles of association, which the young seamstresses in Vera Pavlovna's collective had grasped so readily, evoked confusion and hostility in real life. Trained seamstresses and laundresses brought in to provide a core of experienced workers distrusted all employers and demanded an established salary. Moreover, many of the gentlewomen who joined the shops were more interested in principles than in sewing eight to ten hours per day. One shop, managed by a competent and businesslike woman with some progressive ideas, proved more successful than many others. However, the members of the men's circle that had originally backed it were troubled because it appeared no different from ordinary shops. In an effort to make it more "principled," the men's circle bought three prostitutes free from brothels and sent them to her to be reformed by productive labor. The three refused to work, insulted the customers, and eventually drove away all the business. Thus, ideology and practicality, which had worked so well together in *What Is to Be Done?,* often conflicted directly in real life.

The conflict was exacerbated by the need for men to help implement many of Chernyshevskii's ideas on the "woman question." It was men who married women fictitiously and gave the financial and moral support necessary for the establishment of workshops and collectives. In the early sixties, men gave their support willingly because of the importance of the "woman question." Yet, even in this early period the seeds of a future conflict can be detected, for their primary goal was to demonstrate the superiority of collective principles over capitalist ones. Men conceived of women's liberation as but one stage in the overall process of regenerating Russia, and almost all of them assumed that, once freed from the bonds of the past, the women they assisted would take their place alongside them in this larger struggle. Thus, there existed a potential conflict between male and female interests: men strove for broad social change, while most women sought personal liberation first and foremost.

Such women, individualistic feminists, aimed primarily at their own autonomy and freedom. They were young, usually in their late teens or early twenties, and most came from provincial gentry families that had been impoverished by the emancipation of the serfs in 1861. But, although individualistic feminists predominated in the early sixties, the number of feminist radicals was growing. These women, also young, impoverished gentlewomen, shared the goals of the individualistic feminists but were becoming increasingly attracted to the ideas of the men who supported them.

Both groups were easily distinguished by their appearance: their very dress and demeanor declared their independence. They dispensed with elegant clothing and donned plain, dark-colored wool dresses. They cut their hair short at a time when a woman's hair was considered her crowning glory; they wore blue glasses, and many of them smoked in public. At a time when people expected women to be reticent and retiring, they talked loudly in public and went about the streets alone and unchaperoned. In general, they scandalized their contemporaries, receiving the name "nihilistki" — the feminine form of nihilist, as the entire radical generation of the sixties was called.

For both feminist radicals and individualistic feminists, however, emancipation involved far more than dress. Their struggle for autonomy had begun with a painful break from home and family, with little hope for return. They often depended totally on their own meager resources. Feminist radicals could turn to men of the left for support, but individualistic feminists tended to be suspicious of men and hostile to sexual overtures. Their sexuality had imprisoned them in the past, and now they denied or minimized it. Ekaterina Zhukovskaia, for example, encountered typical problems in her struggle for autonomy. Zhukovskaia had been born to a moderately wealthy, provincial gentry family. She finished boarding school at seventeen, in the late 1850s, at a time when Russian society had already begun to anticipate change. Like other young women, Zhukovskaia learned of these changes through journals, which aroused her desire to participate. Feeling stifled by the stagnant existence of her provincial family, she formulated great plans: she would teach the peasants to read and write, would help them to improve their farming methods, and would set up hospitals for them. Lacking other alternatives, she anticipated marrying a like-minded man, who would assist her and enable her to escape from her family. Educated in a cloistered boarding school and sheltered by her family, Zhukovskaia remained totally ignorant of the relations, sexual and otherwise, between men and women. She accepted the first man who courted her. Over the protests of her parents, who felt she was choosing too hastily, she insisted upon an early engagement.

But she soon had misgivings. As she got to know her fiancé better, she realized that he had less sympathy for her plans than she had first believed. Furthermore, as his sexual demands on her increased, she found herself thoroughly revolted. She tried to break off the engagement, but her parents forbade it, fearing social disapproval. Her husband raped her on their wedding night. Henceforth, her sole concern became freeing herself from that hated marriage. After overcoming many difficulties, she finally succeeded and set off for St. Petersburg. There, she discovered that jobs were scarce and decent lodging difficult to find. Shortly after her arrival, Zhukovskaia was introduced to Vasilii Sleptsov, a writer and activist of some note, who had been involved with women's as well as with radical causes. Sleptsov offered to help Zhukovskaia find work and suggested that she become a member of a commune he had organized. Sleptsov had originally intended to organize it entirely on socialist principles. Zhukovskaia reacted suspiciously to his offer. Although members were expected to pay only according to their ability, she insisted on paying her full share of the commune's upkeep, unwilling to risk depending on anyone. She also demanded to know if Sleptsov planned to implement the French Utopian socialist Charles Fourier's ideas on free love. Assured that she would be free to live as she chose, and convinced that the communal arrangement would be less expensive than any other, she agreed to join, despite her lack of sympathy with communal principles.

Three other women entered the commune, and two of them, Alexandra Markelova and Ekaterina Makulova, can be categorized as feminist radicals. Markelova came from an impoverished gentry family. She had run off with an artist a few years earlier and had kept their illegitimate child even after the father abandoned her, an unusual and courageous act for a gentlewoman of her day. She supported herself by doing translations. Makulova, who came from a similar background, had learned to pare her physical needs to a minimum; she spent all her free time at the library and worked as a governess or companion whenever her money ran out. Both women had joined the commune as much from commitment to Chernyshevskii's ideas as from economic need. Of the four women in the Sleptsov commune, only Masha Kopteva received money from her parents. Spoiled and self-indulgent, she was an unlikely addition to a socialist commune.

The commune experienced difficulties from the beginning, largely because of the disparity between Sleptsov's conception of the arrangement and that of the other members, especially Zhukovskaia. Ironically, women like Zhukovskaia, who most needed the assistance of collectives and communes, helped to destroy them by refusing their full cooperation. She refused to participate in group decisions, refused to eat the humble fare that others had chosen, and finally, refused to do her own housework after the other members had voted to dispense with servants. This, and Sleptsov's own extravagances — he loved flowers and insisted on buying them, loved entertaining and served his own guests lavishly — eventually brought about the demise of the whole endeavor. It failed for the same reasons that collective workshops failed. Nihilism was by no means a monolithic movement: there were class differences as well as sex differences between its members. While the women came from the gentry, the men had diverse class backgrounds. Such men, more humbly born, had long since grown accustomed to a spartan life, but gentlewomen had great difficulty adjusting to it. The demands of socialist cooperation weighed heavily on them, and they (like a number of well-born male nihilists) tended to be less dedicated to fulfilling them. This weakened the collectives, which required maximum commitment and self-discipline, particularly in a society that had not even reached the stage of capitalism.

As the decade wore on, political changes exacerbated the difficulties faced by women seeking autonomy. The initial optimism following serf emancipation and the promise of other reforms had been particularly conducive to social and personal experimentation, but by 1863 reaction had already begun to set in, starting with the bloody suppression of an uprising in Poland that winter. Soon afterward, the government arrested a number of the radicals who had espoused the cause of an independent Poland. As government reaction grew, numerous individualistic feminists, along with many of the people who had toyed with the previously fashionable nihilism, began to disassociate themselves from an ideology that had become suspect. Other women came to rely more heavily on the support of radical men's circles. Those who continued to dress, to behave, and to think as nihilists did so from far greater commitment than before; their activities now involved real risk. And as the hopes generated by the Era of Great Reforms began to wane, many on the left thought increasingly of political revolution.

In 1866 Dmitrii Karakozov, a member of the radical Ishutin circle, attempted to assassinate the czar, Alexander II. Following Karakozov's shot, dozens of people were arrested, tried, and exiled; surveillance of radical and student organizations increased dramatically. The individuals arrested in connection with Karakozov's assassination attempt included a number of women, members of a sewing collective supported by the Ishutin circle. Of them all, only Maria Krylova knew of the circle's aims and endorsed them. Krylova, then in her early twenties, was a feminist radical. She had fled her gentry family because of a yearning for education and independence, and in her first years away from home she read everything she could get her hands on. Under the influence of radicals in Moscow, her desire for knowledge grew into a concern for educating others as well, and she taught in the evening and Sunday schools for workers that proliferated in the sixties. She also worked on behalf of other women, and joined a number of collectives. Perhaps as a result of her frustration with their failure, Krylova by 1865 had become thoroughly committed to revolution, "insofar as it would improve the position of women." [6] She affiliated with the Ishutin sewing workshop solely because of its political aims: she had no idea of how to sew and took no part in the work, paying rent instead for her maintenance in the commune associated with the shop. In short, Krylova became one of the first feminist radicals to go beyond socialist experimentation to full political involvement.

By the second half of the sixties, most individualistic feminists had either become feminist radicals or ceased to be active: political repression forced women as well as men to choose sides. Feminist radicalism, however, rapidly became more radical than feminist. In the early sixties the two movements had been complementary, as demonstrated by women's participation in collectives, communes, and other radical efforts at social experimentation. After 1863, however, the two orientations began to conflict. As the left moved toward political action, men's concern with the "woman question" greatly declined, and their assistance to women became increasingly rare.

Yet, the decline of concern with the "woman question" on the left did not end male efforts to recruit women into their organizations. They needed women as revolutionaries and for the particular moral attributes men assumed that women possessed. For the most part, women responded eagerly; they joined men's circles, frequently abandoning feminist projects in order to do so. But their sacrifice was not rewarded. In this period, men not only excluded women from decision making and leadership positions in radical organizations, they also used women sexually, and sometimes quite casually. Perhaps the most dramatic example of such treatment is the case of Liudmila Radetskaia. In the late 1860s, Radetskaia entered a fictitious marriage to escape a marriage her parents had arranged. She lived with her new husband for a year, in a radical commune composed of remnants of the Ishutin circle. Radetskaia enthusiastically supported the group's aims: "I advocated heroic deeds and felt possessed by the desire to give myself up to serving the people," she later wrote, adding, "I loved everyone so, and wanted so much to be useful to everyone in our circle." [7] When poverty threatened the very existence of the group, her husband asked Radetskaia and one other woman to prostitute themselves in order to obtain the funds to keep it going. The two women agreed, and Radetskaia became the mistress of a banker, turning all the money she received over to her husband, who in turn used it to maintain the commune. She stopped only after she became pregnant, at which point she left both husband and banker to seek work. She was nineteen.

In the late sixties, very few women chose radical action directly; most became involved through men they liked and trusted, and whose goals they shared. Like Radetskaia, such women often proved politically naive and, as a result, somewhat insecure around men, though extremely eager to be of service to the cause. But because they never gained responsibility for any major undertaking, their involvement remained indirect, channeled largely through the men who had first drawn them into the groups. Consequently, when the men were captured or exiled, the women either dropped out or followed them to Siberia, putting an end to whatever contributions they might have made as individuals.

In 1869–1870 the revolutionary movement in Russia began to take a new direction. Most of those who had been active earlier had fled abroad or been imprisoned or exiled, and younger men and women filled their ranks. This new generation of radicals, called populists, although heavily influenced by the ideas of the previous decade, reacted strongly against its individualism. Rejecting the earlier system of organization, which had rested on the leadership of powerful individuals, they formed egalitarian groups based upon mutual trust and shared responsibility. Populists aimed at creating a broad social movement with the Russian peasantry at its center. Within these new, egalitarian organizations, women played an important role.

The year 1869 had brought an unprecedented influx of women to Moscow and St. Petersburg, where advanced courses for them had finally been opened. Although many of the finest professors came to lecture at the schools, the program, intended to supplement women's superficial education, awarded no degree. But so great was the desire of Russian women for any form of education that they flooded the courses in Moscow and St. Petersburg as soon as they opened. These young auditors appeared to be little different from the nihilistki of a decade earlier, but beneath the superficial similarities important changes had already occurred. Significantly, this new group had a more varied class background. In the sixties, virtually all the women who fled their families belonged to the gentry, while the auditors of the courses in St. Petersburg and Moscow came from merchant, petty bourgeois, and clerical families. And while some of them had come to the cities against their parents' will, most had parental approval and even parental support for tuition. Many of these auditors went on to become revolutionaries, but in 1869 most of them remained ardent feminists. In daily meetings, from which they barred men, women exchanged their views on marriage and the family, on women's position in society, and on their purpose in life. The majority felt that even the most foolish men would try to gain intellectual ascendancy over them, and they wanted to define their own views and to develop their own personal and political consciousness. By excluding men, they postponed the inevitable choice of priorities between feminism and radicalism. Since the late 1860s, when the "woman question" had lost its importance as a separate issue on the left, women as well as men had ignored the radical implications of feminism. Giving it strictly a personal, rather than a social perspective, they sought to come to grips with the problems facing them as individuals and as women. Simultaneously, they addressed themselves to broader social issues, but they did not do so as feminists. They saw this as a job for radicals. As a result, however, when their reading of European and Russian socialists convinced them of the need for action, they faced a painful choice between continuing separatism or affiliation with male radicals.

By the winter of 1870, some women had already grown impatient with self-education. While they were reading and discussing, many of the young male students they knew had already begun to act, and they tried to convince women to join them. Within a year, they had largely succeeded. During the winter of 1870–1871 Sofia Perovskaia and Alexandra Kornilova, two of the most ardent feminist separatists, had joined the Chaikovskii circle, a group of medical students then spreading socialist literature among students.

Most women found the transition from feminism to radicalism painful, but for Sofia Perovskaia it was particularly difficult. Only sixteen when she arrived in St. Petersburg, the "woman question" already had great personal significance for her. Born to a wealthy and respected gentry family, Perovskaia from earliest childhood had witnessed violent quarrels between her parents and had invariably taken her mother's side. Her love and sympathy for her mother were matched only by her hatred and distrust of her father; indeed, for the rest of her life she remained more comfortable with women than with men. At sixteen, Perovskaia planned to devote her life to the struggle for women's rights. She made friends easily in St. Petersburg, quickly gathering a circle of like-minded young women around her. A good student and an excellent mathematician, Perovskaia briefly considered enrolling in engineering school. She also participated frequently in the women's circles, and as one of the most vocal advocates of separate women's groups, argued cogently and often that men's and women's groups must not be merged, despite her own growing concern with political and social questions.

Yet, in less than two years she had reversed herself and joined the Chaikovskii circle. Late in the winter of 1870–1871 a special meeting of women confronted Perovskaia and her friend, Alexandra Kornilova, and demanded that they explain their action, but the two women refused to do so. Although their refusal deprives us of any easy interpretation, at the source of their decision lay an earlier conception of feminism. Its goals consisted mainly of freedom from family oppression and economic independence; it offered no solution to the exploitation of factory workers or the oppression of peasants. Because the women had obtained their parents' permission to study and a few opportunities for advanced training, the "woman question" no longer seemed so pressing to them, and they grew increasingly concerned with other social problems. Separatist feminism had enabled them to develop a social analysis of their own, but once they had formulated one, they no longer needed separatism. Having become radicals, they wanted action, and men, eager to recruit them, had begun to act.

The character of their future comrades also served as an important factor in the women's decision to affiliate with men. The men of the Chaikovskii circle differed from the nihilists of the sixties. Indeed, their thinking had developed partly in reaction to the tactics of their predecessors. Instead of a hierarchical organization dominated by a single leader, the men of the Chaikovskii circle stressed the values of comradeship and equality in a group committed to the raising of worker and peasant consciousness through a carefully organized program of propaganda and education. In theory, therefore, and to a striking degree in practice, the men treated their female comrades respectfully and as equals. The men of the Chaikovskii circle had assimilated the feminist ideas of the 1860s into their ideological framework. They demonstrated this not only by treating all comrades equally but also by incorporating feminist issues into the socialist propaganda they conducted in the factories of St. Petersburg. Alone among the populists of the seventies, the Chaikovskii circle devoted some attention to women as a separate group. Of the thirty active members of the circle, seven were women, and from the beginning they participated in the circle's activities on an equal basis with the men. Together they held night classes for workers, conducted propaganda, and built the basis for the first workers' organization in Russia. And for the first time, women began to initiate projects on their own. During the summer of 1872, Perovskaia went to Stavropol, in the south of Russia, where first she assisted a village schoolteacher and then traveled on foot around the countryside, vaccinating peasants against smallpox and disseminating socialist propaganda on her way. That same summer, Alexandra Obodovskaia, another member of the group, worked alone in the countryside propagandizing. Within the organization they had joined, these women retained their identity and initiative. Unlike the women of the sixties, who had participated for the most part indirectly through men, the women of the Chaikovskii circle acted as far more than female auxiliaries: they were radicals independently committed to the cause of the Russian people.

Even more than the women of the Chaikovskii circle, however, the Fritsche group, named after the house in which its members lived, proved that radicalism had become as much a woman's as a man's province. The first radical organization to be made up exclusively of women, the group was first formed in Zurich, where, unlike in Russia, professional education was available to them. Originally, all thirteen members planned to become physicians, hoping thereby to combine their desire for a profession with their wish to serve the Russian people. Strictly speaking, these women did not think of themselves as feminists, but the influence of the earlier women's movement showed both in their desire to pursue a profession and in their willingness to travel abroad to do so. Of the thirteen women in the group, all but Alexandra Toporkova, a tradesman's daughter, belonged to gentry or wealthy families. Many of the families actually agreed to support their daughters while they were in Zurich, and the women had all received the permission of their parents to travel: without it they would have been unable legally to leave Russia. Their very presence in the classroom served as evidence of the changing attitudes of parents to their daughters' professional aspirations.

When they arrived in Zurich early in 1872, the future members of the Fritsche group found a flourishing émigré colony, with a well-endowed library devoted almost exclusively to works on socialism and revolution. A hothouse of Russian radicalism, the colony boasted two of the leading populist theorists of the time, Michael Bakunin and Paul Lavrov. In 1872–1873, populists debated the relationship they should have to the peasantry.

In those debates, Bakunin and Lavrov stood at opposite poles. In 1868, Lavrov had published his *Historical Letters,* in which he declared that the intellectual, whose privileges had been purchased at the expense of the peasantry, had a duty to educate himself as fully as possible in order to use his knowledge for their benefit. Bakunin, on the other hand, believed that education could only increase the separation between intellectuals and the Russian peasantry. Therefore, he argued that intellectuals must abandon their own education and go to "the people," to learn from them and to help bring about the inevitable revolution.

The debate between Lavrov and Bakunin was not merely abstract theorizing: for women in particular, it had enormous practical significance. If women adhered to Lavrov's views, they could acquire an education without appearing selfish. If they followed Bakunin, they would have had to abandon the university immediately, return home, and become professional revolutionaries. This typified the dilemma of their entire generation. The Russian intelligentsia (both men and women) had believed in the capacity of education and knowledge to transform society. Yet, their very education made them strangers in their own land, unable to communicate with the Russian peasantry, who comprised over three-quarters of the population and who were crucial to any revolution. During the 1870s, every socially concerned individual had to contend with this problem. Most eventually chose the Bakuninist path. Originally, the Fritsche group had been closer to Lavrov. Indeed, they had come to Zurich mainly to gain the education that would make them useful. But during their stay, the Bakuninist library and the émigré colony itself gradually transformed their ideas until almost all of them felt ready to abandon their professional education for radical activity.

In the spring of 1872, some of the women students of the colony attempted to set up a circle exclusively for women, so that they could learn to speak well in public. A dispute broke out almost immediately: second- and third-year students, far less radical, objected strenuously to the exclusion of men, insisting that women had nothing to fear from them. By contrast, the younger students wanted to develop their ideas on their own, and they recognized that the presence of men would make this difficult. The two sides held to their positions adamantly, and after a brief moratorium, during which the advocates of separatism prevailed, the group dissolved. Nevertheless, during the short period of its existence, a number of debates had taken place, giving the members an opportunity to take each other's measure and form alliances. By the time of the dissolution, the Fritsche circle had taken on a life of its own.

This group proved crucial to the development of its members, because it answered both their personal and intellectual needs. The members were remarkably young; not one was over twenty, and two were only sixteen. Sonia Bardina, affectionately called "Auntie" by the group, as the oldest and most sophisticated served as its leader. In strange and often intimidating surroundings, confronted by new social and political ideas, the group clung together like a tightly knit family, with Bardina in the position of mediator between them and the rest of the world. This gave Bardina an enormous amount of influence. She had become a socialist while still in Russia, and in Zurich she initiated the political education of her circle. Between 1872 and 1873 the group held formal readings and discussions almost daily, trying to familiarize themselves with all the outstanding works of European socialism, while pursuing their regular studies with discipline and zeal. They might have maintained this dual focus until they finished their course of studies, but at the close of the spring semester in 1873, the Russian government ordered them to return home. It accused them of using their studies abroad to get involved with radical causes, to engage in free love, and to perform abortions on each other.

This infuriated the women. Not only had the government prevented them from completing their studies, it had impugned their morality as well. They made a final, unsuccessful attempt to unite for a public protest, but the divisions between the various groups of women could not be overcome. The younger women insisted on protesting, but the older and more conservative threatened a counterprotest, fearing that the public would associate them with the radicals. The Fritsche group departed without protest, but with greatly increased hostility toward the government. Its members soon realized that they could enroll elsewhere, like Paris or Bern, but before leaving Zurich they drew up a statute and regulations, formalizing their organization and committing themselves to revolutionary goals — if not immediately, then after they had completed their education. Influenced by the socialist atmosphere of Zurich, they resolved to become laborers, to conduct propaganda in factories, and to live among the workers of Russia as equals. After this formalization, a few of the women returned to Russia, but five of them went to Paris and five to Bern to continue their studies. In Paris the Russian government intervened once again, forcing the women to leave the university. Government intervention only hastened the women's decision to become full-time radicals. The entire Paris group and most of the Bern contingent soon joined the Fritsche group in Russia. Only two members, Dora Aptekman and Vera Figner, stayed abroad.

By 1874, when the others had returned to Russia, the composition of their group had been thoroughly changed. While in western Europe, the women had become acquainted with a circle of like-minded young men from the Caucasus. After a series of negotiations, the men and women resolved to merge their groups, taking the name Pan Russian Social Revolutionary Organization and drawing up a new statute and regulations. Celibacy proved a major source of contention: the women wished the organization's rules to bar any sexual relations but the men eventually overruled them. Both men and women agreed, however, that they would be equal within the organization. As in the Chaikovskii circle, members of this new group treated each other with honesty and respect. They resolved to place the goals of their group above family, friends, and self. They intended to spread propaganda for a socialist revolution in Russia. The strategy was for the members to enter factories to convert the workers to socialism. The workers in turn would propagandize their peasant brothers and sisters when they made their periodic trips back to their homes in the countryside. In theory, therefore, every member of the organization had to become a laborer. In fact, however, only the women actually undertook factory labor. They fanned out to the industrial centers of Russia, where, disguised in simple peasant clothing, they applied for jobs.

From the beginning, they were in a dangerous position. Because everyone in Russia had to carry a passport, listing, among other things, social class, they had to begin their jobs with false documents that stated that they were peasants.[8] Furthermore, try as they might, they did not look like the peasant women who worked alongside them: their hands were soft, their complexions delicate and clear — they obviously had never toiled in the fields under a burning sun or done factory work before. Despite these handicaps, the women never hesitated. Most of them entered textile factories, where they labored for thirteen to fourteen hours a day, working with piles of rags on filthy floors, breathing dusty, unventilated air. Most of them lived in the factories, too. The owners provided "dormitories," where women slept on boards attached to the walls by chains and barely wide enough to lie down on. These "dormitories" were also unventilated, filthy, and crawling with insects. The women could leave the factories only on holidays.

At first, they tried to educate their coworkers, but with little success. The women workers preferred to talk of clothing and of men, to eat quickly, and then go to sleep. After a day of work they felt too exhausted to listen to readings or discuss socialist ideas. Eventually, each of the propagandists despaired and attempted to educate the male workers instead. Entering the men's quarters, which were forbidden to women, they took the greatest risks. On the one hand, if caught by the factory authorities the women would immediately be fired and perhaps turned over to the police. On the other hand, the peasant men often did not comprehend the purpose of their visits, and made sexual advances. Only their literacy afforded the women some protection: most peasant men had never seen women who could read and were impressed.[9] When the young women began reading to them, a few workers actually stayed awake to listen, but just as they started organizing, the government closed in. The police uncovered the group in Moscow when the girlfriend of one of the propagandized workers informed in order to save him after he was caught carrying illegal literature. Once the police discovered the administrative center, it proved relatively easy for them to locate the organization's provincial cells as well. By the fall of 1874, all the members of the Fritsche group then in Russia were in prison. For almost three years they awaited their trial in solitary confinement. At approximately the same time, the police arrested the women of the Chaikovskii circle for propagandizing the workers of St. Petersburg.

The relative political calm that followed was shattered in January 1878. Vera Zasulich, a member of a revolutionary circle from the south of Russia, shot General Trepov, the governor general of St. Petersburg, because he had ordered a political prisoner beaten for not removing his cap in the governor's presence. Zasulich, who had become involved with radical circles in the late 1860s, had already suffered imprisonment and exile. Her shot heralded a new stage in the revolutionary movement: henceforth, revolutionaries would meet violence with violence. It marked the failure of the populists' efforts to educate the peasants and to conduct peaceful propaganda in the factories and in the villages. The ignorance of the peasantry, their distrust of an intelligentsia with speech and lifestyle so different from their own, had made political work extraordinarily difficult. Any sustained contact required time and patient effort, but government repression made organization in the countryside virtually impossible. No sooner did the populists settle in a village and establish tentative relations with the peasants than the government swooped down to arrest and imprison them. Although Vera Zasulich was acquitted by a jury that shared her outrage over the beating of a political prisoner, most defendants in the political trials of 1877–1878 received harsh sentences for the mildest of crimes. Almost everyone was imprisoned or exiled, and Zasulich herself had to be spirited out of Russia by her comrades when the czar ordered her held pending further instructions.

Populists divided over the question of how to react. During the summer of 1879 a split occurred in the major populist organization, Land and Liberty. One faction, taking the name the People's Will, chose to pursue terror as the most direct method of bringing about social revolution in Russia. The other group, Black Repartition, preferred to continue working in more traditional ways, conducting propaganda peacefully in the countryside. Women played a prominent role in both of these organizations, but female participation reached its peak in the People's Will, one-third of whose members were women. The People's Will valued its members primarily for their dedication: they pledged to relinquish all personal concerns, all other ties, until its goals were fulfilled. This type of organization served to foster equality for women, because it stressed traditionally "feminine" qualities as the norm for both men and women. In Russia, as elsewhere in the nineteenth century, women were raised to be devoted and self-sacrificing. The women of the People's Will brought their socialization as women to their revolutionary work. In an organization requiring total commitment and self-sacrifice for the cause, the traditional feminine qualities of devotion and selflessness rendered the women of the People's Will outstanding revolutionaries. As such, their male comrades genuinely respected them. In the People's Will, however, devotion and self-sacrifice did not mean passivity; the women expressed their loyalty through action, and in their willingness to risk their very lives to fulfill the goals of the party.

Inequities in role divisions did exist in the People's Will, but they resulted in part from having to operate conspiratorially in a sexist society. Whatever other role a woman might fulfill for the organization, most of them were also *khoziaiki,* housekeepers for conspiratorial apartments registered in their names. Society expected every proper apartment to have a woman running it. While a few people attempted to overcome these traditional sterotypes by sharing housekeeping tasks behind this facade, the party never committed itself to such equality, and the majority of men found it easier to lapse into traditional roles and be served by women. In other areas, however, no real distinctions existed between men's work and women's work. Men and women set type and ran illegal printing presses together. Women prepared bombs, forged documents, and helped to plan and execute all six assassination attempts against Alexander II. Although women did little writing for the party's leaflet, *The People's Will,* they participated actively in the debates over policy. Sofia Perovskaia became one of the most important and powerful members of the People's Will. After the capture of Andrei Zheliabov, who had been coordinating the sixth assassination attempt against Alexander II, Perovskaia took over Zheliabov's responsibilities. She arranged the observation of the czar's movements, organized the agents involved, and on March 1, 1881, she gave the signal for the successful assassination.

Within a month, most members of the People's Will had been captured. For the majority, their trial proved the last public act of their lives. On trial, too, the women displayed a self-sacrificing courage that amazed the court. Accustomed to equality with men in their organization, they refused to accept the benefits of laws that treated women more leniently. A number of them exaggerated the extent of their revolutionary activities or took responsibility for others' acts in order to share the punishment of the men. Not a single one of them shamed themselves or their cause by expressing any regret at the last moment — as a few of the men did. Sofia Perovskaia was hanged for her crimes, along with four of the men. The rest were imprisoned or sent into Siberian exile. Although the People's Will lingered on for four more years, it never again rose to its former importance. When its activities ceased in 1884, an unusual example of revolutionary egalitarianism ended as well.

Women's equal role within the populist movement as a whole, and within the People's Will in particular, resulted from an unusual set of historical circumstances never again reproduced in Russia. In the first place, the populist movement followed the feminist upsurge of the 1860s, which had sensitized the next generation to the "woman question." Second, the radical movement of the sixties had served to awaken women to the need to define their own political consciousness independently of men. Third, one of the distinguishing features of the movement of the seventies was its relative lack of concern for intellectual preparation and its emphasis on activism. Populists became profoundly ambivalent about education because they believed that knowledge would only serve to create greater distance between themselves and the peasantry. Since the educational level of most women remained vastly inferior to that of most men and their theoretical preparation far less thorough, activism gave women a chance to excel. There can be no doubt that, as activists, Vera Zasulich, Sofia Perovskaia, and a number of other women proved indispensable to the movement of the seventies.

Besides valuing women as activists, men viewed their female comrades as special beings, with qualities that elevated them to near sanctity. The populist movement in general, and the People's Will in particular, placed a very high value on the traditional nineteenth-century feminine qualities of devotion, of selflessness, of self-sacrifice. Those who worked with women in this organization, where absolute devotion to the cause was of primary importance, idealized them as nearly perfect revolutionaries. No such extravagant praise is to be found in the memoirs of the women who wrote about each other. What emerges, however, is a powerful sense of sisterhood, uniting these women more closely and strengthening them for the arduous work they undertook. A remnant of family life and a consequence of the early feminism experienced by almost all of them, this solidarity remained, giving the women a special reserve of support. Although the Fritsche group is our only example of a full-fledged revolutionary circle composed exclusively of women, this solidarity emerged even in mixed organizations. During the height of the activity of the People's Will, for example, Perovskaia made special efforts to gather together her women comrades for meetings at the theater, where they could be safe from police surveillance; these meetings always barred men. And long after the People's Will had faded out, women in prison and in exile suffered less illness and insanity than men — because they took better care of each other.

Nevertheless, despite women's solidarity, in the 1870s strictly feminist goals had no place in populist visions of the future. Only philanthropic feminist organizations, which did not challenge the existing social structure, continued to pursue earlier feminist goals of jobs, housing, and education for women. But most younger women who chose to break with tradition were more aware of the inequities of Russian society as a whole and saw themselves as privileged in comparison to the peasantry. This awareness made it extremely difficult for them to pursue exclusively feminist goals — that is, their own autonomy. Even women who did not become revolutionaries, who completed their education and worked as teachers, doctors, or medical aides, often did so in the countryside, serving the peasantry. Others, who chose the path of populist revolution, might have tried to express their feminism directly by organizing peasant or working women as a separate group. But such women, frightened, suspicious, and overworked, proved most difficult to organize, and in any case, populists, both men and women, saw the problem of the peasantry as the overriding issue. Consequently, the problem of the peasant woman was subordinated to that of the peasantry as a whole. Nor could women impose a feminist perspective on the ideal society that would emerge after a revolution. Populists believed that once revolution had done away with the existing power structure, the peasants themselves would determine their social system and form of government. Thus, until it became possible to raise the economic and cultural level of the workers and peasants, feminism would remain a movement of the privileged.

Notes

1. N. A. Dobroliubov, *Russkie klassiki,* Moscow, 1970, pp. 174–176.
2. E. A. Slovtsova-Kamskaia, "Zhenshchina v sem'e i obshchestve," *Istoricheskii Vestnik* (August 1881), 779–780.
3. Nikolai Trubitsyn, *Obshchestvennaia rol' zhenshchiny v izobrazhenii noveishii russkoi literatury,* Moscow, 1907, p. 29. The feelings of uselessness and boredom that impelled them to leave are powerfully conveyed in a number of Anton Chekhov's plays.
4. A *klassnaia dama* worked in a boarding school for girls. Not a teacher, she was responsible for the work and behavior of the girls.
5. Olga Bulanova-Trubnikova, *Tri pokoleniia,* Moscow and Leningrad, 1928, p. 89.
6. R. V. Filippov, *Revoliutsionnaia narodnicheskaia organizatsiia,* Petrozavodsk, 1964, p. 164.
7. E. Ia. Polivanov, "Teni proshlogo," *Ist. Vestnik,* 117 (1909), 761.
8. The law did not recognize a working class.
9. The women explained their literacy by claiming to be Old Believers, the only Orthodox sect in which peasant women learned to read and write.

Suggestions for Further Reading

Aksakov, S. T. *The Family Chronicle.* E. P. Dutton, New York, 1961.

Breshkovsky, Catherine. *Hidden Springs of the Russian Revolution.* Oxford University Press, London, 1931.

Chernyshevskii, N. *What Is to Be Done?* Vintage, New York, 1961. (Originally published 1862.)

Engel, Barbara Alpern, and Clifford N. Rosenthal. *Five Sisters: Women Against the Tsar.* Knopf, New York, 1975.

Figner, Vera. *Memoirs of a Revolutionist.* International Publishers, New York, 1927.

Kovalevskaia, Sonia. *Sonia Kovalevsky: Her Recollections of Childhood.* Century, New York, 1895.

Meijer, J. M. *Knowledge and Revolution.* Van Gorcum, Assen, 1955.

Satina, Sophie. *Education of Women in Pre-Revolutionary Russia.* New York, 1966.

Venturi, Franco. *Roots of Revolution.* Grosset & Dunlap, New York, 1966.

Vodovozova, Elizaveta. *A Russian Childhood.* Faber & Faber, London, 1961.

16

Love on the Tractor: Women in the Russian Revolution and After

Bernice Glatzer Rosenthal

After the Russian Revolution, what became of feminists' aspirations for a totally restructured society that would liberate women? In this essay, Bernice Rosenthal perceives mainly the failures of feminism after 1917. Early efforts to legislate major reforms in family law failed because the nation was in a state of civil war and the government could not begin to provide adequate social services to accommodate such a sweeping transformation. Under Stalin, there was a gradual return to tradition and an emphasis on a pronatalist policy. This emanated from the exigencies of foreign policy, war, and the requirements of socialist industrialization rather than from an explicit decision to preserve women's second-class status. Rosenthal chronicles the shifts of policy and the progression of laws, but we can only guess how Russian women responded to their double identity as worker and wife. She points to the large participation of women in the Soviet economy, but also notes that this has not given women commensurate control over the conditions under which they live and work. Once again we see that political change without an explicit feminist program is insufficient to liberate women.

Foreman at the Gorki Auto Works teaching a young peasant girl to work a vise. The Gorki Auto Works was one of the many new plants established during the first Five-Year Plan. (Sovfoto)

. . . But how in reality to free the child, the woman, and the human being? For that we have as yet no reliable models. All past historical experience, wholly negative, demands of the toilers at least and first of all an implacable distrust of all privileged and uncontrolled guardians.

LEON TROTSKY

Equality of the sexes was a tenet of the Russian revolutionary movement, which culminated in the Bolshevik Revolution of 1917 and whose goal was a classless society. Shortly after assuming power, the new Bolshevik regime eliminated the legal barriers to women's equality and moved to create conditions facilitating the economic, social, intellectual, and cultural equality of the sexes. Transforming women's role from housewife to worker was an intrinsic aspect of Bolshevik plans for the complete transformation of the entire society; their seizure of political power was only the first step in a long revolutionary process.

This chapter will focus on the evolution of Soviet policy toward the women of European Russia and the effects of that policy on women themselves. Following the usual division of Soviet history into three periods: a pre-Stalin period of improvisation (1917–1928), the Stalin period (1928–1953), and the post-Stalin period (1953 to the present), it will be seen that in each period the policy toward women was a by-product of a general and overall policy, with the position of women conforming to a general pattern of expectations for all citizens. For women specifically, initial Bolshevik policy aimed to destroy the bourgeois family, bring women into the labor force, and improve living conditions almost simultaneously. As this proved impossible, policy makers shifted to emphasizing one or the other. Thus, the pre-Stalin period emphasized the destruction of the bourgeois family; the Stalin, bringing women into the labor force; and the post-Stalin, the improvement of living conditions. The crucial factor in determining state policy remained constant: the needs of society as perceived and defined by the Communist party.

Tracing the many modifications made in the original Bolshevik program for women in the half-century since 1917 reveals two basic issues of interest to women everywhere: the priority or lack of priority given women's needs by policy makers and the subjective issue of what women themselves want.

Women and the "Woman Question" Before the Revolution

On the eve of the Revolution, Russia was primarily a peasant society. Peasant women worked hard and bore many children; their husbands, brutalized by poverty, often beat them. The extended patrilineal family prevailed, its division of labor strictly defined by sex. High infant mortality (273 per 1,000 in 1913) resulted from abysmal sanitary conditions and the absence of proper medical care. Strict laws made divorce almost unobtainable. But it hardly mattered; an unhappy woman had no place to go. Domestic service or prostitution (40,000 registered prostitutes in 1913) presented the main alternatives to marriage. Wives of noblemen or rich merchants had more comforts than the wives of peasants, but not much more freedom. The passport laws forbidding women to work, establish residence, or travel without consent of husband or father were not modified until 1912–1914. The mass of Russian women were too poor to utilize their legal right to own property or engage in trade. Some noblewomen played outstanding roles in local assemblies, but even they voted through a male proxy. And all women, regardless of class, sacrificed their own desires for the sake of their husbands and children; religion taught them to expect their rewards in heaven.

Industrialization and urbanization, accelerating in the 1890s, began to undermine the traditional system. In both city and countryside, the extended family began to separate into individual households. In 1897 women comprised less than 2 percent of the labor force; of these 55 percent were servants, 25 percent field hands, 17 percent industrial workers (chiefly textiles), and 4 percent in educational and health services — the only fields open to educated women. By 1906 women comprised 5 percent of the industrial labor force and by 1913, 26 percent. They averaged only 47.7 percent of the daily earnings of men. Pregnancy meant automatic dismissal.

The 1897 census reported 79 percent illiteracy — 71 percent of the men and 87 percent of the women. (For both sexes, literacy varied with class and location; rural areas lagged far behind.) By 1914, due to a massive educational drive beginning in 1905, the illiteracy rate had fallen to roughly 60 percent — with *twice* as many men as women literate and *three times* as many boys as girls in school. (As the economic value of education became obvious, parents sent their sons, but considered education a luxury for their daughters, who would marry.) Women who utilized the expanding opportunities for higher education were primarily from the privileged classes. In the seventies, university-level courses, the "higher women's courses" were established in St. Petersburg, Moscow, Kiev, and Kazan. Authorized by the government, they were instituted by private initiative and dependent on private support. In 1872 the first medical school for women opened in Moscow and others followed. Graduates, called "learned midwives," could practice only on women and children. (The University of Moscow Medical School did not admit women until 1916.) None of these degrees carried the prestige of a degree from a regular university. Furthermore, higher education for women remained a touch and go affair, with many courses shut down in the period of reaction after 1881 and only some reopened. Thus, many women continued to study abroad. Nonetheless, on the eve of the Revolution, Russia was far ahead of western Europe in the number of women university graduates and, together with the United States, led the world in the production of women doctors.

These educated women, chafing at their lack of opportunity, developed a feminist movement strongly influenced by English feminism and unaffiliated with any political party. City based, comprised mainly of professional women and the intelligentsia, it stressed legal rights. One such group, the Mutual Philanthropic League, founded in 1895 by a woman doctor, gave scholarships to poor girls and combated prostitution. A League for Women's Equality, founded in 1905 by a group of Moscow professional women, joined the Union of Unions, a coalition of opposition groups dominated by the liberal party (the Cadets, or Constitutional Democrats), whose activities led directly to the Revolution of 1905; by 1907 the league comprised eighty branches. Prominent members included Anna Milyukova and Adriadna Tyrkova, both wives of Cadet leaders. Through the efforts of such women the Cadets supported female suffrage. Also in 1905, a woman physician founded a separate political party, the Women's Progressive Party.

Feminism grew rapidly after 1905. In 1908 the first All-Russian Conference of Feminists met. Called by the relatively conservative Mutual Philanthropic League, it encompassed a broad spectrum of opinion, from monarchist to socialist, but was basically liberal. The 1,045 delegates included only 45 workers and 1 peasant. Alexandra Kollontai, the leading Marxist feminist and the daughter of a Ukrainian nobleman, attended as a worker because of her role in unionizing women workers.

Most feminists demanded legal equality, equal access to education and employment, divorce reform, and birth control. Some favored female separatism while others urged their sisters to eschew materialism and power altogether and to work toward a society based on love and aesthetic creativity. The conference focused on suffrage, however, and by 1912 feminists had prevailed upon the Duma (Parliament) to enfranchise women. Though the bill, turned down by the Cabinet, never became law, women did gain equality in inheritance and modification of the passport system. In 1913 the Duma named International Woman's Day as a holiday, the female counterpart to Labor Day. The idea for the holiday originated at a 1910 International Socialist Conference in Copenhagen; its adoption by "bourgeois" feminist groups indicates their willingness to ally with others. In contrast, women workers placed less emphasis on legal reform and more on economic issues. They tended to see the "woman question" as a "struggle for bread" (Kollontai's words). In a wave of strikes from 1910 to 1914, organized independently of the major parties, they demonstrated their growing militance. Yet Marxist writings of the period persisted in referring to women workers as the "most backward stratum" of the proletariat, incapable of developing a revolutionary consciousness without party guidance. But, prodded by Kollontai, they did begin to realize the revolutionary potential of women.

Russian Marxism developed in the 1890s; heir to the populist revolutionary tradition, it also accepted the equality of women. But women were less prominent among the Marxists than they had been among the populists. True, Vera Zasulich, who had shot the governor general of St. Petersburg in 1878, helped to found the Social Democratic Workers' party in 1898, which split into Bolshevik (revolutionist) and Menshevik (gradualist) wings, but she was exceptional. Women terrorists tended to gravitate to the aegis of the neopopulist Socialist Revolutionaries, where they made themselves particularly prominent as assassins. Through terror they could express their rage as well as prove their revolutionary mettle. The Social Democrats condemned terror per se. (For some reason, teachers of both sexes supported the Socialist Revolutionaries.) E. D. Kuskova's *Credo* (1899), a statement emphasizing reform rather than revolution, remained the most important statement by a woman Marxist, and Kuskova herself later became a Menshevik.

The Bolsheviks lagged far behind the Mensheviks in organizing women workers; Kollontai was a Menshevik until 1914. The Bolsheviks concentrated on the militant, and almost uniformly male, metal and railroad workers and printers, considering the female textile workers "hopelessly backward." As an open party, the Mensheviks were more interested in numbers. The centralized and disciplined Bolshevik party structure may also account for their comparative lack of interest in women workers; men made policy and gave orders while women did routine work, thus institutionalizing preexisting biases. Nadezhda Krupskaya, one of the few women in high party circles, owed this to her position as Lenin's wife. As first secretary of Iskra, she handled much party correspondence. Lenin himself often relied on her judgment. Krupskaya called attention to the working women as early as 1900, but cannot be considered a feminist. The expertise she developed was in child care and education — traditional women's fields.

Marxists of both camps based their views on women on Engels's statement that as long as the man supports the woman "within the family, he is the bourgeois and the wife represents the proletariat." They agreed with Engels's conviction that household work was unproductive by definition (because it produces no commodities for exchange) and that the bourgeois family based on male supremacy must be destroyed. Only with economic independence can women be equal; society must be reconstructed to enable women to engage in productive work. But until pressed by feminists such as Inessa Armand and Alexandra Kollontai, Marxists had no specific program for woman workers.

Though Lenin was suspicious of feminism, before the war he came to recognize the revolutionary potential of women. Fearing the cooptation of the women's movement by bourgeois or reformist parties, he accepted the need to develop a concrete program designed to win women workers over. The first International Women's Day in 1913 served as a catalyst for Bolshevik feminism. A group of Bolshevik women marched in the parade and *Pravda,* the Bolshevik newspaper, ran an article entitled "Woman's Day and the Woman Worker." The following year, Lenin, Krupskaya, and Inessa Armand founded a newspaper, *Rabotnitsa* (*The Woman Worker*), which exhorted women to fight for socialism alongside "their" men. After this point, while feminist issues always remained secondary to Lenin, and he continued to oppose separate organizations for them, he became more responsive to women's problems. Most of the essays in his well-known pamphlet, *The Emancipation of Women,* date from this time. Though under pressure of civil war, he reluctantly consented to establishing a separate woman's section within the party, but he insisted that party discipline required all groups (women, trade unions, national minorities) to subordinate themselves to the center.

The program the Bolsheviks eventually adopted aimed to reorganize society so that women would not be forced to choose between "creative work" (outside the home) and motherhood. Assuming that women would desire many children, Lenin regarded birth control as an expression of "bourgeois defeatism" and Kollontai, in substance, agreed. They also believed that women's "biological infirmities" required protective legislation; it is not equality when women are forced to work beyond their strength, Kollontai insisted. To further equalize women workers, Bolsheviks planned communal facilities, such as dining rooms, child-care centers, laundries, and dormitories to free women from domestic drudgery and give them time for self-development. Whether these communal facilities would be staffed by men or women was not clear; the important thing was, in Kollontai's words, "the separation of the kitchen from marriage." The party took no stand on monogamy but most Bolsheviks lived conventional family lives. Most of them assumed that after the Revolution some form of marriage would prevail, but based on love rather than economic calculation. Divorce laws would be changed so marriage would last only as long as both parties desired. Alimony and child-support payments would be abolished. Instead, women would support themselves and society would assume the burdens of childrearing. Given all these conditions, the Bolsheviks concluded, complete sexual equality is only a matter of time. Instead of combating one another, men and women must realize their shared interests and fight for socialism together.

Basing their program on an egalitarian ideal, the Bolsheviks failed to discuss authority, hierarchy, and political power with reference to women; they expected that after a brief transition period classes would disappear and the state wither away. Similarly, they did not discuss who would do what work, nor who, if anyone, would become the experts; since all society would become "one big factory . . . with equality of work and equality of pay," it didn't really matter. Assuming that under communism productivity would increase and, sharing the ascetic lifestyle of their populist predecessors, they foresaw no problem in an equal distribution of the basic necessities of life. Sacrificing personal comfort, risking their lives for the sake of the Revolution, they expected others to do the same, at least until the economic basis of communism had been laid.

By the beginning of World War I, all the major parties were committed to women's equality; their disagreement consisted in what equality meant and on how to attain it. While the mass of peasant women remained untouched by feminism, women workers were conscious of the issues, and educated women were psychologically ahead of their western counterparts. Because of women's sacrifices during the war, the czarist government promised them the suffrage. More important, with their men drafted and poorly paid as soldiers, women were forced into the factories; by 1917 women made up 43 percent of the industrial labor force. The high casualty rate among soldiers (half of the 7,500,000 mobilized were killed, wounded, taken prisoner, or missing in action) created increasing numbers of women supporting entire families on their own low pay; inflation- and shortage-induced black markets rendered soldiers' pensions almost worthless.

The militance of 1910–1914 reviving, in the cities women began to organize, to strike, and to demonstrate. Indeed, women triggered the February Revolution of 1917. On International Woman's Day, women textile workers decided, against the advice of all parties, including the Bolsheviks, to call a general strike. Calling on women workers and on housewives standing on the bread lines, they appealed to the militant metalworkers of the Putilov works for support. Only reluctantly and after it became clear that the army would not fire, did men join them. By March 12 (February 27 O.S.) Czar Nicholas II had to abdicate. The Provisional Government formed to rule until the election of a Constituent Assembly became the first government of a major power to grant women the vote. Throughout 1917 women continued to organize into groups concerned with defending women's interests (variously defined). Recognizing the broad support these groups enjoyed, all the major parties, including the Bolsheviks, attempted to recruit women for their own ranks. In fact, the success of these groups was a factor in Lenin's decision to tolerate a separate women's bureau in the party and also, under pressure of civil war, Zhenotdel' (to be discussed subsequently). But the Provisional Government failed to solve the vital questions of peace, bread, and land;

its power disintegrated. Meeting scarcely any resistance, the Bolsheviks, on November 7 (October 25 o.s.) achieved an almost bloodless victory.

Women in a Period of Improvisation: 1917–1928

Very soon after assuming power, the Bolsheviks took steps to implement their program. For women this meant removing the legal props of male supremacy. In December 1917, the new government repealed all the czarist marriage and divorce laws and deprived the clergy of its power to perform marriages. After that date only registered civil marriages were valid. This reform also aimed to weaken the power of the Orthodox Church, since the Bolsheviks considered religion the major barrier to the spread of enlightened attitudes. Other legislation mandated equal pay for equal work (then unknown in the rest of the world), forbade the dismissal of pregnant women, and instituted paid maternity leave and nursing breaks. Elaborate labor codes designed to protect women's health prohibited hot, heavy, or hazardous work, night work, and overtime.

The Family Code of October 1918, a truly revolutionary document, abolished all distinctions between children born in or out of wedlock (the main distinction, inheritance rights, had already been abolished for everyone) and prohibited adoption. Within the home, man and woman each controlled his or her own earnings. A wife could retain her own name, establish her own residence, and have her own passport. Conjugal rights and community property no longer existed and each parent had equal authority over the children, who themselves had rights vis-à-vis their parents. Divorce could be obtained easily, and alimony was abolished except in the case of physical disability; men also qualified. The code specifically stated that women were expected to work.

The first commissar of social welfare, Alexandra Kollontai, devoted special attention to establishing model nurseries and prenatal care facilities. But a fire destroyed her Pre-Natal Care Palace and Model Nursery. Rumors were circulating, fed by extreme statements such as that of Zinaida Lilina, head of the Petrograd Education Department ("We have to take account of every child, we candidly say we must nationalize them") that the Bolsheviks would take children away from their parents by force. Kollontai herself hoped to persuade women to use the child-care centers by providing superior facilities, but all the Bolsheviks were agreed on the necessity of blunting the influence of the home. Kollontai resigned in March 1918. Economic disaster precluded the expenditure of funds for the communal facilities she considered essential for women.

All dreams of progress were thwarted by two years of bloody civil war beginning in June 1918. Women took jobs to support themselves while their men fought. Employment qualified them to receive extra food rations. Some communal agencies did develop, but as unavoidable crisis measures: instead of communal restaurants — soup kitchens; instead of especially designed dormitories — requisitioned homes where workers slept on the floor; instead of model nurseries — emergency shelters for homeless children where many died. In November 1920 desperation led to the legalization of abortion. The decree explicitly viewed abortion as a "necessary evil" and looked to improved conditions to obviate the need for it. In the interim, the regime urged the populace to use contraceptives, which, however, remained unknown and unavailable.

Civil war caused cities to empty out; the entire nation reverted to a primitive mode of life. De facto anarchy particularly harmed women because of the premium lawlessness placed on physical strength. Soldiers raped enemy women and even women on their own side. Half-educated Communists interpreted the attack on the bourgeois family to mean they could have any woman they chose. In at least two cities, Saratov, in agrarian southern Russia, and Vladimir, an industrial city not far from Moscow, local soviets proceeded to nationalize women. Saratov prohibited the "private ownership of women" and made it a crime to "refuse a Communist." Vladimir required all single men and women to register at a central marriage bureau and to select partners once a month. It declared all women over eighteen state property and gave all men the right to select any registered girl "even without her consent in the interests of the state." All children of such unions became state property. Though the party in Moscow revoked both decrees, they show the problems women faced before being regarded as equals. Under such conditions, and with the Bolshevik regime fighting for its life, the Bolsheviks had no choice but to defer the solution of the "woman question" until more peaceful times.

Comparatively few women became active combatants. Of the 63 women decorated for heroism and the 2,000 killed or wounded in action, most had been politically active before the Revolution. Among the opposition to Lenin, Maria Spiridonova led the "left" Socialist Revolutionaries, who attempted a coup against him in the summer of 1918, and Fanny Kaplan, an erstwhile terrorist, actually shot him on August 30, 1918, leaving a bullet lodged in his brain. Most women concentrated on the struggle for survival. Protective legislation became a dead letter and the prohibitions against night work and mining were formally repealed in 1919. Throughout the country, illiterate and unskilled women clustered in menial, dirty, and often dangerous jobs and were conscripted along with men for the labor armies formed by Trotsky in 1920; these detachments did work under conditions of military discipline that civilian labor avoided. Recognizing that illiteracy doomed women to the least desirable jobs, the Bolsheviks decreed compulsory education through the primary grades for both sexes but lacked the money to implement it.

The civil war ended in 1920; it cost 13,000,000 casualties (out of a total population of 136,000,000), 5,000,000 deaths from the famine of 1920–1921 alone, and left 7,000,000 homeless children to roam the countryside. Factories closed for lack of supplies, a "workers' opposition" developed within the Communist party, and revolutionary sailors of the Kronstadt garrison demanded "soviets without Communists." In 1921, in a startling about-face, Lenin instituted a New Economic Policy (NEP) of limited private trade in order to provide incentives for production. Rebuilding the shattered economy took first priority and absorbed all resources. Thus, the social support women needed in order to be truly equal remained unavailable. Most makeshift communal facilities were disbanded and their loss not particularly lamented in any case. Only women with no other choice used the few children's centers still operating. Women who worked did so out of necessity. Because they were still illiterate and unskilled, they worked primarily at menial jobs. Finally, protective legislation backfired; cost-conscious managers did not want to hire or train women (men were also unskilled) because paid maternity leave and nursing breaks made them more expensive to employ. Male workers resented maternity leave as a paid vacation. All during the NEP period unemployment persisted. Women were the last hired and first fired.

By 1928 women comprised 24 percent of the labor force — overwhelmingly widows, divorcées, and unmarried girls. Prostitution, though illegal, spread in the cities, testifying both to women's lack of alternatives and to the persistence of old mores. Under these conditions women who could stay home did so. On the other hand, the female illiteracy rate had dropped to 70 percent from the 1919 high of 90 to 95 percent (total illiteracy having risen due to decimation and emigration of the educated classes) and women constituted half the medical students.

Since the economic conditions for women's emancipation did not yet exist, Bolshevik policy focused on raising women's political and social consciousness. Traditional domesticity, the Bolsheviks realized, was the enemy of the new order; "reactionary" or "superstitious" (they meant religious) women tainted their children with their own attitudes. In the absence of jobs, other means of getting women out of the house and into public life were necessary. Thus, Lenin enjoined women to be politically active, to run for election to local soviets, and to take the initiative in social change. "Root out old habits," he said, "every cook must learn to rule the state." Lenin also exhorted his male comrades to practice at home the equality they preached outside. Anatole Lunacharsky, the commissar of enlightenment (education) stated, "A true Communist stays home and rocks the cradle" so that his wife can attend a party meeting or go to night school. But enforcing these views lay outside the capacities of the party. Instead, it urged women to make their own communal arrangements, to pool their efforts, and stressed the economic inefficiency of the individual household.

To facilitate the politicization of women, *Zhenotdel'* (Woman's Department) was formed as a division of the party. It originated at the November 1918 All-Russian Conference of Proletarian and Peasant Women. Under Kollontai's leadership, it concerned itself with the education and socialization of children, the recruitment of women for the Communist movement, and women's role in building socialism. Active in the civil war effort, Zhenotdel' later organized women workers and peasants. In the factories, the *delegatka* functioned as a combination shop steward, grievance counselor, and big sister — the latter being particularly important to the timid new arrivals from the countryside. The single most common grievance handled by Zhenotdel' dealt with male managers who used their plants as a harem.

Zhenotdel' also took women's side against male management, set up factory arbitration committees, and combated the tendency to fire women first. In addition, they selected some women for advanced training, sponsored outstanding women for election to local soviets, and helped women file applications for divorce. By helping women with their problems, the delegatka hoped to gain their confidence in order to form discussion groups, indoctrinate women in Marxist ideology, and recruit the most promising ones for party membership. Zhenotdel' was less effective in the countryside. The few women who could be persuaded to become activists were usually widows or divorcées. Younger women feared to flout their husband's or father's authority or to alienate potential suitors. Very dedicated, often trekking to remote villages on foot to set up "reading cabins," the delegatka accrued no material advantage from her activities. By the mid-twenties, half a million activists labored to raise the social consciousness of their sisters.

The most popular novel of the NEP period, Fedor Gladkov's *Cement!* features a delegatka as heroine. Attempting to lead her fellow peasant women out of domestic isolation, she sets an example by placing her own child in a children's shelter. Conditions there are abominable; waifs forage in the garbage for food, and her own child soon dies from neglect. Suppressing her personal feelings, she continues to regard communal childrearing as the only correct solution. Ultimately, she leaves her good but stupid husband because the party needs her more than he does. The novel depicts the human dimensions of a society in transition. "All is broken up, changed, and confused," she tells her husband, "somehow love will have to be arranged differently." In the meantime, the novel suggests, both men and women must focus on their work. Other novels of the NEP period carried a similar message; deliberately challenging traditional stereotypes, they describe a "new woman": serious, intelligent, independent, and completely dedicated to her work. Explicitly described as "not beautiful," she wears no make-up and is indifferent to fashion. Husband, lover, and children all take second place to her work in building socialism.

The existence of Zhenotdel' within the party remained precarious. Never sufficiently funded, it was twice rebuked for "overzealousness" in complaining about the material conditions oppressing women. Many male Communists also objected to the departments that dealt with women's affairs attached to party committees at every level and usually staffed by Zhenotdel'. Frequent changes in leadership diminished its clout in party circles. Furthermore, without the authority to make arrests or to impose fines, it depended on mobilizing public opinion by shaming or ridiculing the offender. In 1930, Stalin dissolved it.

Very different problems confronted the Bolsheviks in Central Asia. In 1923 the party launched a special effort to liberate Moslem women. The reasoning, too complex to be detailed here, was that liberating women was the best means to break up traditional Moslem society in order to facilitate greater party control. A series of laws prohibited bridal purchase, raised the marriage age to sixteen, discouraged polygamy, and gave women equal rights in marriage, divorce, inheritance, education, property, judicial proceedings, and positions in public service. Cadres of dedicated women activists went out to enforce the new law and to agitate among the women. The party commanded local functionaries to take the lead by removing their wives' veils and bringing the wives to public meetings, and activists urged women to divorce husbands who mistreated them. But the campaign failed. The party had not allocated resources sufficient to enable women to make the transition from seclusion to independence. Completely unskilled, many women who left their husbands became prostitutes in order to survive. Men used the laws against polygamy to cast out their older wives, whose own families, feeling disgraced, would not take them in. Most important, the party had seriously underestimated the ferocity and fanaticism of male resistance. Men killed their own wives for removing the veil and local courts did not punish them for it. Local party functionaries dragged their feet on implementing the laws. In 1927, a campaign of terror began against independent women — 200 of them were kidnapped, raped, and even murdered in Uzbekistan alone. By 1928, a powerful counterrevolutionary movement emerged led by the Moslem priests called *cadis*. The common desire to keep women subjugated transcended class conflict and soon threatened party control of the area itself. In 1929, Stalin personally called a halt to the campaign because he needed the cooperation of local authorities for the Five-Year Plan.

The "Sexual Revolution"

Relations between men and women changed. High war casualties had created a shortage of men, and the new morality of free love made husbands hard to find. Easy divorce laws enabled a man to "walk off, happily whistling," leaving woman and children behind. Men suffered no financial penalty in divorce, and women lagged far behind economically, socially, and psychologically. Trying to get or to keep husbands, they tended to defer to men. On the other hand, among young Communists, a crude form of Kollontai's theory that the sexual act carries no more significance than "drinking a glass of water" prevailed. Promiscuity came to signify emancipation from traditional mores; a girl who rebuffed a man's advances could be accused of "bourgeois prudery." Both the birthrate and the number of abortions rose markedly. In the countryside, men would sometimes assent to a religious ceremony, which, naive girls failed to realize, lacked legal validity. Lenin himself denounced the "glass of water" theory before his death. "No sane man," he said, "would lie down to drink from a puddle in the gutter or even drink from a dirty glass." Communists must apply their energies to building socialism instead of dissipating them in "libertine habits." Free love he considered a form of "bourgeois hedonism," not a proletarian demand. But during the twenties Kollontai's theory had more influence on the young. Kollontai herself, because of her involvement with the "workers' opposition" of 1921 was persona non grata to Lenin; her appointment as ambassador to Norway really meant exile.

By 1925, the bourgeois family was clearly disintegrating. Many Bolsheviks welcomed its demise as the symbol of the old order. But the socialist family held together by love had not materialized (whether the "socialist family" meant voluntary permanent monogamy, serial monogamy, or communal living remained unclear), and the number of destitute women and children rose rapidly. Letters to the press decried the sexual exploitation of the most vulnerable members of society as unsocialist. One cited the phenomenon of "spongers" living off the earnings of working girls. And Sofia Smidovich, who headed Zhenotdel' from 1922 to 1924, demanded the restoration of family stability.

Though accurate statistics are unavailable, by 1926 the increasing number of destitute women and children caused alarm in party circles and engendered a revision of the Family Code. Aiming to protect the women and children of broken unions, the 1926 code sanctioned common-law marriage. For support purposes, cohabitation meant marriage. Recognizing the difficulty women faced in getting jobs, alimony could be granted for one year, whether or not the marriage was registered, and the man had to support the children. Illegitimate children had the same right to support, and all women could file paternity suits. If a woman did not know who the father was, she could name all the possibilities and each would then be partially responsible for the child. In other words, a child could have several legal fathers. The same code instituted the "postcard divorce" (a postcard constituted sufficient notice to the other party); court proceedings dealt only with financial arrangements and could not deny the divorce itself.

After the 1926 revision, divorce rose rapidly — 450 percent in Petrograd and 300 percent in Moscow alone. Women initiated over 60 percent of divorce actions in the hope of getting support from men who had abandoned them. In the countryside, however, peasant women rarely sued for divorce. But there were cases of peasants taking wives for a season, using their field labor, and then divorcing them after the harvest. Since few peasants had personal property, the courts fixed support payments in terms of food, but collection was nearly impossible. In the cities, men simply disappeared. The courts tended to allot one-third of a man's earnings for support. But as the incidence of multiple divorce rose, meaningful support for two or more former wives became impossible. In one case, a man's entire earnings went to his three former wives and their children while he lived with a fourth wife on alimony from her five previous husbands. Another man had twenty former "wives," each with a child. As the concept of what constituted a family became blurred, the words "husband" and "wife" tended to be used quite loosely.

Kollontai's "glass of water" theory must be understood in the context of the above situation. Man-woman relations, she believed, were still in a state of transition; men did not yet recognize women as equals. They used romance to bend the woman to their will and for her, love became a fetter. As a sensual person herself, Kollontai did not expect women to live without sex. She believed the double standard must end; women must learn to treat sex as a purely physical need and avoid emotional involvement. "If love begins to enslave [the woman], she must make herself free; she must step over all the love tragedies and go her own way." The heroines of her novels are all career women who find fulfillment in work and do not depend on any one man. The heroine of *Love of Three Generations* considers monogamy a form of bourgeois possessiveness; no one belongs to anyone. Pregnant, possibly by her mother's lover, her only regret is that the abortion will cause her to lose time from work. The heroine of *Red Love* is a party worker who leaves her career for marriage but chafes at domesticity. Her husband, however, leaves her for a more traditional woman who caters to him. Despite the approaching divorce, this heroine bears her child. Having found fulfillment in motherhood and work (she has returned to her job with the party), she overcomes the sentiment of jealousy and truly regards the "other woman" as a sister.

Kollontai believed that once pure communism had been attained, both the egoism of men and the submissiveness of women would disappear. Romantic love and sex could then be reunited. "Maternal egoism" (placing one's own child before other's) would also end. All society would be one happy family.

Party leaders, however, thought her optimism premature. By 1927, David Riasanov, then the leading Marxist theoretician, began to fulminate against the "libertinism" of the younger generation, arguing that a "light and casual attitude toward marriage" fosters general social irresponsibility. Marriage, he said, is not just a personal act but has deep social significance. Still uncomfortable with the idea of legislating personal morality, the party began to promulgate an image of Marx and Engels as exemplary family men and to give couples whose marriages were officially registered priority in the allocation of scarce housing. Apart from these measures, the party simply did not know what to do.

Students of law are themselves divided over whether law merely reflects the social consensus or can be a factor in creating it, but there is no question that the legal policy of the Bolsheviks aimed to destroy the bourgeois family, as the prime social institution of the old regime and very much bound up with the religion they were also combating, in order to bring up the younger generation in the spirit of communism, utilize the productive capacities of women in building socialism, and create a new socialist consciousness. The hardships endured by women during this period did not, however, result solely from changes in the family law but from a combination of several factors, including brutalization of the population by the ferociousness of the civil war, a continuing struggle for existence on the economic level, and contempt for "bourgeois morality." (The latter was strongest among young Communists; the older generation lived conventional family lives.) The easy divorce laws, however, exacerbated the situation, and even after the harm to women and children became obvious, the destruction of the bourgeois family continued to have high priority for many Bolsheviks. The vagueness of their own conceptions of what kind of family, if any, would replace it militated against a more aggressive effort on behalf of those caught up in the throes of the transition period.

Women in the Stalin Period: 1928–1953

Stalin's accession to power brought the institution of a totally planned economy. Bolsheviks had long viewed massive industrialization as the means to equality. The first Five-Year Plan (1929–1934) aimed to build the infrastructure of a modern Communist society. Featuring heavy industry and collectivization of agriculture, it skimped on consumer goods. Subsequent plans followed the same pattern of deliberately holding down consumption in order to maximize resources for investment.

Until mechanization could occur, hands still had to be used, thus creating a demand for labor. In order to enlist women, the party drew up lists of occupations deemed especially suitable for them (assembly-line work in factories) and strengthened protective legislation. Each year the percentage of women in the labor force increased: from 24 percent in 1928 to 26.7 percent in 1930, 31.7 percent in 1934, 35.4 percent in 1937. Though many women were peasants displaced by collectivization, they made good workers, registering fewer absences, latenesses, and industrial accidents than men did and showing more amenability to factory discipline.

Stalin's first Five-Year Plan had the aura of a military campaign. The slogan "Catch up to and surpass America!" implied that through struggle and sacrifice, Russians could realize their dream of universal prosperity. Despite a sharp drop in the standard of living, they were enthusiastic and believed the privation to be only temporary. In this atmosphere protective legislation was often ignored. Women filled the most arduous jobs: pulling, hauling, digging ditches, maintaining roads. Illiterate and unskilled, they did not qualify for the most attractive positions. Many were simply drafted and sent to work in the wilderness without proper tools, shelters, and food. In four years, young workers, most of them girls, built over 1,500 industrial plants. Popular literature glorified muscular heroines who could do anything a man could do: the idea of "woman's work" became obsolete.

In 1931 efforts were made to upgrade the skills of the entire labor force, including women. Wage differentials for skilled workers replaced identical wages for all workers. The factory training schools established female quotas; by 1934 women comprised 50 percent of their students. In 1935, on a technical proficiency test compulsory for all workers, women outperformed men in the younger age groups. Women were promoted to supervisory positions and, after 1934, became Stakhanovites (workers who markedly exceed their production norms and are held up as models). On the new collective farms, where model statutes decreed that women be paid in their own name, women became tractor drivers, section managers, brigade leaders, and even chairpersons.

An intensified drive to eradicate illiteracy increased opportunities for both sexes. By 1934 a network of primary schools covered the countryside, and the number of secondary schools increased rapidly. Female quotas in technical training institutes and universities made higher education more accessible to women. Each university department reserved 25 percent of its places for women, particularly benefiting women applicants in science, mathematics, engineering, and agricultural technology. Though accurate statistics on the number of women before the quotas are unavailable, it is clear that previously few women applied for these fields and even fewer had been admitted.

The party itself made sustained efforts to recruit women and to place them in prominent positions on local soviets, people's courts, and factory committees. Though exact figures are unavailable, women did begin to work their way up. We know that the percentage of women in the party rose from 8.2 percent in 1925 to 15.9 percent in 1932 and that by 1933 girls comprised half the members of the *Komsomol* (Young Communist League).

The impact of all these changes varied. For younger women, work provided the means to independence, and increased opportunities for training created the possibility of upward mobility. Many chose not to marry. Jobs and child-care centers in which unmarried women had priority permitted any woman to have children. As a result, some men accused women of flaunting their independence. Older women, on the other hand, expressed bitterness and confusion. They disliked assembly-line work, but for them it was too late to learn new skills. Child-care facilities were included in the first Five-Year Plan, but did not expand rapidly enough to keep pace with demand. Even by 1936 only a small percentage of preschool children could be accommodated, and most married women still did not work. Moreover, the original plan to have twenty-four-hour child-care facilities could not be implemented, so working women could not attend night school or take correspondence courses. As shortages developed, plant managers tended to shift funds from child-care facilities to direct investment in production. By 1935 the hours had been reduced to cover the mother's working time only. Combining work and motherhood became increasingly difficult, and the birthrate plummeted.

Primitive housing conditions may also account for women's increasing reluctance to bear children. The plan did not provide sufficient new housing for the millions of workers flooding into the cities. Often entire families crowded into one room. Few houses had running water or electricity. Hot water and central heating were almost unknown. Carrying water in buckets, chopping wood, hauling fuel for the stove, consumed the woman's time and energy. Factory cafeterias served lunch only. As late as 1935 only 180 laundries existed in all of Russia. Doing the weekly washing involved a full day's work, so working women did it on their day off or at night. Laborsaving devices, like most consumer goods, were not manufactured, and most men refused to help at home with "woman's work." In the newer industrial areas, worse conditions prevailed. At Magnitogorsk, a steel city in the Ural Mountains, tents and dugouts provided the only shelter against the bitter winter winds. Visitors reported waitresses at the workers' cafeteria picking lice out of each other's hair, an example of the absymal sanitary conditions. At the Dnepestroi Dam site, single women slept on plank beds, in crowded barracks, surrounded by wailing infants.

The family continued to disintegrate. No correspondence existed between formally registering a marriage and its stability, and marriage entailed little status or material advantage for either sex. Being a housewife was condemned, and inflationary pressures created a need for the wife's salary. The economic advantages of shared living expenses, plus sex, were attainable without formal marriage. And marriage did not necessarily denote companionship; industrial plants operated around the clock with no common day off, so a couple working different shifts rarely saw each other. At home, overcrowding frayed the nerves. By 1934, unsupervised children constituted a serious juvenile delinquency problem.

The sexual counterrevolution of the mid-1930s promoted a return to a conventional family structure, a pronatalist policy, and the promotion of a puritanical sexual morality. It resulted from several factors: the hardship suffered by abandoned wives and their children, official dismay at sexual permissiveness, and the precipitous decline in the birthrate after 1934. Sexual individualism and personal hedonism conflicted with the collectivist attitudes desired by the regime.

The 1930 official rehabilitation of the family as a socialist institution turned out to be a harbinger of the new policy. Party theoreticians now emphasized the necessity of a stable family structure but continued to oppose bourgeois patriarchal authority based on women's economic dependence. In 1934, Stalin with great publicity visited his aged mother in the Caucasus and that same year a new law held parents legally liable for the vandalism of their children and gave the entire family collective responsibility for the treason, defection, or state crime of any of its members. Homosexuality became a criminal offense punishable by hard labor. Circular letters had restricted abortion since 1931. At the clinic in Kuznetsk, in eastern Siberia, abortion could be performed only to save the mother's life. The 1936 decrees restricting divorce and abolishing legal abortion culminated the return to traditional morality. "The foul and poisonous idea of the liquidation of the family," Stalin announced in 1936, "is a false rumor . . . spread by enemies of the people." High fees introduced for divorce rose steeply for a second and third instance, and records of divorce were included in the labor books of both parties. The decree abolishing legal abortion stated that since the conditions necessitating the original decree of 1920 had been overcome, "mass abortions for egoistic reasons cannot be tolerated." *Izvestia* and *Pravda* editors scolded women who wrote letters of protest. They denied that childbirth was a personal matter and implied that women who failed to bear many children lacked faith in the socialist future. In a sense, this policy was a logical conclusion of earlier attitudes. Even Kollontai regarded childbearing as a social duty. She believed that a pregnant woman "does not belong to herself . . . she is working for the collective . . . from her own flesh and blood she is producing a new unit of labor." To meet some of the specific protests, Stalin promised increased maternity leave, more and better child-care centers, and improved housing, but not contraceptives. Since Russian women had been using abortion *instead* of birth control, the new law resulted in a steep rise in the birthrate: 18 percent for Russia as a whole, 100 percent in Moscow. However, in 1938, military preparedness led to the reduction of maternity leave to the pre-1936 level.

Women still worked but the new emphasis on motherhood hampered their upward mobility. Anticipating women to be frequently pregnant, managers hesitated to train them. Unallayed domestic responsibilities deflected women's time and energy away from activities leading to promotion. Also, in 1936, Stalin terminated the 50 percent female quotas in the factory training schools and technical institutes. Since women were now equal, he said, special measures were no longer necessary. By 1938 the number of women in technical institutes had dropped to a startling 27 percent; after 1938 these figures ceased to be published. The doors opened to women during the first Five-Year Plan were shut, except to a minority. Only universities made no serious attempt to limit women and their number continued to rise. In 1941 women composed 57 percent of the student body (already reflecting mobilization for the war); they studied teaching, medicine, law, mathematics, agronomy, economics, engineering, and all the sciences. But the majority of women still worked in the lowest-skilled, most easily replaceable job categories, including arduous physical labor.

Literature reflected the new emphasis. Earlier heroines had been almost sexless, the plot being girl meets tractor. Married couples when depicted in bed discussed the Five-Year Plan, their children, if any existed, nowhere in evidence. But the post-1936 female, a kind of superwoman, not only made a "serene home" for her husband but had many children and still equaled her husband's performance on the job. Novels and speeches lauded the joys of motherhood and pitied the childless, while posters of happy, large families appeared all over the Soviet Union. The popular child-care manual, Anton Makarenko's *A Book for Parents,* lauded the large family as the place where collective attitudes are first learned and castigated men who abandoned their wives and children. His pedagogy, stressing discipline and subordination to the group, replaced the more individualistic pedagogy of Lunacharsky, who had been dismissed as commissar of enlightenment in 1931. Makarenko's philosophy emphasized the responsibility of all age groups to society.

Article 122 of the Soviet Constitution of 1936 reads:

> Women in the USSR have equal rights with men in all branches of economic, cultural, social, and political life.
>
> The implementation of these rights of women is assured by granting women the same rights as men to work, to pay, to social insurance and education and by government protection of mothers and children, by

> paid maternity leave, and by a wide network of maternity homes, children's *crèches,* nursery schools and kindergartens.

Like the entire constitution, this article bore little relation to Soviet reality; at best it can be considered a statement of a still remote ideal. In 1936 the "great terror" began. Women, too unimportant to be purged, numbered only 10 percent of the victims. But this 10 percent included women working their way up the hierarchy and almost all the older generation of women activists, thus removing all but a few women from the higher levels of Soviet society. Moreover, women whose husbands were arrested suffered heavy secondary pressures, such as being fired from their jobs or evicted from their lodgings unless they got divorced.

Mobilization, with its new demands for workers, brought about a renewed effort to recruit women into the work force. Once again they were urged to improve their skills, and after 1941 figures on the number of women in key segments of the economy again became available. For example, in one year, 1941–1942, the percentage of women steam engine operators rose from 6 percent to 33 percent and similar dramatic increases occurred among tractor drivers, locomotive engineers, steam compressor operators, electricians, and welders — all highly paid occupations. By 1945 women composed 56 percent of the labor force, a majority of the miners and a third of the workers in the Baku oil fields. Crucial to the home front, women worked fourteen to eighteen hours a day, often under severe conditions, as in factories hastily evacuated to Siberia with roofs but no walls. Asked if she were tired, a young girl replied: "Tired? Our men are giving their lives for us. How dare I be tired?" Meanwhile, Grandma kept house and minded the children. Women also engaged in actual combat for the Red Army, most often in guerrilla units but also as machine gunners and snipers; no unit lacked women altogether. Women joined the medical and signal corps and several air regiments consisted entirely of women. The unit that captured Hitler's chancellery had a woman major.

After the war, the loss of 20,000,000 men, out of a total population of 170,000,000, severely disrupted the Soviet demographic balance. A woman recalls, "I know of no one — no one — who did not lose a husband, a son, or a lover." Desire to replenish population added to the party's fear of a postwar relaxation of morality and discipline caused a revision of the Family Code in 1944 along still more conservative and pronatalist lines. To prevent wholesale abandonment by returning soldiers in search of younger women, divorce became extremely difficult. As an incentive for the man to stay in the family, other changes made him de facto head of household and favored him in inheritance, which had been gradually reintroduced since the twenties. A reversal of previous policy deprived illegitimate children of inheritance rights and stigmatized them by a line drawn through the space for "father's name" on their identity cards. Women lost their right to file paternity suits. All this was aimed at creating the stable social climate deemed conducive to large families. For women who did not have husbands, however, to stimulate them to bear children and to prevent recourse to illegal abortion, the state assumed direct responsibility for illegitimate children's support at a fixed rate. Two years later, however, the rate was halved, thus shifting the major burden to the mothers. Special honors were provided, including cash subsidies, for large families. Ten children made a woman a Mother Heroine and seven entitled her to an Order of Maternal Glory. The same law introduced family allowances for three or more children and halved their fees for crèches (for children under three), nursery schools, and kindergartens, all financed by a new tax levied on single persons and couples with fewer than three children.

After the war, reconstruction absorbed all resources. The industrial heartland of European Russia lay in ruins and huge tracts of formerly fertile farmland had become scorched earth. Much of the existing housing had been destroyed by the war, and both communal facilities and consumer goods remained unavailable. A significant number of women became doctors, engineers, and scientists; indeed, the shortage of men worked to their advantage professionally. Others continued to be skilled workers; the labor shortage prevented their wholesale displacement by returning war veterans. But these women constituted a small proportion of the total female labor force; the overwhelming majority of women remained concentrated in the lower echelons of the economic ladder. They built the roads, dug the ditches, shoveled the snow, labored on the construction sites, and worked in the fields. As late as the 1950s, women made up four-fifths of the unskilled laborers. And the male deficit militated against equality in personal life as women catered to men.

The experience of Soviet women during the Stalin era brings the question of priorities into sharp focus. True, the planners could not create the material conditions for equality overnight. But they had a choice — between forced-draft industrialization (including collectivization) and a slower but more balanced scheme of economic development that included consumer goods. Despite the fact that stinting on consumer goods and communal amenities weighed particularly heavily on women, they chose forced-draft industrialization for military, ideological, and political reasons. Well before the success of Hitler, Stalin aimed to increase the military might of the Soviet Union. Ideologically, gradual economic development (Bukharin's plan) meant continuing the mixed economy that benefited peasants far more than workers. And the political factor, the tremendous power accruing to those who control the economy, must not be discounted as a reason for Stalin's choice. Not only did women's well-being have low priority in the original plan, but as necessity dictated cuts in the budget, women's needs (length of maternity leave, hours of child-care-center operation) were cut first. And there is no evidence that the sexual counterrevolution, which negated so many of the women's gains, was unpopular in the higher echelons of the party; the planners themselves, apparently, were ambivalent about the equality they preached.

Women in the Period Since Stalin: 1953–1974*

An era ended suddenly with Stalin's death in 1953. His successors, committed to raising the standard of living and to partial liberalization, legalized abortion in 1955, eased the strict divorce law in 1968, built vast quantities of new housing, and markedly increased the number of child-care centers. Consumer goods, while still expensive, are now slowly becoming available. Women have made important gains over the prerevolutionary period and in comparison to other industrial nations but many complex problems remain.

Most impressive perhaps is the high number of Soviet professional women; in 1970 they comprised 73 percent of the doctors, 35.4 percent of the lawyers, a third of the engineers, well over a third of all scientists, and over half the technicians and certified specialists. Some of the top mathematicians are women, and one of the recent astronauts was a woman. Women work in all segments of the economy. The educational gap between the sexes has been eradicated; indeed, more women than men complete secondary school. Almost all births now occur in hospitals, and infant mortality figures rank among the world's lowest. Soviet women get fifty-six days paid maternity leave before and after childbirth, and the leave can be extended to a year (without pay) without loss of job, pension rights, or seniority. Stringent antirape laws exist, defining various degrees of rape. A male manager, for example, who uses his position to pressure a woman into sexual relations can be charged with taking advantage of her economic or occupational dependency.

Yet Soviet women are still not total economic and political equals. The top echelons of Soviet society, providing the greatest power and financial rewards, remain predominantly male. Within the professions, women's fields have emerged. Medicine is not a well-paid profession, possibly because it has become a woman's profession. The best-paid specialty, surgery, is predominantly male. Law does not pay well either, and the judges and prosecutors of the higher courts are usually men. The pattern can be found

* Since this essay was written, certain statistics may have changed.

in all the professions and occupations; women cluster at the middle and lower ranges. Among skilled workers, for example, women comprise 37 percent of the machinists and metalworkers, but of these 73 percent operate simple machines such as drills. Even in engineering, a particularly prestigious profession in the USSR, women are concentrated in food and consumer goods technology. No woman holds a high office in the Soviet Academy of Science and only very recently have any begun to head research and university departments. In industry, women are 6 percent of the factory directors and 12 percent of the chief engineers. However, women managers tend to supervise other women. In agriculture, the number of women heads of collective farms has remained constant since 1939.

In the political hierarchy, women constitute over a third of the top legislative bodies, the Supreme Soviet and the Council of Nationalities. But an analysis of their personnel reveals a high turnover rate, suggesting tokenism. Until Khrushchev appointed Ekaterina Furtseva (who began her career as a mineralogical engineer), no woman sat on the Presidium of Ministers. After her death, her place was taken by a man. Khrushchev, lamenting the fact that "men administer and women do the work," advocated the promotion of women in all areas of Soviet life. Women comprise 45 percent of local soviets, but all these bodies tend merely to rubber-stamp decisions already made by the Communist party. Though women constitute 20 percent of party members, they number only 4 percent of high officials, and no woman sits on the Central Committee. Indeed, since 1917, only eighty-four women, most of them first-generation Bolsheviks, have risen high enough to fill any of the 4,600 possible positions in leading bodies. Women remain scarce in politically sensitive positions, such as the diplomatic corps and radio and television commentary. They constitute 12.3 percent of the Writers' Union; nonmembers do not have access to publication.

The fact that comparatively few women have reached the top reflects the educational late start of Soviet women. But if not for the impetus given women by the demand for trained personnel during the first Five-Year Plan and World War II (mobilization and then high war casualties forced the lifting of restrictions on training women) their number might well be lower. Women in the thirty to forty age range now moving up are also the beneficiaries of the low birthrate during the war years. Current figures reveal younger women work at dead-end jobs in the middle ranges of the job hierarchy. The subject "what kind of work should women do?" appears frequently in articles in the Soviet press, with no consensus among either women or men yet evident. And differential education sometimes tracks boys and girls.

Moreover, women are overrepresented at the lower economic levels. In 1969, women comprised half the labor force but earned only a quarter of the total wages. Many women do piecework, for which wages often fall below the official minimum. The 1969 Labor Code excludes pregnant women from overtime and all women from certain highly paid categories considered unhealthful or dangerous, night work, and out-of-town assignments. Women who wish these jobs, however, may sign a statement absolving management of responsibility for damages. Heavy physical labor for women, now regarded as a relic of a more backward era, seems to be disappearing. Increasingly, women predominate in clerical work, light assembly-line jobs, the postal service, and public transportation. The low-paid textile industry is almost exclusively female.

Women's unequal achievement is now openly recognized and the reasons for it discussed. Most frequently blamed is the "dual burden" of domestic responsibilities and job. Housekeeping continues to be considered "woman's work" despite constant exhortations from the media for men to help. The Official Principles of Marriage and the Family (1968) holds up the ideal of domestic equality — complete sharing of domestic responsibilities. Soviet women have neither the adequate communal facilities envisioned by the old Bolsheviks nor the appliances of the West. In 1970, according to Soviet figures only 38 percent of apartments in the highly industrialized Moscow-Leningrad area had refrigerators. Poor storage facilities necessitate daily shopping, and food distribution remains inefficient, with long queues that consume an incredible amount of time the norm. Laundry is done in the bathtub and cooking on a one-burner stove. Twenty-five percent of the city dwellers share kitchen and bath; this represents an improvement, since fifteen years ago the figure was 70 percent with hot water in only 2.2 percent of urban apartments. Women tend to spend their evenings and weekends on domestic chores while men are free; they also, according to a recent survey, get one hour less sleep a night. A vicious cycle results; tired women produce less on the job, thereby providing apparent justification for the reluctance to train or promote them. Women themselves opt out of the competition for the top jobs and avoid demanding ones.

Other factors also affect women's occupational choice and limit their ambition. Most important is abiding male resistance to women in authority. Often alluded to but rarely discussed explicitly, it poses a difficult barrier. Men of all social strata are reluctant to take orders from women. Soviet women managers report great personal strains; under constant pressure to prove themselves, they feel they dare not make a mistake. To be treated as equals, they claim, women must be better.

Child care poses the most complex problem of all. Child-care facilities, expanding very rapidly in recent years, still fall short of demand. In Moscow 50 percent of preschool children are accommodated; throughout the Union, 20 percent (1970 statistics; by now they are higher). Facilities close for the summer, however, and only children over seven are eligible for camp. And increasingly sophisticated Soviet parents, mindful of the importance of early childhood for the formation of personality, now demand quality care. While more money can help solve these problems, it does not solve the problem of the children under three, only 10 percent of whom are in crèches. Plans to build more crèches have been dropped because existing ones report empty spaces. Reluctant to place an infant in an institution, many Soviet parents leave it with a grandmother or a neighbor. But increasingly Grandmother works also, and her daughter returns to work as soon as her paid leave expires. A recent study demonstrated that the mothers who take a full year off are the affluent and educated. This discontinuity still leaves them with the problem of keeping up with developments in their field. As a result, in European Russia, even in the rural areas, the one-child family prevails. In general, child-care facilities and consumer goods are far less available in the countryside, and the standard of living far lower.

Raising the low birthrate is still a goal of the regime. In the late fifties, academician Stanislav G. Striumilin proposed placing all children in separate children's cities with provision for parental visits on weekends. Among other advantages, he said, women would be free for real careers. The proposal provoked such an outcry, from both women and men, that Khrushchev personally disavowed it. Since then, proposals have focused on reducing the woman's working day with a proportionate decrease in pay, raising family allowances to cover the actual cost of childrearing, and paying the mother (but not the father) to stay home until the child reaches three. The latter is already policy in Poland, Hungary, and Czechoslovakia. Some women object to the above proposals because they place women at a competitive disadvantage in hiring and promotion; these critics insist that fathers should do their part. Other women, believing that the infants need their mother, support such measures. The man is still regarded as the primary breadwinner. Wives of high officials rarely work and 10 percent of all women are officially classified as housewives (a low figure compared with the United States, but high compared with the recent Soviet past). On the other hand, a recent survey indicated that while many men preferred their wives to stay home, the wives themselves chose working over having another child. A higher standard of living, the bargaining power of an independent income, and for some, job satisfaction, prevail over the supposed joys of motherhood.

A single image of the ideal Soviet woman no longer exists. Articles in the press call for a "return to chivalry," for putting women "on a pedestal," for the "special equality of socialist humanism." The latter means recognition of women's special needs, i.e., protective legislation. One writer maintained "female beauty is not a bourgeois prejudice" and one result of the high divorce rate is governmental injunctions for women to pay heed to their appearance. Beauty parlors are proliferating, and the use of cosmetics has doubled in the past ten years. Possibly a new image of women combining conventional femininity with employment is in process.

The official policy remains conventional, with the family regarded as the basic social cell. An actual marriage ceremony became compulsory in 1968 as did a one-month waiting period before issuance of the license. Younger women will not tolerate unsatisfactory husbands; for them no male deficit exists. Better educated than their mothers, they can support themselves. Though official pronouncements on sexual morality are almost prudish, a survey in Odessa revealed that young men and women both considered sex a physical need and saw no point to waiting for marriage. Indeed, many did not intend to marry at all.

In the cities, younger women have achieved a negative equality, a veto power in personal life. But the positive equality of marriages characterized by love and equal domestic responsibilities remains elusive. In the countryside, change proceeds more slowly. And in both cases, the larger contours of women's world continue to be shaped by a male elite.

Conclusion

The early Bolsheviks assumed that women's subordination was a product of economic backwardness. Once the economic basis of communism had been laid, they expected full equality to follow as a matter of course. They underestimated the difficulties involved in changing consciousness (including their own). Their technological orientation plus Soviet isolation in a hostile world led them to give first priority to economic development. Thus, the Bolsheviks implemented only part of the program. As it worked out, they liberated women more for their labor power than for their personal fulfillment; women became workers but remained housewives and mothers under extremely difficult conditions. The barriers to women's achievement came down precisely in those areas where brains and skills were scarce, hence, women advanced most during labor shortage. Only recently has a concentrated effort begun to improve women's conditions of life. Whether this will lead to true equality as the shortage of labor ends remains to be seen. More than any other single factor, the regime's present pro-natalist policy makes predictions difficult.

Most important, the possibility that noneconomic factors created a predisposition to slight women's needs must not be overlooked. Of these, two are especially important, the premium socialism places on self-sacrifice and the monopolization of power by a male elite. Like their populist predecessors, the Bolsheviks exalted self-sacrifice; they regarded egoism as a sin and comfort as bourgeois. But because traditional Russian society raised women to be altruists, revolutionary values rendered women particularly vulnerable to exploitation. During the twenties, Bolshevik women were often charged with being more feminist than Marxist; once they accepted altruism, they had difficulty defending their own interests. Even Kollontai, the most militant of the Marxist feminists, spoke approvingly of women's "special proneness" to make sacrifices. The same social conditioning led men to expect self-sacrifice from women. As the planners they were in a position to enforce their views. Thus, little was done to assuage the hardships suffered by women in the twenties. In the thirties women's needs, considered luxuries, were last in the budget and likely to be cut first. Even today, the sectors of the economy affecting women, such as the food-distribution system, are among the least efficient of Soviet society.

Today's Soviet women, finally beginning to demand attention to their needs, are themselves in disagreement over what those needs are. Basic issues, such as the kind of work women should do and whether or not women should stay home while the children are young, are still in the discussion stage. Furthermore, different conditions of life in today's highly stratified Soviet society may well give rise to different objective needs. Planning for the needs of all women is more difficult in a variegated society than a simple one, particularly if the attempt be made to allow scope for choice of lifestyle on an individual level. Simply admitting women to the ruling elite may not solve the problem. Elite status, with its special privileges and comforts, may itself create different interests, may itself change the perception of its members; the view from the top is different from that at the bottom. One cannot assume that women who "make it" will be less susceptible to the callousness of power, more sensitive to the needs of ordinary people, both women and men, than male elites have been in the past.

Suggestions for Further Reading

This chapter is based primarily on Russian sources; the purpose of this selected bibliography is to provide suggestions for further reading. Because of the highly controversial nature of much of the material, a variety of views are included.

Books

Benet, Shula, ed. *The Village of Viriatino: An Ethnographic Study of a Russian Village from Before the Revolution to the Present.* Doubleday, New York, 1970.

Brown, Donald, ed. *Women in the Soviet Union.* Teachers College Press, New York, 1968.

Dodge, Norton. *Women in the Soviet Economy.* Johns Hopkins, Baltimore, 1966.

Feifer, George. *The Girl from Petrovka.* Curtis, New York, 1971.

Geiger, Kent. *The Family in the Soviet Union.* Harvard University Press, Cambridge, 1968.

Hollander, Paul. *Soviet and American Society.* Oxford University Press, New York, 1973.

Kollontai, Alexandra. *Autobiography of a Sexually Emancipated Communist Woman.* Herder & Herder, New York, 1971.

Lenin, V. I. *On the Emancipation of Women.* Progress, Moscow, 1972.

Madison, Bernice. *Social Welfare in the Soviet Union.* Stanford University Press, Stanford, 1968.

Mandel, William. *Soviet Women.* Doubleday, New York, 1975.

Massell, Gregory. *The Surrogate Proletariat.* Princeton University Press, Princeton, 1974.

St. George, George. *Our Soviet Sister.* Luce, Washington, D.C., 1973.

Schlesinger, Rudolf. *The Family in the U.S.S.R.: Documents and Readings.* Routledge and Kegan Paul, London, 1949.

Serebrennikov, G. F. *The Position of Women in the U.S.S.R.* V. Gollancz, London, 1937.

Trotsky, Leon. *Women and the Family.* Pathfinder, New York, 1970.

Winter, Ella. *Red Virtue.* Harcourt Brace, New York, 1933.

Zetkin, Clara. *Lenin on the Woman Question.* International Publishers, New York, 1933.

Articles

Bobroff, Anne. "The Bolsheviks and the Working Woman, 1905–1920." *Soviet Studies* (October 1974), 540–567.

Dunham, Vera. "The Strong Woman Motif in Soviet Literature." *The Transformation of Russian Society,* ed. C. E. Black. Harvard University Press, Cambridge, 1970, pp. 459–483.

Goldberg, Marilyn Power. "Women in the Soviet Economy." A Warner-Modular Publication Reprint, no. 42, 1973.

Jancar, Barbara Wolfe. "Women in Soviet Politics." *Soviet Politics and Society in the 1970's,* ed. Henry W. Morton and Rudolf L. Törkes. Free Press, New York, 1974.

Lennon, Lotta. "Women in the U.S.S.R." *Problems of Communism* (July-August 1971), 47–58.

Luke, Louise E. "Marxian Women: Soviet Variants." *Through the Looking Glass of Soviet Literature.* Columbia University Press, New York, 1953, pp. 27–109.

McNeal, Robert. "Women in the Russian Radical Movement." *Journal of Social History* (Winter 1971–1972), 143–163.

Mandel, William. "Soviet Women and Their Self-Image." *Science and Society,* 35 (Fall 1971), 286–310.

Massell, Gregory. "Law as an Instrument of Social Change in a Traditional Milieu: The Case of Soviet Central Asia." *Law and Society Review,* II (February 1968), 179–228.

Mickiewicz, Ellen. "The Status of Soviet Women." *Problems of Communism* (September-October 1971), 59–62.

Stites, Richard. "The Women's Liberation Movement in Russia." *Canadian-American Slavic Studies,* 7 (Winter 1973), 460–474.

Tweedie, Jill. "How Liberated Are Soviet Women?" *New Statesman* (September 21, 1973), 376–377.

The student is also referred to the periodical *Current Digest of the Soviet Press.*

17

Other Scenarios: Women and Spanish Anarchism

Temma Kaplan

In most of western Europe, reformers and revolutionaries addressed themselves to problems raised by industrialization. Spain presents us with an interesting departure, because it remained preindustrial well into the twentieth century and yet was the scene of considerable political protest. Movements dedicated to the liberation of mankind from oppression by the rich, the state, and the church do not usually attract masses of women, who are among the most exploited by these institutions. Temma Kaplan asks why. In her answer, she notes that these institutions often mask their oppressiveness by providing some vital ameliorative services. Furthermore, she points out that custom and the Catholic religion shaped even anarchist ideology, which itself then continued to cast women in traditional passive roles. Finally, she suggests that in the anarchist movement, women were most radical and most unified when they formed their own sexually separate associations — a hypothesis that seems applicable to other revolutionary movements as well. A recurrent dilemma for political leaders is the need to unify men, whose identity derives from their work, and women, whose identity derives from their families.

(From *Tierra y Libertad,* August 16, 1902)

THE REVOLUTION
Principle: Meaningful work for everyone
Means: Collectivization of resources
End: Social harmony and plenty

The Spanish anarchists were more sensitive to the connections between socialism and the liberation of women from tyrannical sexual and family relationships than any other European political group. Libertarian ideology, espoused by the anarchists, effectively induced certain women to raise their own demands even when they conflicted with those of the largely male movement. But what female anarchists won for themselves, they won by themselves, and they were better anarchists for their feminism.

In Spain as elsewhere women were victimized by two institutions — the Catholic Church and the family. Between 1868 and 1939 Spanish anarchists struggled to destroy the tyranny of these and all oppressive institutions. It might seem, therefore, that women would have been especially attracted to the anarchist cause. In fact, the reverse was true. When anarchists attacked the family and the church, women were offended. However exploitative the family and the church may have been, these institutions provided women with a sense of stability, status, and dignity. From the family women received protection, some degree of security, and the experience of cooperative activity. The Catholic Church was more than a place to commune with God and the saints. It was a gathering place where women could reassert female community norms through gossip and commiseration. Daily mass formed the core of poor women's society just as the local bar or café was the center of poor men's social life. Working-class men never would have tolerated a demand for the abolition of their cafés; working-class women did not tolerate the anarchist demand for the destruction of their church. But male anarchists persisted in their attacks on both church and family without offering alternatives. Anarchists did not provide or promise desperately needed social services that women might control themselves. Unless male anarchists could create new opportunities for communalism to replace the old social structure and until they could create enclaves of power for women within the movement, there was no way to win masses of women supporters.

But male anarchists seldom even promised greater female participation in the struggle. They never specified how females, whom they considered victims of traditionally oppressive relationships, would break free to become revolutionary comrades. In fact, reading anarchist publications, one has the distinct impression that male anarchists never seriously considered making women equals. Harangues designed to gain women's support perpetuated old stereotypes and incorporated previous attitudes into the revolutionary movement. They demanded, for example, that anarchist women follow their husbands' orders without regard for their own needs. This callousness toward women seems especially ironic in this movement, which dedicated itself to achieving the autonomy of all human beings. Anarchists' repeated references to women as victims of traditional society implied the view that women were somehow retarded or not fully human. From this followed the opinion that women were incapable of overcoming their own oppression either individually or collectively with other women. Despite the call for valiant deeds by anarchist heroines, one discerns echoes of the condescending voice of the Catholic Church in most anarchist discussions of ordinary women.

When male anarchists addressed the problem of poor men, they generally spoke about them as oppressed people who, though inhibited by circumstances caused by the church and the state, were capable of acting spontaneously in their own interests once these constraints were removed. To tutor men's consciousness, anarchist ideology depended upon the transitional psychological mechanism of voluntarism, enlightened by secular education. Throughout the history of Spanish anarchism, the movement's leaders argued that will, catalyzed by a smattering of natural science and natural law, could overcome the brutalization caused by poverty. Then human beings could live in harmony with nature. Lurking behind this argument seems to be the traditional Catholic emphasis on free will. But, whereas the church had granted women the same ability and responsibility as men to understand what was correct and do it, Spanish anarchists seemed to believe that women were too ignorant and oppressed to understand what was right.

In part, male anarchists' failure to envision women in more aggressively revolutionary roles, and their general failure to make Spanish anarchism responsive to women's needs, was due to the movement's organization. The syndicate, a union of skilled and unskilled workers organized around their productive unit, formed the basic structure of anarchism. These syndicates were first and foremost economic and political bodies; social service and education played a less important role. At some time in the future, all the local Spanish syndicates would declare a general strike, thereby overthrowing capitalism and the state. Once the enemies of poor people had been overcome, the syndicates would become workers' collectives, which would be the only political or economic institutions in the anarchist society of the future. This vision of revolutionary change spoke to the condition of male workers and peasants. In traditional Spanish society, even an unemployed and unskilled male still considered himself to be a worker. If nothing else, he occasionally was a mason or carpenter — the careers most often listed by casual laborers on censuses.

But a woman, despite years of permanent work in the labor force, defined herself and was defined by others primarily in terms of her familial status. Anarchists were never able to deal with women in terms of that dual status, and therefore they sought to organize them around their work — in women's case as housewives — just as they organized other workers. Since housewives were isolated, in almost every town where anarchist trade unions existed, they attempted to gather women into the "miscellaneous" category of syndicates. The needs of these women, anarchists assumed, were the same as those of all other workers. But anarchist insensitivity to the actual situation of women, for whom work such as drawing water, washing clothes, and physically caring for children was subordinate to preserving the social institution of the family, led anarchists to attack the family. They did not understand that the emotional relationships provided by the family gave justification to poor women's lifelong struggle against poverty and hardship. Such women simply would not heed the call to join a movement that promised to obliterate the family as a social unit.

Behind the anarchists' fiery rhetoric about the destruction of the family lingered a romantic vision. What anarchists hated was the bourgeois family, whose members were tyrannized by ties of money and paternalistic authority. One issue upon which early Marxists and anarchists agreed was that "the family should be based on love, liberty and equality." [1] The anarchists believed that their families ideally served to inculcate antihierarchic notions about cooperative behavior. It was generally believed that the authoritarian family provided the model for the authoritarian state. Natural cooperative relationships were perverted as women and children learned to acquiesce to the tyranny of the father. Having learned submissiveness literally at their mothers' knee, poor people became docile before authorities such as the church and state. However simplistic anarchists may have been about the mechanisms of power and authority, they were among the earliest theorists to grasp the relationship between family psychology, revolutionary personality, and political freedom.

When anarchists suggested an alternative to the bourgeois family, they proposed "free love," which was not as radical as the term may have sounded. They did not condone promiscuity but meant rather (in the words of Juan Montseny, writing at the turn of the century) that a couple ought to live together, each with equal rights, until such time as one or the other partner cared to end the relationship. This pattern of common-law marriage was quite common among the Spanish poor, who could not always raise the necessary money to marry in the church and, even if they had married officially, could never obtain a divorce. The notion of free love was consistent with anarchist principles about maximum individual freedom. But without birth control and without child-care facilities — which were established only when a strong female anarchist federation emerged during the Spanish Civil War — the women in free love matches were little better off than if they had been formally married. In fact, they often suffered because convents, the chief source of home work for many women, frowned upon "wanton" women with their illegitimate children and withheld work from them.

Anarchists, therefore, frequently took up the cudgel by calling for the abolition of the distinction between legitimate and illegitimate children and urging an end to discrimination against unwed mothers. This appeal had little impact on contemporary society. But anarchists argued that after the revolution, all babies, whatever the circumstances of their birth, would be considered members of the community. They would be nurtured and supported simply because they were natural beings. The 1902 drawing at the beginning of this chapter portrays life under anarchism and accurately indicates anarchist goals. Rather than the life of leisure and eroticism some historians have attributed to this utopian view of the future, one discovers a scene in which a woman performing hard work seems well fed and clothed because she receives the product she has created. Men work, too, and profit from their own labor. Children prosper as charges of the entire community.

The anarchists' utopia was a romanticized vision of traditional small-town Spanish life with the church, the state bureaucracy, and the rich people removed. In this ideal community all citizens would be equal and no administrative structures would be necessary to guarantee equitable distribution of resources. After the revolution, the anarchists argued, institutional change would occur automatically and power would be destroyed. Hence, by implication, once the church and the family were crushed, an egalitarian, sexually democratic collectivity would emerge and miraculously liberate women from fear and ignorance. In the tradition of Rousseau, anarchists believed that human beings would be basically magnanimous and harmonious if only institutional constraints that promoted greed and competition could be removed.

Anarchists like Ricardo Mella, one of the leading turn-of-the-century theorists, argued that the abolition of the church, state, and bourgeois family would automatically end all power relations. Since power would be destroyed, never to emerge again, anarchists had no need to plan for its distribution. Such views caused anarchists to overlook the necessity of moving from traditional roles to more revolutionary ones by sharing decision making in the present. This combination of naiveté and traditionalism was largely responsible for anarchism's difficulty in dealing with poor Spanish women. It also helps to account for women's general lack of interest in anarchism except in those instances where female anarchists tried to create new institutions that couched revolutionary goals in terms of old norms.

Certain female anarchists, realizing that without an alternative community women would fight to defend the only one they had, attempted to create new institutions for women within anarchism. While the most notable female anarchist leaders, such as Soledad Gustavo (pseudonym for Teresa Mañé), her daughter Federica Montseny, and Teresa Claramunt, were as oblivious as anarchist men to this need, others were more responsive. Female anarchists like Amparo Poch y Gascón, Eulalia Prieto, Lucía Sánchez Saornil, and Mercedes Comaposada, whose experience in anarchist politics came from organizing poor women, realized that anarchism could not achieve its own libertarian goals of human autonomy without giving power to poor women. Women alone drew upon anarchist ideology to teach other women to be self-reliant, to create paramedical institutions, child-care centers, and vocational training programs within anarchist municipal centers. Women thereby could learn to be creative by performing services from which they themselves would immediately benefit.

Male anarchists responded to social changes such as the increased entrance of women into the labor force by uncritically reasserting traditional views about women's capabilities. Male anarchists' initial response to an increase of women in the work force came in 1871, when the Congress of Valencia went on record as supporting women's return to the household in future anarchist society. Though some representatives like Francisco Mora objected, calling this idea sentimental and blind to women's creative faculties, it recurred periodically among male Spanish anarchists. If girls and women were to be returned to the home, there was no need to train them to perform services useful to themselves nor to prepare them to exercise power in the larger community. The housewife remained the model of anarchist womanhood.

Examination of the actual conditions of women in the work force, analysis of how the anarchists tried to dissolve women's links to the church, and a review of women's collective attempts to work for a revolution that would meet some of their own self-determined needs will show how the reality of Spanish women's condition conflicted with the traditionalism of Spanish anarchism. Paradoxically, male anarchists' sharp break with tradition in demanding the destruction of church and family repulsed many potential female supporters. But the few women who did manage to enter the ranks, because they were attracted by other qualities in anarchism, were in turn repulsed by male traditionalism with regard to women's potential role in society.

By the first part of the twentieth century, roughly 10 percent of all Spanish women over fourteen were in the labor market long enough and regularly enough to be counted (see table). In Barcelona in 1905, 15 percent of the female population over fourteen worked outside their homes; they constituted 28 percent of Barcelona's work force.[2] The chart indicates only a partial view of the work force since occasional female laborers and those who worked in the sweated trades were not always listed.

Females worked in almost every kind of industry in Spain at the turn of the century. Numerous women in Burgos and Mallorca manufactured straw shoes — the finished cost of which was so low that they dominated the markets of impoverished Asian nations such as India, China, and Japan. In Medina del Campo and Palencia, women produced burlap bags, cloaks, gloves, and playing cards; they also picked and preserved fruits. Where conditions were worst of all, in Galicia and Asturias, women were employed as construction workers.

While most labor statistics focus upon the activities of urban workers, the percentage of women employed in Spanish agriculture far exceeded the proportion in industry until 1930. The trend toward employing women and children in agricultural work increased at the end of the nineteenth century. As male wages in agriculture improved, partly in response to the strength of anarchist trade unions, growers turned to women and children, who could be paid half salary. Men continued to dominate reaping, which was thought to demand more strength and skill than most women had. But women and children, who had always been employed to hoe and weed, began to work in forestry. They also planted and harvested olives, chickpeas, cotton, sugar cane, grapes, and beans. Harvesting was the most ardu-

TABLE 17–1
DISTRIBUTION OF WOMEN IN THE SPANISH LABOR FORCE

YEAR	TOTAL WOMEN WORKING	AGRICULTURE	INDUSTRY	SERVICE
1910	917,970	359,429 (39.15%)	178,443 (19.44%)	380,093 (41.41%)
1920	1,012,937	321,184 (31.71%)	277,146 (27.36%)	414,607 (40.93%)
1930	1,105,443	263,511 (23.84%)	314,496 (28.45%)	527,436 (47.71%)
1940	1,116,554	262,082 (23.47%)	296,241 (26.53%)	558,231 (50.00%)

SOURCE: María Laffitte, *La mujer en España: Cien años de su historia, 1860–1960*, Aguilar, Madrid, 1964, p. 357.

ous agricultural employment, since speed was the critical factor. Women collected ripe fruit in Murcia, Valencia, Zaragoza, and Alicante, generally working eighteen hours a day and more without breaks, eating their meager food on the run.[3]

Chickpea harvesting was a task almost exclusively performed by women, who still do this work today. Harvests generally occurred at the end of June. Women arose at 3 A.M. and arrived in the fields by dawn. Before the sun was fully up, they worked briskly, in silence, under the gaze of male supervisors. By 11 A.M., the sun had dried the plants to such an extent that harvest, which required pulling out the entire plant, became torturous. With only head scarves or narrow hats to protect them from the blazing sun, the women moved slowly along the rows of chickpeas, which became so dry and razor sharp that, despite gloves and socks, the women's hands and legs were bruised and lacerated by the plants. Some women preferred to return home to their families each evening. Others remained in the fields, sleeping on straw but receiving their meals during the two-week-long harvest. A seventy-year-old woman recently recounted how she and other female harvesters had often worked for nothing more than two weeks' worth of meals: cold soup at 11 A.M., mixed vegetables at 3 P.M., and soup again at night. Their meager wages might be paid in any form the owner chose. One employer paid his workers with combs because he inherited a comb factory that season.

Urban married women who needed work generally produced garments at home for piece rates. Even at peak times, wages were very low. For instance, the 1915 going rate for Barcelona's sweated trades was 1.25 pesetas for a dozen men's shirts. Women's blouses brought 1.50 pesetas a dozen. Women who made slacks or jackets could earn 3 to 4.50 pesetas a dozen, but it was a rare seamstress who could earn more than 1.50 pesetas a day, a sum government reports acknowledged to be insufficient to put food on the table. A 1918 government survey explained that

> often women's wages are the only support of poor families now that many workers are widows or abandoned women with children to support or spinsters, with ailing old parents or a thousand other circumstances which could be cited to persuade one that women's wages are the only means of life for many families, so that they ought to be sufficient for that purpose. . . . They should not be less than male workers' wages.[4]

The report reflected a European-wide phenomenon, that women in home work, industry, and agriculture received proportionally lower salaries than men: In 1873, Spanish women were paid one-half to two-thirds the salaries paid to men for equal work, and in 1913 they were still receiving only one-half to three-fifths.[5]

Female factory workers were generally young, single, and sickly. Workers under fourteen seem to have been especially prone to tuberculosis as a result of poor ventilation in their workshops. Many women suffered from anemia and general malnutrition, which made them more susceptible to scarlet fever and other contagious diseases. They also experienced severe menstrual pain because of uterine deformities caused by crouching at machines; such women often had miscarriages later in life.

Given these execrable conditions, it is no wonder that the image of the female as victim predominated over that of female as autonomous human being among Spanish anarchists. However, men in industrial production and agricultural work gangs suffered many of the same kinds of exploitative conditions. Spanish anarchists tried to organize men into revolutionary trade unions that would give them power over their work and their own circumstances, but they failed to do this for women. In general, male anarchists stressed the detrimental effect female workers had on the syndicalist movement. In Spain, where few men held jobs all year round, even fewer women were regularly employed. Women in need of work could often be used as strikebreakers. While official anarchist policy demanded an end to pay differentials between men and women, individual anarcho-syndicalist leaders such as Juan Martí of Barcelona complained in 1913 that women stole men's jobs in the textile industry because they were willing to work for less. Those men who could find work, he lamented, had to work for women's wages. Traditional male prejudices about women's work persisted despite far reaching anarchist theoretical commitments to the liberation of all human beings.

Anarchists along with all other progressive groups were shocked by prostitution. Until the middle of the nineteenth century, it was quite common for poor widows or seasonally employed single women to engage in occasional prostitution. Also, as was seen earlier, common-law marriage — later called "free love" among the anarchists — was the norm in poor communities although, after 1870, the government even considered women in such permanent monogamous relationships to be prostitutes. One sociologist estimated that in 1872 there were as many as 17,000 clandestine prostitutes in Madrid. By the turn of the century, critics of that city claimed that there was one prostitute for every thirteen or fourteen men and that about 6 percent of the female population of the city were prostitutes. But many of these women worked as seamstresses, milliners, and garment workers when such work was available.

Virtually all liberals and radicals in Spain opposed prostitution, but the anarchists believed that it was unreformable because it was an integral part of capitalism, another way people sold their labor. For anarchist men like Juan Ortega, the degradation of whores was part and parcel of the oppression of the poor in society as a whole. Was it any worse to sell one's time or one's good health working under exploitative conditions? Furthermore, anarchists claimed, authoritarian marriages in which women submitted sexually and psychologically to their husbands in return for economic support were a form of prostitution. They viewed prostitution as another form of victimization under the capitalist state and said it would disappear with the collectivization of property and resources. In their view of prostitution, as in so many other opinions, male anarchists reflected traditional Spanish culture, in which occasional prostitution was recognized as one of the ways, like taking in washing, that poor women might support themselves and their families.

Anarchists responded to female working conditions and widespread prostitution in a manner consistent with their general views about reform. They ambivalently opposed it. Where protective legislation was developed for working-class women in Spain, it resulted from the efforts of liberal bourgeois and aristocratic reformers. Spanish social legislation lagged far behind that of Germany or Great Britain. The first laws concerning factory work passed only in 1873 and applied only to children under seventeen. No laws regulated work done by female miners, cigar manufacturers, or lace makers, for example, until the twentieth century. But by World War I, important statutes officially protected working women. A 1912 decree required employers to provide chairs for women whose jobs forced them to stand; and legislation in the twenties allowed release time for nursing mothers. Night work was outlawed for women. In 1931, the Second Republic passed compulsory maternity insurance and the eight-hour day.

Spanish protective legislation, like similar liberal reforms elsewhere in Europe, was doomed by an inadequate supply of inspectors, general apathy toward working women, and the inapplicability of the laws to the majority of women, who worked as domestic servants, washerwomen, seamstresses, lace makers, or harvesters. Women who worked in their own homes were excluded from laws governing working conditions. Factory inspectors lacked enforcement powers. Where they could coerce owners into meeting codes, the cure was often worse than the ailment when employers decentralized their shops to avoid the expense of providing the protection required by law. Women who desperately needed employment were often forced to do the same work in their dimly lit, badly ventilated garrets that they had done in unhygienic factories. Furthermore, by introducing piece rates for home work in place of the hourly wages formerly paid in factories, employers effected a speedup.

Anarchists vigorously opposed all piecemeal reforms because they believed that so long as the state and the bourgeoisie were in control, there could be no true democracy, no workers' control, and therefore no genuine changes in workers' lives. Piecemeal reforms only reinforced capitalism. Therefore, the Spanish anarchists tried to keep their constituency from participating in struggles for protective legislation. But individual anarchist women such as Eulalia Prieto found that even anarchist workers needed immediate though short-term improvements in their daily lives. Prieto and others therefore attended assemblies of workers to urge them to fight for workers' control over production as well as for protective legislation.

Despite their many difficulties, some anarchist men and women did attempt to create a revolutionary community through independent women's organizations within anarchist locals. Spanish anarchism was the coordinating body for anarchist syndicates and a system of cultural and intellectual organizations, schools, and newspapers geared to the poor. The two movements were coordinated by local anarchist councils in hundreds of towns and cities predominantly in Catalonia, Andalusia, Valencia, and Aragon. Each local was a federation of the important anarchist trade unions in town and of agricultural organizations in the surrounding countryside.

For about half its history, Spanish anarchism was a legal economic and political organization composed of federations of revolutionary labor syndicates, but not a political party. Between 1868 and 1873, 1881 and 1905, 1911 and 1923, and 1931 and 1937, anarchists were relatively free to function. However, police might always sweep into a workers' district or an anarchist town and arrest large numbers of local men, for while the right to associate was sometimes permitted, the right to be an anarchist was not. During the relatively free periods, Spanish anarchism tended to stress syndical organization toward a general strike that would destroy the state and bring about libertarian society or anarchism. In the intervening years, however, when the movement was underground, the local councils re-emerged as workers' and peasants' cultural societies, mutual aid associations, or popular schools. Often no more than the back room of a bar in a small and impoverished town, the center served as a meeting place where members could discuss political and scientific tracts and hear the latest news from outside. Anarchist husbands encouraged their wives to attend such meetings in part to keep them away from the church. Although the centers functioned whether or not syndicalism was outlawed, stress on such issues as the democratization of the family, the development of new interpersonal relations, and the separation of women from the ideological control of the Catholic Church varied inversely with the relative strength of the syndical movement: When labor activity was legal, systematically organized, and therefore strongest, women received less attention; dreams of a revolutionary, egalitarian community also diminished in importance. The economic and political realities confronted by syndicalism conflicted with social aspirations about the future. Revolutionary ideals found better expression in anarchist cultural activities.

The movement's most profound cultural onslaught came in its attempt to spread what it called "integral education" to replace religious precepts. Throughout most of the seventy-year period of Spanish anarchism, education was in church hands. The poor received few scholarships, but the church did prepare poor children for communion and confirmation. Therefore, religious instruction was often the only formal education anarchist youths received. For girls, this meant that, if they attended school at all, they generally learned sewing, decorum, and religious ritual from nuns, who tied them to the church by a mixture of benevolence, power, and fear. In this context, Spanish anarchists advocated pedagogical views that seemed radical even though they owed a debt to traditional rationalist thought. As early as 1870, national anarchist groups called for free, public, secular coeducation for all children below the age of thirteen. The core of Spanish anarchist pedagogical theory was offered by Trinidad Soriano in 1873 when he presented his program for integral education, a curriculum that defined all subsequent male anarchist educational theory until 1939. The sequence was quite simple. All learning would proceed from the study of natural history and scientific method to psychology and logic and then to evolutionary theory. This sequence roughly organized human knowledge into secular categories of nature, mind, and change.

Such a theory attempted to replace a supernatural Catholic universe, interpreted by church dogma, with an anarchist cosmology that posited the continuity between nature and egalitarian society. Human beings, women included, were creatures of nature. Human consciousness was subject to the scientific laws of nature rather than to God and the church. Integral education thus substituted evolution for the will of God, since, as anarchists were fond of saying, revolution was just the speeding up of evolution. Because egalitarian, libertarian society was preordained by nature, history was on the side of the anarchists. The pace of evolution remained to be influenced by anarchist politics, since the development of anarchism could be retarded by ignorance. Anarchist educational programs, therefore, attempted to challenge religious beliefs. The anarchist educational proposals challenged church-state authority, since it was widely assumed that adherence to religious precepts assured social order and the status quo. Even more important, anarchists tied the issue of secular education to revolutionary consciousness. Scientific education, they said, could tutor volition by liberating men from fear of the supernatural. But male anarchists never alluded to the possibility of tutoring female will, strengthening it to withstand exhortations by the clergy and to overcome internal fear based on superstition, let alone to confront their fathers and husbands over psychological or political issues. It seems as if they assumed an androgynous will and then behaved as if it were an exclusively male apparatus.

The anarchists did, however, pay lip service to providing formal coeducation, and failed more because of inadequate funds than because of simple prejudice. From 1873 on, anarchist locals tried to organize coeducational schools, buy books, and establish museums and laboratories wherever possible, but most locals could provide only meager resources. While individual women may have benefited from all this, and while little girls sometimes attended classes, there is no evidence that the predominantly male anarchist locals actively recruited female children.

Yet some anarchist theorists emphasized female education as a means of reprogramming poor women, who anarchists believed were in the clutches of the Catholic Church. Anarchist José Torres Molina wrote in 1889 that his movement's female education program was designed "to transform women's social and moral priorities . . . to win them from religious superstition and apathy." But win them to what?

Some female anarchists made use of the potential communal opportunities offered by the anarchist locals to secure their own needs and to help win over their religious sisters by offering them institutionalized alternatives through the apparatus of anarchism. For instance, as a substitute for baptism, it was quite common for newborn infants to be initiated into the movement in the meeting place of the anarchist local council. In 1873, the Sanlúcar de Barrameda local initiated a boy called Gateway to Human Progress and a girl named Anarchist Europe. This practice continued among Spanish anarchists into the twentieth century. On Sunday, February 26, 1902, Electra (named for the Greek princess who challenged the state), the natural child of anarchist parents, was ceremonially introduced to the assembled anarchist women at the Metal and Iron Workers' Headquarters in Cádiz. The child received books, money, and several choruses of anarchist medlies.[6]

Anarchist women realized that people do not change their lives overnight. Social habit may be more important than ideology in governing people's behavior. The social life connected with the church was as important as religion per se in binding women to Catholicism. So if the practice of secular baptism seems rather religious, it is because the anarchists adopted the forms of the old to teach the new. Anarchist men, however, appear to have been less successful than anarchist women in transforming church doctrine into progressive social theories. Consciously or not, male anarchists used religious arguments they had learned as catechumens to try to win women to anarchism. For example, anarchist Manuel Rioja, writing in 1903, suggested — in an adaptation of St. Augustine's advice to male and female Christians married to heathens — that if a spouse was more interested in the priest's opinion than in good politics, her mate should try to reason her out of religion. Failing that, he should leave her! At the same time as they attacked the institutional church, male anarchists overlooked the force traditional Catholic doctrine had even upon themselves. Unconscious attitudes and prejudices undercut official anarchist doctrines of human equality and dignity. Male anarchists often tried to dominate and direct the behavior of women for the purpose of building anarchism just as priests tried to orient them in the name of preserving Catholicism.

Still, some anarchist women did find ways to adapt labor organization to their needs. Women of all trades and interests entered federations that came under the anarchist umbrella. Syndicates of miscellaneous occupations with women's sections have already been mentioned. For example, in Arcos de la Frontera in 1882 there was a female unit within the local. Other anarchist women's associations, such as Liberated Women, founded in Valencia in 1892, and the 1902 Feminine Society of Cádiz are only two of many women's organizations within the anarchist fold. Some women may also have been concerned with establishing feminist consciousness within the labor movement. Thus, in 1882 two women textile workers, Manuela Daza and Vicenta Durán, claimed to represent Seville's female work force regardless of trade. Women in the labor force did not eschew the syndical movement; they simply tried to run their portion of it themselves and tended to emphasize social needs more than the male sector of the anarchist labor movement did.

The most militant women in the anarcho-syndicalist movement were seamstresses, esparto grass workers, straw shoemakers, embroiderers, and olive pickers. In these occupations, women worked in isolation from men. The only male with whom they came into contact was a foreman or supervisor. His presence tended to forge an alliance of opposition among the women, whereas the presence of male coworkers encouraged females to defer to the men. Spanish anarchism, like other western trade union movements, may have had some trouble winning women to sexually integrated unions, but it seems to have been successful in forming sexually segregated female unions even among seasonally employed female agricultural workers or mill girls. Once unionized, female anarcho-syndicalists faced conflicts with the national anarchist organizations similar to those confronted by men. On principle, anarchists opposed short-term strikes for improved working conditions, higher wages, or reduced hours. However, once they organized into anarchist syndicates, female and male workers for the first time held some bargaining power vis-à-vis their employers, power that prompted them to try to win immediate improvements. Anarchist national or local organizations could not prevent local syndicates from making demands upon their employers and from going out on wildcat strikes if their demands were rejected. A "council of 40,000 organized male and female factory workers" sent a set of proposals to the Cortes in 1873. Included in it were demands for equal salaries for women, minimum wages, the eight-hour day, factory safety procedures, and the introduction of mixed juries of workers and employers to govern labor disputes. The reformist proposals remained essentially the same up through the Spanish Civil War period. National anarchist organizations discouraged such narrow demands hoping, instead, to win workers to the view that nothing short of the revolution would solve their problems.

Even so, male and female wage laborers affiliated with Spanish anarchism went on strike for a variety of reasons. Women workers frequently declared sympathy strikes with men in town although male workers seldom reciprocated. Like men, female anarchists carried on strikes for reduced hours and increased wages. In 1873, sixty Palma de Mallorca seamstresses formed a union and affiliated with the anarchists. At the time, they worked a sixteen-hour day for about 18 cents. Once their own organization was relatively stable, the seamstresses helped unionize women who made the uppers for esparto shoes and those who plaited esparto grass, one of the lowest-paying occupations in Spain. Three groups, the seamstresses, the esparto grass finishers, and the plaiters, struck that year for higher wages, and only the plaiters won their strike.[7] Female agricultural workers in Alcalá del Valle and throughout Andalusia joined in attempts to carry on a general strike in 1903. When there was an upsurge of labor activity following World War I, significant victories were won by female olive pickers in Alcalá de Guadiara, Seville, and by female cigarette makers in Gijón, Oviedo. Further work in Spanish labor history may well demonstrate an extraordinarily high degree of militant activity by anarchist women.

The most important of all the women's associations formed under the auspices of the Spanish anarchists was undoubtedly the Mujeres Libres or Liberated Women group.[8] In the spring of 1936, before the outbreak of the Spanish Civil War, a well-established female anarchist association in Madrid began to publish a newspaper called *Mujeres Libres*. The periodical was dedicated to many of the same issues the organization tried to promote, adult education, particularly vocational training, health care, including contraception and abortion information, and trade union protection for women.

The newspaper caught the imagination of other women's anarchist and feminist groups throughout Spain. Women, chiefly from Madrid and Barcelona but with a few representatives from outlying areas, came together in an umbrella association within the anarchist movement and continued to publish *Mujeres Libres,* the name they also adopted for their own organization. By 1938, Mujeres Libres was a 20,000-member women's federation with branches throughout the republican sector of Spain.

The Civil War (1936 to 1939) transformed Mujeres Libres in many of the same ways it transformed other anarchist groups. Convinced that the war was the initial stage of the revolution, female anarchists, like their male comrades, wanted to proceed as if they were living in revolutionary society. This meant that besides introducing women into the labor force Mujeres Libres tried to help women gain power within the anarchist movement, participate in decision making, and win better working conditions. Female anarchists were not content, as was the Spanish fascist women's organization directed by Pilar Primo de Rivera, merely to encourage women to do the civilian work men had abandoned when they entered the army. This difference is significant, because while other groups in Spain attempted to mobilize women, only Mujeres Libres consistently argued that winning the Civil War and winning their rights as women workers were mutually dependent.

Still more important, Mujeres Libres fought to maintain separate women's organizations even where anarchist revolutionaries seemed to be in control, in Barcelona and Valencia, for example. Mujeres Libres perceived that there was no autonomy for anyone, male or female, without power. To achieve that power they established paraprofessional schools and independent trade unions for women. Many of their adult education projects trained women in health techniques, including midwifery. They tutored women in new agricultural methods so that they could increase production, but they also insisted that all women engaged in such activities be given control over conditions of work, hours, and compensation through producers' cooperatives. If they had ever heard the myth of female self-sacrifice to the revolution, they did not seem to have been affected.

As women became more active in the public sector of the economy — either through the auspices of Mujeres Libres or because of government recruitment, Mujeres Libres concerned itself with protecting these women and with promoting their own control of their work. For instance, in the spring of 1937, Mujeres Libres organized trade unions for female food and transport workers. Even in anarchist agricultural collectives in the province of Valencia, for example, Mujeres Libres insisted on maintaining separate women's associations. Perhaps this resulted not so much from a distrust of their male comrades as from women's continued shyness in integrated public meetings. When women were sexually segregated, as they often had been in the church, anarchist women were quite outspoken.

Mujeres Libres established parent-controlled child-care centers wherever they organized women into industrial, agricultural, or service jobs. They encouraged parents to help raise their children collectively, although there is little evidence that anarchist men actively engaged in child care. Amparo Poch y Gascón, a female physician and founder of Mujeres Libres, traveled throughout the country lecturing on prenatal care and treatment of infants. Mujeres Libres' notion of child and health care seems to have been that control over life, attainable through the acquisition of health-care skills, could provide a base for further independent behavior and female autonomy.

For Mujeres Libres, as for many integrated and male-dominated anarchist groups during the Civil War, it may have seemed as if the old order was crumbling. Therefore, what seemed important was the creation of new social relations. However, Mujeres Libres promoted the additional notion that women as a group required protection against the force of the collectivity. Because anarchists were defeated first by the Communists and finally by General Francisco Franco, we cannot know how this insight might have been applied if the anarchists had succeeded in dominating a victorious

Spanish Republic. But the persistence of traditional norms in anarchists' attitudes leads one to believe that had the anarchists triumphed, female anarchists as well as other women would still have faced a struggle.

It appears that the history of Spanish anarchism up to 1939 was the history of slowly changing attitudes about social and personal matters. While positing the most revolutionary programs for the reorganization of society, male anarchists remained ambivalent about how those changes would or should affect them as individuals. This failure was especially notable in Spanish anarchist writings and decrees about working-class women.

All through its history, the Spanish anarchist press displayed ambivalent views about poor women. Theorists such as Ricardo Mella exaggerated their degradation and portrayed them as ignorant, superstitious, servile drones. On the other hand, anarchists also believed in the pedestal and romanticized certain "feminine" virtues. One anarchist praised the spirit of the lioness defending her cubs and hoped that this "female" sense of loyalty could be communalized. Many anarchists claimed that once the bourgeois family, maintained by patriarchal authority, was destroyed, love would replace force and power as means of preserving revolutionary anarchist society. Their arguments implied that love was somehow a female trait. In practice, however, some female anarchists had an instrumental view of women's relationship to anarchism. Teresa Claramunt, for example, was a popular trade union leader in the Catalan textile industry at the turn of the century. She and her comrade José Prats talked about women as mothers of future revolutionaries but seldom, if ever, as revolutionary comrades who might transform society through personal insights and collective action. None of the other anarchists quite made the theoretical jump to explain the connection between overcoming the state, creating workers' collectives, and transforming people's personalities. Aside from their faith in secular, scientific education and their belief in poor men's potential to develop a will, anarchists could not explain how that process might take place.

Anarchist theorists could not translate their own insights about the relationship between power and revolutionary psychology into political practice. Consuelo Bernardo and Doña B. Montefiore argued that a family was a microcosm of the state in which men, as economic providers who earned greater wages for equal work, held psychological as well as economic power over their wives and children insofar as they could threaten to withdraw support. All the poor were frightened into submission for fear of police repression if they struck against employers and of clerical sanctions, such as withholding home work from poor women, if they seemed to have strayed from the religious path. Anarchists like Milagro Rodríguez were perceptive in viewing sexual relations as a form of domination, but the male anarchists' mistake was to argue that free love without birth control or cooperative child care would redress the balance. Only Mujeres Libres viewed instruction in contraceptive techniques as a necessary part of female liberation.

The decentralization of the anarchist movement makes it difficult to determine just what the prevailing opinion was on any subject. But it is still more difficult to discover what the women prior to Mujeres Libres thought. Yet, from scattered references in anarchist papers and from the literature published under the auspices of Mujeres Libres,[9] it is possible to say that the women seemed to push harder on social-psychological issues, such as teaching women to function politically, to assume leadership positions, and to develop new self-images as potentially autonomous people, than on labor issues. Male anarchists generally gave low priority to social and psychological matters, especially when the trade union movement was most active — a tendency that demonstrates that syndicalism seldom confronted the special condition of women who occupied dual roles as wives and workers. Failure to recognize the rewards women received from their position in the family and the social reasons for their attachment to the church led anarchist men to emphasize their victimization rather than their strength. Victimization denotes the need for charity, even for reprogramming, but not for the reallocation of power and influence. The Spanish anarchists, like other revolutionaries, often implied that since the revolution would ultimately improve the condition of women, good anarchist females would want to subordinate their individual and short-term psychological and social needs to the long-term economic and political benefits they might receive in future anarchist society.

Over the years between 1868 and 1939, the response from women seems to have been fourfold. Many women in anarchist enclaves or married to anarchist men emotionally supported male kin but remained faithful to the church, which regarded them as victims and breeders but gave them a place to meet and a reason for living. Others organized into women's social and intellectual circles within the anarchist local councils, providing themselves with some support in their struggle to continue fighting for survival against tyrannical husbands, excessive childbirth, and possible abandonment. Those who could work sometimes formed labor syndicates that affiliated with the largely male anarchist associations, but there is little evidence to show that their alliance with the male syndicalists won them any benefits they did not win for themselves. Finally, the most compelling response came in the institution of Mujeres Libres, which made a valiant effort to use the ideological force of anarchist doctrine for the benefit of women by giving them power. But more important, because Mujeres Libres seems to have had no illusions about the help they could expect from the great mass of anarchist men, they were not afraid of alienating them by their insistence on the primacy of social issues over economic and political matters even within the revolution. Moreover, by developing the talents of untutored, often illiterate poor Spanish women, by training them to speak out in public, first in small meetings of women, then in friendly anarchist mass meetings, Mujeres Libres in effect taught women how to express their needs and how to share their personal insights about society with the larger movement.

Ironically, women in Mujeres Libres and in many of the less well-known female syndicates and associations went further in implementing anarchist ideals than most sexually integrated anarchist institutions were willing or able to go. In part, their success lay in their ability to see beyond victims and to encourage strong, capable women who had a keen sense of what they needed. Moreover, since traditional village organization offered women virtually no chance to participate actively in any institutions other than the family and the church, women, once mobilized, had fewer illusions about the desirability of transforming the old society into the new merely by removing the rich people, the church, and the state. Mujeres Libres and perhaps some of the earlier women's groups seemed to realize that if they were to break from the church, the source of much comfort and collective support as well as much misery and injustice, they needed a community that was equally powerful emotionally as well as economically. It appears as if Mujeres Libres, for one, was able to establish such a community, if only for a little while.

Notes

The research for this paper was carried out primarily at the Institute of Social History, Amsterdam, Holland, with grants in 1971 from the American Council of Learned Societies and in 1972 and 1973 from the Academic Senate of the University of California. I am grateful to both organizations, to Rudolf de Jong and Thea Duijker of the institute, and to Nancy Fitch and Claudia Koonz for the help they have provided.

1. Cited in Anselmo Lorenzo, *El proletariado militante,* Editorial del Movimiento Libertario Español, C.N.T. en Francia, Toulouse, 1947, vol. 2, p. 196.

2. Albert Balcells, "Condicions laborals de l'obrera a la indústria catalana," *Política i economia a la Catalunya del segle XX: 2 Recerques. Història, economia, cultura,* Eidcions Ariel, Esplugues de Llobregat, Barcelona, 1972, p. 141.

3. Eliseo Bayo, *Trabajos duros de la mujer,* Plaza & Janés, Barcelona, 1970, pp. 109, 114–118.

4. "Preparación de un proyecto de ley sobre el trabajo a domicilio," Instituto de Reformas Sociales, Secciones Técnicos Administrativas, Madrid, 1918, pp. 419, 446.

5. Carlos Seco Serrano, ed., *Actas de los consejos y comisión federal de la región*

española 1870–1874: Asociación internacional de los trabajadores: Colección de documentos para el estudio de los movimientos obreros en España en la época contemporánea, Facultad de Filosofía y Letras. Universidad de Barcelona, Publicaciones de la Cátedra de Historia General de España, Barcelona, 1969, vol. 1, p. lxlx; Balcells, p. 141.

6. "Movimiento Social," *Tierra y libertad,* Barcelona, February 8, 1902; *El condenado,* Madrid, March 27, 1873.
7. *El condenado,* March 8, March 21, March 27, 1873.
8. Temma Kaplan, "Spanish Anarchism and Women's Liberation," *Journal of Contemporary History,* 6, no. 2 (1971), 101–110. *"Mujeres Libres". La doble lucha de la mujer.* Edición a cargo de Mary Nash, Tusquets Editor, Barcelona, 1975. The Nash volume came to our attention after this essay was completed.
9. The Hemeroteca of Barcelona and the Institute of Social History, Amsterdam, are the outstanding places to study Mujeres Libres. Institute holdings in the R. Louzara (R. Lone) collection indicate the kinds of issues with which Mujeres Libres was involved: Amparo Poch y Gascón, *Niño,* n.p., Publicaciones Mujeres Libres, n.d.; Lucía Sánchez Saornil, *Horas de revolución,* n.p., Publicaciones Mujeres Libres, n.d.; and *Como organizar una agrupación,* n.p., Comité Nacional de Mujeres Libres, n.d.

Suggestions for Further Reading

Claramunt, Teresa. "La mujer: Consideraciones generales sobre su estado ante las prerogativas del hombre." Imprenta de *El Porvenir del Obrero,* Majón, 1905.

Fredricks, Shirley Fay. "Social and Political Thought of Federica Montseny, Spanish Anarchist, 1923–1937." Ph.D. dissertation, University of New Mexico, 1972.

Gustavo, Soledad (Teresa Mañé). *El amor libre.* Biblioteca *El Obrero,* Montevideo, Uruguay, 1904.

Kaplan, Temma. *Anarchists of Andalusia, 1868–1903.* Princeton University Press, Princeton, 1977.

Laffitte, María. *La mujer en España: Cien años de su historia, 1860–1960.* Aguilar, Madrid, 1964.

Lida, Clara. *Anarquismo y revolución en la España del XIX.* Siglo Veintiuno, Madrid, 1972.

Montefiore, Dora B. "La independencia económica de la mujer en el Siglo XX," trans. Palmiro de Etruria. *La revista blanca: Sociología, ciencia y arte,* VI (July 1903), 1–11.

Nash, Mary. *La mujer y los anarquistas* and *Los anarquistas ante la cuestión sexual.* Tusquets Editor, Barcelona, 1976.

Nettlau, Max. *La Première Internationale en Espagne, 1868–1888,* ed. Renée Lamberet. 2 vols. D. Reidel, Dordrecht, Holland, 1969.

Peirats, José. *La C.N.T. en la revolución española.* 3 vols. Ruedo Ibérico, Paris, 1971.

Prat, José. "A las mujeres: Conferencia leída en el 'Centro Obrero' de Sabadell y el 'Centro Fraternal de Cultura' de Barcelona los dias 18 y 24 de Octubre de 1903." Biblioteca Juventud Libertaria XII, Imprenta *La Activa,* Barcelona, 1904.

18

Something Old, Something New: Women Between the Two World Wars

Renate Bridenthal

The twentieth century prided itself on gains in women's rights. Suffrage was attained in many countries, and World War I brought women into new fields of work, some of which remained accessible to them after the war. However, as has been demonstrated so often in this volume, legislation and political events had less influence than slow-moving but powerful economic and social forces, and these were not always beneficial to women. Renate Bridenthal indicates that profit maximization led to merger and new technology in agriculture and industry, displacing the smaller enterprises in which women could play a leading role. Rationalization and mechanization created new unskilled jobs and mushrooming bureaucracies while commercial distribution created low-level office and sales jobs. All of these recruited women for their acceptance of low wages and docility. This new female labor force was younger than before and more stereotypically feminine. Appearance and pleasing demeanor were important new attributes in these jobs, which depended so heavily on extensive social contact. Thus, women experienced contradictions. They had greater economic independence, but it depended on age and behavior. New sexual attitudes allowed them greater freedom but also commercially exploited female sexuality in the media. In their family role, women experienced a similar contradiction. Birth control spared them from a constant cycle of childbearing, but their energies were redirected by more professional notions of parenting. Finally, women gained more equality in companionate marriage, but this itself was a mere remnant of the premodern productive and politically important family. Modernization appears here as a problematic advance, welcomed by some and feared by others.

Courtesy Janus Films

Courtesy *Inland Printer*

Reality and the dream. In the 1920s and 1930s, the ideal of glamor, stressing women's sexuality, contradicted and masked women's increasingly routine work lives. This polarization, along with changes in the family as an institution, created a new identity crisis among women. *Above:* Marlene Dietrich in *The Blue Angel,* a German film of 1930. *Below:* Women office workers collating papers, as shown in an ad in *The Inland Printer,* October 1923.

Women's efforts at peace keeping may have seemed like Sisyphean tasks, but their contributions once war broke out were clear and simple. As national populations drew together in 1914 to fight in a common cause, a temporary truce was declared in the war between the sexes. Most of the women's organizations, such as the International Council of Women and its national affiliates, turned dutifully into "ladies' auxiliaries." They organized home front activities, trained and counseled housewives, coordinated job placement for women, organized policewomen and patrols, did relief work and helped evacuate people from threatened areas, set up kindergartens and orphanages. For the sake of the greater cause, they countenanced the shelving of the woman suffrage issue and the suspension of protective legislation. Middle-class women took up white-collar jobs, working-class women moved into better-paid industrial jobs, farm girls flocked into factories, and peasant women took charge of farms. It all seemed natural, under the circumstances. Nobody expected it to last.

Yet, the move of womanpower from some sectors of the economy to others simply accelerated a trend well under way before the war. Postwar attempts to halt and reverse it failed, though they did manage to create hardship and ill will. In many other ways, too, women seemed after the war to have suddenly acquired equality. They won the vote in Germany, Sweden, Russia, the successor states of the Austro-Hungarian empire, the Baltic countries of Latvia, Lithuania, and Estonia, and, after long struggle, in Great Britain. France and Italy held back, their clerical and socialist parties fearing each others' potential gains. Sexual liberty seemed to be in the air as girls crowded the popular dance halls and movie theaters. Many people saw this use of leisure as the first step down the ladder of vice. And women would not disappear from factories, stores, and offices; indeed, they seemed more visible every day. Champions of women's equality cheered each apparent advance; opponents dreaded what they perceived as the decline of Western civilization. Both were wrong. Women had a far more complicated experience. Their situation revealed some of the growing contradictions of modern capitalist Europe; they were personally torn between an old form of life and a new.

The trend, for women of the advanced industrial European nations in the twentieth century, was to move with growing rapidity out of a mutually reinforcing into a conflictual relationship between work and family activities. Increasingly, as business and government took over the family's historical functions of production and socialization, it became a unit of consumption and an emotional fortress. For women, this meant that their traditional domain shrank. Yet, they recaptured that domain, in part, by becoming wage earners in the very institutions that eroded family functions. In the factories, they made products for the home under male supervisors and for male employers; in education and social services they carried out the ameliorative policies of male statesmen. An independent income gave women the bargaining power needed for greater participation in decision making in the family. As wage earners, they won some freedom from their husbands' authority, where family law allowed. However, a layer of institutionalization intervened between women and their work, depersonalizing it and legitimizing male authority even more than before. And their total life options were limited by discriminatory hiring and pay.

Women both gained and lost. But that in itself is not the whole story. It is not simply that women faced new tensions with the double burden of home and work, exacerbated by the spatial division of the two. Rather, the tensions were dynamic and demanded a new synthesis, though they also carried the dangers of a reaction. The new synthesis, envisaged by a few of the boldest feminists, was androgyny — sex-free role determination allowing individuals of whichever sex to fulfill themselves in love, work, and parenthood. The reaction expressed a yearning for restoration of a lost world; it often seemed easier to fall into stereotypical behavior considered feminine than to explore uncharted areas of work and sexual demeanor.

In this chapter, we will examine the elements of this creative tension as they emerged out of World War I. Mainly, we will analyze changes in the structure of work and how these affected women. Then, we will look at changes in family patterns and note some correlations.

To begin with the economic factors, we note that postwar reconversion was in many ways a gruesome experience. Veterans, women, and youth competed for available jobs after factories had tooled down from arms manufacture. Thousands of women lost their jobs in the metal and chemical industries, in construction and engineering, in civil service and transport. They were even dismissed from waiting on tables. Some remained, though often at lower levels of skill and pay. Soon the employment pattern of women in the major western European countries stabilized at one-fourth to one-third of the total working population. It shrank, in most cases, from prewar levels of employment among women, as Table 18–1 shows.[1]

TABLE 18–1

COUNTRY	PERCENTAGE OF ECONOMICALLY ACTIVE WOMEN OUT OF TOTAL FEMALE POPULATION			PERCENTAGE OF ECONOMICALLY ACTIVE WOMEN OUT OF TOTAL ECONOMICALLY ACTIVE POPULATION (SAME CENSUS YEARS)		
	PREWAR	1920S	1930S	PREWAR	1920S	1930S
Belgium	28.6 (1910)	21.3 (1920)	24.1 (1930)	30.9	25.0	26.3
Denmark	27.2 (1911)	24.1 (1921)	26.9 (1930)	31.3	29.7	30.5
France	38.7 (1911)	42.3 (1921)	34.2 (1936)	36.9	39.6	36.1
Germany	26.4 (1907)	35.6 (1925)	34.2 (1933)	30.7	35.9	35.5
Great Britain	25.7 (1911)	25.5 (1921)	26.9 (1931)	29.5	29.5	29.8
Ireland	19.5 (1911)	23.5 (1926)	24.3 (1936)	23.7	26.3	26.2
Italy	29.1 (1911)	27.2 (1921)	24.8 (1936)	31.3	28.7	28.7
Netherlands	18.3 (1909)	18.3 (1920)	19.2 (1930)	23.9	23.2	24.1
Norway	23.0 (1910)	21.9 (1920)	22.0 (1930)	30.1	27.8	27.1
Sweden	21.7 (1910)	25.8 (1920)	28.7 (1930)	27.8	29.8	31.0
Switzerland	31.7 (1910)	31.4 (1920)	29.0 (1930)	33.9	33.9	31.5

SOURCE: Based on P. Bairoch, *La population active et sa structure* (Institut de Sociologie de l'Université Libre de Bruxelles, 1968), pp. 27–34.

What was going on? Briefly, and excluding marginal errors due to census procedures, male employment expanded even more and women were changing their occupations rather than first entering the work force, a process that continued throughout the interwar period. The major shift was from agriculture into the industrial and service sectors. In the course of this transition, many women dropped out of work altogether.

The Agricultural Sector

In the European experience, the larger agriculture figures in an economy, the greater the percentage of women active in the economy. In the postwar period, rural exodus reached such striking proportions that it became a matter of national concern to many states. In some cases, women seemed to be hastening away from the country even more rapidly than men. Thus, in Germany, where the war had left women in the majority of the agricultural labor force, about 320,000 of them had fled the country by 1933, compared to 99,000 men. In France, roughly 1,040,000 women dropped out of agricultural work between 1921 and 1936, compared to 848,000 men. In Italy, from 1921 to 1936, 326,000 women left the agricultural sector compared to 228,000 men. By 1935, the rural exodus had become primarily a feminine phenomenon. The drop in the percentage of women in agriculture was dramatic: in Italy it fell from 59 percent to 45 percent of economically active women from 1921 to 1936; in France, from 46 percent to 40 percent from 1921 to 1936; in Germany, from 43 percent to 38 percent from 1925 to 1939.[2]

Of course, there were reasons unique to each country and to each class. In Germany, a democratic socialist government brought improved labor legislation to the industrial working class, which lured relatively disadvantaged rural labor into the cities. In France, modernization lagged altogether and a particularly inefficient method of agriculture spurred members of the rural population to leave. In Italy, the countryside was partly "deproletarianized" as agricultural workers became owners or tenants by seizing landed estates or by settling newly cleared lands. Others fled virtual serfdom for the towns. In most economies of Europe, agriculture was the least attractive sector, and women would not stay on the farm after so many veterans who "had seen Paree" failed to return.

The country housewife had to work harder than ever before, as her hired help sought out industrial jobs. Her daughter, disinclined to follow her example, left also, especially since the prior male rural exodus had reduced her choice of marriage partners. And she had few alternatives: where agriculture modernized, it offered few careers to women. Indeed, the landowning countrywoman's source of independent income from her chickens, dairy, and garden produce slowly gave way to male-dominated big business. Here women filled only lower-ranking positions because they lacked expertise in the new technology and were denied entry into agricultural schools to acquire it and because men would not accept supervision from them. For the female hired help, the disadvantages of the country far outweighed those of the city. Women agricultural laborers still earned only about 50 percent of the male wage. Why stay, when in industry they could earn 60 to 70 percent of the male wage and have a wider selection of husbands besides?

There were other alternatives to leaving, however. Both the propertied and the employed women tried to improve their positions by organizing, though their interests conflicted with each other. In 1929, the International Council of Women sponsored a conference of national organizations of propertied rural women in London. The organization's Scotch president, the Marchioness of Aberdeen and Temair, presided in stout majesty, her very person breathing the ideals of ladies with landed property. She noted that the precursor of the Women's Rural Institutes in her own country had been the Onward and Upward Association, whose purpose was to create common interests between mistresses and their servants in rural districts. Officially, the international organization claimed to be nonpolitical. In fact, however, the goal of consensus between classes was enunciated by most national representatives, who included a sprinkling of aristocracy — a countess from Germany and another from France and a princess from Rumania — and many well-to-do estate owners from the major countries of Europe and their imperial possessions abroad.

Most of them represented organizations formed before the war, though they began to flourish only afterward. Belgium's women farmers' circles, begun in 1906, aimed to keep people on the land and educate them. For similar purposes, the English Women's Institutes enjoyed support from the Ministry of Agriculture, while several of the French groups were affiliated with religious organizations. The German Association of Agricultural Housewives, dating back to 1898, focused on what came to be called home economics, which in agriculture included farm management.

The war had given these landed countrywomen a sense of their own importance and strength, since the reduction in trade had forced most nations to rely on internal resources. Now they anxiously held their ground, literally and figuratively. From the time of their first meeting to World War II, they defended their interests. These included raising the standards of homemaking and agriculture to higher professional levels, standardizing produce and controlling and improving its marketing, stemming the drift into towns, and influencing legislation that affected them. The last revealed such "unwomanly" positions as that of the German countess who opposed child labor legislation by arguing that goose herding was not very strenuous. Her idealized version overlooked the reality of exploited children deprived of play and education. But few of the countrywomen sounded so sinister. For the most part, the Rural Women's Organization acted as an information exchange and as a social nexus to overcome rural isolation. The Canadian representative said her organization preserved the sanity of women on the prairies, and the Norwegian one recounted an incident in which two old women rowed in an open boat for three hours each way to attend a housewives' get-together.

By 1933, the international association had grown to 1,000,000, of which about 800,000 were North American. But by that time, apparently despairing of having much effect on large-scale agriculture, it became quaint. Toward the end, it looked nostalgically at local costumes and customs. Its last book — a collection of national recipes — showed how far it had abdicated economic and political effectiveness.[3]

The hired female help these landed proprietors so desperately tried to keep had quite different problems. Their only voice was a feeble one in the International Landworkers' Federation, which for the most part represented men. In the 1920s, with employers and governments fearing socialism and famine, the threat of landworkers' strikes could compel the extension of some industrial labor legislation to agriculture. Generally, this meant some regulation of hours, wages, and conditions of work. For women, the most basic protective measures, like maternity leave, were granted. However, equal pay for equal work was not even discussed at the international congress. Not even the women there stressed it. At the first meeting in Amsterdam in 1920, Argentina Altobelli, a firebrand from Italy, presented resolutions condemning war, urging socialization of the land and rejection of nonsocialist unions by the federation. By 1924, however, the Italian landworkers' organization had been dismantled by the fascist government and Altobelli disappeared from the records. The agricultural and industrial depression of the 1930s finally destroyed the federation itself.[4]

If the landworkers' federation was too weak to do much for female agricultural workers, the Women's Bureau of the International Labor Office in Geneva did not do much more. In 1921, it adopted a recommendation that maternity benefits guaranteed to women in industry under the convention of 1919 be extended to women in agriculture. By 1939, sixteen nations had ratified a draft convention to that effect. The main motive, however, was not the political pressure exercised by women but fears of a falling birthrate. Even so, a formal convention was not passed until 1952, because governments and agricultural interests recoiled at the financial burden.[5]

In summary, women had little incentive to stay on the land and demonstrated little sisterhood across class lines. Daughters of propertied families moved into middle-sized cities and either took respectable jobs in public administration or social service or else married and became full-time bourgeois wives and mothers. Daughters of agricultural laborers sought work in factories or shops, where at least they could hope for higher wages and better regulation of work conditions. About half of them also married and at least temporarily dropped out of the economically active population. Rural exodus, a by-product of industrialization, narrowed the horizons of many women to their homes and to their roles as consumers, wives, and mothers.

Some women, however, continued as producers. Let us follow them as they joined their sisters on the assembly line.

The Industrial Sector

The ranks of industrial labor were swelled not only by country girls but also by former domestic servants. During the war and after, hundreds of thousands of women left private service. A combination of new work opportunities and declining middle-class wealth accounted for this phenomenon. Yet, the percentage of women's employment in industry as a percentage of women's total employment remained remarkably stable. From another perspective, the proportion of women in the total manufacturing work force actually fell. Table 18–2 tells the story.[6]

What this means is that economies industrialized and deployed their working populations differently from before, absorbing reduced proportions of women into industry. Yet, male workers complained continuously that women were taking away jobs. What was the trouble about?

The answer lies in an analysis of the changes within industrial work itself, for modernization meant not only more jobs but quite different jobs. An overview shows that the branches of manufacturing traditionally occupied by women declined more rapidly than the new areas that employed them expanded. Thus, textiles and clothing manufacture dropped off faster than metallurgy, chemicals, and electronics picked up. At the same time, the newest industries organized along rationalized lines, that is, by producing standardized parts on assembly lines timed for maximum productivity. The system created jobs for unskilled, patient, precise workers; the qualifications spelled "women." The women thus employed had to keep up with high-speed, often dangerous, mind-numbing work at barely subsistence wage levels, while men grew hostile at the "unfair" competition.

In Germany, where American loans primed the pump of postwar recovery, consumer industries grew after 1925. The chemical industry, supplying everything from synthetic fibers to dyes, flourished. The electronics industry turned out light bulbs and radios. The paper and carton industry, an important concomitant of consumerism and bureaucracy, burgeoned. Metallurgy, including unobtrusive rearmament, grew apace, and optical instruments became Germany's pride. In all of these, women, who in some

TABLE 18–2

	FRANCE		GERMANY		ITALY	
	1921	*1936*	*1925*	*1939*	*1921*	*1936*
% Women in industry / Women employed	22.2	21.6	24.7	27.0	23.6	24.1
% Women in industry / Total population in industry	31.2	27.6	22.2	21.1	27.2	25.0

cases had first entered during the war, stayed and increased their numbers. Less visibly, other changes took place. The textile industry, in which women traditionally predominated, began to languish from competition with synthetic materials. In the clothing industry, large-scale production sharply reduced the number of small female-directed businesses. The same held true of the food and beverage industry. Throughout the economy, the trend toward merger and monopoly edged out small entrepreneurs, especially women. Rarely did they find the same kind of work in industrial management. Leadership in large hierarchical corporations was reserved for men.[7]

In France, a similar development occurred. The number of women employed in textiles and clothing fell, while those in tanning, metalworks, motor car manufacture, chemicals and paper, and electric apparatus rose. The war had brought women into armament manufacture and metallurgy, but here, as elsewhere, they were not trained for postwar skills. Rather, work was reorganized into elementary operations supervised by male foremen. The gap between men's and women's work in industry widened. As in Germany, small, independent businesswomen lost out rapidly, while white-collar employees, usually younger women in nonmanagerial capacities, grew in numbers. Thus, the number of small entrepreneurs who were female declined from about 1,243,000 to 835,000 from 1921 to 1936, while the number of female salaried workers rose from 855,000 to 1,034,000 in the same period. This meant a net increase of about 179,000 office workers for a net loss of about 408,000 independents.[8]

Both Germany and France showed considerable regional variation in their economic development, but in Italy the differences were more dramatic. Here, the south was still virtually enserfed, while the north resembled other advanced industrial nations. Here also, the drop in the number of women in industry accompanied the decline of some traditional industries that had employed them, such as straw manufactures and textiles, where automation displaced many workers. On the other hand, the food industry increased its employment of women, as did shoes and chemicals. Since industrialization in Italy generally lagged behind that in France and Germany, the tendency for women's work in industry to decline became clear only after World War II. Then, women lost about 60,000 jobs in "female" sectors to men, while taking about 35,000 in "male" sectors. The absorption of women into Italian industry was retarded because scarcity of capital prevented investment in the kind of machinery that would have produced changes in the mode of production.[9]

Job competition provoked conflict between the sexes on a continent-wide scale. The hostility often carried over into workers' organizations. Unions in the interwar period showed a mixed record of cooperation and competition between women workers and organized labor. Individual unions and union federations varied in their official attitudes toward women workers, and much of the rank and file only reluctantly acknowledged the legitimacy of their presence. In itself this was understandable, given the historical tendency of employers to hire women to undercut wages. In addition, antifeminism reinforced organized labor's inclination to give low priority to women's demands for equal pay for equal work and for protective legislation. On the other hand, women were hard to organize. Many had internalized the ideology that placed them in the home and they anticipated only temporary participation in the work force. As girls, they had been raised to be docile; hence, employers could dissuade them from joining unions. Even when they accepted their role as workers, union dues were often too steep for their low wages. At union meetings, women often found themselves patronized, if heard at all, so potential female leadership was lost. Finally, for those who did make it into meetings, continued attendance was difficult, since most women also had household duties. As a result, female union membership was discouragingly low.

Women were most unionized in Germany. Thanks to vigorous left-wing political parties, workers' consciousness was relatively high. From here, after all, had come Marx and Engels, who predicted women's emancipation as a by-product of industrialization, and August Bebel, whose *Woman Under Socialism,* first published in 1883, had gone through fifty German editions and at least fifteen foreign-language editions by World War I. The Christian unions, which aimed to protect artisan labor from industrial incursion and to prevent socialist unions from monopolizing labor, also attracted many women.

The French labor movement was divided on the "woman question." The "free" or non-Christian unions, especially the Marxist ones, upheld the revolutionary and utopian socialist tradition, which theoretically espoused sex equality. However, another wing, influenced by the nineteenth-century anarchist Pierre Joseph Proudhon, clung to the view that women belonged in the home. The Christian unions joined in this attitude, echoing Vatican pronouncements on the matter. Pope Leo XIII in 1891 issued an encyclical, *De Rerum Novarum,* which clearly stated:

> Women, again are not suited to certain trades; for a woman is by nature fitted for home work and it is this which is best adapted at once to preserve her modesty, and to promote the good bringing up of children and the well-being of the family.

And the same sentiment was repeated forty years later by Pope Pius XI in his encyclical, *Quadrigesimo Anno.* As for the Italian movement, it was soon swallowed up by the fascist corporate state.

Relations between women and men unionists got off to a bad start immediately after World War I. Demobilization caused severe competition for fewer jobs and brought out the worst in most people. Again and again, women union leaders protested when their male colleagues collaborated with employers in phasing them out of work rather than joining in collective defensive action. Afterward, over the span of the interwar period, discussions on women's work and women's membership in unions reflected the economic cycle. Predictably, during recession, debate intensified over women's physiological and psychological fitness. During the "normalcy" of the later 1920s, meetings tended to run out of time when women's issues arose.

Yet, the picture was not entirely bleak. At best, unions won reductions in the wage gap between men and women, maternity provisions, and protective legislation. The last raised new problems of its own: it increased the costs of female labor and hence sometimes disemployed women. Given the conditions of work, however, it constituted a sufficient advantage to be a major priority of female unionists. Also, unions, especially the socialist ones, selected women union officials and continually recruited with lectures, slide shows, social gatherings, and special newspapers. Militant women often joined in job actions and strikes, initiating some and supporting others, including sympathy strikes with male workers.

Another source of labor reform was the International Labor Organization, a specialized agency of the League of Nations. While the ILO had no enforcement powers, it did have prestige and it set minimum standards of treatment. From 1919 on, it held annual conferences at which it issued conventions and recommendations, building up an international labor code intended to equalize working conditions in member countries as far as national differences would allow.

In 1919, trade union women from Europe, America, and Asia convened the first International Congress of Working Women in Washington. To begin with, they requested the International Conference of Labor to require women representatives. Then followed proposals for labor standards: an eight-hour day or forty-four-hour week for all workers regardless of sex, weekly rest of at least one and a half days, minimum daily rest of half an hour. The minimum age for child labor was to be sixteen. Maternity benefits should include free medical care and a monetary allowance sufficient for six weeks before and after childbirth. The word "sufficient" masked a controversy over the amount and its relation to the woman's wage. The congress also proposed protective legislation, such as limitations on night work and on the use of poisonous materials like lead. The women strongly demanded that protective legislation be extended to all workers regardless of sex, not only in the interests of fairness but also because special legislation for women often limited their scope of work, excluding them from certain industries. Finally, in a somewhat utopian vein, the congress asked for international conventions for equal distribution of raw materials in the world — a still elusive goal.[10]

By 1931, the number of states officially providing benefits for six weeks' leave after childbirth had risen to twenty-two from twelve in 1921, and fifteen others provided for from three to five weeks. Under the best schemes, maternity benefits generally came to only 50 to 60 percent of basic wages, which in the first place often fell below the requirements for a reasonable standard of living. Many categories of wage earners were not covered and of those that were, many had difficulty retaining their jobs after pregnancy. Finally, the European nations did not extend these meager gains to the women in their colonial possessions.

By 1939, the ILO reported that protective labor legislation applicable to all workers had grown considerably, but it also noted that new circumstances — meaning the depression — had raised to prominence the problem of the right to employment. The two observations were not unrelated. The encouragement of maternity as jobs got scarcer made sense. It reduced two anxieties at one time: that about population decline and that about women competing for work. Even the unpolitical ILO finally admitted that women did constitute a reserve of labor from which state and private employers drew freely during periods of exceptional activity and with which they dispensed during downturns. Thus, in Nazi Germany, the Unemployment Act of June 1, 1933, offered marriage loans of up to 1,000 reichsmark on condition that the bride leave her job and not return until the loan was repaid. As a further incentive, the loan was reduced by 25 percent with the birth of each child. In Italy, a law of 1934 allowed women to be replaced by men even in work normally done by women. Companies set quotas for female employees in commerce, banking, and insurance. Not only in the fascist countries but in France, Belgium, the Netherlands, and Great Britain there were similar schemes and laws against double-income families, especially in civil service.[11]

Thus, the changing structure of industry shuffled many women from one branch of manufacturing to another, often giving the wrong impression that they were taking men's jobs. In times of economic crisis, hostility between male and female workers peaked. During relatively stable periods, women workers made important gains by organizing. Their share of manual labor remained relatively stagnant, however. The future of women's employment lay elsewhere.

The Service Sector

In the growing areas of commerce and public and private administration, the influx of women was greatest. The fast-growing service sector included a wide variety of occupations essential to a modern economy: transport, communications, office and sales work, social work, and even some professions sometimes loosely labeled "services." Because it was a relatively undeveloped sector, the sexual division of labor within it had not yet been clearly defined. Furthermore, women had entered it relatively easily during the manpower shortages of World War I. The return of "normalcy" brought expanded consumer production and with it new mass distribution techniques, providing thousands of counters and cash registers for women to staff. Economic dislocation and fears of Bolshevism led to a mushrooming of ameliorative services, such as social work and nursing, considered particularly well suited for women. Technological needs for a more educated work force and the threat of youthful unemployment increased the school population and lengthened the time it spent behind desks, providing new jobs for teachers.

Work in the service sector had certain obvious advantages: it was clean, it paid better than unskilled industrial women's work, and it carried more prestige than other kinds of employment. However, the overall move of women within the employment structure from agriculture to industry to service rarely affected a single individual in the course of her work life or even several generations of the same family. Class limited an individual's options.

Typically, agricultural workers moved into domestic service or factory work; second-generation industrial workers might enter new branches of industry or sales or office work. Almost an equal number of saleswomen and clerks, however, came from the lower and middle echelons of the middle class. They worked for several reasons: war casualties had produced a "surplus" of women who had to support themselves; large businesses and industries displaced smaller shops and artisan establishments, impoverishing some members of this group and forcing their daughters into paid employment; and economic crises eroded the real income of the salaried middle class, with the same result. Women of middle-class origin, however, groomed for leisure or possibly a career, suffered status incongruity. Now, standing next to girls from the lower class waiting on customers or typing and filing, they often felt like the governesses of the nineteenth century — declassed — though only temporarily, they hoped. They waited for Prince Charming in a business suit. If and when he appeared, they eagerly left work.

Everywhere, the "new" female work force was considerably younger than the previous one, and a far smaller proportion of married women worked than in the premodern economy. The vast majority of women in the service sector were under thirty. Several circumstances accounted for this. For one thing, they had little opportunity to rise through the ranks of commerce or government into more interesting and responsible positions. Discrimination kept them in dead-end jobs, bias colored recognition of their abilities, men would not accept their authority in superior positions, and they were expected to marry and drop out. Therefore, women lost whatever confidence they possessed, underachieved sometimes, and were bored into leaving as soon as they could afford to. Employers also preferred younger women in work involving public relations for their attributes of docility, gratitude, and sexual attractiveness. When their youth faded, their employability diminished. Soon these jobs were stereotyped: the cute secretary and the flighty salesgirl became stock figures of cartoons. The governments themselves, on whom the ILO depended for execution of equitable labor legislation, became prime culprits when budgets were cut. They provided models of discriminatory behavior by reserving certain civil service posts for men, by firing married women, and by turning guidance counseling and placement into tracking.

In Germany, the percentage of women in the service sector out of all economically active women rose from 18.8 percent to 24.6 percent between 1925 and 1933. Their proportion of the sector as a whole during the same period rose from 29.4 percent to 32.7 percent. In France, between 1921 and 1936, the percentage of working women who were salaried employees rose from 27.2 percent to 34.3 percent, but their share of the sector remained about the same at 40 percent. In Italy, 25 percent of all employed women worked in nonagricultural and nonindustrial pursuits in 1936, compared to 18.3 percent in 1921, while for this occupational category as a whole, their share grew from 28 percent to 30 percent.[12]

There was not, however, an even exchange in numbers of women from traditional parts of the economy to modern parts. Women tended to lose their independent positions in the former faster than the latter could absorb them. Thus, in France from 1921 to 1936, the number of female small proprietors dropped by 408,000 while the number of female salaried employees rose by only 179,000. Male proprietors, by contrast, increased by 156,000, and over 100,000 men became salaried employees. Germany had a similar pattern: from 1925 to 1933, women independents in such branches as clothing, food and beverages, industry and crafts, inns and taverns, fell by over 300,000, while women white-collar workers in the same period increased by about 250,000. In Italy, as we have seen, female disemployment resulted from a quickly shrinking agricultural sphere, a relatively slowly expanding industrial sphere, and a lagging service sector. Chronic unemployment and underemployment ensured that most new jobs were filled by men.[13]

If the development of the lower levels of the service sector did not bring unalloyed improvement to women employed in it, neither did the higher levels, which shaded off into the professions. The most promising areas for those in the middle class who could afford the education were teaching, nursing, and social work. These were mostly civil service jobs. Here, discrimination often took the form of differential job classification.

In France, the number of women in public service and the professions, including teaching, increased from about 417,000 to 507,000 from 1921 to 1936, a fairly large gain numerically. However, their proportion of the whole expanding category increased a scant 1 percent, from 30 to 31. In Germany, the number of women teachers actually fell between 1925 to 1933, from 97,675 to 94,140, and their share in the profession fell from 32 to 30 percent. The number of nurses rose from 117,128 to 131,794 in the same period, and nursing remained a predominantly female profession. In social welfare, in contrast, while the number of women rose from 54,582 to 69,895 between 1925 and 1933, their predominance became precarious as men swarmed in: women's share fell from 82 to 67 percent of the profession. In Italy, the trend was again retarded. The number of women teachers rose between 1921 and 1931, from 128,266 to 134,985, making a proportional gain of 70 to 73 percent. However, by 1961 the trend reversed itself as the sector grew and attracted more men: women's share fell to 67 percent. The number of nurses increased from about 14,200 to 19,000 from 1921 to 1931, but nursing was only a little over half female. After World War II, those parts of the Italian service sector that expanded most rapidly had a shrinking proportion of women. It rose only where an insignificant number of them were employed at all: in banking, insurance, finance, and transportation.[14]

In short, men and women jostled each other for work in the "helping professions." These jobs represented state institutionalization of traditional family functions such as household management, education, and health care, which the family could no longer effectively fulfill in modern society. Previously, women had performed this kind of work in the family. After professionalization, these activities offered a minority of women opportunities in a modern economy, while leaving the majority alienated from these aspects of their traditional role.

A still smaller minority had higher aspirations. The few hundreds of women whose families both cared to and could afford to send them to the university encountered different sorts of difficulties. Besides the taunts of teachers, colleagues, and public opinion, they suffered material hardships. Girls often got smaller allowances than boys, and many of them could not afford books. They could not rent rooms as easily and received worse medical care. Nor did they find much warmth in comradeship. One German woman law student wrote that in class women were laughed down whether they answered correctly or not; in discussions of family law, male students waxed enthusiastic over prereform legislation, which had subjugated wives, and once held up the lecture for ten minutes in indignation when the teacher stated that women could now become judges in commercial courts. Socially, male and female students did not know how to act toward each other. Male students recognized only two kinds of girls: virginal marriage candidates and "other," usually sought in the town on evenings out. Independent girls nonplused them. Women students had few role models and sometimes fell into one of two patterns. Each bore its own stigma: if they dressed attractively, they were not taken seriously, if they dressed "seriously," they were not considered attractive. A comfortable identity remained elusive.[15]

For the successful graduates, there were further obstacles. Medical associations put quotas on female entry into the profession (a favorite among women students), antiquated legislation restricted female lawyers' range of possibilities, female engineers and chemists found jobs only in the lowest ranks of industry and science, and female university professors were as rare as diamonds. For these lucky few, the road ahead was still less smooth than for their male colleagues. Women doctors did not enjoy the full confidence of the public and had difficulty establishing a private practice. More women doctors than men ended up working in clinics, hospitals, and public health institutions. Dentists had a better time of it; for a while it even seemed as if odontology might become a feminine field. As always, in such cases, women's "special qualities" were noted: their precision, dexterity, patience, and personal sensitivity, especially with children. Indeed, in Europe today, women dentists are not uncommon, while many Americans still cringe before the image of a woman with the drill. Women lawyers faced problems more like those of doctors. Few had their own practice and most of those dealt with family law or protective factory legislation for women. One perceptive French observer recorded the subtle bonding in exchanges of glances between male judges and lawyers on cases involving female lawyers. Similarly, male collusion kept female journalists from news scoops and interviews. Some women's ambitions in these new and open fields seem quixotic today: in aviation, for example. In France, one woman aviator held a world record for distance and another one held it for looping. They joined Amelia Earhart among history's curiosities. Flying did not become a woman's job.

Legal emancipation and technical breakthroughs seemed to promise so many new vistas. The full strength of the reins of custom had yet to be tested. These consisted not only of men's bias but also of women's own internalized feelings of inferiority and responsibility. Hence, women's work lives suffered repeated interruptions. Whatever else they might be, women had to be not only good wives and mothers but also good daughters and sisters, putting family needs above their own at all times. Avoiding marriage did not always free women for single-minded pursuit of their work. The resulting discontinuity in their work lives blunted their career trajectories, especially where seniority and keeping up to date was crucial. If they did give their careers priority, they suffered caricature as cold-blooded, hard-bitten, pinched-face old maids. The image frightened another whole generation into the waiting shelter of conformity.

The Family: Dissolution or Reconstruction?

Conformity meant marriage and children. Even professional women were not exempt from the first female "duty." Statesmen and observers watched the declining birthrate with dismay bordering on panic. Demographers' calculations indicated that key European populations were not replacing themselves. England, Denmark, France, Germany, Sweden, Austria . . . all had birthrates below the acceptable minimum. Alarmists spoke of race suicide and misogynists were not the only ones to ascribe the phenomenon to women's purported new liberties. Quiet sabotage was implied in such titles as *The International Birth Strike* by Ernst Kahn and *Revolt of Women* by Hamilton Fyfe. Increasing numbers of miscarriages, in some cases exceeding live births, looked suspiciously like abortions, which were illegal. Illicit birth-control clinics and information offices spread, and Margaret Sanger took her battle for contraception to an international level. Popularized Freud reached the masses via movies and cheap literature announcing: women could and did have pleasure. It was a complex message, which easily shaded back into an older stereotype: women *are* pleasure. The celluloid sexpot was born. But so was a new type: the bachelor girl.

She was best described in a widely read novel of 1922, *La Garçonne,* by Victor Margueritte. The heroine, Monique Lerbier, wore her hair and skirts short; she danced, played sports, took courses at the Sorbonne, found an interesting job, drove her own car, and treated her boyfriends like studs. Her straightforward manner, her direct gaze, her vigorous handshake bore witness to a change unimaginatively called masculinization. The novel enjoyed an instant success. Twenty thousand copies sold in advance and it was grabbed off the shelves at the rate of 10,000 a week soon after its appearance. By 1929, 1,000,000 copies had been sold. Nor did it remain quarantined in France: translated into a dozen languages, La Garçonne made her way through Europe. Her notoriety derived from the fact that she approximated some real people, though the French conservative press denied it vigorously. The centrist democratic press recognized but deplored it, and the feminist and socialist press exhibited mixed feelings about it. Her creator shared the ambivalence: in the end he wrote her safely into marriage.

In any case, Monique Lerbier and her sisters were not responsible for the declining birthrate. The upper and middle classes had been limiting their families for several centuries. What caused alarm was the working-class emulation of this pattern. On the one hand, a large, dissatisfied working class with rising demands could be politically threatening. On the other hand, a large pool of labor could keep wages competitively low, and manpower was also needed for armies. Class divisions underscored the ambivalence toward sexual liberty for women in general. Simple racism compounded it as sober demographers worried about Europe becoming unable to carry on the "right breed" in the face of the yellow and black perils multiplying in Asia, Africa, and India. Most voiced concern about their immediate neighbors; each country counted the others' populations anxiously, measuring off potential armies. Would-be guardians of public morality predicted the crumbling of all human relationships following the decline of female chastity. To them, an obvious symptom of moral decay was the disregard of the law shown by the purchase of contraceptives and procurement of abortions in the face of stiff penalties. Finally, the whole thing smacked of Bolshevism to those who, in the 1920s, looked across to the Soviet Union, where free love was institutionalized for a time.

Feminists and other proponents of birth control succeeded in winning over some conservative opinion by arguing the case for eugenics and poverty control. Neo-Malthusian Leagues had formed in Great Britain, Holland, France, and Germany in the 1870s and had held international conferences since 1900. Part of their appeal lay in the alternative they proposed to socialism, namely, to diminish the birthrate among the lower classes so that these could fit themselves to their wages rather than trying to fit their wages to their needs. This offered several advantages: it would keep the poor from demanding a redistribution of wealth, it would keep the upper and middle classes from being swamped numerically and perhaps politically, and it would "improve the quality of the race." However, no one explained who was to select "the best" or how. If birth control offered an alternative to civil war, it similarly offered an alternative to revolution and international war. It could obviate the need, so some thought, for a radical redistribution of wealth and power, nationally and globally. Not everyone shared this view. The British, with their empire, were relatively satisfied with the status quo and accepted the idea that nations should live within their means. The Germans, ambitious newcomers to global imperialism, resented it.[16]

While public opinion slowly shifted, family size continued to shrink. There were many reasons for this. Women's employment outside the home was by far not the only one, though it does correlate with lower fertility. Full-time housewives, however, also reduced the number of their children. For one thing, more children survived infancy, so sheer quantity of progeny was no longer necessary for family continuity. Related to this was the hope for social mobility. Families concentrated on having fewer children, who would not merely survive but rise to a higher socioeconomic level. This meant prolonged training for a skill or profession; family resources went toward grooming one or two, usually boys, rather than toward propagating many. Furthermore, urbanization itself made a difference; in the country, children helped with farm work; in the city, they became liabilities, mouths to feed for increasingly long periods of time as the age for leaving school rose. Finally, the postwar period brought new attention to family functions;

with the decline of other of its functions, the focus sharpened on intrafamilial relations and personality development. Fewer children with longer lives entailed stronger emotional commitment to each one and heightened concern for the quality of child care. Expert opinion converged to professionalize motherhood. Thus, while some forces freed women from the endless cycle of childbearing, traditionalism crept in by another door in another guise.

Family sociology began to move in the direction of Talcott Parsons, who after World War II categorized men's role in the family as "instrumental" (manipulating the environment for the benefit of the family) and the wife's role as "expressive" (facilitating emotional interactions within the family). Educators, psychiatrists, sociologists, and social workers all studied the failures of the family with a view to saving it. They were conservative, in that they tried to halt the apparent dissolution of the family. Some researchers, drawing their empirical evidence mainly from welfare cases and broken homes, concluded from their untypical samples that lack of family cohesion was the cause of many social problems. They also traced school failures and a rising crime rate to the absence of working mothers from the home. True, others faulted endemic under- and subemployment and instabilities resulting from social injustice. But the professional opinion of family sociologists joined the chorus of medical experts and psychologists, who advised women not to deny their purported biological and psychological make-up by slighting their families. Duty underscored nature.[17]

The majority of women, of course, were ill equipped for sophisticated motherhood. Many of them were barely literate greenhorns from the country. They could hardly fulfill their function as socializing agents in a rapidly changing world, especially if they lacked contact with it through work and remained ghettoized in their communities. If anything, they would lose status as traditional authorities for their daughters and sons and be woeful role models for the former. Trained female educators stepped in to fill the vacuum. They worked in kindergartens, as the child development theories of the educational reformers Johann Heinrich Pestalozzi and Friedrich Wilhelm August Froebel were revived, and they continued through elementary school. Middle-class women found careers in child care and teaching, often at the cost of their own family lives, as we have seen, and others became distanced from their children. Thus, while some people began to express fears about the feminization of education, women came to be a step removed from children at both ends of the process, as parents and as teachers. A layer of male-directed institutionalization intervened between them and children.

Not only parent-child relationships but also husband-wife relationships were examined more closely. What shape those really took must remain a matter for conjecture, given the immature state of the discipline of family sociology then. However, we can extrapolate a tendency from existing studies. A pioneering work by Theodor Adorno and Max Horkheimer, *Authority and the Family,* begun at the Institute for Social Research in Frankfort on the Main, Germany, and published in Paris in 1936 after its authors fled Nazism, examined family interaction in order to find clues to political behavior. On the basis of a questionnaire, crude by today's standards, they found links between patriarchal authoritarianism and the development of personalities prone to totalitarianism. From a different, psychoanalytic perspective, Wilhelm Reich, in his *The Mass Psychology of Fascism* of 1933, drew similar conclusions. German sociologists emerged from World War II on the defensive and claimed instead a growing equalization of power distribution within the family. Cross-national research now confirms that egalitarian companionate marriage tends to replace patriarchy when women work outside the home.[18]

Less remarked upon is the fact that the arena thus more equitably shared has itself become smaller. The family has been reduced in many of its historical functions: as a unit of production, as the transmitter of economically significant property such as land or small independent artisan or trade establishments, and as the main socializing agent. Production, socialization, and many supportive services are now carried on by big business and big government. The family provides little besides companionship and mutual self-help when larger social institutions fail. Even this began to dwindle as early as the interwar period and before. Young people drifted away to their peer groups, leaving parents to relate to each other as best they could. The "generation gap" was noticed. In sum, companionate marriage, whatever its rewards, was a remnant. Women had made gains in a declining sphere.

Must we conclude, then, that between the two world wars, women's emancipation, so highly touted, was a hoax? Or may we look for glimmers of progress and future promise? The answer is a qualified yes to both. The thrust of change consisted of such diverse currents and crosscurrents that analysis is difficult at best. Each of the two main strands of women's lives, work and family, developed in ways that heightened the tension between them. Women's traditional role was relieved in some respects and made more time-consuming in others, as motherhood changed in quality. Women's work lives provided novel opportunities for self-development, but under conditions and according to terms that severely restricted fulfillment. Some women suffered under the double burden, others chose one or the other, a few "superwomen" lived out the contradictions successfully.

For the majority, however, the difficulties proved too much. Nostalgia fostered reaction, worldwide depression lent it encouragement, conservative political parties throve on the growing reactionary mood. People spoke of the "failure" of the women's movement. Soon another war created another generation of ladies' auxiliaries — helpmeets rather than independent actors. The traditional ideology of women's role triumphed again for a time.

Notes

1. Paul Bairoch, *La Population active et sa structure,* Editions de l'Institut de Sociologie, Université Libre de Bruxelles, Institut de Sociologie, Centre d'Economie Politique, Brussels, 1968, pp. 27–34.
2. Henri Fuss, "Unemployment and Employment Among Women," *International Labor Review,* 31 (1935), 490; Renate Bridenthal, "Beyond *Kinder, Küche, Kirche:* Weimar Women at Work," *Central European History,* 6 (June 1973), 151–2; Françoise Guelaud-Leridon, *Le Travail des femmes en France,* Institut National D'Etudes Démographiques, Travaux et Documents, Cahier no. 42, Presses Universitaires de France, Paris, 1964, p. 25; Rosa Anna Perricone, *L'Inserimento della Donna nelle Attivitá Economiche in Italia,* Nuova Serie, Società Italiana di Economia Demografia e Statistica, Rome, 1972, p. 18.
3. Rural Women's Organization, *What the Country Women of the World are Doing,* vols. 1–5, International Council of Women, London, 1929–1936.
4. International Landworkers' Federation, Reports of the Congresses, *Report of the First Congress,* Amsterdam, 1920; *Report of the Fourth Congress,* Geneva, 1926; *Report of the Fifth Congress,* Prague, 1928; *Report of the Sixth Congress,* Stockholm, 1931.
5. International Labor Organization, *Studies and Reports,* Series I, no. 1, Geneva, 1921, p. 11, and Series I, no. 4, Geneva, 1939, pp. 19, 33.
6. Table 18–2 represents a compilation of data from a number of sources: Germany, Statistisches Amt, *Wirtschaft und Statistik,* vol. 14 (1934), Sonderbeilage 24, p. 4; Perricone, *L'Inserimento,* pp. 18, 35; Guelaud-Leridon, *Le Travail;* Pierfrancesco Bandettini, "The Employment of Women in Italy, 1881–1951," *Comparative Studies in Society and History,* vol. 2 (1959–1960), p. 374.
7. Bridenthal, "Beyond," pp. 159–161.
8. Jean Daric, *L'Activité professionnelle des femmes en France,* Institut National D'Etudes Démographiques, Travaux et Documents, Cahier no. 5, Presses Universitaires de France, Paris, 1947, p. 43.
9. Franco Archibugi, "Recent Trends in Women's Work in Italy," *International Labor Review,* 81 (1960), 290–295.
10. International Congress of Working Women, *Resolutions adopted by the First Congress of I.C.W.W. in Washington, U.S.A., October 28 to November 6, 1919,* National Women's Trade Union League of America, Chicago, 1919.
11. International Labor Organization, *Studies and Reports,* Series I, no. 4, Geneva, 1939, pp. 346–347, 359, 362.
12. *Wirtschaft und Statistik*; Guelaud-Leridon, *Le Travail,* pp. 14, 25; Perricone, *L'Inserimento,* p. 35.

13. Daric, *L'Activité,* p. 43; Bridenthal, "Beyond," p. 161; Nora Federici, "Evolution et caractéristiques du travail féminin en Italie," *Cahiers de l'Institut de Science Economique Appliquée,* 122, series AB2, Institut de Science Economique Appliquée, Paris, February 1962.

14. Guelaud-Leridon, *Le Travail,* p. 25; Bridenthal, "Beyond," pp. 163–164; Perricone, *L'Inserimento,* pp. 39, 89; Archibugi, "Recent Trends," p. 296.

15. Michael H. Kater, "Krisis des Frauenstudiums in der Weimarer Republik," *Vierteljahrschrift für Sozial- und Wirtschaftsgeschichte,* 59, 2 (1972).

16. Sixth International Neo-Malthusian and Birth Control Conference, vol. 1: *International Aspects of Birth Control,* ed. Margaret Sanger, The American Birth Control League, Inc., New York, 1925, pp. 13, 132.

17. Georg Schwägler, *Soziologie der Familie, Ursprung und Entwicklung,* Heidelberger Sociologica, 9, Mohr (Siebeck), Tübingen, 1970, pp. 86–108.

18. Robert Blood and Donald Wolfe, *Husbands and Wives,* Free Press, New York, 1960; William J. Goode, *World Revolution and Family Patterns,* Free Press, New York, 1970; Günther Lüschen and Eugen Lupri, *Soziologie der Familie,* Westdeutscher Verlag, Opladen, 1970; *Journal of Marriage and the Family,* vol. 31, no. 2, is a special issue about cross-cultural family research.

Suggestions for Further Reading

There are few English works available on European women in the interwar period. The best surveys on twentieth-century changes in women's work, family, and political roles, and legislation affecting women, are Evelyne Sullerot, *Woman, Society and Change* (McGraw-Hill, New York, 1971); Raphael Patai, *Women in the Modern World* (Free Press, New York, 1967); and Edmund Dahlström, ed., *The Changing Roles of Men and Women,* trans. Gunilla and Steven Anderman (Beacon Press, Boston, 1971).

Family research has advanced considerably in recent years. Good guides to that field are Joan Aldous and Reuben Hill, eds., *International Bibliography of Research in Marriage and the Family, 1900–1964* (University of Minnesota, Minneapolis, 1967); Lutz K. Berkner, "Recent Research on the History of the Family in Western Europe," *Journal of Marriage and the Family,* vol. 35 (August 1973); and Andrée Michel, ed., *Family Issues of Employed Women in Europe and America* (Brill, Leiden, 1971).

Two consciousness-raisers from then and now make fruitful comparative reading. August Bebel, *Woman under Socialism,* trans. Daniel de Leon, 1903, from the thirty-third edition (Schocken Books, New York, 1971) makes significant strides toward a feminist awareness but remains rooted in some traditional concepts and never fully breaks with a male point of view. Sheila Rowbotham, *Woman's Consciousness, Man's World* (Penguin, Baltimore, 1973), by contrast, adopts an entirely new perspective on the changes affecting women in the modern period.

19

Mothers in the Fatherland: Women in Nazi Germany

Claudia Koonz

Temma Kaplan asked why Spanish women most often remained unmoved by appeals to join radical movements that promised liberation from all oppression. In this essay, Claudia Koonz investigates Nazi women who vigorously opposed progressive social change. Fears of modernization, exacerbated by the depression of 1929, galvanized them into active defense of traditional values. As we have seen, when a political or religious movement is struggling to gain hegemony amid chaos, every member of that movement, male or female, participates in some vital way. After the victory, women's function is transferred from a disruptive to a stabilizing role, usually in the family. In the early years of the Third Reich, Hitler established a huge corps of women officials to restore the traditional family. As he prepared his nation for war, still another trend developed. Women were recruited out of their homes and into the work force. Thus, throughout the Nazi period, women were called upon to defend tradition in some untraditional ways. This paradox is explained by the recognition that economic need, not prevailing ideology, determines women's entry into and retreat from the work force. During the dramatic shifts of policy, women's loyalty to the Nazis was enhanced by official efforts to raise their self-esteem. However, they never exerted the slightest influence over the major decisions affecting their lives.

The ideal mother and her ideal son: the cover of a Nazi women's periodical. (With permission of Institut fuer Zeitgeschichte, Muenchen)

The ideal Nazi man was a fighter; the ideal Nazi woman, his mother. Women were not to aspire to great achievements in the competitive, masculine worlds of politics, government, industry, and the military. Rather, women's lives ought to revolve around their true calling, motherhood. Apparently this doctrine appealed to both men and women in postdepression Germany. In the last free elections before the Nazi seizure of power, about one third of both male and female voters supported the Nazis. Just after the 1933 elections, Adolf Hitler boasted to an American woman, "Women have always been among my staunchest supporters. They feel that my victory is their victory. They know I serve their cause."

Feminists wondered how German women could vote to disenfranchise themselves. How, they asked, could women oppose the new emancipation granted to them in the Weimar Republic? Nazi politicians pointed out that anyone who voted Nazi voted to disenfranchise himself *or* herself and to undo the liberal reforms inaugurated after World War I. Yet this response is at best only a half-truth. The male voter for National Socialism may have been voting to end elections — but he could still envisage himself as a trooper in the Sturm Abteilung (SA), party official, or civil servant. And he could identify with the blatantly masculine élan of the party. Nazi men did not vote to remove themselves from all aspects of political life. Nazi women did. We cannot explain women's support for Hitler by assuming they were ignorant of National Socialist attitudes toward women, nor can we attribute the popularity of the Nazis among women to vague psychological propensities such as female passivity. To understand why women voted for and sometimes joined the Nazi party we will have to consider their criticisms of the emancipation of women in the Weimar Republic and to evaluate the changes they anticipated in the Third Reich. On the "woman question," as on so many other issues, early party supporters frequently expressed disillusionment with the realities of post-1933 society.

Although Nazi leaders consistently emphasized the primacy of motherhood for all women, their definition of that role expanded and contracted according to the needs of the Nazi party and state. In a first phase, before 1933, women in the Nazi movement struggled shoulder to shoulder with their male comrades in whatever capacity the situation demanded. After the seizure of power, Hitler ordered employed women to relinquish their jobs and dedicate their full energies to rearing large families. By 1937, this policy was reversed as Hitler prepared for war: mothers, he decreed, must now also work in factories, offices, and fields. During all three phases, Nazi leaders saw women as ancillary, yet crucial to their cause. Leafletting amidst a hostile crowd, altering national consumption patterns, or building bombers could all be reconciled with motherhood. One policy, however, remained consistent. At no time could Nazi women expect to exert the slightest influence over the policies that affected their lives. Except within their own organizations, women could not hope to attain positions of leadership or control. From the foundation of the party through the defeat of the Nazi state, the needs of women — like the needs of all citizens — remained subservient to the demands of the Nazi elite. Girls learned to "Be brave! Be pure! Be German!" while boys in the Hitler Youth marched to the slogan, "Be brave! Be strong! Die smiling!" Traditional sex-role stereotypes were preserved to the detriment of men and women alike.

Yet, unaware of the consequences, women welcomed the apparent return to tradition. While men formed their own Nazi fighting groups, women joined a host of organizations dedicated to home economy, child care, and *volkish* culture. Comradeship and same-sex solidarity reinforced loyalty among women as well as among men. Moreover, there were always women who welcomed the opportunity to organize other women, at first to struggle for Nazi victory then to help in establishing a harmonious Nazi state, and finally to participate in the Nazi war effort. They were the heroines, the traditionalists, and the opportunists — in that order.

The Heroines

In the early 1920s women comprised about 20 percent of the Nazi party membership. Although they played virtually no role in policy making, they did contribute money and moral support to the movement. Years later Hitler thanked the women of the party who had preserved party unity during his imprisonment. However, at the time neither Hitler nor the other Nazi men had paid much attention to their women colleagues. Not even at election times did they campaign for the female vote; and no woman ever held any party office. Because they were deemed so unimportant, women were unintentionally given the opportunity to organize their own relatively independent associations, edit their own newsletters, pamphlets, and broadsides, proselytize among other women, and discuss their views on the "woman question." While no Nazi orthodoxy on the "woman question" emerged, it is possible to discern some trends in the writings of women who joined or supported the Nazi movement prior to 1933.

Like their male counterparts, Nazi women expressed contempt for democracy, liberalism, individualism, and decadence. But in addition they deplored the emancipation of women. The Weimar Constitution of 1919 stipulated that "men and women shall have basically the same rights and duties." This meant that women were eligible to vote, hold public office, and pursue whatever career they wished. In fact, one-third of the labor force was female; between 70 and 90 percent of all eligible women voted in Weimar elections; between 6 and 9 percent of the parliamentary delegates elected were women; and about 20 percent of all university students were women.

These signs of emancipation, which so greatly impressed foreign observers, did not reflect the realities faced by most German women. Nazi critics complained that though the Weimar reforms may well have meant personal emancipation for a few well-educated, privileged women, the average woman merely felt more exploited. Paula Siber, an early adherent of National Socialism, noted that while the women's movement produced a few women judges and parliamentarians, it "forced hundreds of thousands of German women out into the streets of the big cities and produced thousands of wage slaves to the capitalist economic order." Nazi women argued that it was unjust to force women into a man's world in which they were unwanted and for which they were unprepared. Instead of reforming that male world, they urged women to return to the security of their traditional spheres of activity. In these roles women could exercise control over their lives and command respect from society. Besides the personal rewards of such a life, traditional women could have the additional satisfaction of knowing they contributed to the national cause by raising a loyal, decent future generation.

Women who supported the Nazis hoped to stem the tide of decadence they believed was engulfing their society. Unable to explain what appeared to be the demise of all morality and order, these women often blamed foreign influence and women's emancipation. A new English "girl type," a "movies-sport-jazz-flirt," behaved so scandalously that women in general came to be regarded as mere sex objects. Liberty, claimed one Nazi supporter, had been a French import in the first place and naturally produced only libertinism and prostitution. Another author blamed the increasing "materialism, naturalism, and Americanism" on the emancipated women who abandoned their homes and joined women's organizations. These "emancipationists," claimed Nazi women, had declared a "sex war" that promised to become as damaging to national solidarity as the socialists' class war. Nazi women, like Nazi men, came from predominantly lower-middle-class backgrounds. Whereas working-class women had long been accustomed to working outside their homes and upper-middle-class women often received educations that equipped them for careers or charitable social work, lower-middle-class women were unprepared to benefit from the changes initiated by Weimar Germany. Many had worked as sales clerks or servants prior to marriage, but these were not jobs to which they wished to return. Similarly, the intellectuals' Weimar culture, so often praised by literary critics and historians, only represented chaos and decadence to them. To counter the modernity they feared, Nazi women worked for a return to a largely mythical past in which they might win respect and feel secure.

Women Nazis did not, however, argue that patriotic, traditional German women ought to surrender to the masculine will and become the servants of men. Like the "emancipationists," they fervently believed women and men were equal. The path to achieving this equality, however, lay not in snatching away male occupations and professions but in restoring honor to traditional womanly responsibilities. Nazi women dreamed of a future in which men and women would be separate but equal. One Nazi woman leader claimed that women had been subjugated for centuries and declared the time had come for women to stop being "half-human beings." She urged women to return to the ancient Nordic traditions in which men and women were equal. Male historians, she continued, had deliberately obscured this truth for centuries. But now that she and other women historians had begun to rewrite history, the truth would be known. A Nazi woman who was interested in anthropology claimed that in ancient Germanic civilizations women were biologically equal to men. Recently discovered skeletons proved this conclusively, she said. The author did not, however, explain just how this biological equality would lead one to conclude that women ought to remain in their separate sphere. In the late 1920s a "racial scientist" concluded that women of "inferior" or "Mediterranean" races might well be inferior to the men of those races, but Germanic women and men had always been equal. Transferring this racial elitism to domestic politics, she declared that the Nazi state of the future would have to depend upon the skill of its very best qualified citizens, whether male or female. As society became more stratified along racial and class lines, talented members of both sexes would be recruited into the leadership. Elitism and racism, in the view of many Nazi women leaders, would replace sexism.

Many of these complaints about Weimar Germany emerged in other conservative writings as well as in Nazi works. It was their vehemence that differentiated Nazi women from other traditional and religious German women. While conservatives generally assumed that most problems would somehow be solved, Nazi women firmly believed that only a Nazi revolution could save the situation. Nowhere is this more obvious than in the speeches and autobiographical accounts of rank-and-file women who supported the party prior to the seizure of power.[1] These women — like their male counterparts — tended to be relatively young. Most joined in their twenties and thirties. Although their accounts abound in phrases like "we women," Nazi women viewed themselves as Nazis and Germans first and as women second. "We don't care about women's or men's rights — we are concerned solely with Germany's salvation!" wrote one woman. Not surprisingly, the family backgrounds of the women were characterized by a religious childhood and a generally conservative education. The threat of socialism terrified them — as is indicated by their anxious and exaggerated accounts of the 1918 German revolution. One woman had vivid memories of "street brawls, the mass graves, plundering, murder, and untold horrors of Bolshevik terror." Contrary to the assumptions of historians, women did not merely follow their husbands, fathers, or sons into the ranks of the Nazi party. One woman recalled, "Frequently it was the woman in a family who first understood the great ideas of Adolf Hitler and then — to her own personal misery — joined the Party against her family's wishes." In several cases women who joined the party noted that they created hardships for other members of their families — and sometimes husbands lost their jobs because of their wives' pro-Nazi activities.

Women in the early Nazi movement, like the men, were usually fanatic and dedicated. Frequently, these women expressed their scorn for passive, conservative, and traditional women. Nazi women viewed themselves as revolutionaries and proudly declared their "determination, joy at sacrifice [*Opferfreude*] and fanatical faith." But while autobiographical accounts by Nazi men emphasize violence, brawling, and paramilitary activities, the women's stories are characterized by an almost religious faith. Religious adjectives and metaphors color the narratives, and many women report joining the party as the result of a conversion experience. Said one woman,

> I had very little political experience [in the early 1920s] but then I heard Hitler speak and saw his pictures on so many posters. From then on I was converted into a fascist fighter and joined the German Freedom Movement [Nazi party].

Another "awaited the dawn of a new era," and believed that Hitler had been sent by God to usher in that new age. Some compared Hitler's life of hardship and faith to the life of Christ, and many early party members reported their impressions of Hitler in religious terms. "Quiet and sincere was his face, but a shining fire burned in his eyes!" wrote one woman. Another recalled, "I do not any longer remember how to describe it. When one had the great experience of looking the man in the eyes one simply became a fanatic!" This impression was confirmed repeatedly.

"This simple man, with the true, steady, honest gaze that streamed like rays of the sun into the 22,000 enthusiastic people," renewed one woman's faith in her ideals. In the writings of these women Hitler appeared to be the messiah of a secular religion.

As dedicated followers of a messiah, women Nazis did not worry about whether they were respected as women. They were needed for the work at hand and participated enthusiastically in a variety of roles during those "glorious days of struggle." They "worked to the point of exhaustion" and frequently risked arrest or attack for putting up illegal posters after dark, caring for fugitive and wounded SA men, and smuggling illegal campaign literature throughout Germany. "We women could not merely stand aside and let the men do all the work. We wanted to call out in a feminine way, 'Germany awake!' " recalled a woman from a small town. One mother justified her frequent absences from home by saying, "The Nation is in peril! I cannot remain happy and carefree at the supper table when Mother Germany weeps — and her children might die. Germany must live on — even if we must sacrifice our lives!" These women may have been behaving like "typical" women in their adoring attitude toward Hitler, but in their day-to-day party activities they were courageous and spirited — and certainly did not behave like the stereotype of the passive, meek woman. Proudly they noted that their sex did not prevent them from being harassed by the enemies of National Socialism. A woman from Göttingen commented, "We were so convinced of the righteousness of our cause, that we scarcely noticed the jeering and insults hurled at us." As Nazi women walked down the street, proudly wearing their armbands, they were met by calls of, "Hitler whore!" "Nazi bloodhound!" "Brown pig!" "Nazi creep!" and "Nazi goose!" One woman recalled an encounter in a park where she was leafletting:

> A proper citizen who felt I disturbed his peace, told me I was a bad person, and observed that I ought to go home and cook dinner for my family or else get myself elected to the Reichstag. But I told him, "With so many people like you, we women can't afford to step back and cook . . . I don't want my children ever to be able to say to me 'Mother, where were you when disaster threatened Germany?' "

Perhaps there was truth in one woman's comment, "Harassment is the best teacher of political solidarity." Similarly, another early Nazi woman observed, "The time of struggle forged a unity among us that no power on earth could have rent asunder!"

Although the early Nazi women recalled the splendid days of struggle, they were usually content to leave street violence, rallies, and anti-Bolshevik harassment to the men. Typically, women would address small political gatherings, conduct door-to-door campaigns, hand out leaflets, and organize women's clubs to support Nazi activities. In addition, they collected used clothing and food for the poorer party members, sewed clothing for unemployed SA men, organized children's parties, set up rest homes for the SA, and prepared food and refreshments for party rallies. The women were engaged primarily in the feminine activities for which they had been socialized, but they noted no feeling of inferiority on that account. Whether man or woman, it was victory that counted, they believed. Women's duties were not the same as those of the SA or SS, but they were equally important in the eyes of Nazi women. Moreover, the party leadership allowed women considerable organizational and ideological autonomy.

Naively, women anticipated that this relatively high degree of independence would persist after the victory of National Socialism. They failed to see that their autonomy resulted not so much from anyone's belief in the basic dignity or importance of women but from the Nazis' disregard for women altogether. Naturally, Nazi leaders would not refuse the women's contributions—whether those contributions were "comradeship or motherly love." But not for a moment did any Nazi leader seriously consider allowing women to pursue an independent policy or have a voice in policy making after the establishment of a Nazi state. As in so many other areas, the Nazi elite did not lay down a strict orthodoxy or establish a tight, centralized organization prior to 1933. Loyalty to Hitler alone constituted sufficient grounds for acceptance by the party. Thus, women who professed loyalty to Hitler were tolerated in the movement whether they wished to wear or to sew brown shirts.

Typically, women who supported the Nazis gathered together in local groups without national affiliation. The local histories of these groups tell the story of tiny circles of women who spontaneously began to meet in support of Nazi ideals and activities. Often there were only five or six women in the earliest groups, but membership increased rapidly after 1930. Fanatical dedication compensated for small numbers. The history of the pro-Nazi organization in Nuremberg, the Patriotic Women's League, comments, "146 women is surely not very many; but if each woman selflessly devotes herself to the service of a great ideal, then the women of Germany can do their part!" The district leader of Kurhessen reported that no women's support groups existed until early in 1930, when 10 women formed an association. By 1931 they counted 158 women members and by 1932 there were 2,020. As these organizations expanded they tended to affiliate with one of the national pro-Nazi women's organizations, which had been founded in the 1920s.

The oldest of these organizations was founded several years before the Nazi party itself and only gradually shifted its allegiance to National Socialism. Guida Diehl founded the Newland Movement in 1917 to further the practical application of Christian ideals to daily life. By the mid-twenties the organization claimed 200,000 members. Although Diehl and her followers admired Hitler's ideals, they deplored the uncouth image of the SA men. The chaos of the depression, however, motivated them to reconsider their position. Crisis required a strong party, Diehl decided. In Hitler they saw a "genuine German hero — honest, God-fearing, and righteous." As in wartime, Germany needed warriors. So the members of Newland dedicated their energies to helping the SA men from 1932 on. In return for her loyalty, Diehl was selected to become the leader of the Fighting Women's Union for Nazism.

In 1923 Elsbeth Zander formed the Red Swastika (Rotes Hackenkreuz) specifically to work with the SA men. Under the slogan "Faith, Hope, Love" the women of the Red Swastika established rest homes for SA men, collected money and clothing for them, and prepared food for Nazi families without incomes. In the mid-1920s Zander renamed her organization the Order of German Women. Starting in 1930 she published her own newsletter. Police records estimated their membership at 4,000 in 1930 (distributed among 160 local clubs), and Zander claimed they counted 10,000 members in the following year. Zander, unlike Diehl, controlled her organization with true Nazi authoritarianism. On the front page of the organization's newsletter appeared the drawing of a large megaphone with the message "ELSBETH ZANDER SPEAKS!" coming out of it. Frequently the paper closed with a prayer, "May the Lord God protect Elsbeth Zander, the leader of the women's order!"

Zander viewed herself as Hitler's right-hand woman. Since the Führer seemed to be ignoring the feminine half of the population, Zander appears to have decided that she ought to assume authority over it. Never, however, did Zander dream of challenging Hitler's absolute authority. Not only did her paper contain hundreds of laudatory articles about Hitler, but her organization collected large amounts of money and provided many useful services. The primary emphasis in the Order of German Women was on motherhood. But the tasks of motherhood, as Zander defined them, included not only rearing children but preparing the way for a new future by inculcating all members of the German nation with new values and ideals. After the Nazi seizure of power women would be needed more than ever because only women could redirect Germans' attitudes. Zander often quoted Hitler to illustrate her point. "Our goal is not only to create a new party, but to create new human beings!" Men might have to battle to destroy the old culture, but only women could educate the new Nazi believer.

Women who supported Nazism were free to organize in local circles, regional associations, and national unions. Nazi leaders accepted their support without making any demands other than that the members profess loyalty to Hitler. While pro-Nazi men always received encouragement to become party members, no similar effort was made to recruit women into the ranks of card-carrying Nazis. And while Nazi leaders tolerated a variety of women's organizations, one view on women's position in the movement was not tolerated. This view, as expressed in the party newspaper in 1926, argued that women needed no special organization of their own. The author criticized the Nazi revolutionary organization because it liberated only one-half of the human race and kept the other half enslaved — as either "a luxury item" or "producer of many children." She railed against the "crass egotism" that led men to view women as breeders and urged Nazi men to struggle for the elimination of all distinctions based on class, sex, and birth. The Nazi leadership lost no time in pronouncing this view heretical. Women could organize support for Hitler, but their participation could never exceed that of a ladies' aid.

By late 1931 Nazi leaders began to pay attention to their organized women followers. As it became clear that the party could not seize power by coup or revolution, the leaders began to redirect the party toward electoral activities. This included efforts to win the female vote. Local women's circles now came under the jurisdiction of the district leaders (*Gauleiter*), and regional associations were brought under the supervision of the newly created National Socialist Women's League. Women greeted this change with mixed emotions. On the one hand, the increased attention from the Nazi elite flattered them, but on the other hand, they regretted losing much of their original independence. Under the leadership of Elsbeth Zander women had joined wholeheartedly in the campaign battles of the early 1930s. After 1932 Hitler himself realized the importance of attracting women voters and introduced two new elements into his speeches. He warned that Bolshevism would destroy the family; and he promised that if elected his party would find jobs for all husbands and husbands for all unmarried women. While the percentage of women party members decreased to under 5 percent, membership in women's organizations soared and the female vote for the Nazi party increased dramatically.

We may deplore the Nazi solution to Germany's problems, but it is clear that Hitler spoke to real needs. His promise to provide a husband for every woman, for example, had great appeal. Because of the staggering loss of life in World War I, about 2,000,000 German women would not be able to find husbands. Although the war had been begun by men and been fought by men, this shortage of men was commonly referred to as the "woman surplus." A bitter opponent of Nazism recalled that Hitler's promise of a husband and home "had an enormous effect, touching deeply as it did the innermost feelings and desires of millions of women for whom equal rights had 'til then meant merely the right to be exploited." [2]

In addition to the anxiety about marriage experienced by single women or widows, Hitler played on a more universal anxiety — the depression. He promised that all employed women with husbands or fathers who could support them would be removed from the labor market. This, declared the Nazis, would eliminate all families with double incomes and distribute jobs among male workers. With 6,000,000 women employed (10 percent of the total population, or nearly 20 percent of the labor force), it was understandable that there would be concern about this issue. The situation was exacerbated by the fact that while almost 30 percent of the male work force was unemployed, only about 10 percent of all employable women were out of work.[3] Women workers were blamed for stealing men's jobs because they would work for lower wages. A refugee from Nazi Germany looked back on those days and recalled that women became the breadwinners while their men sat idle. This, she said, created deep psychological depression in men, women, and children. In reality, however, women did not steal men's jobs. The sectors of the economy that both were better paid and employed mostly men (i.e., heavy industry and construction) were the hardest hit by the economic crisis. Still, pervasive antifeminism led the general public to make scapegoats of women workers for the conditions they could neither control or comprehend.

Anxiety prevailed over analysis and people longed for "the good old days" when mothers stayed at home. The household for the German woman was like the small business, farm, or shop for the middle-class man. The home provided the wife with dignity, status, and security. Even when women had not yet been forced by economic necessity to take in washing, seek work in an office or store, or offer their services as housekeepers, they expressed great anxiety that such a fate might befall them. Middle-class women had been socialized to be wives. When this role appeared to be threatened, they fought to defend it rather than seeking new alternatives. Thus, Nazi women proselytized among their peers by using appeals to revive the traditional women's tasks.

It may be that the women who so adoringly worshiped Hitler did anticipate returning to a life centered on the home after the Nazi revolution. But the leaders of the Nazi women's movement had learned to speak in public, organize meetings, campaign, lobby, write political pamphlets, and direct welfare projects. They took great pride in their independence and accomplishments. Certainly, they considered themselves to be the equals of Nazi men. The women did not anticipate returning meekly to their homes after 1933. In Hitler's "second revolution" women would participate actively in the creation of a new society. They did not think this would necessitate their participation in politics. Political power, they believed, would remain in male hands while cultural power would fall under their jurisdiction. After 1933 women leaders did indeed make an important contribution to the new regime. But they contributed service to the Nazi state without gaining any influence over its basic policies. Early in 1933 Nazi policy became unmistakably clear:

> There is no place for the political woman in the ideological world of National Socialism. . . . The intellectual attitude of the movement on this score is opposed to the political woman. . . . The German resurrection is a male event.[4]

The Traditionalists

With the seizure of power came a dramatic change in the Nazi women's movement — and in official Nazi policy toward women. The earlier feelings of elitism and esprit de corps disappeared with the rapid influx of new members. Courage and loyalty diminished in importance after the struggle for power had been won, while more "feminine" virtues like obedience and motherliness took on a new importance. Official recognition converted the women's organization into another branch of the bureaucracy and imposed an unprecedented orthodoxy on the "woman question." Persistent unemployment, combined with fears of depopulation, produced widespread scapegoating of women in the labor force. Too late, female Nazi leaders began to hear the misogynistic overtones in their male colleagues' statements.

Despite scattered protests, the women's section of the party had been reorganized by the party elite in 1931–1932. That process continued after 1933, and the women's organizations were "purified" as part of a general policy to eliminate all potential dissidents. Less attention has been paid to the reconstitution of the women's organization than to the dramatic purge of the SA or the bureaucratic housecleaning of radical elements in the German Labor Front, but all proceeded from Hitler's determination to eliminate any potential threat to his absolute power. The Order of German Women was renamed the National Socialist Women's Association (NS Frauenschaft). After a brief tenure in office, Zander was replaced by a man. Within a year, most of the earlier leaders and writers in the pro-Nazi women's movement were retired from prominent positions. All women's organizations, whether charitable, social, professional, or political, were ordered either to submit to Nazification or dissolve themselves. The nationwide Union of Women's Organizations chose the latter course, but nearly all of the smaller organizations associated with it decided to add "NS" to their titles, accept Nazi-approved leaders, and participate in Nazi activities. By 1936 nearly 11,000,000 women were associated with the nationwide Frauenschaft. In addition to whatever a group's original purpose was, its members pledged themselves to "fight for the Germanic ideals," to aid economic recovery, to fight for "the purification of the

Aryan race," to rear a healthy younger generation, to "search for a new, genuine solution to the woman question," to fight decadence, and to "combat in word and deed the Jewish Marxist spirit." Each woman promised to "SPREAD THESE DOCTRINES OPENLY AND EVERYWHERE. TO LOYALLY AND TIRELESSLY PLEDGE OURSELVES TO THIS BATTLE, THAT WE SOLEMNLY SWEAR TO OUR LEADER ADOLF HITLER!" Meanwhile, official propaganda emphasized women's responsibilities to remain at home and raise families.

Almost at once, female Nazis who had hoped to be included in the Nazi state protested. Several supporters of Nazism contributed essays to a volume entitled *From German Women to Adolf Hitler,* in which they alternately demanded and requested a share in policy making in the Nazi state. They argued strongly for the admission of women into all fields — including the military and the diplomatic service, asked men of good will to realize that a "people's state [*Volksgemeinschaft*] cannot be a state for men only," and claimed that the exclusion of women from government was a carry-over from the decadent Weimar democracy. One bitter opponent of democracy claimed that an exclusively male democratic state would favor the worst man over the best woman. A strong dose of nationalism runs through all these essays. Typical was a reminder to the Führer that if he wanted a generation of strong men, strong women would have to produce them. Some argued that all women ought not be forced into motherhood, just as not all men were required to become soldiers. These women demanded an important role in the Nazi state and affirmed their deep loyalty to Hitler.

These and other protests did not halt or even retard the transformation of official policy on women in the Third Reich. Prior to 1933, Hitler expressed no objections to accepting aid from enthusiastic Nazi women, nor had he found it expedient to discourage the most outspoken women leaders; and after 1933 he welcomed into the new state all those women who had been recruited by Zander, Diehl, and other leading Nazi women. But the original women leaders disappeared from important positions. As in other branches of the state, idealistic, fanatic, determined women were replaced by bureaucrats with connections. Hitler now needed a different kind of woman.

Gertrud Scholtz-Klink was the ideal Nazi leader in the new state. Her most important attribute, absolute subservience, was reinforced by her public image. The mother of four, a widow, former civil servant in the state of Baden, a party member from before 1933, blond, blue-eyed, and Aryan — Scholtz-Klink seemed perfectly suited to take over the leadership of the Frauenwerk (Women's Bureau). Within a few years of accepting this position, Scholtz-Klink married her superior, the director of Nazi welfare. In return for her cooperation with the Nazi hierarchy Scholtz-Klink was given ever larger areas of jurisdiction. Within two years of her appointment as director of the Women's Bureau, she became the director of all voluntary women's organizations, the Red Cross, the Women's Office of the Labor Front, the national Women's Labor Front, and the motherhood service. Yet, after four years in office Scholtz-Klink complained that while she had marched with Hitler and often appeared on the same speakers' platform, never once had she been allowed to discuss any aspect of his policy on women. Scholtz-Klink and the women in her office received ever-increasing bureaucratic responsibilities over their followers and employees, but they exerted virtually no influence upon policy making. Like so many leaders of Jewish ghetto communities in the Third Reich, women gained the illusion of power but lost control over the major decisions that affected their lives. Administrative autonomy was no substitute for real authority over basic policy making. American historian Mary Beard was impressed at the fact that in 1941 Scholtz-Klink controlled with "dictatorial authority" 30,000,000 German women and 20,000,000 women in occupied territory. But Beard misjudged. Hitler was correct when he wrote in 1942 that women had never possessed any political influence. "In no local section of the Party has a women ever had the right to hold even the smallest post."

Another indication of Hitler's lack of esteem for the Frauenwerk was reflected in the low percentage of party members in its leadership. Of about 37,000 women leaders only 5.7 percent belonged to the party; and only about 2 percent of all high Nazi officials worked under the Women's Bureau.[5] Only the Labor Front included so few party members. Whereas employment in any of the other governmental departments could be a steppingstone to advancement into the higher echelons of the party or state, no woman ever was promoted beyond the Women's Bureau. Women could aspire to status *within* the women's bureaucracy.

This was, of course, the logical consequence of the Nazis' separation of society into masculine and feminine spheres. The women's spheres remained inferior in many respects, but the Nazi policy did create employment opportunities for many women and filled the spare time of hundreds of thousands of volunteers. Every community with over 3,500 inhabitants was assigned one full-time, paid director of women's affairs; each of about 18,500 communities had a special head of home economics; 770 regional leaders coordinated women's activities; and in each of 32 districts a woman leader was appointed as the counterpart of the (male) district leader.[6] In addition to these salaried officials, there were thousands of part-time and volunteer workers, so that the Frauenwerk included 2,700,000 women by 1935. Moreover, women worked in other divisions of the government as well, such as the welfare division, the women's section of the Labor Front, and the lower levels of the educational hierarchy. Thus, in 1935 one out of every ten civil servants was a woman. While German women were not encouraged to join the Nazi party, every woman was urged to belong to one of the women's organizations or services. Wives of SA and SS men and party officials were all but required to join one; others were lured into Nazi activities by promises of reduced prices for certain commodities; any woman who was employed by the state could not keep her job unless she joined and participated actively in at least one organization.

Scholtz-Klink's first task was to elevate the status of the woman who wished only to raise a family and not seek employment outside the home. One of the most obvious methods to accomplish this in a literate society was to launch an educational campaign to professionalize the role of housewife. Under Scholtz-Klink's supervision the Nazis began an educational blitz to educate women in nutrition, interior decoration, economic management of household finances, child care, efficient cleaning methods, and sewing. Two hundred and seventy-nine schools were established to train mothers, and 1,000 teachers with 2,000 volunteers were recruited to staff these schools. Financing for this program came from the sale of commemorative badges sold on the German mothers' day — Hitler's mother's birthday. Over 1,500,000 women per year enrolled in nearly 84,000 motherhood courses. This, one woman Nazi pointed out, was more than the Weimar Republic had offered during the fourteen years of its existence. Fifteen thousand cooking courses attracted over 300,000 women per year and over 1,500,000 women enrolled in courses in home economy.[7] These courses were not included in the regular secondary curriculum but were intended for women who had already completed their formal schooling.

For women who seemed especially talented a leadership training school was established and conducted along similar lines to the elite training schools for SS men. For upwardly mobile careerist women, the Nazis offered a program in household science that led to a master's degree (*Meisterin*). The women's schools were well funded and provided with newly constructed buildings, special equipment, audiovisual aids, and the latest household machines. In addition, the programs sponsored outings, cultural evenings of music or speeches, and exhibitions of women's work. Textbooks glorified women's work and women's history. Typical of this genre was a collection of biographies entitled *Of Brave, Cheerful and Educated Housewives* (1937). For women who were not enrolled in courses, the state radio network offered thousands of hours per year of instruction in women's work, news about well-known women, and readings of literature that would appeal to women listeners. It may be true that German women have never had so little political power in the twentieth century as under the Nazis, but it is also true that women have never been the object of so much official solicitude.

The motives of the Nazi leadership were not altruistic; women's activities fulfilled many functions for the Nazi state. Scholtz-Klink told German women that their first duty was to raise a new generation that would be loyal to the Third Reich. To do this, German mothers had to be converted to Nazi ideology. Every course, every pamphlet on housekeeping, every radio broadcast contained propaganda. Rebecca West recalled a conversation she had with a German hairdresser's assistant who was worried that she might have failed the exam for admission into the profession. West assured her that she seemed competent in her profession and ought not worry. But the young woman responded, "Yes I am good at my work! Shampooing I can do, and water waving I can do, and hairdyeing I can do; but I keep mixing up Goering's and Goebbels' birthdays." The Nazis set out to permeate all aspects of life with their ideology.

In keeping with this policy, they devoted a great deal of attention to the youth. Just as all German boys were recruited into the Hitler Youth, all German girls were pressured into joining one of the organizations for girls and young women. Either because girls resisted more than boys or because boys were more actively forced into their organizations, there were always greater proportions of boys in Nazi youth organizations than girls. In 1936–1937, for example, of 3,500,000 young people in official organizations only 37 percent were female. An American observer noted that the Nazis lavished more attention and publicity on boys' activities than on girls'.

For girls and young women between seventeen and twenty-five years of age, the government offered an alternative to school and work — the labor year. Under this plan girls from the countryside were to live in an urban area and learn about city life through working for schools, hospitals, and social agencies there; city girls were to go into the countryside and join with the farmers in their work; a third type of camp was designed to help new settlers on recently reclaimed land. Although the labor year was made compulsory for male and female youth in 1936, over twice as many young men as young women participated. Only young women who desired to go on to a university education were absolutely required to put in their time with the labor year program. Two-thirds of all placements were in rural areas to offset the rural exodus. Frequent complaints marred the record of these camps. Some observers claimed that the girls merely provided free servants for overworked farm women. Others said that girls too often seduced farmers — or that farmers behaved indecently toward the girls. A few critics asserted that the entire purpose of the project was to remove 30,000 women and girls from the labor market each year and maintain them in work camps. But the project leaders insisted on the ideological and psychological importance of their effort. Women ought, they said, to experience the same kind of comradeship as men. Just as men formed warrior bands, women ought to form motherhood associations. Peer group solidarity would replace competitiveness among women and simultaneously deepen women's loyalty to the state. Organized mothers would produce dedicated Nazi children.

Behind ideology and propaganda lay the true goal of the Nazi women's program. By urging women to return to full-time motherhood, Nazi leaders planned to reverse the falling birthrate. In 1913 the crude birthrate was 27.5 live births per 1,000 (or a net gain in population of 12.4 per 1,000 when the death rate was figured in); by 1933 the crude birthrate had fallen to 14.7 per 1,000 (with a net population increase of 3.5 per 1,000).[8] Only a year after the seizure of power, the crude birthrate dramatically increased to 18.0 per 1,000 (with a net population increase of 7.1 per 1,000).

The Nazis succeeded where earlier politicians had failed by passing legislation to outlaw birth control and encourage marriage. While they could not produce husbands for each of the "surplus women," the Nazi planners did succeed in making marriage economically attractive. Each couple who wished to marry received an automatic marriage loan of 550 marks with which they purchased household furnishings. In an economy where about one-third of all workers earned less than 1,500 marks per year, this sum appeared attractive indeed. The 1933 marriage rate jumped by 24 percent over the previous year. Between August 1933 and the spring of 1935 over 500,000 couples took advantage of this scheme. To be eligible for a loan each couple had to demonstrate that neither partner was a Jew and to promise that the wife would not seek employment outside the home. If the marriage produced children, the principal would be reduced 25 percent for each child born. Couples who participated in this program produced nearly 200,000 children during the first three years of its operation.[9]

To further encourage marriage and childbearing the Nazis offered psychological incentives as well. For example, parents who bore nine children (or seven sons, whichever happened first) were allowed to choose any official of the state to be the next child's godfather. By 1936 Hitler could claim over 12,000 such godchildren — but Hindenburg had 27,000! Mothers with many children received special medals every Mother's Day. Those with over four children were rewarded by bronze medals; over six, by silver; and more than eight by gold. After 1939 all party youth were required to salute women who wore these medals. These propagandistic measures were reinforced by legislation that lessened the stigma attached to illegitimate children and the women who bore them. During the Weimar Republic socialists had long campaigned for such a reform, but their efforts met with failure because of vehement conservative opposition. In a nation where the illegitimacy rate varied between 8 and 11 percent, this reform was important. But Nazi legislation did not stop there. Immediately after they seized power, Nazis closed all birth-control education centers and increased the prison sentences for anyone convicted in an abortion case.

Nazi policy endeavored to end the double standard in sexual morality by allowing men and women equal freedom. But instead of achieving this goal by reducing the chance of unwanted pregnancy, the Nazis wanted to end the negative consequences of unwed motherhood.

Women not only produced German children, but, economists discovered, spent 75 percent of all German wages. It followed that they ought to be organized as consumers. Accordingly, posters, pamphlets, recipes, and radio commercials urged women to buy what was plentiful and adjust eating habits to harvest times. In a year that produced an especially large apple harvest, for example, propaganda exhorted women to "Think of the Fatherland! Cook with Apples!" The Women's Bureau organized boycotts of Jewish department stores and other "non-Aryan" businesses. Perhaps the best-publicized and most effective consumer campaign was the weekly "stew meal," when all German families were exhorted to eat a "one-pot, one-course" main meal and donate the money saved to a Nazi charity. Posters extolled the virtues of "stew — the meal of sacrifice for the Reich!" Foreigners may have scoffed as they read Scholtz-Klink's speech to the Nuremberg party rally in 1937 in which she extolled the humble soup ladle as a weapon as powerful as other weapons, but the mobilization of the German consumer was impressive.

In still another respect the Nazis redirected women's activities to serve their own ends. Women's charity work was expanded to become a vital factor in National Socialist welfare policy. Just as women had previously collected money for charity, the Nazi women launched several campaigns each year to raise money to support a wide range of welfare programs. By far the largest of these drives was the Winter Relief program, which helped poor families during the cold winter season. Women collected money on street corners, by door-to-door canvassing, and by direct appeals to large corporations and businesses. Donors received badges to wear on the lapels of their coats or to display in their shop windows. In 1937 women sold 118,700,000 badges — which had been made by poorly paid seamstresses in their homes. Although these drives remained primarily the responsibility of women, the party leaders also did their share by exerting pressure on potential contractors. Hermann Göring himself in the winter of 1934 appeared on a Berlin street corner holding a Winter Relief collection box saying, "It is more blessed to give than to receive." On another occasion a truckload of SS men rode through the city streets jokingly warning people that if they failed to contribute generously they would find themselves facing prison terms for high treason. The Winter Relief raised sufficient funds to finance a welfare program that benefited between 16 and 20 percent of the population annually.[10] This impressive sum resulted partly from party pressure on individuals to contribute generously, but it was women's volunteer work that accounted for the fact that only 2 percent of the total collected was required for overhead.

Under the slogan "Put the common good ahead of individual gain," women administered the Nazi welfare program and collected the funds to pay for it. Although the leadership of the Welfare Bureau was exclusively male, it was the women's efforts that provided National Socialism with a thin veneer of "socialism." Hitler made virtually no effort at any genuine socialist reform. Instead, the term "socialism" came to be synonymous with "sacrifice." Women accepted this task for which their upbringing had already prepared them. After the ideal of socialism lost any chance of realization, it was relegated to the women's sphere. Feminine spirit and morale substituted for genuine change.

Hitler's first major action on the "woman question" directly involved women's "joy in sacrifice." All women employed outside the home were exhorted to give up their jobs so that unemployed men would receive greater job opportunities. Posters demanded, "Get ahold of pots and pans and broom and you'll sooner find a groom!" "Not for you the business life; rather learn to be a wife!" "A job will not bring happiness near. The home alone is your proper sphere!" But some women did not willingly retreat into their homes. What could not be accomplished by propaganda, economic incentives, or socialization was enforced by decree. In June 1933, legislation mandated the immediate dismissal of all women whose husbands were employed by the government. Further, it stipulated that no woman under thirty-five years of age could be granted permanent tenure in office — on the assumption that she ought to marry and bear children.

These laws had precedents in the Weimar Republic. After the 1923 inflation, legislation prevented women from holding civil service jobs if their husbands also worked for the government. Although this law expired in 1928, a similar measure passed the Reichstag in 1932 — with only the Communist party opposing it. But Nazi legislation against "double-income families" received great publicity. Private employers were told that women could be dismissed without further justification if their husbands or fathers could support them. Quotas of 10 percent were imposed on women students in higher education; women doctors were allowed to practice only if they merged their practices with those of their physician husbands; women lawyers were removed from judgeships and high state offices, and women teachers were often dismissed in favor of men.

The impact of this legislation is difficult to assess. At one extreme, a Nazi women's paper claimed that after only one year the number of women employed outside their homes dropped from 11,000,000 to 6,000,000 — leaving no options but suicide or prostitution for hundreds and thousands of women and girls, according to the editor. However, at the other extreme an American scholar estimated that only about 300,000 women were actually dismissed. Labor statisticians calculated that women's participation in the labor force dropped from 30 percent in 1933 to 24 percent in 1935. As the economy recovered from the depression the absolute number of women in the labor force increased steadily. The decrease of women relative to men resulted from the fact that men had been more severely affected by unemployment in the first place. Economic recovery, based as it was on heavy military expenditures, meant a speedy reemployment of men and did not indicate massive dismissals of women. When one examines long-term trends in the composition of the labor force, Hitler's much-publicized expulsion of women had only minimal effects on the absolute numbers of women employed. By 1939 women comprised approximately 30 percent of the work force — just as during the last normal years of the Weimar Republic. Women in the professions, likewise, did not suffer as severely as contemporaries believed, although hundreds of women professionals were harassed for their liberal political beliefs.[11]

Moreover, the Nazis' sharp distinction between male and female sectors of employment produced an ironic result. If women's work were really separate, then educated women physicians, officials, lawyers, economists, and educators would be required to staff the "women's world." After 1936, quotas against women in higher education were quietly overlooked, and women were even encouraged to become lawyers and physicians. Thus, a sex-segregated society produced opportunities for women in traditionally masculine occupations. But despite education or professional status, women could not advance into male realms of decision making.

After 1933, no Nazi woman could cherish the illusion that she would be esteemed in any but a subservient position. Despite shifts in official policy, one principle remained intact: women must never exert any influence over major policy making. Women were allowed horizontal mobility to work in the home, factory, office, or field — as national priorities or personal necessity dictated. But, except within the women's organizations, all vertical mobility remained closed to them. Women were expected to provide a steady supply of obedient children and also to work whenever they were needed and to provide the image of social cohesion. It was the woman's task to create harmony and maintain high morale — while SA and SS men applied terror and coercion to enforce obedience. Both roles were traditional. Men were powerful and women nurturant. The Nazis were not simply "prowoman" or "antiwoman" — they were pro-Nazi.

The Opportunists

As Nazi leaders began to dream of conquest and plan for war, their attitude toward women's proper sphere underwent a dramatic reversal. Modern, "total" war inexorably incorporates large numbers of women into public sectors — regardless of political systems or ideology. Realizing this,

Nazi planners no longer asked *are* women capable of holding jobs outside their homes but *how* can we enable women to enter the labor force? Nazi historians investigated women's economic role and concluded that from the Middle Ages through the early stages of the Industrial Revolution women had played a major part in production. It was time, they declared, for women to return to productive activities. "Tradition" was thereby redefined and women were urged to be traditional by reclaiming their economic importance. Industrial psychologists investigated the methods by which office and factory work might be made more pleasant for women workers. Coffee breaks, free soup at lunchtime, brightly painted work areas, day-care centers, free household helpers, and an extra day off for doing the family washing every two weeks were introduced in many areas. Experiments ascertained that women work and learn best when supervised by female personnel, so women were recruited into these positions. Discussion groups were formed to give women employees an opportunity to overcome their conflicts, anxieties, and guilt about working outside their homes in previously masculine occupations. Psychologists continued to maintain that masculine and feminine work would never be the same, but they expanded their conception of appropriate women's employment. Selling, for example, required "womanly understanding and intuition." Salesmen who expressed anxiety that they would be fired were assured that men in feminized fields would never be laid off, even though no more men would be hired in these areas. Economists investigated women's work during World War I in the hope of ascertaining just how women could best be deployed in industry. All restrictions against married women employees were quietly dropped — as were quotas against female students, teachers, and other professionals. Even wives who had received marriage loans on the condition that they not seek employment were encouraged to look for work.

This reversal of policy on the "woman question" was accompanied by a vigorous propaganda drive to revise women's self-image. Pamphlets proclaimed a renaissance of women's work, while the official Nazi woman's magazine announced, "We see the woman as the eternal mother of our people, but also as the working and fighting comrade of the man!" One woman wrote that women still belonged primarily in the home, but then proceeded to redefine "home" to include "wherever Germany may need us!" Magazine articles praised Germany's outstanding film director (Leni Riefenstahl) and leading test pilot (Hannah Reitsch) for their service to the fatherland. Hitler glorified women who "with iron discipline entered into the fighting German community." After the outbreak of World War II the Women's Bureau even declared that men and women were equal. Everywhere women were urged to join organizations and to form strong bonds with other women. Comradeship on the assembly line and in women's associations, they were told, contributed just as much to victory as soldiers' comradeship at the front.[12]

Yet despite this publicity drive, misogyny persisted among party officials. In letters and memos Nazi leaders referred to women as "geese," "dumb prattlers," and "simple-minded ravers." In newsletters they accused women of ruining morale because they cluttered the streets by standing in line waiting to purchase food. At no time did anyone consider equalizing male and female wages for the same work. Nor were women advanced to decision-making positions in industry, politics, or business. The Ministry of Labor established its official policy in 1939 — after receiving complaints about discrimination from women workers. "There can be no basic equality with the man." Wages would remain at about 75 percent of male wages (although by 1941 the guideline rose to 80 percent). Wages, they asserted, depended not only on productivity but on the needs of individual workers. Thus, women with large numbers of dependents received a small monthly subsidy, but women in general were assumed to require less money. Further, Nazi officials declared that equalizing male and female salaries would disrupt the harmony within the home and between men and women workers.[13] Other regulations supported this harmony — such as the rule that male workers must always be addressed by their official titles (Doctor or Director, for example), while women were called simply Miss or Mrs. Nazi harmony depended upon male supremacy.

After the minister of propaganda, Joseph Goebbels, made his famous declaration of "total war" in 1943, all women were required to register with the employment office. By the end of the war more German women than German men were employed — and the number of foreign laborers totaled half the number of women workers. However, only about 40 to 50 percent of all German women were employed during the Third Reich. This means that women's paid participation in the war effort never equaled their participation in the World War I economy. Observers reported that women in Nazi Germany responded to labor conscription by evading it wherever they could. Wives of high-ranking party officials were hired for fictitious jobs; women with influence managed to find relatively pleasant part-time office jobs; many women adopted several children so they would not be required to work full time, and over half the women conscripted after 1943 failed to meet health standards that would have required them to hold full-time jobs. While the women who entered the labor market in the late 1930s may well have been genuinely happy to receive greater occupational opportunities, the same cannot be said of the women who found themselves forced into employment after the war began.

With increasing labor shortages, all earlier rules about a division of labor based on sex disappeared. Women worked in construction, armaments factories, shipyards, and foundries. Official propagandists ignored these

FIGURE 19–1
COMPOSITION OF THE LABOR FORCE IN GERMANY, 1914–1945[14]

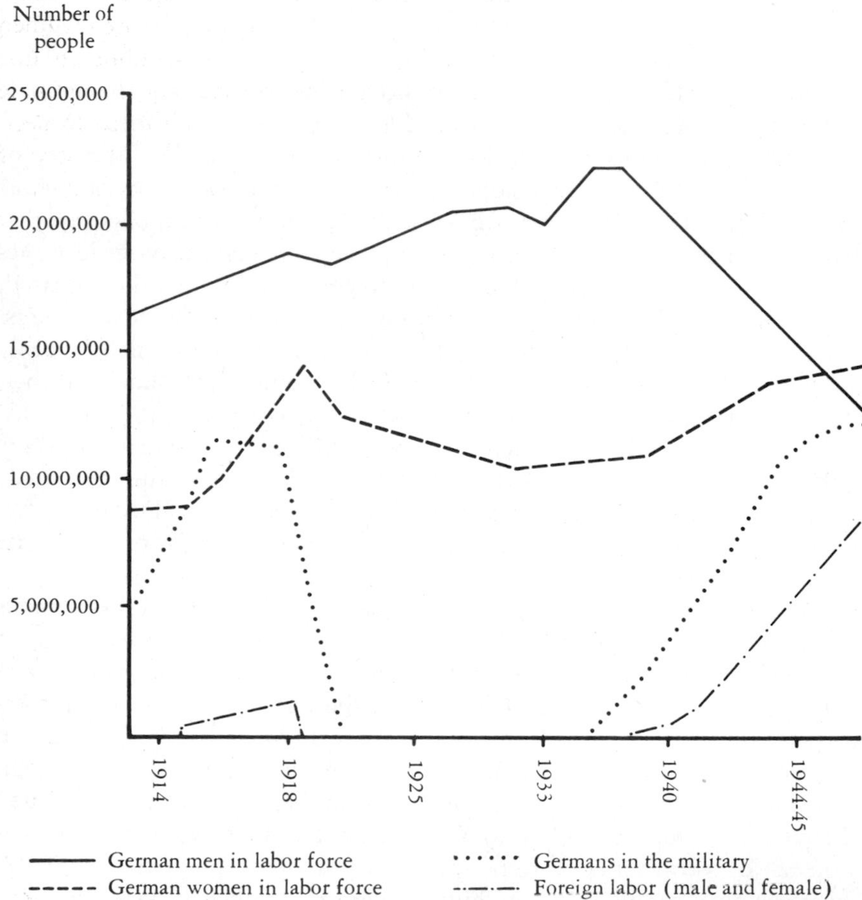

women in "inappropriate" jobs, because they worried that male workers would feel demoralized if they found that women with so little training and experience could do male work. Instead, women's role in colonizing newly conquered areas received great attention. The Welfare Bureau proudly announced that for the first time in world history women social workers marched into defeated nations with the troops. A press release praised the women who followed the military cannons with "their own goulash cannons." Under the title "Living Socialism!" another article described how the women would redistribute the wealth of the "plutocrats" among the poorer segments of the "liberated population." Once again women provided the illusion of socialism and justice within a brutal context.

Despite the hardships of war, German women were expected to continue bearing many children and to indoctrinate those children with fanatic faith in the Nazi state. Mothers who failed to do this risked being reported by their own children. Social scientists have often observed that a fascist state, with its emphasis on a strong family life, offers security and status to women. Not only does such a view ignore the oppression of women within the patriarchal family but it misrepresents fascist society. While Nazi propaganda praised the strong family, Nazi policy undermined family solidarity. Children were recruited into Nazi youth organizations, and Nazi education formed their world view from an early age. During the last years of the Third Reich it became clear that the ideal Nazi society of the future would not encourage family-centered bonds but same-sex peer-group associations.

By the late 1930s Nazi planners had begun to suggest that unwed motherhood provide an institutionalized alternative to marriage. One physician put it crudely, "Round up a thousand German girls of the purest stock, isolate them in a camp, and let a hundred German men of equally pure German stock join them. You will have a thousand children at one stroke!" In 1939 Heinrich Himmler, the head of the elite SS, exhorted each of his soldiers to leave a child behind before marching off to battle. Young women, he hoped, would cooperate with this policy from a "sense of profound moral seriousness."[15] Specially selected young women and men received state sponsored vacations at camps for unmarried people with the understanding that sexual taboos would be ignored. Women who returned from these camps as "heroic mothers" then lived in special homes for unwed mothers. These young women attended lectures, lived communally, participated in group outings, and studied courses related to motherhood and childrearing. Some observers tell us that some of these mothers welcomed the opportunity to bear children "for their fatherland" without the inconvenience of marriage. Compared to factory work or life in labor camps, the home for unwed mothers may not have appeared so oppressive. Whatever the attitudes of these women, these so-called "breeding camps" resulted from male fantasy, not concern for women's well-being. This preoccupation with breeding is illustrated dramatically by Hitler's schemes for repopulating Germany after the war. In the last months of the war, with Allied bombers destroying Berlin, Hitler and the Nazi elite lived in a bunker deep under the city. There Hitler devised a plan whereby every decorated soldier would be allowed to marry more than one woman after German victory. Women, like medals for bravery, would be the Nazi hero's reward.

Meanwhile, the Women's Bureau disintegrated. Scholtz-Klink divorced her second husband and married a high-ranking SS general. Complaints poured in to party headquarters that she and her husband cared only about amassing a fortune so they could purchase a country estate in Poland. Speakers from the Women's Bureau failed to appear to give much-publicized speeches to raise women's morale. Women's role in policy making remained utterly insignificant. Of over 1,400 Nazi leaders in 1944 only 9 were women. Still, radio broadcasts instructed women to bear with courage the loss of their sons, fathers, and loved ones. As bombs destroyed their homes, women were supposed to welcome the opportunity to become civil defense "heroes" (not "heroines"). With neither uniforms or weapons, women were recruited into the military as scouts, saboteurs, medics, communications aides, and messengers. As in the early days of the party, this was again a "time of struggle." When sacrifice was the order of the day, women were allowed to contribute equally with men. As both "spiritual mothers" and "fighting comrades," women once again were expected to embody a myth that every day became more remote from reality.

Yet, there were German women who courageously resisted Nazi rule. Many socialist and Communist delegates to the Reichstag in the Weimar Republic went to labor camps or to the scaffold along with their male comrades. The Nazis established five concentration camps especially for women who were arrested for resistance activities. Sophie Scholl and Liselotte Hermann were among the most publicized martyrs of the German resistance. Unfortunately, we know about only those women who were ultimately unsuccessful and therefore were captured. Successful members of the resistance escaped arrest — and have largely disappeared from the historical record. Women utilized the sexist attitudes of male Nazis to their own advantage. Chatting flirtatiously with the guards, they calmly wheeled their baby buggies past checkpoints — and once out of sight removed forged passports or illegal pamphlets from under their infants' blankets. Or the honest German mother would soberly reassure the Gestapo officer (over a cup of hot tea) that *she* would never harbor a Jewish refugee. Because Nazi men believed women to be incapable of independent action, some women could resist courageously the policies they deplored.

Conclusion

Although the Third Reich failed to endure for 1,000 years, as Hitler predicted it would, it did survive for twelve. An important factor in its survival was the Nazis' ability to manipulate traditional masculine and feminine role stereotypes. While storm troopers and soldiers brought terror first to Germany and later to all Europe, women were supposed cheerfully to make sacrifices and perform whatever functions the state required. Throughout, they were expected to remain idealistic, optimistic, and domestic. When the commandant at the Auschwitz concentration camp returned to his family after a day's work, he could assuage whatever conscience he had left with the secure knowledge that he was a decent family man. Except for the women in the resistance, German women made ideal collaborators. Naively anticipating that their womanly sphere would one day be elevated to prominence, they mistook propaganda for reality. But cultural power without economic power is empty. Although women joined the vast array of women's organizations and heard themselves praised by hours of propaganda, they remained only privates in a civilian army commanded by Nazi men.

Notes

1. In 1934, Theodor Abel, a professor at Columbia University, posted announcements in all Nazi party meeting places to publicize an essay competition. He asked that the competitors describe their activities in the Nazi party before 1933 and emphasize "family life, economic condition, education, membership in other organizations, participation and important thoughts, experiences and feelings about events and ideas of the post-war period" (T. Abel, *Why Hitler Came to Power: An Answer Based on the Original Life Stories of 600 of His Followers,* Prentice-Hall, New York, 1938, pp. 1–4). Of the 683 answers, 48 were written by women. All of the essays are in the Manuscript Collection in the Hoover Institution at Stanford University, Stanford, California. Peter Merkl recently subjected these data to new analysis, and the results of his study appear in his book, *Political Violence under the Swastika: 581 Early Nazis,* Princeton University Press, Princeton, 1975.

   For help in researching this material, I am greatly indebted to Mrs. Agnes F. Peterson of the Hoover Institution. Permission to quote was kindly granted by the Hoover Institution, from Hoover Institution on War, Revolution and Peace, Theodore F. Abel Collection.

   A second source of information is a collection of local histories of pro-Nazi women's organizations assembled by the Nazi Party Archives in 1936. These essays are available on microfilm from the NSDAP Hauptarchiv, Hoover Institution.

2. Hilda Browning, *Women Under Fascism and Communism* (Lawrence, London, n.d.), pp. 1–2.

3. The Nazi statistical argument is best expressed in Richard Peikow, *Die soziale und wirtschaftliche Stellung der deutschen Frau in der Gegenwart,* Ph.D. dissertation, Humbolt University, Berlin, 1937. For the statistics on employment, see "Die erwerbstätigkeit der Reichsbevölkerung," *Statistik des deutschen Reiches,* vol. 453, Heft II, Berlin, 1936.

4. Engelbert Huber, *Das ist Nationalsozialismus,* quoted in George Mosse, *Nazi Culture,* New York, 1966, p. 47.

5. Robert Ley, ed., *Parteistatistik,* n.p., Berlin, 1935, vol. 3, pp. 15–16.

6. Eva Zuberbier, *Die nationalsozialistische Auffassung vom häuslichen Dienst,* Ph.D. dissertation, Leipzig, 1939, pp. 17–20.

7. These and similar statistics are frequently cited in the German literature, but appear also in two pieces of propaganda in English: Gertrud Scholtz-Klink, *Tradition Is Not Stagnation But Involves a Moral Obligation,* 1938, and Charles W. Domville-Fife, *This is Germany,* London, 1935, pp. 196–212.

8. *Wirtschaft und Statistik* (February, 1940), 66–67.

9. Friedrich Burgdörfer, *Bevölkerungsentwicklung im Dritten Reich,* Kurt Vonwinckel, Heidelberg and Berlin, 1935, pp. 34 ff. Peikow, *Die Soziale,* claims that 350,000 children were born as a result of the scheme, pp. 19–20.

10. Hanna Rees, *Frauenarbeit in der NS Volkswohlfahrt,* Eher, Berlin, 1938, pp. 22–42; Richard Grunberger, *The 12-Year Reich,* Holt, Rinehart & Winston, New York, 1971, pp. 86–87, 108–109, 208.

11. *Die deutsche Kämpferin,* July 1934; Robert Brady, *The Spirit and Structure of German Fascism,* Viking, New York, 1937, p. 211; David Schoenbaum, *Hitler's Social Revolution,* Doubleday Anchor, New York, 1967, pp. 184–185; Jill McIntyre, "Women and the Professions in Germany, 1930–40," A. Nicholls and E. Matthias, *German Democracy and the Triumph of Hitler,* London, 1971, pp. 178 ff; *Statistik des deutschen Reiches,* vol. 453, Berufszählung, vol. 2, "Die Erwerbstätigkeit der Reichsbevölkerung," Berlin, 1936, pp. 5 ff. When national insurance statistics are used instead of the census tracts the rate of male employment increased by 70 percent as compared to a female increase of 30 percent from 1933 to 1938. "Frauenerwerbsarbeit," *Soziale Praxis,* 47 (September 1, 1938), 1079; Clifford Kirkpatrick, *Nazi Germany: Its Women and Family Life,* Bobbs-Merrill, Indianapolis and New York, 1938, pp. 231 ff.

12. Ruth Kohler-Irrgang, *Die Sendung der Frau in der deutschen Geschichte,* Hase & Koehler, Leipzig, 1938, p. 235; Friedrich Syrup, "Ersatz von Männerarbeit durch Frauenarbeit? *Soziale Praxis,* 47 (September 15, 1938), 1094; *NS Frauenwarte,* Nr. 18 (1935–1936), 565; Ursula von Gersdorff, ed., *Frauen im Kriegsdienst,* Stuttgart, 1969, pp. 294 ff.

13. "Frauenlöhne," Reichsarbeitsminister, BA Koblenz, R 41/69, and Gersdorff, *Frauen,* pp. 330 ff., both contain fascinating discussion of women's wages. For Nazi correspondence on the subject, see Institut für Zeitgeschichte microfilm, MA 468/T89, Reel 159, 525717 ff.

14. This figure is based on sources previously noted and Gustav Stolper, *The German Economy,* Harcourt Brace World, New York, 1967, pp. 168 ff; Magda Menzerath, *Kampffeld Heimat: Deutsche Frauenleistung im Kriege,* Allemannen, Stuttgart, 1941, pp. 35–40; Angela Meister, *Die deutsche Industriearbeiterin,* Munich, 1938.

15. The Himmler quotation is reproduced in Jans Joachen Gamm, *Der braune Kult,* Hamburg, 1962, p. 145; Kirkpatrick, *Nazi Germany,* quotes the physician, p. 143; and for a discussion of sociologists and the family question, see Kate Millett, *Sexual Politics,* Avon, New York, 1971, pp. 157 ff.

Suggestions for Further Reading

Abel, Theodor. *Why Hitler Came to Power: An Answer Based on the Original Life Stories of 600 of His Followers.* Prentice-Hall, New York, 1938.

Brady, Robert. *The Spirit and Structure of German Fascism.* Viking, New York, 1937.

Browning, Hilda. *Women under Fascism and Communism.* Lawrence, London, 1943.

Dornemann, Louise. *German Women under Hitler Fascism: A Brief Survey of the Position of Women up to the Present Day.* Allies Inside Germany, London, 1943.

Douie, Vera, ed. *Women: Their Professional Status; A World Survey Immediately Preceding World War II.* British Federation of Business and Professional Women, London, 1947.

Folsom, Joseph K. *The Family and Democratic Society.* Wiley, New York, 1943.

Guillebaud, C. W. *The Social Policy of Nazi Germany.* Cambridge University Press, Cambridge, 1941.

Kirkpatrick, Clifford. *Nazi Germany: Its Women and Family Life.* Bobbs-Merrill, Indianapolis and New York, 1938.

McIntyre, Jill. "Women and the Professions in Germany, 1930–1940." Anthony Nicholls and Erich Matthias, *German Democracy and the Triumph of Hitler.* Allen & Unwin, London, 1971.

Puckett, Hugh Wiley. *Germany's Women Go Forward.* Columbia, New York, 1930.

Seydewitz, Max. *Civil Life in Wartime Germany: The Story of the Home Front.* Viking, New York, 1945.

Stephenson, Jill McIntyre. *Women in Nazi Society.* Barnes & Noble, New York, 1976.

Thomas, Katherine. *Women in Nazi Germany.* Gollancz, London, 1943.

20

Family Models of the Future

Andrée Michel

We have seen that forms of the family and women's role in them have undergone major transformations. During periods when the family exercised a degree of public influence, women's status was fairly high relative to that of men. But as expanding, specialized public institutions assumed many functions previously provided by the family, the role of both the family and women diminished. Throughout, however, one factor has remained constant: women's roles are limited by family needs. Andrée Michel proposes that we now live on the threshold of an unprecedented departure from this social fact. She predicts that a few societies will see the development of a new family ideal. In coming generations, the family will serve its members according to their individual needs and abilities, rather than vice versa. If this happens, we will see the end of what sociologist William Goode has called "the classic family of Western nostalgia" and the birth of a new human-centered set of social arrangements. Michel's optimism is based on faith in two forces: a democratic trend in society, and the responsiveness of major institutions to the articulate and vehement demand of an aroused populace. Whether or not one agrees, it is appropriate to close with speculations about the future and the family.

Some contemporary trends point toward more sharing and less sexual division of labor in families of the future. In this bronze entitled *Family Group,* Henry Moore captured the spirit of companionate marriage. (From *Henry Moore, Sculptures and Drawings*, ed. David Sylvester. Reproduced by courtesy of the publishers, Lund Humphries, London.)

One generally thinks about the future with the assumption that technological and economic modernization will produce social progress. However, certain European schools of philosophy contend that social progress stands in a dialectical relationship with technological advance rather than proceeding from it. According to this point of view, social progress may at times initiate technological progress while at other times it may follow. Human involvement is necessary, since the most perfect computer is able to provide solutions only in terms of alternatives that have been suggested to it.

Too many sociologists, particularly in North America, believe that economic and technological developments shape society. Arguing deterministically, an American book entitled *The Next Five Hundred Years,* which was written several years ago, predicts that developed countries such as the United States and Russia will have women heads of government prior to the year 2000. It also projects that a third of the religious leaders and most of the doctors in the Protestant countries will be women. And yet Jessie Bernard, in *Academic Women,* tells us that between 1930 and 1964 the percentage of American women with a Ph.D. diminished.

Now, there are many measures of social progress; number of women in way of obtaining influential positions is only one. Still, setting predictions aside and relying on facts, we cannot blithely assume that technological advance in itself will foster social progress. Sociologists can propose alternatives within the limits of any given stage of development; but individuals — in this case, women — must be willing to overcome obstacles.

The role of women in the family is a vital area of contemporary debate. Our epoch is characterized by a heightened tension between the traditional and the modern images of the family. We will examine this problem in three stages. The first defines these two images or patterns of the family. The second evaluates various pressure groups upholding both images and describes the methods used by one group to maintain the traditional image and by the other to convert society to a modern family model. The third section analyzes the chances of promoting a more human conception of the family by the year 2000.

Modern and Traditional Images of the Family

What characterizes the traditional image of the family? First of all, in this image, the role of each member of the family group is narrowly defined according to his or her status as father or mother, son or daughter. A role is a cluster of rights and obligations attached to the status of an individual or to his or her position in a group. In the traditional family, these roles are assigned, with little regard for the aptitudes or aspirations of the individual, according to the predetermined criteria of sex or age. The husband fulfills the family's economic needs and functions as the authority with regard to the wife and children. The wife, a full-time spouse and mother, acts as emotional facilitator. She comforts and consoles and remains at home to raise the children and do the housework. Each of these roles is complementary to the other.

In addition to actual roles, we have a second dimension: the mystique of the traditional family. This mystique includes several components. There is first of all what Betty Friedan calls the feminine mystique. In her book she shows how the maternal role is glorified, exploited, and eventually diverted from its primary purpose. It overpowers all other feminine roles and subordinates them. Thus we see that the other roles the woman is capable of fulfilling are devalued in preference to the maternal role. To make the woman forget what she has renounced, the maternal role is glorified. Imprisoned in the domestic routine, she becomes economically and psychologically dependent on her husband. Having sacrificed her educational and economic options, she faces an empty existence when the children have grown up and left home. At forty, she realizes that she has a life expectancy of seventy or seventy-five and that it will be very difficult for her to make a meaningful life for herself. One must emphasize that in this image of the family, the feminine mystique of the full-time mother is a very recent phenomenon. This bourgeois ideal was not appropriated by the majority until quite recently. The full-time housewife and mother came into being after the middle of the nineteenth century.

This feminine mystique has its complement in the masculine mystique, which has been less analyzed. In it, the man is the superior being by virtue of his intelligence, courage, and initiative. To make this acceptable to the woman there is a third mystique of equality in complementarity. Because men and women are defined by different roles, the housewife's economic dependence is camouflaged. She is told that her role is not identical but complementary to his. However, even in theory these roles are not symmetrical. In this traditional conception, if a man is assigned the role of family provider, he nevertheless may differentiate himself within the masculine gender by his profession. He is a mason, a doctor, a salesman, and so on. Meanwhile, his wife has only a vicarious individuality. She has only a mediated identity as the mother of a certain child or the wife of a Mr. Somebody who has a certain profession and whose name she bears. From this point of view, as Betty Friedan has indicated, the wife lives only by proxy. Her own identity and personality are submerged.

The final component in the traditional image of the family consists of respect for the conventions and institutions associated with marriage. Premarital sex, adultery, and divorce are condemned in the interests of sexual monopoly. In addition, the woman relinquishes her individual choice concerning maternity, contraceptives, and abortion in the supposed interests of the family. Thus, the traditional family restricts all its members through its role ascriptions but is especially detrimental to women's individuality.

At the other extreme, we have the modern image. Here again, it consists of three elements. First of all, stereotyped roles disappear in the modern conception of the family: the family is no longer a small group in which the members play roles predetermined as a function of their sex or age. The concept of person replaces that of role. The individual is viewed as a person regardless of sex or age. Each human being freely develops all potentialities and must not be restricted and forced to develop according to prescribed rules to fulfill predetermined roles.

According to this conception, the man or woman may cross the barrier of sex-role stereotypes and assume the role of the other. Even the child is able to play certain nontraditional roles. Children, for example, may aid in the socialization of their parents and not be uniquely socialized by them. Certain American psychologists have shown that parents learn a great deal from their children even though, in the traditional conception of the family, learning is supposed to proceed only in the opposite direction. If certain roles remain, they are so flexible that they may be fulfilled either by the husband or the wife according to the situation. These roles may also vary according to the social class, the family cycle, or other circumstances.

The second element in this modern conception of the family is the replacement of the notion of family obligation by a eudemonical conception of the family. The individual does not think that she or he exists for the institution of marriage or the family but that these institutions exist for her or him. Each individual assumes a moral right to happiness and expects to find it in the marriage or the family. This attitude entails a certain pragmatism. One accepts conventions when they are useful but does not feel obliged to submit to them under all circumstances. This attitude is apparent in the behavior of today's students when they form free unions. When someone questions them, many respond: "Why get married? We'll wait until we have children." This exemplifies the eudemonical conception of marriage: one marries when it seems useful for the conjugal group. Others remain unmarried although they are eventually considered married by common law.

Other departures from tradition include the double career family, analyzed by two English sociologists, Rhona and Robert Rapoport. In the double career family, both the husband and wife have professions and participate more or less equally in the domestic tasks. Husbands as well as wives perform a double role, domestic and professional. Still another alternative is adopted when individuals find it absurd to live in a separate domicile with an individual car, television, etc., when they could share these with other people in a commune, thus diminishing their consumer needs and dividing the responsibilities for child care. Many individuals are presently experimenting with this method.

The third element is the freedom to dissolve a marriage. Divorce rates are high in countries such as the United States and even Russia, which has now almost overtaken the United States in the number of divorces granted. This is one of the consequences of the eudemonical conception of marriage, but divorce also results from women's new perception of their needs. Women demand changes in the masculine and feminine roles because they reject the double burden of employment and housework. Not only does the wife refuse the authority of her husband, but she wants him to assume a full share of all domestic tasks. This situation may result in tensions. Research conducted by William Goode reveals that one of the principal causes of divorce is the authoritarianism of husbands. In the Soviet Union, one of the main reasons for divorce invoked by women is the husband's "lack of cooperation" in the family. The women and the youth have become the most sensitized to the modern conception of the family. Men, as the relatively privileged sex, tend not to perceive inequities in the traditional family.

The Methods Used to Support Both Images of the Family

These images are supported by the mass media or by various groups and associations that often constitute pressure groups to impose their conception of the family on family and social legislation. Both the traditional and the modern conceptions of the family have their supporters and their opponents.

What are these pressure groups? The list includes political parties, labor unions, professional associations, industrial firms, commercial enterprises, religious groups, feminine and family associations, mass media, and so on. Although the division of these groups might be rather predictable as concerns their adherence to a particular view of the family, they all contain many ambiguities. No group adheres exclusively to a traditional image of the family. Each group contains elements of modernism and of traditionalism.

Family and social legislation provide one of the most effective props of the status quo. Several years ago, an American sociologist, Judith Blair, studied the family and social legislation of the contemporary world. She concluded that most of these laws upheld the traditional model of the family and were based on the conception of the family as an ensemble of roles assigned according to sex and age. A further reinforcement comes from the mass media. Women's magazines, radio, television, and films tend in the direction of traditionalism. In addition, sociologists have studied children's books and found that the family models presented to four- and five-year-olds are traditional ones. The woman is a good cook, housekeeper, and mother; or when she has a profession, she is either a nurse or a primary school teacher; whereas, the man is a doctor, farmer, engineer, etc. More important, children are depicted in ways that prepare them to assume male and female roles: boys play interesting games, encounter challenging adventures, and solve problems; girls stay near home, obey authority, and play protomaternal roles. Advertisements also enhance traditional conceptions of the family. A recent poster advertising Brandt washing machines proclaims "Brandt is a part of the family" and shows the happy triad: the housewife filling a washing machine with a child at her side. One might inquire as to whether or not the husband is also a part of the family thus depicted.

Political parties and pressure groups also manipulate the symbols of the traditional family to gain their own objectives. In France this strategy dates from the Old Regime. When the French kings wished to increase their power, they mandated family legislation making the husband head of the nuclear family. These laws were aimed at weakening the large, clanlike feudal families that opposed the accumulation of royal power and the centralization of the monarchy. When the monarchy disappeared, this reliance on the traditional family to maintain a degree of social order persisted. One was led to believe that if the family crumbled, everything would collapse. However, we are not told that this prediction concerns only the traditional, patriarchal image of the family and society; for it is possible to imagine a family and a society that are more egalitarian. Thus, pressure groups manipulate symbols and ideas of the family in order to attain goals extrinsic to the family, such as maintenance of the social order, sale of products, and recruitment into the labor force.

Similarly, the schools reproduce the stratification of sex roles and maintain a traditional conception of the family. During the last hundred years, the social and life sciences (biology, sociology, psychology, psychoanalysis) have committed themselves to this traditional ideology and furnished justifications for the traditional family models. Societies always tend to justify what they produce; and after all, each society has the sociologists and psychologists it deserves.

The above-mentioned measures, however, will no longer be effective once individualism becomes pervasive enough to inspire youth and women to free themselves from the traditional family image. When these minority groups (that is, demographic majority groups lacking power) abandon the traditional image, they begin to mobilize for change, through organized movements and legal action.

Institutionally, this change in consciousness coexists with important developments in corporate capitalism. No longer does demand govern production; rather, consumer needs are now created by the producers. More women and men believe that it is impossible to live without comfort, cars, electrical appliances, and holidays. To meet these new needs, married women must participate increasingly in the labor force. Today in France and in the United States, working women comprise about 40 percent of the total labor force. According to Marx and Engels, confirmed by contemporary empirical research, the economic participation of women has freed them from subordination to the husband's authority. But it has not freed women from household tasks and from discrimination at work and in society. A conflicting situation arises from women's aspirations to be equal partners with men. Hence the creation of new feminist movements.

Thus, Frenchwomen organized to circumvent and change legal restrictions against abortion. In the last several years, they formed a nationwide network to provide information concerning abortion and to organize centers where women can obtain abortions. Finally, in January 1975, women won the right to legal abortion.

Another obstacle being overcome is the single-salary tax deduction, which encourages women to stay at home. Women often find work without declaring it so that the couple can maintain a single-salary status, or else they simply surrender the advantage it offers and seek full-time employment. Statistics show that in France, as well as in the United States and Sweden, many more women between the ages of twenty and thirty with young children are working than ten years ago. For instance, in 1968, about half of all Frenchwomen in their twenties and with children of preschool age were employed. Since there are very few day nurseries in France, French mothers take their children to a nursemaid. These nursemaids are usually themselves mothers of young children, who prefer to stay at home and get some extra money by looking after additional children. After infancy, French kindergartens provide extensive care. Statistics indicate that 22 percent of all French children under the age of three attend; 72 percent of those between three and four; 92 percent of those between four and five, and fully 100 percent of those between five and six.

As the world changes, so do the social sciences. Sometimes they respond to change and foster it. Where myths about the traditional family are collapsing, a new type of psychologist and sociologist appears, with more rigorous methods and criteria, no longer content with approximation. For example, social scientists are discovering that the criteria for judging child development are not related solely to the mother's employment — that other variables such as social class, personality, education, and income are significant as well. A new generation of sociologists, psychologists, and psychiatrists now are rethinking the problems and challenging the basic postulates of the conservative social science that has reigned during the last hundred years. The theses of René Spitz, John Bowlby, and Benjamin Spock, emphasizing the role of mothering in early childhood, are now considered outdated among young women in the social sciences, as is the popularization of Freud that describes women as inferior, able to find achievement only in motherhood.[1] The renewal of social science is possible thanks to the collaboration of women researchers, just as the restructuring of society will be possible only if women are afforded equal opportunities to participate fully. Men, by and large, are too conservative to change and adopt new perspectives. They use social science as a foil to hide some unpleasant realities and protect their vested interests. For instance, they endeavor to highlight conflicts between social classes or ethnic groups as the basic sociological issue. Young women students and female researchers assert that the social stratification by sex with the exploitation of women at work and in the family are equally important.[2]

It is necessary, however, to point out that the dichotomy between the two images of the family that we have schematized is not so clear in reality. One does not always find on one side pressure groups supporting either the traditional or the modern image. In each social group as well as in each individual, one finds a mixture of these two images, which are superimposed, sometimes in conflict. One might say that among the most tradition-minded, there is an 80 percent traditional and 20 percent modern image of the family; whereas, among the modernists or radicals the proportion would be reversed. Between the two, there are all varieties of attitudes. For example, one French political party promotes legislation favoring divorce and abortion but upholds traditional sex roles. This traditionalism blinds them to the advantages that could be accorded both sexes if a different perspective were adopted. Take the example of the leave granted to the mother when the children are ill. In Sweden this leave of absence has been replaced by parental leave. This permits the parents to choose which person should remain at home to care for the infant. In that country, the conception of the family rests on the person and not on a role attached to a particular sex. Thus, in a variety of ways, women are circumventing and bringing to an end some of the traditional constraints on their freedom.

The Chances of Attaining the Modern Image by the Year 2000

Geographic, structural, economic, and cultural factors all help to determine the future of a society. These factors have been clearly identified by Germaine Tillion in *The Harem and the Cousins.*[3] The author contends that traditional, patriarchal conceptions of the family developed about 4,000 years ago around the Mediterranean basin with the invention of large-scale agriculture. With the disappearance of small family plots, accumulation occurred and eventually there were surpluses. With this accumulation, the patriarchal family appeared, based on the servitude of women. The farther one moves away from the Mediterranean basin, where our present civilization originated, and the farther north one goes, the more family model number one (the "traditional" one) recedes and model number two (the "modern" one) is approximated.

Schematically, the Mediterranean countries, Spain, southern Italy, Greece, and northern Africa (but not Yugoslavia), maintain, either by custom or legislation, some version of family model number one. Not too long ago, in northern Africa and Greece, women who had sexual relations prior to marriage were put to death, and their lovers sometimes encountered the same fate. In certain large cities of northern Africa, parents choose their daughter's husband, an act that provokes epidemics of suicide in young girls, many of whom no longer accept the traditional model to which they are constrained. Out of fear and veneration wives and children obey the paterfamilias. Family and social legislation is still archaic in these countries. There is little chance of seeing them adopt model number two by the year 2000.

A second group of countries may be distinguished that are in transition, but where conception number one still dominates over conception number two. One could provisionally include France, northern Italy, Belgium, Austria, and West Germany among these countries. Here individuals are still viewed in terms of their traditional roles. The Napoleonic Code has had considerable influence, particularly in Italy, France, and Belgium, although the situation is at present better in Belgium than in France. In the elaboration of family legislation, traditional patriarchal mystiques still predominate. These mystiques are embodied in legislation that in certain aspects is still archaic: just ten years ago family planning was still outlawed in France. Not until 1970 did parental control replace paternal authority. But in order for this change to be incorporated into daily life, all organizations concerned with families (family assistance centers, Social Security agencies, police departments, public authorities, etc.) have yet to be notified. When a married Frenchwoman requests the family assistance or aid to which she is entitled, the social worker still asks to see the "head of the family." Other examples demonstrate de facto inequality in spite of legal equality. If the wife is not employed, she can make use of her husband's social security to obtain medical treatment, but the unemployed husband cannot use her social security benefits to obtain medical care. In addition, unemployed wives can benefit from their husband's retirement fund following his death, but the husband receives no such assistance when his wife dies, even if she had been employed for many years. Only in the civil service can a widower obtain a part of his wife's retirement fund at her death. French people are still far from equality, because the family mystique that accompanies model one is still at the base of French law.

Part-time employment, granted mainly to women, is still another measure envisioned to serve model number one. If there is no reason to consider the woman as the person primarily responsible for housework and child care, part-time employment should be given to men more often. There are certainly times in the life of a family or couple when the man would like to remain at home and the woman would prefer to work outside the home. On the other hand, wages for housework, if adopted, would transform the woman into a domestic civil servant, paid by the state, and would greatly inhibit the development of her creative faculties.

What are the chances that the countries in this second group will succeed in attaining family model number two by the year 2000? This will depend on the orientation of women's movements: these groups may remain attached to the traditional family model or feminist women may motivate them in other directions. Similarly, social planners and legislators must make conscious choices about family models before they adopt a course of action.

The third group of countries is composed of those that embody transitional models but where conception number two, founded on respect for the person, is already widely accepted. The Soviet Union, the United States, England, and China might be classified in this group.

In the United States, family and social legislation is presently undergoing considerable transformation. Divorce is considered a matter between two adults; no-fault divorce laws are becoming more widespread. In abortion laws, repression has been challenged by freedom of choice. The Supreme Court of the United States has declared that state legislation prohibiting abortion is a limitation of individual liberty and is therefore unconstitutional.

In the Soviet Union, according to Urie Bronfenbrenner,[4] the child is taught to fulfill certain responsibilities. For example, the older child may be responsible for small brothers and sisters in the home or for the younger children at school. Soviet women have succeeded in highly qualified professions such as medicine and architecture to a degree unequaled in other countries. They are also engineers, economists, social planners, and are numerous in administrative and policy-making positions.

What are the chances that these countries will attain family model number two by the year 2000? The prospects are fairly hopeful, but here as elsewhere this depends on the continuing struggles of women and young people as well as on the options of social planners. Numerous obstacles remain. In the Soviet Union, a powerful state limits the freedom of women to organize under their own leaders without the control of a political party or external organization. One recalls the vicissitudes concerning the abortion law authorized after the Russian Revolution, which was suppressed during the 1930s and not reinstated until 1958. The laws concerning divorce have also undergone several changes; however, it has become easy to obtain a divorce in the Soviet Union during the last few years.

In the United States, women's victories remain precarious because the enforcement of federal legislation is hampered by the individual state governments and weak federal agencies. The pressures of the market economy and the large monopolies are always ready to violate antidiscrimination laws and even constitutional rights for their own purposes. Only a strong feminist movement will achieve family model number two.

In the Scandinavian countries one has the best chance of seeing the triumph of the modern family model. In these countries, a family policy is being constructed according to this model. These are the only countries where laws are not consistently based on traditional roles. The woman is viewed as a whole person existing in her own right. All measures that are constraining or repressive, such as those concerning divorce and abortion, are undergoing analyses, revisions, or transformations. The explicit social policy of the Swedish government suppresses sex roles and allows individuals to organize their own lives.[5] Research by psychologists reveals that children of three or four have already assimilated the male and female stereotypes. Therefore, early intervention in childhood is necessary if traditional stereotypes are to be transformed. A Scandinavian intergovernmental commission has been established to define the policies to be followed. This commission studies school books with a view to censuring those that emphasize masculine and feminine roles. Primary schools in Finland, Norway, and Sweden offer courses in child care, cooking, and sewing that are taught equally to girls and boys during the seven years of primary school.

While the Scandinavian countries appear to be the most serious about creating the basis for an androgynous lifestyle, certain obstacles remain even in these countries.[6] In Sweden, for example, men predominate in the parliament and among the social planners. These men, who are legislators and planners, are also husbands who perhaps find the traditional situation quite advantageous and hesitate to risk loss of status in both the family and society at large if the sexes were equalized.

Yet the Scandinavian countries are in the best position to attain family model number two by the year 2000. In them, the trends for change are more developed because women use the political and cultural values of the countries. Socialism and peace, tolerance and secularism encourage women to fight for their rights. In Oslo, I met bright women who for twenty years had been fighting to rid school books of sex-role stereotyping. In Sweden, Alva Myrdal is working to obtain improvement in the status of women. The situation in Scandinavian countries seems to indicate that women can be promoted more easily in peaceful countries than where a strong military structure exists.

In conclusion, one might say that there is no absolute determinism. There are merely certain options from which policy makers must choose. To the extent that women and young people push society in the direction of the modern model, resistances will undoubtedly develop against it. Here we should cite the prognostications of an American futurologist who predicts that social tensions will arise due to these changes.

The women's liberation movements are not, as some would like to believe, merely temporary, but rather just beginning. Tactics may change, but we are witnessing the rejection by women of the traditional feminine and family mystiques. At the same time, young people are departing from traditional roles in the family and society. Where family and social legislation aid them, people will be freed from narrowly prescribed family roles and their potential for full humanity will be liberated.

NOTE: Since the writing of this article in 1974, French women have obtained a law freeing abortion (1975) and a law allowing divorce by mutual consent (1976).

Notes

This chapter is a revised version of a paper read at the Eighth World Congress of Sociology of the International Sociological Association, Toronto, August 18 to 24, 1974.

1. John Bowlby, *Attachment and Loss,* 2 vols., Hogarth Press, London, 1969–1973; René Arpad Spitz, *The First Year of Life,* International Universities Press, New York, 1965; Benjamin Spock, *Baby and Child Care,* 3rd ed., Hawthorn Books, New York, 1968.
2. "Libération des femmes, année zéro," *Partisans* (July–October 1970).
3. Germaine Tillion, *Le Harem et les cousins,* Editions du Seuil, Paris, 1966.
4. Urie Bronfenbrenner, *Two Worlds of Childhood: U.S. and U.S.S.R.,* Russell Sage Foundation, New York, 1970.

5. The Swedish Institute, *The Status of Women in Sweden, Report to the United Nations,* 1968.
6. Joy and Howard Osofsky, "Androgyny as a Life Style," Carolyn C. Perrucci and Dena B. Targ, *Marriage and the Family,* McKay, New York, 1974.

Suggestions for Further Reading

Beckwith, Burnham Putnam. *The Next Five Hundred Years.* Exposition Press, New York, 1967.

Bernard, Jessie. *Academic Women.* Pennsylvania State University Press, University Park, Pa., 1964.

———. *Women, Wives, Mothers: Values and Opinions.* Aldine, Chicago, 1975.

Bluh, Bonnie Charles. *Woman to Woman: European Feminists.* Starogubski Press, New York, 1974.

Bronfenbrenner, Urie. *Two Worlds of Childhood: U.S. and U.S.S.R.* Russell Sage Foundation, New York, 1970.

Friedan, Betty. *The Feminine Mystique.* Norton, New York, 1963.

Goode, William J. *World Revolution and Family Patterns.* Free Press, New York, 1963.

Perrucci, Carolyn C., and Dena B. Targ, *Marriage and the Family.* McKay, New York, 1974.

Rapoport, Rhona and Robert. *Dual-Career Families.* Penguin Books, Middlesex, England, 1971.

Skolnick, Arlene S. and Jerome H. *Family in Transition.* Little, Brown, Boston, 1971.

Notes on Contributors

MARYLIN BENTLEY ARTHUR received her Ph.D. in classics from Yale University in 1975 and is currently assistant professor of Greek and Latin at Columbia University, where she also teaches a course on women in antiquity. She has published and lectured on Greek misogyny and on the changing representation of women from the Homeric to the classical period. She is at work on a book about women in Greek law, life, and literature.

RENATE BRIDENTHAL received her Ph.D. in history from Columbia University in 1970. She is assistant professor of history at Brooklyn College, The City University of New York, where she also co-administers the Women's Studies program; and she is affiliated with The Institute for Research in History. She has published articles on theories of women's history, German women, and German intellectual history. She is interested in developing a Marxist-feminist synthesis of contemporary European women's history.

BARBARA ALPERN ENGEL received her Ph.D. in Russian history from Columbia University. After teaching for two years in the Women's History program at Sarah Lawrence College, she is currently assistant professor of history at the University of Colorado in Boulder. Co-editor of *Five Sisters: Women Against the Tsar,* she is now engaged in research on the female intelligentsia in Russia.

RUTH GRAHAM received her Ph.D. in history from The City University of New York in 1971. She taught at Queens College (C.U.N.Y.) for seven years and is now a member of The Institute for Research in History. She has written articles on the revolutionary clergy and on women in the French Revolution and is currently working on a book about the ecclesiastical deputies to the National Convention of France in 1792–1795.

EDITH F. HURWITZ has taught at several colleges and universities. She was a National Endowment for the Humanities research fellow at Yale University and a visiting scholar in the history department at Wesleyan. She became interested in the international women's movement while doing research for her book *Politics and the Public Conscience: Slave Emancipation and the Abolitionist Movement in Britain.* With Samuel J. Hurwitz she co-authored *Jamaica — A Historical Portrait.* Recently she prepared a three-part bibliographical survey of the Caribbean area for *Choice: Books for College Libraries.*

TEMMA KAPLAN, associate professor of history at the University of California, Los Angeles, received her Ph.D. from Harvard University in 1969. Since then she has written widely on three overlapping topics: comparative European labor and peasant history, women in Europe and the Third World, and Spanish social history. An attempt to deal with all three can be found in her recent book *Anarchists of Andalusia, 1868–1903.*

JOAN KELLY-GADOL is concerned with recent theoretical developments in feminism and women's history. She holds a Ph.D. from Columbia University, and has published articles on women's history, as well as a book and several articles on the Italian Renaissance. She is professor of history at The City College, The City University of New York, and is affiliated with the Sarah Lawrence College Program in Women's History and The Institute for Research in History.

ABBY KLEINBAUM received her Ph.D. in history from Columbia University in 1970. As associate professor of history at the Borough of Manhattan Community College, The City University of New York, she is also serving on the Board of Directors of The Institute for Research in History. She is author of several articles and reviews on women's history and is working on a book tracing the idea of Amazons in history.

CLAUDIA KOONZ received her Ph.D. from Rutgers University and is now associate professor of history at Holy Cross College. Her major research interest centers on German industrialization in the early twentieth century. In earlier work on women's history, she studied the impact of suffrage on women in the Weimar Republic. Currently she is examining the role of German women during two world wars and the 1929 Depression.

ELEANOR LEACOCK, who holds a Ph.D. in anthropology from Columbia University, is professor of anthropology at The City College, The City University of New York. Her research has included studies of schooling in New York and Zambia, the social history of native Americans, and women cross-culturally. Her publications include *Teaching and Learning in City Schools, The Culture of Poverty: A Critique,* and *North American Indians in Historical Perspective.*

THERESA M. MCBRIDE is assistant professor of history at Holy Cross College in Worcester, Massachusetts, and author of *The Domestic Revolution: The Modernization of Household Service in England and France, 1820–1920.* Her fields of interest are comparative labor history, family history, and modern French history; future research projects include investigations into women's participation in protest, occupational expectations, and choices, and the rise of white-collar employment before 1930.

MARY LYNN MCDOUGALL received her Ph.D. in history from Columbia University in New York in 1974 and is now assistant professor of history at Smith College. She has done research on Lyonnais workers in the first half of the nineteenth century and edited a book of readings entitled *The Working Class in Modern Europe.* She is currently completing a monograph on Lyon during the Second Republic.

JOANN MCNAMARA holds a Ph.D. in history from Columbia University. She is presently an associate professor at Hunter College, The City University of New York, and a member of The Institute for Research in History. After the publication of a book, *Gilles Aycelin, The Servant of Two Masters,* she turned to the history of women in the Middle Ages and has published several articles on the subject independently and with Suzanne Wemple.

ANDRÉE MICHEL received her Ph.D. in sociology from the University of Paris, Sorbonne, in 1959. She is director of a research group on sex roles, the family, and human development at the National Center of Scientific Research in Paris, as well as Co-chairperson of the International Research Committee on Sex Roles of the International Sociological Association. She has recently published *Travail Féminin: un point de vue* and is now editing *Women, Society, and Sexism.* Both books deal with the status of women as members of the work force.

E. WILLIAM MONTER received his Ph.D. in history from Princeton University in 1963 and is presently professor of history at Northwestern University. Originally a specialist in the history of Calvin's Geneva, he has been occupied with the history of European witchcraft for several years. Currently he is working on the history of women in Geneva, 1500–1800.

BARBARA CORRADO POPE, a Ph.D. candidate at Columbia University, is working on a study of women in nineteenth-century France. At present she is the instructor of women's studies at the University of Oregon, married and the mother of a daughter, and an active member of the New American Movement, a democratic socialist organization.

RUBY ROHRLICH-LEAVITT received her Ph.D. in anthropology from New York University in 1969, and she is an associate professor at the Borough of Manhattan Community College, The City University of New York. Her book *The Puerto Ricans: Culture Change and Language Deviance* merged speech pathology, which she formerly practiced, with anthropology. She edited and contributed essays to the anthology *Women Cross-Culturally: Change and Challenge,* and has published several articles on women from a feminist anthropological perspective.

BERNICE GLATZER ROSENTHAL received her Ph.D. in history from The University of California, Berkeley, in 1970 and now teaches history at Fordham University. She has published articles and an educational cassette on Russian women and a book on the intellectual history of Russia between 1890 and 1917. Her future plans include further research on the intellectual and cultural history of Russia in the years before the revolution and a comparative study of women in socialist countries.

RICHARD T. VANN is currently professor of history and letters at Wesleyan University. His major field of research is English social history in the preindustrial era. He is executive editor of the journal *History and Theory,* author of *The Social Development of English Quakerism, 1655–1755,* and compiler of *Century of Genius: European Thought 1600–1700.*

SUZANNE WEMPLE is associate professor of history at Barnard College and holds a Ph.D. from Columbia University. Her specialization is social and intellectual history of the early Middle Ages. She has published articles on medieval women's history and is presently working on a study of women in Frankish society.

SHERRIN MARSHALL WYNTJES received her Ph.D. from Tufts University in 1972 and is now assistant professor of history at the University of Massachusetts at Boston. Her research has focused on family history in the sixteenth-century Netherlands.

Index

FGHIJ-A-8987654321O